Foundations of Economics

Fifth Edition

Foundations of Economics

Fifth Edition

David Begg

London   Boston   Burr Ridge, IL   Dubuque, IA   Madison, WI   New York
San Francisco   St. Louis   Bangkok   Bogotá   Caracas   Kuala Lumpur
Lisbon   Madrid   Mexico City   Milan   Montreal   New Delhi
Santiago   Seoul   Singapore   Sydney   Taipei   Toronto

Foundations of Economics

David Begg
ISBN-13 9780077145606
ISBN-10 0077145607

Published by McGraw-Hill Education
Shoppenhangers Road
Maidenhead
Berkshire
SL6 2QL
Telephone: 44 (0) 1628 502 500
Fax: 44 (0) 1628 770 224

Website: www.mcgraw-hill.co.uk

British Library Cataloguing in Publication Data
A catalogue record for this book is available from the British Library
Library of Congress Cataloging in Publication Data
The Library of Congress data for this book has been applied for from the Library of Congress

Executive Editor: Natalie Jacobs
Development Editor: Kiera Jamison
Marketing Manager: Vanessa Boddington
Senior Production Editor: James Bishop

Text Design by Hard Lines
Cover design by Adam Renvoize
Printed and bound in Great Britain by Ashford Colour Press

ISBN-13 9780077145606
ISBN-10 77145607

Dedication

For my beloved Jen

Brief Table of Contents

Detailed Table of Contents

Preface

Useful foundations need to be reliably up to the job, help you understand the rest of your life, and be fun enough to make you want to bother.

Foundations of Economics is specially designed for students studying introductory economics in a single term or semester. The book streamlines the arguments that make its parent text *Economics* the 'student's bible' for economics (BBC Radio 4).

Foundations of Economics covers only the core topics but trains students to think for themselves, using a wide range of data and examples, and offers authoritative commentary on topical issues.

Learning by doing

Few people practise for a driving test just by reading a book. There is no substitute for finding out if you can actually do a hill start. We give you lots of examples and real-world applications in order to help you master economics for yourself. Try to do the examples at the end of every chapter, and compare your answers with those we give at the end of the book.

Don't read on 'cruise control', highlighting a few sentences and gliding through paragraphs that we worked hard to simplify. Active learning is much more efficient. When the text says 'clearly', ask yourself 'why' it is clear. See if you can construct diagrams before you look at ours. For more help with study skills, please visit our website: **http://www.openup.co.uk/studyskills**.

To assist you in working through the text, we have developed a number of distinctive features. To familiarize yourself with these features, please turn to the Guided Tour on pages x–xi.

Key changes to the fifth edition

The fifth edition has been updated to meet the needs of today's busy students on whom pressures are greater than ever. Key changes include:

- Completely rewritten, action-oriented Learning Outcomes provide clearer goals for students' development
- Extensive coverage of the crash of 2008, the European financial crisis and recent policy updates
- Thorough updating of real-world examples, case studies and applications

In addition, the website for the new edition is fully updated and includes a wealth of supplementary resources for both students and lecturers. Please see **www.mcgraw-hill.co.uk/textbooks/begg** for more information.

Guided Tour

Learning Outcomes

Learning outcomes present the key skills that you should develop by reading this chapter.

Learning outcomes

By the end of this chapter, you should be able to

- Explain the price elasticity of demand
- Analyse the revenue effect of a price change
- Appreciate why bad harvests help farmers
- Understand the cross-price elasticity of demand
- Explain the income elasticity of demand
- Distinguish inferior, normal and luxury goods
- Explain the price elasticity of supply
- Analyse the revenue effect of a price change

 Measuring demand responses

Chapters 2 and 3 introduced the basic ideas of demand and supply. Sometimes, it is sufficient to have a qualitative idea of how things will work out. For example, we may be content to be able to deduce that an increase in demand will make prices go up. But on other occasions we need to know not just the general direction of a change but its magnitude. If you are asked to invest £10,000 in a friend's business, you will

Finally, holding constant the own-price of a good and the prices of relat of the quantity demanded to changes in consumer incomes. As in Cha saving. For the moment, we assume that a rise in the income of consum equivalent increase in total consumer spending.

In Chapter 2 we introduced the concepts of normal and inferior go These described, other things equal, how quantity demanded respond responses to price changes, it is helpful to quantify the magnitude of t

The **income elasticity of demand (ied)** measures the change i response to a 1 per cent rise in income. The ied is given by

ied = [% change in quantity demanded]/[corresponding

The income elasticity of demand measures how far the demand curve change. Figure 4-1 shows two possible shifts caused by a given percenta

Key Terms

These are highlighted where they first appear in the text, so that you can note the new term and the definition that accompanies it.

Boxes and Case Studies

These provide examples, illuminating ideas and theories presented within the chapter, and offer an insight into how economics applies to the real world.

Case study Good news! A bad harvest!

There's an awful lot of coffee in Brazil, which supplies a big share of the world market. experienced the most severe frost of the last 20 years, which wrecked the 1995 coff table below shows what happened to coffee exports from Brazil. As a result of the cris prices (measured in US dollars) more than doubled from 90 cents per pound weight pound. This price increase reflected not a rise in demand but a fall in supply to the worl second row of the table below shows the sharp drop in Brazilian exports, which by 199 cent below their level of 1993. What happened to Brazilian export revenue from coffe by 70 per cent, despite the 'bad' harvest and lower export quantities. The demand for c – very inelastic. New Yorkers, and many other coffee addicts, cannot do without th

Brazilian coffee exports 1993–95		1993
P	Price (US cents/pound weight, 1995 prices)	90
Q	Export quantity (1990 = 100)	113

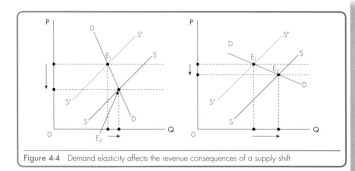

Figure 4-4   Demand elasticity affects the revenue consequences of a supply shift

Graphs, Tables and Figures

These are presented in a simple and clear design to help you understand key economic models and to absorb relevant data.

Recaps

These sum up the ideas that have been discussed in each chapter, reviewing the concepts and topics that you should now comprehend.

Recap

- The price elasticity of demand (sometimes simply called the elasticity of demand) is the percentage change in quantity demanded when the price of that good or service increases by 1 per cent.
- Demand is elastic (inelastic) when a 1 per cent price fall induces a rise in the quantity demanded by more (less) than 1 per cent.
- Price cuts raise (lower) total spending and producer revenue when demand is elastic (inelastic). Spending and revenue are unchanged if demand is unit-elastic.
- The cross-price elasticity of demand shows how the quantity demanded of one good responds to a change in the price of a related good.
- The income elasticity of demand shows the percentage change in quantity induced by a 1 per cent rise in income and total spending. Higher income increases demand for normal goods and reduces demand for inferior goods.
- Luxuries have an income elasticity above 1. Necessities have an income elasticity below 1. Inferior goods have a negative income elasticity.

Review Questions

Found at the end of every chapter, these provide questions and problems to test your understanding of the material. Questions are graded by level of difficulty so you can assess your progress. Solutions to the exercises are available at the end of the text so you can check your progress.

Review questions

To check your answers to these questions, go to page 334.

1 Why is demand more elastic in the long run than in the short run? Could it ever be less elastic in the long run?

2 Which of the following statements refer to the income elasticity of demand and which to the price elasticity of demand? (a) A Mercedes is a luxury, (b) I am addicted to nicotine, (c) bread is cheap and so attractive to poor students, (d) only the rich have servants, (e) the minimum wage has increased the cost of employing servants, so nowadays few people can afford them.

3 The price of a service rises and people demand more of it. Is the service normal or inferior? Why?

4 Suppose London introduces a congestion charge for Londoners but also gives £500 a year subsidy to all Londoners so that the average Londoner is neither better nor worse off from the combined effect of the two measures. Answer true or false for each of the following statements: (a) People's behaviour will change because of the income effect of

EASY

Online Resources

Online Learning Centre

Visit **www.mcgraw-hill.co.uk/textbooks/begg** today.

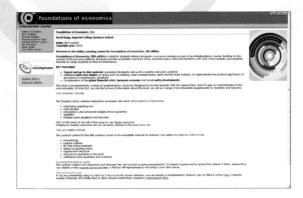

After completing each chapter, log on to the supporting Online Learning Centre website. Take advantage of the study tools offered to reinforce the material you have read in the text, and to develop your knowledge of economics in a fun and effective way.

Resources for students include:

- Basic MCQs
- Advanced MCQs
- Graphing Tool
- Case Studies
- Practice Exam Questions with Answers
- Web Links

Also available for lecturers:

- Lecture Outlines
- Solutions to Questions in the Book
- PowerPoint Slides
- Artwork
- Testbank
- Additional Exam Questions and Solutions
- Videos and Teaching Notes

Test Bank available in McGraw-Hill EZ Test Online

A test bank of over 1400 questions is available to lecturers adopting this book for their module. A range of questions is provided for each chapter, including multiple choice, true or false, and short answer or essay questions. The questions are identified by type, difficulty and topic to help you to select questions that best suit your needs, and are accessible through an easy-to-use online testing tool, **McGraw-Hill EZ Test Online**.

    McGraw-Hill EZ Test Online is accessible to busy academics virtually anywhere – in their office, at home or while travelling – and eliminates the need for software installation. Lecturers can choose from question banks associated with their adopted textbook or easily create their own questions. They also have access to hundreds of banks and thousands of questions created for other McGraw-Hill titles. Multiple versions of tests can be saved for delivery on paper or online through WebCT, Blackboard and other course management systems. When created and delivered through EZ Test Online, students' tests can be immediately marked, saving lecturers time' and providing prompt results to students. To register for this FREE resource, visit www.eztestonline.com.

Make our content your solution

At McGraw-Hill Education our aim is to help lecturers to find the most suitable content for their needs delivered to their students in the most appropriate way. Our **custom publishing solutions** offer the ideal combination of content delivered in the way which best suits lecturer and students.

Our custom publishing programme offers lecturers the opportunity to select just the chapters or sections of material they wish to deliver to their students from a database called CREATE™ at

www.mcgrawhillcreate.co.uk

CREATE™ contains over two million pages of content from:
- textbooks
- professional books
- case books – Harvard Articles, Insead, Ivey, Darden, Thunderbird and BusinessWeek
- Taking Sides – debate materials

Across the following imprints:
- McGraw-Hill Education
- Open University Press
- Harvard Business Publishing
- International material

There is also the option to include additional material authored by lecturers in the custom product – this does not necessarily have to be in English.

We take care of everything from start to finish in the process of developing and delivering a custom product to ensure that lecturers and students receive exactly the material needed in the most suitable way.

With a **Custom Publishing Solution**, students enjoy the best selection of material deemed to be the most suitable for learning everything they need for their courses – something of real value to support their learning. Teachers are able to use exactly the material they want, in the way they want, to support their teaching on the course

Please contact **your local McGraw-Hill representative** with any questions or alternatively contact Warren Eels e: **warren_eels@mcgraw-hill.com**.

Acknowledgements

The author would like to thank all those students, former students and lecturers who have made suggestions on how this and previous editions could be improved. These comments have been invaluable to the ongoing development of the text. The usual highly professional support from the editorial and production team at McGraw-Hill should not go unmentioned, and particularly Natalie Jacobs, whose editorial initiative and personal support were outstanding.

The publisher and author would like to thank the following reviewers who provided their comments and suggestions for developing the new edition of this book:

Michael Brookes, Middlesex University
Catherine Dolan, University of Leeds
Carole Doyle, Glasgow Caledonian University
Conchita Garcia-Iglesias, University of Helsinki
Piotr Marek Jaworski, Napier University
Chunxia Jiang, Middlesex University
Chris Jones, Aston University
David Kraithman, University of Hertfordshire
Munacinga Simatele, University of Hertfordshire
Yoke Eng Tan, Canterbury Christ Church University
Mark Whitford, Canterbury Christ Church University

Our thanks also go to those who have contributed in any way to previous editions of this text. We would also like to thank all contributors to the Online Learning Centre website resources: Snæfríður Baldvinsdóttir for the Lecture Outlines and Additional Exam Questions and Solutions; Ian Belshaw for the Testbank, Weblinks and Multiple Choice Questions; Piotr Jaworski for the PowerPoint presentations; Pavan Vasireddy and Edwin Acheampong for the Practice Exam Questions and Answers.

About the Author

David Begg is Professor of Economics at Imperial College Business School.

Born in Glasgow, David went to Cambridge in the hope of playing cricket for England but became fascinated with economics. After also studying at Oxford, he won a Kennedy Scholarship to the Massachusetts Institute of Technology. He returned to jobs at Oxford then London universities.

An expert on monetary and exchange rate policy, David has advised the Bank of England, HM Treasury, the IMF and the European Commission. He is a fellow of the Royal Society of Edinburgh, a fellow of the City and Guilds of London Institute and a non-executive director of Imperial Innovations, which invests in technology start-ups from Imperial College, University of Cambridge, University of Oxford and UCL.

David has always been committed to showing how useful economics is in making sense of the world around us. His other books include *Economics* (co-authored with Gianluigi Vernasca, now in its 10th edition) and *Economics for Business* (co-authored with Damian Ward, now in its 4th edition).

What is economics?

Learning outcomes

By the end of this chapter, you should be able to:

- Explain why economics is the study of scarcity
- Show how opportunity cost reflects scarcity
- Understand how society rations scarce goods and services
- Discuss the pros and cons of relying on the market
- Distinguish positive and normative economics
- Differentiate microeconomics and macroeconomics
- Appreciate why theories deliberately simplify reality

- Distinguish nominal and real variables
- Understand a simple theoretical model
- Draw scatter diagrams
- Use the 'other things equal' assumption to let key influences be ignored but not forgotten
- Explain demand and supply
- Understand what is meant by market equilibrium
- Discuss how markets resolve what, how and for whom things are produced
- Analyse the effect of price controls

 ## What economists study

Economics is much too interesting to be left to professional economists. It affects almost everything we do, not merely as students but as parents, voters and workers. It influences climate change, whether we can make poverty history and the resources we have to enjoy ourselves.

The formal study of economics is exciting because it introduces a toolkit that allows a better understanding of the problems we all face. Everyone knows a smoky engine is a bad sign, but sometimes only a trained mechanic can give the right advice on how to fix it. This book is designed to teach you the toolkit and give you practice in using it.

Nobody carries a huge toolbox very far. Like Swiss army knives, useful toolkits are small enough to be portable but have enough proven tools to deal with both routine problems and nasty surprises. With practice, you'll be surprised at how much economic analysis can illuminate daily living.

Every group of people must solve three basic problems: what goods and services to make, how to make them, and who gets them.

Economics is the study of how society decides what, how and for whom to produce.

Goods are physical commodities such as steel and strawberries. Services are activities such as massages or live concerts, consumed or enjoyed only at the instant and in the location that they are produced. If you attend Glastonbury Festival, you enjoy a service: you were there at the time. If you video it on your mobile phone, the Glastonbury video is a good that you can enjoy later or post on the Internet for friends elsewhere.

Society has to resolve the conflict between people's limitless desire for goods and services, and the scarcity of resources (labour, machinery, raw materials) with which goods and services are made. Economics is the analysis of these human decisions, about which we aim to develop theories and test them against the facts.

As a student, you can afford the necessities of life – a place to live, food to eat, a brilliant textbook such as this one – and some extras, such as summer holidays and visits to clubs. You are richer than some people, poorer than others. Income distribution across people is closely linked to the 'what', 'how' and 'for whom' questions. Table 1-1 shows that in poor countries, average income per person is only £314 a year. In the rich industrial countries, income per person is £23 837 a year, 76 times larger. For whom does the world economy produce? Mainly, for the 16.5 per cent of its people in the rich industrial countries. What is produced? What people in those countries want to buy!

The large differences in income between groups reflect *how* goods are made. Poor countries have little machinery, and their people have less access to health and education. Workers in poor countries are less productive because they work in less favourable conditions.

Income is unequally distributed within each country as well as between countries, and this affects *what* goods and services are produced. In Brazil, where income is unequally distributed, rich people can afford domestic servants who work for low wages. In egalitarian Denmark, few people are sufficiently rich to afford to hire servants.

Table 1-1 World population and income, 2009

	Country group		
	Poor	Middle	Rich
Income per head £	314	2071	23 837
% of world population	12.5	71	16.5
% of world income	1	27	72

Source: World Bank, *World Bank Development Report 2012*

Table 1-2 The composition of national output

% of national output	UK	USA	France	China	India
Agriculture	1	1	2	10	17
Industry	24	21	20	46	28
Services	76	77	78	43	55

Source: World Bank, *World Bank Development Report 2012*

Scarcity and opportunity cost

Economics is the study of scarcity. When something is so abundantly available that we get all we want, we don't waste time worrying about what, how and for whom it should be produced. In the Sahara, there is no need to worry about the production of sand.

Although it may surprise you, most output is services not goods. Table 1-2 shows that in rich countries agriculture is usually about 1 per cent of national output. Manufacturing is rarely over 20 per cent. Manufacturing plus mining gives us total industrial output, usually below 25 per cent of national output in the developed economies. The remaining 75 per cent or more is services (banking, transport, communications, tourism, entertainment, defence, education, health).

The Industrial Revolution of the nineteenth century was largely about the move from agriculture to the production of industrial goods. The rise of the service economy is more recent. Hence, emerging markets, such as China and India, that have yet to become fully modernized, have larger agricultural and industrial sectors (and a smaller service sector) than Europe and the USA.

How can transport be a service? Boeing and Airbus produce goods (aeroplanes) but Virgin and British Airways operate an airline service – if you miss the flight, you don't get the service.

Next time you hear about the loss of jobs in manufacturing, remember that in rich countries it is only a small part of national output, and still in trend decline. More and more of manufacturing is being outsourced to cheaper locations in the global economy.

> For a **scarce resource**, the quantity demanded at a zero price would exceed the available supply.

When resources are scarce, society can get *more* of some things only by having *less* of other things. We must *choose between* different outcomes, or make trade-offs between them.

> The **opportunity cost** of a good is the quantity of *other* goods sacrificed to get another unit of *this* good.

As a country, we can have more education only if we have less of something else, perhaps less defence or less food. Governments may make these tough choices, but markets also play a role.

The role of the market

> A **market** uses prices to reconcile decisions about consumption and production.

Markets and prices are one way in which society can decide what, how and for whom to produce. During the British beef crisis, caused by fears about 'mad cow disease', pork prices rose 30 per cent while beef prices fell. This provided the incentive to expand pig farming, and stopped too many shoppers switching to pork until the new piglets were ready for market.

Box 1-1

Scarcely a hospital bed

In 2012, the UK government was struggling to introduce controversial reforms to the National Health Service, whose budget seems to get bigger every year. In fact, in almost every advanced economy, health spending keeps on rising, whatever the government in power. The chart below shows health spending (public and private sector) as a percentage of national output in a range of countries since 1960. Health spending has risen most quickly in the United States, where health care is largely privately provided, but the upward trend is clear in all countries.

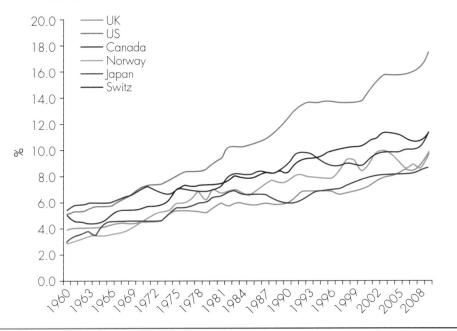

Health spending as a percentage of national output, 1960–2009

Source: OECD

Why do people want even more money spent on health? First, we are all living longer, and older people need more health care. Second, medical advances have led to successful but very expensive treatments. Making these available to some people reduces the resources left for others. With an ageing population, health spending must rise *faster* than national output if people are to get the same standard of care as in the past. And to get every new treatment, however expensive, health spending has to rise *much faster* still. To pay for this within a National Health Service, taxes would have to rise a lot.

The real issue is *scarcity*: on what taxes to spend our limited resources? Do we have fewer teachers and televisions in order to pay taxes and divert more resources to health? If not, we can't avoid rationing health care. This rationing can be done via markets (charging for health care so people choose to have less) or by rules (limiting access to treatment). Society's decision affects what is produced, how it is produced and, dramatically in this example, for whom it is produced.

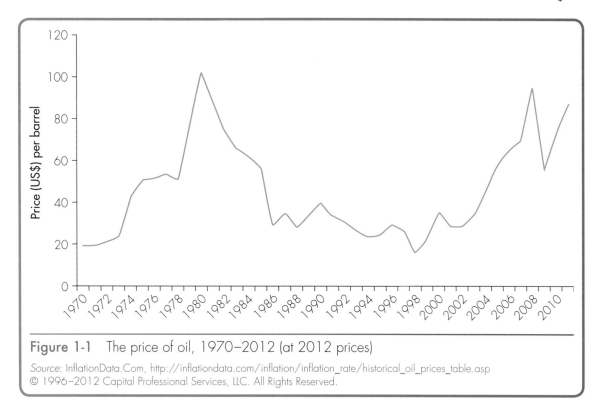

Figure 1-1 The price of oil, 1970–2012 (at 2012 prices)

Source: InflationData.Com, http://inflationdata.com/inflation/inflation_rate/historical_oil_prices_table.asp
© 1996–2012 Capital Professional Services, LLC. All Rights Reserved.

Everybody knows that oil prices have risen rapidly in the last few years. Figure 1-1 shows the history of oil prices since 1970. To remove the effect of inflation, we adjust oil prices for changes in the prices of goods and services as a whole, isolating how oil prices have moved relative to other goods and services.[1] The answer is shown in Figure 1-1.

Figure 1-1 shows that oil prices are much higher than in the 1990s. Is disaster around the corner? We can learn from what happened last time oil prices were higher, in the early 1980s. What we know is that such high prices induced changes in people's behaviour. Consumers found ways to economize on expensive energy (smaller cars, relocation to reduce commuting distances, more effort on insulating the roof to save energy) and producers looked harder for new sources of oil and to invent alternative energy sources as substitutes for oil. Figure 1-1 showed that the market 'solved' the problem of high oil prices in the early 1980s. As behaviour changed, demand for oil fell and supply increased. The price came down again.

Although booming demand from China and India has bid up oil prices sharply in recent years, oil prices are unlikely to remain near $100/barrel indefinitely. Many new energy sources become profitable if they are competing with oil prices over $50/barrel. It may take a decade to get these onstream, but the more confident people are that high oil prices are going to last, the greater will be the incentive to discover and introduce alternative forms of energy, thereby reducing the price of oil again. It is this self-correcting feature of markets that is their greatest strength.

---

[1] Figure 1-1 happens to use 2012 as the baseline for the price of goods and services as a whole, but we could have used any other year instead provided we use the same year throughout the sample. That is why the figure refers to measuring things 'at 2012 prices'. It takes the actual price of oil, for example in 1990, then scales it up proportionately to reflect the rise in general prices of goods and services between 1990 and 2012. The fluctuations shown in Figure 1-1 therefore reflect the scarcity of oil rather than general inflation.

Figure 1-2 Market orientation

How might resources be allocated if markets did not exist?

In a **command economy,** government planners decide what, how and for whom goods and services are made. Households, firms and workers are then told what to do.

Central planning is complicated. No country has ever made all decisions by central command. However, in China, Cuba and the former Soviet bloc there used to be a lot of central direction and planning. The state owned land and factories, and made key decisions about what people should consume, how goods should be made and how much people should work.

Imagine that you had to run the city where you live. Think of the food, clothing and housing allocation decisions you would have to make. How would you decide how things were made, and who got what? These decisions are being made every day in your own city, but chiefly through the mechanism of markets and prices.

The opposite extreme from central planning is a reliance on markets in which prices can freely adjust. In 1776, Adam Smith's *The Wealth of Nations* argued that people pursuing their self-interest would be led 'as by an invisible hand' to do things in the interest of society as a whole.

In a **free market economy**, prices adjust to reconcile desires and scarcity.

Hoping to become a millionaire, you invent the mobile phone. Although motivated by self-interest, you make society better off by creating new jobs and using existing resources more productively. In a free market, people pursue their self-interest without government restrictions. A command economy allows little individual economic freedom, since decisions are taken by the state. Between these extremes is the mixed economy.

In a **mixed economy**, the government and private sector interact in solving economic problems.

The government affects economic activity by taxation, subsidies and the provision of services such as defence and the police force. It also regulates the extent to which individuals may pursue their own self-interest. All countries are mixed economies, though some have freer markets than others, as Figure 1-2 shows.

Box 1-2

Stagnation under central planning versus crashes under market capitalism

During 1989–91, the Soviet bloc abandoned Marxist central planning and began transition to a market economy. The Soviet bloc grew rapidly before the 1970s, but then stagnated. Economic failure brought down the Berlin Wall. Whereas Russian Prime Minister Nikita Kruschev had boasted to President J.F. Kennedy that the Russian model would bury western capitalism, it was the latter that survived. The euphoria of pro-marketeers was typified by the publication in 1992 of *The End of History and the Last Man* by Francis Fukuyama, which argued that historical evolution had converged on western liberal democracy which was now here to say. The subsequent success of India and China as they increase the role of the market only seems to confirm the diagnosis.

Key difficulties that emerged under central planning were:

- **Information overload** Planners could not keep track of all the details of economic activity. Machinery rusted because nobody came to pick it up, crops rotted because storage and distribution were not co-ordinated. The further planned economies got away from the original baseline of the market, the greater these problems became.

- **Bad incentives** Complete job security undermined work incentives. Since planners could monitor quantity more easily than quality, firms met output targets by skimping on quality. Without environmental standards, firms polluted at will. Central planning led to low-quality goods and an environmental disaster.

- **Insufficient competition** Planners believed big was beautiful. One tractor factory served the Soviets from Latvia to Vladivostok. But large scale deprived planners of information from competing firms, making it hard to assess managerial efficiency. Similarly, without electoral competition, it was impossible to sack governments making economic mistakes.

If market economies make a mistake, the sharp change in the price then provides an incentive to rectify that mistake; under central planning, the mistake can be perpetuated indefinitely. Conversely, when we continue to argue for centuries about which system is better, it is useful because each have some merits and no system in unambiguously superior in all circumstances. The triumphalism of the pro-market economists and politicians took a bit of a knock after the financial crash of 2007–08 and the subsequent period of austerity and slow growth that we have yet to escape. What caused the crash?

Why did markets not see it coming? And why can they not reverse more quickly its lingering consequences? Case study 1-2 later in this chapter explains in detail the origins of the crash. Essentially, it derived from overconfidence in lending that was subsequently shown to have been based on unjustifiable optimism about the value of houses and other long-term assets. Since US housing mortgages had been traded around the world in a second-hand market, the collapse in their value affected financial institutions in almost every country, even where they had had no initial connection to the US housing market. Panic set in, and banks that had lasted a century or more were suddenly in trouble. The famous US investment bank Lehman Brothers went bust in September 2008, causing a worldwide financial crisis. UK banks also had to be rescued by the government.

If central planning can get further and further divorced from reality, are not markets vulnerable to the same accusation? For most goods and services, the market price provides a crucial signal about scarcity that is a reliable guide to the adjustment now required. When things get dear, we need to make more and buy fewer. When things get cheap, we can buy more and want to produce fewer.

If central planning can get further and further divorced from reality, are not markets vulnerable to the same accusation? For most goods and services, the market price provides a crucial signal about scarcity that is a reliable guide to the adjustment now required. When things get dear, we need to make more and buy fewer. When things get cheap, we can buy more and want to produce fewer.

▶

Having explained why asset prices are so volatile in a market economy, we can also explain why the subsequent recovery has been painful and protracted. The value of all outstanding assets is much larger than the annual flow of income or output of the economy per annum. Hence, a serious downgrading of asset values is a large number relative to national output. Where people, banks or governments find themselves with debts that are now large relative to their smaller asset valuation, it takes years of extra saving out of income to restore the desired relationship between assets and debts. It is a long hard slog, taking a decade or more in the case of a deep crisis.

Market capitalism has always been vulnerable to speculation and occasional crashes in asset prices – famous historical examples include the South Sea Bubble (a company trading in the colonies) and the Dutch tulip mania (when the price of bulbs briefly exceeded the price of houses) – but it is also the case that over centuries capitalism has proved resilient and successful.

Positive and normative

> **Positive economics** deals with scientific explanation of how the economy works. **Normative economics** offers recommendations based on personal value judgements.

Positive economics aims to explain how the economy works, and thus how it will respond to changes. It formulates and tests propositions of the form: if cigarettes are taxed, their price will rise. In this sense, positive economics is like natural sciences such as physics, geology or astronomy.

Many propositions in positive economics are widely agreed to be correct. As in any science, there are some unresolved questions where disagreement remains. Research in progress will resolve some of these issues, but new issues will arise, providing scope for further research.

Normative economics is based on subjective value judgements, not on the search for objective truth. Should resources be switched from health to education? The answer is a subjective value judgement, based on the feelings of the person making the statement. Economics can't show that health is more or less desirable than education. However, it can answer the positive question of what quantity of extra health could be achieved by giving up a particular quantity of education.

Micro and macro

Economics has many branches. Labour economics deals with employment and wages, urban economics with housing and transport and monetary economics with interest rates and exchange rates. However, a different classification cuts across these branches.

> **Microeconomics** makes a detailed study of individual decisions about particular commodities.

For example, we can study why individual households prefer cars to bicycles and how firms decide whether to make cars or bicycles. Comparing the markets for cars and for bicycles, we can study the relative price of cars and bicycles and the output of these two goods.

However, in studying the *whole* economy, such detailed analysis gets very complicated. We need to simplify to keep the analysis manageable. Microeconomics offers a detailed treatment of one part of the economy – for example, what is happening to cars – but ignores interactions with the rest of the economy in order to keep the analysis manageable.

However, if these wider interactions are too important to be swept under the carpet, another simplification must be found.

> **Macroeconomics** analyses interactions in the economy as a whole.

To be able to study the economy as a whole deliberately simplifies the individual building blocks of the analysis. Macroeconomists don't divide consumer goods into cars, bicycles, TVs and iPods. Rather, they study a single bundle called 'consumer goods' in order to focus on the interaction between household shopping sprees and firms' decisions about building new factories.

Case study 1-1   'Making poverty history'?

Rock stars, such as Bono and Bob Geldoff, sometimes organize concerts to demonstrate that people in the world's rich countries want their politicians to intervene in the world economy to help the poor of the world, particularly in Africa. Key parts of this are getting the debts of the poor countries written off, more aid for the poor, and a new deal on world trade. How would these changes affect what, how and for whom things are produced in the world?

The effect of debt write-offs and more aid

Debtors are supposed to pay interest and repay the money they originally borrowed. So, poor indebted countries have to use a big part of their national income just to pay foreign creditors, reducing what is left to spend on food and other necessities of a decent life, to say nothing of resources to invest in enhancing future productivity. Since poor countries are often subsistence farmers, this means less money for irrigation and livestock, and less money to invest in building decent housing and providing clean water. Conversely, rich countries not only enjoy their own high output, they also get interest income from their loans to poor countries. So, people in rich countries can afford more BMWs and flat screen TVs.

Writing off debt of poor countries will not merely mean that the poor can afford a little more and the rich a little less, it will also mean that the world produces fewer BMWs but digs more wells in Africa. Also, transferring production from mechanized rich countries to labour-intensive poor countries will affect not merely for whom goods are produced and what goods are produced, but also how production is undertaken.

Increasing aid to poor countries has similar effects. By transferring resources from rich to poor, it affects the *for whom* question directly. In turn this affects *what* is produced: more of what the poor want, and less of what the rich want. Highly mechanized production in rich countries will be a little less, whereas labour-intensive production by poor countries will expand.

Trade reform

In rich countries — such as those in the EU, and the US and Japan — domestic farmers are heavily subsidized and there are large taxes on foreign imports of food. Developed countries tell themselves that they are protecting their rural environment and ensuring a national food supply in time of war. But they are also destroying food producers in poor countries.

The World Trade Organization exists to negotiate and implement agreements on the rules and tariffs governing international trade. In the last 50 years, the WTO has agreed many reductions in import tariffs, but has yet to secure agreement to cut trade protection of farmers in rich countries.

Poor countries rely greatly on agriculture. If they cannot sell their output in rich countries, their produce fetches only low prices, trapping poor farmers in poverty. Worse still, if they raise agricultural productivity by the use of better seeds, irrigation or mechanization, they simply bid down the price of their crops, because they have to sell even more agricultural food output to the same poor countries as before.

Suppose the rich countries now allow imports of foreign food on equal terms with those enjoyed by farmers in rich countries. Now African farmers can sell in London and Paris. This has two effects. Food prices fall in London and Paris, where food is now less scarce. But these prices still greatly exceed the prices African farmers previously received when selling only in poor countries. So European consumers are better off (lower food prices) and African farmers benefit (much higher prices than before for their output).

This argument applies whatever the barriers faced by African farmers. It does not matter whether these are import duties into rich countries or subsidies by rich countries to their own farmers. Trade reform has to eliminate both if African agriculture is to prosper, and that might be the largest single contribution that the rich countries could make to ensuring sustainable improvements in the world's poorest countries. Without trade reform, neither aid nor debt relief is likely to make poverty history.

Conversely, the threat to poor countries as a result of the global financial crisis of 2008 is not merely that rich countries may feel less generous in providing aid but that they may be tempted to restore greater levels of trade protection.

Globalization

Globalization has had other effects. For example, the surge in demand for food and raw materials by India and China has bid up commodity prices throughout the world. This effect has meant that poor farmers in Africa and elsewhere have benefited. However, higher prices also reflected lower supply as well as greater demand. Adverse effects of global warming have impoverished areas of rural agriculture in many poor countries. Where this has been the cause of higher food prices, it has been the destruction of rural food producers that has accompanied the rise in food prices. Regardless of the reason for higher food prices, consumers, in poor countries as well as rich countries, have faced a dramatic increase in their cost of living.

 ## How economists think

It is more fun to play tennis if you can serve, and cutting trees is easier with a chainsaw. Every activity or academic discipline has a basic set of tools, which may be tangible, like the dentist's drill, or intangible, like the ability to serve in tennis. To analyse economic issues we use both models and data.

A **model** or **theory** makes assumptions from which it deduces how people behave. It deliberately simplifies reality.

Models omit some details of the real world in order to focus on the essentials. An economist uses a model as a traveller uses a map. A map of London omits traffic lights and roundabouts, but you get a good picture of the best route to take. This simplified picture is easy to follow, yet provides a good guide to actual behaviour.

Data are pieces of evidence about economic behaviour.

The data or facts interact with models in two ways. First, the data help us quantify theoretical relationships. To choose the best route we need some facts about where delays may occur. The model is useful because it tells us which facts to collect. Bridges are more likely to be congested than six-lane motorways.

Second, the data help us to test our models. Like all careful scientists, economists must check that their theories square with the relevant facts. The crucial word is *relevant*. For several decades the number of Scottish dysentery deaths was closely related to the UK inflation rate, but this was a coincidence not the key to a theory of inflation. Without any logical underpinning, the empirical connection eventually broke down. Paying attention to a freak relationship in the data increases neither our economic understanding nor our ability to predict the future.

Economic data

To gather evidence, we can study changes *across groups or regions* at *the same point in time*; or for a single group or region *over time*. Table 1-3 shows a *cross-section* of unemployment rates in different countries in 2012. All European countries are suffering from the after-effects of the financial crash, but Mediterranean countries have been hit particularly hard. Table 1-4 shows a *time-series* of UK house prices between 1960 and 2012.

Table 1-3 Unemployment by country (percentage of labour force), 2012

UK	France	Spain	Greece
8.8	8.0	22.7	18.7

Source: OECD, *Economic Outlook*

The average price of a new house rose from £3100 in 1963 to £216 000 in 2011. Are houses really 70 times as expensive as in 1960? Not once we allow for inflation, which also raised incomes and the ability to buy houses.

Nominal values measure prices at the time of measurement. **Real values** adjust nominal values for changes in the general price level.

In the UK the consumer price index (CPI) measures the price of a basket of goods bought by a typical household. Inflation caused a big rise in the CPI during 1963–2011. The third row of Table 1-4 calculates an index of real house prices, expressed as if the CPI had always been at the level it attained in the year 2011. It shows how house prices would have changed if there had been no general inflation in the price of goods as a whole.

An **index number** expresses data relative to a given base value.

Comparing 1963 and 2011, but allowing for inflation in the price of goods and services in general, real house prices rose sixfold, from £33 800 to £190 000. Most of the 70-fold rise in nominal house prices in the top row of Table 1-4 was actually caused by inflation.

Table 1-4 UK house prices (average price of a new house)

	1963	1983	2011
House price (£000s)	3.1	32.9	216
CPI (2007 = 100)	9.3	57.4	114
Real price of houses (2007 £000s)	33.3	57.3	190

Source: ONS, *Economic Trends*

Box 1-3

Economic thinking down the ages

Classical economists of the nineteenth century assumed that prices adjusted pretty quickly to balance supply and demand. This meant that scarcity reflected an appropriate balance between our ability to produce and our desire to consume. This argument appeared to apply not just to markets for goods and services but also to the market for labour, balancing the wish to work and the need for workers. In such a world, the principal roles for the government were to provide stability and to ensure a modicum of fairness through the tax system.

Stability was provided in part by the Gold Standard, which linked the printing of money to the available supply of gold, which could be augmented only slowly by goldmining. Over 100 years there was no systematic tendency to inflation since there was no flood of money being created. The Gold Standard also fixed exchange rates between countries, in effect an early form of monetary union. Countries in trouble in the nineteenth century – just like Greece and Spain today within the Eurozone – were supposed to pursue austerity, bidding down their prices and wages, until they became competitive again and recovered. As today, this adjustment often took a long time.

During the First World War, the Gold Standard was suspended and countries printed money to pay for the war, creating lots of inflation and by different amounts in different countries. Restoring the Gold Standard in the 1920s was no easy matter. Countries like the UK experienced general strikes as they tried (too hard) to bash down wages in order to enhance international competitiveness within the restored fixed exchange rate system. After the US stock market crash of 1929, countries abandoned the Gold Standard, floated their exchange rates, but could not all gain competitiveness at the expense of each other. The interwar period convinced many that free markets were not necessarily the best answer.

The British economist John Maynard Keynes argued that markets did not always change the price of goods and services quickly enough to restore the balance of supply and demand at a point compatible with full employment. He argued that the government should step in to improve the performance of markets, boosting demand when it was insufficient. This they could do by cutting interest rates, cutting taxes or boosting government spending. In response to those who argued that markets would get it right eventually, he acidly retorted 'in the long run we are all dead'.

Keynes' views dominated postwar thinking in the 1940s and 1950s, as governments aimed to manipulate overall demand close to the level of full capacity and full employment. For a couple of decades this appeared a remarkable success. But gradually inflation started to rise, and unemployment also began to increase.

The American economist Milton Friedman argued that too much focus on output manipulation had meant that policy makers had forgotten that, in the absence of growing output, printing money was likely simply to bid up the price of goods. Of equal importance, Keynes had focused so much on demand that he had rather tended to take supply for granted – overall output would drift up by 2–3 per cent a year because of population growth and productivity improvements.

What actually happened in the late 1960s and early 1970s was that the economy's ability to supply became reduced. Policy makers noted the falling output and incorrectly diagnosed the cause as too little demand. Policies that boosted demand when supply had already fallen simply caused a big inflation, for which the 1970s is famous. The rest of the century was devoted to policies that gradually tried to improve supply through better incentives and greater investment, coupled with a framework for creating demand stability.

Politicians themselves do not always make the best policy makers – too frequently narrow political advantage gets in the way of sound economic judgement. Economists thought they had cracked the problem by making central banks – such as the Bank of England and the US Federal Reserve – independent of political influence. The benevolent technocrats used interest rate policy to stabilize demand around full capacity, giving steady output growth and low inflation. For more than 10 years, the formula worked wonderfully.

It also created a false sense of security. It was precisely this belief that everything was being safely kept under control that encouraged bankers to take bigger and bigger risks in the pursuit of profit, leading to the crash of 2007–08.

Economic models

After a career in business, you become head of the London Underground. The Tube is losing money. You want to change the level of fares to get more revenue. Revenue is the P, the price of a Tube fare, multiplied by Q, the number of passengers. You can set the fare, but what determines the number of passengers?

The number of passengers will fall if the Tube fare is higher, but will rise if passengers have more income to spend. You now have a barebones model of the demand for Tube journeys. It depends on Tube fares and income.

Higher Tube fares *add* directly to revenue, by raising P and hence revenue per passenger, but also *reduce* revenue by reducing Q as fewer people take the Tube. Theory alone can't tell you the best fare to maximize $P''Q$. The answer depends on how much Q falls when you raise P.

Some empirical research may establish the facts. Experimental sciences, including many branches of physics and chemistry, conduct controlled experiments in a laboratory, varying one input at a time while holding constant all the other relevant inputs. However, like astronomy and medicine, economics is primarily a non-experimental science. Astronomers can't suspend planetary motion to study the earth in isolation, and doctors rarely poison people just to see what happens. Similarly, economists don't create 50 per cent unemployment to see if wages will then fall.

Most economic data are collected while many of the relevant factors are simultaneously changing. We need to disentangle their separate influences. To make a start, we can pick out two of the variables in which we are interested, pretending the other variables remain constant.

A **scatter diagram** plots pairs of values simultaneously observed for two different variables.

Suppose we measure the Tube fare (pence per passenger kilometre) on the vertical axis, and Tube revenue on the horizontal axis (£m in total revenue), both adjusted for inflation by using constant prices. Figure 1-3 shows how this might look. We plot a scatter diagram in which each point represents a different year. Years of low fares tend to be years of low revenue. On average, higher revenue is associated with higher fares.

It seems that higher fares *cause* lower revenue, but we should not jump to conclusions. Theoretical reasoning suggests other things, such as the introduction of the congestion charge for vehicles in central London, might have led to a sharp rise in people's willingness to use the Tube; and simple inspection of the data shown in Figure 1-3 suggests that fares alone are not the only explanation. If fares were the whole story, we would expect to see the data points lying neatly along a line or curve showing the relationship between fares and revenue.

Other things equal

When one 'output' is affected by many 'inputs' we can always draw a two-dimensional diagram relating the output to *one* of the inputs, treating the other inputs as given. Moving along this line shows how the highlighted input affects the output. However, if any *other* input changes, we need to show this as a shift in the relationship between output and our highlighted input.

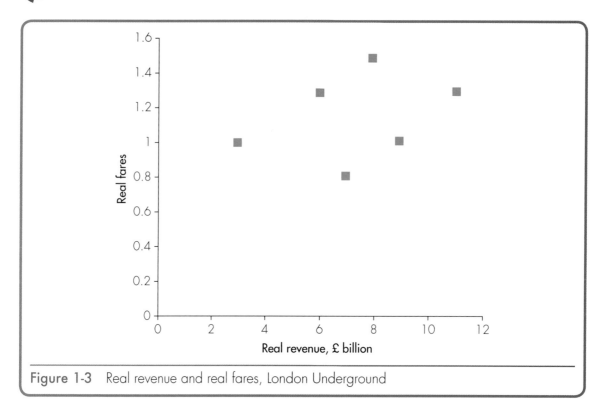

Figure 1-3   Real revenue and real fares, London Underground

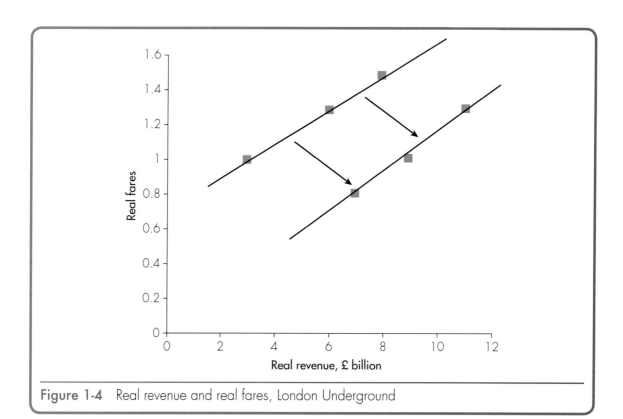

Figure 1-4   Real revenue and real fares, London Underground

Other things equal is a device for looking at the relation between two variables, but remembering other variables also matter.

Figure 1-4 reinterprets the data in Figure 1-3 as showing two parallel lines, one before the introduction of the congestion charge and the other, further to the right, after the introduction of the charge. Now the observed data fit the theory much more neatly, and reverses out previous conclusions: now it becomes apparent that higher fares are positively correlated with higher revenue, once we control for non-price factors influencing Tube usage.

Other things equal, higher fares go with higher revenue. Changing the congestion charge alters one of these other things, and we have to show this as a shift in the entire relationship between fares and revenue.

Case study 1-2   The crash of 2008

The credit crunch has its roots in the US housing market, where poor families were encouraged to buy their homes with mortgages whose terms were initially easy but then became tougher. These mortgages were then securitized – aggregated into bundles and resold to other creditors who had no direct knowledge of the households doing the borrowing. When the households got into trouble making the repayments, many financial firms around the world owned assets whose value started to tumble. House prices fell, causing further fears, and wiping out the value of yet more assets on financial balance sheets.

As panic spread, banks became reluctant to lend, causing problems for other borrowers who in normal times would have had no difficulty borrowing. The market for new mortgages almost completely dried up, and banks became reluctant to lend to other banks in case they too were in trouble. The first chart shows the collapse of mortgage lending, which has yet to show any signs of recovery. The second chart shows the collapse of the share price of Barclays Bank, from around £8 to around £3 per share between February 2007 and September 2008, before eventually recovering to between £2 and £3. Barclays was one of the banks that did not need a government bailout; others, such as Royal Bank of Scotland (RBS), Lloyds TSB and Halifax Bank of Scotland, fared even worse, and continued to make losses as late as 2012.

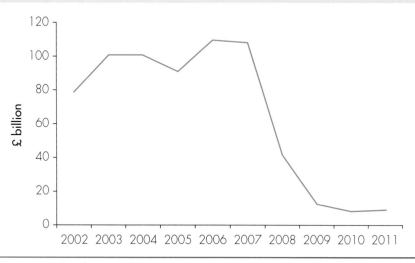

Net UK mortgage lending, £ billion

Source: Bank of England

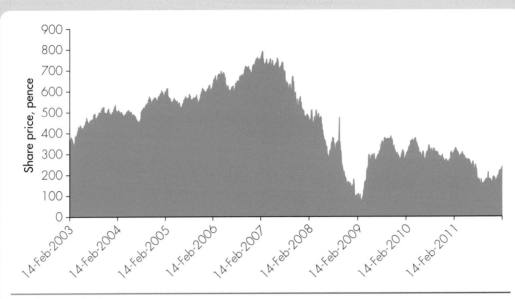

Barclays Bank share price, pence

Source: www.yahoo.co.uk/finance

By autumn 2008, a surge of failures took place: the entire US investment banking industry was eliminated, the largest US insurance company went bankrupt, and the largest retail banking failure in US history occurred. In the UK, Bradford & Bingley (the market leader in buy-to-let mortgages) was wound up, with its deposits being taken over by Abbey (part of the Santander group), HBOS had to be rescued by Lloyds TSB, and the government became the majority shareholder in RBS. High-profile banking failures also occurred throughout the rest of Europe. Even the Archbishop of Canterbury wrote an article in the *Spectator* defending the views of Karl Marx on the evils of unbridled capitalism. What does this example tell us about the market economy?

First, financial markets and asset valuations can be very volatile – they depend on what people guess other people guess other people think things are worth.

Second, healthy markets require some regulation to prevent excessive swings of optimism and pessimism to which human beings are sometimes subject, especially when acting in groups (just think of the average football crowd!). After the financial crash of 1929, US regulators decided to make their banking system less risky by preventing deposit-taking institutions from actively speculating for their own direct gain. Over the next 80 years, these regulations were dismantled with the aim of promoting greater competition. Thus, a second lesson of the crash is likely to be that banks are more tightly regulated in future.

Why can't we simply decide the right amount of regulation and then stick to it forever? In part, it is because each generation is not very good at learning the lessons that its predecessors had to learn. Bright, ambitious young traders quickly appreciate the potential gain from taking greater risks without fully appreciating the costs also entailed, conclude that their superiors are be coming old-fashioned and gradually their appetite for risk increases. It may be no accident that we have one big financial setback in each generation, since that is all that cools things down again.

Nor is this anything new. During the Dutch tulip mania of 1637 speculation in tulip bulbs reached amazing heights, prices reaching up to 20 times the annual income of a skilled craftsman, before subsequently crashing back to reality. President Bush remarked in July 2008 that Wall Street got drunk and then had a hangover. What are the elements of an intelligent solution to the problem?

The banking system needs to function; without it market capitalism does not work. This means that banks need an injection of new assets to make them solvent again. What are the possible sources of this injection? The private sector solution is that banks invite people to buy additional shares, thereby injecting much needed financial capital. This may work if it is believed that the crisis is temporary – for then share prices can be expected subsequently to increase – but is unlikely to work if the crisis deepens, for then people will worry that share prices may fall further. If the private sector will not volunteer to inject the required money into bank finances, the only remaining source is the public purse. Taxpayers may resent bailing out rich bankers but the reason that it has to be swallowed is that the cost to the rest of us will be even higher if we allow a collapse of the banking system.

In addition, the Bank of England can cut interest rates on its lending to banks, not merely in the hope that banks will then cut interest rates that they charge to borrowers but also in the knowledge that banks may increase their profit margins and thereby restore their own solvency. However, this is a slow process.

Finally, to the extent that swings in confidence are reversible later, acquisition by the government of the bad debts of banks is not entirely taxpayers' money down the drain. Once the crisis is over, some of these assets will gain value again. In principle, the government could even make a profit by temporarily holding assets that subsequently recover in value. This is more likely the shorter the duration of the crisis. The longer it drags on, the more values are likely to erode as the real economy is affected, and the larger the ultimate burden on taxpayers. At today's share prices, the value of the UK government's stake in RBS is still well below the value of the bailout that the bank received from the government in 2008.

How markets work

Some markets (shops, fruit stalls) physically bring together the buyer and seller. Other markets (the Stock Exchange) operate through intermediaries (stockbrokers) who transact business on behalf of clients. E-business is conducted on the Internet. These markets perform the same economic function. Prices adjust to equate the quantity people wish to buy and the quantity people wish to sell. By making the price of a Ferrari ten times the price of a Ford, the market ensures that the output and sale of Fords greatly exceeds the output and sale of Ferraris. Prices guide society in choosing what, how and for whom to produce.

To think about a typical market we need demand, the behaviour of buyers, and supply, the behaviour of sellers. Then we can study how a market works in practice.

Demand is the quantity buyers wish to purchase at each conceivable price.

Demand is not a particular quantity but a full description of the quantity buyers would purchase at each and every possible price. Even when food is free, only a finite amount is wanted. People get sick from eating too much. As the price of food rises, the quantity demanded falls, other things equal.

Supply is the quantity sellers wish to sell at each conceivable price.

Again, supply is a full description of the quantity that sellers would like to sell at each possible price. Nobody would supply anything at all if the price was zero and they got no revenue from sales. At higher prices, people are able and willing to supply more. The quantity supplied rises.

The **equilibrium price** clears the market. It is the price at which the quantity supplied equals the quantity demanded.

Suppose the price is below the equilibrium price. With a low price, the quantity demanded is high but the quantity supplied is low. There is a shortage, or *excess demand*, a shorthand for the more accurate statement 'the quantity demanded exceeds the quantity supplied *at this price*'.

Conversely, at any price above the equilibrium price, the quantity supplied is high but the quantity demanded is low. Sellers have unsold stock. To describe this surplus, economists use the shorthand *excess supply*, meaning 'excess quantity supplied at this price'. Only at the equilibrium price are quantity demanded and supplied the same. The market clears. People can buy or sell as much as they want at the equilibrium price.

Is the market automatically in equilibrium? Suppose the price is initially too high. There is unsold stock and excess supply. Sellers have to cut the price to clear their stock. Cutting the price has two effects. It raises the quantity demanded, and reduces the quantity supplied. Both effects reduce the excess supply. Price-cutting continues until the equilibrium price is reached and excess supply is eliminated.

Conversely, if the price is too low, the quantity demanded is large but the quantity supplied is small. With excess demand, sellers run out of stock and charge higher prices. Prices rise until the equilibrium price is reached, excess demand is eliminated and the market clears. Prices adjust until equilibrium is reached, after which things settle down at that level.

By behaving in this way, prices help resolve the basic questions of economics – what, how and for whom goods are produced. The goods (and services) produced are those that people are prepared to buy at the equilibrium price, which is also necessary to induce producers to supply those goods. Until recently, most households could only envy the plasma screen TVs they occasionally saw in airports or TV newsrooms. At the price that they cost to produce, there was little household demand apart from that from popstars and footballers' wives. However, technological advances, affecting how LCD screen TVs are made, are steadily reducing the equilibrium price, making them increasingly affordable. In 1985, mobile phones had yet to arrive. By 2011, almost every student had one, not merely for ringing their friends but also for taking photos and accessing the Internet. Lower prices had brought them within everyday reach.

Price controls

Price controls may be floor prices (minimum prices) or ceiling prices (maximum prices).

A **price control** is a government regulation to fix the price.

Price ceilings may be introduced when a sharp fall in supply occurs. Wartime scarcity of food would mean high prices and hardship for the poor. Faced with a national food shortage, a government may impose a price ceiling on food so that poor people can afford some food.

Suppose, due to a shortage of wheat and flour, the equilibrium price of a loaf of bread would have been £15. Not a good time to be a student or a pensioner. To try to help out, the government imposes a price ceiling of £2 a loaf. Compared with the equilibrium, the quantity demanded is now much higher, but, at £2 a loaf rather than £15, bakers are bound to want to produce even less.

With a higher quantity demanded but a lower quantity supplied, there is now excess demand, long bread queues, and two outcomes. The lucky people who manage to buy a loaf at £2 get cheaper bread than before, but with fewer total loaves for sale, some people actually get less than before. Also, illegal markets emerge as bakers find willing buyers for bread at prices above the legal price ceiling of £2.

Whether or not this system is 'fairer' than the free market system depends in part on how society responds to this bread rationing. If everyone abides by the rules, bread may be distributed more evenly across people than in a free market when the advantage of being rich would be enhanced in times of food scarcity. However, it is also possible that bread rationing becomes corrupt, and bakers favour their friends or take bribes. Since excess demand means that some people may get nothing, it is possible that it is always the poor and the disadvantaged who get nothing. In an effort to avoid this, ceiling prices may be accompanied by government-organized rationing, to ensure that available supply is shared out fairly, independently of ability to pay. Provided the government itself is not corrupt, this may be a reasonable compromise in times of acute food shortage.

A *ceiling price* aims to reduce the price for consumers. Conversely, a *floor price* aims to raise the price for suppliers. A national minimum wage is a floor price for labour. If this is set above the equilibrium wage that would equate the quantity of labour supplied and demanded in a free market, the minimum wage will have two effects. It will raise the quantity of labour that workers wish to supply, but reduce the quantity of labour that firms wish to demand. There is excess supply of labour, total work falls, but the fortunate workers who obtain work will earn a higher wage than they would have done in a free market.

Many governments also set floor prices for agricultural products, and then buy up the excess supply unwanted by the private sector. European butter prices are set above the free market equilibrium price as part of the Common Agricultural Policy. European governments have bought massive stocks of butter that otherwise would have been unsold at the floor price. Hence the famous 'butter mountain' – and of course it has been necessary to prevent African producers accessing the EU agricultural market to take advantage of these artificially high food prices.

Case study 1-3   Green piece

Our planet is running out of rainforests and fish stocks. Environmental campaigners, such as Greenpeace, aim to raise awareness and encourage voters to demand that their politicians take action to save the planet before it is too late.

Why do we manage the environment so badly? An economist's response is 'because we don't price the environment like other commodities'. Earlier, we discussed how the market 'solved' the problem of scarcity after oil producers in OPEC (Organization of Petroleum Exporting Countries) collectively restricted oil production after 1973 in order to make oil more scarce, and then raise its equilibrium price (see again Figure 1-1).

But the high price did not stick for long. We explained that users of oil found ways to use less and non-OPEC oil producers – firms such as Shell, BP and Exxon – increased their exploration activity and found it worthwhile extracting oil from deep fields previously considered too expensive.

If market pricing worked for oil, why not price the environment, using markets and high prices to encourage people to look after the environment once it starts to get scarce?

Until now, the reason has been technology. Anyone can walk in a field, dump rubbish after dark, pump chemicals into a river, or drive down a public street. Gradually, however, electronic monitoring of usage is getting easier and cheaper. It will then be possible to treat the environment as another commodity to be marketed. This will give rise to a vigorous debate about the 'what, how and for whom' questions.

We know how to charge cars for using a particular street at a particular time. A smart card in the car could pick up signals as it passed various charge points. The driver would get a monthly bill like an itemized phone bill. Rush-hour traffic would pay more when congestion was severe. The 'for whom' question could also be addressed. Residents could get a flat-rate annual payment, in exchange for supporting road pricing. Pricing the environment has a big advantage. It introduces a feedback mechanism, however crude, so that when society makes mistakes an alarm bell rings *automatically*. The price of scarce things rises.

Many economists think that a 'carbon tax' on emission of the gases that induce climate change is an important part of the solution to global warming. In one sense, it does not matter whether UK oil prices are high because the UK government deliberately levied a tax or because the Chinese boom bid up the world price of oil. Either way, UK consumers will economize on the use of oil. To that extent, when world prices for oil increase, the UK government could reduce fuel taxes a bit, as the transport industry often argues. But the two situations are not identical. When the Chinese boom bids up oil prices, industrial activity in China is adding further to global warming and environmental deterioration. If anything, European governments need to redouble their environmental efforts rather than ease up by reducing fuel taxes.

- Economics is the study of what, how and for whom society produces. The central economic problem is to reconcile the conflict between people's unlimited wants and society's limited ability to make goods and services to meet these demands.
- Industrial countries rely extensively on markets to allocate resources. Prices reconcile production and consumption decisions.
- In a command economy, central planners decide what, how and for whom things are produced.
- Modern economies are mixed, relying mainly on the market but with a big dose of government intervention.
- Positive economics studies how the economy actually behaves. Normative economics makes prescriptions about what should be done.
- Microeconomics gives a detailed analysis of particular activities. Macroeconomics focuses on the entire economy, but simplifies the building blocks in order to keep track of the main interactions.
- A model is a deliberate simplification of reality.
- Data or facts suggest relationships to be explained. Having formulated theories, we use data to test our hypotheses and to quantify the effects implied.
- Index numbers express data relative to a base value. The consumer price index is the average price of things bought by consumers. Inflation is the annual growth rate in the CPI.
- Nominal (current price) variables are valued at the prices when the variable was measured. Real (constant price) variables adjust nominal variables for changes over time in the general level of prices.
- Scatter diagrams plot the relation between two variables. A line through these points shows their average relationship, other things equal. If a relevant 'other thing' changes, we need to plot data separately for the different subperiods.
- Demand is the quantity that buyers wish to buy at each price. Other things equal, the lower the price, the higher the quantity demanded.
- Supply is the quantity that sellers wish to sell at each price. Other things equal, the higher the price, the higher the quantity supplied.
- The market clears, or is in equilibrium, when the price equates the quantity supplied and the quantity demanded. At prices below the equilibrium price, excess demand (shortage) then raises the price. At prices above the equilibrium price, excess supply (surplus) then reduces the price. In a free market, deviations from the equilibrium price are self-correcting.
- An effective price ceiling must lie *below* the free market equilibrium price. It then reduces the quantity supplied, raises the quantity demanded and creates excess demand. An effective price floor must lie *above* the free market equilibrium price. It then reduces the quantity demanded and raises the quantity supplied, creating excess supply. The government may buy up this excess supply.

Review questions

To check your answers to these questions, go to pages 374–5.

1 How are the problems what, how and for whom settled within your own family?

2 Which of the following are scarce: (a) water in the desert, (b) water in a rainforest, (c) economics textbooks, (d) hours a day for work, rest and play?

3 An economy has five workers. Each worker can make four cakes or three shirts. (a) How many cakes can society get if it does without shirts? (b) How many shirts can it get if it does without cakes? (c) What is the opportunity cost of making a shirt?

4 Which statements are positive and which are normative? (a) Taxing cigarettes reduces the quantity sold. (b) Cigarettes should be highly taxed. (c) Brits earn more than Poles. (d) Poles should work harder. (e) All Africans earn high salaries.

5 If markets are so good, why do sergeant majors give orders rather than buy military services from private soldiers?

6 Society abolishes higher education. Students have to find jobs immediately. If there are no jobs available, how do wages and prices adjust so that those who want jobs can find them?

7 At the start of the twenty-first century, Europeans are richer than Africans. Give three reasons for this, and propose one policy change that could help close the gap.

8 The table below shows a student's annual income and the number of times that she visits a club each year. (a) Plot a scatter diagram. (b) Try to fit a line through these points. (c) Suggest a relation between income and clubbing. (d) Which causes which?

EASY

Income £	1000	2000	3000	4000
Number of club visits	17	23	32	38

9 You are hired as a consultant to advise on whether the level of crime is affected by the fraction of people unemployed. (a) How would you test this idea? What data would you want? (b) What 'other things equal' problems would you bear in mind?

10 If economics can't conduct controlled laboratory experiments, can it be a science? Can all sciences conduct controlled experiments?

11 Use the data in Table 1-4 to plot a scatter diagram of the relation between nominal house prices and the consumer price index. Is this time-series data or a cross-section relationship?

12 Madonna charges high prices to get into her concerts. (a) Why can she charge such high prices? (b) Does this mean that if she charged higher prices still, even more people would want to come?

13 Why are these statements wrong? (a) The purpose of a theory is to let you ignore the facts. (b) People have feelings and act haphazardly. It is misguided to reduce their actions to scientific laws.

14 Given the data for mobile phones, find the equilibrium price and quantity.

Price	10	12	14	16	18	20
Quantity demanded	10	9	8	7	6	5
Quantity supplied	3	4	5	7	8	9

EASY

15 What is the excess supply or demand when price is (a) £12 or (b) £20? (c) In which case would you have a long queue at the music shop?

16 Suppose the government raises the minimum wage a lot. (a) What effects do you expect to see in the market for workers? Will employment rise or fall? (b) Could trade unions still be in favour of the policy? (c) Is it likely employers would favour the policy?

17 Why are these statements wrong? (a) Manchester United, being a more famous football club than Wrexham, will always find it easier to fill its stadium. (b) The European 'butter mountain' shows how productivity can be improved when farmers are inspired by the European ideal.

18 Here is a 'for whom' question. Suppose Greek banks owe banks in the UK and Germany £5 billion but can repay only £2 billion. The UK and German governments offer Greece a gift of £1 billion to help them. (a) Does this help Greece? Why or why not? (b) Suppose instead that the £1 billion gift had been to banks in the UK and Germany. Would the outcome be the same as in (a) or different? Explain.

INTERMEDIATE

19 Imagine trying to create a market in 'safe streets'. Someone knocks on your door and asks you to contribute £1000 a year towards the police force. What is your answer? Does this tell us anything about your attitude to safe streets? What amount of safe streets would the market supply through this mechanism?

20 Suppose it is possible in five years' time to make as much energy as we want from biofuels provided the price is the equivalent of at least $80/barrel for oil. (a) What does this imply about the eventual price of oil in, say, ten years' time? (b) Is it possible for oil prices to be substantially above $80/barrel for the next few years? (c) Do higher oil prices in the short run increase or reduce the incentive to look for alternative energy technologies?

DIFFICULT

21 Profitable speculation should stabilize financial markets – successful speculators are those who buy when the price is below the equilibrium price and sell when it has risen, or sell when the price is above the equilibrium price and buy when it has fallen. Why, then, are financial market prices so volatile?

22 **Essay question** Suppose the UK government changes the planning laws to allow the building of 3 million new homes by 2020. Discuss what this is likely to mean for: (a) the price of houses for first-time buyers and (b) the demand for country houses in areas adjacent to new housing developments. (c) Does your answer to (b) depend upon whether new houses are accompanied by new infrastructure (better roads, shops, train services, flood protection)?

DIFFICULT

23 **Essay question** Should the Internet be free? Discuss arguments for and against.

Online Learning Centre

To help you grasp the key concepts of this chapter check out the extra resources posted on the Online Learning Centre at www.mcgraw-hill.co.uk/textbooks/begg.

There are additional case studies, self-test questions, practice exam questions with answers and a graphing tool.

Thinking with diagrams and graphs

Economists use three kinds of logical reasoning – words, graphs and mathematics. In this book, we mainly use words. As you can see, even in Chapter 1 it is sometimes necessary also to use diagrams and graphs. This appendix provides a basic toolkit for those unfamiliar with these tools.

Reading diagrams

You need to be able to read a diagram and understand what it says. A two-dimensional diagram plots the values of one variable on the horizontal axis and values of the other variable on the vertical axis. If there are no other relevant variables, this relationship will usually look like a straight line or a smooth curve. Figure A1-1 shows a hypothetical relationship between two variables: P for price and Q for quantity. We measure quantity values in the vertical Q direction and price values in the horizontal P direction. It is up to us which variable we use on which axis; we could, and often do, show quantity on the horizontal axis and price on the vertical axis instead.

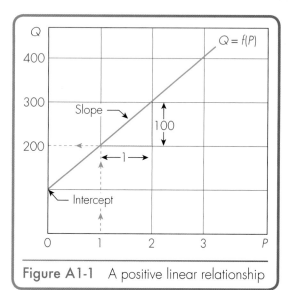

Figure A1-1   A positive linear relationship

In this hypothetical relationship, quantity Q is a function of price P, for which we could use the shorthand $Q = f(P)$. This means that knowing the value of P always tells us the corresponding value of Q. We need to know values of P to make statements about Q. In Figure A1-1, Q is a *positive* function of P. This means that higher values of P imply higher values of Q.

When, as in Figure A1-1, the function is a straight line, only two pieces of information are needed to draw in the entire relationship between Q and P. We need the *intercept* and the *slope*. The intercept is the height of the line when the variable on the horizontal axis is zero. In Figure A1-1 the intercept is 100, the value of Q when $P = 0$.

Lots of different lines could pass through the point at which $Q = 100$ and $P = 0$. The other characteristic is the *slope* of the line, measuring its steepness. The slope tells us how much Q (the variable on the vertical axis) changes each time we increase P (the variable on the horizontal axis) by one unit. In Figure A1-1, the slope is 100. By definition, a straight line has a constant slope. Q rises by 100 whether we move from a price of 1 to 2, or from 2 to 3, or from 3 to 4.

Figure A1-1 shows a *positive* relation between Q and P. Since higher P values are associated with higher Q values, the line slopes *up* as we increase P and move to the right. The line has a positive slope. Figure A1-2 shows a case in which Q is a *negative* function of P. Higher values of P imply smaller Q values. The line has a negative slope.

Economic relationships need not be straight lines or linear relationships. Figure A1-3 shows a nonlinear relationship between two variables Y and X. The slope keeps changing. Each time we raise X by one unit, we get a different rise (or fall) in Y. Consider the relationship between the income tax rate X and income tax revenue Y. When the tax rate is zero, no revenue is raised. When the tax rate is 100 per cent, nobody bothers to work and revenue is again zero. Beginning from a zero tax rate, rises in tax rates initially raise total tax revenue. Beyond some tax rate, further rises in tax rates then reduce tax revenue, which becomes zero by the time the tax rate is 100 per cent. Diagrams display the essence of real-life problems.

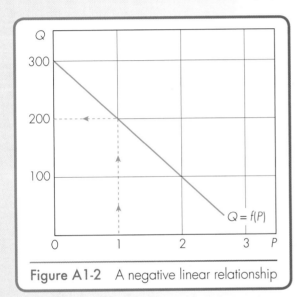

Figure A1-2 A negative linear relationship

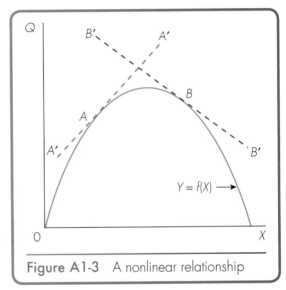

Figure A1-3 A nonlinear relationship

Microeconomics

Demand

A market reconciles the wishes of buyers and sellers. To understand how markets work, we need to examine separately the behaviour of buyers and sellers. In this chapter we explore what determines the choices made by buyers. Once we understand how they make decisions, we can predict how demand will change in response to changes in the environment faced by buyers.

2-1 The demand curve

In 2000, the Mayor of London introduced a congestion charge of £5 a day to drive into central London. Subsequent studies concluded that the effect of this had been to reduce demand for road use in London by up to 20 per cent *relative to what it would otherwise have been*. Of course, as income rose, more and more people could afford cars and booming businesses needed more deliveries by lorry. So vehicle use and congestion did not change a lot *relative to what it had been before*.

However, the correct way in which to judge the impact of a policy change is to compare the subsequent outcome with what would have happened if the policy change had not taken place. Comparison with the past is the wrong comparison. The congestion charge did indeed make a difference.

This success led the mayor to raise the charge to £8 in 2005, and to £10 by 2012. But price is not the only determinant of demand. Demand depends on more than the price of the good or service itself. We need to develop a framework in which to think things through.

In this chapter we explore demand, the behaviour of buyers, in detail. Chapter 3 will discuss supply, the behaviour of sellers. Combining the analysis of demand and supply, we can then deepen our understanding of how markets work.

Demand is the quantity buyers wish to purchase at each conceivable price.

Demand is not a particular quantity but a full description of the quantity buyers would purchase at each and every possible price. We can show this relationship between price and quantity demanded as a *demand curve, DD* in Figure 2-1. This relationship may happen to be a straight line, as shown in the figure, but may often instead be a curve, not a straight line. We use the term demand curve to cover both possibilities.

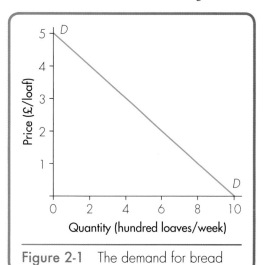

Figure 2-1   The demand for bread

In Figure 2-1, we plot price on the vertical axis. The vertical distance measures the price of the good or service. The horizontal distance measures the corresponding quantity demanded. Thus, each point on *DD* indicates a price and corresponding quantity demanded at that price.

A **demand curve** shows the quantity demanded at each possible price, other things equal.

Even when bread is free, only a finite amount is wanted: beyond 1000 loaves a week, everyone is stuffed with bread and can't eat any more. As the price of food rises, the quantity demanded falls, other things equal. In Figure 2-1, this corresponds to moving *along* the line *DD* – leftwards and upwards – buying less and less bread as the price is increased, until buyers demand no bread at all once the price reaches £5 a loaf.

We can use a similar figure to think about the congestion charge. Think of the vertical axis as measuring the congestion charge (the price of using London roads), and the horizontal axis as measuring the extent of vehicle traffic in London. Initially, drivers did not have to pay any direct charge for using London streets. They paid for petrol, but there was no additional fee for driving down Oxford Street rather than going round London on the M25 ring road. So drivers simply used London streets as much as they wanted. They were free. With a zero price, daytime demand for London streets exceeds the capacity of London streets to cope with this amount of traffic.

Figure 2-2 shows the demand curve *DD* for daytime car use in London. Initially, with no congestion charge, the outcome is at point *A*. Traffic is heavy and Piccadilly Circus is congested because the quantity of car and lorry trips demanded is so large. Introducing the congestion

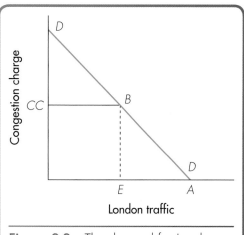

Figure 2-2   The demand for London road use

charge at the level *CC* shown in Figure 2-2 raises the price of car use, and moves buyers up the demand curve from *A* to *B*. As a result, traffic falls from point *A* to point *E*. The purpose of the congestion charge was therefore to make people demand less use of London streets, and in so doing to reduce congestion, allowing traffic to flow more freely. How much a given price increase reduces the quantity demanded depends principally on how easily buyers can find alternative goods and services that perform a similar function. With brilliant public transport available, a modest congestion charge on cars might induce large numbers of people to switch to buses. The demand curve *DD* for car travel is then relatively *flat*, showing that small price rises reduce the quantity demanded a lot. If public transport is unreliable, slow and dirty, a big rise in the price of road use may reduce the demand for road use by only a little. We would then draw a *steep* curve *DD* to show that car use is fairly insensitive to the level at which the congestion charge is set.

If higher prices make demanders move upwards *along* a given demand curve, how then do we represent the surge in demand for car travel after the London bomb explosions on public transport?

Box 2-1

Consumer surplus

How much do consumers value what they buy? Since they are able to choose what quantity to purchase – nobody is forcing them – if they value the last unit purchased by more than its price they ought to buy even more. Conversely, if the last unit purchased was worth less to them than its cost, then they have already bought too much. Consumers should buy up to the quantity at which the marginal benefit of the last unit bought equals its extra cost (see figure).

Suppose consumers can buy as much of the good as they wish at the fixed price of 11. The consumers like and value the good differently from one another. The person most desperate for the very first unit would in fact have paid a price of 14 – the demand curve

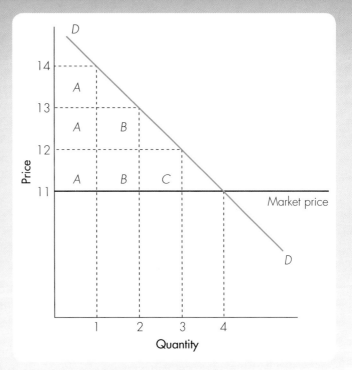

tells us that, if only one unit is sold, the price is 14. That is the valuation the most desperate consumer, with the highest valuation, places on the first unit. The valuation on the second unit sold is 13, because the demand curve tells us that is how much the price has to fall to ensure that two units are sold. The valuation on the third unit is 12, and so on.

If the lucky producers could sell different units at different prices, they would charge the first person most and then gradually cut the price so as to entice additional purchasers. If goods could be sold

▶

in very small quantities, the *area below the demand curve* would then measure the total valuation by, and benefit to, consumers.

Charging different prices to different people usually creates an incentive for consumers to trade among themselves, undermining the attempt by producers to charge different prices to different people. Most of the time, there is a single price for everyone. In the diagram, consumers can buy as much as they want at the price of 11.

The person who bought the first unit would have paid as much as 14 but only paid 11. For the first unit, the consumer surplus is (3 × 1) = 3, which is the extra valuation times the quantity of 1. It is shown by the three areas marked *A* in the diagram.

> The **consumer surplus** is the amount by which the benefit to the consumer exceeds the cost of buying that unit.

For the second unit bought (whether by the same consumer or by another person), the demand curve says that the valuation on the second unit is 13, but the price paid is only 11. The consumer surplus on this one unit is therefore 1 × 2 = 2, shown by the two areas marked *B* in the diagram. For the third unit, the valuation is 12 and the consumer surplus is 1, shown by the area *C* in the diagram.

Consumers will buy up to the point at which the demand curve *DD* crosses the market price line. The total consumer surplus is therefore the area between the horizontal price line and that part of the demand curve lying above the line. When the fourth unit is bought, its valuation is 11 and its cost to the consumer is 11, so there is no more consumer surplus. Buying any more would create a consumer deficit – the valuation, as given by the height of the demand curve, would be lower than the price that consumers have to pay. Because consumers pursue their self interest and are free to choose how much to buy, one implication is that their decision to buy four units in total maximizes the total consumer surplus. Buying fewer would leave some consumer surplus available but unexploited, and buying more would cause consumer surplus unnecessarily to be reduced.

Maths 2-1

Consumer surplus

For those of you who like maths, imagine that the demand curve is given by $q = \alpha - \beta p$, where q and p are the quantity and price, and α and β are positive constants. Suppose the market price p^* is fixed. Before reading on, try to work out (a) the quantity purchased and (b) the consumer surplus.

The quantity purchased is $(\alpha - \beta p^*)$. If this is positive, the market exists. If it is negative, it implies that consumers do not value the good as highly as its production cost and the good will never be made. Assuming the market exists, consumer surplus is the area of the triangle between the demand curve and the price line. The width of this triangle is simply the quantity $(\alpha - \beta p^*)$, and its height is the vertical distance between the maximum price α/β paid as the quantity is almost zero and the actual price is p^*. The area of a triangle is half its height times width. Hence, assuming the good can be purchased in tiny individual units, the total consumer surplus is $\frac{1}{2}(\alpha - p^*)(\alpha - \beta p^*)$.

2-2 Behind the demand curve

Other things equal, lower prices are accompanied by higher quantities demanded, and vice versa. But prices are not the only determinant of demand. Other things do not always remain constant. We now study three other influences: the price of related goods, the income of buyers, and tastes or preferences of buyers.

1 **The price of other goods** *Higher* bus fares may *raise* the quantity of car travel demanded at each possible price of car use. In everyday language, buses are a substitute for cars. Higher prices for substitutes for cars make people switch towards more car use. Conversely, petrol and cars are not substitutes but complements. You can't use a car without using fuel. A *rise* in the price of petrol tends to *reduce* the demand for cars since it raises the price of using a car.

A rise in the price of one good raises the demand for **substitutes** for this good, but reduces the demand for **complements** to the good.

Most goods are substitutes for each other. If the price of food rises, you will generally demand a little less food and a little more entertainment. Complementarity is usually a more specific feature (mobile phones and SIM cards, coffee and milk, shoes and shoelaces). If milk becomes more expensive, fewer people will buy a cappuccino.

2 **Consumer incomes** When incomes rise, the demand for most goods rises. Typically, richer consumers buy more of everything. Compared with what you demand, Elton John buys more cars, more restaurant meals, more holidays, larger houses and more legal advice. However, there are exceptions. You probably buy more baked beans and use more launderettes than he does.

For a **normal good**, demand rises when income rises. For an **inferior good**, demand falls when income rises.

Most goods are normal goods. As we have got richer over the last 100 years, we have bought more food, more travel and more household goods. Inferior goods are cheap, low-quality goods that people would prefer not to buy if they could afford to spend a little more. Students buy cheap cuts of meat but graduate to steaks when they get a good job. The Queen does not have to take her clothes to a public launderette. She can afford to install expensive washing machines or even employ people to hand wash everything.

3 **Tastes** Tastes or preferences of consumers are shaped by convenience, custom and social attitudes. The fashion for the mini-skirt reduced the demand for fabric. The emphasis on health and fitness has increased the demand for jogging equipment, health foods and sports facilities but reduced the demand for cream cakes, butter and cigarettes.

So why did people buy fewer barbeques during the UK summer of 2011? Not because the price of barbeques changed. The lower quantity of barbeque use demanded was *not* a movement downwards along a given demand curve *DD* in response to a lower price of barbeques. The only other possibility was that the wet summer – 20 per cent more rainfall than average – *shifted* the *entire* demand curve to the left, leading to lower barbeque demand. Figure 2-3 shows this as a shift from the original demand curve *D'D'* to the new demand curve *DD*. At any price (a given vertical distance), buyers now wish to purchase a lower quantity (smaller horizontal distance) than before. In particular, at the original price *P'*, the quantity demanded now falls from *G* to *E*.

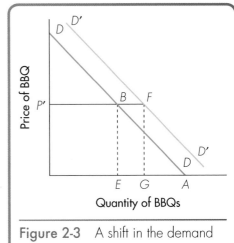

Figure 2-3   A shift in the demand curve

Changes in the price of the good (or service) move us *along* a *given* demand curve: other things equal, higher prices reduce quantity demanded. But other things do not always remain fixed. When they change, we have to shift the entire demand curve. Changes in other determinants of demand (changes in the price of substitutes or complements, changes in incomes or changes in tastes) *shift* the demand curve. Such changes that *increase* demand *shift* the demand curve to the *right* (from DD to D′D′ in Figure 2-3). Such changes that *reduce* demand *shift* the demand curve to the *left* in Figure 2-3 (from the demand curve D′D′ to DD).

When the wet summer reduced the demand for barbeques form D′D′ to DD, which of the 'other things equal' behind the demand curve then changed? There was no significant change in consumer incomes during the rain, so it must have been one of the other two potential channels.

The most obvious solution is to say that the rain changed consumer tastes for outdoor barbeques, the demand for which fell as a result. The entire demand curve shifted to the left in Figure 2-3.

To sum up, the quantity demanded reflects four things: its own price, prices of related goods, incomes and tastes. We could draw a two-dimensional diagram relating quantity demanded to any one of these four things. The other three would be the 'other things equal' for that diagram. In drawing demand curves, we always choose the price of the commodity itself to put in the diagram with quantity demanded. The other three things become the 'other things equal' for a demand curve.

Why single out the price of the commodity itself to plot against quantity demanded? Because, once we add supply, we can show the self-correcting mechanism by which a market reacts to excess demand or excess supply, by changing the *price* to restore equilibrium. We want to show how quantities are affected by prices as the market does its job. But when one of the other important determinants of demand changes, we have to show these as shifts in the demand curve. Things that increase demand shift the entire demand curve to the right (more quantity at any price). Things that reduce demand shift the entire demand curve to the left (less quantity at any price).

Here is a chance to see if you have understood. Try completing Table 2-1, describing what happens to the demand curve for UK higher education in response to each of six important events.

The effect of income on demand

Having studied changes in prices, we now study changes in income. For the moment, we neglect saving and assume higher income is all spent. This tends to raise the quantity demanded of most individual goods. However, quantities demanded don't all change by the same amount, so budget shares change with income.

Table 2-1 Shifts in the demand curve (please tick the appropriate box in each line)

Event	Demand curve for UK university places	
	Shifts left	Shifts right
1 UK university tuition fees abolished		
2 Other EU countries raise university fees		
3 UK gets richer		
4 Young people lose faith in education, and instead volunteer for a lifetime of service in Africa		
5 Bill Gates subsidizes all UK university places		
6 An earthquake destroys five UK universities		

(Answers provided on page 38, but complete the table before skipping to them)

Table 2-2   Budget shares, 2001–10

	Real consumer spending (2005 £bn)	% budget share	
		Food and drink	Recreational goods
2001	733	10	1
2010	850	9	3

Source: ONS, UK National Accounts

The **budget share** of a good is the spending on that good as a fraction of total consumer spending.

Table 2-2 shows the share of UK consumer spending devoted to (a) food and drink, and (b) recreational goods, such as computer games and sports equipment, between 2001 and 2010. Real consumer spending rose over the period, from £733 billion to £850 billion (both measured at 2005 prices). The budget share of food and drink fell from 10 per cent to 9 per cent. Even so, the absolute amount spent on food and drink must have risen: 9 per cent of £850 billion is a lot more than 10 per cent of £733 billion. The budget share of recreational goods increased strongly (more golf clubs, music systems and computer games as people felt richer).

Does the quantity demanded always increase when a person's income increases? The answer is usually but not always. The few exceptions are called inferior goods: quantity demanded actually falls when income rises. Inferior goods are low-quality goods for which higher quality but more expensive alternatives are available. Poor people buy fish fingers and polyester shirts. With more income, they buy seafood and comfortable cotton shirts. Higher income reduces the demand for fish fingers and polyester shirts. These are inferior goods.

The demand for an inferior good (or service) falls when consumer income rises. The demand for a normal good increases when consumer income rises. For luxuries, quantity demanded rises even faster than income, so that the budget share of this good or service increases with income. Goods or services that are not luxuries are called necessities, which are therefore either inferior goods (or services) or else they are normal goods (or services) but not luxuries. Necessity is a technical term in economics – higher incomes lead to a lower budget share – not to be confused with the everyday meaning that you cannot do without it.

Case study 2-1   High prices take lamb off the menu

According to an article in *The Telegraph* (12 March 2012), British households are abandoning the traditional Sunday favourite of roast lamb, consumption of which had fallen by 20 per cent in the previous 12 months. Did this reflect a reduction in the demand for lamb? If so, what are the possible reasons for this change in behaviour?

One reason why demand might fall is if the public have become more health conscious and have heeded warnings that too much red meat causes a higher risk of heart attacks. If so, we would expect to see a corresponding rise in the demand for lean meats such as chicken or vegetarian alternatives such as tofu. Like Sherlock Holmes, in trying to diagnose what is going on, we have to search for every piece of available evidence. A rise in the price of chickens would be one useful piece of evidence in support of this particular explanation.

▶

A second possibility is not that there was any change in the absolute desirability of lamb but rather a rise in the wish to eat some alternative. All these episodes of *River Cottage Veg* had alerted people to how nice vegetarian main courses could be. Given a limited budget and only 52 Sunday lunches a year, any increase in the demand for a substitute for lamb reduces the demand for lamb itself.

Both these explanations imply that the demand curve for lamb shifts downwards. What do you think then happens to the price of lamb, other things equal? With less lamb demanded, producers have to cut their prices to sell lamb. A fall in the demand for lamb should be associated with a lower price of lamb.

But this is not what actually happened. *The Telegraph* article goes on to say that, during the year in which the quantity of lamb consumption fell by 20 per cent, the price had risen from £7.33 to £8.56 a kilo, a price rise of 17 per cent. With annual inflation of around 3 per cent, almost all the increase was a rise in the real price of lamb. Since a fall in demand was not the explanation, the explanation must instead have been a fall in supply, reasons for which we explore in detail in the next chapter. Lamb became scarcer because less was supplied, driving up the price of lamb. For a given demand curve for lamb, this moved consumers up the given demand curve, buying a lower quantity at a higher price. In fact, they bought 20 per cent less quantity at a real price that was about 14 per cent higher.

The article goes on to explain some of the reasons for the fall in lamb supply. In particular, New Zealand farmers – suppliers of most UK lamb – were diverting their acreage from lamb to beef, where the profits had become larger because of what had happened to beef prices. Why had beef prices risen in New Zealand?

We now get a sense of how complicated the world is, but how simple our reasoning can be. Economic growth in Asia led to higher incomes, raising the demand for most commodities but particularly for beef. This led to a rise in the relative price of beef. This induced agricultural suppliers to move out of lamb production into beef production, making lamb more scarce. Higher lamb prices then caused UK households to put less lamb on the Sunday table, not because the demand for lamb had fallen but because a higher price was reducing the quantity demanded along a given demand curve.

Luxury goods are high-quality goods for which there are lower-quality, but adequate, substitutes: Mercedes cars not small Fords, foreign not domestic holidays. Inferior goods are low-quality goods that people readily abandon as they get richer. Necessities that are normal goods lie between these two extremes. As incomes rise, the quantity of food demanded rises, but only a little.

Table 2-2 showed that recreational goods are luxuries whose budget share rose with UK income after 2001. Food and drink are not a luxury; their budget share fell as income rose. Nor are they inferior goods. At constant prices which adjust for the effects of inflation, during 2001–10 real food spending *increased* from £73.3 billion (10 per cent of £733 billion) to 76.5 billion (9 per cent of £850 billion).

Table 2-3 summarizes the demand responses to higher income, holding constant the prices of all goods. Lower income has the opposite effect.

These patterns of demand response are vital to business and government in forecasting the changing pattern of consumer demand as the economy grows and people get richer. Suppose incomes grow at 3 per cent a year for the next five years. The demand for luxuries, such as restaurants, will rise strongly. In contrast, the demand for some necessities such as bread may hardly rise at all, and the demand for cheap cuts of meat, such as tripe, will fall. The growth prospects of the three industries are very different.

Table 2-3 Demand responses to a rise in income

Good	Quantity demanded	Budget share	Example
Normal	Rises with income		
Luxury	Rises strongly with income	Rises	BMW
Necessity	Rises weakly with income	Falls	Food
Inferior	Falls	Falls	Bread

Inflation and demand

Chapter 1 distinguished *nominal* variables, measured in prices at the time, and *real* variables, measured in constant prices to adjust for inflation. If all nominal variables double, every good costs twice as much, but all incomes are twice as high. Nothing has really changed. Quantities demanded are unaltered.

This does not contradict our analysis of price and income elasticities of demand. The former shows the effect of changing one price, holding constant other prices and nominal income. This is not relevant when all prices and incomes rise at the same rate. The latter shows the effect of higher real income. But real income does not change under pure inflation.

 ## 2-3 Demand and consumer choice

Measuring past behaviour is a good guide to the future when nothing dramatic changes. Sometimes, however, we need to think about what people might do in a future situation which is completely different from the past. To predict demand behaviour, we need a *theory* of how consumers make choices. A successful theory is consistent with past behaviour but also helps predict responses in new situations.

Effects of a price change: substitution and income effects

As the price of a good falls, people buy more of it, so surely demand curves slope down? Unfortunately, things are not this simple. Suppose the price of bread falls. For the rest of your life, you need to remember this has two quite different effects.

The **substitution effect** says that, when the relative price of a good falls, quantity demanded rises.

Your intuition will always discover the substitution effect, the bit that is obvious. You have to train yourself to look for, and find, the second effect.

The **income effect** says, for a given nominal income, a fall in the price of a good raises real income, affecting the demand for all goods.

If bread is a normal good, the demand for bread will rise when real income (spending power) rises. Hence, when the price of bread is lower, the quantity demanded rises both because (a) it is now relatively cheaper than before (the substitution effect) and (b) with bread costing less, the consumer's income has more purchasing power; being richer as a result, the consumer buys more of all normal goods, including more bread. Both the income effect and the substitution effect raise the quantity of bread demanded when the price of bread falls. Bread is relatively cheaper, so people buy more. Moreover, cheaper bread raises the purchasing power of the given nominal income; this also raises the demand for bread.

Hence, for normal goods, our theory says the demand curve must slope down. Price cuts lead to a higher quantity demanded.

Answers to Table 2-1

| Event | Demand curve for UK university places | |
	Shifts left	Shifts right
1 UK top-up fees abolished	Demand curve shifts neither left nor right – reducing the price of UK university education moves us downwards along the original demand curve. Quantity demanded increases, but only because the price fell.	
2 Other EU countries raise university fees		The demand curve for UK university education shifts to the right. At each and every price, the quantity of UK university places demanded is larger than it would have been before.
3 UK gets richer		At any price, people demand more UK university places than before; demand curve shifts right.
4 Young people lose faith in education, and instead volunteer for a lifetime of service in Africa	Change in tastes reduces demand for UK university places; demand curve shifts left.	
5 Bill Gates subsidizes all UK university places	Price falls and moves downwards along a given demand curve – unless the fact that Bill is cool after his Live 8 appearance means more young people become interested in university, in which case the change in tastes also shifts the demand curve to the right.	
6 An earthquake destroys five UK universities	Loss of universities is a change in supply not a change in demand. If greater scarcity then drives up the price, this moves people up a given demand curve. If the loss of university professors implies that total income falls, this may shift the demand curve down (but not by much – professors don't get paid a lot).	

Now consider an inferior good, perhaps the pot noodles beloved of students but rarely eaten by investment bankers. A fall in the price of pot noodles makes them relatively cheaper than before. Other things equal, this makes people buy more pot noodles (the substitution effect). However, the lower price of pot noodles raises the real income or purchasing power of everyone who previously bought any pot noodles at all. Being richer, consumers buy *more* normal goods but *fewer* inferior goods, including fewer pot noodles (the income effect of the price cut in pot noodles). If the income effect is strong enough, it can outweigh the substitution effect so that the net effect is that cheaper pot noodles reduce the quantity demanded – this happens when people are desperate to give them up as soon as they become rich enough to afford something they like better.

Thus, for inferior goods, theoretical reasoning alone cannot deduce which of the two effects is larger, and hence whether price cuts lead to a higher or lower quantity demanded. It will vary from good to good and we need empirical evidence to resolve the issue. In practice, demand curves for goods and services usually slope down. Inferior goods and services are rare.

In other markets, the 'perverse income effect' that outweighs the 'obvious substitution effect' is more common. Here is a quick taster of things to come. Higher interest rates increase incentives to save, don't they?

Saving means not spending all today's income, reducing consumption today to raise consumption later.

Think of the interest rate as the price of time, the cost of consuming today instead of later. When the cost of consuming today rises, you choose less of it. Surely?

Your intuition has found the substitution effect. Consuming today has got relatively more costly, and you consume less, thus saving more. Where is the income effect lurking? To afford that foreign holiday next year, you don't have to save so much if interest rates are higher and your assets cumulate more quickly! This makes you save less. Empirically, it is very hard to find whether interest rates have much effect on total saving. Politicians think higher interest rates boost saving, and are always devising schemes like ISAs to provide tax breaks, hoping that higher after-tax interest rates will boost national saving. Economists are pessimistic that this will work. Much of it is just a subsidy to the rich – something to remember if you become Chancellor of the Exchequer!

Effects of income changes

Real income can rise either because nominal income increases while prices are constant, or because the price of a commodity falls while nominal income is constant. The former leads to a pure income effect; the latter must be decomposed into separate income and substitution effects.

Successive rises in real income lead to large increases in the quantity demanded if the good (or service) is a luxury with a large income elasticity of demand. Quantity demanded increases less quickly for normal goods or services with smaller, but still positive, income elasticities. For inferior goods, higher income reduces quantities demanded. Poor students give up beans on toast once they become rich bankers.

Tastes and demand

Different people may have different tastes, making different choices even when facing the same prices and enjoying the same income.

> **Tastes** describe the utility a consumer gets from the goods consumed. **Utility** is happiness or satisfaction.

Tastes depend on culture, history, familiarity, relationships with others, advertising, and so on. Explaining these influences is the role of other social sciences, like psychology and sociology. Economists treat them as an 'other things equal' assumption behind a particular demand curve.

However, tastes can change, with important effects. In the past few decades there have been big changes in social attitudes to organic food and the formality of dress. The demand curve for organic food shifted outwards, but the demand curve for top hats shifted inwards. We shift demand curves when there are changes in the 'other things equal'.

Marginal utility and demand

Fred goes clubbing and drinks lager. Initially, he goes to one club but has no lager. Fred is thirsty and can't enjoy himself. With a lager, he'd be a lot happier.

> The **marginal utility** of a good is the *extra* utility from consuming one more unit of the good, holding constant the quantity of other goods consumed.

Fred's first lager gives him high marginal utility. A second lager gives him extra utility, but not as much extra utility as the first one did. A third and fourth lager add less and less extra utility.

> Tastes display **diminishing marginal utility** from a good if each extra unit adds successively less to total utility when consumption of other goods remains constant.

Figure 2-4 shows Fred's marginal utility, which falls the more he drinks. It also shows the price of each lager. If a

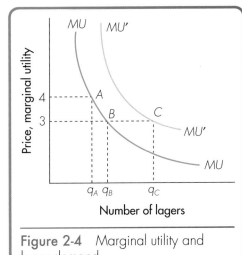

Figure 2-4 Marginal utility and lager demand

lager costs £4, and Fred gets £6 of marginal utility from it, he should buy another one. If he only gets £2 of marginal utility from his last lager, he has bought too many. He should buy lager up to the point at which the marginal cost (£4 for the last lager) equals the marginal benefit or marginal utility. Figure 2-4 shows Fred choosing point A when lagers cost £4 each.

Figure 2-4 suggests that, if the price of lager falls from £4 to £3, Fred will definitely buy more lager because of diminishing marginal utility. But the figure only shows the substitution effect! The marginal utility curve assumes quantities of other goods remain constant. However, as the price of lager falls, Fred can afford more club nights too. Whether this shifts Fred's marginal utility curve up or down depends on whether lager is a normal or an inferior good, which is the income effect at work.

If lager is a normal good, the income effect shifts the marginal utility curve outwards to MU, in Figure 2-4. This also makes Fred consume more lager (point C). Income and substitution effects go the same way. The demand curve for lager, drawn through A and C, slopes down. If lager was an inferior good, the MU curve might have shifted *inwards* enough to make Fred consume less lager when its price fell.

So far, marginal utility analysis merely reinforces our earlier and simpler discussion of income and substitution effects. However, it was worth learning, as Box 2-3 confirms.

Box 2-2

Bend it like Beckham

Maria Sharapova has made more from advertising than from winning Wimbledon, and LA Galaxy wanted David Beckham as much for what the Beckham brand could do for its marketing as it did for his ability to bend free kicks. For many years, Thierry Henry was the suave image of the Renault Clio. Why do the manufacturers pay superfees to superstars to promote their wares? They are trying to change your tastes. There are lots of small cars, but only one has va-va-voom. It's the one to die for. No other will do.

You could buy a car magazine and find out whether the Clio's suspension geometry really is different. But

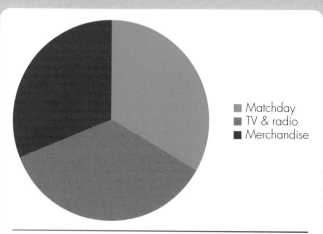

Manchester United revenue composition, 2011 (%)

Source: Deloitte, *Football Money League 2012*

that's not the point. This advertising is about *style*. Not what you think is nice, but what *other people* think is nice. Renault is assuring you that other people, stylish people, think it's cool to drive a Clio. Do so and you can be cool too. This *interdependence* of tastes is what opens the door for so much advertising and PR. Clubs such as Manchester United fully understand the value of marketing their merchandise. The chart above shows that they make roughly the same from selling the brand (replica shirts, etc.) as from gate receipts or broadcasting revenue.

Box 2-3

The water–diamond paradox

Here's a riddle for your friends who don't study economics. Why is the price of water, essential for survival, so much lower than the price of decorative diamonds? Diamonds are scarcer than water. Yet consumers clearly get more total utility from water, without which they die.

Marginal utility solves the puzzle. The marginal benefit of the first unit of water is enormous. But we each consume lots of water. Since water is relatively abundant, the supply curve for water lies well to the right and the equilibrium price is low. Consumers have moved a long way down their marginal utility of water curve.

If water is supplied free, consumers should use water up to the point at which its marginal utility is zero. May as well wash the car again. Even a small rise in price may lead to a large cutback in usage – demand is very elastic in this region of the demand curve.

Diminishing marginal utility also explains our earlier discussion of consumer surplus. The first unit consumed is the most valuable, then the next unit, and so on. Depending on the commodity, the marginal utility of a large quantity may be near zero or actually negative. Too much alcohol makes people ill, and that last drink may have a negative valuation, at least in the cold light of day.

From individual to market demand curve

How do we aggregate individual demand curves to get the total demand in a particular market?

The **market demand curve** is the horizontal sum of individual demand curves in that market.

We always plot price on the vertical axis. All consumers in a market face the same price P. Suppose at a price of £2 the first consumer demands a quantity of A and the second consumer a quantity of B; the market demand is a quantity of C = A + B when the price is £2. Repeating this procedure at each and every possible price we trace out the market demand curve. Figure 2-5 shows how two individual demand curves D_1 and D_2 are horizontally aggregated to get the market demand curve D. In most markets, where there are lots of purchasers, the market demand curve is obtained by adding horizontally the demand curves of every individual in the market.

The market demand curve is important because, together with the market supply curve, it determines the price that clears the market in equilibrium. Having seen how the individual demand decisions can be aggregated to derive the market demand curve, we turn next to a more detailed analysis of supply decisions.

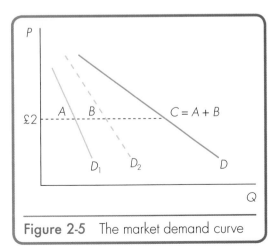

Figure 2-5   The market demand curve

Case study 2-2   Conspicuous consumption

This chapter has introduced the theory of demand, and examples of how the theory can be applied to real-world behaviour and the data that it generates. By now we hope you are convinced that the theory makes sense and is consistent with the facts. But are there important exceptions that we have glossed over?

Here is an example for you to think about. The next time a new generation of Nike trainers appears, you know that you will simply have to have them. In fact, the more they cost, the more exclusive they will seem and the more you will probably be determined to have them. Your parents may feel the same about Gucci shoes or the Porsche Boxster. So have economists got it wrong?

Question for discussion: *Do demand curves really slope up for such goods: the more they cost, the larger the quantity demanded?*

Try to formulate an answer before you read on. We will however give you one clue – the answer is nothing to do with income effects and inferior goods. One thing on which we can all agree is that Gucci and Porsche brands are bought only by rich people, not poor people.

The phenomenon of *conspicuous consumption* – demanding goods precisely because they are expensive and therefore exclusive – was first discussed by US economist Thorstein Veblen (1857–1929), after whom they are sometimes referred to as 'Veblen goods'. They are goods designed to create envy among others.

However, this need not pose any difficulty for our theory of demand. Indeed, Box 2-2 above already contains the beginning of the answer, the interdependence of preferences. The diagram below

shows two demand curves, *MM* for a mass-produced version of a good and *EE* for an exclusive version that is highly admired by the trendy elite. The elite version is more desirable for two reasons. First, it may be innately better. On most objective tests, a Boxster outperforms a Mondeo. Second, however, it is also more fashionable, more esteemed by the in-crowd, and therefore more desirable, whatever its objective characteristics. For both reasons, the demand curve *EE* lies above the demand curve *MM*. At any given quantity (a distance to the right in the horizontal quantity direction), people will pay more (higher vertical distance) for the exclusive good than the mass-market good.

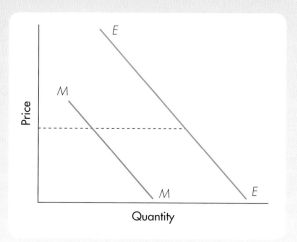

Conditional on the attributes of the exclusive good – in Nike's case how comfortable they are and how your friends think they look – the less you had to pay, the more of them you would buy. Your demand curve *EE* is high up because of the attributes that make them exclusive, but still slopes down – other things equal, you will buy more if they are cheaper.

Believing that Veblen goods are evidence of an upward-sloping demand curve is to make the mistake of confusing movements along a given demand curve with shifts in the demand curve itself. When a good is more exclusive, its demand curve has shifted further upwards. But the demand curve still slopes downwards. If other things remain equal, cutting the price then means sliding downwards along the given demand curve.

- The quantity demanded depends mainly on four things: the price of the good itself, the price of substitutes and complements for that good, income and spending of buyers, and tastes of buyers.
- A demand curve highlights the relation between the quantity demanded and one of these four things, namely the price of the good itself, holding constant the other three influences on quantity demanded.
- When one of the other three influences changes, we have to reflect this as a shift in the demand curve. When the price of the good itself changes, we show this as a movement along a given demand curve.
- For inferior goods, quantity demanded falls as income rises. Goods that are not inferior are normal goods.
- For luxury goods, quantity demanded rises more than 1 per cent when income rises by 1 per cent. Hence, their budget share increases as income increases. Goods that are not luxuries are necessities, whose budget share falls as income rises. All inferior goods are necessities. Normal goods are necessities only if they are not luxuries.
- Doubling all nominal variables has no effect on demand since the real value of incomes and the real price of goods are unaltered.
- A price change has a substitution (relative price) effect and an income (purchasing power) effect. Intuition usually locates the substitution effect. You must also find the income effect.
- Demand curves slope down for normal goods. A sufficiently inferior good could have an upward-sloping demand curve; such goods are very rare.
- Because of the income effect, higher interest rates need not encourage more saving.
- Marginal utility is the extra benefit of consuming the last unit of a good, holding constant consumption of other goods. Tastes display diminishing marginal utility. This explains the water–diamond paradox.
- At each price, the market demand curve is the sum of the quantities demanded by different people facing that price.

Review questions

To check your answers to these questions, go to pages 375–77.

1 Suppose the demand for peaches is not very sensitive to price: to sell 10 per cent more you have to cut the price by 20 per cent. You are the only fruit seller in town, and your fruit stall has 100 ripe peaches that can usually be sold for £1 each. You now discover ten of your peaches are rotten and can't be sold. (a) What quantity do you now wish to sell at once? (b) What is the new equilibrium price? (c) Do you get more or less revenue than the £100 you had originally expected to earn?

2 Two possible ways to reduce global warming are: (a) a tax on emissions of carbon dioxide from cars and power stations; and (b) a ban on driving cars except at the weekend. Which policy works by shifting the demand curve for energy to the left, and which works by moving consumers leftwards along a given demand curve for energy?

3 For vegetables, quantity demanded rises 0.2 per cent when the price falls 1 per cent, but rises 0.9 per cent when income rises 1 per cent. For catering, quantity demanded rises 2.6 per cent when the price falls 1 per cent but rises 1.6 per cent when consumer incomes rise 1 per cent. Are vegetables and catering luxuries or necessities?

4 During 1975–2010, UK households' spending on bread and cereals rose from £1.5 million to over £6 million. Does this mean bread is a normal good? Could it be an inferior good? Which seems more likely to you?

5 Why are these statements wrong? (a) Because cigarettes are a necessity, tax revenue on cigarettes must rise when the tax rate is raised. (b) Farmers should insure against bad weather that might destroy half the crops of all farmers. (c) Farmers should not insure against events that affect their crops alone.

6 Do higher consumer incomes always benefit producers?

7 'A higher hourly wage makes people want to work longer by making work more attractive than leisure.' 'A higher wage makes people better off, raising the quantity of leisure demanded, and thereby reducing the length of time people wish to work.' Which is the income effect, and which is the substitution effect?

8 Suppose Glaswegians have a given income, and like weekend trips to the Highlands, a three-hour drive away. (a) If the price of petrol doubles, what is the effect on the demand for trips to the Highlands? Discuss both income and substitution effects. (b) What do you expect to happen to the price of Highland hotel rooms?

9 Explain the concepts of: (a) utility, (b) marginal utility and (c) diminishing marginal utility.

10 Name a good for which your marginal utility falls so much that you get negative marginal utility when you consume too much of this good.

EASY

11 Could the marginal value of the second unit ever exceed the marginal value of the first? If you think so, provide an example. How would the demand curve then look? Could this still be true for the aggregate demand curve over all consumers?

12 Explain (a) the concept of consumer surplus for an individual; and (b) the concept of total consumer surplus for a particular good. If producers could charge a different price for every unit sold, what would be the relationship between total revenue and consumer surplus?

INTERMEDIATE

13 Air conditioners are luxury goods. (a) Name two countries that you expect to have the highest per capita demand for air conditioners at present. (b) If people continue to get richer and global warming continues to increase, what is likely to happen to the quantity of air conditioners demanded? And what will this do to global warming? And hence to the demand for air conditioners? (c) Could this process spiral out of control?

14 Why are these statements wrong? (a) Inflation reduces demand since prices are higher and goods are more expensive. (b) Abolishing income tax on the income from saving must make people save more.

DIFFICULT

15 **Essay question** We observe a person behaving differently in apparently similar situations. Either the situations were not similar or the person is 'irrational'. Which approach would an economist take? Why? Is it realistic to think that we can account for behaviour in every situation?

16 **Essay question** What prevents producers charging different prices for different sales of the same product? Is it more likely that we will observe differential pricing for goods or for services? Why?

Online Learning Centre

To help you grasp the key concepts of this chapter check out the extra resources posted on the Online Learning Centre at www.mcgraw-hill.co.uk/textbooks/begg.

There are additional case studies, self-test questions, practice exam questions with answers and a graphing tool.

CHAPTER 3

Supply and market equilibrium

Learning outcomes

By the end of this chapter, you should be able to:

- Understand that supply describes the behaviour of sellers
- Show the effect of price on quantity supplied
- Illustrate how supply curves depict this relationship
- Analyse other determinants of supply
- Explain when supply curves shift
- Relate revenue, economic cost and economic profit
- Distinguish stocks and flows
- Discuss whether profit maximization is plausible

- Analyse how a firm chooses the output to supply
- Distinguish total revenue and marginal revenue
- Distinguish total cost and marginal cost
- Derive the output level that maximizes supplier profits
- Show how prices reconcile demand and supply
- Analyse equilibrium in a market
- Assess the effect of shifts in demand or supply curves

Having understood the behaviour of buyers, we next examine the behaviour of sellers. What motivates suppliers? How do they make choices? What happens when their economic environment changes? Once we can answer these questions, we can then combine supply and demand to see how markets reconcile supply and demand.

The supply curve

Much of the world's cocaine began as a coca plant in Columbia, and poppies in Afghanistan are the source of most of the heroin that finds its way into European countries. American and European governments keep pressurizing politicians in Columbia and Afghanistan to eradicate the problem by stopping their farmers producing the raw materials for the drugs trade. From time to time the BBC and CNN show flaming hillsides as helicopters attack peasant farmers. But the following year, the same crops are back in bloom. Why is the supply of coca and poppies so hard to stamp out?

An economist's answer is that the incentive to produce this crop is large. When poor farmers get much higher prices for one crop than for the alternative crops that they could produce instead, they will be very keen to supply the most profitable crop. French farmers could also produce poppies, but, within the Common Agricultural Policy, they have other crops which also yield them high returns.

In contrast, frozen out of the markets of rich countries by high external tariffs, farmers in developing countries do not have profitable opportunities to engage in legal trade with the world's rich countries. Illegal trade is relatively more attractive to farmers. The quantity supplied is high because farmers get a high price for their crops. As international travel has become easier, transporting drugs has become easier too. In turn, this has raised the price that drug traffickers will pay poppy growers, making poppy growing even more attractive to farmers.

Moreover, in comparison with the government of Afghanistan, the French government has more incentive and greater ability to stamp out illegal crop production. It has more incentive because, as a member of the EU, it has more to lose by upsetting its partner countries. It has greater ability because it is richer and technically more sophisticated. Identifying and eradicating illegal crops is easier.

This example illustrates many of the themes of this chapter. What determines the incentive to produce and supply to the market? How sensitive is production to the price being offered? Must prices be reduced in order to diminish the incentive to supply or can supply be reduced through other means?

> **Supply** is the quantity producers wish to offer for sale at each conceivable price.

Supply is not a particular quantity but a full description of the quantity producers would sell at each and every possible price. We can show this relationship between price and quantity supplied as a *supply curve, SS* in Figure 3-1.[1] The vertical distance measures the price of the good or service. The horizontal distance measures the corresponding quantity supplied. Thus, each point on *SS* indicates a price and corresponding quantity supplied at that price.

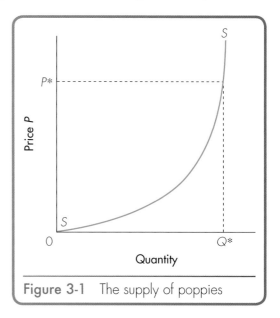

Figure 3-1   The supply of poppies

> A **supply curve** shows the quantity supplied at each possible price, other things equal.

When the price of poppies is zero, nobody will bother to grow them for sale. As the price of poppies rises, the quantity supplied rises, other things equal. In Figure 3-1, this corresponds to moving *along* the line *SS* – rightwards and upwards – offering more and more poppies for sale as the price is increased, until every Afghan hillside is saturated with poppies and no more can be produced. In Figure 3-1, the maximum possible supply is Q^*, and any price above P^* has no further effect in raising the quantity supplied.

We can use a similar figure to think about UK clean energy from wind power in the early twenty-first century. At a low price, it is not worth UK producers producing energy from wind farms (which are not

---

[1] As with demand curves, supply curves may be a straight line or a curve, but in either case must slope upwards as we move to the right. If, unlike Figure 3-1, the supply curve was a straight line, this would imply that the quantity supplied could be increased without limit provided the price was high enough.

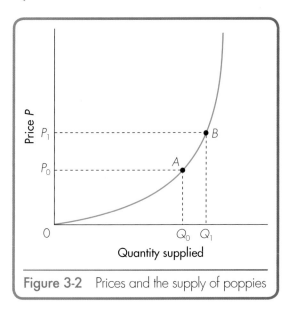

Figure 3-2　Prices and the supply of poppies

very efficient and, being noisy and ugly, cause a lot of local resentment that is not worth incurring for low levels of energy production). If energy prices were to remain high for a long time, it would then become worth bearing these costs and producing more UK energy in wind farms. But there is only so much physical wind in the UK in any one year. Beyond some output Q^*, the UK cannot currently produce any more energy from wind no matter how high the price. The supply curve becomes vertical at that point, just as it did for poppies in Figure 3-1.

Figure 3-2 shows what happened to poppy production when the advent of cheaper and faster travel made smuggling easier, raising the price that smugglers were prepared to pay for poppies. Initially, the poppy market was at point A, with a price P_0 and quantity Q_0 supplied. Once smuggling became easier, the price rose to P_1 and farmers responded by raising quantity supplied to Q_1. They moved upwards along a given supply curve, from A to B, in response to the higher price they were being offered by drug smugglers.

Conversely, if Western countries adopt better surveillance techniques that eradicate smuggling, the prices being offered to Afghan poppy growers will fall: without the drug dealers, only a few poppies can be sold in their next best use, to flower shops. In Figure 3-2, we can imagine that we begin at point B, with a price P_1 and quantity Q_1. The consequence of eradicating drug smuggling is to reduce the price to P_0 and poppy farmers respond by reducing the quantity supplied to Q_0.

If changes in prices make suppliers move *along* a given supply curve, how then do we represent more effective policing of illegal poppy production by the Afghan government?

Behind the supply curve

Recall our discussion of demand curves in Chapter 2, in which price changes moved demanders *along* a given demand curve but changes in the prices of related goods, changes in incomes or changes in tastes led to *shifts* in the demand curve. In exactly the same way, movements in price move suppliers *along* a given supply curve, but changes in any of the 'other things equal' have to be depicted as *shifts* in the supply curve.

The three principal 'other things' that affect supply are technology available to producers, the cost of inputs (labour, machines, fuel and raw materials), and government regulation. Holding these three things constant, movements *along* a particular supply curve show the effect of prices on quantity supplied. A change in any of these 'other things equal' shifts the supply curve, changing the amount producers want to supply at each price.

Technology

Better knowledge of fertilizers or improvements in irrigation technology make it profitable to supply more poppies than before at any particular price being offered, just as electronic or information technology has made it possible to supply more televisions and computers at any price than was the case ten years ago.

As a determinant of supply, technology must be interpreted broadly. A technological advance is any improvement in knowledge that allows more physical output from the same quantity of physical input as before. It is this productivity increase that means that producers are willing to supply more than before at any particular price. This improvement might come from better science, but it might also arise from better psychology.

When Japanese car producers first established car plants in the UK, they achieved much higher productivity levels than traditional car producers. This was due in part to workforce motivation and organization. Rather than taking lunch alone in a directors' dining room, those running the company ate in the same cafeteria as workers, making the workers feel more valued and allowing insights from the factory floor to be fed into senior management.

Technical progress can reflect better teamwork as well as better science. Either way, a supplier gets more output from given input quantities, and hence can supply more at any particular price. The supply curve shifts to the right (because we measure quantities in the horizontal direction, a rightward shift implies a greater quantity supplied at each price). Conversely, if we ever had a collective memory lapse and forgot how to do something, the supply curve would shift to the left.

Input prices

A particular supply curve is also drawn for a given level of input prices. Lower input prices (lower wages, lower fuel costs) induce firms to supply more at each price, shifting the supply curve to the right. When world oil prices fell to $10/barrel for several years in the late 1980s and early 1990s, the airline business was profitable and lots of new airlines sprang up supplying more airline flights than before. The supply curve for flights shifted to the right. Conversely, when oil prices rose to over $100/barrel, the cost of running an airline increased dramatically, and the supply curve for flights shifted sharply to the left. Some airlines even went bankrupt and quit the industry entirely. Things were no longer so easy for easyJet.

Government regulation

Given a free choice, suppliers choose the lowest-cost production method from their viewpoint. If regulations make suppliers use a different production method, this must be more costly for suppliers. It shifts the supply curve to the left, reducing the quantity supplied at each price. More stringent safety regulations prevent chocolate producers using the most productive process because it is dangerous to workers. Anti-pollution devices raise the cost of making cars. More effective prosecution of poppy growers raises the cost of supplying poppies. When regulation prevents producers (legal or illegal) from selecting the cheapest production method, regulation shifts the supply curve to the left. See Table 3-1.

Table 3-1 Shifts in the supply curve (tick the appropriate box in each line)		
	Universities' supply curve for student places	
Event	Shifts left	Shifts right
1 UK top-up fees abolished		
2 UK lecturers get big pay rise		
3 New law requires wheelchair access to every classroom		
4 Young people lose faith in education, and instead volunteer for a lifetime of service in Africa		
5 Bill Gates donates e-Learning packages to all UK universities		
6 An earthquake destroys five UK universities		

(Answers provided on page 52, but complete the table before skipping to them)

3-3 Introducing the theory of supply

So far, we have described supplier behaviour, but in order to develop a better simulation model that allows us to predict how suppliers respond in hypothetical situations, we need to develop an explicit theory of supply. For each possible output level, a firm compares what this output costs to make and what revenue it earned from sales. Profits are the excess of revenue over costs. Our theory of supply assumes each firm chooses the output level that maximizes its profit. This is the key to our theory of supply.

A firm's accounts

Although illegal poppy growers may not bother to keep accounts, legitimate businesses are required to keep and submit them. Moreover, once a business attains any level of sophistication, those running it will want to know all the details of how it is operating, in order to take the best decisions possible.

In modern economies, firms report two sets of accounts, one for stocks and one for flows.

Stocks are measured at a point in time; **flows** are corresponding measures over a period of time.

The quantity of water flowing out of a tap is different per second and per minute. The measurement requires a time interval to make sense. The stock of water in the basin at any instant is a number of litres, and requires no time dimension. A firm reports profit-and-loss accounts per year (flow accounts) and a balance sheet showing assets and liabilities at a point in time (stock accounts). The two are related, as they are for the basin of water. The inflow from the tap is what changes the stock of water over time, even though the latter is only measured in litres at each point in time.

Flow accounts (profit and loss)

A firm's **revenue** is income from sales during the period, its **costs** are expenses incurred in production and sales during the period, and its **profits** are the excess of revenue over costs.

This sounds very easy, but there are a few tricky complications. Economists and accountants adopt different definitions because they are interested in different things. Accountants have to certify that nobody is stealing cash from the business. They care about cash flow.

Cash flow is the net amount of money received by a firm during a given period.

Economists care about what, how and for whom goods are produced. Accountants keep track of actual cash spent. Economists focus on opportunity cost.

Opportunity cost is the amount lost by not using resources in their best alternative use.

You quit a job as a teacher of ICT and start an Internet business, paying out £5000 in the first year as you camp in an Internet cafe, and spend the least you can on running your business. An accountant treats your costs as £5000. An economist stresses that your time was not free – you could have earned £20 000 a year teaching ICT. It only makes sense to switch your labour resources into the Internet job if you can earn at least £25 000. For an economist, interested in incentives to allocate resources, a revenue of £25 000 is merely break-even; for an accountant, it is £20 000 profit after paying the Internet cafe.

Normal profit is the accounting profit to break-even after all economic costs are paid.
Economic (supernormal) profits in excess of normal profit are a signal to switch resources into the industry. **Economic losses** mean that the resources could earn more elsewhere.

Here is a second case in which economists' and accountants' definitions are different. The Internet start-up also requires the ICT teacher to use £2000 of her savings to cover everyday expenses. The accountant treats this personal financial injection by the owner as free, but an economist recognizes the opportunity cost. If the money could have earned £100 in interest during the year, that is another economic cost to deduct in calculating economic profit.

Suppose the Internet start-up company does so well that it buys its own office.

Physical capital is any input to production not used up within the production period. Examples include machinery, equipment and buildings. *Investment* is additions to physical capital.

This capital is a stock and not a flow, but we cannot exclude it entirely from the firm's flow accounts. The capital becomes less valuable during the period for which flow accounts are drawn up. This depreciation is a proper charge on the flow accounts.

Depreciation is the cost of using capital during the period.

It reflects both wear and tear, and gradual obsolescence. Capital has a second economic cost in flow accounts: the money tied up when the capital was bought. The interest this could have earned is an economic cost to the flow accounts of the firm.

Stock accounts (balance sheet)

The balance sheet shows at a point in time the assets and liabilities that the firm has built up as a result of flows in all preceding periods.

Assets are what the firm owns. **Liabilities** are what it owes. **Net worth** is assets minus liabilities.

Assets include cash in the bank, money owed by customers, inventories, and physical capital such as plant and machinery. Liabilities are debts the firm still has to repay to suppliers and its bankers. Net worth includes not just these tangible assets minus liabilities, but also an estimate for the value of its reputation, customer loyalty and a host of intangible assets that economists call *goodwill*.

Box 3-1

The value of a good name

Goodwill affects the ability of the firm to make money in the future and is just as valuable an asset as physical assets cumulated from past behaviour. The consultancy Interbrand tries to calculate goodwill by comparing the stock market value of companies with the identifiable physical and financial assets they own: the more its stock market value exceeds the direct value of its physical and financial assets, the higher is the residual value of the brand itself. US giants such as Coca-Cola, IBM and Microsoft top the worldwide list, but Mercedes and IKEA are well up on it. Banks have taken a tumble since the financial crisis.

Rank	Company	Industry	Brand value ($bn) 2011
1	Coca-Cola	Drinks	72
2	IBM	Computers and software	70
3	Microsoft	Software	59
4	Google	Internet	55
6	McDonald's	Fast food	36
8	Apple	Computers	34
12	Mercedes	Cars	27
31	IKEA	Furniture	12
32	HSBC	Banking	12
79	Barclays	Banking	4

Source: www.interbrand.com

You are considering switching resources between uses. Should you study the flow accounts for the year, or the stock accounts at the time of your decision? The former shows recent behaviour, the latter shows the long-run position. If you can afford to take a long-run view, you may be more interested in the stock accounts. If you have to worry about short-term considerations, the flow accounts may be more informative.

Do firms really maximize profits?

Economists assume that firms make supply decisions to maximize profits. Some business executives, and even some economists, question this assumption. A sole owner is accountable only to herself and may have other aims (nice location, popularity with the local community, doing good). When Anita Roddick started Body Shop, she cared about its ethical and environmental policies as well as the narrow objective of making money. Richard Branson has taken evident pleasure out of running his airline as well as simply making money.

Answers to Table 3-1

Event	Supply curve for UK university places	
	Shifts left	Shifts right
1 UK top-up fees abolished	Alters the price and moves universities along a given supply curve; no shift.	
2 UK lecturers get big pay rise	Lower quantity supplied at each level of fees.	
3 New law requires wheelchair access to every classroom	Lower quantity supplied at each level of fees.	
4 Young people lose faith in education, and instead volunteer for a lifetime of service in Africa	Affects demand not supply.	
5 Bill Gates donates e-Learning packages to all UK universities		Makes supplying universities easier and cheaper; hence entire supply curve shifts right.
6 An earthquake destroys five UK universities	Lower capacity to supply, so supply curve shifts left.	

Most business is done by large companies. Most large companies are public companies with large numbers of shareholders, who cannot all be involved in every management decision. Thus, most large companies are not run directly by their owners. Instead, the shareholders appoint company directors to act on their behalf and review the directors' performance at regular intervals. Directors have day-to-day discretion and only account formally to shareholders at the annual shareholders' meeting. In practice, shareholders rarely dismiss the directors, who have inside information about the true prospects of the firm. It is hard for shareholders to be sure that new directors could do better.

Given this separation of ownership and control, shareholders want maximum profits but directors have some scope to pursue their own agenda. This may include executive perks, such as nice cars and a company jet. If status depends on size, directors may pursue size rather than profits, advertising too much or holding prices lower than is ideal for profits and shareholders' interests.

Even so, profit maximization is a good place to start in developing a theory of supply. First, even if shareholders are kept partly in the dark, other firms in the industry are better informed. Companies not pursuing profits have low profits, and hence low share prices. A takeover raider can buy the company cheaply, change the policy, make extra profits and cash up as the share price soars. Fear of takeovers may force the directors to pursue profit maximization.

Second, shareholders provide incentives for managers to do what shareholders want. They offer directors profit-related bonuses and share options. The total value of these is small relative to company profits but big relative to what directors earn in salary alone. Directors then maximize profits, as the shareholders want.

Box 3-2

Bankers' bonuses

By 2012, public opinion had begun to turn against enormous 'bankers' bonuses'. The chief executive officer of state-owned Royal Bank of Scotland had enjoyed a bonus of £2.5 million in 2011. Despite a solid year of improvement in performance at RBS, this award was cut to £1 million in 2012, provoking a public outcry that forced Stephen Hester to announce he would give up entirely his bonus entitlement that year. Nor did pressure arise only in the public sector. Bob Diamond of Barclays Bank had his annual bonus reduced from £6.5 million in 2011 to £2.7 million in 2012. Shareholder anger at the proposed size of executive pay led to the departure of the chief executives of insurance group AVIVA and Trinity Mirror, owner of the *Daily Mirror* newspaper.

Public displeasure was linked less to the adverse incentive effects that such bonuses might have on excess risk taking than to the view that large payments were 'unfair' or 'unjustified by the performance of the bank' in that year. This was exacerbated by the widespread feeling that the rest of the economy was being made to suffer for years because of the past actions of a few bankers: never in the field of economic history had so much pain been inflicted on so many by so few.

Concerns about fairness usually become more acute at times of economic stress. In the good times, when almost everyone is enjoying a better living standard, there is less concern about all being in it together.

Corporate pay packages are set by 'remuneration committees' usually made up of non-executive directors. Non-execs are not the full-time board members engaged in the everyday running of the company; rather, they are part-time outsiders who bring external experience to challenge constructively how the full-time management is conducting the company's affairs. Often these non-execs will themselves be full-time executive directors of other companies. This allows senior managers in one industry to bring their experience to bear on the management of companies in other industries.

Some people think that this benefit may be overshadowed by the danger that a cosy remuneration culture evolves. You agree to big bonuses in my company, expecting similar non-executive directors then to agree to big bonuses in your company. If most of the major players are in the same system, who challenges the system itself? Moreover, most remuneration committees set themselves targets such as 'paying in the top half of salaries for the industry in order to attract the best talent'. But everyone cannot be in the top half. It gives rise to a remuneration race.

Why pay bonuses at all? Why not just pay high salaries to good people? The case for bonuses hinges on their ability to target and encourage particular behaviour that the company's shareholders wish to see. Much of the time, however, bonus criteria depend quite crudely on things like profits and share price growth. Can bonuses *over-incentivize* the management, for example causing them to take too many risks in the pursuit of profits or growth?

In 2007, Northern Rock became the first British bank to fail for many decades. The Rock had been borrowing short term in order to invest in mortgage lending from which it could not easily get its

▶

money back quickly. When the credit crunch took hold and banks became scared to lend to each other, Northern Rock suddenly found it impossible to borrow the new money that it required to keep its operation going.

Eventually, Chancellor Alistair Darling concluded that the least worst option for the government was to nationalize the Rock. Allowing it to go bankrupt risked provoking a general panic and self-fulfilling stampedes against other banks that were perfectly sound. Allowing private consortia, such as that led by Sir Richard Branson, to have bought the Rock and kept it operating as a going concern would have been an attractive solution in principle. However, the private bidders realized what a pickle the government was in and therefore submitted low bids for the Rock, hoping to make a lot of money once they had sorted out the bank. In the circumstances, the government preferred to make the killing itself, taking over the Rock and hoping to sell it later once its business had been sorted out.

The case of Northern Rock provides interesting evidence about the traditional solution to the problem of the separation of ownership and control in a public company. Recognizing that directors did have the scope to behave in part in the interests of directors rather than in the interests of shareholders, shareholders traditionally responded by giving the directors bonus schemes and stock options linked to the value of the company.

In a £1 billion company, offering the directors additional incentives of £10 million if the company does well takes only a tiny amount away from shareholders but makes a huge difference to the focus of the behaviour of directors. If big bonuses are at stake, they might as well behave the way shareholders wish. Hence, the argument went, smart use of incentives could make directors behave in the true interests of shareholders.

Many influential commentators, not least Mervyn King, the Governor of the Bank of England, argued that this process had gone too far. Incentives were no longer the solution to but the cause of the problem. A corporate leader who pockets a couple of £5 million bonuses may not care about the longer-run implications of the policies he has adopted for the company, and may in any case get a further payoff if he has to leave the company because his strategy unravels. When the Rock's chief executive Adam Applegarth finally departed, he collected a payoff of £700 000 in addition to the bonuses he had previously earned.

The Rock was the bank most exposed to the credit crunch because it had been the most aggressive bank, borrowing substantial amounts of short-term money in order to grow very quickly. While the environment was benign, the strategy worked and the Rock looked a big success story. Its management team was well rewarded. But the strategy was vulnerable to a drying up of credit. When this eventually happened, the Rock was doomed.

Although dramatic, this was not an isolated incident. Most of the largest financial institutions – US giants such as Merrill Lynch, Morgan Stanley and Citigroup, but also European banks such as the Royal Bank of Scotland, Barclays, HBOS and UBS – suffered horrible losses from over-optimistic lending during 2004–06. Big name chairmen, such as Stan O'Neal (Merrill Lynch), Charles Prince (Citigroup) and Marcus Ospel (UBS) all resigned or retired early.

Why did they all get so overextended during the boom? It would be wrong to blame everything on the effect of personal incentives, whether at board level or further down the organization. Shareholders have to take their share of the blame. In the boom years, they congratulated their management for doing so well and taking such well-judged risks. Any management team that had behaved more prudently was accused of lacking imagination and sometimes dismissed in favour of a more aggressive team. It is hard to be a responsible manager when the shareholders have joined the bandwagon.

3-4 An overview of the supply decision

We begin with production costs. Each output level can be made in several ways. A field of wheat can be farmed by lots of workers with few tools, or by one worker with a lot of machinery.

Given the price of each input and the different production techniques available, the firm calculates the lowest-cost way to make each possible output level. This may entail different techniques at different outputs.

> The **total cost curve** shows the lowest-cost way to make each output level. Total cost rises as output rises.

Table 3-2 shows different outputs and the corresponding total cost. At any output, the firm has a fixed cost of 10, perhaps the cost of paying interest on old debts. As output rises from 1 to 4, total cost rises from 18 to 54. Extra output incurs extra costs. The third column shows marginal cost.

> **Marginal cost** is the change in total cost as a result of producing the last unit.

The marginal cost of the first unit of production is 8, the rise in total cost from 10 to 18. Similarly, the marginal cost of producing the fourth unit of output is 14, the rise in total cost from 40 to 54. Having considered cost, now think about revenue. Column 4 shows total revenue from selling the output produced. With no output, the firm gets no revenue. One unit of output can be sold at a price of 20, giving a total revenue of 20. This is also the marginal revenue of going from zero to one unit of output sold.

> **Total revenue** is the output price times the quantity made and sold. **Marginal revenue** is the change in total revenue as a result of making and selling the last unit.

As output and sales rise, column 4 shows that revenue rises for a bit but eventually gets smaller as sales increase. To sell more and more output, the firm has to cut prices to induce buyers to demand this output. Since all output is sold for the same price, cutting the price to sell new units reduces the revenue earned on previous units. This second effect eventually outweighs the first. Beyond three units, extra sales actually cut revenue. Column 5 does the sums for you, showing the marginal revenue from the last unit sold, which takes into account the effect on total revenue of bidding down the price that previous units have been sold for. By the bottom row of Table 3-2, marginal revenue is actually negative.

Armed with the first five columns of Table 3-2, you advise the firm what output to make and sell. One method is simply to subtract total cost from total revenue to obtain economic or supernormal profits. Column 6 shows that profit-maximizing output is 2, at which profits are 3. This is similar to the method used by a mountaineer who checks the top has been reached by making sure he can look down on all surrounding sides.

There is another way to check you are at the top. Work out the slope you are standing on. If it is not flat, take the upwards direction. At the very top, the slope is zero. There is no direction you can move in order to get any higher. This is the marginal principle.

Table 3-2   The supply decision

Output Q	Total cost TC	Marginal cost MC	Total revenue TR	Marginal revenue MR	Economic profits	MR – MC
0	10	–	0	–	–10	
1	18	8	20	20	2	12
2	28	10	31	11	3	1
3	40	12	36	5	–4	–7
4	54	14	35	–1	–19	–15

The **marginal principle** says that, if the slope is not zero, moving in one direction must make things better; moving the other way makes things worse. Only at a maximum (or a minimum) is the slope temporarily zero.

Economists use the marginal principle a lot. Profit is maximized at the output at which marginal profit is zero. Otherwise, a different output can add to profit. Marginal profit is simply marginal revenue minus marginal cost. Column 7 uses this decision rule. If marginal revenue exceeds marginal cost, the firm made a marginal profit on the last unit, and should make even more. If marginal revenue is less than marginal cost, the firm made a marginal loss on the last unit, and already made too much. With a marginal profit of 1, it was a good idea to make as much as 2 units. However, with a marginal loss of 7 from making a third unit, it is best to stop at 2 units. This, of course, is the same answer we got by calculating total profit from total revenue and total cost. Sometimes it is an easier method to implement.

Plotting MC and MR curves

Table 3-2 is an artificial example. Output does not have to be a whole number. Dairies can make 1284.8 litres of milk if this is the best output level. Figure 3-3 plots continuous curves for marginal cost *MC* and marginal revenue *MR*. The *MR* curve steadily falls as output rises: price cuts are needed to get customers to buy more. For most of its range, the *MC* curve rises: making the last unit gets harder and harder. For example, a coal mine has to go ever deeper to find more coal.

A profit-maximizing firm chooses to supply the output q^*, at which marginal profit is zero. Marginal revenue exactly equals marginal cost. At any lower output, *MR* exceeds *MC* and the firm adds to profits by expanding. At any output above q^*, *MC* exceeds *MR* and the firm adds to profits by contracting output.

We can also use Figure 3-3 to examine changes in costs or revenue curves. Anything that shifts the *MC* curve up (such as wage increases, or tougher pollution controls) means that *MC* crosses *MR* at a lower output. This makes perfect sense: when costs rise, the firm supplies less. Conversely, a change in demand behaviour that shifts the *MR* curve up increases the output that the firm supplies: with better revenue opportunities, the firm chooses to supply more output.

You probably thought you knew that already. However, Figure 3-3 is also making a point that is less obvious. What induces a profit-maximizing firm to reduce output is an increase in *marginal* cost. If you ask your friends who are not studying economics, they might reply that it is higher average costs or higher total costs that make firms wish to cut back production. Actually, neither of these assertions need be correct.[2] But if the marginal revenue curve *MR* is unaltered, you now know that an upward shift in marginal cost curve *MC* always makes firms wish to supply less.

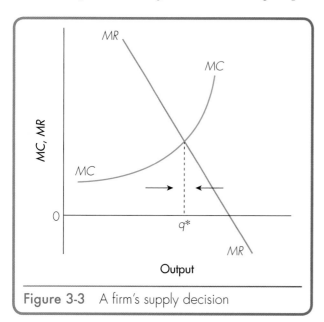

Figure 3-3 A firm's supply decision

---

[2] If you wish to show off your new economic understanding, here is a simple example. To help finance disaster relief, the government imposes a tax of £50 000 on every firm, whatever output they produce. At all positive output levels, the cost and benefit of raising output are unaffected by this tax, and hence *MC* and *MR* are unaffected. The firm will not cut back output despite the fact that average and total costs have risen. It might as well get the biggest surplus possible from production and sale, whether or not it then has to pay a disaster levy to the government.

Do firms know their MC and MR curves?

There are two ways in which to maximize profits. The first is by having a highly professional management with access to excellent management information. Marginal cost and marginal revenue are what they are trying to discover. Alternatively, a firm may simply be run by an intuitive genius who gets things right without going through all the laborious steps above.

Competition means that most surviving bosses are good at such decisions. If they get things right, they are maximizing profit, which ensures that *MC* must equal *MR* whether anyone in the firm knows it or not. Using the marginal principle is how mere mortals keep track of what proven business leaders do instinctively.

Maths 3-1

The calculus of profit maximization

A firm faces a revenue schedule $R(q)$, which tells it how much revenue R it receives by producing and selling a quantity q. It also faces a cost schedule $C(q)$, which relates total costs to quantity produced. Its profit is therefore $R(q) - C(q)$ and its decision problem is to choose output q in order to maximize profits. Differentiating profits with respect to output, marginal profit is $dR(q)/dq - dC(q)/dq$. The first term is just marginal revenue and the second term marginal cost. Profits are maximized when further changes in output generate no additional profit, which occurs when

$$dR(q)/dq - dC(q)/dq = 0 \quad \text{so} \quad MR - MC = 0 \quad \text{or} \quad MR = MC$$

So we've mastered the supply decision?

We have found the principle from which all else follows. There are still some details to fill in. First, both revenue and costs may differ in the short run and in the longer run. A firm may have to react to a marginal revenue schedule which changes over time. Even more important, a firm's cost curves change over time. We also have to aggregate individual supplies to get the market supply curve. This depends on how many suppliers there are, and how they react to one another. The ensuing chapters explain different forms of market structure and what this means for the supply decision.

 ## Combining supply and demand

Now that we have developed the theories of demand and supply, and understand how to reflect behaviour in demand and supply curves, we can provide a deeper analysis of the role of markets that we introduced in Chapter 1. Prices adjust to equate the quantity people wish to buy and the quantity people wish to sell. In so doing, these prices influence what goods are produced, how they are produced and for whom they are produced. The upward-sloping curve *SS* in Figure 3-4 shows how much sellers wish to sell at each price. The downward-sloping curve *DD* shows how much consumers wish to purchase at each price. The market is in equilibrium at point *E*, where the two curves intersect. The equilibrium price is P^*, at which a quantity Q^* is supplied and demanded.

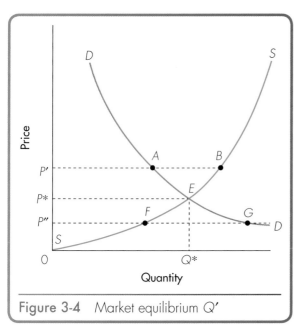

Figure 3-4 Market equilibrium Q'

The **equilibrium price** clears the market. At this price, the quantity supplied equals the quantity demanded.

At any price P' above $P*$ (a higher vertical distance in the price direction in Figure 3-4), the quantity supplied exceeds the quantity demanded. There is excess supply at this price and suppliers have unsold stock. To sell this unsold stock, suppliers have to reduce the price. This keeps happening until the market returns to equilibrium at point E.

Conversely, at any price P'' below $P*$ (a lower vertical distance in the price direction in Figure 3-4), the quantity demanded now exceeds the quantity supplied. There is excess demand at this price, and buyers cannot find all the goods they would like to purchase.

Buyers offer to pay more than suppliers are asking for, and the price is steadily bid upwards until the equilibrium is restored at point E.

Case study 3-1

Without access to demand, higher productivity can hurt producers

The case of world agriculture

Rich countries have spent years accumulating physical capital, such as factories and buildings, and human capital, the stock of knowledge and skills that makes the workforce productive. In rich countries, few people still farm the land. There are more profitable things to do. Chapter 1 showed that agriculture is now less than 2 per cent of national output in countries such as Japan, France and the UK.

Poor countries are poor precisely because they have accumulated less physical and human capital. They have to make do with their labour and the land available to them. Agriculture is a much larger share of their national output. Fifty years ago many people thought that the best way to help poor countries was to provide aid and technical assistance to improve their agricultural productivity. Since this was such a large share of their output, it offered the best opportunity to increase people's living standards.

Some countries, such as Sudan, have remained ravaged by civil war and little progress has been made. But in many countries – India is a good example – there has been a Green Revolution. With better fertilizer, better irrigation and, importantly, better varieties of crops that are faster growing and more disease resistant, agricultural output has soared. However, this has not led to the increase in national income that was expected.

The first figure shows what has happened to the real (inflation-adjusted) price of crops in the last 50 years. Prices are now only about a third of what they were 50 years ago. World markets have been flooded by extra supply, both because farmers in rich countries became more productive and exported to world markets, and because emerging market producers also became much more productive than they used to be.

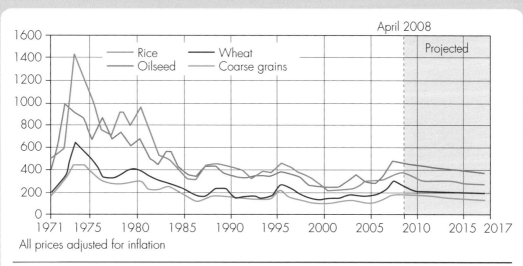

World food commodity prices (US$/ton), 1971–2017

Sources: FAO; OECD

The figure on the real price of food shows recent developments in more detail. As globalization boomed in the period leading up to the crash of 2008, there was a very sharp rise in the real price of foodstuffs. The crash then led to recession and a fall in demand, bidding prices downwards sharply. However, leading agricultural forecasters believe that real prices will now stabilize at higher levels than in the 1990s.

This case study also makes a crucial second point, not about levels of prices but about changes in prices in response to increases in supply. For a given rightward shift in the supply curve, the induced *change* in prices in the two following diagrams depends not on the height of the demand

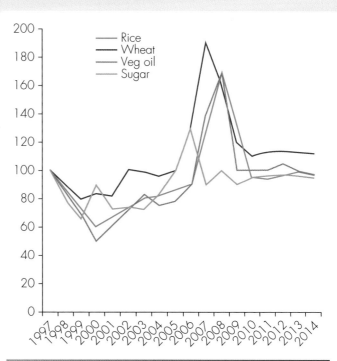

The real price of food (1997 = 100 for each commodity)

Source: OECD-FAO Agricultural Outlook 2009–2018

curves but on their *slope*. It is because the demand curve is flatter in the right-hand diagram that the same shift in supply induces a smaller fall in price (and therefore has to be reflected in a larger change in equilibrium quantity).

Developing world producers have mainly had to sell their extra supply in *poor* markets that have a limited capacity to absorb the extra quantity being supplied. There is a limit to how much extra poor people wish to buy, no matter how much the price is reduced. If emerging market producers had access to markets of the rich developed countries, they would find demand was higher and hence they would get higher prices for their agricultural output.

The two figures below illustrate the same increase in world food supply, and hence the same right-ward shift in the two supply curves, in each case from $S'S'$ to SS. However, in the left-hand figure, demand is not price sensitive and the demand curve is steep. Producer revenue (price × quantity) actually falls when supply increases. Initially, revenue is the sum of the rectangles A and C. After the supply increase, it is the sum of B and C. Since B is smaller than A, producer revenue actually falls when producers get more productive and supply increases from SS to S'S'.

In the right-hand figure, demand is higher and more price sensitive: the demand curve is much flatter. The same increase in supply bids down the price much less in the right-hand diagram, and the rightward shift in the supply curve now increases producer revenue (price × quantity). Initially, it is the rectangles A + C, and subsequently the rectangles B + C. If only emerging market producers had free access to the markets of the rich countries, the productivity revolution in emerging market agriculture would be the solution to a great deal of world poverty.

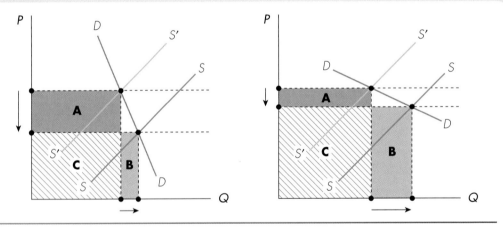

The revenue effects of a supply shift

We can also consider shifts in demand rather than supply. Some countries, especially in sub-Saharan Africa, are very dependent on a single crop (see figure overleaf), which, once harvested, has to be sold for whatever price it will fetch. Such countries have a very steep supply curve in the short run. With a near-vertical supply curve, the effect of demand fluctuations is to cause large fluctuations in the equilibrium price.

In the next diagram, we consider a downward shift in demand from the curve labelled D to that labelled D'. When the supply curve S_1 is almost vertical, the demand shift induces a large fall in price (from P_1 to P_2) but only a small increase in quantity (from q_1 to q_2), whereas when the supply curve is much flatter, as shown by S_2, the same fall in demand leads to a much lower fall in price but a much greater fall in quantity.

Thus, countries whose exports are inelastic in supply face large price fluctuations when international demand conditions for their exports fluctuate, whereas countries whose exports are inelastic in supply face large quantity fluctuations when international demand fluctuates.

So far, the argument has been that the twentieth-century agricultural revolution in emerging markets succeeded in achieving a huge increase in agricultural output without achieving a similar increase in incomes in these countries. Much of the higher output was offset by lower prices. In 2007, this began to change. The large demand for food in successful emerging markets such as China led to a dramatic increase in world prices for food, and in some cases speculators then piled in, exacerbating the sharp rise in food prices.

Why does rapid growth in countries such as China and India lead to a rise in world food prices? It must be because, at least for now, these countries are adding more to the demand for food than to the supply of food. People move from the countryside to the cities during this phase of economic development. And we know from Chapter 1 that rich developed countries devote only 1 or 2 per cent of their output to agriculture. Rising productivity may increase the absolute output of agriculture in emerging market economies but this output will probably grow less quickly than their demand for food. We often talk about the days of cheap oil being over; the same may be true for food. If so, this will have a major impact on the what, how and for whom questions that lie at the heart of economics.

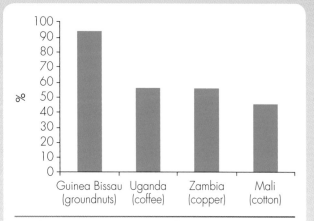

Single crop as percentage of export revenue

Source: IMF

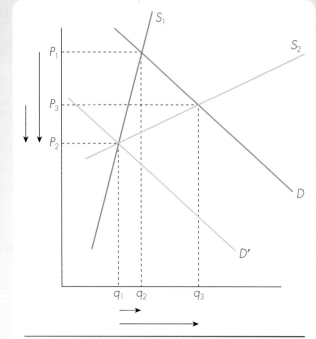

The revenue effects of a demand shift

Recap

- Supply describes how much producers wish to sell at each possible price.

- A supply curve plots quantity supplied against price, other things equal. Changes in price move suppliers along a given supply curve.

- The principal other things equal are technology, input price and the extent of regulation. Technical progress makes inputs more productive and allows producers to produce more at each possible output price. The supply curve shifts to the right. Lower input prices have a similar effect. Tougher regulation makes life harder for producers and the supply curve shifts to the left.

- An increase in supply shifts supply curves to the right, which also implies downwards. This is because quantity is measured in the horizontal direction, and supply curves slope upwards. We can interpret an increase in supply either as a rightward shift (more quantity at each price) or as a downward shift (does not require such a high price to produce any particular quantity). It is the same thing.

- Flows are measured over time; stocks at a point in time. Profit is the difference between the flow of revenue and cost.

- Economic costs include all opportunity costs. Normal profit is the accounting profit that just covers all economic costs. Supernormal profits are any profits above this level.

- Firms are assumed to maximize profits even if shareholders cannot directly observe the behaviour of directors. Maximizing profits automatically entails marginal cost equals marginal revenue.

- Marginal cost is the extra total cost entailed in producing an extra output unit. Marginal revenue is the corresponding change in revenue from selling that extra unit of output.

- An upward shift in the *MR* schedule, or downward shift in the *MC* schedule, raises the output supplied. Lower marginal revenue or higher marginal cost schedules have the opposite effect.

- The equilibrium price equates the quantity demanded and supplied. It is the point at which supply and demand curves intersect.

- Above this price, there is excess supply, which puts downward pressure on prices to restore equilibrium. Below this price, there is excess demand, which puts upward pressure on prices to restore equilibrium.

- The steeper the supply curve, the more a shift in demand will lead to changes in price rather than quantity. The steeper the demand curve, the more a shift in supply will lead to changes in price rather than quantity.

Review questions

To check your answers to these questions, go to pages 377–78.

1 Which of the following represents an increase in supply by supermarkets: (a) The invention of the Internet, which makes it possible for supermarkets to sell online and reduces their distribution costs? (b) A reduction in the wages of supermarket workers because their trade union becomes less powerful? (c) Deregulation of supermarkets that ends the ban on opening on Sundays? (d) Higher prices for supermarket goods because families are stocking up for their annual parties?

2 You are a sheep farmer in the Welsh hills. Give three examples of a change that would reduce your supply. Was one of your answers a change in the price of wool? Why or why not?

3 The table below shows two demand curves DD and $D'D'$ and two supply curves SS and $S'S'$. Each row shows a price, and the quantities supplied or demanded at that price on each of the different curves. (a) What are the equilibrium price and quantity when demand is DD and supply SS? (b) What if demand is DD and supply $S'S'$? (c) Now suppose demand increases by 3 units at each price so that DD becomes $D'D'$. Repeat your answers to (a) and (b). (d) Which of the two supply curves will be associated with smaller price fluctuations for any given shift in demand?

Price	DD quantity demanded	D'D' quantity demanded	SS quantity supplied	S'S' quantity supplied
1	7	10	4	5.5
2	6	9	6	6
3	5	8	8	6.5
4	4	7	10	7
5	3	6	12	7.5

EASY

4 Why might firms, such as accountants and lawyers, where the trust of the customer is important, choose to be partnerships with unlimited liability?

5 Should a firm care about its profits in the short run or its profits in the long run? Could there ever be a conflict between the two objectives? Provide an example of why a firm might not wish to maximize profits in the short term.

6 A firm's consultants report that, at the current level of operations, marginal cost exceeds marginal revenue. What output decision should the firm take? What should it do if marginal cost is less than marginal revenue?

7 Which of the following are flows and which are stocks: (a) income, (b) output, (c) a factory building, (d) labour input?

8 Examine the following table and deduce what is the profit-maximizing level of output:

Output (units)	1	2	3	4	5	6
MC	4	5	6	7	8	9
MR	8	7	6	5	4	3

9 To check your answer to Question 8, complete the table below. Assume that it costs 5 to be in business at all, even if you produce no output, but that you get zero revenue if you produce zero output. [Hint: to get total cost of making 1 unit, take the *TC* of 0 units and add the marginal cost of the first unit. The *TC* of 2 units is simply the *TC* of 1 unit plus the marginal cost of the second unit, and so on.] What output maximizes total profits? Is this what you got in Question 8?

Output (units)	0	1	2	3	4	5	6
Total cost *TC*	5						
Total revenue *TR*	0						
Total profits = *TR* − *TC*							

10 Explain when an increase in output can leave producers with lower income. What does this imply about the price elasticity of demand? Would reducing output in these circumstances lead to higher incomes?

11 At the very top of a hill, what is the slope? Suppose on your walk you always move in the upward direction: will you eventually find the top of the hill? Now think of the hill as a representation of a firm's profit. Marginal profit on the next unit of output, the slope of the profit hill at this level of production, is simply marginal revenue *MR* minus marginal cost *MC*. What is marginal profit when the firm is maximizing profits? What does this tell you about *MR* in comparison with *MC* at that point?

12 Why are these statements wrong? (a) Firms with an accounting profit must be thriving. (b) Firms don't know their marginal costs. A theory of supply can't assume that firms set marginal revenue equal to marginal cost. (c) The biggest profit comes from the largest sales.

13 (a) Unexpectedly, the government levies a once-off 'windfall' tax on the profits of a company making large profits. What is the company's optimal output response? (b) Suppose the company is worried that there will also be future 'unexpected windfall taxes'. If its cost and revenue schedules are given, should its behaviour be affected? (c) If the company had been intending to invest, spending money today to shift down cost curves in the future, could its present investment decision be affected by fears of future windfall taxes?

14 **Essay question** The industrial revolution was built on the ability of entrepreneurs to float companies and obtain funding. But modern stock exchanges force firms to focus too much on the short term, hampering the ability of new businesses to raise money and get going. Do you agree?

DIFFICULT

15 **Essay question** Is the payment of large bonuses to senior management in the interest of shareholders? Describe at least one reason it is and one reason it is not. Why would shareholders tolerate any situation that was not in their collective interest?

Online Learning Centre

To help you grasp the key concepts of this chapter check out the extra resources posted on the Online Learning Centre at www.mcgraw-hill.co.uk/textbooks/begg.

There are additional case studies, self-test questions, practice exam questions with answers and a graphing tool.

Elasticities of demand and supply

 ## 4-1 Measuring demand responses

Chapters 2 and 3 introduced the basic ideas of demand and supply. Sometimes, it is sufficient to have a qualitative idea of how things will work out. For example, we may be content to be able to deduce that an increase in demand will make prices go up. But on other occasions we need to know not just the general direction of a change but its magnitude. If you are asked to invest £10 000 in a friend's business, you will want to know not just that it is going to make profits but also the size of these profits.

Moreover, sometimes what appear to be qualitative conclusions still need quantitative analysis. Will cutting the price of your output give you more revenue or less revenue? The answer depends on whether the quantity of your output demanded rises by more or less than enough to compensate for the lower price that you are charging. This is intrinsically a quantitative question. Answering questions like this requires us to discuss further the ways in which we quantify demand and supply responses.

Table 4-1 shows the demand for beer. At £10/pint, nobody buys beer. As the price falls, the quantity of beer demanded increases. At £1/pint, 90 pints are demanded.

Table 4-1   The demand for beer

Pints						
£ price P	10	8	6	4	2	1
Quantity demanded Q	0	20	40	60	80	90

By how much does the quantity of beer demanded rise when the price is cut by £1? The answer is by ten pints. So the price responsiveness of beer demand is 10 pints per £. What happens if we switch to litres? Since a pint is about 1.8 litres, the answer is now that the quantity of beer demanded rises by 18 litres for every £1 fall in the price. Suppose we are in New York. Now we need to use dollars not pounds. If $2 exchanges for £1, then instead of saying quantity demanded rises by 10 pints for every £1 fall in the price, we have to say that it rises by 5 pints for every $1 fall in the price.

Even though behaviour is the same in each case, our answer about the price responsiveness of beer demand keeps changing its numerical value depending on the units in which we measure quantity and the currency in which we measure price. Even within a single currency such as sterling, we get different answers depending on whether we measure responsiveness to a £1 price cut or to a 1p price cut. The answer to this dilemma is to work with measures that are unit free. They do not depend on the units in which we measure prices of quantities, so the numerical answers don't change when we change the units of measurement.

To accomplish this, we work with percentage changes. If we explore the effects of cutting the price by 1 per cent, it does not matter whether we are dealing with pounds sterling, US dollars or euros. Similarly, if we say the quantity demanded increases by 1 per cent, this answer again is independent of the units in which we measure this. If you are still unsure why this is the case, the following example should help.

Suppose the initial quantity is 100 tons. As a result of a price cut, quantity demanded rises to 110 tons. The absolute rise in quantity demanded is 10 tons. This depends on the units in which quantity is measured. In the Imperial system of weights and measures, there are 2240 pounds per ton. So the increase of 10 tons is also an increase of 22 400 pounds. Now examine the effect of percentages. We begin in tons:

$$\% \text{ increase} = 100 \times [(\text{final amount} - \text{initial amount})/\text{initial amount}]$$
$$= 100 \times [(110 \text{ tons} - 100 \text{ tons})/100 \text{ tons}]$$
$$= 100 \times [10 \text{ tons}/100 \text{ tons}] = 10\%$$

The key point is that tons enter in both the numerator and denominator of the percentage calculation and hence the units cancel out. Just to check, we can do it in pounds, too:

$$\% \text{ increase} = 100 \times [(246\ 400 \text{ lb} - 240\ 000 \text{ lb})/240\ 000 \text{ lb}]$$
$$= 100 \times [24\ 000 \text{ lb}/240\ 000 \text{ lb}] = 10\%$$

Exactly the same reasoning applies to percentage changes in prices, whether we measure in pence, pounds, euros or dollars.

Equipped with this insight, we can now revert to our question: how do we measure the responsiveness to demand and supply with respect to various changes in variables that affect them?

The price responsiveness of demand

When a cut in the price of a good or service has a large effect on the quantity of that good or service demanded, we say that demand for the good or service is *price elastic*. Consumers are very responsive to prices. When the same size of price cut has a small effect on quantity demanded, we say that demand is *price inelastic*. Consumers are not very responsive to prices.

> The **price elasticity of demand (ped)** measures the *responsiveness* of quantity demanded to changes in the price of that good or service. The ped is given by the formula
>
> **ped = [% change in quantity demanded]/[corresponding % change in price]**

Table 4-2 presents a simple example, applied to football tickets.

How do we measure the responsiveness of the quantity of tickets demanded to the price of tickets? Each price cut of £1 raises ticket sales by 8000. But we want to work in percentages.

Suppose a 1 per cent price cut raises the quantity demanded by 2 per cent. The demand elasticity is the percentage change in quantity (+2 per cent) divided by the percentage change in price (−1 per cent) and is thus given by −2. The minus sign tells us quantity *rises* when price *falls*, or vice versa. Quantity and price are moving in opposite directions as we move along a downward-sloping demand curve. If a price fall of 4 per cent increases the quantity demanded by 2 per cent, the demand elasticity is $-\frac{1}{2}$ since the quantity change (+2 per cent) is divided by the price change (−4 per cent). Since demand curves slope down, price and quantity changes always have opposite signs. The price elasticity of demand tells us about movements along a demand curve. The demand elasticity is a negative number.

For further brevity, economists often omit the minus sign. It is easier to say the demand elasticity is 2 than to say it is −2. When the price elasticity of demand is expressed as a positive number, it is implicit that a minus sign must be added (unless there is an explicit warning to the contrary). Otherwise, it implies that demand curves slope up, a rare but not unknown phenomenon.

The price elasticity of demand for football tickets is shown in column (3) of Table 4-2. Examining the effect of price cuts of £2.50, we calculate the price elasticity of demand at each price. Beginning at £10 and 20 000 tickets demanded, consider a price cut to £7.50. The price change is −25 per cent, from £10 to £7.50, the change in quantity demanded is +100 per cent, from 20 000 to 40 000 tickets. The demand elasticity at £10 is (100/−25) = −4. Other elasticities are calculated in the same way, dividing the percentage change in quantity by the corresponding percentage change in price. When we begin from the price of £12.50, the demand elasticity is minus infinity. The percentage change in quantity demanded is +20/0. Any positive number divided by zero is infinity. Dividing by the −20 per cent change in price, from £12.50 to £10, the demand elasticity is minus infinity at this price.

We say that the demand elasticity is *high* if it is a large negative number. The quantity demanded is sensitive to the price. The demand elasticity is *low* if it is a small negative number and the quantity demanded is insensitive to the price. 'High' or 'low' refer to the size of the elasticity, ignoring the minus

Table 4-2 The demand for football tickets

(1) Price (£/ticket)	(2) Tickets demanded (000s)	(3) Price elasticity of demand
12.50	0	−∞
10.00	20	−4
7.50	40	−1.5
5.00	60	−0.67
2.50	80	−0.25
0	100	0

sign. The demand elasticity falls when it becomes a smaller negative number and quantity demanded becomes less sensitive to the price.

When demand is elastic, a 1 per cent price cut raises quantity by more than 1 per cent. Hence total spending by buyers (and hence total revenue of sellers) increases. Quantity rises more than prices fall. Conversely, when demand is inelastic, a 1 per cent price cut leads to a rise in quantity by less than 1 per cent. For such goods, a price cut reduces consumer spending and producer revenue. Quantity rises less than prices fall. In the intermediate case between elastic and inelastic demand, we say that demand is unit elastic: a 1 per cent fall in prices induces exactly a 1 per cent rise in quantity, leaving spending by buyers and revenue of sellers unaffected.

Why do we care whether demand is elastic or inelastic? We look first at an example about farmers. Suppose a harvest failure reduces by 30 per cent the crop supplied to market. Since the demand elasticity for food is low – people need to eat and if necessary can sacrifice holidays and nights out – it may take a price rise of 60 per cent to reduce quantity demanded by 30 per cent in line with the lower supply. However, if prices rise twice as much as quantity falls, farmers' incomes will *rise* when the harvest is *bad*!

Conversely, a bumper harvest that adds 30 per cent to the quantity of food being sold at market may require a 60 per cent price reduction to induce buyers to buy all this extra quantity. Farmers will then make *low* incomes when the harvest is *good*. This paradox only arises because the demand for food is inelastic – it takes large price changes to induce small changes in quantity demanded.

Box 4-1

What determines demand elasticities?

The price elasticity of demand depends on consumer taste. If everyone must have an iPad, higher iPad prices have little effect on quantity demanded. If tablet computers are thought a frivolous luxury, the demand elasticity is much higher. Psychology and sociology help explain why tastes are as they are. Taking these tastes as given, the easier it is to find a substitute that fulfils the same need, the higher is the demand elasticity.

This also explains why companies advertise so much. If Apple and Samsung can convince you that a tablet is essential, demand will be more inelastic, allowing the makers to raise prices without losing so many consumers. This raises profit margins. Apple have spent a lot on advertising to raise awareness of their brand.

Taking a different example, IBM used to be known as the world's most successful producer of computers. Founded in 1911, it was renamed International Business Machines in 1924 and made large computers but also moved into laptops. It still holds more patents than any other US-based technology company and its employees won five Nobel prizes. Despite this stellar record, by 2000 it had concluded that the computer hardware business was likely to become commoditized – standardized production, many competitors, large volume, low profit margins. If one computer was ultimately much like another, the elasticity of demand would be high and profit margins would be low.

Bravely, IBM quit the hardware business and moved into software instead. Its PC business was sold to Lenovo, and it purchased PricewaterhouseCoopers consulting to help it build its service business. Nowadays, IBM designs computer programs, promotes new applications in the digital economy, and is famous for its Smarter Planet initiative. In 2011 it overtook software giant Microsoft in market

▶

value. As a market leader in services software, it earns profit margins of over 20 per cent, considerably higher than in the commoditized computer hardware business. Demand for bespoke business services, such as specially designed software, is much less elastic – companies that come up with good solutions can charge higher prices than their competitors. IBM's strategic change of direction looks to have paid off.

Incidentally, if you are wondering whether Apple is a hardware or a software company, it is often remarked that the basic technology in, for example, the iPhone is really quite simple – it is in design, understanding of its customers and ability to supply the app services that they desire that Apple leads the world. Fundamentally, it is a service company, which explains its high markups. Other companies have to struggle to compete. In mobile phones, the 1990s pioneer Nokia is now languishing and Samsung now threatens to overtake Apple. Apple is already on to the next thing. This makes a second point – demand elasticities for new products or services are likely to be lower than for well-established products or services.

A third related issue is the distinction between a generic category and a particular brand within that category. If the price of *all* cigarettes rises, addicted smokers buy cigarettes anyway. However, if the price of a single brand of cigarettes rises, smokers switch to other brands to meet their nicotine habit. Thus, for a particular cigarette brand the demand elasticity is quite high, but for cigarettes as a whole it is low. Similarly, if all clubs raise ticket prices, dedicated football fans will probably pay up reluctantly. But if Chelsea alone raise prices, some supporters might switch to other clubs in London. Tottenham and Arsenal are not that far away.

In all these examples, it is the strength of consumer desire and the ease or difficulty of finding substitute ways in which to fulfil this desire that determine whether demand elasticities will be low or high.

Here is another application of the use of the price elasticity of demand. Suppose Mercedes has 10 000 cars for sale but 20 000 customers eager to buy at the current price. Knowing the price elasticity of demand for Mercedes cars lets its executives in Stuttgart work out how much they can raise the price while still selling all the cars that they have produced. Without this information, they may underprice their cars (creating long queues of willing customers who would have been prepared to pay more) or overprice their cars (piling up large stocks of unsold Mercedes). Although Mercedes can react subsequently to the evidence about shortages or unsold cars, it is better to get things right at the first attempt. Research on the price elasticity of demand helps them do this.

Price, quantity and revenue

Reducing the price P boosts the quantity demanded Q. The effect on sales revenue, $P''Q$, depends on how quantity responds to price cuts. When demand is elastic, quantity rises by more than the price falls, so revenue rises. When demand is inelastic, price cuts lower P more than it boosts Q. Hence revenue falls.

In Table 4-3, demand for Stella Artois is elastic but demand for beer as a whole is inelastic. Falls in the price of Stella alone raise spending on Stella by increasing its sales a lot, whereas falls in the price of all beer reduce spending on beer. Table 4-4 relates these results to demand elasticities.

By collectively restricting oil supplies, the oil-producers' organization OPEC made oil prices soar. This raised oil producers' revenue since oil demand was *very* inelastic. Oil users had few alternatives to oil in the short run. Cuts in oil supply caused a big price rise and vast revenue gains for OPEC members.

Table 4-3   Price changes, spending and revenue

Price P	Stella		All beer	
	Q	P × Q	Q	P × Q
2	5	10	30	60
1.5	10	15	32	48
1	20	20	34	34

Table 4-4   Demand elasticities and spending changes

Change in total spending caused by	Price elasticity of demand is		
	Elastic (e.g. 3)	Unit-elastic (1)	Inelastic (e.g. 0.3)
Price rise	Fall	Unchanged	Rise
Price cut	Rise	Unchanged	Fall

Case study 4-1   Good news! A bad harvest!

There's an awful lot of coffee in Brazil, which supplies around one-third of the global coffee market. In 2011, adverse weather conditions in Brazil reduced its planting and production of coffee. Volume fell from 2.86 million tons in 2010 to 2.67 million tons in 2011, a reduction of about 7 per cent. As a result, the global supply of coffee fell – one reason why the price of coffee more than doubled between 2009 and 2011. What happened to Brazilian exports of coffee? Export values rose substantially. The higher price of coffee more than compensated for a disappointing export volume.

The global demand for coffee is inelastic; in fact, very inelastic. New Yorkers, Londoners, Parisians, and many other coffee addicts, cannot do without their coffee fix.

This example illustrates a general result. If demand is inelastic, farmers earn more revenue from a bad harvest than from a good one. The demand elasticity is low for many components of our staple diet, such as coffee, milk, bread, tea and meat.

When demand is inelastic, suppliers *taken together* are better off if supply falls. However, if a fire destroys the crop of a single farmer, that farmer's revenue falls. It would not make sense for a farmer deliberately to set fire to her own crops. Lower output from a single farm has almost no effect on total supply. The market price is unaffected. The single farmer sells less output at the same price as before. The individual producer faces an elastic demand – consumers can switch to the output of similar farmers – even if the demand for the crop as a whole is very inelastic.

In contrast, if farmers as a whole could reduce their total output, they would earn more revenue not less. This of course is precisely what OPEC has accomplished in the market for oil, another commodity in inelastic demand.

This sharp contrast between the individual and the aggregate is sometimes called the *fallacy of composition*. What is true in the aggregate need not be true for individuals, and vice versa.

Table 4-5 UK price elasticities of demand

Good (broad type)	Demand elasticity	Good (narrow type)	Demand elasticity
Fuel and light	−0.5	Bread	−0.4
Food	−0.6	Fish	−0.8
Clothing	−0.6	Expenditure abroad	−1.6
Services	−0.7	Catering	−2.6

Sources: R. Blundell, P. Pashardes and G. Weber, 'What do we learn about consumer demand patterns from micro data?', *American Economic Review*, 1993; *National Food Survey 2000*

Short run and long run

In the *short run*, customers may be unable to adjust much to changes in prices. For example, when fuel prices rise, people still need to drive their cars and heat their houses, so there is little immediate change in the quantity of fuel demanded. However, as time passes, smaller cars can be designed and built, and people can move back into city centres to save commuting costs, and more is invested in insulating houses to reduce heating bills. In the *long run*, the demand for fuel is more elastic.

This result is very general. Even if addicted smokers can't quit when cigarette prices soar, fewer young people start smoking. In response to a price increase, quantity demanded gradually falls as time elapses.

Measuring price elasticities

Table 4-5 confirms that the demand for broad categories of basic commodities, such as fuel, food and clothing, and services, is inelastic. As a category, only services such as haircuts, the theatre and sauna baths have an elastic demand. Households simply do not have much scope to alter the broad pattern of their purchases.

In contrast, there is a much wider variation in the demand elasticities for narrower definitions of commodities. Even then, the demand for some commodities, such as dairy produce, is very inelastic. However, particular kinds of services such as foreign expenditure and catering have much more elastic demand.

Box 4-2 provides an opportunity for you to see if you have mastered the calculation of price elasticity of demand.

Maths 4-1

Expressing elasticities using calculus

Suppose the demand curve is linear and given by $q = \alpha - \beta p$, where α and β are positive constants, p denotes the price and q the quantity demanded. For a small change in price, the corresponding quantity change dq/dp in this case equals $-\beta$, reminding us that the negative slope is constant for this linear demand curve. The price elasticity of demand, measuring percentage changes, is given by

$$(p/q)dq/dp = -\beta(p/q) = -\beta(\alpha - q)/q = 1 - (\alpha/q)$$

At low quantities (caused by high prices), the demand elasticity is large and negative (very elastic). As prices fall and output rises demand becomes less elastic.

Demand curves are not usually straight lines. Suppose instead that demand is given by $\log q = -\alpha \log p$. Hence, $(1/q)dq/dp = -\alpha/p$, so whatever the level of prices and quantities, the demand elasticity is simply $-\alpha$.

The cross-price elasticity of demand

The (own-) price elasticity of demand tells us about movements along a given demand curve holding constant all determinants of demand except the price of the good itself. We now hold constant the own-price of the good and examine changes in the prices of *related* goods. The cross-price elasticity tells us the effect on the quantity demanded of the good i when the price of good j is changed. As before, we use percentage changes.

The cross-price elasticity may be positive or negative. It is positive if a rise in the price of good j increases the quantity demanded of good i. Suppose good i is tea and good j is coffee. An increase in the price of coffee raises the demand for tea. The cross-price elasticity of tea with respect to coffee is positive. Cross-price elasticities tend to be positive when two goods are substitutes, and negative when two goods are complements. We expect a rise in the price of petrol to reduce the demand for cars because petrol and cars are complements.

Table 4-6 shows estimates for the UK. Own-price elasticities for food, clothing and travel are given down the diagonal of the table, from top left (the own-price elasticity of demand for food) to bottom right (the own-price elasticity of demand for travel). Off-diagonal entries in the table show cross-price elasticities of demand. Thus, 0.1 is the cross-price elasticity of demand for food with respect to transport. A 1 per cent increase in the price of travel increases the quantity of food demanded by 0.1 per cent.

The own-price elasticities for the three goods lie between −0.4 and −0.5. For all three goods, the quantity demanded is more sensitive to changes in its own price than to changes in the price of any other good.

Table 4-6   Cross-price and own-price elasticities of demand in the UK

% change in quantity	Caused by a 1% price change in demand of		
	Food	Clothing	Travel
Food	−0.4	0	0.1
Clothing	0.1	−0.5	−0.1
Travel	0.3	−0.1	−0.5

Source: R. Blundell, P. Pashardes and G. Weber, 'What do we learn about consumer demand patterns fom micro data?', *American Economic Review*, 1993

Box 4-2

Practising calculating price elasticity of demand (ped)

P = price (£)	1	2	3	4	5	6
Q = quantity demanded	10	8	6	4	2	1

The rows in Table 4-2 give price and quantity data for a particular demand curve. The table below shows five columns, labelled *a–e*, each corresponding to a situation in which the price changes by £1 and there is a corresponding change in the quantity demanded.

In column *a*, a 100 per cent price rise (from £1 to £2) induces a –20 per cent fall in quantity demanded (from 10 to 8), implying a price elasticity of demand of (–20/100) = –0.2. Similarly, in column *c*, a 50 per cent price reduction (from £2 to £1) induces a 25 per cent rise in quantity demanded (from 8 to 10), implying a price elasticity of (25)/(–50) = –0.5.

Try to complete columns *b*, *d* and *e* for yourself.

	a	*b*	*c*	*d*	*e*
(1) Initial P and Q	P = 1	P = 2	P = 2	P = 4	P = 5
	Q = 10	Q = 8	Q = 8	Q = 4	Q = 2
(2) New P and Q	P = 2	P = 3	P = 1	P = 3	P = 6
	Q = 8	Q = 6	Q = 10	Q = 6	Q = 1
(3) % change in P	100*(2 – 1)/1 = 100		100*(1 – 2)/2 = –50		
(4) % change in Q thus induced	100*(8 – 10)/10 = –20		100*(10 – 8)/8 = 25		
(5) ped = (4)/(3)	–0.2		–0.5		

The response of demand to income changes

Finally, holding constant the own-price of a good and the prices of related goods, we examine the response of the quantity demanded to changes in consumer incomes. As in Chapter 3, we neglect the possibility of saving. For the moment, we assume that a rise in the income of consumers will typically be matched by an equivalent increase in total consumer spending.

In Chapter 2 we introduced the concepts of normal and inferior goods, and of necessities and luxuries. These described, other things equal, how quantity demanded responds to an increase in income. As with responses to price changes, it is helpful to quantify the magnitude of these responses.

The **income elasticity of demand (ied)** measures the change in the quantity demanded in response to a 1 per cent rise in income. The ied is given by

ied = [% change in quantity demanded]/[corresponding % change in income]

The income elasticity of demand measures how far the demand curve shifts horizontally when incomes change. Figure 4-1 shows two possible shifts caused by a given percentage increase in income. The income elasticity is larger if the given rise in income shifts the demand curve from DD to $D''D''$ than if the same income rise shifts the demand curve only from DD to $D'D'$. When an income rise shifts the demand curve to the left, the income elasticity of demand is a negative number, indicating that higher incomes are associated with smaller quantities demanded at any given prices.

In Chapter 2 we distinguished *normal* goods, for which demand increases as income rises, and *inferior* goods, for which demand falls as income rises. Thus, normal goods have a positive income elasticity (since income and quantity demanded change in the same direction as one another), whereas inferior goods have a negative income elasticity (showing that income and quantity demanded change in opposite directions).

We also distinguished luxury goods and necessities. All inferior goods are necessities, and have negative income elasticities of demand. However, necessities also include normal goods whose income elasticity of demand lies between zero and one. Luxuries have an income elasticity of demand in excess of one.

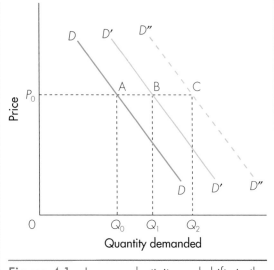

Figure 4-1   Income elasticity and shifts in the demand curve

These definitions tell us what happens to budget shares when incomes are changed but prices remain unaltered. The budget share of inferior goods falls as incomes rise. Higher incomes and household budgets are associated with lower quantities demanded at constant prices. Conversely, the budget share of luxuries rises when income rises. Because the income elasticity of demand for luxuries exceeds one, a 1 per cent rise in income increases quantity demanded (and hence total spending on luxury goods) by more than 1 per cent. Rises in income *reduce* the budget share of normal goods that are necessities. A 1 per cent income rise leads to a rise in quantity demanded but by less than 1 per cent, so the budget share must fall.

Table 4-7 summarizes the demand responses to changes in income, holding constant the prices of all goods. The table shows the effect of income increases. Reductions in income have the opposite effect on quantity demanded and budget share.

Table 4-8 reports income elasticities of demand in the UK, for broad categories of goods in the first two columns and narrower categories in the last two columns. Again, the variation in elasticities is larger for narrower definitions of goods. Higher incomes have much more effect on the way in which households eat (more prawns, less bread) than on the amount they eat in total. Food is a normal good but not a luxury. Its income elasticity is 0.45.

Table 4-7   Demand responses to a 1% rise in income

Good	Income elasticity	Quantity demanded	Budget share	Example
Normal	Positive	Rises		
Luxury	Above 1	Rises more than 1%	Rises	BMW
Necessity	Between 0 and 1	Rises less than 1%	Falls	Food
Inferior	Negative	Falls	Falls	Bread

Table 4-8 UK income elasticities of demand

Broad categories	Income elasticity	Narrower categories	Income elasticity
Tobacco	0.5	Coal	2.0
Fuel	0.3	Bread and cereals	0.5
Food	0.5	Dairy produce	0.5
Alcohol	1.1	Vegetables	0.9
Clothing	1.2	Travel abroad	1.1
Durables	1.5	Leisure goods	2.0
Services	1.8	Wines and spirits	2.6

Sources: J. Muellbauer, 'Testing the Barten model of household composition effects and the cost of children', *Economic Journal*, 1977; A. Deaton, 'The measurement of income and price elasticities', *European Economic Review*, 1975

The last column indicates that, within the food budget, higher income leads to a switch towards vegetables (whose income elasticity is higher than that for food as a whole) and away from bread, for which the quantity demanded declines. Rich households can afford to eat expensive salads to avoid getting fat. Poor people need large quantities of bread to ward off the pangs of hunger. Notice that tobacco is an inferior good, with its largest budget share among poor people. Richer people get their kicks in other (more expensive) ways.

Income elasticities help us forecast the pattern of consumer demand as the economy grows and people get richer. Suppose real incomes grow by 15 per cent over the next five years. The estimates of Table 4-8 imply that tobacco demand will rise by 7.5 per cent but the demand for wines and spirits will rise by 39 per cent. The growth prospects of these two industries are very different. These forecasts will affect decisions by firms about whether to build new factories and government projections of tax revenue from cigarettes and alcohol.

Similarly, as poor countries get richer, they demand more luxuries such as televisions, washing machines and cars.

Box 4-3

Store wars in an age of austerity

Since 2008, families have faced a substantial squeeze. Many incomes have failed to keep pace with inflation, and there have been large increases in the real cost of food and fuel. Taxes have been raised, and welfare benefits reduced, as the government struggles to get the budget deficit under control. As supermarkets battle it out for supremacy, or just for survival, how has the change in the economic climate affected competition?

Our theory predicts that, other things equal, a fall in real income should lead to a reduction in demand for all normal goods (having a positive income elasticity of demand) but a rise in demand for inferior goods (having a negative income elasticity of demand). Let's think first of all about cloth-ing. By 2012, upmarket Aquascutum had gone bust as the demand for its high-quality clothes collapsed. Aquascutum fits the theory nicely. But why, then, has Burberry, another business with a flagship store in London's Regent Street, done so well? Burberry managed to diversify out of the UK, becoming a global brand, and recently taking advantage of the huge growth of the affluent middle class in China. During 2011, Burberry sales to China alone grew by 30 per cent.

For poorer UK households, some of whom have experienced dramatic falls in family purchasing power, we should expect this loss of real income to lead to a search for cheaper goods with a negative income elasticity of demand. This is easily confirmed in the market place. Budget clothes retailer Primark enjoyed a 16 per cent increase in sales during 2011, whereas clothing sales in UK family favourite Marks and Spencer fell over the same period. With less to spend, people generally cut back on clothes spending, but the switch towards budget clothing was sufficiently strong that companies like Primark benefited considerably.

Like M&S, Tesco sells clothes as well as food. Tesco tried to respond to the austerity squeeze with a major price discounting campaign over the 2011 Christmas period. The price drop proved a big flop. Struggling consumers had to go somewhere even cheaper than Tesco if they wanted to buy clothes.

A similar story emerges in food retailing. German budget supermarket Aldi experienced a 25 per cent increase in UK sales during 2011, not because people were feeling richer but because they were feeling poorer. Tesco, previously the huge success story of the last ten supermarket years, lost out in its food business as well as its clothing business, and its price drop campaign failed to stem the tide. People deciding to tighten their belts went somewhere else entirely.

The same phenomena can be observed in other industries. Think of the success of the budget hotel chains Travelodge and Premier Inn, and the plight of package tour operators who have been victim of people deciding to stay in the UK for their vacation. Consumers have also switched from smart restaurants to ready meals, delayed home improvements and made the ageing car last a bit longer.

Thinking about the income effect on demand is useful not only in understanding how demand patterns change during recession and recovery, but also in thinking about the consequences of major global transformations. In China there are now 1 million millionaires and 600 billionaires. In the aggregate, the Chinese economy is making the equivalent of a new Italy every year. Similar effects, at a slower pace, are taking place in India, Brazil and Russia. These changes will profoundly affect the pattern of global demand. Companies able to plug into this demand growth – such as Mercedes, BMW and Burberry – will do very well indeed.

Measuring supply responses

The price responsiveness of supply

When a price rise has a large effect on quantity supplied, we say that the supply of the good is *elastic*. Suppliers are very responsive to prices. When the same size of price rise has a small effect on quantity supplied, we say that supply is *inelastic*. Sellers are not very responsive to prices.

> The **elasticity of supply** measures the *responsiveness* of quantity supplied to the price that suppliers receive. The (price) elasticity of supply is measured by
>
> **Supply elasticity = [% change in quantity supplied]/[% change in price]**

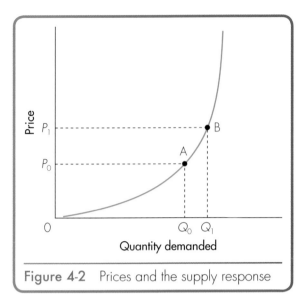

Figure 4-2   Prices and the supply response

When supply is elastic, a 1 per cent price rise increases quantity supplied by more than 1 per cent. Supply is price responsive. When supply is inelastic, a 1 per cent price rise increases quantity supplied by less than 1 per cent. Supply is less responsive to price. In the extreme cases, a horizontal supply curve means that quantity supplied is infinitely responsive to the price: the elasticity of supply is infinity. Conversely, a completely vertical supply curve means that producers supply the same quantity whatever the price. The price elasticity of supply is zero.

In the previous chapter, whether demand was elastic or inelastic affected whether revenue (price × quantity) fell or rose when the price increased. Because demand curves slope down, prices and quantities change in opposite directions, which is why it is important to know which effect dominates the other. For supply, there is no such conflict. Supply curves slope upwards. Prices and quantities always change in the same direction: high prices go with high quantities, low prices with low quantities. Hence, a price increase always raises the total revenue received by sellers (both price and quantity increase), and a price fall always reduces the revenue of sellers since both price and quantity are lower. In Figure 4-2, a price increase from P_0 to P_1 increases total revenue received by suppliers from OP_0AQ_0 to OP_1AQ_1.

Let us try to put our knowledge of supply elasticities to work. As we showed in Chapter 1, oil prices have shot up to all-time record levels. Truckers and fishermen are on strike around Europe, protesting at the high cost of fuel. We know that emerging economies are continuing to add to the demand for energy: they want cars, air travel, central heating, air conditioning, and power for their factories, all on a scale never seen before. So we can safely assume that the demand for energy is very strong. It will stay strong unless the global economy has an implosion. Possible sources of an implosion include a worldwide banking crisis, wars caused by rising food prices or scarce water, and fights over energy resources themselves.

But suppose none of these catastrophes occur. Emerging markets continue to prosper and world economic growth continues. What do you think will happen to oil prices. Will those who were amazed to see oil rise above $100/barrel next have to cope with oil at $200/barrel?

This is where supply elasticities get into the story. Recall the oil price hikes of 1973 and 1981. For a short time, oil prices were very high but then market forces got to work. Oil firms explored ever more costly and remote environments, and they did discover more oil. Lots of it. The supply elasticity of oil turned out to be much higher in the long run than in the short run. And as this extra quantity supplied came on stream, scarcity diminished and the price of oil came down. In fact, at one point it had fallen back to only $8/barrel.

Box 4-4

What determines supply elasticities?

The elasticity of supply is determined by how profitable it is for suppliers to increase quantity supplied when they are offered higher prices for their output. In part, this reflects technology. With a mass production line, it may be relatively easy to respond to opportunities to sell at higher prices, but doubling the TV revenue money for football clubs is no guarantee that another Lionel Messi will emerge.

As with demand, we need to distinguish between supply to the market as a whole and the behaviour of individual suppliers. If prices rise, a particular supplier may or may not be able to increase output by much. Some, such as a supplier of online services, may be able to increase supply by a lot. Others, such as a copper mine operating near full capacity already, may have little ability or willingness to increase the quantity supplied.

But increasing the supply of existing producers is not the whole story. Higher prices may entice new suppliers into the market, thereby enlarging total supply. Total supply is then more elastic than the supply of individual producers. The rise in air passengers in the last two decades reflected the growth of easyJet and Ryanair, rather than a major expansion by British Airways and Air France.

As with elasticity of demand, elasticity of supply is higher in the long run than the short run. Given more time, it is easier for producers to respond to a price change. It may take time to build new production capacity to respond to a price increase. A period of sustained high oil prices has finally made it profitable for energy companies to extract shale gas. So spectacular has this been in North America that it is now forecast that the United States will be self-sufficient in energy over the next two decades, a far cry from its energy dependence on OPEC producers in the 1970s. To take an even more obvious example, suppose energy prices ever became so high that the world concluded that the only feasible solution was nuclear power. It would probably take 20 years to build these nuclear power stations.

Similarly, closing factories or laying off workers is not something producers undertake on the first day that prices fall. They wait a bit to see if the price reduction is permanent, and even then it takes time to organize a production and employment response. Overnight, supply can be pretty inelastic.

Europe has far too many car producers. Elite brands such as BMW and Mercedes are enjoying the demand created in booming emerging markets, but the volume car business continues to struggle. Can a country such as France really support Citroen and Peugeot and Renault in a global industry in which large scale and a global supply chain is the key to delivering quality at reasonable prices? Recently, SAAB went bust, but further rationalization had been predicted for the last decade at least. Achieving exit by long-established players takes time. In the meantime, supply is quite inelastic.

To sum up, supply curves are often steep in the short run, showing that price changes have only small effects on quantity supplied. In the longer run, supply is more elastic and supply curves become flatter, indicating that quantity supplied varies more with price changes. Some of the longer run response is achieved by incumbent companies adjusting their output, but some is achieved by entry of new firms or exit of old ones.

What about this time round? Unlike 30 years ago, when OPEC curtailed supply, this time it is a surge in demand that has initiated the process. Last time, supply only had to rise back to its initial level to redress the balance; this time, a sustained increase in supply will be needed. From where is it to come?

It is important to realize that it is really the market for energy not oil that we are discussing. And there are many potential sources of new energy – solar, wind, nuclear, biofuels – in addition to ways of adding to the supply of oil itself (e.g. from shale deposits not previously exploited). These new technologies share one thing in common – they were not economic to exploit when the price of oil was low. At oil prices below \$30/barrel, it was much more profitable to rely on oil to supply our energy needs. But if prices are sustained above \$60/barrel, many of these alternative technologies begin to become attractive; at prices above \$100/barrel, they are even more lucrative. The more energy analysts depict a scenario of sustained high oil prices, the more people will decide to invest in alternative technologies.

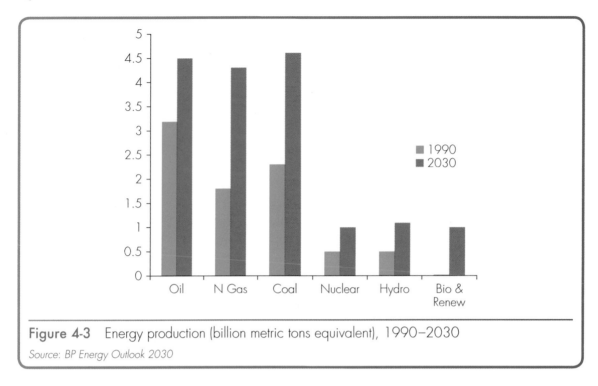

Figure 4-3   Energy production (billion metric tons equivalent), 1990–2030

Source: BP Energy Outlook 2030

Some are still experimental and will take years to perfect. Other technologies are already perfected but it will still take years to build the required capacity to produce on a sufficient scale to bid energy prices down again. And therein lies the catch. If investors believe someone else may invest in the capacity to increase energy supply significantly, they may start to doubt how long high energy prices are going to remain. This may make their own planned investment in additional supply less profitable. Yet if everyone draws the same conclusion, nobody will invest in the capacity needed to increase supply and prices will remain high!

This is probably too pessimistic an outcome. The prospect of high energy prices is probably robust enough to encourage a considered effort being devoted to increasing future energy supply. The supply elasticity will prove higher in the long run than it has been in the short run. It has been the surge in demand, coupled with the near-vertical short-run supply curve for oil, that has caused such a surge in oil prices. But don't bet on $200/barrel in 2030. The odds are that important new energy sources, viable at much lower prices than this, will be on stream by then. Some of these sources have the potential for considerable quantities of supply and should be able to cope with substantial rises in world demand for energy.

Figure 4-3 shows the forecast by BP in 2012 of how the energy market will evolve until 2030. Oil remains important, coal and natural gas grow even more, and the fastest growth is in biofuels and renewable energy, but from a tiny baseline.

Summing up

Price changes move a market along given supply and demand curves. Provided prices are free to adjust, the market gets to an equilibrium in which quantity supplied equals quantity demanded. Starting from this equilibrium, the consequences of a given shift in the one curve depend on the elasticity of the *other* curve. Figure 4-4 shows a supply shift from SS to $S'S'$ as a result of an increase in supply, shifting equilibrium from E_1 to E_2.

When demand is inelastic, price falls a lot but quantity hardly rises. Revenue falls, from the rectangle whose diagonal is OE_1 to the rectangle whose diagonal is OE_2, as in the left-hand part of Figure 4-4. Conversely,

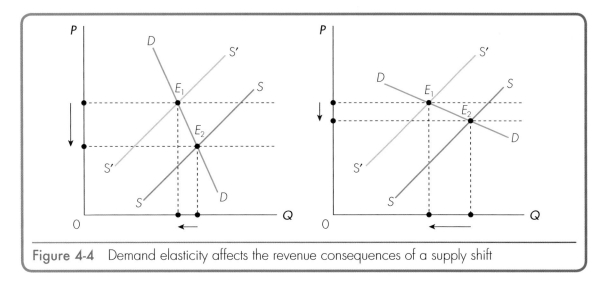

Figure 4-4   Demand elasticity affects the revenue consequences of a supply shift

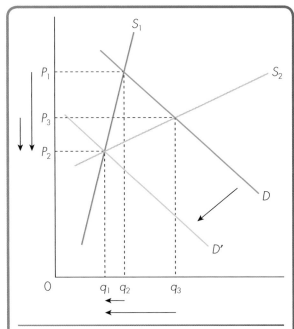

Figure 4-5   How supply elasticities affect the consequences of a demand shift

when demand is elastic, as in the right-hand part of Figure 4-4, the same supply shift from SS to $S'S'$ leads to a large quantity increase and only a small price decrease. Now the revenue rectangle whose diagonal is OE_2 exceeds the original revenue rectangle whose diagonal is OE_2.

The same type of reasoning can be applied to a shift in demand. Now the consequences depend on the elasticity of the supply curve. In Figure 4-5, we consider a downward shift in demand from the curve labelled D to that labelled D'. When the supply curve S_1 is almost vertical, the demand shift induces a large fall in price (from P_1 to P_2 but only a small fall in quantity from q_1 to q_2, whereas when the supply curve is much flatter, as shown by S_2, the same fall in demand leads to a much lower fall in price but a much greater fall in quantity.

Thus, producers with an inelastic supply curve experience larger price changes when demand shifts, but they face smaller quantity changes, so the implications for revenue rectangles are much affected by the elasticity of supply.

Recap

- The price elasticity of demand (sometimes simply called the elasticity of demand) is the percentage change in quantity demanded when the price of that good or service increases by 1 per cent.
- Demand is elastic (inelastic) when a 1 per cent price fall induces a rise in the quantity demanded by more (less) than 1 per cent.
- Price cuts raise (lower) total spending and producer revenue when demand is elastic (inelastic). Spending and revenue are unchanged if demand is unit-elastic.
- The cross-price elasticity of demand shows how the quantity demanded of one good responds to a change in the price of a related good.
- The income elasticity of demand shows the percentage change in quantity induced by a 1 per cent rise in income and total spending. Higher income increases demand for normal goods and reduces demand for inferior goods.
- Luxuries have an income elasticity above 1. Necessities have an income elasticity below 1. Inferior goods have a negative income elasticity.
- Supply is elastic if quantity supplied is very responsive to price and inelastic if quantity supplied is not very responsive to price. Provided the supply curve remains given, revenue of suppliers always changes in the same direction as price, since price and quantity change in the same direction as we move along a given supply curve.
- Supply elasticities are never negative. An elasticity above 1 means that a 1 per cent increase in the price leads to an increase in quantity supplied by more than 1 per cent. Supply is elastic. An elasticity below 1 means that a 1 per cent increase in the price leads to an increase in quantity supplied by less than 1 per cent. Supply is inelastic. A vertical supply curve has a supply elasticity of 0; a horizontal supply curve has an infinite supply elasticity.

Review questions

To check your answers to these questions, go to pages 378–79.

1 Why is demand more elastic in the long run than in the short run? Could it ever be less elastic in the long run?

2 Which of the following statements refer to the income elasticity of demand and which to the price elasticity of demand? (a) A Mercedes is a luxury, (b) I am addicted to nicotine, (c) bread is cheap and so attractive to poor students, (d) only the rich have servants, (e) the minimum wage has increased the cost of employing servants, so nowadays few people can afford them.

3 The price of a service rises and people demand more of it. Is the service normal or inferior? Why?

4 Suppose London introduces a congestion charge for Londoners but also gives £500 a year subsidy to all Londoners so that the average Londoner is neither better nor worse off from the combined effect of the two measures. Answer true or false for each of the following statements: (a) people's behaviour will change because of the income effect of the combined policies. (b) People's behaviour will change because of the substitution effect of the combined policies. (c) Demand for driving vehicles in London will fall compared to what it would otherwise have done. (d) Whether demand falls or not depends on whether the alternative (public transport) is normal or inferior.

5 Complements are goods for which there is a joint demand (shoes and shoelaces, right shoes and left shoes), whereas substitutes are alternative goods that satisfy a similar need (tea and coffee, bread and potatoes). (a) Do you think the cross-price elasticity of demand for shoes and shoelaces is positive or negative? (b) Do you think the cross-price elasticity of demand for tea and coffee is positive or negative? (c) Does this suggest a way to define complements and substitutes?

6 Unit-elastic demand is the special case in which a price change has no effect on the spending of buyers and the revenue of sellers. Is there a corresponding interpretation of unit-elastic supply? Why or why not?

7 You harvest your fresh but delicate strawberries and set up a market stall to sell them. It is a hot day. What is your elasticity of supply? Describe the shape of your supply curve for strawberries.

8 Why are rail fares higher during the rush hour? Comment on the following justifications: (a) total demand is higher at these times, (b) business people have to get to work at those times and have no alternative but to pay, (c) otherwise the train operators would have to buy more trains, which would be completely unused outside the rush hour.

9 If during austerity a budget clothes retailer grabs market share from a mid-market clothes retailer, why does the latter not completely copy the behaviour of the former when times are tough, selling only cheap and cheerful clothing?

10 A new government imposes a ceiling on rents in order to help poor students. (a) If you are a private landlord, what is the immediate effect on the quantity of student flats that you supply? (b) If the ceiling persists for ten years, what do you think has now happened to the total supply of student flats? (c) Is the supply elasticity of student flats higher in the short run or in the long run?

11 (a) If the government wants to maximize revenue from cigarette tax, should it simply set a very high tax rate on cigarettes? (b) If the government achieves its objective, what is the elasticity of demand for cigarettes at the price corresponding to this tax rate? (c) If you want not merely to get tax revenue but also to make people healthier, should you set a tax rate above or below that which maximizes revenue from cigarette taxation?

EASY

INTERMEDIATE

DIFFICULT

DIFFICULT

12 **Essay question** Suppose climate change causes flooding that wipes out much of UK agriculture. Discuss what happens to the price of food in the UK: (a) in the short run and (b) in the long run. Did you assume that the UK made and consumed all food itself or did you allow for international trade? How does the outcome differ in these two cases?

13 **Essay question** The operation to sell tickets for the 2012 Olympic Games in London was widely criticized. What process would you have set up? What objectives would you be trying to accomplish?

Online Learning Centre

To help you grasp the key concepts of this chapter check out the extra resources posted on the Online Learning Centre at www.mcgraw-hill.co.uk/textbooks/begg.

There are additional case studies, self-test questions, practice exam questions with answers and a graphing tool.

CHAPTER 5

Costs, supply and perfect competition

Learning outcomes

By the end of this chapter, you should be able to:

- Relate total, average and marginal cost
- Explain the law of diminishing returns
- Assess costs in the short run
- Define technology and production techniques
- Relate returns to scale and average cost curves
- Distinguish long-run and short-run costs
- Analyse a firm's supply decision in the short run and long run
- Understand temporary shutdown and permanent exit

- Show how minimum efficient scale and market size together determine market structure and the number of firms that can survive in the industry
- Explain the concept of perfect competition
- Show why a perfectly competitive firm's output equates price and marginal cost
- Examine incentives for entry and exit
- Derive the supply curve of a perfectly competitive industry
- Analyse the effect of shifts in demand or costs

In this chapter, we explore the costs that a firm faces, and examine how this affects its decision to produce. In the short run, a firm can vary some inputs to production, but is stuck with some things inherited from the past. In the long run, it can eventually change all the inputs to production and the production techniques used to combine these inputs. It has more flexibility in the long run. For a given set of demand conditions, we explore how different costs lead to different output decisions of suppliers.

We then examine how demand and cost structures interact to determine the type of competition that exists in a market. In some cases, individual firms have little or no effect on the price of the products that they produce and sell; in other cases, the price received is very sensitive to the output decisions of individual firms. Some firms are tiny, others huge. We analyse why this is the case.

We conclude the chapter by studying one particular form of competition, in which individual firms have no effect at all on the price of their products. The following chapter examines all other forms of competition, which share the feature that each firm recognizes that, by producing more, it will bid down the price that it receives.

5-1 How costs affect supply in the short run

Chapter 3 introduced the bare bones of a theory of supply, which depended on both costs and revenue. Now we need to put more flesh on this theory. Chapters 5–6 deal with two ideas. First, adjusting production methods takes time. Given time, firms may be able to reduce costs by choosing more appropriate methods of production. This leads to a distinction between optimal behaviour in the short run, when some things cannot be changed, and in the long run when everything can be changed.

Second, the revenue obtained from selling any particular output depends on the extent of competition in that market. This means that the general theory of supply is affected by the context of the degree of competition in which firms find themselves. To begin the analysis of the general theory of supply, this chapter deals with the special case of perfect competition. Chapter 6 then examines the theory of supply in other market environments in which competition is more restricted.

New companies, such as Orange and Amazon, lost a lot of money before eventually starting to make profits. Existing companies, such as British Airways and British Telecom, made big losses in the cyclical downturns of 2001–02 and 2008–09, despite previous periods of healthy profits; and banks made huge losses in 2007–08 as a result of over-optimistic lending decisions. But most kept going nevertheless. Firms don't always close down when they are losing money. They may keep going because they expect demand to rise, or costs to fall. We need to distinguish between the *short-run* and the *long-run* supply decisions of firms. In the short run, a firm can't fully adjust to new information. In the long run, full adjustment is possible. In this section, we focus on how costs affect the supply decision. We then turn to the influence of demand and revenue on supply decisions.

> An **input** (sometimes called a **factor of production**) is any good or service used to make output. A **production technique** is a particular way of using inputs to make output. **Technology** is the list of production techniques known today.

Inputs are labour, machinery, buildings, raw materials and energy.

> **Land** is the input supplied by nature; **capital** is the input that exists because of a previous production process, and still exists at the end of the production process. **Raw materials** are the physical inputs used up during the production process.

Thus, machinery and buildings are capital, because they were made previously, but now supply input services to the production processes in which they are now used; and they will still be there again next year. Power stations supply capital input services to making electricity and trains supply capital input services to the production of train journeys. For simplicity, economists often treat land as fixed in supply (even though meticulous application of fertilizer may increase its effective input a little). Capital services are usually fixed in the short run, but variable in the long run. Eventually we can produce more buildings and machinery (thereby increasing their input to future production), or allow them to depreciate (thereby reducing their input to future production).

Raw materials are things such as fertilizer in agriculture or hops in the beer industry, inputs that are entirely used up during the production process. We get some raw materials largely from nature (fresh water, plants, easily collected minerals) but devote considerable amounts of production to making some raw materials for subsequent production processes (high-octane fuel for aircraft, specialist steel for buildings, silicon for computer chips).

Labour is the production input supplied by workers.

With slavery now abolished, firms don't own workers any more, but they do rent or hire the labour services of workers. We usually assume that labour is the most easily variable input in the short run. How productive these workers are depends on the quantities of other inputs with which they can work. In some countries, wheat is produced with few people using lots of machinery: these workers will produce a lot of output per worker. In other countries, the same crop is produced with lots of workers using little machinery: now output per worker will be lower because they have a lower quantity of non-labour inputs with which to co-operate.

Both are possible techniques with which to produce wheat. Which one is adopted will depend on the prices of the different inputs and the chosen scale of production.

Short-run costs and diminishing returns

In the short run, the firm has some fixed inputs.

A **fixed input** can't be varied in the short run. A **variable input** can be adjusted, even in the short run.

The short run varies from industry to industry. It may take ten years to build a new power station, but only days to create a new market stall. Having built a power station, the electricity supplier must treat this input as fixed in the short run – the input of power station services cannot quickly be augmented nor quickly reduced. The existence of fixed inputs in the short run has two implications.

First, in the short run the firm has some fixed costs, which must be paid even if output is zero. It has to pay rent on its premises even if it decides not to produce anything this month. Second, because the firm cannot make all the adjustments it would like, its short-run costs must exceed its long-run costs. If it behaves differently in the long run, this can only be because it prefers to switch to a cheaper production method once this opportunity arises.

Variable costs are the costs of hiring variable factors, typically labour, raw materials and energy. Although firms may have long-term contracts with workers, and with material or energy suppliers, in practice most firms retain some flexibility through overtime and short time, hiring or non-hiring of casual and part-time workers, and purchases of raw material and energy in the open market to supplement contracted supplies.

Fixed costs don't vary with output levels. **Variable costs** change with output.

Chapter 3 introduced the theory of supply. Marginal revenue is the extra revenue obtained from selling another unit of output. Marginal cost is the extra cost of producing another unit of output. A firm will increase its profit if it expands output further whenever marginal revenue exceeds marginal cost, and will also increase its profit if it contracts its output whenever marginal revenue is less than marginal cost. Hence, profits are maximized at the output at which marginal revenue is equal to marginal cost. This was summarized in Figure 3-3, which we show again here as Figure 5-1.

We now wish to understand in more detail what determines the costs of a firm in the short run. For simplicity, we will think about a firm whose only variable input in the short run is labour. To show we are explicitly focusing on the short run, we now draw the short-run marginal

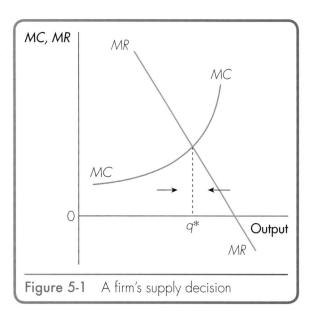

Figure 5-1 A firm's supply decision

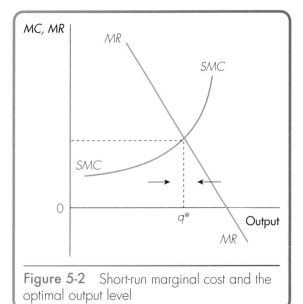

Figure 5-2 Short-run marginal cost and the optimal output level

cost curve *SMC* available to the firm while it has to treat its other inputs as fixed. It can increase output only by using more and more labour to work with fixed amounts of capital and other inputs.

> The **marginal product** of a variable input (labour) is the *extra* output from *adding* 1 unit of the variable input, holding constant the quantity of all other inputs in the short run.

The first worker has a whole factory to work with and has too many jobs to do to produce much. A second worker helps, a lot, and so does a third. Suppose the factory has three machines and the three workers are now specializing in each running one of the factory's machines. The marginal product of a fourth worker is lower. With only three machines, the fourth worker gets a machine only when another worker is resting. A fifth worker only makes tea for the other four. By now there are diminishing returns to labour.

> Holding all inputs constant except one, the **law of diminishing returns** says that, beyond some level of the variable input, further rises in the variable input steadily reduce the marginal product of that input.

Output is varied by using more labour input. Changes in the marginal product of labour affect the marginal cost of making output. The more productive a worker, the lower is the cost of making output. Figure 5-2 shows that, as output rises, short-run marginal costs initially fall as we move to the right along *SMC*; however, beyond some output, diminishing returns set in, additional workers add less and less to extra output, and hence marginal cost becomes higher and higher as the firm raises output further by adding to its variable labour input. While the marginal product of labour is rising, each worker adds more to output than the previous workers, and marginal cost is falling.

> **Short-run marginal cost SMC** is the extra cost of making one more unit of output in the short run while some inputs are fixed.

Once diminishing returns to labour set in, the marginal product of labour falls steadily as output is expanded, and marginal costs therefore rise with the level of output. This is the basic insight behind the shape of the marginal cost curve in Figure 5-2. Because other inputs are limited, it takes more and more extra workers to make each extra unit of output.

In Figure 5-2, the output *q** is the most profitable output to produce because it is the point at which *SMC* = *MR*. If *SMC* exceeded *MR* at that output, the firm could make even more profit by contracting output a little (the last unit of production cost more to produce than it added to revenue); if *MR* exceeded *SMC*, the firm could make even more profit by expanding output a little further (thereby making more in revenue than it costs to produce for that extra unit of production).

Sunk costs

If certain costs have *already* been incurred and can't be affected by your decision, ignore them. They shouldn't influence your future decisions. In deciding how much to produce in the short run, the firm ignores its fixed costs which must be incurred anyway.

It may seem a pity to abandon a project in which a lot of money has already been invested. Poker players call this throwing good money after bad. If you don't think it will be worth reading the rest of this book, you should not do it merely because you put a lot of effort into the first four chapters. Your optimal decision of how to spend your time, from now on, is to decide whether the benefits of reading the rest of the book outweigh the costs of reading the rest of the book.

A firm's supply decision in the short run

The firm only has one thing left to check. Should it be producing at all? To answer this question, the firm calculates its total revenue from production and compares this with its total costs in the short run.

Total costs are **total fixed costs** plus **total variable costs**.

In the short run, the firm has to pay the costs of its fixed inputs whether or not it produces any output and earns any revenue. The only decisions it can make are whether to incur variable costs and, if so, how much to produce. (Total revenue *minus* variable costs) is therefore the financial benefit to the firm from deciding to produce, and producing at q^*, at which $SMC = MR$ is guaranteed to maximize this financial benefit.

The firm's short-run supply decision is therefore simple to describe:

(a) If at output q^*, total revenue *exceeds* total variable costs, then produce output q^*.

(b) If, even at output q^*, total revenue is less than total variable costs, then produce zero output: shut down in the short run and hope for better times later.

Two final remarks. First, in the short run, even if the firm decides to produce, it may not be making profits. It is stuck with its fixed costs whatever it does. Ignoring these, it produces if it at least makes a profit on the variable part that it can affect. Either the profit from production is large enough to cover the fixed costs too, in which case the firm is in overall profit, or the profit from production is positive but less than the fixed costs, in which case the decision to produce is partially reducing the losses from the fixed (overhead) costs, even though in total the firm is still losing money.

Second, instead of comparing total revenues and total costs, we can divide both by output to get average revenues and average costs.

Average revenue is total revenue divided by output. But revenue is just output multiplied by price. So average revenue *is* the price the firm receives for its output. **Average cost** is total cost divided by output.

Since total cost = total fixed cost + total variable cost, dividing everything by the same output level we get

Average cost = **average fixed cost** + **average variable cost**

We can therefore restate the firm's supply decision as follows:

(a) If at the best production level q^*, price (hence average revenue) > average variable cost, then choose to produce q^*.

(b) If at output q^*, price < average variable cost, then shut down temporarily and produce 0.

Of course, private firms cannot be compelled to lose money indefinitely – they would rather quit the industry entirely. To examine when temporary shutdown makes sense and when permanent exit makes sense, we need to think about the long run as well as the short run.

Box 5-1

General Motors survives the slump, but only just

In the good times, well-run companies invest for the future and use the opportunity to think about their strategic direction for the future. Less well-run companies allow cost to creep upwards, get into businesses some way from their core competence and are surprisingly vulnerable when the downturn comes.

For years, General Motors was the pride not just of Detroit but of America. An early convert to global thinking, it had bought Vauxhall in 1925, Germany's Adam Opel in 1928 and Sweden's SAAB in 1989. By 2006 it had 200,000 employees and earned over $200 billion a year, but it had quite expensive labour contracts, had not led the trend towards much smaller cars, had been drawn into ancilliary businesses such as GMAC, its financial services division, and had failed to invest as much as the competition – whereas Ford had turned around Jaguar and Volvo by investing heavily in new model development, SAAB had been left with old models. Despite its $200 billion revenue in 2006, General Motors was barely breaking even.

In 2007 the US housing market fell by around 10 per cent, marking the end of the house price bubble and the beginning of trouble for mortgages secured against housing assets. As households and firms began to perceive the problem, their appetite for costly new vehicles declined abruptly. Loss of confidence also threatened the GM loans business in GMAC.

General Motors declared losses of $38 billion in 2007 and $31 billion in 2008, by which time the company was effectively bust. Significant losses in the financial services business had compounded the losses from car production itself. US presidents were unwilling to allow the pride of Detroit to go under, taking the entire region with it. Even market-oriented George W. Bush provided $14 billion in government support; Barack Obama injected another $39 billion.

If there had been no way in which GM could survive, these injections would merely have been largely a waste of money, and would merely have postponed the inevitable. It was critical, both for GM and the US government, that a successful recovery plan was devised and delivered.

GM managed to implement many of the textbook remedies. It renegotiated its labour contracts, convincing workers and unions that a lower wage in a sustainable company was preferable to a high wage that led to unemployment or bankruptcy. In the global business of auto production, more and more of the world's car supply is being manufactured in countries with lower wage costs. Detroit had to take a big step in this direction or go under.

GM also shrunk its labour force: whether or not it had been inappropriately high in 2006, GM had to prepare for a new slimline operation in which the volume of its car sales would be permanently lower. Having sold 4.5 million vehicles as late as 2006, by 2009 its sales were down to 2 million, a fall of 55 per cent in three years. GM also began to attack more vigorously the small car market with new products such as the new Chevrolet Aveo, more in tune with a world with oil prices at record highs. Leaving aside luxury brands, such as BMW and Mercedes, the brands that have grown during the European recession are Hyundai, Kia and Chevrolet.

What was the combined result of the repositioning of the company and the partial recovery of the US economy after 2009? GM declared a much smaller loss of $4 billion in 2009, but then profits of $4 billion in 2010 and over $7 billion in 2011. Taking a purely short-run view, the company would have been closed in 2007. Since then, it has begun to pay back the investments that were made in it. If the profits continue, the decision may be justified by GM profits alone; taking into account the wider cost to the Michigan economy if GM had folded, the US government probably considers its investment money well spent.

Costs and supply in the long run

A technique is said to be **technically efficient** if no other technique could make the same output with fewer inputs. **Technology** is all the techniques known today. **Technical progress** is the discovery of a new technique that is more efficient than existing ones, making a given output with fewer inputs than before.

Technology relates volumes of inputs to volume of output. But costs are values. To deduce the cheapest way to make a particular output, the firm needs to know input prices as well as what technology is available. At each output level, the firm finds the lowest-cost technique. When labour is cheap, firms choose labour-intensive techniques. If labour is expensive, the firm will switch to more capital-intensive techniques that use less labour.

Faced with higher demand, the firm will want to expand output, but adjustment takes time. In the long run, the firm can adjust all input quantities and the choice of technique. In the short run, the firm can't change all inputs, and may also be unable to change technique. It may be years before a new factory is designed, built and operational.

Long-run total cost LTC is the total cost of making each output level when a firm has plenty of time to adjust fully and produce this output level by the cheapest possible means. **Long-run marginal cost LMC** is the rise in total cost if output permanently rises by one unit. **Long-run average cost LAC** is LTC divided by the level of output Q.

In the long run, most firms face the U-shaped average cost curve shown in Figure 5-3. At higher output levels, the firm achieves efficiency gains and lower average costs. However, beyond some output level Q^*, life gets more difficult for the firm, and its average costs increase if output is higher.

There are **economies of scale** (or increasing returns to scale) if long-run average cost LAC falls as output rises, **constant returns to scale** if LAC is constant as output rises, and **diseconomies of scale** (or decreasing returns to scale) if LAC rises as output rises.

The U-shaped average cost curve in Figure 5-3 has scale economies up to point A, where average cost is lowest. At output levels above Q^*, there are decreasing returns to scale. Since LAC is horizontal at point A, there are constant returns to scale when output is close to Q^*.

Other shapes of cost curve are possible. Later, we shall see that in some industries with large-scale economies, LAC may fall over the entire output range. Conversely, the output Q^* may be so tiny that the LAC curve slopes up over most normal output ranges.

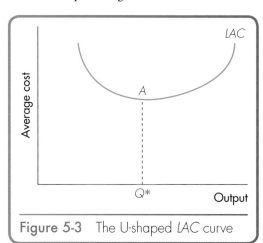

Figure 5-3   The U-shaped LAC curve

Maths 5-1

Average costs and marginal costs

For those of you familiar with calculus, here is a neat example of its elegance. Suppose total costs depend on output through the cost curve $C(q)$. Average cost $A(q)$ is therefore given by $C(q)/q$, which simply divides total cost by the quantity of output produced. The slope of this average cost curve is computed by differentiating with respect to q, which yields $(dC/dq)/q - C/q^2$ and average cost is at a minimum when this slope is zero, which implies $(dC/dq) = C/q$. This says that marginal cost dC/dq = average cost C/q when output q is at the level that attains minimum average cost.

Scale economies

There are three reasons for economies of scale. Production may entail some *overhead costs* that do not vary with the output level.[1] A firm requires a manager, a telephone, an accountant and a market research survey. It can't have half a manager and half a telephone if output is low. From low initial output, rises in output allow overheads to be spread over more units of output, reducing average cost. Beyond some output level, the firm needs more managers and telephones. Scale economies end. The average cost curve stops falling.

A second reason for economies of scale is *specialization*. At low output levels, each of the few workers has to do many jobs and never becomes very good at any of them. At higher output and a larger workforce, each worker can focus on a single task and handle it more efficiently. The third reason for economies of scale is that large scale is often needed to take advantage of better machinery. Sophisticated but expensive machinery also has an element of indivisibility. A farmer with a small field may as well dig the field by hand. With a larger field, it becomes worth buying a tractor.

Diseconomies of scale

The main reason for diseconomies of scale is that management is hard once the firm is large: there are *managerial diseconomies of scale*. Large firms need many layers of management, which themselves have to be managed. Co-ordination problems arise, and average costs begin to rise. Geography may also explain diseconomies of scale. If the first factory is sited in the best place, a second factory has to be built in a less advantageous location, and the third in a less advantageous location still.

The shape of the average cost curve thus depends on two things: how long the economies of scale persist, and how quickly the diseconomies of scale occur as output rises.

The lowest output at which all scale economies are achieved is called **minimum efficient scale**.

In heavy manufacturing industries economies of scale are substantial. At low outputs, average costs are much higher than at minimum efficient scale. High fixed costs of research and development need to be spread over large output to reduce average costs. Hence, large markets are needed to allow low costs to be attained.

High transport costs used to mean that markets were small. For industries with large fixed costs, this meant that average costs were high. Globalization is partly a response to a dramatic fall in transport costs. By selling in bigger markets, some firms can enjoy large-scale economies and lower average costs.

In other industries, minimum efficient scale occurs at a low output. Any higher output raises average cost again. There is a limit to a hairdresser's daily output. A larger market makes little difference. Globalization has not had a big impact on hairdressing; but the Internet has always been global – admitting another user to Google hardly costs anything at all. Almost all the costs are fixed costs, the costs of setting up the website in the first place. Marginal cost is very low. And average cost falls as more users are admitted and the fixed costs are spread across more and more users.

We begin by discussing the output decision of a firm with a U-shaped average cost curve. Then we show how to amend this analysis when firms face significant economies of scale.

---

[1]   Some textbooks refer to these as fixed costs, because they must be paid anyway. We prefer to call them overhead costs, reserving the term 'fixed costs' for those which cannot be varied in the short run but could be altered if there is sufficient time to adjust production methods. In contrast, overhead costs have to be paid by any firm that remains in business, no matter how long it has to adjust.

Box 5-2

Scale economies, sharing platforms and dancing with the devil

The job of competitors is to compete with one another. Yet increasingly we see examples of firms, supposedly in competition, developing co-operative agreements for some of their activities. What lies behind this is often the search for economies of scale.

Car makers have long collaborated on vehicle engines or the car chassis, in order to share expensive costs of R&D and spread them over greater total sales, thereby reducing the cost per car. Recent examples include agreements between Peugeot Citroën and Toyota to share components of a city car – simultaneously sold as the Peugeot 107, the Toyota Aygo and the Citroen C1; between BMW and Fiat to share costs on the platform for the Mini and the Alfa Romeo MiTo; and between Nissan and Renault to share the new platform for the Renault Modus, Renault Clio, Nissan Cube and Nissan Micro.

So prevalent are these agreements in the motor industry, driven by the need for scale economies, especially in the volume car business in which brand and design are a little less important than value for money, that it is increasingly the case that producers either have to forge such links with rivals or else themselves be a massive global producer (such as Ford or VW) where these scale economies can be achieved within the company itself. The days of small, or even medium-sized, independent producers are over, except in niche markets such as sports cars.

A similar example is the proliferation of airline networks, such as *Star Alliance* (including Air Canada, Air China, Lufthansa, Singapore Airlines, United Airlines) and *One World Alliance* (including BA, Cathay Pacific, Iberia, Japan Airlines and Qantas). In part this again entails sharing expensive platforms – new customer reservation systems to handle airline bookings, for example – to enjoy scale economies but it also provides a mechanism for eliminating wasteful duplication and wasteful competition. Instead of all these airlines feeling obliged to operate a route on which they will have half empty planes, a single flight can simultaneously be badged with the flight details of several members within an alliance, allowing that plane to operate much closer to full capacity while leaving each member airline able to claim it offers a wide range of routes on its service.

These examples all entail co-operation between firms at a similar stage in the chain of production, what one might call co-operation between producers making substitute products for one another. They co-operate in some dimensions and then compete like crazy on other dimensions.

Such co-operation has the potential to be in the social interest when it allows society access to services or products at lower cost than could be supplied by an individual company acting alone. However, regulators have to watch out for such alliances merely becoming a vehicle for co-operative price fixing by firms, raising profit margins by negotiating away competition without having any offsetting benefit in cost reduction.

During the last decade, there has been increasing co-operation between logistics giants such as parcel-delivery companies DHL and UPS. For example, UPS, which had some excess capacity in its American air-freight network, carried DHL's packages on its planes inside the US – and between the US, Canada and Mexico – thereby earning from DHL a fee of up to $1 billion a year. This practice then proliferated across companies and regions. In 2012, the EU concluded that some of these arrangements were merely cartels to fix prices at unnecessarily high levels. It concluded that

▶

▶
there had been a 'gardening club' in which the names of vegetables such asparagus and courgettes were used as code words by the price fixers. The Commission fined 13 firms, including UPS, a total of €169 million. Interestingly, DHL, which blew the whistle, was let off the fine.

Co-operation deals among rivals are tricky because firms need to be very clear about what will and will not be covered by them. For example, newspapers differentiate themselves by their editorial content and the quality of their advertising-sales operations. Editorial and advertising departments of rival papers must be kept separate if they are to retain their distinctive identities. But distribution, printing and back-office operations may be easier to consolidate without blurring brands.

Average cost and marginal cost

As output rises, average cost falls whenever marginal cost is below average cost; average cost rises whenever marginal cost is above average cost. Hence average cost is lowest at the output Q^* at which LAC and LMC cross. Figure 5-4 illustrates.

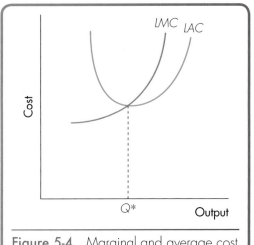

Figure 5-4 Marginal and average cost

This relation between average and marginal is a matter of arithmetic, as relevant to football as to production. Suppose Wayne Rooney scores 3 goals in his first 3 games, thus averaging 1 goal per game. Two goals in the next game, implying 5 goals from 4 games, raises the average to 1.25 goals per game. In the fourth game the marginal score of 2 goals exceeded the average score of 1 goal in previous games, thus raising the average. But if Wayne had not scored in the fourth game (a marginal score of 0), this would have dragged down his average per game from 1 (3 goals in 3 games) to 0.75 (3 goals in 4 games).

Similarly, when the marginal cost of making the next unit of output exceeds the average cost of making the existing units, making another unit *must* raise average cost. Conversely, if the marginal cost of the next unit is below the average cost of existing units, another unit *must* reduce average cost. When marginal and average cost are equal, making another unit leaves average cost unchanged.

Hence, in Figure 5-4, average and marginal cost curves cross at minimum average cost. At outputs below Q^*, LMC is below LAC, so average cost is falling. Above Q^*, LMC is above LAC, so average cost is rising. At output Q^*, average costs are at a minimum. As in Wayne's world, this relation rests purely on arithmetic.

Box 5-3

Scale economies and the Internet

Producing information products such as films, music and news programmes has a high fixed cost, but distributing these products digitally has almost a zero marginal cost and no capacity constraint. Scale economies are vast. Moreover, if marginal cost is close to zero, smart suppliers will price their products so that marginal revenue is also tiny.

EMI, a legend of the music industry, was formed in 1931. Its Abbey Road studios in London hosted giants such as the Beatles, at one time making it the fourth-largest record label and one of the top 100 companies on which the FTSE stock market index was based. Competition from Internet downloads gradually undercut this business completely. In 2011, deep in debt, it was taken over by the US bank Citigroup, which then sought to break up EMI and sell it off in pieces to consortia led by Sony, Vivendi and others.

The viable surviving parts of the business operate largely online, with records and CDs becoming obsolete.

The firm's long-run output decision

We can now describe how a firm chooses its output level in the long run. This is a two-part decision. First, the firm evaluates its marginal cost and marginal revenue, thereby telling the firm the best output at which to produce in the long run. It should produce the output at which $LMC = MR$. If marginal revenue exceeds marginal cost at any particular output, the firm is still making a marginal profit by producing more, and should therefore raise production. If marginal cost exceeds marginal revenue, the firm has made a marginal loss on the last unit of production and should produce less. Only when marginal revenue equals marginal cost is there no scope to increase operating profits by changing the output level. The marginal condition tells us the best positive output level for maximizing profit, namely, where marginal revenue equals marginal cost.

However, the firm also has to check that it should be in business at all. Given that it has chosen the most advantageous output level, is it making profits at this output? Or does it make losses at every output level, in which case the marginal condition has merely identified the least bad output to produce? It might be even better to give up completely and eventually make zero rather than lose money forever.

Suppose Q^{**} is the output at which $LMC = MR$. If, at this output, the price for which this output can be sold (which we deduce from the demand curve) exceeds the average cost LAC of making this output, the firm is making permanent profits and should remain in the industry. However, if at the 'best' output Q^{**} the firm is losing money because LAC exceeds the price for which Q^{**} can be sold, the firm is better off by closing down completely.

Notice the two-stage argument. First we use the *marginal condition* ($LMC = MR$) to find the best output, *then* we use the *average condition* (comparing LAC at this output with the price or average revenue) to determine if the best output is good enough for the firm to stay in business in the long run. If the firm's best output yields losses, it should close down.

It is important to realize that the best output Q^{**} is not, in general, the same as the output Q^* in Figure 5-4 at which long-run average costs are minimized. Figure 5-4 is purely an analysis of costs. What the firm wishes to do depends both on costs and revenues. If demand is strong enough, it is profitable to produce more than the minimum efficient scale Q^* because at this output level there are still further profits to be exploited by producing even more. Conversely, demand may be so weak that the firm chooses to produce less than minimum efficient scale. Any attempt to produce more would drive prices down too much. The

Table 5-1 A firm's supply decisions

Output decision	Marginal condition: output at which	Produce this output unless
Short run	MR = SMC	P < *Short-run average variable cost*; if it is, shut down temporarily
Long run	MR = LMC	P < *LAC*; if it is, quit permanently

firm would lose more from lower prices than it would gain from being able to reduce average costs. This completes our analysis of the supply decision, as demonstrated in Table 5-1.

Short-run and long-run costs

Even if losing money in the short run, a firm will stay in business if it at least covers its variable costs. In the long run it must cover all its costs to stay in business. A firm may reduce its costs in the long run, converting a short-run loss into a long-term profit. In the short run, its technique of production is fixed and it has some fixed inputs to production. In the long run, it can vary everything.

The firm will only wish to vary things where, by doing so, costs are reduced and hence profitability is increased.

Case study 5-1   Gone today but steel here tomorrow

Thirty years ago, British Steel was a state-owned monopoly, selling largely in the UK. Then the firm was privatized and its market became global, in which British Steel was a relatively small player. It merged with a Dutch steel maker to form a new company, Corus, which also failed, and was then taken over by an Indian company, Tata Steel.

© Alistair Forrester Shankie

Despite all these changes, the UK plants struggled to break even. Partly, as with the car industry in Detroit, this reflected globalization. UK labour costs in steel manufacture are now six times those in Brazil and ten times those in India. If the UK wishes to be a high-wage producer within the global economy, it needs either to have massive investment to make UK factories ultra-modern and technically sophisticated or else to recognize that more basic production will be undertaken in lower-wage countries than the UK. The industry tried to move into niche hi-tech steel, which entailed shutting down more basic capacity that was being outcompeted by cheaper producers abroad.

As competitive pressures mounted, the UK steel industry faced the classic choice: undertake expensive investment to restore competitiveness, shut down temporarily and hope for better demand conditions in the future, or exit the industry in order to avoid making permanent losses. If you had been a shareholder, would you have thought it worth contributing more money in the hope of saving the business, or concluded that it was more prudent to contract, saving your money for other, more profitable ventures with a greater prospect of international success?

Whoever owned the UK steel industry, they always concluded that it needed to shrink yet further to become commercially viable. Even Tata Steel, a huge global success, concluded that further parts of the UK steel industry needed to be closed. This was not just a cyclical decision reflecting temporary recession, but a longer-run view that UK costs did not justify the major investment needed for ongoing success.

Just when Teesside had almost given up hope of retaining its steel-making economy, SSI Industries of Thailand re-opened the plant in April 2012, having bought the Teesside Cast Products plant from Tata for £400 million in 2010. The plant will produce steel slabs for export to Thailand.

5-3 How market structure affects competition

We now explore how market structures differ in the type of competition they exhibit, and how this relates to the underlying determinants of cost and demand. We begin by looking at different types of competition.

> A **perfectly competitive** firm faces a horizontal demand curve at the going market price. It is a price-taker.

A perfectly competitive firm is insignificant relative to the market demand that it faces. Its output decisions have no effect on the price that it faces.

Perfect competition is a useful benchmark, and represents one extreme in the spectrum of possible market structures. What determines the structure of a particular market? Why are there 10 000 florists but only a handful of chemical producers? How does the structure of an industry affect the behaviour of its constituent firms?

In any market structure other than perfect competition, each firm faces a downward-sloping demand curve for its product and is therefore an *imperfectly competitive* firm.

> An **imperfectly competitive** firm recognizes that its demand curve slopes down. To sell more of its own output, it needs to reduce its own price.

Within this general category are three particular examples.

> For a **pure monopoly**, the demand curve for the firm is the industry demand curve itself. There is only one firm in the industry and it has no fear of entry by others.

Table 5-2   Market structure

Form of competition	Number of firms	Ability to affect price	Entry barrier	Example
Perfect competition	Many	Nil	None	Fruit stall
Imperfect competition				
Monopolistic competition	Many	Small	None	Corner shop
Oligopoly	Few	Medium	Some	Cars
Pure monopoly	One	Large	Huge	Post Office

An industry with **monopolistic competition** has many sellers making products that are close but not perfect substitutes for one another. Each firm then has a limited ability to affect its output price.

Between these two lies **oligopoly**, an industry with only a few, interdependent producers.

Table 5-2 offers an overview of market structure. As with most definitions, the distinctions can get a little blurred. How do we define the relevant market? Was British Gas a monopoly in gas or an oligopolist in energy? Is Network Rail a monopoly in train lines or an oligopolist in transport infrastructure competing, for example, with the British Airports Authority?

We also have to be careful about the relevant definition of the market. When a small country trades in a competitive world market, even the sole domestic producer may have little influence on market price, which may be determined in the world market.

Why market structures differ

We now develop a general theory of how the economic factors of demand and cost interact to determine the likely structure of each industry. The car industry is not an oligopoly one day but perfectly competitive the next. It is long-run influences that induce different market structures. In the long run, one firm can hire another's workers and learn its technical secrets. In the long run, all firms or potential entrants to an industry essentially have similar cost curves.

Earlier in this chapter, we discussed minimum efficient scale, *MES*, the lowest output at which a firm's long-run average cost curve bottoms out. This is shown as the output Q^* in Figure 5-5.

When *MES* is tiny relative to the size of the market, the industry demand curve is drawn a long way to the right in Figure 5-5. There is room for lots of little firms, each producing Q^* but trivial relative to the output of the whole industry – a good approximation to perfect competition. Conversely, when *MES* occurs at an output nearly as large as the entire market – imagine drawing a demand curve only just to the right of point A in Figure 5-5 – there is room for only one firm. A second firm trying to squeeze into the remaining space would have room only to produce a small output; but then its *LAC* curve would imply much higher average costs

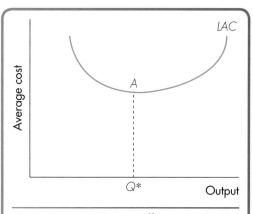

Figure 5-5   Minimum efficient scale Q*

because it enjoys inadequate scale economies. So there is no room for a second firm to enter and make a profit. A natural monopoly enjoys sufficient scale economies to have no fear of entry by others.

When *MES* occurs at, say, a quarter of the market size as reflected by the position of the demand curve, the industry is an oligopoly, with each firm taking a keen interest in the behaviour of its small number of rivals.

Monopolistic competition lies midway between oligopoly and perfect competition. There is room for many small firms but, unlike perfect competition, the firms are not identical to one another. Each corner shop is slightly closer to some customers than others. So each small firm has a little scope to affect the price it charges for its products.

Market structure thus reflects the interaction of two things: the shape and position of long-run average cost curves (and in particular the output corresponding to minimum efficient scale for a single firm) and the size of the market (as determined by the output levels consistent with the industry demand curve as a whole). Together, these determine how many firms are likely to survive in the industry and hence the type of competition that will then take place between them.

Perfect competition is one end of this spectrum, with *MES* so small relative to industry demand that each firm is insignificant. Next we look at the opposite case, in which only a single firm can survive.

Box 5-4

Facing the music

Operating in every major music market, three firms now dominate the global music industry – Sony Bertelsmann, Vivendi SA and AOL Time Warner. Each of the three (a) owns a large collection of labels that were formerly independent companies, and (b) also operates in other aspects of entertainment such as publishing or telecommunications.

Why are there so few companies in the global music business? Because most of it is now digital and the marginal cost of connecting another user is tiny, whereas the fixed costs of developing playlists are large. These costs are independent of the subsequent number of users. This is a classic case in which economies of scale are huge. There is no point being a small producer. Actually, life is not that easy for the giants either: the value of the global recorded music market is falling every year because of price competition and endemic Internet piracy.

Global recorded music sales fell by almost 9 per cent in 2010 and a further 3 per cent in 2011 as digital piracy continued to take its toll on the industry, with the UK overtaken by Germany as the second-largest music market after 'physical' sales of CDs collapsed by almost a fifth. Global recorded music revenues fell by £10 billion in 2011, according to the annual report by the IFPI, which represents the international music industry.

Digital revenues grew by 8 per cent year-on-year to account for 31 per cent of all recorded music revenues. However, the growth of digital is impeded by piracy and winning consumers over to legal download models.

Sources: bbcworldservice.com; www.guardian.co.uk

We conclude this chapter by studying the case of perfect competition in more detail. In the next chapter we explore the various types of imperfect competition.

5-4 Perfect competition

The previous two sections have explored how costs vary in the short run and in the long run, and how the firm therefore chooses whether to supply any output and, if so, what quantity of output is best. Throughout this analysis of costs and supply, we treated demand conditions as given.

We now switch our attention from costs to demand and revenue, for which we need to know about the structure of the industry in which the firm operates.

An **industry** is the set of all firms making the same product.

The output of an industry is the sum of the outputs of its firms. Yet different industries have very different numbers of firms. The UK has thousands of florists but only one producer of nuclear energy. We begin with perfect competition, a hypothetical benchmark against which to assess other market structures.

In **perfect competition**, actions of individual buyers and sellers have no effect on the market price.

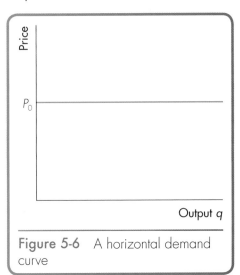

Figure 5-6   A horizontal demand curve

This industry has many buyers and many sellers. Each firm in a perfectly competitive industry faces a horizontal demand curve, shown in Figure 5-6. Whatever output q the firm sells, it gets exactly the market price P_0, and the tiny firm can sell as much as it wants at this price. If it charges more than P_0, the firm loses all its customers. If it charges less than P_0, it attracts all the vast number of customers of other firms. This horizontal demand curve is *the* crucial feature of a perfectly competitive firm. We sometimes say such a firm is a *price-taker*. It has to treat the market price as given, independent of any decisions made by the individual firm. Next time you visit a fruit market, in which there are many stalls selling identical onions, you can think of each stall as a price-taker in the market for onions.

For each firm to face a horizontal demand curve, the industry must have four characteristics. First, there must be many firms, each trivial relative to the industry as a whole. Second, the firms must make a standardized product, so that buyers immediately switch from one firm to another if there is any difference in the prices of different firms. Thus, all firms make essentially the same product, *for which they all charge the same price.*

Why don't all the firms in the industry do what OPEC did, collectively restricting supply to raise the market price of their output? A crucial characteristic of a perfectly competitive industry is *free entry and exit*. Even if existing firms could organize themselves to restrict total supply and drive up the market price, the consequent rise in revenues and profits would attract new firms into the industry, raising total supply and driving the price back down. Conversely, when firms in a perfectly competitive industry are losing money, some firms close down. This reduces total supply and drives the price up, allowing the remaining firms to survive.

The firm's supply decision

We have already developed a general theory of the supply decision of a firm. First, the firm uses the marginal condition ($MC = MR$) to find the best positive level of output; then it uses the average condition to check whether the price for which this output is sold covers average cost. *The special feature of perfect competition is the relationship between marginal revenue and price.* Facing a horizontal demand curve, a competitive firm does *not* bid down the price as it sells more units of output. Since there is no effect on the revenue from existing output, the marginal revenue from an additional unit of output *is* its price: $MR = P$.

The firm's short-run supply curve

Firms in any industry choose the output at which short-run marginal cost *SMC* equals marginal revenue *MR*. In perfect competition, *MR* always equals the price *P*. Hence, a competitive firm produces the output at which price equals marginal cost, then checks whether zero output is better.

Figure 5-7 illustrates the firm's supply decision in the short run. P_1 is the shutdown price below which the firm fails to cover variable costs in the short run. At all prices above P_1, the firm chooses output to make $P = SMC$.

> A competitive firm's **short-run supply curve** is that part of its short-run marginal cost curve above its shutdown price (the price that just covers its short-run average variable costs).

This shows how much the firm wants to make at each price it might be offered. For example, at a price P_4, the firm chooses to supply Q_4.

The firm's long-run supply curve

Similar reasoning applies in the long run. Figure 5-8 shows the firm's average and marginal costs in the long run. Facing a price P_4, equating price and long-run marginal cost, the firm chooses the long-run output Q_4 at point D. Here it makes profits, since it is earning a price P_4 in excess of its average cost; equivalently, its total revenue exceeds its total cost.

In the long run, the firm exits from the industry only if, at its best positive output, price fails to cover long-run average cost *LAC*. At price P_2, the marginal condition leads to point B in Figure 5-8, but the firm is losing money and leaves the industry in the long run.

A competitive firm's long-run supply curve is that part of its long-run marginal cost *above* minimum average cost. At any price below P_3, the firm leaves the industry. At price P_3, the firm makes Q_3 and just breaks even after paying all its economic costs.

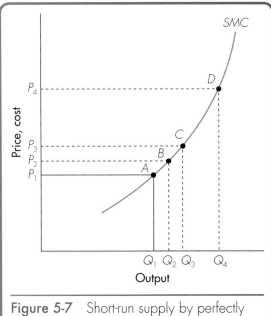

Figure 5-7   Short-run supply by perfectly competitive firm

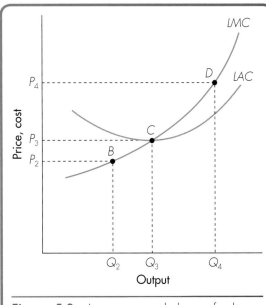

Figure 5-8   Long-run supply by perfectly competitive firm

Entry and exit

The price P_3 corresponding to the minimum point on the *LAC* curve is called the *entry or exit price*. There is no incentive to enter or leave the industry. The resources tied up in the firm are earning just as much as their opportunity costs – what they could earn elsewhere. Any price less than P_3 will induce the firm to exit from the industry in the long run.

Entry is when new firms join an industry. **Exit** is when existing firms leave.

We can also interpret Figure 5-8 as the decision facing a potential entrant to the industry. At a price P_3, an entrant could just cover its average cost if it produced an output Q_3. Any price above P_3 yields economic profits and induces entry by other firms in the long run.

Industry supply curves

A competitive industry comprises many firms. In the short run, two things are fixed: the quantity of fixed factors used by each firm, and the number of firms in the industry. In the long run, each firm can vary all its factors of production, but the number of firms can also change through entry and exit.

The short-run industry supply curve

Just as we can add individual demand curves by buyers to get the market demand curve, we can add the individual supply curves of firms to get the industry supply curve. In Figure 5-9, at each price we add together the quantities supplied by each firm to get the total quantity supplied at that price. In the short run, the number of firms in the industry is given. Suppose there are two firms, A and B. Each firm's short-run supply curve is the part of its *SMC* curve above its shutdown price. Firm A has a lower shutdown price than firm B, perhaps because it has modern machinery. Each firm's supply curve is horizontal up to its shutdown price. At a lower price, no output is supplied.

The industry supply curve is the horizontal sum of the separate supply curves. Between P_1 and P_2 only the lower-cost firm, A, is producing. At P_2, firm B starts to produce too. When there are many firms, each with a different shutdown price, there are many small discontinuities as we move up the industry supply curve. Since each firm in a competitive industry is trivial relative to the total, the industry supply curve is in effect smooth.

The long-run industry supply curve

As the market price rises, the total industry supply rises in the long run for two distinct reasons: each existing firm moves up its long-run supply curve, and new firms find it profitable to enter the industry.

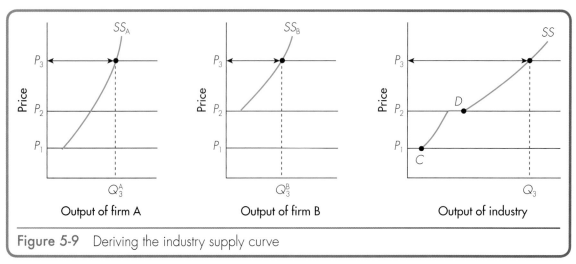

Figure 5-9   Deriving the industry supply curve

Thus, total quantity rises both because each existing firm makes additional output and because new firms enter the industry and produce. Conversely, at lower prices, all firms move down their long-run supply curves, producing less output because prices are lower, and some firms may also leave the industry because they can no longer break even at the lower prices.

At any price, the industry supply is the horizontal sum of the outputs produced by the number of firms in the industry at that price. Hence, the long-run supply curve is flatter than the short-run supply curve for two reasons: each firm can vary its factors more appropriately in the long run; and higher prices attract *extra* firms into the industry. Both raise the output response to a price increase.

For each firm, the height of the minimum point on its *LAC* curve shows the critical price at which it can just survive in the industry. If different firms have *LAC* curves of different heights, they face different exit prices. At any price, there is a marginal firm only just able to survive in the industry, and a marginal potential entrant just waiting to enter if only the price rises a little.

The *long-run* industry supply curve normally slopes up, but in one special case it is horizontal. Suppose all existing firms and potential entrants have *identical cost curves*. In particular, they have the same long-run average cost curves *LAC* and thus the same price, shown as P_3 in Figure 5-8, at which they will enter or exit the industry in the long run. In this special case, if the market price ever exceeds P_3, new firms will enter the industry since they can make profits at any price above P_3. This flood of new entrants creates extra output, reduces scarcity and bids down equilibrium prices until the price reverts to P_3, at which price there is no longer any incentive for firms to enter the industry. Conversely, if the price ever falls below this critical price, firms leave the industry, which makes output scarcer and raises the equilibrium price, until prices rise again to P_3, at which price there is no longer any pressure on firms to leave the industry.

Thus, in the long run, if all firms face identical cost curves, industry supply entails each individual firm producing at the output corresponding to the bottom of its average cost curve, and changes in industry output would be entirely accomplished by changes in the number of firms, via entry and exit. The industry supply curve in the long run is then *horizontal* at price P_3 corresponding to minimum average cost.

But this is a very special case. Normally, firms will have slightly different cost curves from one another for a whole host of reasons – differences in location, in expertise and knowledge, and in materials. Perfect competition does not require that firms are identical, merely that each firm is tiny relative to the market as a whole. Once firms are different, there is no possibility of expanding industry output indefinitely merely by attracting yet more of these identical firms.

On the plausible assumption that the lowest-cost producers are *already* in the market, inducing a rise in the quantity that an industry supplies generally requires higher prices, for two reasons: to induce existing firms to move along upward-sloping *LMC* curves and to attract new firms able at least to break even now that prices are higher than previously. Saying that higher prices are needed to induce the industry to supply more output is just to say that the industry supply curve slopes upwards.

Equilibrium in a competitive industry

Although each individual firm faces a horizontal demand curve for its output, the industry as a whole faces a downward-sloping demand curve for its total output. People will only buy a larger total quantity if the price is lower. To induce people as a whole to buy more flowers from flower stalls, the price of flowers needs to fall. Only then will romantic partners buy fewer boxes of chocolates and instead take home more roses for Valentine's Day.

Industry demand obeys the general laws of demand that we discussed in Chapter 2. Having now also discussed the industry supply curve, we can examine how supply and demand determine equilibrium price in the short run and the long run in a perfectly competitive industry.

In short-run equilibrium, the market price equates the quantity demanded to the total quantity supplied by the given number of firms in the industry when each firm produces on its short-run supply curve. In long-run equilibrium, the market price equates the quantity demanded to the total quantity supplied by the number of firms in the industry when each firm produces on its long-run supply curve. Since firms

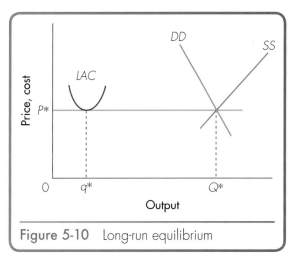

Figure 5-10   Long-run equilibrium

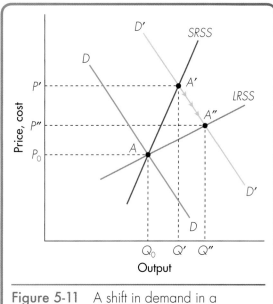

Figure 5-11   A shift in demand in a competitive industry

can freely enter or exit from the industry, the marginal firm must make only normal profits so that there is no further incentive for entry or exit.

Figure 5-10 shows long-run equilibrium for the industry. Demand is *DD* and supply is *SS*. At the equilibrium price P^*, the industry as a whole produces Q^*. This is the sum of the output of each tiny producer. At price P^*, the marginal firm is making q^* at minimum *LAC* and just breaks even. There is no incentive to enter or exit.

A rise in costs

Beginning from this equilibrium, suppose a rise in the price of raw materials raises costs for all firms in the industry. The average cost curve of every firm shifts up. The marginal firm is now losing money at the old price, P^*. Some firms eventually leave the industry. With fewer firms left, the industry supply curve *SS* shifts to the left. With less supply, the equilibrium price rises. When enough firms have left, and industry output falls enough, higher prices allow the new marginal firm to break even, despite an upward shift in *LAC*. Further incentives for entry or exit disappear.

Notice two points about the change in the long-run equilibrium that higher costs induce. First, the rise in average costs is eventually passed on to the consumer in higher prices. Second, since higher prices reduce the total quantity demanded, industry output must fall.

A rise in industry demand

The previous example discussed only long-term effects. We can of course discuss short-run effects as well. And we can examine changes in demand as well as changes in cost and supply. Figure 5-11 illustrates the effect of a shift up in the industry's demand curve from *DD* to *D'D'*.

The industry begins in long-run equilibrium at *A*. Overnight, each firm has some fixed inputs, and the number of firms is fixed. Horizontally adding their short-run supply curves (the portion of their marginal cost curves above the shutdown price), we get the short-run industry supply curve *SRSS*. The new short-run equilibrium is at *A'*. When demand first rises, it needs a big price rise to induce individual firms to move up their steep short-run supply curves, along which some inputs are fixed.

In the long run, firms adjust all factors and move on to their flatter long-run supply curves. In addition, economic profits attract extra firms into the industry. The new long-run equilibrium is at *A"*. Relative to *A'* there is a further expansion of total output, but, with a more appropriate choice of inputs and the entry of new firms, extra supply reduces the market-clearing price.

| Case study 5-2 | Globalization and potential competition make firms price takers |

The key feature of perfect competition is that each individual producer understands that it cannot affect the price by its production decisions. So what are these industries populated by trivially small firms? Some service industries provide good examples. There are no haircut hypermarkets. Most hairdressers are small because the technology does not yield large-scale producers any cost advantage. Because each operates on a small scale, but the market in the aggregate is large, each is therefore small relative to the market as a whole.

Perfect competitors can be producers of goods as well as services. There are also lots of small sheep farmers, each with a small patch of hillside, and lots of car washes, each having to charge similar prices.

Farms cultivating wheat usually operate on a much larger scale nowadays. If there were only 100 UK wheat farmers, would this mean that they would no longer be price takers? Each is surely large enough to affect the price of UK wheat. Does this mean that wheat should not be viewed as a perfectly competitive industry? This argument would make sense if the UK did not trade with the rest of the world. But, for the national economy, international trade is increasing all the time, as shown in the table below.

Imports as percentage of national output	1967	2012
Belgium	36	79
Netherlands	43	72
UK	18	31
France	14	30

Source: OECD, Economic Outlook

UK firms have to compete not just with other UK firms but also with foreign firms who actually export to the UK or would like to do so. Potential entrants to the UK market are not only UK firms but foreign firms that can sell to UK consumers not merely by building factories in the UK but simply by exporting goods from their factories abroad.

In theory, we could have a situation in which the entire UK market is supplied by a single UK firm but that firm is still a price taker, and has no effect on UK prices at all. Suppose the whole of Norfolk became a giant wheat field supplying wheat to every UK bakery. If this superfarm thinks it faces no competition, it will be tempted to raise prices in order to make larger profits. It will try to do to wheat what OPEC did to oil: harvest a little less, make the good more scarce, force up the price (as with oil, the demand for wheat is inelastic – we all need our daily bread). So the superfarm has a small bonfire of its wheat crop to make the remaining wheat scarce. Imagine its disappointment when it subsequently discovers that high wheat prices then induce a flood of wheat imports as French and German farmers see profitable opportunities to sell their wheat in the UK!

Perhaps in the original situation, the UK superfarm faced only slightly cheaper costs of supplying the UK market than the costs faced by French and German farmers. For example, the only difference arose from the slightly higher transport costs of bringing wheat through the Channel Tunnel. Once UK wheat prices rise by more than the initial cost advantage of UK producers, suddenly there is a flood of new supply from abroad.

▶

The more globalization takes place – national markets are increasingly integrated into a single world market – the more the relevant definition of the market is that global market itself and the prices that prevail in that market. We may therefore see situations in which even large UK firms have little ability to affect the price of their output because these firms are tiny *relative to the world market that sets the price*.

The fact that a UK firm looks large relative to the size of the UK market may not be an indication that the industry cannot be perfectly competitive. When products are standardized and can be shipped relatively easily (and therefore cheaply) from one country to another, national prices may in fact be set by international market forces.

UK firms drilling for oil in the North Sea do not set the world price of oil, nor do UK coal miners set the world price of coal. Whenever a commodity is easily traded internationally, it is in the world market that the price is set. American and Chinese supply may affect world prices, but in most cases the output from a small country such as the UK has a negligible effect on the price.

Some commodities, such as concrete, are so expensive to transport – relative to their intrinsic value, that the relevant market is much more localized. It is then important to think about the number of *domestic* firms in relation to the size of the domestic market. Similarly, although there are lots of golf courses in the UK, most people do not want to drive 400 miles for a weekend golf game. Again, the market is more localized. Learning to judge the size of the relevant market is one of the skills you will develop as you read this book.

Recap

- The main production inputs are labour, capital, land, raw materials and energy. Land is supplied by nature and often treated as fixed in quantity. Capital is the input previously produced by people, and not used up during the current production process to which it is an input. Raw materials are used up during the production process to which they are an input. Labour is the service provided by use of workers.

- The short run is the period in which some inputs are fixed but some (especially labour, but perhaps also energy and raw materials) are variable. The production technique may also be fixed in the short run. In the long run, all input quantities and the choice of production technique can be varied if the firm wishes.

- The short-run marginal cost curve (*SMC*) rises because of diminishing returns to the variable input as output rises. Diminishing returns arise because more and more of the variable input(s) must be added to given quantities of the fixed input(s).

- Short-run total cost is short-run fixed cost + short-run variable cost. Hence, short-run average cost is short-run average fixed cost + short-run average variable cost, since in each case we simply divide the relevant total cost by the same output level.

- The firm sets output in the short run to equate *SMC* and *MR*, provided price covers short-run average variable cost. In the short run, the firm may produce at a loss if it recoups part of its fixed costs. Otherwise, it shuts down temporarily.

- In the long run, a firm can adjust all its inputs. In the short run, some inputs are fixed.
- The long-run total cost curve is the cheapest way to make each output level, when all inputs and the production technique are adjusted. It depends on technology and input prices. Technology is the set of all production techniques currently known.
- Average cost is total cost divided by output. The long-run average cost curve *LAC* is typically U-shaped. There are economies of scale on the falling bit of the U. The rising part reflects diseconomies of scale. Where the curve is horizontal, there are constant returns to scale and average cost is neither rising nor falling as output increases.
- When marginal cost is below average cost, average cost is falling. When marginal cost is above average cost, average cost is rising. Average and marginal cost are equal only at the lowest point on the average cost curve.
- In the long run, the firm supplies the output at which long-run marginal cost *LMC* equals *MR* provided price covers *LAC* at that output. If price is lower, the firm goes out of business.
- Market structure refers to the relative size of minimum efficient scale and the total size of the market as reflected by the position of the industry demand curve.
- Market structure is also affected by the shapes of these curves. The steeper the industry demand curve, the more an entrant's extra output will bid down the price, making it harder to enter; and the steeper the *LAC* curve at outputs below minimum efficient scale, the harder it is for an entrant to enter and produce a small output.
- In an imperfectly competitive industry, each firm faces a downward-sloping demand curve. The more output it produces, the lower the price it receives.
- In a perfectly competitive industry, each buyer and seller is a price taker, and cannot affect the market price.
- Perfect competition is most plausible when a large number of firms make a standard product, there is free entry to and exit from the industry, and customers can easily verify that the products of different firms really are the same.
- For a competitive firm, marginal revenue and price coincide. Output is chosen to equate price to marginal cost. The firm's supply curve is its *SMC* curve above its short-run average variable cost. At any lower price, the firm temporarily shuts down. In the long run, the firm's supply curve is that part of its *LMC* curve above its *LAC* curve. At any lower price, the firm exits the industry.
- Adding, at each price, the quantities supplied by each firm, we get the industry supply curve. It is flatter in the long run both because each firm can fully adjust all factors and because the number of firms in the industry can vary.
- A rise in demand leads to a large price increase, but only a small rise in quantity. Existing firms move up their steep *SMC* curves. Price exceeds average costs. Profits attract new entrants. In the long run, output rises further but the price falls back a bit. In the long-run equilibrium, the marginal firm breaks even and there is no further change in the number of firms in the industry.
- A rise in costs for all firms reduces the industry's output and raises the price. In the long run, a higher price is needed to allow the firm that is now the marginal firm to break even. The price rise is achieved by exit from the industry, and a reduction in industry supply.

Review questions

To check your answers to these questions, go to pages 379–81.

1 (a) Is it sufficient for a firm to know the set of available production techniques? (b) What other information is needed to run a firm?

2 (a) Why might scale economies exist? (b) The table below shows some production techniques. The cost of a worker is £5. A unit of capital costs £2. Complete the table and calculate the least-cost way to make 4, 8 and 12 units of output. (c) Are there increasing, constant or decreasing returns to scale in this output range? Which applies where?

Units of	Method 1	Method 2	Method 3	Method 4	Method 5	Method 6
Labour input	5	6	10	12	15	16
Capital input	4	2	7	4	11	8
Output	4	4	8	8	12	12
Total cost						
Average cost						

EASY

3 Suppose the cost of capital rises from 2 to 3 in the question above. (a) Would the firm change its method of production for any levels of output? Say which, if any. (b) How do the firm's total and average costs change when the cost of capital rises?

4 From the total cost curve shown below, calculate marginal and average cost at each output. Are these short-run or long-run cost curves? How can you tell?

Output	0	1	2	3	4	5	6	7	8
Total cost	12	25	40	51	60	70	84	105	128

5 Why does a marginal cost curve always pass through the minimum point on the average cost curve?

6 Why are these statements wrong? (a) Firms making losses should quit at once. (b) Big firms can always produce more cheaply than smaller firms. (c) Small is always beautiful.

7 The domestic economy has only one firm, but faces a flood of imports from abroad if it tries to charge more than the world price. Is this firm perfectly competitive?

8 Suppose an industry of identical competitive firms has a technical breakthrough that cuts costs for all firms. What happens in the short run and the long run? Explain for both the firm and the industry.

9 If every firm is a price taker, who changes the price when a shift in demand causes initial disequilibrium?

10 Which industry has a more elastic long-run supply curve: coal mining or hairdressing? Why?

11 Suppose average cost falls whenever output is increased, no matter how large output becomes. Draw the average and marginal cost curves. Does marginal cost pass through the point of minimum average cost? How many firms do you expect to find in such an industry? Explain your answer.

12 You observe a competitive industry that has been in equilibrium for a long time. (a) What is happening to the price and total quantity produced? (b) You now observe a large fall in the price accompanied by a small reduction in quantity; some time later, the price partially recovers but output falls even more. In terms of supply and demand curves, what happened?

13 Since Ford and Vauxhall are very competitive with one another, should we view them as perfectly competitive firms?

14 Why are these statements wrong? (a) Since competitive firms break even in the long run, there is no incentive to be a competitive firm. (b) Competition prevents firms passing on cost increases.

15 **Essay question** 'Globalization means a larger market, less market power, and hence the increasing relevance of the economist's model of perfect competition.' Do you agree? What might prevent perfect competition being established in all industries?

16 **Essay question** If firms in a competitive industry make only normal profits, why is there any incentive to invest in research and development in such industries?

Online Learning Centre

To help you grasp the key concepts of this chapter check out the extra resources posted on the Online Learning Centre at www.mcgraw-hill.co.uk/textbooks/begg.

There are additional case studies, self-test questions, practice exam questions with answers and a graphing tool.

CHAPTER 6

Imperfect competition

Learning outcomes

By the end of this chapter, you should be able to:

- Define and distinguish forms of imperfect competition
- Analyse pure monopoly
- Discuss how a monopolist chooses output
- Compare this output with that in a competitive industry
- Show how a monopolist's ability to price discriminate affects output and profits
- Define and analyse monopolistic competition

- Explain the tension between collusion and competition within a cartel
- Explain oligopoly and interdependence
- Analyse games between interdependent firms
- Define commitment and credibility
- Show why there is little market power in a contestable market
- Distinguish innocent entry barriers and strategic entry barriers

In the previous chapter, we explored the costs faced by a firm, how these interact with its demand curve to determine the output decision of the firm, and how cost structure and market demand determine the degree of competition in a market. In particular, we then analysed the case of perfect competition in which each firm believes that it has no effect on the price of its output and therefore acts as a price taker.

We now discuss all the other forms of competition, in which firms believe they face a downward-sloping demand curve and therefore have to assess how their marginal revenue differs from the price that they face, because additional output bids down the price received on all previous units of output.

It is helpful to recall the different types of imperfect competition that we introduced in the previous chapter.

For a **pure monopoly**, the demand curve for the firm is the industry demand curve itself. There is only one firm in the industry and it has no fear of entry by others.

An industry with **monopolistic competition** has many sellers making products that are close but not perfect substitutes for one another. Each firm then has a limited ability to affect its output price.

Between these two lies **oligopoly**, an industry with only a few, interdependent producers.

We now analyse each of these in turn. The larger the output of minimum efficient scale (lowest point of long-run average cost curve), relative to the market size (output on the industry demand curve), the smaller will be the number of firms that the industry can support.

 ## Pure monopoly

The perfectly competitive firm is too small to worry about the effect of its own decisions on industry output. In contrast, a pure monopoly *is* the entire industry.

A **monopolist** is the sole supplier or potential supplier of the industry's output.

A sole national supplier need not be a monopoly. If it raises prices, it may face competition from imports or from domestic entrants to the industry. In contrast, a pure monopoly does *not* need to worry about competition from either existing firms or from firms that could enter.

Profit-maximizing output

To maximize profits, a monopolist chooses the output at which marginal revenue *MR* equals marginal cost *MC*, then checks that it is covering average costs. Figure 6-1 shows the average cost curve *AC* with its usual U-shape.

Marginal revenue *MR* lies below the downward-sloping demand curve *DD*. The monopolist recognizes that, to sell extra units, it has to lower the price, even for existing customers. The more units the firm is already making and selling, the more any price reduction to sell a new unit has the effect of depressing revenue earned on existing units produced. Hence, as we move to the right and output increases, the marginal revenue schedule lies increasingly below the demand curve. Indeed, marginal revenue can become negative. In cutting the price to sell an additional output unit, the firm can lose more revenue on existing units than it gains in revenue by being able to sell an extra unit.

It is implicit in this argument that the firm has to charge a single price to all purchasers, and therefore has to reduce the price for which existing units are sold in order to sell an extra unit by inducing buyers to move downwards along their demand curve. Later, we analyse what happens when the monopolist can charge different prices to different customers. Initially, however, we assume that this is impossible.

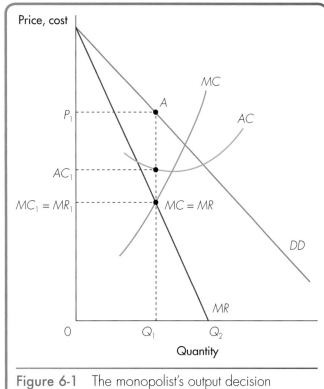

Figure 6-1 The monopolist's output decision

Any firm maximizes profits choosing the output at which marginal revenue MR equals marginal cost MC. In Figure 6-1, the monopolist thus chooses the output Q_1. The demand curve DD implies that the monopolist sells Q_1 at a price P_1 per unit. Profit per unit is thus $[P_1 - AC_1]$, price minus average cost at the output Q_1. Total profit is the area $(P_1 - AC_1) \times Q_1$.

Even in the long run, the monopolist *continues* to make these monopoly profits. By ruling out the possibility of entry, we remove the mechanism by which profits are competed away in the long run by additional supply.

Price-setting

A competitive firm is a *price taker*, taking as given the price determined by supply and demand at the industry level. In contrast, the monopolist is a *price setter*. Having decided to make Q_1, the monopolist quotes a price P_1 knowing (from the demand curve) that the output Q_1 will be bought at this price.

When demand is elastic, lower prices increase revenue by raising quantity demanded a lot. When revenue rises, the marginal revenue from the extra output is positive. Conversely, when demand is inelastic, marginal revenue is negative. To raise output demanded, prices must be cut so much that total revenue falls.

To maximize profits, a monopolist sets $MC = MR$. Since MC is always positive, MR must also be positive at the profit-maximizing output. But this means that demand is elastic at this output. Hence, in Figure 6-1, the chosen output must lie to the left of Q_2. *A monopolist will never produce on the inelastic part of the demand curve where* MR *is negative, for then* MR *could not equal* MC, *which can never be negative.*

Monopoly power

At any output, price exceeds a monopolist's marginal revenue since the demand curve slopes down. In setting $MR = MC$, the monopolist sets a price above marginal cost. In contrast, a competitive firm equates price and marginal cost, since its price is also its marginal revenue. A competitive firm cannot raise price above marginal cost. It has no monopoly power.

Monopoly power is measured by price *minus* marginal cost at any output level.

Changes in profit-maximizing output

Figure 6-1 may also be used to analyse the effect of changes in costs or demand. Suppose higher input prices shift the MC and AC curves up. The higher MC curve must cross the MR curve at a lower output. The cost increase must reduce output. Since the demand curve slopes down, lower output induces a higher equilibrium price.

Similarly, with the original cost curves, an upward shift in demand and marginal revenue curves means that MR now crosses MC at a higher output. The monopolist raises output.

Monopoly versus competition

We now compare a perfectly competitive industry with a monopoly. Facing the same demand and cost conditions, how would the *same* industry behave if it organized as a competitive industry or as a monopoly? Cost differences are often the reason why some industries become competitive while others become monopolies. Only in special circumstances could the same industry be either perfectly competitive or a monopolist.

One case in which the comparison makes sense is when an industry has lots of *identical* firms. From Chapter 5 we know that, as a competitive industry, its long-run supply curve *LRSS* is then horizontal. It can always expand or contract output by changing the number of firms, each producing at the bottom of its long-run average cost curve. If run as a competitive industry, long-run equilibrium occurs where this horizontal supply curve crosses the industry demand curve. In Figure 6-2 this occurs at A, where output is Q_C and the price is P_C.

Now suppose two things happen. The different firms come under a single co-ordinated decision maker, and all future entry is prohibited. Perhaps the industry is nationalized (but told to keep maximizing profits). Long-run costs, both marginal and average, are unaffected, but now the industry supremo recognizes that higher output bids down prices for everyone.

In the special example, *LRSS* is also the marginal cost of output expansion by the multi-plant monopolist. In the long run the cheapest way to raise output is to build more of the identical plants, each operated at minimum average cost. Hence, equating marginal cost and marginal revenue, the multi-plant monopoly produces at *B*. Output Q_M is lower under monopoly than competition, and the price P_M is higher than the competitive price P_C.

The monopolist cuts output in order to create scarcity and raise the equilibrium price. In Figure 6-2 average cost and marginal cost are equal, since each plant is at the bottom of its *LAC* curve, where it crosses *LMC*. Hence, the monopolist's profits are the rectangle $P_M P_C BF$.

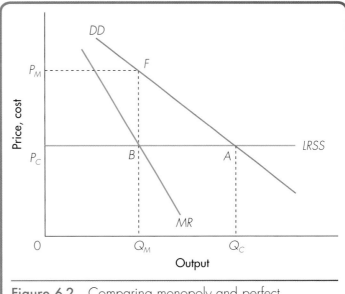

Figure 6-2   Comparing monopoly and perfect competition

Without fear of entry, the consequent profits last forever. Notice the crucial role of blocking competition from entrants. Without this, the attempt to restrict output to raise prices is thwarted by a flood of output from new entrants.

Box 6-1

Barriers at the checkout

When the Morrisons supermarket chain took over its rival Safeway, Morrisons was catapulted from the supermarket minnow, with a 6 per cent market share, to a big league player with 17 per cent of the UK market; only marginally less than Sainsbury's, one-time leader of the supermarket industry. Since the merger, Morrisons has continued to prosper.

The takeover of Safeway was contested, with Tesco, Asda and Sainsbury's all mounting rival bids to Morrisons'. At one stage, Philip Green, the owner of high-street retailer British Home Stores, also registered an interest in Safeway. Safeway was such an attractive target because it provided the last chance to enter the supermarket industry. Without

Market share of UK supermarket revenue, 2011	%
Tesco	31
Asda	17
Sainsbury's	16
Morrisons	12
Big 4	**76**

Source: 'Supermarkets: changing market share', 16 August 2011, www.guardian.co.uk

access to land sites, and facing difficulty getting planning permission for new supermarkets, the only way in which to become a successful supermarket chain was to enter the industry by taking over a chain that already had all the distribution outlets required. With Safeway in the hands of Morrisons, and the industry consolidated into large players, the next takeover will be that much more difficult. The entry barriers are steadily rising.

▶

If the abuse of monopoly power is not to be controlled by having more firms in competition, we need closer scrutiny of the conduct of the small number of powerful firms that remain in the industry. The UK Competition Commission has therefore taken an ongoing interest in monitoring aspects of their behavior to ensure that consumers get a reasonable deal.

Online grocery sales are also booming, and are expected to rise from 3 per cent of the market in 2011 to 6 per cent by 2016. IGD's *ShopperTrack* research found that, while 17 per cent of UK adults now shop online, 44 per cent intend to do so in the next five to ten years. The research also showed that online shopper loyalty was somewhat illusory, with 64 per cent buying from two or more online supermarkets and 47 per cent saying they would like to try another. Smartphone applications were expected to have the greatest impact on future shopping behaviour.

A key issue for competition will be whether the incumbent firms with the largest and best existing stores automatically dominate the online business as well. The table below shows that current web traffic is pretty highly correlated with grocery market share of sales from physical shops. To the extent this continues, there will remain a premium on the best high-street locations.

Grocery and alcohol websites ranked by share of UK visits

Rank	Website	Share of visits (%)
1 Tesco	www.tesco.com/groceries	21.25
2 ASDA	http://groceries.asda.com	11.46
3 Morrisons	www.morrisons.co.uk	9.95
4 Sainsbury's Online Groceries	www.sainsburys.co.uk/groceries	8.86
5 Waitrose	www.waitrose.com	5.94
6 ALDI UK	http://uk.aldi.com	5.69
7 Lidl UK	www.lidl.co.uk	5.01
8 mySupermarket.co.uk	www.mysupermarket.co.uk	4.50
9 Ocado	www.ocado.com	4.24
10 Tesco Wine	www.tesco.com/winestore	1.88
11 Hungry House	www.hungryhouse.co.uk	1.13
12 Milk and More	www.milkandmore.co.uk	0.99
13 Naked Wines	www.nakedwines.com	0.99
14 Waitrose Wine Direct	www.waitrosewine.com	0.94
15 Riverbed Organic Vegetables	www.riverbed.co.uk	0.93

Source: Experian Hitwise

We should also remember the effects of the recession, which are subtly changing the locational advantage of incumbents. First, squeezed households are trading down to budget supermarkets wherever they are located – hence the rise of ASDA, ALDI and Lidl. Second, as more and more shops in other retail sectors go bust and vacate the high street, opportunities to grab useful sites have become a little easier.

Source: www.Internetretailing.net

Discriminating monopoly

Thus far, all consumers were charged the same price. Unlike a competitive industry, where competition prevents any individual firm charging more than its competitors, a monopolist may be able to charge different prices to different customers.

A **discriminating monopoly** charges different prices to different buyers.

Consider an airline monopolizing flights between London and Rome. It has business customers whose demand curve is very inelastic. They have to fly. Their demand and marginal revenue curves are very steep. The airline also carries tourists, whose demand curve is much more elastic. If flights to Rome are too dear, tourists can visit Athens instead. Tourists have much flatter demand and marginal revenue curves.

The airline will charge the two groups *different* prices. Since tourist demand is elastic, the airline wants to charge tourists a low fare to increase tourist revenue. Since business demand is inelastic, the airline wants to charge business travellers a high fare to increase business revenue.

Profit-maximizing output will satisfy two separate conditions. First, business travellers with inelastic demand will pay a fare sufficiently higher than tourists with elastic demand that the marginal revenue from the two separate groups is equated. Then there is no incentive to rearrange the mix by altering the price differential between the two groups. Second, the general level of prices and the total number of passengers are chosen to equate marginal cost to both these marginal revenues. This ensures that the airline operates on the most profitable scale, as well as with the most profitable mix.

When a producer charges different customers different prices, we say it *price discriminates*. There are many examples in the real world. Rail operators charge rush-hour commuters a higher fare than midday shoppers whose demand for trips to the city is much more elastic.

Price discrimination often applies to services, which must be consumed on the spot, rather than to goods, which can be resold. Price discrimination in standardized goods won't work. The group buying at the lower price resells to the group paying the higher price, undercutting the price differences. Effective price discrimination requires that the submarkets can be isolated from one another to prevent resale.

Figure 6-3 illustrates *perfect price discrimination*, where it is possible to charge every customer a different price for the same good. If the monopolist charges every customer the same price, the profit-maximizing output is Q_1, where MR equals MC and the corresponding price is P_1.

If the monopolist can perfectly price discriminate, the very first unit can be sold for a price E. Having sold this unit to the highest bidder, the customer most desperate for the good, the next unit is sold to the next highest bidder, and so on. In reducing the price to sell that extra unit, the monopolist no longer reduces revenue from previously sold units. The demand curve *is* the marginal revenue curve under perfect price discrimination. The marginal revenue of the last unit is simply the price for which it is sold.

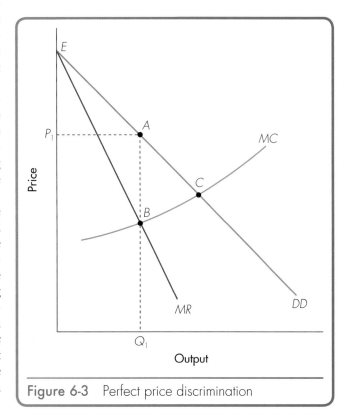

Figure 6-3 Perfect price discrimination

A perfectly price discriminating monopolist produces at C, where $MC = DD$, which is now marginal revenue. Price discrimination, if possible, is always profitable. In moving from the uniform pricing point A to the price discriminating point C, the monopolist adds the area ABC to profits. This is the excess of additional revenue over additional cost when output is higher.

The monopolist makes a second gain from price discrimination. Even the output Q_1 now brings in more revenue than under uniform pricing. The monopolist also gains the area EP_1A by charging different prices, rather than the single price P_1, on the first Q_1 units. Economic consultants often earn their fees by teaching firms new ways in which to price discriminate.

Notice, too, that whether or not the firm can price discriminate affects its chosen output by affecting its marginal revenue. In the extreme case, perfect price discrimination leads to the same price and output as under perfect competition, since in both cases the firm then sets $MC = MR = P$.

Maths 6-1

Price discrimination

Consider the linear demand schedule $p = \alpha - \beta q$, which related price to quantity produced, and that α and β are positive constants. Suppose for simplicity that there is a constant average and marginal cost of production γ per unit. Total revenue is $qp = q(\alpha - \beta q)$. If the firm has to charge the same price to all customers, its marginal revenue is $d[q(\alpha - \beta q)]/dq = \alpha - 2\beta q$. Equating marginal cost γ and marginal revenue, the optimal choice of q is given by $q^* = (\alpha - \gamma)/2\beta$, at which point the demand curve shows the corresponding price is $p^* = \alpha - [\beta(\alpha - \gamma)/2\beta] = (\alpha + \gamma)/2$. Hence, maximized revenue p^*q^* is $[(\alpha - \gamma)/2\beta][(\alpha + \gamma)/2] = (\alpha^2 - \gamma^2)/4\beta$. Intuitively, revenue is stronger when demand is stronger (large α) and when costs are lower (small γ).

Suppose now that the firm can sell every unit at a different price. As it increases sales, the demand curve now shows the marginal revenue from each unit sold (since the price of all smaller units of output is no longer bid downwards by the requirement to charge a uniform price). Equating marginal revenue $\alpha - \beta q$ and marginal cost γ now yields $q^* = [\alpha - \gamma]/\beta$, which for this particular demand curve is precisely twice the optimal output compared with the uniform pricing case. The price p^* of the last unit sold is therefore $\{\alpha - \beta [\alpha - \gamma]/\beta\} = \gamma$, which makes sense since the demand curve is the marginal revenue curve here and γ is marginal cost.

In addition to the revenue $p^*q^* = \gamma [\alpha - \gamma]/\beta$, the producer also gets the extra revenue of having sold all units below q^* at a price higher than γ. This extra revenue is given the area of the triangle between the horizontal line at height γ and the portion of the demand curve above this line. The area of this triangle is half its base times its height, which is $(\alpha - \gamma)q^* = (\alpha - \gamma)^2/2\beta$.

Hence, the extra revenue from price discrimination, compared with uniform pricing, is

$$R(PD) - R(UP) = \{[\gamma [\alpha - \gamma]/\beta] + [\alpha - \gamma]^2/2\beta\} - \{(\alpha^2 - \gamma^2)/4\beta\}$$
$$= (\alpha^2 - \gamma^2)/4\beta$$

This is positive provided only that α, the maximum height of the demand curve, exceeds γ, the marginal cost of production. This proves that price discrimination yields higher revenue than uniform pricing. Notice that the gain arises from two sources. First, for the output produced under uniform pricing, the price discriminator gets more revenue by charging higher prices to more desperate customers. Second, the price discriminator produces additional output on which a profit is also made, whereas the uniform pricer does not find this profitable because it drags down the price too much on previous units.

Monopoly and technical change

Joseph Schumpeter (1883–1950) argued that, even with uniform pricing, a monopoly may not produce a lower output and at a higher price than a competitive industry because the monopolist has more incentive than a competitive firm to shift its cost curves down. Technical advances reduce costs, and allow lower prices and higher output. A monopoly has more incentive to undertake research and development (R&D), necessary for cost-saving breakthroughs.

In a competitive industry a firm with a technical advantage has only a temporary opportunity to earn high profits to recoup its research expenses. Imitation by existing firms and new entrants soon compete away its profits. In contrast, by shifting down all its cost curves, a monopoly can enjoy higher profits forever. Schumpeter argued that monopolies are more innovative than competitive industries. Taking a dynamic long-run view, rather than a snapshot static picture, monopolists may enjoy lower cost curves that lead them to charge lower prices, thereby raising the quantity demanded.

This argument has some substance, but may overstate the case. Most Western economies operate a *patent* system. Inventors of new processes acquire a *temporary* legal monopoly for a fixed period. By temporarily excluding entry and imitation, the patent laws increase the incentive to conduct R&D without establishing a monopoly in the long run. Over the patent life the inventor gets a higher price and makes handsome profits. Eventually the patent expires and competition from other firms leads to higher output and lower prices. The real price of copiers and microcomputers fell significantly when the original patents of Xerox and IBM expired.

Case study 6-1   The value of a good patent

Why has Nestlé cleaned up on the espresso coffee business? Not because potential competitors don't know where to find good coffee or how to manufacture home espresso machines. Rather, they have been defeated by the series of patents taken out by Nestlé.

The best cup of coffee requires that all coffee grounds are the same size, are stored in containers that do not allow the coffee to oxidize before it is used, and that it is brewed in hot water of exactly the optimal temperature and pressure. Nestlé's patents for grinding, packaging and delivering coffee through their famous Nespresso system (now licensed and retailed by other brand names) have effectively wiped out the competition. Nestlé's patent lawyers managed to pre-empt the key processes so accurately that Nestlé's competitors gave up trying to challenge the Nestlé monopoly. Now they are simply waiting for the patents to expire. Patents have become a key part of competitive strategy in the knowledge economy. You are probably aware of two other hotly contested patent issues in today's global economy.

© Nestlé Nespresso SA

The first is the patents of incumbent music companies who argued, successfully eventually, that Napster and other free Internet download music services were infringing the patent (usually called a copyright when it applies to music, writing and the arts) held over the artistes that they had produced. Without such protection, there is no incentive to remain in the industry: expensive investment never has any payback since Internet companies subsequently compete away all the profits. Foreseeing this, recording studios would go bankrupt and there would be no music for the Internet to download. This issue has now been resolved, and the music industry has received sufficient protection that it can now coexist with Napster and iPods, which have to pay a fee for the music to which they have access.

Another contentious issue is the price of drugs that combat HIV/Aids. Global pharmaceutical companies, such as GlaxoSmithKline (GSK), Pfizer and Merck, always argue that drug development is hugely costly, and that many drugs fail to succeed in the testing phase, so that the occasional winner has to earn lots of money to cover the cost of all the ones that fail, just as successful gamblers recognize that their winnings on the occasional horse that they pick has to cover all the losses on the plausible horses that nevertheless failed to win as expected. Yet poor countries, such as those in sub-Saharan Africa where HIV/Aids is a major social and economic problem, argue that they should not be forced to pay drug prices considerably in excess of current production costs merely so that pharmaceutical companies can repay their failed investment in other drugs that did not work out as planned.

Both sides of course are simultaneously correct. If pharmaceutical companies are deprived of profits on their winners, they will have to exit the industry since they will no longer be able to pay for their inevitable losers. Since the latter lose big, it also takes big winnings just to keep pharmaceutical companies in the industry. However, if they charge prices that poor Africans cannot afford, not only do many people find this ethically unattractive, it may even diminish the profits of drug companies themselves. You already know enough economics to appreciate that, if the world price of drugs is substantially above the current production cost, then even a lower price would yield a profit. If Africans could then afford to buy at this lower price, total drug company profits would rise *provided they did not have to reduce the price for which the drugs were sold in rich countries.* Hence, if all countries support this form of price discrimination – and if those allowed to import at lower prices undertake not to attempt to resell to richer countries at higher prices – poor countries will get the cheaper drugs that they need, and drug producers will find that they get the same revenue as before from the rich countries (where prices have not changed), plus some new sales to poor countries that were not taking place before because poor countries could not afford the high prices previously charged to them.

Monopolistic competition

The theory of monopolistic competition envisages a large number of quite small firms, each ignoring any impact its own decisions might have on the behaviour of other firms. There is free entry and exit from the industry in the long run. In these respects, the industry resembles *perfect* competition. What distinguishes monopolistic competition is that each firm faces a *downward*-sloping demand curve in its own little niche of the industry.

Different firms' products are only limited substitutes. An example is the location of corner grocers. A lower price attracts some customers from other shops, but each shop has some local customers for whom local convenience matters more than a few pence on the price of a jar of coffee. Monopolistically competitive industries exhibit *product differentiation*. For corner grocers, differentiation is based on location. In other cases, it reflects brand loyalty or personal relationships. A particular restaurant or hairdresser can charge a slightly different price from other producers in the industry without losing all its customers.

Monopolistic competition requires not merely product differentiation, but also few economies of scale. Hence there are many small producers, ignoring their interdependence with their rivals. Many examples of monopolistic competition are service industries.

Each firm produces where its marginal cost equals marginal revenue. If firms make profits, new firms enter the industry. That is the competitive part of monopolistic competition. As a result of entry, the downward-sloping demand curve of each individual firm shifts to the left. For a given market demand curve, the market share of each firm falls. With lower demand but unchanged cost curves, each firm makes lower profits. Entry stops when enough firms have entered to bid profits down to zero for the marginal firm.

Figure 6-4 shows long-run equilibrium once there is no further incentive for entry or exit. Each individual firm's demand curve DD has shifted enough to the left to just be tangent to its LAC curve at the output q^* the firm is producing. Hence, it makes zero economic profits. Price P^* equals average cost. For a perfectly competitive firm, its horizontal demand curve would be tangent to LAC at the minimum point on the average cost curve. In contrast, the tangency for a monopolistic competitor lies to the left of this, with both demand and LAC sloping down. The firm chooses output such that marginal revenue equals long-run marginal cost. That is the monopolistic part of monopolistic competition.

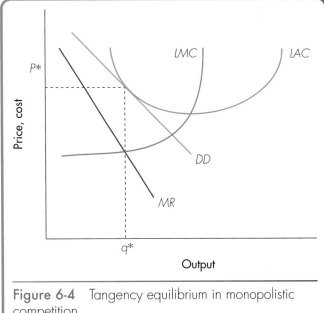

Figure 6-4 Tangency equilibrium in monopolistic competition

Notice two things about the firm's long-run equilibrium. First, the firm is *not* producing at the lowest point on its average cost curve. It could reduce average costs by further expansion. However, its marginal revenue would be so low as to make this unprofitable.

Second, the firm has some monopoly power because of the special feature of its particular brand or location. Price exceeds marginal cost. Hence, firms are usually eager for new customers prepared to buy more output at the *existing* price. It explains why we are a race of eager sellers and coy buyers. It is purchasing agents who get Christmas presents from sales reps, not the other way round.

 ## Oligopoly and interdependence

Under perfect competition or monopolistic competition, there are so many firms in the industry that no single firm need worry about the effect of its own actions on rival firms. In pure monopoly the firm has no rivals. In contrast, the essence of an oligopoly is the need for each firm to consider how its actions affect the decisions of its relatively few rivals. The output decision of each firm depends on its guess about how its rivals will react. We begin with the basic tension between competition and collusion in such situations.

Collusion is an explicit or implicit agreement between existing firms to avoid competition.

Initially, for simplicity, we ignore entry and exit, studying only the behaviour of existing firms.

The profits from collusion

The existing firms maximize their *joint* profits if they behave like a multi-plant monopolist. A sole decision-maker would organize industry output to maximize total profits. By colluding to behave like a monopolist, oligopolists maximize their *total* profit. There is then a backstage deal to divide up these profits between individual firms.

Having cut back industry output to the point at which $MC = MR < P$, each firm then faces a marginal profit $(P - MC)$ if it can expand a little more. Provided its partners continue to restrict output, each individual firm now wants to break the agreement and expand!

Oligopolists are torn between the desire to collude, thus maximizing joint profits, and the desire to compete, in the hope of increasing market share and profits at the expense of rivals. Yet if all firms compete, joint profits are low and no firm does very well.

Cartels

Collusion between firms is easiest when formal agreements are legal. Such *cartels* were common in the late nineteenth century. They agreed market shares and prices in many industries. Such practices are now outlawed in Europe, the US and many other countries. However, secret deals in smoke-filled rooms are not unknown even today.

The kinked demand curve

In the absence of collusion, each firm's demand curve depends on how competitors react. Firms must guess these reactions. Suppose that each firm believes that its own price cut will be matched by all other firms in the industry but that an increase in its own price will induce no price response from competitors.

Figure 6-5 shows the demand curve DD each firm then faces. At price P_0, the firm makes Q_0. Since competitors do not follow suit, a price rise leads to a big loss of market share to other firms. The firm's demand curve is elastic above A at prices above P_0. However, a price cut is matched by its rivals, and market shares are unchanged. Sales rise only because the industry as a whole moves down the market demand curve as prices fall. The demand curve DD is much less elastic for price reductions from the initial price P_0.

Thus, marginal revenue MR is discontinuous at Q_0. Below Q_0 the elastic part of the demand curve applies, but at Q_0 the firm hits the inelastic portion of its kinked demand curve and marginal revenue suddenly falls. Q_0 is the profit-maximizing output for the firm, given its belief about how competitors will respond.

The model has an important implication. Suppose the MC curve of a single firm shifts up or down by a small amount. Since the MR curve has a discontinuous vertical segment at the output Q_0, it remains optimal to make Q_0 and charge a price P_0. The kinked demand curve model may explain the empirical finding that firms do not always adjust prices when costs change.

It does not explain what determines the initial price P_0. It may be the collusive monopoly price. Each firm believes that an attempt to undercut its rivals induces them to cut prices to defend market share. However, its rivals are happy for it to charge a higher price and lose market share.

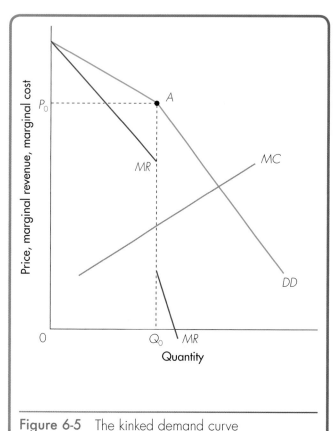

Figure 6-5 The kinked demand curve

There is a difference between the effect of a cost change for a single firm and a cost change for all firms together. The latter shifts the marginal cost curve up for the industry as a whole, raising the collusive monopoly price. Each firm's kinked demand curve shifts up since the monopoly price P_0 rises. Thus, we can reconcile the stickiness of a single firm's prices with respect to changes in its own costs alone, and the speed with which the entire industry marks up prices when all firms' costs are increased by higher taxes or wage rises in the whole industry.

Game theory and interdependent decisions

A good poker player sometimes bluffs. Sometimes you make money with a bad hand that your opponents misread as a good hand. Like poker players, oligopolists have to try to second-guess their rivals' moves to determine their own best action. To study how interdependent decisions are made, we use *game theory*.

A **game** is a situation in which intelligent decisions are necessarily interdependent.

The *players* in the game try to maximize their own *pay-offs*. In an oligopoly, the firms are the players and their pay-offs are their profits in the long run. Each player must choose a strategy.

A **strategy** is a game plan describing how the player will act or move in each situation.

Being a pickpocket is a strategy. Lifting a particular wallet is a move. As usual, we are interested in equilibrium. In most games, each player's best strategy depends on the strategies chosen by other players. It is silly to be a pickpocket in a police station.

In **Nash equilibrium**, each player chooses his best strategy, *given* the strategies chosen by other players.

This description of equilibrium was invented by John Nash, who won the Nobel Prize for Economic Science for his work on game theory, and was the subject of the film *A Beautiful Mind*, starring Russell Crowe. Sometimes, but not usually, a player's best strategy is independent of those chosen by others. If so, it is a *dominant strategy*. We begin with an example in which each player has a dominant strategy.

Box 6-2

Michael Porter on competitive advantage

Harvard Business School professor Michael Porter is renowned as a guru on competitive strategy, whose advice is sought by prime ministers and corporate chief executives. Porter advises clients to be clear on what they are trying to accomplish. The diagram helps understand his advice.

First, it is important to understand which part of the market – which customers – are being targeted. A firm can pursue a niche market strategy or chase after most of the entire market. Second, whichever market it is trying to pursue, the firm needs to be clear on whether its competitive advantage will arise because its products (whether goods or

	Uniqueness competency	Low cost competency
Narrow market scope	**Segmentation strategy**	
Broad market scope	**Differentiation strategy**	**Cost leadership**

▶

services) will be distinctive in attributes or because the firm has refined its production to the extent that it can undercut its competitors making the same thing.

Where a firm decides to pursue a niche market – examples include BMW in cars, Louis Vuitton in luggage, the *Financial Times* in journalism – the key to success is to limit scope for competition by convincing customers that this market niche really is different. The *Financial Times* is not a differentiated seller of general material – its coverage of the arts may indeed be excellent, but people who buy the *FT* have to be pretty interested in financial affairs in the first place. By convincing more people to take an interest in financial markets, the *FT* can build the niche and its strong position within it. The fewer the substitutes, the less elastic is demand and the more the firm can raise prices without losing too much volume, a sure recipe for enhancing profits.

A second type of product differentiation is not in convincing customers that the market segment is different but in convincing customers that the product has unique attributes even though the market being pursued is broad. Mobile phones and hand-held devices are huge – Apple's success is primarily based on differentiating its product within this generic sector. Apple devices offer brilliant design, are customer friendly and use high quality graphics. Given these attributes, Apple can charge premium prices. Demand is inelastic. Many people simply have to have, and be seen to have, an iPad.

The third source of potential competitive advantage is cost advantage and hence the ability to undercut competitors. For example, the Ford Focus and Ford Mondeo are regularly held up as examples of great value for money packages. The basis for such a cost advantage might be scale, learning through repetition, locational advantage or unique technology.

Collude or cheat?

Figure 6-6 shows a game that we can imagine is between the only two members of a cartel like OPEC. Each firm can select a high-output or low-output strategy. In each box, the first number shows firm A's profits and the second number, firm B's profits for that output combination.

When both have high output, industry output is high, the price is low and each firm makes a small profit of 1. When each has low output, the outcome is more like collusive monopoly. Prices are high and each firm does better, making a profit of 2. Each firm does best (a profit of 3) when it alone has high output; for, then, the other firm's low output helps hold down industry output and keep up the price. In this situation we assume the low-output firm makes a profit of 0.

Now we can see how the game will unfold. Consider firm A's decision. If firm B has a high-output strategy, firm A does better also to have high output. In the two left-hand boxes, firm A gets a profit of 1 by choosing high but a profit of 0 by choosing low. Now suppose firm B chooses a low-output strategy. From the two right-hand boxes, firm A still does better by choosing high, since this yields it a profit of 3, whereas low yields it a profit of only 2. Hence firm A has a dominant strategy. Whichever strategy B adopts, A does better to choose a high-output strategy. Firm B also has a dominant strategy to choose high output. Check for yourself that B does better to go high whichever

		Firm B output			
		High		Low	
Firm A output	High	1	1	3	0
	Low	0	3	2	2

Figure 6-6 The Prisoners' Dilemma game

strategy A selects. Since both firms choose high, the equilibrium is the top left-hand box. Each firm gets a profit of 1.

Yet both firms would do better, getting a profit of 2, if they colluded to form a cartel and both produced low – the bottom right-hand box. But neither can afford to take the risk of going low. Suppose firm A goes low. Firm B, comparing the two boxes in the bottom row, will then go high, preferring a profit of 3 to a profit of 2. And firm A will get screwed, earning a profit of 0 in that event. Firm A can figure all this out in advance, which is why its dominant strategy is to go high.

This is a clear illustration of the tension between collusion and competition. In this example, it appears that the output-restricting cartel will never get formed, since each player can already foresee the overwhelming incentive for the other to cheat on such an arrangement. How, then, can cartels ever be sustained? One possibility is that there exist binding commitments.

A **commitment** is an arrangement, entered into voluntarily, that restricts one's future actions.

If both players could simultaneously sign an enforceable contract to produce low output, they could achieve the co-operative outcome in the bottom right-hand box, each earning profits of 2. Clearly, they then do better than in the top left-hand box, which describes the non-cooperative equilibrium of the game. Without any commitment, neither player can go low because then the other player will go high. Binding commitments, by removing this temptation, enable both players to go low, and both players gain. This idea of commitment is important, and we shall meet it many times. Just think of all the human activities that are the subject of legal contracts, a simple kind of commitment simultaneously undertaken by two parties or players.

This insight is powerful, but its application to oligopoly requires some care. Cartels within a country are illegal, and OPEC is not held together by a signed agreement that can be upheld in international law! Is there a less formal way in which oligopolists can commit themselves not to cheat on the collusive low-output solution to the game? If the game is played only once, this is hard. However, in the real world, the game is repeated many times: firms choose output levels day after day. Suppose two players try to collude on low output. Furthermore, each announces a *punishment strategy*. Should firm A ever cheat on the low-output agreement, firm B promises that it will subsequently react by raising its output. Firm A makes a similar promise.

Suppose the agreement has been in force for some time, and both firms have stuck to their low-output deal. Firm A assumes that firm B will go low as usual. Figure 6-6 shows that firm A will make a *temporary* gain today if it cheats and goes high. Instead of staying in the bottom right-hand box with a profit of 2, it can move to the top right-hand box and make 3. However, from tomorrow onwards, firm B will also go high, and firm A can then do no better than continue to go high too, making a profit of 1 for evermore.

However, if A refuses to cheat today it can continue to stay in the bottom right-hand box and make 2 forever. In cheating, A swaps a temporary gain for permanently lower profits. Thus, punishment strategies can sustain an explicit cartel or implicit collusion even if no formal commitment exists.

It is easy to say that you will adopt a punishment strategy in the event that the other player cheats; but this will affect the other player's behaviour only if your threat is credible.

A **credible threat** is one that, after the fact, it is still optimal to carry out.

In the preceding example, once firm A cheats and goes high, it is then in firm B's interest to go high anyway. Hence B's threat to go high if A ever cheats is a credible threat.

Entry and potential competition

So far we have discussed imperfect competition between existing firms. What about potential competition from new entrants? Three cases must be distinguished: where entry is trivially easy, where it is difficult by accident and where it is difficult by design.

Contestable markets

Suppose we see an industry with few incumbent firms. Before assuming it is an oligopoly, we must think about entry and exit.

A **contestable market** has free entry and free exit.

Free exit means that there are no *sunk* or irrecoverable costs. On exit, a firm can fully recoup its previous investment expenditure, including money spent on building up knowledge and goodwill. A contestable market allows *hit-and-run* entry. If the incumbent firms, however few, are pricing above minimum average cost, an entrant can step in, undercut them, make a temporary profit, and exit. If so, even when incumbent firms are few in number, they have to behave as if they were perfectly competitive, setting $P = MC = AC$.

The theory of contestable markets is controversial. There are many industries in which sunk costs are hard to recover, or where expertise takes an entrant time to acquire. Nor is it safe to assume that incumbents will not change their behaviour when threatened by entry. But the theory does vividly illustrate that market structure and incumbent behaviour cannot be deduced by counting the number of firms in the industry. We were careful to stress that a monopolist is a sole producer *who can completely discount fear of entry*.

Innocent entry barriers

Entry barriers may be created by nature or by other rivals.

An **innocent entry barrier** is one made by nature.

Absolute cost advantages, where incumbent firms have lower cost curves than entrants, may be innocent. If it takes time to learn the business, incumbents have lower costs in the short run.

Scale economies are another innocent entry barrier. If minimum efficient scale is large relative to market size, an entrant cannot get into the industry without considerably depressing the price. It may be impossible to break in at a profit. The greater the innocent entry barriers, the more we can neglect potential competition from entrants. The oligopoly game then reduces to competition between incumbent firms, as we discussed in the previous section.

Where innocent entry barriers are low, incumbent firms may accept this situation, in which case competition from potential entrants prevents incumbent firms from exercising much market power, or else incumbent firms will try to design some entry barrier of their own.

Strategic entry deterrence

The word 'strategic' has a precise meaning in economics.

Your **strategic move** influences the other player's decision, in a manner helpful to you, by affecting the other person's expectations of how you will behave.

Suppose you are the only incumbent firm. Even if limited scale economies make it feasible for entrants to produce on a small scale, you threaten to flood the market if they come in, causing a price fall and big losses for everyone. Since you have a fat bank balance and they are just getting started, they will go bankrupt. Entry is pointless. You get the monopoly profits. But is your threat credible? Without spare capacity, how can you make extra output to bid down the price a lot.

Seeing this, the potential entrant may call your bluff. Suppose, instead, you build a costly new factory which is unused unless there is no entry. If, at some future date, an entrant appears, the cost of the new factory has largely been paid, and its marginal cost of production is low. The entrant succumbs to your credible threat to flood the market and decides to stay out. Provided the initial cost of the factory (spread suitably over a number of years) is less than the extra profits the incumbent keeps making *as a result of having deterred entry*, this entry deterrence is profitable. It is strategic because it works by influencing the decision of *another* player.

Strategic entry deterrence is behaviour by incumbent firms to make entry less likely.

Is spare capacity the only commitment available to incumbents? Commitments must be irreversible, otherwise they are an empty threat; and they must increase the chances that the incumbent will fight. Anything with the character of fixed and sunk costs may work. Fixed costs artificially increase scale economies, and sunk costs have already been incurred.

Box 6-3

Banking on entry deterrence

Retail banking is a key activity in a modern market economy. As in other countries, British banks have taken a pasting since 2007. Northern Rock had to be nationalized, Royal Bank of Scotland is now 80 per cent owned by the government, and Halifax Bank of Scotland was bailed out by Lloyds TSB (to the fury of Lloyds' shareholders since to date it has proved a lousy investment). By 2010 the UK Office of Fair Trading (OFT) was worrying about how to stimulate renewed competition in the sector, both by enticing in new entrants and in order to find new bidders to buy up assets being sold off by the state or being forcibly removed from private banks in order to leave them less in the position of being 'too big to fail' (and thereby being able to rely on government assistance even when they screw up).

The OFT report of November 2010 assessed four potential sources of entry barrier to new retail banking entrants. First, incumbents might enjoy a considerable advantage in already having regulatory approval for banking licences and customer credit provision. The OFT concluded this was logically possible but in practice nothing much to worry about. Potential new banks could get these approvals without too much trouble.

Next, the OFT worried about banking infrastructure – access to the IT systems needed to run the payment systems, track customers and operate effectively. Here, the OFT concluded that incumbents do have a major advantage – this big investment is a sunk cost that does not need to enter their marginal costing and pricing decisions, whereas an entrant has to finance it and worry about how to get a return on that investment. IT makes up around two-thirds of the start-up cost of entering the retail banking business.

Third, the power of existing brands may prevent customers switching to new banks. This is less likely to be a problem if the incumbent brands have been damaged by the financial crisis. It is also less of a problem if the entrant is itself an established brand. For example, in November 2011 the UK government sold Northern Rock to Virgin Money for £747 million. Virgin may not have been all that well known for its previous activities in financial services, but both its airline and its train business are well established. Similarly, by 2012 RBS had sold 318 branches to Santander, which was already established in the UK banking business after taking over Abbey National in 2004.

Finally, the OFT considered barriers to exit from the industry. The theoretical model of perfect competition requires free exit as well as free entry to the industry. Why? Because if a potential entrant has to worry about costs of exit in the future, this will restrict their willingness to enter today. What are these exit costs in banking? Principally that a bank is likely to want to exit during a financial crisis, which is precisely the time at which other banks are likely to be in trouble too. It will therefore be difficult to sell off the assets – the bank branches, the IT system, the customer network – for a price anywhere near the cost for which these assets had to be built up.

How tough is it to enter the retail banking business? Pretty tough for a complete newcomer. Less tough for a firm already established in banking elsewhere. In the last few decades, the UK has seen entry by Santander from Spain, and from HSBC from East Asia.

Summing up

Few industries in the real world closely resemble the textbook extremes of perfect competition or pure monopoly. Most are imperfectly competitive. Game theory in general, and notions such as commitment, credibility and deterrence, let economists analyse many of the practical concerns of big business.

What have we learned? First, market structure and the behaviour of incumbent firms are determined *simultaneously*. At the beginning of the section, we argued that the relation between minimum efficient scale and market size would determine market structure, whether the industry was a monopoly, oligopoly or displayed monopolistic or perfect competition. However, these are not merely questions of the extent of innocent entry barriers. Strategic behaviour can also affect the shape of cost curves and the market structure that emerges.

Second, and related, we have learned the importance of *potential* competition, which may come from domestic firms considering entry, or from imports from abroad. The number of firms observed in the industry today conveys little information about the extent of the market power they truly exercise. The more globalization takes place, the more relevant this argument becomes.

Finally, we have seen how many business practices of the real world – price wars, advertising, brand proliferation, excess capacity, or excessive research and development – can be understood as strategic competition in which, to be effective, threats must be made credible by commitments.

Case study 6-2   Why advertise so much?

Evan Davis is host of the *Dragons' Den*, and co-presenter of BBC Radio 4's flagship *Today* programme. John Kay writes a fortnightly column on corporate strategy for the *Financial Times*. This case study is based on work they did together at the London Business School over 20 years ago, but which is still just as relevant today.

Advertising is not always meant to erect entry barriers to potential entrants. Sometimes, it really does aim to inform consumers by revealing inside information that firms have about the quality of their own goods.

When consumers can tell at a glance the quality of a product, even before buying it, there is little gain from advertising. Black rotten bananas cannot convincingly be portrayed as fresh and delicious. Information is freely available and attempts to deceive consumers are detected rapidly. However, for most goods, consumers cannot detect quality before purchase, and gradually discover quality only after using the good for a while.

The producer then has inside information over first-time buyers. A conspicuous (expensive) advertising campaign *signals* to potential buyers that the firm believes in its product and expects to make enough repeat sales to recoup the cost of the initial investment in advertising. Firms whose lies are quickly discovered by consumers do not invest much in advertising because they never sell enough to recoup their outlay on adverts. Consumers discover the poor quality and refrain from repeat purchasing. Foreseeing this, the firm that knows it will be quickly discovered never wastes money on expensive advertising in the first place.

What about one-off purchases, such as refrigerators, that usually last a decade or more? Consumers would really benefit from truthful advertising but producers of high-quality goods have no incentive to advertise. It would pay producers of low-quality refrigerators to advertise too since it would be ages before gullible consumers needed to return for a repeat purchase. A willingness to advertise no longer signals how much the firm believes in its own product. Since high-quality firms do not bother advertising, and since low-quality firms mimic the behaviour of high-quality firms, low-quality firms do not advertise either.

The table below shows advertising spending as a fraction of sales revenue for the three types of good identified above. The theory fits the facts well.

Quality detected	Time till buy again	Example	Advertising as percentage of sales revenue
Before buy	Irrelevant	Bananas	0.4
Soon after buy	Soon	Biscuits	3.6
Long after buy	Much later	Refrigerator	1.8

Source: E. Davis, J. Kay and J. Star, 'Is advertising rational?', *Business Strategy Review*, 1991

Recap

- Market structure refers to the relative size of minimum efficient scale and the total size of the market as reflected by the position of the industry demand curve.

- Market structure is also affected by the shapes of these curves. The steeper the industry demand curve, the more an entrant's extra output will bid down the price, making it harder to enter; and the steeper the *LAC* curve at outputs below minimum efficient scale, the harder it is for an entrant to enter and produce a small output.

- A pure monopoly is the only seller or potential seller in an industry. The monopolist has a large minimum efficient scale relative to the size of the industry. Economies of scale are important.

- To maximize profits, a monopolist chooses the output at which $MC = MR$. The relation of price to MR depends on the elasticity of the demand curve.

- A monopolist cuts back output to force up the price. The gap between price and marginal cost is a measure of monopoly power.

- A discriminating monopoly charges higher prices to customers whose demand is more inelastic.

- Monopolies have more ability and incentive to innovate. In the long run, this is a force for cost reduction. Temporary patents achieve some of the same effect even in competitive industries.

- Imperfect competition exists when individual firms face downward-sloping demand curves.

- When minimum efficient scale is very large relative to the industry demand curve, this innocent entry barrier may produce a natural monopoly in which entry can be ignored.

- At the opposite extreme, entry and exit may be costless. The market is contestable, and incumbent firms must mimic perfectly competitive behaviour, or be undercut by a flood of entrants.

▶

- Monopolistic competitors face free entry and exit, but are individually small and make similar though not identical products. Each has limited monopoly power in its special brand. In long-run equilibrium, price equals average cost. Each firm's downward-sloping demand curve is tangent to the downward-sloping part of its *LAC* curve.
- Oligopolists face a tension between collusion to maximize joint profits and competition for a larger share of smaller joint profits. Without credible threats of punishment by other collusive partners, each firm is tempted to cheat.
- Game theory describes interdependent decision-making. In the Prisoners' Dilemma game, each firm has a dominant strategy but the outcome is disadvantageous to both players. With binding commitments, both are better off by guaranteeing not to cheat on the collusive solution.
- In Nash equilibrium, each player selects her best strategy, given the strategies selected by rivals.
- Innocent entry barriers are made by nature, and arise from scale economies or absolute cost advantages of incumbent firms. Strategic entry barriers are made in boardrooms and arise from credible commitments to resist entry if challenged.

Review questions

To check your answers to these questions, go to pages 382–3.

1 A monopolist produces at constant marginal cost of £5 and faces the following demand curve:

Price (£)	8	7	6	5	4	3
Quantity	1	2	3	4	5	6

EASY

Calculate the *MR* curve. What is the equilibrium output? Equilibrium price? What would be the equilibrium price and output for a competitive industry? Why does the monopolist make less output and charge a higher price.

2 In addition to the data above, the monopolist also has a fixed cost of £2. What difference does this make to the monopolist's output, price and profits? Why?

3 Now suppose the government levies a monopoly tax, taking half the monopolist's profit. (a) What effect does this have on the monopolist's output? (b) What was the marginal profit on the last unit of output before the tax was levied? (c) Does this help you answer (a)?

4 Why do golf clubs have off-peak membership at reduced fees?

5 Why might a monopoly have more incentive to innovate than a competitive firm? Could a monopoly have less incentive to innovate?

6 Why are these statements wrong? (a) By breaking up monopolies we always get more output at a lower price. (b) A single producer in the industry is a sure sign of monopoly.

7 Vehicle repairers sometimes suggest that mechanics should be licensed so that repairs are done only by qualified people. (a) Evaluate the arguments for and against licensing car mechanics. (b) Are the arguments the same for licensing doctors?

8 An industry faces the demand curve:

EASY

Q	1	2	3	4	5	6	7	8	9	10
P	10	9	8	7	6	5	4	3	2	1

(a) As a monopoly, with $MC = 3$, what price and output are chosen? (b) Now suppose there are two firms, each with $MC = AC = 3$. What price and output maximize joint profits if they collude? (c) Why do the two firms have to agree on the output each produces? Why might each firm be tempted to cheat?

9 Unilever, makers of Walls ice cream, used helpfully to supply, free of charge, freezer cabinets to small shopkeepers, such as newsagents and corner shops, in exchange for the shop stocking Walls ice cream. What has this to do with entry barriers? If you were in charge of competition policy, would you allow this activity or prohibit it? Why, or why not?

10 Proud parents used to buy their children bound volumes of encyclopaedias to put on their bedroom bookshelves. Then CDs came along offering much the same service at a fraction of the cost. Subsequently, the volunteer-based Wikipedia offered free reference search on the Internet. What do you think happened to the production of encyclopaedias in book form? Would anybody still buy them? How can the readers be sure of the quality of Wikipedia information? Would you believe material offered by Google more?

INTERMEDIATE

11 With the industry demand curve in Question 8, two firms, A and Z, begin with half the market each when charging the monopoly price. Z decides to cheat and believes A will stick to its old output level. (a) Show the demand curve Z believes it faces. (b) What price and output would Z then choose?

DIFFICULT

12 Why are these statements wrong? (a) Competitive firms should collude to restrict output and drive up the price. (b) Firms would not advertise unless it increased their sales.

13 **Essay question** A good-natured parent knows that children sometimes need to be punished, but also knows that, when it comes to the crunch, the child will be let off with a warning. Can the parent undertake any pre-commitment to make the threat of punishment credible?

DIFFICULT

14 **Essay question** Why do shops offer price discounts, including 2-for-1 offers or coupons that can be redeemed towards the price, rather than simply cut the price of the product?

Online Learning Centre

To help you grasp the key concepts of this chapter check out the extra resources posted on the Online Learning Centre at www.mcgraw-hill.co.uk/textbooks/begg.

There are additional case studies, self-test questions, practice exam questions with answers and a graphing tool.

CHAPTER 7

Input markets: labour

Learning outcomes

By the end of this chapter, you should be able to:
- Explain the demand for labour
- Analyse labour supply and work incentives
- Show why poverty traps arise
- Discuss what determines wages and employment
- Understand why Wayne Rooney and Adele earn so much
- Distinguish the many different kinds of labour
- Show how human capital adds to skills
- Explain when investment in education and training makes sense
- Discuss the role of trade unions
- Analyse how globalization affects trade unions
- Show the effect of a minimum wage

The next two chapters discuss markets for inputs to production. In this chapter, we discuss the market for labour, examining both the quantity of labour employed and the skills which that labour possesses. The following chapter discusses the market for other production inputs. Once we understand the equilibrium price and quantity of each input, we can ask questions about the distribution of income across people and across inputs.

 7.1 ## The labour market

We turn now from markets for output to markets for the inputs from which output is produced. With a few minor modifications, the tools we have developed over the last four chapters can be used to analyse input markets too.

In winning a tennis tournament, Andy Murray earns more in a weekend than a professor earns in a year. Students studying economics can expect to earn more than students studying philosophy. An unskilled worker in the EU earns more than an unskilled worker in India. Each of these outcomes reflects the supply and demand for that particular type of labour.

The demand for labour

By a single firm, in the long run

A firm's demand for inputs depends on the technology it faces, the price of each input and demand for its output. Technology and input prices determine its costs. Demand determines the revenue from sales. The chosen output equates marginal cost and marginal revenue. In so doing, it determines the inputs that the firm demands.

In the long run a firm can adjust its inputs and the technique it uses to produce output. If the wage rises, the firm substitutes away from labour towards capital that is now relatively cheaper than before. Mechanized farming economizes on costly workers in the UK. However, with cheap abundant labour but scarce and expensive capital, Indian farmers use labour-intensive techniques.

At a given output, a higher wage makes a firm demand less labour and more of its other inputs. However, by raising the cost of making output, a higher wage also reduces the firm's chosen output level. This reduces the firm's demand for *all* inputs. In the long run, both effects reduce the quantity of labour demanded when the wage rises.

The effect of a higher wage on the demand for *other* inputs is ambiguous. The demand for capital rises as firms substitute away from labour, but lower output reduces the demand for all inputs, including capital. Whether or not a higher wage increases the demand for capital depends on whether the substitution effect (change in the relative prices of inputs) is larger or smaller than the output effect (a higher price for any input increases the marginal cost of output and reduces profit-maximizing output, and hence the firm needs lower quantities of inputs).

Similarly, a higher price of capital reduces the quantity of capital demanded. Firms substitute away from capital, and lower output also reduces the demand for capital. However, if the substitution effect is strong, the demand for labour may rise, despite lower output.

In the short run

In the short run, the firm has some fixed inputs. Suppose capital and land are fixed, and we view labour as the input that can be varied.

> The **marginal product of labour MPL** is the extra physical output when a worker is added, holding other inputs constant.

Beyond some point, the *diminishing marginal productivity* of labour sets in. With existing machines fully utilized, there is less and less for each new worker to do, and the marginal product of labour falls. However, profits depend on revenue not just on physical output.

> The **marginal revenue product of labour MRPL** is the change in sales revenue from selling the extra output that arises when an extra worker is employed, holding other inputs constant.

Thus, *MRPL* is the marginal benefit of hiring an extra worker. If the firm is perfectly competitive, it can sell more output without affecting its output price. *MRPL* is then simply *MPL* multiplied by the output price. Figure 7-1 shows the marginal revenue product of labour for a competitive firm. It slopes down because of diminishing marginal productivity. The wage is the marginal cost of hiring another worker. The firm expands workers until the marginal cost of another worker equals the marginal benefit. At a wage W_0, the firm hires N_0 workers. At a wage W_1, the firm hires N_1 workers.

Thus, *MRPL* is the demand curve for labour for a competitive firm, showing how many workers it hires at each wage. It measures the marginal benefit of having another worker. Moving down this schedule shows how the desired quantity of employment by the firm rises as the wage falls.

This theory is easily amended when the firm has *monopoly power* in its output market (a downward-sloping demand curve for its product) or *monopsony power* in its input markets (an upward-sloping supply curve for inputs because the firm's large scale affects the price of inputs).

> A **monopsonist** must raise the wage to attract extra labour.

The marginal cost of an extra worker exceeds the wage paid to that worker: if all workers must get the same wage, extra hiring also bids up the wage paid to the existing labour force.

Similarly, for a firm with monopoly power in its output market, the *MRPL* schedule is no longer the marginal product of labour multiplied by the output price. To sell extra output, facing a downward-sloping demand curve the firm must cut its output price, even on existing output. To calculate the marginal revenue product of labour, it finds the marginal product of labour *MPL*, then calculates the change in total revenue when it sells the extra output.

Figure 7-2 shows the schedules $MRPL_1$ and $MRPL_2$ for two firms with the same technology. Both schedules reflect diminishing marginal productivity – a property of technology – but $MRPL_2$ is steeper because an imperfectly competitive firm must also cut its price to sell more output. The

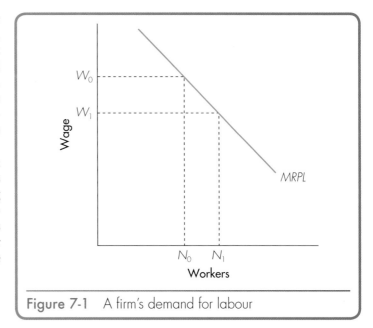

Figure 7-1 A firm's demand for labour

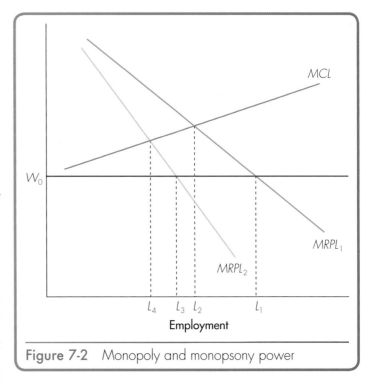

Figure 7-2 Monopoly and monopsony power

marginal benefit of another worker is lower on $MRPL_2$ than on $MRPL_1$. Similarly, although W_0 is the marginal cost of labour for a competitive firm taking the wage as given, a monopsonist faces a marginal cost of labour *MCL* in Figure 7-2.

Profit is maximized when the marginal revenue from an extra worker equals its marginal cost. Otherwise, the firm's hiring is inappropriate. A firm that is a price taker in both its output and input markets hires L_1 workers in Figure 7-2. A firm with market power in its output market hires L_3 workers. A firm with market power in hiring labour input hires L_2 workers. And a firm with market power in both markets hires L_4 workers. For the rest of this chapter we assume both output and input markets are competitive. The analysis is easily amended for other cases.

Changes in a firm's demand for labour

A higher wage moves a firm *along* its *MRPL* schedule, reducing the quantity of labour demanded. If the marginal cost of a worker is higher, the firm has to adjust employment until the marginal benefit of a worker is also higher. Lower employment means that labour encounters fewer diminishing returns when working with a given quantity of other inputs. At this lower level of employment, the marginal benefit of a worker is higher. By reducing employment enough, the firm can raise the marginal benefit of a worker in line with the higher marginal cost of a worker when the wage rises. The firm moves leftwards and upwards along a given *MRPL* schedule.

Box 7-1

The new Youth Contract

In early 2012, the UK Department of Work and Pensions announced a new £1 billion Youth Contract, in response to the challenge of youth unemployment. Aimed at young unemployed people in the 18–24 age group, the scheme will provide nearly half a million new opportunities, including apprenticeships and voluntary work experience placements. It also marks a substantial increase in the support and help available to young people through the Work Programme, Jobcentre Plus and sector-based work academies. Many businesses have already offered support by committing opportunities and vacancies for young people without jobs.

Why should the young experience such trouble finding jobs? First, those who already have successful work experience may seem a safer bet from a firm's standpoint – such workers have already learned the culture of work and shown they can stick at a job, whereas newcomers have a larger range of as yet unknown attributes. Second, workers with experience have learned additional skills during the process, making them more valuable. An economist's answer is in part that workers who are less valuable should be paid lower wages to offset this disadvantage. Society struggles with the conflicting wishes to attain high levels of employment for all and to ensure reasonable fairness in income disparity.

A related way of posing the question is to ask who should pay for the training that young workers need in order to make them valuable employees. Should it be the firm, that may ultimately benefit from higher productivity, or the worker, who will benefit from subsequently higher wages? Young workers are typically not so well off, so asking them to contribute too much to their training may deter them from pursuing costly training and lead them instead to seek less skilled jobs in which their take-home pay is initially greater.

Globalization is providing lots of competition from unskilled workers with lower wages around the world. The future for unskilled workers does not look bright. Hence the government may wish to contribute public money to subsidizing training in order to position the UK as a high-skills economy. There is little point championing the UK's high-tech strategy if our education system and labour markets combine to create lots of unskilled workers who will be outcompeted in the global knowledge economy.

Germany is often held up as a model of how the UK might instead behave. Apprenticeships are part of Germany's dual education system and a key part of many people's working life. Finding employment without having completed an apprenticeship is almost impossible in many technical occupations. A person can undertake an apprenticeship to become a plumber, optician, doctor's assistant and oven builder, for example. While spending over half their time in companies serving an apprenticeship, young workers can simultaneously continue formal academic studies in vocational schools. It is no accident that Germany's manufacturing sector is substantially larger than that of the UK.

Schemes like the new UK Youth Contract may prove useful, but at £1 billion the scheme is still pretty small in comparison with the need. It would require a complete change in culture to embed vocational training in our educational system and provide a more seamless connection between school and workplace.

However, a rise in the output price raises the marginal benefit of labour at any particular wage. It *shifts* the entire *MRPL* schedule upwards, raising its demand for labour. For a given output price, two other things raise a firm's demand for labour. Technical progress makes labour more productive and raises its marginal benefit. So does a greater quantity of other inputs with which labour can work. When a firm gets more capital, this raises the demand for labour by shifting the *MRPL* schedule up. At any wage, the firm hires more workers than before.

For the special case of perfect competition, a firm hires labour until $W = MRPL = [P \times MPL]$. Hence, the marginal product of labour *MPL* equals the real wage W/P. If nominal wages and output prices both double, real wages and employment are unaffected. Nothing real has changed.

Demand for labour by an industry

Since all firms in the industry face the same wage as each other, you might think that we simply add each firm's labour demand schedule horizontally to get the industry demand schedule. This is nearly correct but not quite. At a lower wage, each firm wants to hire more labour. This expands industry output, bidding down the output price. Even a competitive industry must cut its price to induce people to buy its higher total output.

This fall in the output price shifts to the left each individual firm's demand curve for labour. The marginal benefit of a worker is lower. We thus conclude that the industry demand curve for labour, relating the wage and the quantity of labour demand, is *steeper* than the horizontal sum of firms' individual labour demand curves.

Although each firm takes its output price as given, the entire industry bids down its output price when lower wages induce it to expand hiring and output. At industry level, this reduces the sensitivity of labour demand to the wage. Indeed, the more inelastic is the demand for the industry's output, the more inelastic will be the industry's demand for labour, because any given expansion will reduce prices by more, reducing the marginal benefit of hiring workers.

Labour supply

Labour supply depends both on how many people work and on their hours of work. To analyse labour supply, we ask how many hours do people in the labour force wish to work, and what makes people join the labour force at all?

The **labour force** is everyone in work or seeking a job.

Hours of work

How many hours a person in the labour force wants to work depends on the *real* wage, W/P, the nominal wage divided by the price of goods, which measures the amount of goods that can be bought as a result of working. People not working can stay at home and have fun. Each of us has only 24 hours a day for work and leisure. More leisure is nice but, by working longer, we can get more income with which to buy consumer goods.

We can use the model of consumer choice in Chapter 2. The choice is now between goods as a whole and leisure. A higher real wage raises the quantity of goods an extra hour of work will buy. This makes working more attractive than before and tends to increase the supply of hours worked. But there is a second effect. Suppose you work to get a target real income to finance a summer holiday. With a higher real wage, you don't have to work so long to meet your target.

These two effects are the *substitution and income effects* of Chapter 2. A higher real wage raises the relative return on working – a substitution effect or pure relative price effect that makes people want to work more. But a higher real wage also makes people better off – a pure income effect. Since leisure is a luxury good, the quantity of leisure demanded rises sharply when real incomes increase. This income effect tends to make people work less. Lottery winners quit their jobs.

The income and substitution effects pull in opposite directions. We need empirical evidence to see whether higher wages make people supply more hours of work. For most developed economies, this evidence says that, for men and women with full-time careers, the two effects largely cancel out. A change in the real wage has little effect on the quantity of hours supplied.

This conclusion applies to relatively small changes in real wage rates. In most Western countries, the large rise in real wages over the past 100 years has been matched by reductions of ten hours or more in the working week. The income effect has outweighed the substitution effect.

Workers care about take-home pay after deductions of income tax. A reduction in income tax rates thus raises after-tax real wages. Hence, the same empirical evidence implies that lower income tax rates will not lead to a big rise in the supply of hours worked! Tax cuts are not a magic solution to work incentives, and moderate tax rises should not be expected to have a major disincentive effect on hours of work.

Labour force participation

The effect of real wages on the supply of hours is smaller than often supposed. Real wages also affect labour supply by changing incentives to join the labour force.

The **participation rate** is the fraction of people of working age who join the labour force.

Table 7-1 presents UK data on participation rates. Most men are in the labour force, though nowadays when older men lose their jobs they often give up completely and leave it. A smaller but still quite stable percentage of single women are in the labour force. There has been a big rise in the number of mothers in the labour force, from only 25 per cent in 1951 to over 60 per cent today. By 2006, over 75 per cent of all women were in the labour force.

Someone not in the labour force has lots of leisure, but how does she afford consumer goods? She may have inherited wealth, won the National Lottery, be supported by her working partner, or get income support and housing benefit from the government. If she joins the labour force and gets a job, she loses an hour of leisure for every hour she works. However, for every pound she initially earns, she loses over 90 pence in withdrawal of government benefits. Since the Treasury coffers are not limitless, governments help the very poor but claw as much

Table 7-1 UK participation rates (%)

	1971	2011
Men	95	82
Women	59	71

Source: http://www.statistics.gov.uk

money back as they can once people's circumstances improve a little. Moreover, going out to work entails several costs – the right clothes, commuting to work and paying for child care. It may simply not be worth it.

The **poverty trap** means that getting a job makes a person worse off than staying at home.

Suppose the real wage rises. It may now be possible to pole vault over the poverty trap into work that pays. Conversely, lower real wages make the poverty trap worse. Hence, higher real wages increase the incentive to join the labour force.

What happened to income and substitution effects here? These tools compare two situations in which an individual can adjust their behaviour at the margin. The poverty trap is a high wall that entrants must clear to get into the labour force. Analysis of small changes is not the right procedure. Beginning from a low wage, a small rise in the wage makes no difference. As wages keep rising, eventually a person can soar over the wall and want to join the labour force. Different people face walls of different heights. As wages in the economy rise, the aggregate labour supply response is continuous. A few more people join with each rise in real wages.

Why has labour force participation by women risen so much in recent decades? First, there was a social change in attitudes to women working. Second, pressure for equal opportunities has raised women's wages. Third, the opportunity cost of working has fallen. Dishwashers and vacuum cleaners, and some limited assistance from men, have made it easier for women to go out to work.

Box 7-2
Ameliorating the poverty trap to increase those in work

During 1997–2010, the Labour government's policies fell under two main headings, 'Welfare to Work' and 'Making Work Pay'. Both reflected a belief that work allows people to acquire skills and new opportunities: work is a ladder allowing people gradually to climb out of poverty. 'Welfare to Work' had two elements: more help in finding a job and more pressure (threat of loss of social security benefits) on those thought to be making little effort to find work.

Both raised the incentive to participate in the labour force. 'Making Work Pay' dealt with incomes of people once they were in the labour force. The 'Working Family Tax Credit' gave money to workers with children, provided the parent worked a minimum number of hours a week (the limit being set roughly to make it possible for mothers to work while their children were at school).

Both measures tried to attack the poverty trap – the situation in which going out to work leaves people less well off than staying at home and living on welfare benefits.

The trilemma for governments is always the same: how to reconcile (a) a civilized and decent level of benefits for those in need; (b) how to prevent the scheme being prohibitively expensive in budget terms; and (c) how therefore to confine assistance to a relatively small number of people.

Suppose the government paid welfare benefits to all citizens no matter how rich, and simply applied income tax to any income then earned. This would keep disincentive effects of working to a tolerable level – people would not lose benefits by going out to work – but it would make the entire scheme incredibly costly since the rich get benefits too. In order to finance the whole scheme, income tax rates would have to be much higher, creating possible disincentives for everyone in the labour market.

▶

Conversely, suppose people quickly lose welfare benefits as they start to earn income. This can imply a huge marginal tax rate as a result of going out to work. Not only do people become liable for income tax but they also lose more benefits the more they initially work. In such circumstances, it may pay to stay at home. This is particularly the case for people with large levels of housing benefit – either because they have large families or because they live in an expensive area such as London.

There is no easy answer. How has the Conservative–Liberal coalition government tried to tackle things since its election in 2012?

Many of its manifesto proposals had to be put on hold while it tackled the problem of reducing the government debt and budget deficit. The 2012 budget announced that child benefits would be withdrawn for workers earning more than £60 000. This immediately created a public outcry by causing sharp differences between the treatment of those earning just under the threshold and just over the threshold. Since those families are often in the income range consistent with their swinging between political party affiliation, the government had been sensitive to their pain, and had abandoned a previous plan to set the threshold at £50 000.

The government is also exploring a ceiling on the total welfare benefits that a family can enjoy, perhaps at the level of the median after tax income of a UK family. In practice, this would hit unemployed families with many children living in expensive areas.

To sum up, social influences matter and are one of the 'other things equal' that can change. For given attitudes, labour supply to the economy rises with the level of real wages, but not by a lot. It is rather inelastic. Many people are already in the labour force. Offsetting income and substitution effects means that further changes in wages have a small effect on hours worked. The main reason that aggregate supply of person-hours rises when real wages rise is that extra people can leap over the wall and join the labour force.

Labour supply to an industry

Suppose the industry is small relative to the economy, and wishes to hire workers with common skills. It must pay the going rate, adjusted only for the particular non-monetary characteristics of that industry. The *equilibrium wage differential* across two industries offsets differences in the desirability of jobs to workers, removing any incentive for workers to move between industries. Nasty and dangerous jobs have to pay more.

A small industry faces a horizontal labour supply curve at the appropriate wage. Paying this going rate, it can hire as many workers as it wants. In practice, few industries are this small. The construction industry is a significant user of roofers, and the haulage industry a significant user of lorry drivers. When an industry expands, it usually bids up wages for those skills by raising the whole economy's demand for a skill that, in the short run, is in limited supply. In the short run, an industry faces an upward-sloping labour supply curve.

In the long run, the industry's labour supply curve is flatter. When short-run expansion bids up the wages of computer programmers, more school-leavers train in this skill, enhancing the long-run supply of programmers. With more programmers available, an individual industry does not have to raise the wage so much to attract extra workers with this skill.

Case study 7-1   Premiership wages

Premiership footballers earn breathtaking amounts of money. The wage bill in UK Premier League football rose to over £2 billion in 2009–10. Spiralling club incomes reflect not only increasing demand as satellite TV retails football to ever wider (and more profitable) audiences, but also greater proficiency in marketing ancillary products like replica shirts. Manchester United earns 35 per cent of its income from games, 37 per cent from TV rights and 28 per cent from commercial activities. Such breadth and depth to football teams' revenues has led to players trying to get their hands on all of the club's additional revenue.

As clubs lose revenue from TV or commercial deals, downward pressure on wages begins. When teams are relegated to lower divisions, expensive players are offloaded. Any change in the generosity of sponsorship is likely to feed into wages as a whole. The financial success of the Premier League was caused by its ability to sell TV rights and market its products. Its ability to attract top foreign players was the consequence not the cause of this success, though it then reinforced further successes. Conversely, promotion from the Championship to the Premiership for the 2009–10 season was worth about £100 million for the successful clubs.

If you want to understand more about Premier League finances, look at the annual review of football finances by top consultants Deloitte. For 2009–10, they reported that, because of strong wage growth, only Premier League and Bundesliga actually made profits; La Liga and Serie A lost money. In all countries, growth in revenues quickly finds its way into greater spending on players in the attempt to buy success.

When the labour supply curve for top footballers is almost vertical – how many extra Ronaldos, Rooneys and Droghbas do you expect to find by paying a bit more? – any upward shift in the labour demand curve leads largely to higher wages. The entire history of the Premier League bears this out. Booming revenues have gone largely into players' pockets.

However, over the years the annual Deloittes reports have noted a new twist on this, arguing that the wave of new owners at clubs, including Aston Villa and Liverpool, is likely to result in more restraint in spending, with servicing debt and investing in stadia being other key priorities.

'A lot of these new owners have had sporting success but also considerable financial success,' said director of Deloitte's Sports Business group, Alan Switzer. 'A decent chunk of the money will still flow through to the players, but we don't think it will be the same proportion that flowed through previously.'

One way an economist could think about this claim is to say that the gross revenue of football clubs is no longer available only to pay footballers. Some portion has to go on debt interest and building stadia. Only the net revenue affects the demand for footballers. Most of this will still go into wages, but this is a smaller share of total revenue than previously.

Even so, the Premiership wage bill continues upwards as the chart below shows, particularly the recent explosion at Manchester City since it was acquired by Sheikh Mansour in 2008.

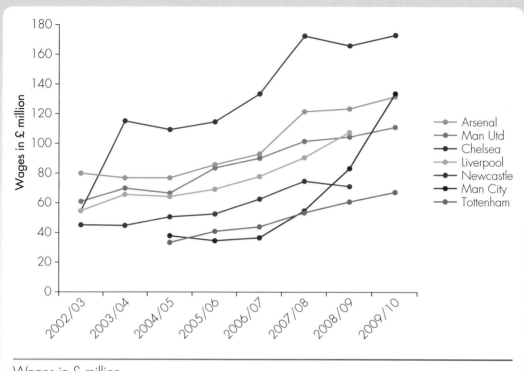

Wages in £ million

Sources: http://abehnisch.com/tag/premier-league; www.deloitte.com

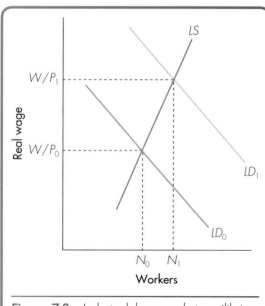

Figure 7-3 Industry labour market equilibrium

Labour market equilibrium in an industry

Figure 7-3 shows labour supply and demand for an industry. In equilibrium, the real wage is W/P_0 and employment is N_0. Shifts in these supply or demand curves change this equilibrium. In the market for Premier League footballers, the labour supply curve LS is steep since it is hard to find more good footballers no matter how much the industry offers to pay.

Football clubs' revenue from TV depends in turn on the revenue that TV can earn from advertising. If the global economy slows down, firms cut back their spending on advertising. When they do, even Wayne Rooney feels the effects.

The arrival of Sky TV, paying vast sums to show games on TV, raised the demand for footballers from LD_0 to LD_1, causing a large rise in their wages. Thus, Premier League footballers get high wages for two reasons. First, the derived demand curve for their labour is high because football clubs can earn massive revenue from the success of their talented footballers. Second, the labour supply curve for people with these skills is very steep. Even by paying a lot more, it is hard to attract many more Beckhams into the football industry. Beckham and Owen have few adequate substitutes. Thus, supply and demand explain the high wages of top stars.

Conversely, football matches in the lower divisions were first shown live on ITV Digital. When this channel went bankrupt, revenues of football clubs outside the Premier League fell sharply, reducing the demand for players in the lower divisions. Their equilibrium wage fell. As you would expect, since Sky TV has begun televising games from the Championship division as well as the Premier League, demand curves for players in the Championship division have started shifting upwards again. These fluctuations illustrate vividly that the demand for footballing labour is derived from the demand for the output of the football clubs, which nowadays depends significantly on whether the games get access to TV revenues.

Different kinds of labour

In most European countries men earn more than women, and whites earn more than non-whites. Is this discrimination, or do different workers have different productivity? Workers differ not merely in gender and race but in age, experience, education, training, innate ability, and in whether or not they belong to a trade union.

Figure 7-4 shows that UK women earned about 83 per cent as much as men in 2011, though the gender gap is closing steadily. Table 7-2 highlights other sources of pay differential.

People with more education and training earn more, whether or not they are in a trade union. Work experience adds

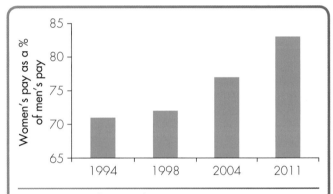

Figure 7-4   The gender gap in pay (women's pay as % of men's pay)

Source: www.statistic.gov.uk/cci

Table 7-2   UK pay differentials

% extra pay for	Sector in which then employed	
	Unionized	Non-unionized
Education and training		
GCSE	+5	+13
A-levels	+16	+21
University degree	+32	+47
Postgraduate degree	+50	+50
Other higher education	+18	+21
Apprenticeship	+11	+9

Source: A. Booth, 'Seniority, earnings and unions', *Economica*, 1996

to earnings, though at a diminishing rate, especially in manual work, where older workers cannot match their strong, young colleagues. But experience still matters, even in manual work. Job characteristics also affect pay. Manual workers, perhaps with fewer skills, earn less than non-manual workers. Firms in the busy (and expensive) South East region, including London, have to pay workers more.

Human capital

Human capital is the stock of accumulated expertise that raises a worker's productivity.

Human capital is the result of past investment in workers. It enhances their productivity and thus their current and future incomes. Education and training involve current sacrifices – both direct costs and giving up opportunities to earn immediate income – but yield the benefit of higher future incomes because productivity is higher. In long-run equilibrium, the extra benefit of acquiring skills must just cover the extra cost of acquiring them. Table 7-2 suggests that the pay-off to education can be large. Don't quit now!

On-the-job training

Human capital can also be accumulated after people get a job. *Firm-specific skills* raise a worker's productivity only in that particular firm. A worker knows how that factory works and what makes these particular teams of workers function effectively. These skills may be worthless in another firm. In contrast, *general skills*, such as knowing how to use Windows or Excel, can be transferred to work in another firm.

A firm will pay for training in firm-specific skills. Its workers' productivity rises, but they are unlikely to move to other firms where their productivity (and hence wages) will be lower. Conversely, the more general or transferable the skill, the more a firm will want the worker to pay the cost of training. No firm will invest in training workers who then move to other firms.

An apprentice works for less than his immediate marginal product, thus paying for his own training. This investment raises his future productivity, raising his future income wherever he works. Firms do not mind if the worker quits, since the worker bore the cost of the training.

Signalling

Human capital theory says that education and training raise worker productivity. An alternative theory of education is the theory of *signalling*. This theory says it could be rational to invest in costly education *even if education adds nothing directly to a worker's marginal product*. This theory may be more helpful in explaining why history graduates earn big money in banking.

The theory assumes that people are born with different innate ability. Some people are good at most things, other people are less smart and less productive. Not all smart people have blue eyes. The problem for firms is to tell which applicants are the smart ones with high productivity. Looking at their eyes is not enough.

Screening

Suppose higher education contributes nothing to productivity. Signalling theory says that, in going on in education, people who know that they are smart send a signal to firms that they are the high-productivity workers of the future. Higher education *screens out* the smart high-productivity workers. Firms can pay university graduates more because they know that they are the high-ability workers.

To be effective, the screening process must separate the high-ability workers from the others. Why don't lower-ability workers go to university and fool firms into offering them high wages? Lower-ability workers could not be confident of passing.

If studying adds to productivity, firms should offer higher wages to people who *attend* university, whether or not they pass the final exam. If university screens out the good people, firms will care not about attendance but *academic performance*.

Some firms hire university students before they sit their final exams. Is this evidence against the signalling theory? Not necessarily. Screening works in a second way. Since most people know their own ability, firms may take it on trust that people who have stuck it out till their final year at university believe themselves to be at the high end of the ability range.

It seems probable that education (even at the highest level) contributes something to productivity. But there may also be an element of screening. Engineering, law and business degrees presumably contribute more to productivity than philosophy, history or medieval French. If education raises productivity directly, it is good for society. It raises the amount of output that the labour force can eventually produce.

What if the only function of higher education is to signal the high-ability workers? It still makes sense for individuals to go to university. It raises their future incomes. Does it make sense for society as a whole? The social gain to learning who are the smart workers is that, by matching smart workers to difficult jobs, society gets higher output. If the only function of higher education is to screen out the high-ability workers, there is a cheaper way for society to achieve the same result. A national IQ test, with results adjusted for disadvantages of background and previous opportunity to learn, might screen as well (possibly even better!) at much less cost to society as a whole.

Asymmetric information

The 2001 Nobel Prize for Economics was shared by three economists who pioneered the analysis of inside information, where people know more about themselves than others can easily discover.

George Akerlof of the University of California at Berkeley first analysed behaviour in the used car market where sceptical buyers fear that sellers may try to offload useless cars about which the seller has much more information than the buyer. Akerlof showed that, in market equilibrium, buyers *assume* all cars are bad. Sellers of good cars cannot get a fair price. If buyers cannot tell the difference between good and bad, the only way in which they can protect themselves from exploitation is to assume the worst. The same analysis helps us understand loan sharks, junk bonds and some forms of discrimination against minorities.

Michael Spence of Stanford University showed that this problem is partly solved if those knowing they have good characteristics take costly actions to reveal credibly that they must be the good guys. Smart people go to university, doing without a salary, to signal that they are smart. There is no point in stupid people trying to mimic this behaviour – they will flunk the exams. His own research emphasized how education can *signal* innate talent. Signalling also explains how firms use dividends to signal their optimism about future profits to the stock market.

Joseph Stiglitz of Columbia University developed an alternative solution to Akerlof's adverse selection problem, relying on *screening* by the uninformed rather than signalling by the informed. By offering a lower premium in exchange for a higher deductible, insurance companies can induce those who know they are low risk to reveal themselves. Similarly, a steep wage–earnings profile for wages, beginning very low but ending very high, is attractive only to workers knowing that they do not intend to quit the labour force early. (For other Nobel Prize winners, see www.nobelprize.org.)

 ## Trade unions

Trade unions are worker organizations that affect pay and working conditions. UK union membership was almost 40 per cent of the workforce in the late 1920s, then collapsed in the depression of the 1930s, before climbing to 50 per cent in 1980. Since then it has been in constant decline, in part because the industrial economy is giving way to the service economy, and because the public sector has shrunk significantly. See Figure 7-5.

The traditional view of unions is that they offset the firm's power in negotiating wages and working conditions. A single firm has many workers. The firm is in a strong bargaining position if it can make separate agreements with each of its workers. By presenting a united front, the workers can impose large costs on the firm if they *all* quit. The firm can replace one worker but not its whole labour force. The existence of unions evens up the bargaining process.

Figure 7-5 Union membership (% of labour force), 1910–2010

A successful union must be able to restrict the firm's labour supply. If the firm can hire non-union labour, unions find it hard to maintain the wage above the level at which the firm can hire non-union workers. Hence, unions are keen on closed-shop agreements with individual firms.

A **closed shop** means that all a firm's workers must be members of a trade union.

By restricting supply and making workers scarce, a union can raise wages for the workers who still have jobs. How far will a union swap lower employment for higher wages in an industry? And what determines union power to control the supply of labour to particular industries?

The more the union cares about its *senior* members, the more it will raise wages by restricting employment. Senior workers are the least likely to be sacked. Conversely, the more a union is democratic, and the more it cares about potential members as well as actual members, the less it restricts employment to force up wages.

The more inelastic the demand for labour, the more a given restriction in jobs raises the wage. The incentive to unionize the labour force is strong when big wage rises are achieved with little loss of employment. Conversely, when labour demand is elastic, forcing up wages costs many jobs. Unions are then less attractive to their members.

Unions and globalization

On the first of May each year, union members are well represented in the big marches against capitalism and globalization. In a small country, big firms may have significant monopoly power. This has two consequences. First, they make substantial profits, a tempting target for unions. Second, facing limited competition, the firms will have little trouble passing on higher costs as higher prices in the event that unions restrict labour supply and raise wages. Thus, a big firm in a sheltered small economy is a fertile environment in which to be a trade union.

Globalization makes domestic firms swim in a much bigger pond with many foreign competitors. Facing this extra competition, the output price is much less sensitive to the output of domestic firms: in the extreme case, domestic firms may be price-takers in the world market and unable to raise prices at all when domestic costs increase. Moreover, this more competitive environment means that entry by others is likely already to have competed away most of the firm's profits.

Hence, when unions now restrict labour supply, they scarcely manage to force up the wage; and if they do, they risk the possibility that their employer will go bankrupt. Globalization weakens the power of domestic trade unions. That is why unions mind about globalization and march against it. Globalization has made labour markets more competitive, undermining the local monopoly power of local unions.

Unions as agents of management

Union wage differentials arise not only from the successful restriction of labour supply. Union work has certain characteristics – a structured work setting, inflexibility of hours, employer-set overtime, and a faster work pace – a whole set of conditions that might be regarded as unpleasant. Higher wages in such industries are partly *compensating wage differentials* for these non-monetary aspects of the job.

Thus, unions tend to emerge in industries where large productivity gains would result from the introduction of unpleasant working conditions. The union exists not to restrict labour supply in total, but to negotiate productivity gains, ensuring that workers receive proper compensating differentials for the unpopular changes in working practices that firms find it profitable to introduce. On this view, the unions do not make separate deals for pay and working conditions; rather, their role is to secure pay increases *in exchange for* changes in working conditions.

From this perspective, unions play an important role in allowing firms to commit to what they promise. Without unions, there is the danger that workers would agree to new technologies and changes in work conditions but then find that the firm failed to honour its promise to offer higher wages in return. The existence of unions helps their members believe that firms will stick to their half of the bargain.

Summing up

We are therefore left with three possible views of the role of trade unions. First, unions may represent the exercise of monopoly power in the labour market by groups of workers who have banded together precisely for that purpose (the equivalent of OPEC in the market for oil supply). We all remember or know of the incessant strikes of the 1970s when unions were very powerful. Their power has been reduced by anti-union legislation, by a shrinking public sector (which was always less able to stand up to union power) and by globalization, which has increased competition and diminished monopoly power of unions.

Second, unions may have been the antidote to extreme power of employers with the local ability to exploit local workers – a levelling of the playing field. More effective competition policy and globalization have reduced the power of firms in labour markets in advanced countries and therefore reduced the need for the union antidote.

Finally, changes in the way in which work is organized, caused largely by the IT revolution that has allowed smaller firms to prosper and market their activities via the Internet, have led to much smaller firms that offer less scope for unions to negotiate complex changes on behalf of large workforces. Nowadays, many services are outsourced around the world and the monolithic large firm has often been disaggregated into its distinct parts.

Case study 7-2   Higher education pays off

Nowadays many students have to contribute to the cost of their own education, and emerge from college and university with the debt millstone round their neck. Of course, compared with 30 years ago, borrowing in general has become a lot easier. Some of the debt millstone of graduates is probably accounted for by a few shopping sprees too many and a rather nice lifestyle while in higher education. Even so, we all know that education has become expensive and most of the debt burden was incurred in the good cause of acquiring a proper education.

But this raises some obvious questions. Why has education become more expensive? Are the gains to having a university education sufficient to justify actually paying for one? And are some subjects better investments than others?

The main reasons that university education has become more expensive for the government are: (a) as a society we have decided that many more young people should go to university, which is no longer something that only the privileged think of doing, and (b) as taxpayers we have been unwilling to raise state support for university education in line with our targets for getting a much higher percentage of the population through university. If the state won't pay, the rest has to be borne by private individuals.

The fairness of who pays for what is not independent of the benefits that education confers. If students are subsequently going to earn enormous salaries, it is not unreasonable that they bear a part of the cost of their own education. If higher education makes hardly any difference to lifetime income, the case for charging students in some form is correspondingly reduced. People with university degrees earn at least a third more than people without such degrees. This may overstate the effect of the degree itself – some people get well rewarded because they are smart and happened to go to university rather than because they went to university.

What about the particular subject that you are studying? Are some better passports to a job than others? The table below shows the results of a major empirical study on determinants of people's wages by the time they are 33 years old. Women who studied humanities at undergraduate level on average gain only 5 per cent on the salary they are subsequently earning at the age of 33. In contrast, if they were studying economics, they would on average add 24 per cent to their salary at age 33. Men also add 20 per cent to their salary by studying economics rather than the arts – in the latter case, a humanities degree is actually associated with below-average salaries at age 33.

Just be glad you are reading *Foundations of Economics*, rather than *Foundations of English*. Notice, too, how poorly chemistry is treated in the market place.

	% extra wage in Britain at age 33 for	
	Men	Women
First degree	+15	+32
Postgraduate degree	+15	+35
Extra effect by subject		
Arts	−10	+5
Economics	+10	+24
Chemistry/biology	−17	−11
Maths/physics	+9	+16

Source: R. Blundell et al., 'Returns to higher education in Britain', *Economic Journal*, 2000

7-4 A minimum wage

First introduced in 1999, the UK minimum wage has subsequently risen by 60 per cent and is now £5.73 an hour for adults, with a reduced rate for young workers. Figure 7-6 shows the demand curve $D_L D_L$ and the supply curve $S_L S_L$ for workers in a particular industry. Free market equilibrium is at E. For skilled workers, the equilibrium wage W_0 exceeds a minimum wage at W_1, which is thus irrelevant.

Suppose the minimum wage is W_2, above the free market equilibrium wage W_0. At W_2, there is excess labour supply $L_2 - L_1$. Since firms cannot be forced to hire workers they do not want, employment is L_1.

A national minimum wage may exceed the free market equilibrium wage for low-skill occupations. If so, those workers lucky enough to find jobs get higher wages than before but the total amount of employment is lower than in free market equilibrium. Minimum wages may explain involuntary unemployment among low-skilled workers. A minimum wage prices some workers out of a job: by raising wages, it slides firms up their demand curves, cutting jobs. Even politicians understand. Right?

The 'proof' relies on a competitive labour market. People's intuition is often based on perfect competition. What happens if there is a sole employer? A monopsonist's new hiring bids up the price of existing workers: the marginal cost of labour exceeds the wage. Figure 7-7 shows the marginal revenue product of labour, the labour supply curve facing the firm and the marginal cost of labour to the monopsonist. In equilibrium, $MRPL = MCL$. Employment is N_1 and a wage W_1 is needed to attract this labour. The vertical gap between LS and $MRPL$ shows workers are paid less than their marginal product. This is called *exploitation*.

At a minimum wage W_2, the monopsonist faces a *horizontal* labour supply at W_2, at least until N_2 people are hired. W_2 is now the marginal cost of labour. The firm hires N_2 workers to equate the marginal cost and marginal benefit of hiring. By offsetting exploitation, the minimum wage boosts jobs from N_1 to N_2.

Beginning at free market equilibrium at a wage W_1, successive rises in the minimum wage *boost* jobs (sliding the firm along the labour supply curve LS) until the minimum wage reaches W_2, at which employment is

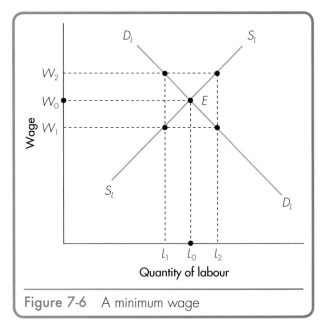

Figure 7-6 A minimum wage

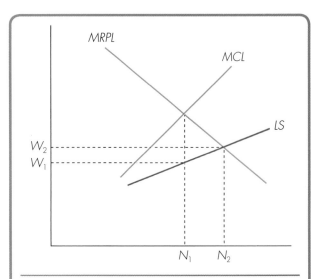

Figure 7-7 A minimum wage for a monopsonist

Source: Dolado et al., 'The economic impact of wages in Europe', *Economic Policy*, 1996

maximized. Still higher minimum wages now move the firm up its demand curve, *reducing* jobs thereafter. When firms have some monopsony power, a minimum wage slightly above the free market equilibrium is good for jobs – it offsets the distortion caused by the market power of employers – but a minimum wage substantially above the free market equilibrium is bad for jobs.

Whether the minimum wage is too high to boost jobs is thus an *empirical* question. A study of EU countries found no evidence that minimum wages cut adult employment, but some evidence they cut youth employment. The productivity of the young and unskilled is low. Minimum wages, even at lower rates for youths, are often above the intersection of LS and $MRPL$.

The minimum wage revisited

Suppose labour demand, the marginal revenue product of a worker, is given by $MRP = 7 - 2n$, where n is the number of workers, and labour supply is given by $n = w - 1$. Industry equilibrium equates the wage and marginal revenue product of labour, at which $7 - 2n = n + 1$. Hence, the equilibrium employment is 2, and the equilibrium wage is 3. Suppose the government imposes a minimum wage. If this is anywhere below 3 it has no effect. If it is higher than 3, it reduces the number of workers demanded but increases the number of workers wanting to work. There is lower employment and an excess supply of workers in the labour market.

Now suppose the situation is a monopsony. The single employer faces a wage bill wn, which is just $n(n + 1)$. The marginal cost of an extra labour is obtained by differentiating this with respect to n, yielding $2n + 1$. Equating this to MRP yields the optimal profit, at which point $7 - 2n = 2n + 1$. So monopsony reduces equilibrium employment to $3/2$. The corresponding marginal revenue product of labour, the marginal benefit to the firm, has risen to $7 - 2(3/2) = 4$, which is also its marginal cost of labour. From the labour supply curve, workers receive a wage of only $[1 + (3/2)] = 5/2$. The gap between the MRP of 4 and the wage of $5/2$ is exploitation.

Now suppose the government imposes a minimum wage of 3. At any employment level up to 2, the marginal cost of employment to the monopsonist is 3 since the wage is unaffected by expansion of employment. But we already know that the firm hires 2 workers when it faces a marginal labour cost of 3, and at that point 2 workers are happy to work (labour supply is then $3 - 1$).

Hence, beginning from monopsony ($n = 3/2$, wage $= 5/2$, $MRP = 4$), imposition of a well-judged minimum wage of 3 can increase employment to 2, and increase take-home pay to 3 by eating into the monopsony profits that would otherwise have been made, thus changing the incentives for the firm to hire workers.

- In the long run, a firm will choose the lowest-cost way of producing its chosen output level. A higher wage has a substitution effect (a switch out of labour into other inputs) and an output effect (higher costs reduce output and the need for inputs). Both reduce the demand for labour.

- In the short run, the firm has some fixed inputs, and varies output by varying its variable input, labour. Labour faces diminishing returns when other factors are fixed. Its marginal physical product falls as more labour is used.

- A profit-maximizing firm produces the output at which marginal output cost equals marginal output revenue. Equivalently, it hires labour up to the point where the marginal cost of labour equals its marginal benefit (its marginal revenue product).

- A firm's *MRPL* schedule shifts up if its output price rises, if its capital stock rises or if technical progress makes labour more productive. All raise the demand for labour by raising its marginal benefit. The converse changes shift the *MRPL* schedule downwards.

- For someone already in the labour force, a higher real wage has a substitution effect that raises the supply of hours worked, but an income effect that reduces the supply of hours worked. The two roughly cancel out.

- Participation rates rise with higher real wage rates, lower fixed costs of working and changes in taste in favour of working rather than staying at home. All three have raised labour force participation, especially by married women.

- Equilibrium wage differentials are monetary compensation for different non-monetary characteristics of jobs across industries.

- When demand is high and supply is scarce, equilibrium wages will be high. Firms can still make profits provided demand continues to be high.

- Different workers get different pay. This reflects personal characteristics such as education, job experience, gender, race and union status.

- Skills or human capital are the most important source of wage differentials. Human capital formation includes both formal education and on-the-job training. Workers with more education and training earn higher lifetime incomes.

- Skilled labour is relatively scarce because it is costly to acquire human capital. Workers acquire human capital if the benefit exceeds the cost. Firms pay for training if there is then little danger of the worker leaving the firm; otherwise, the worker has to pay for it.

- Education may allow innately more skilled workers to signal this skill to future employers. If so, education allows higher future wages even if the education itself makes no direct contribution to productivity.

- Under 30 per cent of the UK labour force now belongs to a trade union. Unions restrict the labour supply to firms or industries, thereby raising wages but lowering employment. Unions move firms up their demand curve for labour. Unions achieve higher wages the more inelastic the demand for labour and the more they are willing or able to restrict the supply of labour. Globalization makes labour demand more elastic and reduces unions' incentive to raise wages.

- Unions also raise wages by negotiating compensation for changes in work practices that raise productivity but reduce the pleasantness of the job. Without unions, workers might never agree to such changes, believing that firms would not honour their promise to raise wages after conditions were irreversibly altered.

- In a competitive labour market, a minimum wage has no effect if it is set below the free market equilibrium wage. If it is set above this level, it will lead to a fall in employment and a rise in wages. Employed workers will benefit but some workers will not have access to jobs that previously would have been available.

Review questions

To check your answers to these questions, go to pages 383–4.

1 Why is a firm's output supply decision the same as its labour demand decision?

2 (a) Why does the marginal product of labour eventually decline as more labour is hired?

(b) A firm builds a new factory, adding to its capital stock and the flow of capital services thereby provided. What happens to the firm's demand for labour as a result?

3 Over the last 100 years, the real wage rose but the working week got shorter. (a) Explain this result using income and substitution effects. (b) Could labour input have risen despite shorter working hours per person?

4 A film producer says that the industry is doomed because Russell Crowe and Julia Roberts are paid too much. Evaluate the argument.

5 When might an industry face a horizontal supply curve for labour?

EASY

6 Why are the following statements wrong? (a) There is no economic reason why a sketch that took Picasso one minute to draw should fetch £1 million. (b) Higher wages must raise incentives to work.

7 Suppose going to university adds nothing to productivity but reveals that you were simply born clever and determined. Would graduates earn more than non-graduates? Would it matter if you studied philosophy or economics? What can be deduced from the fact that arts graduates earn less than economics graduates?

8 A worker can earn £20 000 a year for the next 40 years. Alternatively, the worker can take three years off to go on a training course whose fees are £7000 per year. If the government provides an interest-free loan for this training, what future income differential per year would make this a profitable investment in human capital?

9 Suppose economists form a union and establish a certificate that is essential for practising economics. Would this raise the relative wage of economists? How would the union restrict entry to the economics profession?

10 'Youth unemployment is high so we should reduce the minimum wage for young people.' Evaluate this argument.

INTERMEDIATE

11 A small firm is worried that its young women workers will soon leave to start a family, disrupting the business and wasting the money the firm has invested in their training. The firm does not wish to hire only men and risk falling foul of legislation outlawing discrimination by gender. What advice would you give the owner?

12 Why are trade unions highly visible in industries with monopoly power in their output market but not in competitive industries? What is the likely consequence of globalization for the future of trade unions?

13 Why are these statements wrong? (a) Free schooling from 16 to 18 ensures that the poor can stay on in education. (b) Many low-paid workers belong to a trade union. Hence unions do not improve pay and conditions.

DIFFICULT

14 **Essay question** Young hospital doctors complain that the long hours they have to work are not adequately compensated by their initial salaries. Use the material of this chapter to discuss at least two theories of what is going on.

15 **Essay question** The US has persistently had lower unemployment than Spain and Italy. How would you explain this?

Online Learning Centre

To help you grasp the key concepts of this chapter check out the extra resources posted on the Online Learning Centre at www.mcgraw-hill.co.uk/textbooks/begg.

There are additional case studies, self-test questions, practice exam questions with answers and a graphing tool.

CHAPTER 8

Other input markets and income distribution

Learning outcomes

By the end of this chapter, you should be able to:

- Analyse the markets for capital and land
- Distinguish flows over time and stocks at a point in time
- Understand the markets for renting capital services and for buying new capital assets
- Explain the required rental on capital

- Derive the present value of a future cost or benefit
- Show how land rentals are determined
- Describe the functional distribution of income
- Analyse the personal distribution of income

Chapter 7 examined the market for labour. We now examine some of the other inputs used with labour in the production process. Having completed this analysis of factor markets, we then discuss the *income distribution* in an economy. The price of an input, multiplied by the quantity used, is the income of that input. We need to know the prices and quantities of all inputs to understand how the economy's total income is distributed.

The market for capital

Physical capital is the stock of produced goods used to make other goods and services and not used up in that subsequent production process. **Land** is the input that nature supplies.

Physical capital includes machinery used to make cars, railway lines that produce transport services, and school buildings that produce education services. Land is used in farming, and in the supply of housing and office services. The distinction between land and capital is blurred. By applying fertilizer to improve the soil balance, farmers can 'produce' better land.

Capital and land are both assets. They do not completely depreciate during the time period in which we study output decisions by firms. Raw materials are previously produced but they are used up completely during the subsequent production process. Buildings and machinery live on, contributing to yet more production in the future.

Physical capital

Fixed capital is plant, machinery and buildings. Inventories are stocks of working capital, goods awaiting further production or sale. Over time, the economy is becoming more *capital-intensive*. Each worker has more capital with which to work. Because capital depreciates, it takes some investment in new capital goods merely to stand still.

> **Gross investment** is the production of new capital goods and the improvement of existing capital goods. **Net investment** is gross investment minus the depreciation of the existing capital stock. **Depreciation** is the amount by which capital wears out during the existing production period.

If net investment is positive, gross investment more than compensates for depreciation and the capital stock is growing. However, very small levels of gross investment may fail to keep pace with depreciation; the capital stock then falls.

Stocks and flows

> A **stock** is the quantity of an asset at a point in time. A **flow** is the stream of services an asset provides in a period of time.

Rental payments and asset prices correspond to flows and stocks.

> The cost of using capital services is the **rental rate** for capital services.

Tourists rent a car for the weekend. Building contractors pay a rental rate to lease earth-moving equipment. Sometimes there is no rental market. It is impossible to rent a power station. When firms make a once-and-for-all purchase of a capital asset or stock, they must calculate how much it is implicitly costing them to use their capital.

Unlike labour, capital goods can be bought and have an asset price.

> The **price of an asset** is the sum for which the asset can be purchased outright. The owner of a capital asset gets the future stream of capital services from this asset.

Buying a car for £9000 entitles you to a stream of future transport services. You might even obtain a stream of future rental payments by letting your friend drive it. What will a buyer pay for a capital asset? This reflects the value of the future income from capital services that the asset stock provides. However, we can't simply add the future rental payments over the life of the capital asset to calculate its current asset price or value. We have to pay attention to the role of *time* and *interest payments*.

Table 8-1 stresses two distinctions: between *stocks* and *flows*, and between *rental payments* and *asset prices*. The hourly wage is the *rental payment* to hire an hour of labour. There is no asset price for the asset

Table 8-1   Stock and flow concepts

	Capital	Labour
Flow input to hourly production	Capital services	Labour services
Payment for flow	Rental rate (£/machine hour)	Wage rate (£/labour hour)
Asset price	£/machine	£/slave, if purchase allowed

called a 'worker' because we no longer allow slavery! However, for capital there are markets both to buy and sell capital goods and to lease capital services from other firms.

A stock is the quantity of an asset at a point in time (e.g. 100 machines on 1 January 2013). A flow is the stream of services that an asset provides in a given period. The cost of using capital services is the rental rate for capital. The asset price is the sum for which the stock can be bought, entitling its owner to the future stream of capital services from that asset.

Buying a factory for £10 000 entitles the owner to a stream of future rental payments on the capital services that the factory provides. What will a purchaser pay for a capital asset? If you borrow £10 000 to buy the machine, you face two costs. First, the opportunity cost of the funds tied up, which could instead have earned interest. If the interest rate is 10 per cent a year, this costs you £1000 a year in lost interest. Second, the value of the machine falls each year as it wears out with use and becomes obsolete. Suppose this depreciation is £500 a year. Although it cost £10 000 to buy the asset outright, it is effectively costing you £1500 a year to use the flow of capital services that it generates during its lifetime.

If you enter the leasing business, you will buy the machine only if you can rent it for at least £1500 a year. The required rental is the price that connects the market for capital assets, in which capital goods are bought and sold, and the market for capital services, in which capital is hired out for use. Even where a business buys an asset for its own use, it should calculate whether the asset is covering its economic cost.

The **required rental** is the income per period that lets a buyer of a capital asset break even.

The required rental can change for three reasons. First, a higher price of new capital goods means that required rentals must rise: with more funds tied up, there is more interest and depreciation to offset. Second, a higher interest rate raises the required rental, since the interest forgone by owning the asset has risen. Third, a higher depreciation rate raises the cost per period of holding the asset, and hence the return it must earn to cover its costs.

The demand for capital services

The firm's demand for capital services is very like its demand for labour services. The rental rate for capital replaces the wage rate as the cost of hiring factor services. We emphasize the *use* of *services* of capital. The example to bear in mind is a firm renting a vehicle or leasing office space.

The **marginal revenue product of capital MRPK** is the extra revenue from selling the extra output that an extra unit of capital allows, holding constant all other inputs.

The marginal revenue product of capital *MRPK* falls as more capital is used. First, physically there are diminishing marginal returns to adding more and more capital with other inputs held constant. Second, the firm may have to cut its output price to sell the extra output. The firm rents capital up to the point at which the rental rate equals its marginal revenue product. A lower rental rate makes the firm demand more capital services.

This entire demand curve for capital services shifts up if there is (a) a higher output price, making the extra physical output more valuable, (b) a rise in the quantity of other inputs that makes capital more productive, or (c) a technical advance that makes capital more productive.

Box 8-1

Cashing in on the social network, and other tales of asset pricing

Nowadays everybody knows about Facebook, either because they use it or because they saw the film *The Social Network* which told how Harvard student Mark Zuckerberg created the website. By the first quarter of 2012, Facebook was generating revenues of $1 billion per quarter, and still growing strongly, having risen by 45 per cent year on year. Profits were not doing quite so well, being $205 million for the quarter, a little less than the $233 million in the first quarter of 2011.

Facebook fetched a purchase price of $108 billion when it was sold on the stock market in May 2012. How can the price of the asset be so much larger than its current revenue or profits? Investors must believe that revenue growth will continue to be spectacular, and that future profits will far exceed current profits.

Investors get rewarded through two mechanisms, dividend income and capital gains on the share price. Suppose corporate equities as a whole offer a real return of about 4 per cent. Without any capital gains, it would take a dividend payout of around $4 billion per year to justify an asset valuation for the company of around £100 billion. Facebook's profits are not yet anywhere near this level. If they pay out $1 billion in dividends, then investors must be looking for around $3 billion in capital gains to make the target return of $4 billion for $100 billion invested. Facebook floated on the stock market at $108 billion, so its share price is expected to keep rising strongly thereafter. If it does not, somebody has made a bad mistake.

Another good example is provided by Apple, legendary maker of the iPad, iPhone and MacBook. Apple shares soared from $2.5 per share in October 2010 to over $6 per share in April 2012 as its sales surpassed all expectations, yet until the first quarter of 2012 the company was not paying any dividends at all to investors. People held Apple shares because the capital gains were more than enough to compensate.

Sometimes a company announces losses and yet its share price rises. How can this be? It all depends what the market was expecting, and how much these expectations had already fed into the share price. In 2012, IBM announced higher profits yet immediately its share price fell – the market had been expecting even better.

How would you like to start a company, lose £229 million pounds in your first year of trading, and watch your share price rise on the stock market? Not a bad beginning for Orange, the mobile phone operator. Because telecommunications was a growth area, stock market analysts forecast profits in the future even when the young company made massive losses in its early years. Orange's stock market value reflected guesses about the stream of future profits that shareholders expected to receive.

Even after the 1997 announcement of a big loss, Orange's total share value was £2.6 billion. Shareholders were banking on some pretty big profits in the future. Nor were they disappointed. By October 1999, Orange was worth £20 billion after a takeover by German competitor Mannesmann. After its subsequent sale to France Telecom, Orange's market value reached £21.6 billion, more than that of the whole of its new French parent company. Today, Orange is the global brand under which France Telecom operates.

Because capital lasts a long time, the price of a capital asset has to value the stream of income that it will earn throughout its lifetime, not just the rentals that it is earning today. After the dot.com bust in 2000–01, people became more pessimistic about future profits in telephony, and Orange's share price fell back sharply. Then, like other hi-tech stocks, its share price grew substantially during 2003–07, before the credit crunch caused asset prices to fall again. Since its takeover by Mannesmann and then France Telecom, we no longer get separate share price quotations for Orange on its own.

Asset prices are volatile because they depend on beliefs about the asset's income over its entire future life. When this future life is long, small changes in beliefs about revenue growth can lead to big changes in the capital value of that entitlement.

The industry demand curve for capital services

As with labour, the industry demand for capital services adds together how much each individual firm demands at each rental rate. Again, the industry demand is less elastic than those of individual firms. Even if each firm thinks it has no effect on the output price, the industry as a whole must cut the price to sell more output. This reduces the marginal benefit of more capital, making demand less responsive to a fall in the rental rate on capital.

The supply of capital services

Capital services are produced by capital assets. In the short run, the total supply of capital assets (machines, buildings and vehicles), and thus the services they provide, is fixed to the economy as a whole. New factories cannot be built overnight. The economy's supply curve of capital services is vertical at a quantity determined by the existing stock of capital assets.

Some types of capital are fixed even for the individual industry. The steel industry cannot quickly change its number of furnaces. However, by offering a higher rental rate for delivery vans, the supermarket industry can attract more vans from other industries, even in the short run, and thus faces an upward-sloping supply curve.

In the long run the total quantity of capital in the economy can be varied. New machines and factories can be built. Conversely, with no new investment in capital goods the existing capital stock will depreciate and its quantity will fall. Similarly, individual industries can adjust their stocks of capital.

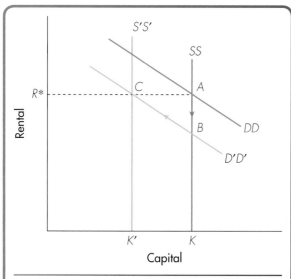

Figure 8-1 Equilibrium and adjustment in the market for capital services

Long-run equilibrium

In Figure 8-1, the inherited stock of capital determines the vertical supply curve for capital services at quantity K in the short run. Given the industry demand for capital services DD, this determines the equilibrium rental on capital services in the industry. If this matches the required rental on capital R^*, this is a long-run equilibrium. Users of capital services are equating their marginal benefit and marginal cost. Owners of capital services are earning streams of income that just cover the cost of buying the capital asset. Likewise, producers of capital assets – the construction and machine tool industries – are selling new assets at a price that just covers the cost of making them.

Adjustment to changes

In Figure 8-1 suppose that greater import competition reduces the demand for domestic textiles. Beginning in long-run equilibrium at *A*, a lower output price shifts the derived demand curve for capital services to the left in the textile industry, from *DD* to *D'D'*. Overnight, the supply of capital services *SS* is vertical at *K*, determined by previous investment in capital assets.

The immediate effect is a big drop in rentals on textile machinery. The industry moves from *A* to *B*. Machine owners no longer get the required rental *R**, and stop building new machines. Depreciation gradually reduces the stock of existing machines. This makes capital services scarcer, and bids up the rental. When capital has fallen to *K'*, the rental returns to the required rental *R** and long-run equilibrium is restored at *C*. Producers of new machines make just enough new machines to cover depreciation of existing machines, and the capital stock remains constant.

This example alerts us to the fact that adjustment of capital is much more difficult than adjustment of other inputs, which is why we treat it as a fixed factor in the short run. Adding to capital can take years if it involves building new specialist factories, and reducing capital can also take years as we wait for capital to depreciate. Of course, a single owner of a building can sometimes sell it to a new owner, but the economy as a whole finds it harder to knock down buildings and decommission power stations. Vehicles, on the other hand, have an active second-hand market, even crossing national boundaries. Otherwise, owners of luxury cars wouldn't find them stolen to order for a drug baron somewhere else in Europe or Africa.

Box 8-2

Interest rates and present values

A lender makes a loan to a borrower, who agrees to repay the initial sum (the principal) *with interest* at some future date. A loan of £100 for a year at 10 per cent interest must be repaid at £110 by the end of the year. The extra £10 (10 per cent of £100) is the interest cost of borrowing £100 for a year. *Interest rates* are quoted as a percentage per annum.

Suppose we lend £1 and re-lend the interest as it accrues. The first row of the table below shows what happens if the annual interest rate is 10 per cent. After a year we have £1 plus an interest payment of £0.10. Re-lending the whole £1.10, we have £1.21 by the end of the second year. Because of *compound interest*, the absolute amount by which our money grows increases every year. The first year we increase our money by £0.10, which is 10 per cent of £1. Since we re-lend the interest, our money grows by £0.11 in the next year since we earn 10 per cent on £1.10. If we lend for yet another year, our money will grow by £0.121 to £1.331 at the end of the third year.

	Year		
	0	1	2
At 10% interest rate			
Value of £1 lent today in	£1	£1.10	£1.21
PV of £1 earned in	£1	£0.91	£0.83
At 5% interest rate			
Value of £1 lent today in	£1	£1.05	£1.10
PV of £1 earned in	£1	£0.95	£0.91

▶

At 10 per cent interest per annum, £1 on year 0 is worth £1.10 in year 1 and £1.21 in year 2. Now ask the question the other way round. If we offered you £1.21 in two years' time, what sum today would be just as valuable? The answer is £1. If you had £1 today you could always lend it out to get exactly £1.21 in two years' time. The second row of the table extends this idea. If £1.21 in year 2 is worth £1 today, then £1 in year 2 must be worth £(1/1.21) = £0.83 today. £0.83 today could be lent out at 10 per cent interest to accumulate to £1 in year 2. Similarly, £1 in year 1 is worth only £(1/1.10) = £0.91 today.

> The **present value** of a future £1 is the sum that, if lent today, would cumulate to £1 by that date.

Compound interest implies that lending £1 today cumulates to ever-larger sums the further into the future we keep the loan and re-lend the interest. Conversely, the present value of £1 earned at some future date becomes smaller the further into the future the date at which the £1 is earned.

The present value of a future payment also depends on the interest rate. The third row of the table shows that a loan of £1 accumulates less rapidly over time if the interest rate is lower. At 5 per cent interest, a loan of £1 cumulates to only £1.10 after two years, compared with £1.21 after two years when the interest rate was 10 per cent in row 1. Hence the fourth row of the table shows that the present value of £1 in year 1 or year 2 is larger when the interest rate is only 5 per cent than in the corresponding entry in row 2 where the interest rate is 10 per cent.

8-2 The market for land

Since land is the input supplied by nature, we often treat its supply as constant, since it cannot be augmented by economic activity. This is not literally true. We can drain marshes, and improve land with fertilizer. However, it is much harder to add to the total supply of land than that of machines or buildings. We capture the key feature of land by treating its total supply as fixed.

Box 8-3

The best address

Since land is in fixed supply, land prices are dearest where demand is greatest relative to this fixed supply. The table below lists the ten dearest places to buy a two-bedroom apartment. Demand is strong in London partly because of the wealth generated in the City of London, partly because so many corporate head offices are in London, and partly because so many of the world's wealthy people own a house in London. Demand for land in Hong Kong is less strong, but the supply of land is very scarce, helping to drive up land prices. The next time you see a table like this, expect to see Shanghai and Beijing. The BRICs – Brasil, Russia, India and China – now have some very rich citizens.

The world's most expensive address 2011

Rank	City	Street	£k per sq foot
1	Hong Kong	Severn Road	78
2	London	Kensington Park Gardens	71
3	Monte Carlo	Avenue Princesse Grace	70
4	Cap Ferrat (French Riviera)	Chemin de Saint-Hospice	63
5	New York	Fifth Avenue	63
6	Paris	Quai Anatole	45
7	Geneva	Rue Bellot	43
8	Porto Cervo (Sardinia)	Via Romazzino	24
9	Sydney	Wolseley Road	21
10	Moscow	Ostozhenka	18

Source: *International Business Times*, Australia

Figure 8-2 shows the derived demand curve *DD* for land services. With a fixed supply, the equilibrium rental is R_0. A rise in the derived demand, for example because wheat prices have risen, leads only to a rise in the rental to R_1. The quantity of land services is fixed by assumption.

Consider a tenant farmer who rents land. Suppose the EU's Common Agricultural Policy (CAP) offers better prices for wheat. Since the demand for using land rises, this will bid up rents, as in Figure 8-2. Despite receiving more for the wheat crop, the tenant farmer is also paying higher rent and may not be better off, complaining that high rentals make it hard to earn a decent living. As in our discussion of footballers' wages, it is the combination of a strong derived demand and inelastic supply that leads to a high equilibrium price for the input's services. Figure 8-2 implies that farm subsidies, earned through the CAP, benefit the owners of land, for whom rentals rise, but may not benefit those who rent land in order to farm it. They are now faced with higher rents that essentially offset the higher subsidies. The true beneficiary is the land owner not the land user.

Since 2000 the price of food has risen dramatically. This is a worldwide phenomenon and we must seek the causes in the global market not in a particular country. What does our analysis of the market for land tell us about what may be happening to the price of food?

First, the demand for food has risen sharply. Industrialization in India and China has seen rural peasants move to the cities, where their productivity has been much higher. With higher incomes, they buy

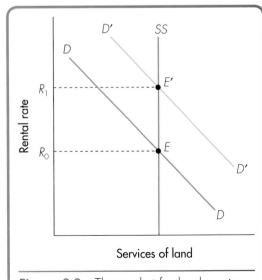

Figure 8-2   The market for land services

more food. As food prices soar, the demand for land increases. That is the first force at work, but it is not the only one.

The supply of land being devoted to food production has been falling. Faced with the problems of climate change, politicians have seen the growth of biofuels as a relatively easy answer. Farmers have been encouraged to withdraw land from food production and devote it instead to growing plants to be used in the production of biofuels. Thus, just at the time the demand for food was increasing, the supply of land devoted to food production fell and thus the supply of food fell.

As if this was not bad enough, national governments then became protectionist and took steps to restrict trade in food. In many of the poor countries that exported food to the world economy, governments restricted exports in order to have cheaper food available to their own citizens. In so doing, the supply of food to the rest of the world was reduced, forcing up world food prices elsewhere.

Maths 8-1

Asset values again

In market equilibrium, the going rate of return on assets is, say, an interest rate of r. We can think of this as per period, and by thinking about shorter and shorter periods we can view r as the instantaneous rate of return in a very short period indeed. Suppose an asset pays an income of y each instant. If the asset price is p, then to match the going return it must be the case that

$$r = (y/p) + (1/p)(dp/dt) \qquad (1)$$

The first term on the right-hand side shows the instantaneous return per pound invested, and the second term the proportional capital gain per instant. The formula says that together these must match the going rate of return r on assets that the market gets elsewhere.

If the price of the asset is constant, the last term is zero, in which case all its return comes from the income it earns. For a share in the company, this is the dividend that the company pays out to shareholders.

Now consider a precious metal such as gold, which pays no financial income. Why would people ever hold gold when they could earn an income on stocks and shares? The financial market can be in equilibrium only if $r = (1/p)(dp/dt)$. Provided the gold price keeps appreciating on average, it can offer a capital gain that generates enough return to keep pace with the market as a whole. Earlier in the chapter, we noted that Apple shares had risen strongly even when the company was not paying a dividend. It would have been more accurate to say that, because Apple was not paying a dividend, the share prices needed to keep rising to keep investors interested.

Consider a government bond whose income (for bonds, this is called the *fixed* coupon payment) is higher than r. For example, today r might be 3 per cent but the bond happens to offer a regular coupon of 10 per cent. If the bond is long lived, and happened to have been issued many years ago when inflation and interest rates were much higher than today, it is quite possible that the coupon is 10 per cent because that looked sensible at the time the bond was originally issued.

If the bond pays a coupon of 10 per cent when the market only needs a return of 3 per cent, how does this remain an equilibrium? Only if the final term in equation (1) is *negative*. The bond is popular because of its high coupon. Investors bid the price to a high level, so high in fact that its price will fall from now on. These anticipated capital losses reduce the expected return back to the level consistent with the rest of the market.

Combining our analysis of input markets

Modern economies are becoming more capital-intensive in production techniques. Why is capital intensity rising in the long run? First, in the long run we can raise the supply of capital more easily than the supply of labour or of land. Hence, rising demand bids up wages and land rentals more than rental rates for capital. Firms substitute away from labour as it gets relatively more expensive than capital. Second, firms then look for inventions to economize on expensive labour. Hence, new technologies often favour more capital-intensive methods that save on the need for lots of expensive workers.

Why does the price of a house in London keep rising, even after adjusting for inflation? The supply of land close to the city centre is fixed. As households and businesses get richer, their demand for land rises. With a fixed supply, the price has to rise to ration scarce land in London. So, low-paid nurses complain that they cannot find affordable accommodation close to their jobs in hospitals located in central London.

 ## Income distribution

The income of an input is simply its rental rate multiplied by the quantity of the factor employed. We now use our discussion of input markets to analyse the distribution of income in the UK.

The **functional income distribution** is the division of national income between the different production inputs.

Table 8-2 shows the income shares of the different inputs in the UK in 2006 and compares these shares of national income with their shares during the 1980s. The functional income distribution has been quite stable over time. As national income rose, the total income of each production input broadly kept pace, though advances in IT made it easier for large companies to outsource specialist activities to small suppliers, which helps explain the rise in self-employment and the decline in the share of capital and land.

The **personal income distribution** shows how national income is divided between people, regardless of the inputs from which these people earn their income.

The personal income distribution is relevant to issues such as equality and poverty within a country. Table 8-3 excludes the very poor, showing data only for those whose incomes are large enough to have to submit a tax return. Even within this group, pre-tax income is quite unequally distributed in the UK. Essentially, the richest 1 per cent of taxpayers earned 13 per cent of all the pre-tax income in 2010–11, and the richest 25 per cent of taxpayers earned more than half the total UK national income. Interestingly, despite all the talk about globalization and increased inequality, Table 8-3 shows only small changes over the last ten years. Even so, why do some people earn so much while others earn so little?

Table 8-2   UK functional income distribution

	% of national income	
Input	1981–89 average	2009
Employment	64	64
Self-employment	6	10
Capital and land	30	26

Source: ONS, UK National Accounts

Table 8-3 UK personal income distribution, 2000–2010

Tax year	% of national income earned by earners in the				
	Top 1%	Top 5%	Top 10%	Top 25%	Top 50%
1999/2000	11	23	33	53	76
2010/2011	13	25	35	55	77

Source: www.hmrc.gov.uk

Table 8-4 UK distribution of marketable wealth, 1976–2005

	1976	2005
Percentage of wealth owned by		
Most wealthy 1%	21	21
Most wealthy 25%	71	77
Most wealthy 50%	92	94

Table applies to adults aged 18 and over
Source: www.statistics.gov.uk

Unskilled workers have little training and low productivity. Workers with high levels of training and education earn much more. Some jobs, such as coal mining, pay high compensating differentials to offset unpleasant working conditions. Pleasant, but unskilled, jobs pay much less since many people are prepared to do them. However, talented superstars in scarce supply but high demand earn big money.

Another reason for the disparities in Table 8-3 is that personal income is not just labour income but also income from owning capital and land. This wealth is even more unequally divided than labour income. One reason why the distribution of personal income is so unequal is that the ownership of wealth, which provides income from profits and rents, is even more unequal. Table 8-4 gives details for 1976–2005 (it takes ages to produce such data, which is always years behind).

After Labour lost the 1979 general election, it moved to the left. This pleased party activists but took the party too far away from the preferences of most voters. The Conservatives were in power for the next 17 years. After heavy defeat in 1983, successive Labour leaders slowly moved the party back to the middle ground. New Labour focus groups interviewed people directly to clarify the majority view on different issues. The result? Labour victories in 1997, 2001 and 2005.

Initially, as Chancellor of the Exchequer, Gordon Brown helped the poor a lot without frightening the middle classes. As a result of his first four budgets, the post-tax income of the poorest 10 per cent of people rose by 9 per cent, the post-tax income of the next-poorest 10 per cent rose by 8 per cent. He did this without raising income tax or VAT.

Some of it was financed by stealth taxes, such as the tax treatment of pension funds, which ordinary voters did not notice or understand. Some was financed by making transfer payments more selective. Instead of a universal benefit, scarce resources were concentrated only on those who really needed them. Some of it was financed by economic growth: as incomes grew, given tax rates yielded more tax revenue, which was mainly given to the poor. What is politically interesting about the Blair–Brown strategy is that they redistributed spending power substantially towards the poor, but did not trumpet their achievement, preferring to continue to make steady cumulative changes without scaring off the floating middle-income voters on whom election results depend.

In 2007–08 this reputation for clever politics was shattered by the abolition of the 10 per cent tax band for low income earners. This was one of many reasons why Labour lost the 2010 election – its core supporters either switched sides or did not vote at all. When David Cameron took office, he too was acutely aware of the need to look after the voters in the middle ground who decide the outcome of elections. For example, when the Treasury suggested saving money by abolishing child benefit subsidies for everyone who earned over £40 000 a year, the Prime Minister vetoed the change because it hurt too many in the 'squeezed middle', voters most likely to change sides at the next general election. Eventually, the 2012 budget removed child benefit completely only for those earning over £60 000 a year, of whom there are many fewer people.

Budget statements rarely go out of their way to draw attention to bad news contained in the fine print. For example, the 2012 Budget trumpeted both the decline in the top rate of income tax from 50 to 45 per cent and the raising of the minimum tax threshold at which income tax is first paid, but kept rather more silent about the fact that the higher 40 per cent rate of income tax now became payable at an income threshold that was £1000 *lower* than in the previous year, thereby taking some extra tax off everyone who earned more than £41 450, dragging an extra 300 000 people into this higher rate band.

Box 8-4

To him that hath shall be given

Postwar politics during 1950–70 saw a big effort to create social cohesion, and an evening up of standards of living, particularly in Western Europe. Welfare benefits, social housing, publicly provided goods, redistributive taxes all played key roles. Since 1980 there has been more diversity of objectives. In the UK, Mrs Thatcher set out to reverse some of these trends; in many of the Mediterranean countries the European social model has remained largely unaltered.

Some of the changes reflect domestic politics but some have been influenced by globalization, the trend towards greater integration of markets and consequently lower degrees of national sovereignty. Since it is harder to tax those who threaten to leave, and harder to subsidize activities that may generate a rapid influx of foreigners hoping to enjoy these subsidies, by and large globalization has acted to reduce taxes on the rich and to reduce subsidies for the poor. It may have enhanced total efficiency but only at the cost of greater inequality.

The following chart was produced by the UK Department of Work and Pensions. It shows, for each decile in the income distribution (lowest 10 per cent, next-lowest 10 per cent, all the way up to the top 10 per cent of income earners), what has happened to their income during the decade from 1998–9 to 2008–9. It shows clearly how much the bottom 10 per cent lost out, and quite how well the top 10 per cent have done.

▶

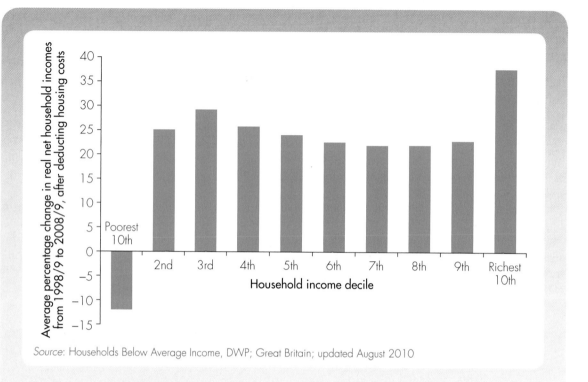

Source: Households Below Average Income, DWP; Great Britain; updated August 2010

The next chart, from the same source, shows the composition of each income decile. The richest 10 per cent are typically working-age adults in working families, or children of such people. For the bottom three deciles, many of these people are either in families without work or are pensioners on pretty inadequate pensions.

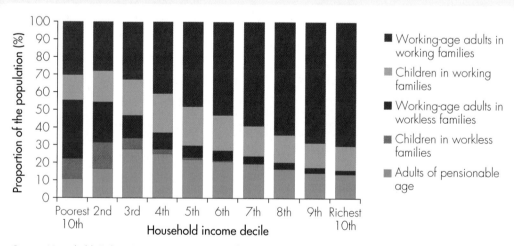

Source: Households Below Average Income, DWP; the data is the average for 2006/07 to 2008–09; UK; updated August 2010

Recap

- Physical capital is the stock of produced goods used to make other goods and services and not used up in that subsequent production process. Land is the input that nature supplies.

- Stocks are measured at a point in time. Flows are measured during periods of time. Flows are the rate of change of the corresponding stock, and a stock is the cumulation of the relevant flows.

- Capital services are input flows provided by capital assets. A firm demands capital services up to the point at which the rental on capital services equals the marginal revenue product of capital. The latter rises if the output price rises, if capital has more of other inputs with which to work or if technical progress makes capital more productive.

- In the short run, the supply of capital services is fixed. In the long run, it can be adjusted by producing new capital goods or by allowing the existing capital stock to depreciate.

- The required rental allows a supplier of capital services to break even in buying a capital asset. The required rental is higher, the higher is the interest rate, the depreciation rate or the purchase price of the capital good.

- In long-run equilibrium, the asset price of a capital good is both the price at which suppliers of capital goods are willing to make new goods and the price at which buyers can earn the required rental.

- The present value of a future sum of money is that sum of money today which could cumulate at compound interest to become that future sum at the future date. Since interest rates are positive, it takes a lower current sum to cumulate to a given future sum.

- The present value of £1 paid in N years' time is therefore lower the larger is N, and lower the larger is the interest rate. With more years during which to cumulate, it takes less today to build up into £1 in N years' time. With a higher interest rate, it also takes less today to build up into £1 in N years' time.

- The value of a capital asset is therefore the present value of the flow of future rentals that it will earn in providing capital services.

- Land is the special capital good whose aggregate supply is fixed even in the long run.

- The functional distribution of income across different inputs reflects equilibrium prices and quantities in input markets. Each input's share of national income is fairly stable over time.

- The personal distribution of income shows how income is distributed across individuals, through whichever input supply they earn this income.

- High incomes reflect ownership of attributes (such as skills) or ownership of assets in scarce supply and high demand. Markets do not produce equality across individuals.

- The bequest of wealth across generations perpetuates advantage and disadvantage. Across individuals, wealth is even more unequally distributed than income.

Review questions

To check your answers to these questions, go to pages 384–6.

1 Classify each as a stock or a flow: (a) a four-bedroom house, (b) the annual output of the UK house-building industry, (c) a painting by Picasso, (d) a training video, (e) a training course with a live presenter.

2 Discuss the main determinants of the firm's demand curve and the industry's demand curve for capital services.

3 The interest rate falls from 10 to 5 per cent. How does this affect the rental on capital services and the level of the capital stock in an industry in the short and long run?

4 Which asset price rises most if interest rates fall permanently from 8 per cent to 4 per cent: (a) the price of cars or (b) the price of office buildings? Will the asset price adjust immediately to its new long-run equilibrium value?

5 A plot of land is suitable only for agriculture. Can the farming industry go bankrupt if there is a rise in the price of land? How would your answer be affected if the land could also be used for housing?

6 How fixed is the supply of land: (a) in the aggregate and (b) to an individual user?

7 If land is fixed in quantity and quality, can land rentals keep pace with other factor incomes in a growing economy?

8 Name three taxes that help equalize the after-tax personal income distribution. Do any taxes have the opposite effect? Did you remember inferior goods?

9 Brazil has an unequal personal income distribution. Suggest at least three reasons for this.

10 How does an increase in globalization affect the domestic income distribution. Does this explain why far-right parties, such as the National Front in the UK or in France, tend to be hostile to globalization?

11 'My company's profits have risen, yet its share price has fallen – financial markets are simply irrational.' Could this assertion be incorrect? In what circumstances? Be as specific as you can.

12 Why are these statements wrong? (a) If the economy continues to become more capital-intensive, eventually there will be no jobs left for workers. (b) Land is freely supplied by nature, and hence land rentals should be zero.

13 Suppose high energy prices lead to a rise in the demand for nuclear power stations. (a) Draw a diagram showing the market for the capital services from nuclear power stations. (b) Use this diagram to describe how the market adjusts to higher demand in the short run. (c) How does the market adjust in the long run?

14 **Essay question** What should be the impact of globalization on assets in fixed supply, particularly land? Can you think of an example in which globalization might induce a fall in land prices?

DIFFICULT

15 **Essay question** In 2012 the UK government reduced the top rate of income tax from 50 to 45 per cent. What economic reasons might justify such a change? What would be the case against such a change?

Online Learning Centre

To help you grasp the key concepts of this chapter check out the extra resources posted on the Online Learning Centre at www.mcgraw-hill.co.uk/textbooks/begg.

There are additional case studies, self-test questions, practice exam questions with answers and a graphing tool.

Governing the market

This chapter discusses why markets do not always allocate outputs efficiently or fairly, creating a need for government to intervene in order to enhance outcome from society's viewpoint. Most issues about fairness and the distribution of income are intrinsically controversial and the subject of ongoing disagreement. In regard to efficiency, some interventions are well understood and widely supported. Few people would favour abolition of taxation on cigarettes. Other issues are more controversial, because there is disagreement about how the market works or about how the intervention would work. Disputes about the best way in which to deliver health care are an obvious example.

Equity, efficiency and market failure

Are markets a good way to allocate scarce resources? What does 'good' mean? Is it fair that some people earn much more than others in a market economy? These are not positive issues about how the economy works, but normative issues based on value judgements by the assessor.

Left-wing and right-wing parties disagree about the market economy. The right believes the market fosters choice, incentives and efficiency. The left stresses the market's failings and how government intervention can improve market outcomes. Generally, outcomes are judged against the criteria of equity and efficiency.

Horizontal equity rules out discrimination between people with similar characteristics and performance. Vertical equity is the Robin Hood principle, taking from the rich to give to the poor.

> **Horizontal equity** is the identical treatment of identical people. **Vertical equity** is the different treatment of different people in order to reduce the consequences of these innate differences.

An economy's *resource allocation* describes who does what, and who gets what. Equity always entails value judgements but Vilfredo Pareto suggested a definition of efficiency that might be free of value judgements.

> For given tastes, inputs and technology, an allocation is **efficient** if no one can then be made better off without making at least one other person worse off.

Suppose we have ten apples to give to Stan and Rudi. Failure to hand out all ten apples is inefficient. A free lunch is available. Stan can get more apples without Rudi having fewer. Giving Stan and Rudi five apples each is efficient. None are wasted. However, giving all ten to Rudi is also efficient, but many would think this unfair; eight for Stan and two for Rudi is still efficient, but fairer.

Taxation and subsidies can redistribute apples, but may waste some in the process. If a free market yields seven for Rudi and three for Stan, suppose by redistribution we could then gain one more for Stan but only at the cost of losing two for Rudi. Reasonable people will disagree on whether this is desirable. It is a pure value judgement.

The invisible hand

Adam Smith suggested that a market economy is efficient 'as if by an Invisible Hand'. Perfect competition may do the job. Each consumer buys goods until his marginal cost (the price of the good) equals the marginal benefit of the good to him. The demand curve shows how much consumers buy at each price. Thus at each quantity in Figure 9-1 the demand curve *DD* is also the marginal benefit to consumers of getting that quantity of films.

Perfectly competitive producers equate price to marginal cost. At each output in Figure 9-1 the supply curve *SS* thus shows the marginal cost of making that amount of the good. At Q_1 films, the marginal benefit to consumers is P_1, above the marginal cost to producers. Society should make more films than Q_1. Where supply and demand intersect,

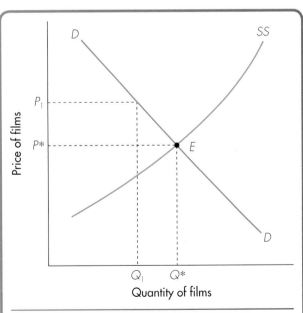

Figure 9-1 Competitive equilibrium and Pareto-efficiency

the social marginal benefit P^* of using resources to make films equals the social marginal cost P^* of films. No free lunch is available by reallocating resources. The allocation is efficient.

No government decided this. Each consumer and each firm pursued their self-interest, buying and selling what made sense to them. Prices co-ordinated their decisions. Because every buyer and seller faced the *same* price, marginal benefits equalled marginal costs. Society got the efficient quantity produced and consumed.

Even so, the resulting allocation may well be very unequal, as the talented are rewarded more highly than the disadvantaged. The Invisible Hand applies to efficiency but not to equity. Quite often, it does not deliver efficiency either.

Market failures

> A **distortion** or **market failure** exists if society's marginal cost of making a good does not equal society's marginal benefit from consuming that good.

There are four principal sources of market failure.

Taxation

Governments levy taxes to finance public spending. A tax creates a gap between the price the buyer pays and the price the seller receives. If there is car tax of £2000, car buyers equate the marginal benefit of cars to the gross price, but car producers equate the marginal cost of cars to the lower net price received by producers. Hence the marginal cost of cars is £2000 less than the marginal benefit of cars. This is inefficient. Society should make more cars. Government spending is needed to offset other distortions in the market economy, and to redistribute income, but taxation itself usually creates a distortion.

Imperfect competition

Facing downward-sloping demand curves, imperfect competitors set marginal cost equal to marginal revenue, which is less than the price they charge. Thus, price exceeds marginal cost, like a privately imposed tax. Again, such industries produce too little from the social viewpoint: in equilibrium, the marginal benefit of more output exceeds its marginal cost.

Externalities

Externalities are spillovers, such as pollution, noise and congestion. A person's decision ignores her effect on other people. There is no market for externalities like noise, secondary cigarette smoke or induced congestion on roads. Without a market in noise, prices cannot equate the marginal benefit of making a noise and the marginal cost of that noise to other people.

Other missing markets

People cannot always insure against the risks that they face, or find a loan on reasonable terms. Like externalities, these are examples of missing markets. The problem is often the fear market participants have of being exploited by others with superior information. Again, with no market, price cannot equate society's marginal costs and benefits of these activities.

We now discuss market failures in more detail, and how policy might solve them. The rest of this section discusses externalities and other missing markets. The next two sections discuss taxation and imperfect competition.

Externalities

> An **externality** arises if a production or consumption decision affects the physical production or consumption possibilities of other people.

A chemical firm pollutes a lake, imposing an extra production cost on anglers (fewer fish) or a consumption cost on swimmers (dirty water). The firm pollutes until the marginal benefit of polluting (a lower cost of making chemicals) equals its marginal cost of polluting, which is zero. It ignores the marginal cost its pollution imposes on anglers and swimmers.

Conversely, you paint your house but ignore the consumption benefit to your neighbours, who now live in a nicer street. You paint up to the point where your own marginal benefit equals your marginal cost, but society's marginal benefit exceeds yours. There is too little house painting.

In both cases, the private costs or benefits differ from social costs or benefits. Figure 9-2 shows the marginal private cost MPC of making chemicals. For simplicity, we assume it is constant. The marginal social cost MSC of chemical production is the marginal private cost plus the *marginal externality* from pollution at each output of chemicals. As chemical production rises, each extra unit of chemical output causes more pollution damage.

The curve DD shows the demand for chemicals. At the equilibrium output Q, the marginal social cost MSC exceeds the marginal social benefit of chemicals (the private demand curve DD, since there are no consumption externalities). The output Q is inefficient. By reducing chemical production, society saves more in social cost than it loses in social benefit. Society could then make some people better off without making anyone worse off.

The efficient output is Q', at which the marginal social benefit and cost of the last output unit are equal. By producing at the market equilibrium E, not the efficient point E', society wastes the triangle $E'EF$, the excess of social cost over social benefit when output rises from Q' to Q.[1]

Production externalities make private and social cost diverge. Consumption externalities make private and social benefit diverge. Again, free market equilibrium is inefficient. Output is too low if externalities are beneficial, as with planting roses in your garden, but is too high if externalities are adverse, as with smoking in restaurants.

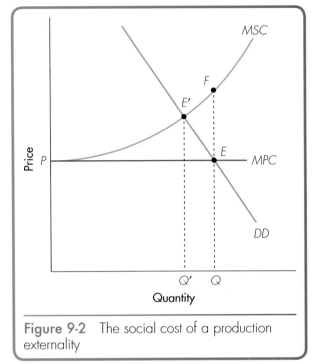

Figure 9-2 The social cost of a production externality

Case study 9-1   The economics of climate change

There is increasing evidence that global temperatures are rising. The science of climate change means that we are also likely to see greater fluctuations in climate as well. Hence, extreme events will become much more frequent. Large parts of Bangladesh may disappear under water forever; and English villages, from Yorkshire to Cornwall, have already experienced flash flooding. Conversely, regions of the world that are currently temperate may become arid and uninhabitable. The figure below shows the dramatic change in global temperatures in recent years.

---

[1] Beneficial production externalities help other producers. Pest control by one farm reduces pests on nearby farms. The marginal social cost of farm output is then *below* the marginal private cost. We could re-label the MSC curve as MPC in Figure 9-2 and re-label MPC as MSC. Free market equilibrium is at E' but E is now the efficient point.

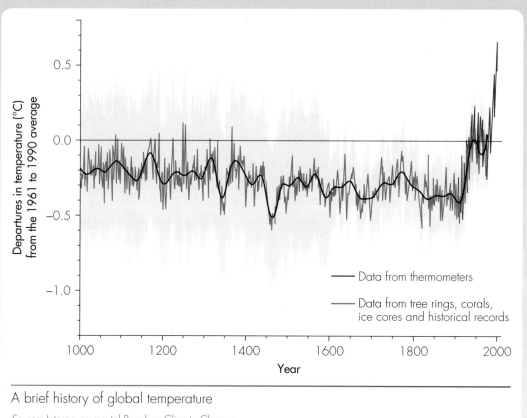

A brief history of global temperature

Source: Intergovernmental Panel on Climate Change

The science of climate change

The earth's climate is affected by many things, from solar radiation to the consequences of human behaviour. The ebb and flow of previous ice ages reminds us that human behaviour is not the only cause of climate change. Even so, there is increasing evidence that we must look to ourselves as a major cause of recent global warming.

Greenhouse gases – including carbon dioxide and methane – shield the earth from solar radiation, but also trap the heat underneath. Without them, all heat would escape and we would freeze to death. But we need just the right amount. Too much greenhouse gas and the earth overheats, causing global warming.

The recent build-up of greenhouse gases reflects large emissions of carbon dioxide from households, from power stations and from transport. This may cause ice to melt, and water to expand, causing sea levels to rise. A catastrophic eventual consequence would be melting of permafrost in Siberia, releasing such volumes of methane that a large rise in temperature would then be inevitable, perhaps threatening human survival.

Carbon, a key constituent of all greenhouse gases, is a useful common denominator. Slowing, let alone reversing, global warming requires the combustion of much less carbon.

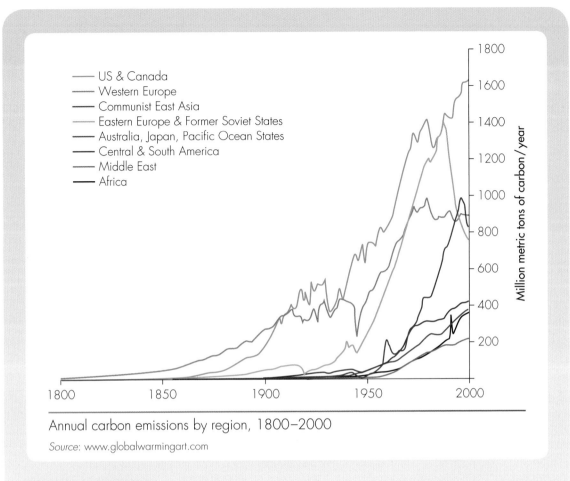

Annual carbon emissions by region, 1800–2000

Source: www.globalwarmingart.com

The Kyoto Protocol

In 1997, a group of countries signed an amendment to the UN International Treaty on Climate Change, committing themselves to cut greenhouse gas emissions. By 2006, 169 countries (though not the US) had signed.

Developed countries accepted the obligation to reduce emissions by 2012 to 5 per cent below the level of their emissions in 1990. Developing countries had not yet any commitment but could take part in the Clean Development Mechanism. Thus, China and India ratified the protocol but were not yet bound by the commitment to reduce emissions: given their population size, rate of economic growth and future energy demands, China and India will have a huge impact on what happens to greenhouse gases.

Within the EU's overall targets, individual members could buy and sell obligations within the EU Emissions Trading Scheme. The Clean Development Mechanism allowed India or China to invest in emissions reduction, such as a cleaner power station, and sell the emissions credit to a UK or German company so that Europe then met its overall emission obligations.

Thus the projected total cutbacks could in principle be achieved efficiently: those most easily able to reduce emissions cheaply would do so; those for whom emissions reduction was expensive could instead purchase a credit from someone else better placed to cut back emissions cheaply.

Updating Kyoto: Copenhagen and Durban accords

In 2009 the Copenhagen Summit attempted to rejuvenate the process of credible and binding cutbacks to greenhouse emissions, but achieved disappointingly little. Developed countries such as the US and Australia remained reluctant to give up a lifestyle that relied heavily on energy use, and many developing countries continued to argue that, like the developed countries before them, they should prioritize growth and tackle emissions reduction only once a greater level of prosperity had been achieved.

After the disappointment of Copenhagen, the 2011 Durban Summit, attended by 190 countries, appeared to make more progress. A 'road map' would guide countries towards a binding deal to cut carbon, agreed by 2015 and becoming effective after 2020. A Green Climate Fund of around $100 million would be created by 2020 to help developing countries reduce pollution without jeopardizing economic development. This outcome was a delicate political compromise – tough enough to be acclaimed by the enthusiasts for emissions reduction, but still vague enough to allow wiggle room for the sceptical countries.

Cost–benefit analysis

Even if we accept the science, what should we do, and how quickly? This gets to the core of the what, how and for whom questions of Chapter 1. The 'for whom' question is particularly acute. How much pain should the current generation take in order to make life nicer for future generations? Can we expect China and India to slow their economic development to make life nicer for citizens in Europe and the US who begin with many more economic advantages?

The emissions reduction targets remain modest, and as yet fail fully to commit the key economies of the US, China and India, on whom much will actually depend. Supporters see these targets as the thin end of the wedge, creating a political dynamic that will allow tougher targets soon; which is precisely why they are opposed by those who would potentially lose out (e.g. the air-conditioned affluent citizens of the US and Australia, whose current energy consumption is enormous).

The UK government commissioned a report on the economics of climate change written by Sir Nicholas Stern, a London School of Economics professor, and ex-chief economist of both the World Bank and the European Bank for Reconstruction and Development. The Stern Review concluded that 1 per cent of global GDP must be invested from now on if we are to head off the worst effects of climate change; and that failure to act now risks a future cost of up to 20 per cent of global GDP.[2]

Property rights and externalities

Can we set up a market in pollution? By pricing pollution itself, people could trade it until private marginal costs and benefits were equal. With nobody now ignored, private and social costs or benefits are the same again. Notice, in passing, that this implies that the efficient quantity of pollution is not zero. Eliminating the last little bit has a huge marginal cost and only a small marginal benefit. It is not worth cutting back to zero.

---

[2] Many of the world's leading economists – including economics Nobel Prize winners Sir James Mirrlees, Amartya Sen, Joseph Stiglitz and Robert Solow, and Professor Jeffrey Sachs, Director of the Earth Institute at Columbia University in New York – have come out strongly in support of the Stern Review. The principal point of subsequent debate has been the appropriate interest rate at which to discount future costs and benefits. The decision about how much to discount the welfare of future generations affects the present value of the benefits of tackling climate change today, and hence both the optimal pace of action and estimates of the cost of inaction. Although the quantitative conclusions change, the qualitative conclusions do not.

Why do we not have a market in pollution? Someone at your door says: 'I am collecting money from people who hate factory smoke in their gardens. We'll pay the factory to cut back. Will you contribute? I'm visiting 5000 houses nearby.' Even though you hate smoke, you pretend not to care and do not contribute. If everybody else pays, the factory cuts back and you get the benefit. If nobody pays, your small payment makes little difference. Whatever others do, you do not pay: you are a *free rider*. Everyone else reasons similarly. Nobody pays, even though you are all better off paying to get the smoke cut back.

> A **free rider**, knowing he cannot be excluded from consuming a good, has no incentive to buy it.

Taxing externalities

Cigarette smokers cause bad consumption externalities for those nearby. Figure 9-3 shows the supply curve SS of cigarette producers, which also shows marginal social cost. DD is the private

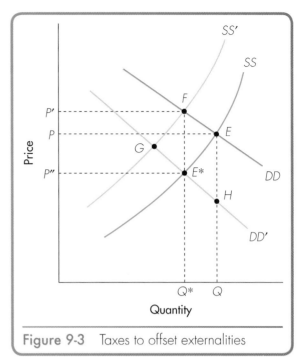

Figure 9-3   Taxes to offset externalities

demand curve, showing the marginal private benefit of cigarettes to smokers. The marginal social benefit DD' of cigarette consumption is lower than DD because of the harmful consumption that smokers inflict on others.

Free market equilibrium is at E, but the efficient point is E^*. The government now levies a tax E^*F per packet of cigarettes. With the tax-inclusive price on the vertical axis, the demand curve DD is unaffected, but the supply curve shifts up to SS', which, subtracting the tax E^*F from each price, returns producers to the original supply curve SS.

A tax rate E^*F leads to market equilibrium at F. The efficient quantity Q^* is produced and consumed. Consumers pay P' and producers get P'' after tax is deducted at E^*F per unit. The tax rate E^*F is exactly the marginal externality on the last unit when the efficient quantity Q^* is produced. Consumers behave as if they took account of the externality, though they look only at the tax-inclusive price. Taxes that offset externalities *improve* efficiency. The fact that alcohol and tobacco have harmful externalities is a reason to tax them heavily.

Box 9-1

Trading carbon credits

Environmental protection has been a mixed success in the last 40 years. Smog has gone, and fish are back in many rivers. But coal-fired power stations still emit sulphur dioxide, and Greenpeace activities highlight many other examples that still cause concern. If we want to reduce pollution further, should we use quotas or taxes?

Facing the same pollution tax rate, each firm would adjust until the marginal cost of cutting pollution is the same across firms, a necessary feature of the efficient solution. However, in an uncertain world, the government might miscalculate, and set the wrong tax rate. If pollution beyond a certain critical level is disastrous, for example irreversibly damaging the ozone layer, direct regulation of the quantity of pollution is safer, even if it fails to cut pollution in the least-cost way.

A clever compromise is possible: an *emissions trading programme* and *bubble policy*. For example, specify a minimum standard for air quality, and impose pollution emission quotas on individual polluters. Any firm below its pollution quota gets an *emission reduction credit (ERC)* that can be sold to other polluters wanting to exceed their pollution quotas. Total pollution is regulated, but firms that can cheaply cut pollution do so, selling their ERC to firms for which pollution reduction is costlier. This reduces the total cost of pollution reduction.

When a firm has many factories, the *bubble policy* applies pollution controls to the firm as a whole, not to individual factories. A firm can cut back most in the plants where pollution reduction is cheapest. The policy combines 'control over quantities' for aggregate pollution where the risk and uncertainty are greatest, with 'control through the price system' for allocating efficiently the way these overall targets are achieved.

This policy is now finding expression in the emissions trading of carbon credits in relation to the pollutants that cause global warming. A carbon credit, a 'permit that allows the holder to emit one ton of carbon dioxide', can now be traded in an international market at the price then prevailing in the market. The mechanism, formalized in the Kyoto Protocol (see Case study 9-1), is similar to the earlier, successful, US Acid Rain Program to reduce industrial pollutants.

Under the Kyoto Protocol, quotas for maximum emission of greenhouse gases were specified for developed, so-called Annex 1, countries. Unused quotes were sold as carbon credits. Since 2005, the Kyoto mechanism has been adopted for CO_2 trading by all the countries within the European Union under its European Trading Scheme (EU ETS), with the European Commission as its validating authority. Since 2008, EU participants must link with the other developed countries who ratified Annex 1 of the protocol, and trade the six most significant greenhouse gases.

Prominent exchanges on which carbon credits can be traded include the Chicago Climate Exchange, European Climate Exchange, PowerNext, and the European Energy Exchange. Many companies now engage in emissions reduction in order to generate credits that can be sold on one of the exchanges.

The chart on the next page shows what has been happening to the market price of carbon credits. Prices fluctuate quite a lot, depending on views about how rigorously the scheme will be enforced (stronger enforcement bids up the price of carbon), on whether the trading regime might be superceded by compulsory reductions (undermining the trading regime and carbon price) and on the future of carbon-free alternatives (principally nuclear).

The chart shows in blue the current price of carbon credits during 2010–12, but also in orange the price of future credits available a year later, and most interestingly, in turquoise, the price during 2010–12 of future credits available for the year 2020. The sharp upward spike in the turquoise graph corresponds to the Japanese Fukushima nuclear disaster and the subsequent decision of the German chancellor, Angela Merkel, to abandon a large German nuclear programme. Without nuclear electricity, conventional power sources were going to be needed more and consequently the price of carbon shot upwards.

Generally, however, prices have been drifting downwards, in part because of increasing pessimism about how long the economic recession will last. What is bad for business is paradoxically good for the environment, since there is less economic activity.

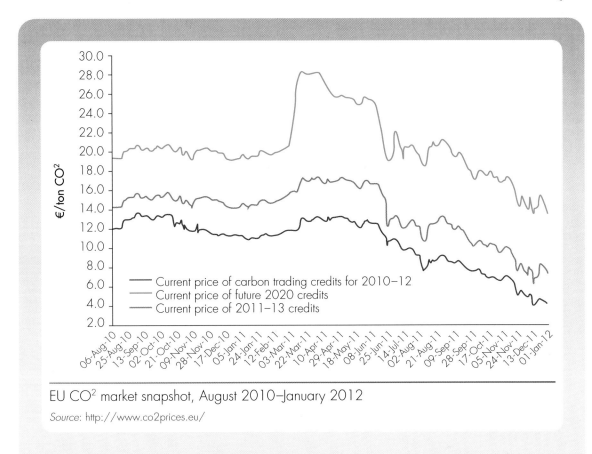

EU CO_2 market snapshot, August 2010–January 2012

Source: http://www.co2prices.eu/

The carbon trading market is forecast to rise to €3 trillion by 2020, and the Swiss bank UBS forecast that carbon credit prices might triple during 2011–13. Raising the price of carbon will achieve four goals. First, it signals to consumers which goods and services are high-carbon ones and should therefore be used more sparingly. Second, it signals to producers which inputs use more carbon (such as coal and oil) and which use less or none (such as natural gas or nuclear power), thereby inducing firms to substitute low-carbon inputs. Third, it gives market incentives for inventors and innovators to develop low-carbon products and processes to replace the current generation of technologies. Fourth, it economizes on the information needed for the first three tasks.

Public goods

Public goods are like a very strong externality. Most goods are private goods. The ice cream in your throat is now unavailable for eating by other people. Not so with public goods, such as clean air and national defence.

A **public good** is necessarily consumed in equal amounts by everyone.

Public goods have this special feature in consumption, in whichever sector they are produced. If the Navy patrols coastal waters, your consumption of national defence does not affect our quantity of national defence. We get different amounts of utility from it if our tastes differ, but must all consume the same quantity. Nobody can be excluded from consuming a public good once it exists, and the act of consumption does not deplete the quantity left for other people.

Public goods supplied in private markets are wide open to the free-rider problem. Since you get it, *whether or not you pay for it*, you never buy a public good that already exists. Private markets do not produce the efficient quantity. We need government intervention. The efficient quantity of a public good equates the marginal cost of making it to the marginal social benefit of having it, which is simply the *sum* of the marginal private benefit of each person consuming that quantity.

Democracies resolve this problem through elections. By asking, 'How much would you like, given that everyone will be charged for the cost of providing public goods?', society tries to identify the efficient quantity of a public good. This may then be produced by the public sector, or contracted out to private suppliers.

Other missing markets

Information is not always free to acquire. People often know more about their own behaviour than others can easily find out. Fear that people will exploit this informational advantage may then prevent markets from developing. Here are two problems that crop up regularly.

Moral hazard

Insurance companies calculate the odds of various risks occurring. Is this how they calculate what premium to charge for house insurance? Sitting in a restaurant, you remember you left some chips frying in a pan. Why leave your nice meal to go home to switch the cooker off? You are fully insured against fire. Similarly, with full health insurance you may not bother with precautionary check-ups. The act of insuring raises the likelihood of the thing you are insuring against. Bailing out failed banks who took too many risks merely encourages the next generation of bankers to take more risks.

Moral hazard exploits inside information to take advantage of the other party to the contract.

With complete information, the insurance company could refuse to pay out if you do not take proper care. With costly information, it is hard for the company to discover this key fact.

Actuarial calculations for the whole population, many of whom are uninsured, are now a poor guide to your behaviour once insured. Moral hazard makes it harder to get insurance and costlier if you get it. Insurance firms at best offer partial insurance, leaving you to bear part of the cost if the bad thing happens. This gives you an incentive to take care, reducing the odds of the bad outcome. Hence, insurance firms pay out less often and can charge you a lower premium.

Adverse selection

People who smoke are more likely to die young. Individuals know if they themselves smoke. If an insurance firm cannot tell who smokes, it must charge everyone the same price. Suppose this reflects mortality rates for the whole country. Non-smokers, with above-average life expectancy, find the price too dear. Smokers, knowing their looming health problems, realize that the price is a bargain.

Adverse selection means individuals use their inside information to accept or reject a contract. Those accepting are no longer an average sample of the population.

The insurance firm cannot distinguish the two groups, but knows that a price based on the national average will attract only smokers, a loss-making proposition. Instead, the firm assumes that all its customers smoke, and charges a suitably high price. It defends against the worst. Non-smokers cannot get insurance at a fair price.

To check the difference between moral hazard and adverse selection, which is which in the following examples? (1) A person with a fatal disease signs up for life insurance. (2) Already having insured his kids, a person then becomes unexpectedly depressed and commits suicide. (The first is adverse selection, the second moral hazard.)

Similarly, borrowers know if they are safe or risky, but this is hard for lenders to discover. Suppose a bank should charge safe borrowers an interest rate of 5 per cent, but risky borrowers an interest rate of 15 per cent. An accountant may tell the bank to charge something in-between, like 10 per cent. An economist knows this will attract only risky borrowers. The only equilibrium is for the bank to charge

15 per cent, attracting only risky borrowers. Safe borrowers are fed up because they cannot get a loan on decent terms. Adverse selection prevents a market for safe borrowers.

Moral hazard and adverse selection prevent some markets developing properly. Without markets, the Invisible Hand cannot equate marginal social benefit and marginal social cost.

Box 9-2

The case of the missing markets

Markets cannot work efficiently if they do not exist in the first place. Many of the public policy problems that we encounter arise from this fact. Let's just see how many examples we can find. A theme of the following discussion is to ask why the markets are missing and whether new technologies can help remedy the problem.

Environmental markets

Already in this chapter, we have dealt extensively with environmental depreciation, whether by small-scale pollution or large-scale damage to the climate. What distinguishes the environment from cornflakes or clothes is that it has so many attributes of a public good. Your walking in a field may not preclude my walking in the field, and the extensive scale of the landscape makes it hard for landowners to charge individual customers even if they wanted to. Clean air is even harder to monitor and trade. Freedom from intrusive noise is another public good that has been expensive to monitor and price. Uncongested city streets are yet another example.

We have already discussed carbon trading, but what would a more general pricing revolution look like?

Imagine every car has a sensor that provides signals about its emissions, its location, its speed, and so on. At the end of the month, the driver could be sent a bill explaining the monthly charges incurred. As a result, people would drive more slowly, reduce peak hour driving and switch to low-emissions cars. The market would be starting to work.

In 1986 the Porsche 959 pioneered computer chips in the tyres, telling the driver about tyre pressures and whether there is a puncture. We have come a long way since then. Technologically, we are close to the point at which the tyres in your car can talk to tyres in a car a mile in front, getting warnings about congestion, accidents and fog. And imagine if your tyres were also talking to your insurance company and affecting the insurance premium you would be charged next year.

Missing markets rely either on the prohibitive cost of charging systems or on prohibitive informational asymmetries between buyer and seller that undermine confidence in trading. The digital revolution is slashing costs, enhancing monitoring technologies, and leveling the information playing field.

Health care markets

Europeans have long been suspicious of using markets to allocate health care – Americans view the European model as socialist, intended as a term of abuse. Health has two important features. First, it is bound up with inequality since becoming unhealthy has a huge effect on living standards, not just by removing opportunities for work and leisure but because treatment and care are expensive. Second, there is huge informational asymmetry between the well-informed doctors and the less well-informed patients. Hence, governments have to get heavily involved in health care.

▶

The first feature need not be an obstacle to using the market. The state could provide or subsidize medical insurance. It is really the informational asymmetry that gets in the way. Attempts to introduce 'a bit more market' may actually be counterproductive if they do not resolve the information problem.

But things are changing. Prospective patients use Google to check their symptoms before even visiting a doctor or hospital. Digital technologies are not only assisting the consumer, they are also providing better monitoring of medical outcomes. Not only can we learn success rates for individual surgeons, we can also use sensors in people's houses to track whether they actually followed their doctors' advice, took their medicines appropriately and laid off the cigarettes. It is possible to start contemplating a world in which markets will play a larger role in the allocation of health care.

Personal credit ratings

When different people embody differing risks of default that are unobservable by the lender, the only sustainable equilibrium is for the lender to treat everyone as a bad risk: the problem of adverse selection in credit markets. Low-risk people cannot borrow at a price that makes sense for them.

But think what happens as we switch from using cash to credit cards, the Internet and mobile phones. Digital data on individual transactions can be captured and centrally processed. Suddenly lenders have a much better idea about people's income and spending patterns, including their existing debt interest and loans recently taken out. Again, this enhances transparency and reduces informational asymmetries.

Increasingly, TV and digital advertising includes adverts from lenders willing to deal with high-risk customers. In part, this is because modern data banks and high-powered computing make it possible to analyse just how high a risk each individual is. There is an appropriate price for everything. Once a lender knows where to set the price, a market can develop. This does not mean that some people will not default on their loans, merely that the interest rate charged will have included a premium that makes appropriate allowance for this risk.

Similarly, the next time you visit your friendly bank manager, you should be aware that modern banks have extensive computer models of personal spending data. The manager may appear friendly and inquisitive about your family, but she will already have scrutinized your spending habits before you even arrive to help form a judgement about your creditworthiness.

These are just some of the ways in which the digital revolution is promoting the use of markets. The more society can rely on markets, the less it needs government intervention to redress market failures. Questions about income distribution, however, will always be matters for politics and governments.

 Taxation

Table 9-1 shows UK government spending over nearly 60 years. Governments buy goods and services – schools, defence, the police, and so on – which directly use resources that could have been used in the private sector. Governments also spend on *transfer payments* – subsidies such as social security, state pensions and debt interest – that do not directly use scarce resources. Rather, they transfer purchasing power to people who then buy goods and services.

Table 9-1 UK government spending (% of GDP), 1956–2012

	1956	1976	2012
Total spending	34	47	43
Goods and services	21	26	27
Transfer payments	13	21	16

Sources: ONS, *UK National Accounts*; HM Treasury, *Budget*, various issues

Table 9-2 UK income tax rates, 1978–2012

Taxable income (£000) (inflation adjusted, 2008 prices)	Marginal tax rate (%)	
	1978/79	2008/09
20	34	20
30	45	20
40	45	40
50	45	40
70	60	40
100	65	40
160	83	45

Note: Taxable income after deducting allowances. In 2008/09+ a single person's allowance was £6035.
Sources: ONS, *Financial Statement and Budget Report*

Between 1956 and 1976, the scale of government got bigger. Since then, the trend was reversed until around 2000. During 2000–10, the Labour government presided over a rapid growth in the state, initially because it thought it was wealthy and that the country could afford it, and then because it sought to stave off the worst effects of the crash of 2007–08. Since 2010, the Conversative government has been cutting the size of the state again to get a grip on the spiralling national debt.

One reason why governments sometimes want to cut back the state is in order to make tax cuts, either to make the electorate feel good or in the hope that this will boost business and enterprise.

If T is the amount paid in tax, and Y is income, then T/Y is the **average tax rate**. The **marginal tax rate** shows how total tax T increases as income Y increases.

Taxes are *progressive* if the average tax rate rises as income rises, taking proportionately more from the rich than from the poor. Taxes are *regressive* if the average tax rate falls as income level rises, taking proportionately less from the rich. Table 9-2 shows that the UK, like many other countries, has cut tax rates in the last two decades, especially for the very rich.

UK government spending, and the taxes that finance it, are now about 40 per cent of national output. Nearly 40 per cent of government spending is transfer payments, such as pensions, welfare payments and debt interest. This share tends to rise in recession because there are more unemployed. Just over half of government spending goes to buy goods and services, especially health, defence and education. Most government spending is financed by taxation, mainly *direct taxes* related to income (income tax itself, national insurance contributions, and corporation tax paid by firms) and *indirect taxes* on expenditure (value added tax (VAT) and excise duties on fuel, alcohol and tobacco).

Direct taxes are taxes on income; **indirect taxes** are taxes on spending.

We now assess the UK tax system against our two criteria: equity and efficiency.

How to tax fairly

In taking proportionately more from the rich than from the poor, income tax reflects the principle of *ability to pay*, based on a concern about vertical equity. In contrast, the *benefits principle* argues that people who get more than their share of public spending should pay more than their share of tax revenues. Car users should pay more than pedestrians towards public roads.

The benefits principle often conflicts directly with the principle of ability to pay. If those most vulnerable to unemployment must pay the highest contributions to a government unemployment insurance scheme, it is hard to redistribute income, wealth or welfare. If the main objective is vertical equity, the ability to pay principle must take precedence.

Two factors make the tax and benefit system more progressive than income tax alone. First, transfer payments actually give money to the poor. The old get pensions, the unemployed get jobseeker's allowance, and the poor get income support. Second, the state supplies some public goods available to the poor even if they do not pay taxes. The rich sunbathe in their own gardens, but the poor sunbathe in public parks.

There are some *regressive* elements that take proportionately more from the poor. Beer and tobacco taxes, and the National Lottery, are huge earners for the government. Yet the poor spend much more of their income on these goods than do the rich. These things effectively redistribute from the poor to the rich!

Tax incidence

The ultimate effect of a tax can be very different from its apparent effect.

Tax incidence is the final tax burden once we allow for all the induced effects of the tax.

Figure 9-4 shows labour demand *DD* and labour supply *SS*. With no tax, equilibrium is at *E*. Now an income tax is introduced. If we measure the gross wage on the vertical axis, the demand curve *DD* is unaltered since the gross wage is the marginal cost of labour to the firm.

However, it is the wage net-of-tax that induces workers to supply labour. *SS* still shows labour supply in terms of this net wage, so we must draw the higher schedule *SS'* to show the supply of labour in terms of the gross wage. The vertical distance between *SS'* and *SS* is the income tax on earnings from the last hour of work.

The new equilibrium is *E'*. The gross wage is *W'*, at which firms demand *L'* hours. The vertical distance *A'E'* is the tax paid on the last hour of

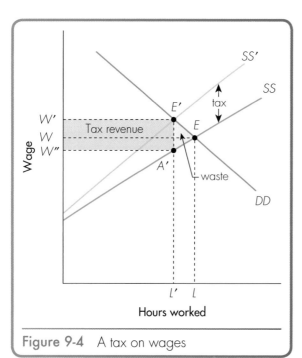

Figure 9-4 A tax on wages

work. At the net wage W''', workers supply L' hours. Relative to the original equilibrium, a tax on wages raises the gross wage to W', but cuts the net wage to W'''. It raises the wage firms pay, but cuts the wage workers get.

The **tax wedge** is the gap between the price paid by the buyer and the price received by the seller.

The incidence of the tax fell on *both* firms and workers even though, for administrative convenience, the tax was collected from firms. The incidence or burden of a tax does not depend on who hands over money to the government. Taxes alter equilibrium prices and quantities. These induced effects must also be taken into account. However, we can draw a general conclusion. The more inelastic the supply curve and the more elastic the demand curve, the more the final incidence will fall on the seller rather than the purchaser.

Maths 9-1

Tax incidence again

Suppose demand is given by $q = a - bp$ and supply is given by $q = cp$, where q and p denote price and quantity, and a, b, c are positive constants. Without any taxation, equilibrium is given by $p^* = a/(b + c)$ and $q^* = ca/(b + c)$.

First, suppose the government levies a tax t per unit on the price paid by buyers. If we interpret p as the price received by sellers, then the supply curve remains $q = cp$ but the demand curve becomes $q = a - b(p + t)$. Hence, in the new equilibrium, $a - b(p + t) = cp$, so

Supplier price $p = a/(b + c) - tb/(b + c)$

Buyer price $p + t = a/(b + c) + tc/(b + c)$

Quantity $q = ca/(b + c) - tbc/(c + b)$

Clearly, if the tax rate is zero, we revert to the previous answer. More generally, the incidence of the tax is as follows: the buyer pays more, the fraction $b/(b + c)$ of every extra unit of tax, and the seller receives less, the fraction $cb/(b + c)$ of every extra unit of tax.

Suppose instead of levying the tax on the buyer, the tax is charged to the seller. The supply curve is now $q = c(p - t)$ and the demand curve is now $q = a - bp$ if p is now the price paid by the buyer. Equilibrium implies $a - bp = c(p - t)$ whence

Supplier price $p - t = a/(b + c) - tb/(b + c)$

Buyer price $p = a/(b + c) + tc/(b + c)$

Quantity $q = ca/(b + c) - tbc/(c + b)$

Thus, although we have now defined p differently, the outcomes are exactly the same. Independently of whether we tax the buy or seller, it leads to the same price for the buyer, the same price for the seller and the same equilibrium quantity. Either way, the relative split of the tax incidence between buyer and seller depends on the relative price sensitivity of the demand curve and the supply curve.

How much fiscal sovereignty?

Before 2001, UK betting tax had been a big earner for the Treasury. It had to be scrapped because of competition from offshore bookies offering online betting without such a tax. The government was forced to change betting tax to stop onshore bookies being wiped out. How the Internet and globalization are changing the nation-state is a key issue of the new millennium. Economics helps you understand better what is going on.

Similar issues arise in the taxation of mobile workers, such as investment bankers. If the government threatens too large a tax, the bankers threaten to go to New York or Geneva where taxation is more favourable. Once the tax base is mobile across countries, governments have to be very careful about the tax rates that they levy. Fiscal sovereignty is undermined by the prospect of the taxed escaping abroad. Conversely, when the person or thing to be taxed cannot escape abroad, the government can potentially set much higher tax rates and therefore has more fiscal sovereignty.

Greater mobility of workers across countries is one aspect of greater globalization. Similar effects arise from competition in the international movement of goods and services combined with a series of free trade agreements that prevents a national government taxing foreign activities differently from domestic ones. The threat of non-domiciled (non-doms are foreigners resident in our country) to quit if taxed too much is an example of the former; the evaporation of the betting tax is an example of the latter.

This of course explains why globalization often leads to greater income inequality. It is the rich, and the activities they provide, that are usually mobile across countries, while the poor, and the more basic goods and services they provide, are trapped at home. Fear that the rich will quit holds down taxes on the rich, leaving poorer people as the only alternative source of tax revenue.

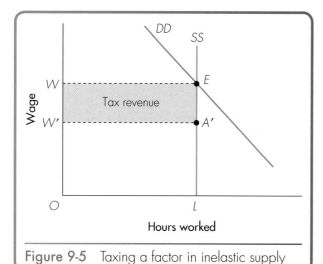

Figure 9-5 Taxing a factor in inelastic supply

Figure 9-5 shows the extreme case of a vertical supply curve. Without a tax, equilibrium is at E and the wage is W. A vertical supply curve SS implies that a quantity of hours L is supplied whatever the net wage. A tax on wages leads to a new equilibrium at A'. Only if the gross wage is unchanged will firms demand the quantity L that is supplied. The entire incidence falls on the workers. To check you have got the idea of incidence, draw for yourself a market with a horizontal supply curve but a downward-sloping demand curve. Show that the incidence of a tax now falls only on consumers.

Dealing with monopoly power

Imperfectly competitive firms with some monopoly power must cut their price to sell more output. Since marginal revenue is less than the price for which the last good is sold, marginal cost is less than price and marginal consumer benefit. Such firms make less than the socially efficient quantity.

Moreover, when a competitive firm gets lazy it loses market share and may go out of business. When a monopoly gets lazy, it simply makes less profit. From the social viewpoint, its cost curves are then unnecessarily high.

Social cost

> There are two **social costs of monopoly power**. The first is too little output; the second is wastefully high cost curves.

Society may not worry just about the inefficiency of imperfect competition. It may also care about the *political* power that large firms exert, and the *distributional* issue of the fairness of large monopoly profits.

Taxing monopoly profits

The way to maximize after-tax profits is to maximize pre-tax profits. Thus, for *given* cost curves, a monopolist's output is unaffected by a tax on monopoly profits. Since the demand curve for its output is unaffected, making the same output means charging the same price. Governments can tax away monopoly profits. High profits are not directly a social cost of monopoly power.

Must liberalization help?

Is more competition always better? Suppose there are big economies of scale and a steadily downward-sloping average cost curve. Suppose the government insists on more competition, say entry of a second producer. Greater competition reduces profit margins, but, with lower output, the firms cannot enjoy scale economies and have high average costs. Society may lose more from the cost increase than it gains from greater competition.

We thus discuss two approaches to policy. Where scale economies are not too big, promoting competition is indeed the answer. But where scale economies are vast, it is better to keep the monopoly but regulate its behaviour.

Competition policy

What do Durex, Valium and Cornflakes have in common with household gas supplies, mobile phones and Heathrow Airport? All were investigated by the Competition Commission, which monitors the behaviour of big firms and checks for the possible abuse of monopoly power.

> **Competition policy** tries to promote efficiency through competition between firms. The **Competition Commission** examines whether a monopoly, or potential monopoly, is against the public interest.

UK businesses operating internationally are increasingly subject to EU competition law, but many businesses still operate primarily within the UK. The latter are governed by UK competition law, chiefly the Competition Act 1998 and the Enterprise Act 2002, which made it a criminal offence, punishable by a jail sentence, to engage in a dishonest cartel.

> The **Office of Fair Trading (OFT)** is responsible for making markets work well for consumers, by protecting and promoting consumer interests while ensuring that businesses are fair and competitive.

In particular, the OFT has the power to refer cases to the Competition Commission for a detailed investigation in cases in which existing monopoly power may be leading to a 'substantial lessening of competition.'

For UK companies with substantial business within the EU, EU competition law takes precedence over UK law. Article 81 of the Treaty of Amsterdam prohibits anti-competitive agreements that have an appreciable effect on trade between EU Member States and which prevent or distort competition within the EU. Article 82 prohibits the abuse of any existing dominant position. Responsibility for enforcement of these Articles lies with the European Commission.

For UK companies operating principally within the UK, it is UK competition policy that matters. Prior to the Enterprise Act 2002, the Commission evaluated whether or not a monopoly was acting 'in the public interest', with no presumption that monopoly was bad. Many previous judgements of the Commission concluded that companies were acting in the public interest – for example, because they had an excellent record of innovation and cost reduction that outweighed the fact that their monopoly position also allowed them to reduce output and raise prices.

The Enterprise Act 2002 focuses more narrowly on competition itself and made the Competition Commission more accountable by defining its objectives more clearly. This also brought UK law more clearly into line with EU competition law, by placing measures of competition at the centre of the evaluation of competition policy.

UK competition policy in practice

The Competition Commission has wide powers, yet few firms have been penalized after its investigation. The Commission has often relied on informal assurances that bad behaviour would stop. For example, after examining charges from fixed phones to mobile phones, it concluded that emerging competition in telecommunications was not yet sufficient to discipline the top suppliers, whose charges were too high. The Commission recommended that top suppliers such as Vodafone and O_2 reduce their prices considerably.

Other recent cases include the investigation into whether 'store cards' issued by particular retailers were substantially reducing competition, and the report on the extended warranties that retailers often offer when you buy a new camera or TV. Annual UK sales of domestic electrical goods are nearly £20 billion, and consumers spend nearly £1 billion a year buying extended warranties (multi-year insurance and service agreements), usually purchased from the retailer of the goods at the time the goods are bought. If you are buying a new camera in one shop, it is difficult for a different supplier simultaneously to be offering you a warranty.

The Commission concluded that this monopoly power led to prices on warranties being up to 50 per cent higher than they would have been in a competitive market. To remedy this, the Commission demanded that retailers provide consumers with much more transparent written information about the cost of warranties, and that consumers should be allowed to cancel warranties (with a full refund) for up to 45 days after their initial purchase.

This judgement illustrates what has long been a distinction between the US and UK approaches to competition policy. US competition law often seeks a structural change in the industry to *prevent* the potential for monopoly power. UK competition law has more frequently sought to *control* behaviour of those with monopoly power rather than to restructure the industry altogether.

Market structure often reflects the tension between the output required for minimum efficient scale and the size of the market as given by demand for the product. Large countries, facing large demand, may have room for many firms operating at minimum efficient scale. Small countries, with smaller markets, have room for fewer firms at minimum efficient scale.

Hence, large countries can break up monopolies more easily, since subdivided firms may still enjoy substantial scale economies. In smaller countries, with smaller markets, breaking up monopolies may sacrifice scale economies and simply raise costs. Developing policies to contain monopoly behaviour may then be preferable to policies that outlaw monopoly itself.

Merger policy

Competition policy also scrutinizes the formation of large new companies.

A **merger** is the union of two companies where they think they will do better by amalgamating.

A *horizontal merger* is the union of two firms at the same production stage in the same industry. A *vertical merger* is the union of two firms at different production stages in the same industry. In *conglomerate mergers*, the production activities of the two firms are essentially unrelated.

A horizontal merger may allow more scale economies. One large car factory may be better than two small ones. Vertical mergers may assist co-ordination and planning. It is easier to make long-term decisions about the best size and type of steel mill if a simultaneous decision is taken on car production for which steel is an important input. Conglomerate mergers involve companies with completely independent products, and have less scope for a direct reduction in production costs.

Table 9-3 UK mergers (annual averages), 1972–2012

Year	Number
1972–85	560
1986–89	1300
1990–2008	580
2009–12	306

Source: www.ons.gov.uk

Merger policy must thus compare the social gains (potential cost reduction) with the social costs (larger monopoly power). Table 9-3 shows merger activity involving UK firms. It shows dramatic merger booms in the late 1980s, and the sharp reduction since the crash of 2007–08.

Merger booms would have been impossible if policy had automatically opposed them. Individual cases were again examined case by case. Until 2010, there were two grounds for referring a prospective merger to an investigation by the Competition Commission: (1) that the merger creates market share of at least 25 per cent, or (2) that the company taken over has an annual turnover of at least £70 million.

Since 2010, the principal reason for referring a merger is that it may lead to a Substantial Loss of Competition (SLC). If, after investigation, the Commission finds this to be the case, it has a wide range of powers to prevent this from occurring.

Since 1965, only 4 per cent of merger proposals have been referred to the Competition Commission. UK policy has largely consented to mergers, reflecting two assumptions. First, cost savings from scale economies are big. Second, as part of an increasingly competitive world market, even large UK firms have little monopoly power.

Regulating natural monopolies

Sometimes, large domestic firms face little foreign competition, and the size of scale economies makes them natural monopolies.

A **natural monopoly**, having vast scale economies, does not fear entry by smaller competitors.

The government can nationalize them, to control their behaviour in the public interest, or can leave them as private firms but appoint independent regulators to supervise their behaviour. After 1945, most European countries chose nationalization. Since 1980, they have increasingly reverted to regulation of private monopolies.

To limit the exercise of monopoly power, regulators sometimes impose a price ceiling. For many years after its privatization in 1984, BT had an '$RPI - X$' price ceiling. Its *nominal* prices could rise with the retail price index, minus X per cent. X is the annual fall in its *real* price that the regulator demands. Since BT enjoyed rapid technical progress, it should have been able to cut costs year after year. And it did: during its first ten years as a private company, BT's real prices fell by 43 per cent.

Telecoms is an interesting industry because competition has increased substantially in the last decade. BT now faces competition from mobile phones, cable TV companies and local providers. For calls made from land lines, regulators have now concluded that it is no longer necessary to place so much emphasis on regulating the price of phone calls themselves. Competition may be adequate provided that other entrants can access the infrastructure of BT's phone lines. Regulation has shifted back up the vertical chain, from regulation of the final price to regulation of access to intermediate networks that then facilitate competition in the final output market.

Unlike telecoms, where greater competition has altered the need for regulation, some industries will always exhibit significant monopoly power. Because transporting water is very expensive, there is always likely to be only one local water company. To contain this monopoly power, the water regulator OFWAT has adopted an annual price ceiling that has allowed the real price of water to *rise* to finance much needed investment in pipes and water purification. Conversely, after criticizing the termination charges that mobile phone companies imposed on calls to other networks, the Competition Commission imposed a price ceiling of '*RPI – 15*' for industry giants Vodafone and O_2, and slightly smaller rates of real price reduction for Orange and T-Mobile.

The general principles have been: (a) where cost efficiencies of scale make monopoly inevitable, regulate conduct, principally by regulating prices; and (b) where regulating access and entry by competitors is feasible – precisely because it is not necessary to have a single superfirm – encourage competition; as this comes about, the need to regulate prices becomes less pressing.

Case study 9-2　The full Monti

The success of Microsoft is partly built on the way it bundles products together, making it hard for competitors to compete on individual components without offering the entire package. If you buy Windows, you get Internet Explorer, Windows Media Player and Microsoft Office. Each program works effectively with the rest of the Windows family. Rival producers complain that their products do not interface easily with the Windows family, which deters customers from buying elsewhere. By refusing to disclose access codes for interoperability in workgroup servers, Microsoft makes it harder for non-Windows programs run on office networks to access Windows systems. Similarly, RealPlayer, offered by RealNetworks, claimed to be disadvantaged in comparison with Windows Media Player.

In March 2004, the EU Competition Commissioner was Mario Monti (who in 2011 became prime minister of Italy). Monti ruled (a) that Microsoft had illegally refused to supply the proprietary information needed for interoperability, and (b) that Microsoft had illegally tied Media Player to the Windows operating system. Microsoft was fined €497 million, and ordered to remedy these deficiencies. During 1998–2002, similar issues (for example, the monopoly position of Windows' Internet browser) were examined by the US Department of Justice, though the case was finally settled out of court. Microsoft continued to

Mario Monti © Stephen Bisgrove/Alamy

appeal against this judgment, but in 2008, the EU fined Microsoft an additional $1.4 billion for failure to comply with the March 2004 anti-trust decision. This represents the largest penalty ever imposed in 50 years of EU competition policy.

The Microsoft case demonstrates why firms operating in global markets need to face competition authorities that operate on a similar scale. Imagine if Microsoft had been investigated separately by national authorities in the UK, France, Germany, Sweden and Ireland, each with its own national rules, and all frightened to be tough in case they lost market share to more lenient regulators in other countries. When global giants deal with fragmented national regulators, it may be impossible for the latter to discharge their responsibility effectively.

Indeed, EU Commissioner Monti revealed that he had been in close discussion with his US counterpart throughout the investigation of Microsoft and subsequent appeal negotiations. Monti noted that the EU had consulted the US authorities more than had been the case in reverse when the US was deciding its attitude to Microsoft, and that the EU happened to be more united than the US, in the sense that this decision had the unanimous support not only of the EU Commission, but also of the individual competition authorities of each of the EU Member States.

Recap

- Horizontal equity is the equal treatment of equals, and vertical equity is the deliberately unequal treatment of unequals.
- A resource allocation says who makes what and who gets what. It is efficient if no reallocation of resources could then make some people better off without making others worse off.
- For given inputs and technology, there are many efficient allocations, differing in fairness.
- If there are no market failures, free markets are efficient. Producers and consumers equate marginal costs and marginal benefits to the same price, and thus to each other.
- Governments face a conflict between equity and efficiency. Redistributive taxes drive a wedge between prices to buyers and sellers, undermining the Invisible Hand.
- Distortions occur if market equilibrium does not equate marginal social cost and benefit, an inefficiency, or market failure. Distortions arise from taxation, imperfect competition, externalities, and other missing markets reflecting informational problems.
- Externalities imply one agent's decisions have direct but neglected effects on others. The free-rider problem usually inhibits markets in pollution or congestion. Imposing taxes (subsidies) to reflect the marginal adverse (beneficial) externality makes people act as if the market existed, restoring efficiency.
- Public goods are a strong externality in which everyone consumes the same amount and cannot be prevented from doing so. Markets cannot handle this well. Having elections to decide the level of public goods is a possible solution.
- Inside information inhibits markets through moral hazard and adverse selection. Where markets are missing, prices cannot equate marginal social cost and benefit.
- Government revenues come mainly from direct taxes on personal incomes and company profits, and indirect taxes on purchases of goods and services. Government spending is partly purchases of goods and services, and partly transfer payments.
- A progressive tax and transfer system takes most from the rich and gives most to the poor. The UK tax and transfer system is mildly progressive.

- By taxing or subsidizing goods that involve externalities, the government can induce the private sector to behave as if it takes account of the externality, thus raising efficiency.
- Except for taxes designed to offset externalities, taxes are generally distortionary. By driving a wedge between the selling price and the purchase price, they stop prices equating marginal cost and marginal benefit.
- The incidence of tax is who ultimately pays the tax. The more inelastic is demand relative to supply, the more a tax falls on buyers not sellers, and vice versa.
- The social costs of monopoly power are too little output and high cost curves that waste resources.
- Competition policy tries to promote competition to discipline monopoly power. In the UK, where the Office of Fair Trading believes that competition is being substantially reduced, it can refer the case to the Competition Commission. The Commission weighs the costs of monopoly power against possible gains from larger scale.
- Anti-competition agreements between firms, such as collusive price-fixing, are illegal.
- Mergers may be horizontal, vertical or conglomerate. Conglomerate mergers have the smallest scope for economies of scale. The recent merger boom consisted largely of horizontal mergers to take advantage of larger markets caused by globalization, European integration and deregulation.
- In principle, mergers can be referred to the Competition Commission if they will create a firm with a 25 per cent market share or the company taken over has a turnover of at least £70 million.
- For both monopolies and mergers, EU competition law takes precedence over UK law if the firms operate within the EU on a significant scale.
- Natural monopolies enjoy such scale economies that effective competition is impossible.
- Governments can nationalize such firms or regulate them as private monopolies. In the latter case, price ceilings help limit the abuse of monopoly power.
- Sometimes, by breaking up companies or by requiring that the owner of a large infrastructure network makes access available to smaller competitors, it is possible to stimulate adequate competition in the final output market.

Review questions

To check your answers to these questions, go to pages 386–7.

1 An economy has ten goods to share between two people. (x, y) denotes that the first person gets x and the second person y. For allocations (a) to (e), say if they are efficient, equitable or neither: (a) (10, 0), (b) (7, 2), (c) (5, 5), (d) (3, 6), (e) (2, 8). Would you prefer allocation (d) or (e)?

2 Driving your car in the rush hour, you slow down other drivers. Is this an externality? How might it be offset efficiently? Discuss the merits of fuel taxes that also penalize rural drivers on deserted roads.

3 Should it be compulsory to wear seatbelts in cars?

4 Which of the following are public goods: a privatized coastguard system, a tolerant society, a state-owned post office? In each case, explain your answer.

5 Why are these statements wrong? (a) Society should ban all toxic discharges. (b) Railways must be made completely safe. (c) Anything the government can do the market can do better.

6 Which of the following are public goods? (a) The fire brigade, (b) clean streets, (c) refuse collection, (d) cable television, (e) social toleration, (f) the postal service. Explain and discuss alternative ways of providing these goods or services.

7 Classify the following taxes as progressive or regressive. (a) 10 per cent tax on all luxury goods, (b) taxes in proportion to the value of owner-occupied houses, (c) taxes on beer, (d) taxes on champagne.

8 There is a flat-rate 30 per cent income tax on all income over £2000. Calculate the average tax rate (tax paid divided by income) at income levels of £5000, £10 000 and £50 000. Is the tax progressive? Is it more or less progressive if the exemption is raised from £2000 to £5000?

9 (a) Suppose labour supply is completely inelastic. Show why there is no social inefficiency if wages are taxed. Who bears the incidence of the tax? (b) Now suppose labour supply is quite elastic. How much of the tax is ultimately borne by firms and how much by workers? Will the tax distort the equilibrium quantity of labour?

10 Why are these statements wrong? (a) Taxes always distort. (b) If government spends all its revenue, taxes are not a burden on society as a whole.

11 With constant $AC = MC = 5$, a competitive industry makes 1 million cars. Taken over by a monopolist, output falls to 800 000 cars, and the price rises to £8. AC and MC are unchanged. By calculating an inefficiency triangle analogous to those in Figures 9-2 and 9-3, quantify the social cost of monopoly in the case of a price ceiling of 5? Would this be efficient?

12 A regulator now imposes a price ceiling of 6. What happens to the social cost of monopoly? Could the regulator impose a ceiling of 5? Would this be efficient?

EASY

13 In 2012, the Australian government decided to impose a carbon tax. How could it decide at what level the tax should be set? Is this safer or riskier than combining quotas with tradeable permits?

14 'Carbon taxes should be delayed until the economic recovery is better established.' 'The whole point of carbon taxes is to reduce something of which we are already doing too much.' Adjudicate.

15 Draw *AC* and *MC* for a natural monopoly that continues to enjoy scale economies as its output rises. What is the socially efficient output if cost curves do not shift? Could the regulator set a price ceiling that would achieve this?

16 Why are these statements wrong? (a) Monopolies make profits and must be well-run companies. (b) Mergers are beneficial; otherwise companies would not merge.

17 **Essay question** Does globalization always reduce the case for merger control?

18 **Essay question** Banks typically operate in many countries simultaneously. What does this imply about how banks should be regulated? Who should be responsible for banks that fail?

Online Learning Centre

To help you grasp the key concepts of this chapter check out the extra resources posted on the Online Learning Centre at www.mcgraw-hill.co.uk/textbooks/begg.

There are additional case studies, self-test questions, practice exam questions with answers and a graphing tool.

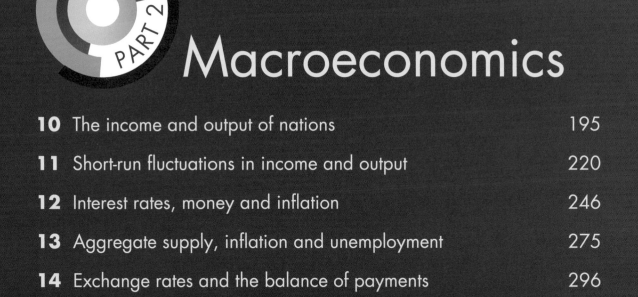

Macroeconomics

CHAPTER 10

The income and output of nations

Learning outcomes

By the end of this chapter, you should be able to:

- Define and explain measures of national income and output
- Analyse the circular flow of resources and payments
- Show why leakages must equal injections
- Discuss what national income fails to measure
- Analyse determinants of economic growth
- Explain why economics was called the dismal science
- Understand evidence about growth rates
- Discuss the costs of growth
- Distinguish trend growth and cycles around this path
- Analyse why business cycles occur

Microeconomics magnifies the detail in order to analyse particular markets. In contrast, macroeconomics simplifies the building blocks in order to focus on how they fit together as a whole. Macroeconomics is the study of the entire economic system and how it interacts.

This chapter introduces the basic building blocks of macroeconomics and how they combine as national income. We then study how national income grows in the long run, and how it may fluctuate in the short run. In so doing, we begin the discussion of the recent financial crisis and its repercussions, the biggest challenge faced by macroeconomics for over 100 years.

Macroeconomic data

The media are always discussing problems of slow growth, inflation, unemployment and the future of national currencies. These issues help determine the outcome of elections, and make some people interested in learning more about macroeconomics.

Table 10-1 National income and income per citizen, 2010

		National income (US$ trillion)	Income per citizen (000s of US$)
G7	US	14.6	47
	Japan	5.5	42
	Germany	3.3	43
	France	2.6	42
	UK	2.2	38
	Italy	2.1	35
	Canada	1.6	43
BRICs	Brazil	2.1	9
	Russia	1.5	10
	India	1.7	1
	China	5.9	4

Source: World Bank, *World Development Report*, 2011

Macroeconomics studies the economy as a whole.

Table 10-1 shows both national income and income per person in the Group of Seven or G7,[1] the largest of the rich industrial countries. In total, Americans earned $14.6 trillion in 2010, or about $47 000 per person. Japanese national income was $5.5 trillion, about $42 000 per person. Although Brazil, China, India and Russia are much less developed, and thus have lower incomes per person, they have such large populations that their total incomes are large. China now has the second-largest national income in the world, although its citizens each earn less than a tenth as much as the average American. What do we mean by the concepts of national income and national output, and how are they measured?

Households and firms

Households own land, labour and capital, whose services they rent to firms as production inputs. Households spend this income buying the output of firms.

The **circular flow** is the flow of inputs, outputs and payments between firms and households.

In Figure 10-1, the inner loop shows the flows of real resources between the two sectors, and the outer loop shows the corresponding flows of payments. This suggests three ways to measure the amount of economic activity in an economy: (a) the net value of goods and services produced, (b) the value of household earnings, and (c) the value of spending on the final output of firms. Whether we measure net output, incomes (including profit) or final spending, we get the same answer for GDP.

Gross domestic product (GDP) measures an economy's output.

---

[1] The G7 are the US, Japan, Germany, the UK, France, Italy and Canada. When Russia is also included, this becomes the G8.

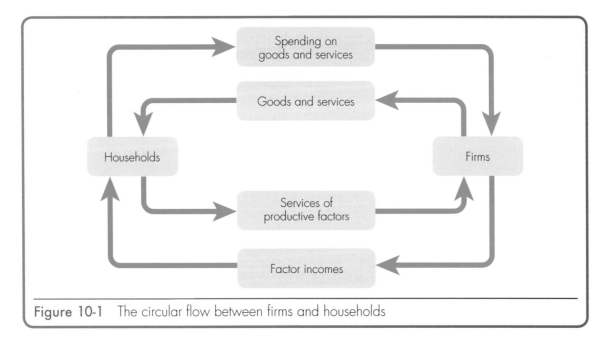

Figure 10-1   The circular flow between firms and households

However, there are several complications. First, the output of firms is not all sold to households. The concept of value added avoids double the output that some firms buy from other firms.

Value added is net output, after deducting goods used up during the production process.

From gross output we deduct the use of raw materials and partly finished goods, but not the cost of labour or capital. The steel in a car door was *already* counted as the output of the steel producer, and must not be counted again as part of the output of the car producer.

We do not deduct the labour of car workers from car output, since car workers were not produced and measured elsewhere in the economy. Nor do we deduct the cost of using the assembly line that made cars. Provided this capital input does not depreciate, it is available next period to make yet more cars, and hence was not used up.

Total value added is the net output of the economy. One way or another, this is paid to households as income and profits, and this income is spent buying the final output that firms sell to end users. So far, households are the only end users.

Leakages and injections

Saving S is the part of income not spent buying output. **Investment I** is firms' purchases of new capital goods made by other firms.

If households earn £7000 but spend only £5000 on consumption *C*, they must save the other £2000. To pay out incomes of £7000, firms must have value added of £7000 which is sold to end users. If £5000 is sold to households for consumption, the other £2000 must have been sold to firms buying new capital goods. These firms are end users because this capital is *not* then used up as a production input.

Saving is a **leakage** from the circular flow, money paid to households but *not* returned to firms as spending. Investment is an **injection** to the circular flow, money earned by firms but *not* from sales to households. Leakages always equal injections, as a matter of definition.

The *only* way to measure saving is the part of income not spent on output, since income equals output, which is either goods for households or investment goods for firms. Saving must equal investment. By definition.

Similarly, suppose firms do not sell all their output. We treat the flow of unsold goods as temporary *investment* by firms to add to their stock of working capital. Household consumption plus *total* investment still equal output and spending. When stocks are run down, this is negative investment, again keeping the accounting straight.

Adding the government and foreign countries

The government is also an end user, buying the output of firms (education, health, tanks). Governments also spend money on welfare benefits B for things such as pensions, jobseeker's allowance and income support. Not being physical output, these subsidies or *transfer payments* are not part of GDP. They get counted later when spent on household consumption. However, government purchases G of final output are part of GDP. Government spending, both on physical goods and services and on monetary transfer payments, is financed by taxes T.

Finally, we add trade with the rest of the world. Net exports add to GDP.

Exports X are made at home but sold abroad. **Imports Z** are made abroad but bought at home.

Domestic output is bought for consumption C, investment I, government spending G and exports X. Subtracting the import content Z in these goods, GDP is $[C + I + G + X - Z]$. This is paid out as incomes and profits to households, who use it for consumption, saving or paying taxes net of benefits received. Thus GDP is also $[C + S + T - B]$. These two measures of GDP must be equal. Deducting consumption from both measures, $[I + G + X - Z] = [S + T - B]$. Hence

$$\begin{array}{cc} \textit{Total leakages} & \textit{Total injections} \\ S + [T - B] + Z \ = & I + G + X \end{array}$$

Total leakages from the circular flow (savings, net tax payments and imports) are money from domestic firms that households do not recycle to domestic firms again. Total injections (firms' investment, government purchases and exports) are sources of firms' revenue not originating from households. Total leakages still equal total injections.

Saving needs no longer equal investment if other elements ensure that total leakages and injections remain equal. But when we remove the government and the foreign sector, we recover the special case that saving must equal injections.

Figure 10.2 illustrates the circular flow in detail. Injections are shown in blue and leakages in red. Investment, export and government spending are injections because they augment the basic circular flow of income between households and firms. Money is withdrawn through leakages to saving, imports and

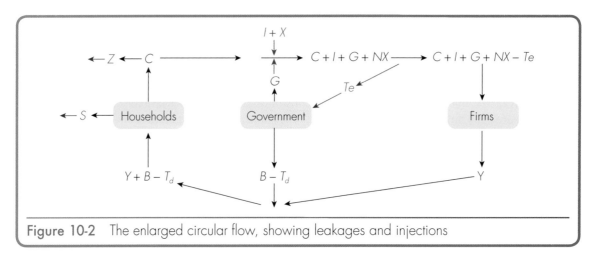

Figure 10-2 The enlarged circular flow, showing leakages and injections

net taxes ($T_e + T_d - B$), where T_e is taxes on expenditure, T_d direct taxes on income, and B welfare benefits paid by government. Saying that $T_d - B$ leaks out is the same as saying $B - T_d$ is injected, which is why we show it in red, as with the other leakages.

From GDP to GNP

To complete the national accounts, we deal with two final problems. First, foreigners own some of our capital and land, and we own some assets abroad. These assets or property earn income unconnected with domestic output.

> **Gross national product (GNP)** is the total income of citizens wherever it is earned. It is GDP plus net property income from abroad.

If the UK has an inflow of £2 billion from foreign assets, but an outflow of £1 billion in property income to foreigners, UK GNP, the income of UK citizens, is £1 billion more than UK GDP, the value of output in the UK.

The final complication is depreciation.

> **Depreciation** is the fall in value of the capital stock during the period through use and obsolescence.

Depreciation is an economic cost, reducing net output in any period. Deducting depreciation from GNP yields net national product (NNP) or national income.

> **National income** is GNP minus depreciation during the period.

Our national accounts are now complete, but can you remember them? Figure 10-3 will help to keep you straight.

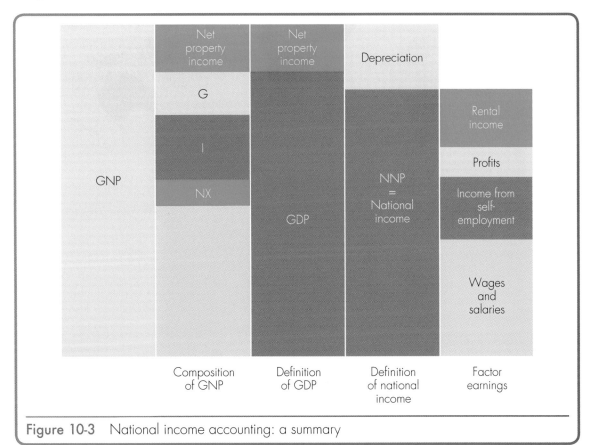

Figure 10-3   National income accounting: a summary

Box 10-1

Easily measured, but not the whole story

When things are traded in a market, or embedded in government tax statistics, they are relatively easy to measure. Many of our difficulties arise precisely because some of the most valuable things are not easily measurable. GDP easily captures the output of washing machines, but not of happiness, health or environmental depreciation.

The United Nations Human Development Index systematically tries to measure three broad dimensions of economic development – health, education and material standard of living – and produces annual statistics for all UN member countries. The map below shows the geographic range of outcomes – no prizes for guessing which colours represent prosperity and which represent poverty as measured by the Human Development Index.

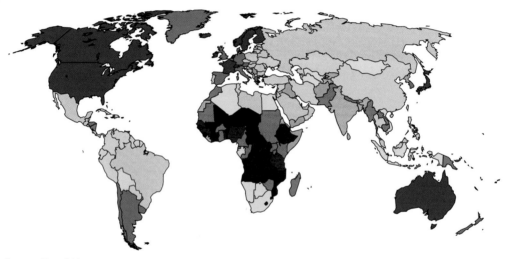

Source: United Nations

Health is crudely captured by life expectancy at birth, education by the proportion of the children enrolled at school and by the proportion of adults who are can read, and material standard of living is crudely captured by per capita GDP.

Some of these indicators are more stable than others. For example, before the financial crash, Iceland came top in the world in the UN measure, and Sierra Leone bottom. But Iceland's banks experienced the biggest crash of all, and so the Icelandic economy is now in serious trouble. This will not immediately affect its adult literacy or the life expectancy of its population, but these will gradually suffer unless economic prosperity can be restored.

Like sausages, economic statistics simply reflect what you put into them. If you care about democracy, equality or environmental sustainability, don't get hung up merely because your country is not doing well on the particular things that GDP does measure.

People who visit France quickly learn that the French have a good quality of life, better than you would expect simply by looking at their GNP. In 2009, President Sarkozy commissioned a panel of economic experts to advise on how to adjust their national statistics better to reflect the benefits of long lunches, long holidays and early retirement.

Think of this as a health warning on GNP and GDP statistics. They measure what they measure. Unless and until electorates want to spend more money collecting more comprehensive statistics, GNP and GDP will use data already being collected annually for other purposes such as taxation.

Source: Adapted from John Kay, 'Do not discount what you cannot measure', *Financial Times*, 22 September 2009

What GNP measures

Depreciation, being hard to measure, is treated differently in different countries. Most international comparisons use GNP, which avoids the need to argue about depreciation.

Nominal GNP is measured at the prices when income was earned. **Real GNP** adjusts for inflation by valuing GNP in different years at the prices prevailing at a particular date.

Since it is physical quantities of output that yield utility or happiness, it is misleading to judge economic performance by nominal GNP. GNP in the UK rose from £25 billion in 1960 to over £1500 billion in 2011. Yet prices in 2011 were nearly 20 times higher than in 1960. Despite the 60-fold rise in nominal GNP, real GNP in 2011was only about 3.2 times its level of 1960. The rest of the increase in nominal GNP was due to the effect of inflation, as shown in Table 10-2.

What GNP omits

In practice, GNP omits some things that ideally should be included. First, some outputs, such as noise, pollution and congestion, reduce true economic output and should be deducted from the usual GNP measure. This is logically correct but hard to implement. These 'bads' are not traded in markets, so it is hard to quantify them or value the costs they impose.

These activities include household chores, DIY activities and unreported jobs. Moreover, deducting environmental depreciation from measures of national output and income would radically alter our view of how well different countries are doing, and might affect the political incentives to pay more attention to such issues.

Leisure is also a valuable commodity. If two countries make the same output of consumer goods but one delivers more leisure for its residents, its net output of relevant economic goodies is higher. Yet conventional measures of GNP and GDP ignore leisure completely. Standard measures are confined to what is easily measured. Often national statistics are the by-product of tax collection or other government activities. As macroeconomists, we have to deal in the statistics that we have, which are not always the ones we would like to have.

Table 10-2 Nominal and real GNP, 1960–2011

	1960	1995	2011
Nominal GNP (current £bn)	25	750	1541
GNP deflator (1995 = 100)	8	100	151
Real GNP (£bn, 1995 prices)	316	750	1022

Sources: ONS; OECD

Case study 10-1 — Tax evasion, crime and the mismeasurement of GNP

Gangster Al Capone, never charged with murder, was eventually convicted of tax evasion. Taxes are evaded by smugglers and drug dealers but also by gardeners, plumbers and everyone else doing things 'for cash'. Since GNP data are based on tax statistics, the 'hidden' economy is unreported. This means that official GNP statistics may substantially understate the true value of GNP.

© Aidart

Economists have various ways to estimate the size of the hidden economy. One way is to count large-denomination banknotes in circulation. People with fistfuls of £50 notes are often engaged in tax evasion. Indeed, when the euro was first launched as a currency, the decision to make the most valuable note €500 (much more valuable than the largest dollar banknote, the $100 bill) led to fierce discussion as to whether the euro would replace the dollar as the preferred currency of crooks.

Another way is to guess people's income by studying what they spend. Maria Lacko has used the stable relationship between household use of electricity and its main determinants – income and weather temperature – to estimate incomes from data on electricity consumption and temperature. She confirms two popularly held views. The hidden economy is large both in former communist economies, where the new private sector is as yet unrecorded, and in several Mediterranean countries with a history of trouble getting their citizens to pay tax. She found that the size of the hidden economy might be around 20–30 per cent of reported GDP in the countries of Eastern Europe and the Mediterranean, but probably only 5–10 per cent of the size of GDP in the US and UK. If we measured this properly, GDP would therefore be much larger.

Another way to estimate the hidden economy is to conduct surveys and offer people immunity if they tell the truth. Recent work by Friedrich Schneider is quoted by the UK National Audit Office (*Tackling the Hidden Economy*, 2008). His estimates are shown below.

The hidden economy (% of national income)

Belgium	Sweden	Canada	Australia	UK	US
22	19	16	14	12	9

Source: National Audit Office, *Tackling the Hidden Economy*, April 2008, The Stationery Office

10-2 Economic growth

During 1870–2000, UK real GDP grew tenfold and real income per person fivefold. We are richer than our grandparents, but less rich than our grandchildren will be. Table 10-3 shows that sustaining a slightly higher growth rate for a long time makes a huge difference. What is long-run economic growth? What causes it?

Table 10-3   Long-run growth, 1870–2000

	Real GDP		Real GDP per person	
	Ratio of 2000 to 1870	Annual growth (%)	Ratio of 2000 to 1870	Annual growth (%)
Japan	100	3.7	27	2.7
US	66	3.4	10	1.8
Australia	45	3.1	4	1.2
France	15	2.2	10	1.9
UK	10	1.9	5	1.3

Sources: Angus Maddison, 'Phases of capitalist development', in R. C. O. Matthews (ed.), *Economic Growth and Resources*, Macmillan, 1979; updated from IMF, *International Financial Statistics*

Economic growth is the rate of change of real income or real output.

Had we been growing for thousands of years, we would be even richer now than we are. It is only in the last 250 years that real GDP per person has been persistently increasing.

Potential output is the level of GDP when all markets are in equilibrium.

Short-run shifts in demand or supply can lead to a temporary period in which output differs from potential output. However, in the long run, changes in output caused by any fluctuations around potential output are swamped by the effect of persistent growth of potential output itself.

Potential output grows either because the quantity of inputs grows, or because a given quantity of inputs makes more output. The main inputs are labour, capital and land (the environment). How much output a given bundle of inputs produces depends on the productivity of these inputs.

Like us, our grandparents had a 24-hour day, but were probably fitter since they got more exercise. Why can we make more output than they could? We must have accumulated lasting advantages in the meantime. These cumulated advantages are physical capital, skills that we call human capital, or technical ideas that we call technology.

Technology is the current stock of ideas about how to make output. **Technical progress** or better technology needs both **invention**, the discovery of new ideas, and **innovation** to incorporate them into actual production techniques.

Major inventions led to spectacular gains in knowledge. The wheel, the steam engine and the modern computer changed the world. Industrialized societies began only when productivity improvements in agriculture allowed some of the workforce to be freed for industrial production. Before then, almost everyone had to work the land merely to get enough food for survival.

Requirements for economic growth
Embodiment of knowledge in capital

To introduce new ideas to production, innovation usually needs investment in new machines. Without investment, bullocks cannot be transformed into tractors even when a blueprint for tractors exists. Major inventions lead to waves of investment and innovation to put these ideas into practice. The mid-nineteenth century was the age of the train. We are now in the age of the microchip.

Learning by doing

Human capital also matters. With practice, workers get better at a particular job. Difficult skills take years to master, whether the skill is bending it like Beckham, using computer software or diagnosing and fixing a mechanical failure. Sometimes productivity and output rise even without more physical capital or new technology. However, eventually we master even difficult tasks. Further output growth then requires the use of more inputs or the application of newer technology.

Growth and accumulation

In 1798, Thomas Malthus' *First Essay on Population* predicting that population growth would drive down living standards to starvation levels suggested that permanent growth in living standards was impossible. This dire prediction led to the branding of economics as 'the dismal science'.

Malthus argued that the supply of land was fixed. As the population expands, more and more labour has to work with this fixed supply of land, leading to diminishing returns to labour productivity, which would steadily fall. Hence, living standards would decline to the point at which starvation then eliminated the population growth that was causing the problem in the first place.

Some of the poorest countries today face this *Malthusian trap*. Agricultural productivity is so low that everyone must work the land to produce food. As population grows but agricultural output fails to keep pace, famine sets in and people die. If better fertilizers or irrigation raise agricultural output, population quickly rises as nutrition improves, and people are driven back to starvation.

Today's rich countries have broken out of the Malthusian trap. How did they manage it? First, by raising agricultural productivity (*without* an immediate rise in population) some workers could be shifted to industrial production. The capital goods then made included better ploughs, machinery to pump water and drain fields, and transport to distribute food more effectively. With more capital input, productivity rose further in agriculture, releasing more workers for industry to make yet more capital. Capital accumulation prevented diminishing returns to population growth.

Second, rapid technical progress in agricultural production caused steady growth in productivity, reinforcing the effect of more capital input. Living standards improved steadily. Hence, even with land in fixed supply, sustained growth is possible. Accumulated capital can grow, substituting for fixed land, and technical progress keeps output growing even when inputs do not increase.

Capital accumulation

By 1960, Nobel Prize winner Robert Solow had worked out a neoclassical theory of growth used in empirical work ever since. By *neoclassical* we mean that it simply assumes that actual output equals potential output, rather than worrying also about whether this is always true in the short run.

In the long run, output labour and capital all grow. Since they cannot be constant, the idea of equilibrium must be applied not to levels but rather to growth rates and ratios.

> Along the **long-run equilibrium path**, output, capital and labour grow at the same rate. Hence output per worker, y, and capital per worker, k, are constant.

For simplicity, consider a closed economy isolated from the rest of the world. Suppose population growth raises labour input at a constant rate n. Assume too that a constant fraction s of income is saved; the rest is consumed. Aggregate investment (public plus private) is the part of output not consumed by either the public or private sector. The neoclassical model assumes that market forces ensure that all saving is invested to increase the capital stock. This investment can be decomposed into two components, capital widening and capital deepening.

> In a growing economy, **capital widening** gives each new worker as much capital as that used by existing workers. **Capital deepening** raises capital per worker for all workers.

Whether or not capital deepening is possible depends on whether investment is more than sufficient to achieve capital widening. For example, with a growing population and labour force, if £1 billion is needed to provide as much capital per head for new workers as is enjoyed by existing workers, then any total investment of less than £1 billion will not achieve complete capital widening, let alone have any investment left over for the purpose of raising capital per head for all workers. Conversely, an investment of £2 billion would not only be enough to contribute the £1 billion needed for capital widening, there would also be a further £1 billion available for capital deepening. Then, all workers would get more capital per head than in the previous period, and capital accumulation would itself be a source of faster output growth.

How much investment is needed simply to achieve capital widening, the threshold beyond which further investment adds to capital per person? The demands of capital widening are larger (a) the faster is population growth n (more new workers for whom new capital is needed), and (b) the more capital per person k that new workers need to match the capital per person k enjoyed by existing workers.

In this long run, labour is growing at the rate n as it always does. Hence capital and output are growing at the rate n, keeping capital per person and output per person constant. The neoclassical growth model thus describes the nature of the steady-state path and explains how the economy converges to this path if it does not begin there. If capital per person is initially too low, it takes only a little investment to accomplish capital widening, so there is investment left over for capital deepening, which raises capital per person towards the steady-state level.

Conversely, if capital per person is initially above the steady-state level, there is insufficient investment to provide new workers with this large amount of capital per person. Hence, capital per person falls back towards the steady-state level.

A higher saving rate

Suppose people permanently increase the fraction of income saved. We get more saving and more investment, but *not* permanently faster growth!

Population continues to grow at the rate n. Hence, in the long run, output and capital *must* eventually grow again at n for this to be a steady state. So what happens to the extra saving? It allows capital deepening, raising capital per worker from its original level (say, k^*) to some higher level (say, k^{**}), after which the new steady state is reached, with capital, output and labour all growing at n. With higher capital per worker, the burden of capital widening – providing enough capital for the growing population – becomes harder. When capital per worker has risen by enough, all the extra saving and investment are taken up with capital widening. Further capital deepening ceases. Only during the temporary transition from the equilibrium path to the new one has capital (and hence output) grown faster than labour. Thereafter, the economy settles down to grow at the rate n again, albeit on a higher parallel path with higher levels of capital and output per worker.

Growth through technical progress

So far, the theory says that output, labour and capital all grow at rate n. Although it is true that capital and output grow at the same rate, in practice both grow more rapidly than labour. That is why we are better off than our great-grandparents. Each generation has more capital per person than the previous generation enjoyed, and hence attains a higher level of income per person than the previous generation.

Of course, capital accumulation is not the whole story. There is also technical progress. Imagine that the creation of new knowledge at the rate t lets each worker do the work of $(1 + t)$ previous workers.

Labour-augmenting technical progress increases the effective labour supply.

Effective labour input now grows at the rate $(t + n)$ because both technical progress and population growth increase the effective labour force. Now, in the long run, capital and output each grow at the same rate $(t + n)$ as the effective labour supply. But actual people continue to grow at the rate n. Hence, capital per worker and output per worker *grow* permanently at the rate t.

With this amendment, our theory of long-run growth now fits all the important facts of the real world. The ratio of capital to output is constant in the long run. Both capital and output grow at the rate $(t + n)$, which exceeds the rate n at which population and the labour force grow. Hence capital per worker and output per worker grow steadily in the long run. And that fits the facts.

Neoclassical growth

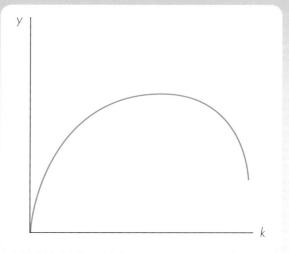

Suppose for simplicity that output per person y is related to capital per person k via the relationship $y = ak - k^2$. When there is no capital, there is no output. Thereafter, raising k initially raises y but at a decreasing rate. The formula is chosen just to keep the maths simple, so we are implicitly interested only in the part of the diagram in which y is still rising as k increases.

Capital deepening occurs at the rate $dk/dt = sy - nk$, the excess of saving per person (at a constant fraction s of output per person) over the capital widening nk required to provide new workers with the same capital per person as existing workers. Hence, in the steady state

$$nk^* = s[ak^* - k^{*2}]$$

which occurs both in the uninteresting case of $k^* = 0$, and in the more relevant case in which

$$k^* = a - n/s$$

Hence, a greater productivity of capital (larger a) or a greater saving rate (larger s) raise the steady state level of capital per worker k^*, and hence also of output per worker y^*. A faster rate of population growth n reduces steady state capital and output per worker because more of gross investment has to go on capital widening, leaving less for capital deepening.

Out of the steady state,

$$dk/dt = s(ak - k^2) - nk = k[(sa - n) - sk]$$
$$= sk[k^* - k]$$

Hence, for all $k < k^*$, capital deepening is occurring and aggregate output is growing more quickly than in the steady state; conversely, when $k > k^*$, aggregate investment is insufficient to cover capital widening and so capital deepening is negative. Wherever the economy begins, it converges to the unique steady state.

Evidence about growth

The Organisation for Economic Co-operation and Development (OECD) is a club of about 30 of the world's richest countries, from industrial giants like the United States and Germany to smaller economies like New Zealand, Ireland and Turkey. Table 10-4 shows the growth of OECD countries since 1950. The table shows the sharp productivity slowdown after 1973 in all OECD countries.

Table 10-4 Average annual growth in real output per worker (%)

	OECD	Japan	Germany	France	UK	US
1950–1973	3.6	8.0	5.6	4.5	3.6	2.2
1973–2010	1.5	1.9	2.2	1.7	1.6	1.0

Sources: S. Dowrick and D. Nguyen, 'OECD comparative economic growth 1950–85', *American Economic Review,* 1989; OECD, *Economic Outlook.*

Why did productivity growth slow down? First, 1973 was also the year of the first OPEC oil price shock, when real oil prices quadrupled. This had two effects. First, it diverted R&D towards very long-term efforts to find alternative energy-saving technologies. These efforts may take decades to pay off and show up in improvements in actual productivity. Second, the higher energy prices made much of the capital stock useless. Energy-guzzling factories, too expensive to operate, were scrapped. The world lost part of its capital stock, reducing output per head. If this explanation is correct, the more recent bout of high oil prices will have the same effect again.

Moreover, increasing regulation and pollution control, although socially desirable, raised production costs and reduced *measured* output and hence *measured* productivity. We return shortly to the mismeasurement of output and hence of output growth.

Having discussed differences in growth across sub-periods, we now discuss differences across countries. The fact that OECD countries move together across sub-periods shows that many aspects of growth are not within a country's control. Technical progress spreads quickly wherever it originates. Countries are increasingly dependent on the same global economy.

The convergence hypothesis

The Solow model has a unique steady state, to which a country converges whatever its initial level of capital per worker. When capital per worker is low, it takes little investment to equip new workers (capital widening), so the rest of investment raises capital per worker (capital deepening). Conversely, when capital per worker is already high, saving and investment are insufficient to give new workers the old level of capital per worker, which therefore falls.

> The **convergence hypothesis** says poor countries should grow quickly but rich countries should grow slowly.

Since this seems plausible, why is sub-Saharan Africa not growing really quickly? Basically, for two reasons. So far, the analysis assumed that a constant fraction of income is saved. But people with low living standards may have to consume *all* their income just to stay alive. With no saving, they then have no resources to invest at all. They are thus unable to begin the virtuous cycle of investment that generates additional output, thereby providing a surplus that can be saved and reinvested in yet more capital accumulation. Also, since a lot of technical progress is made operational through installing new capital equipment that embodies the latest ideas, countries that are not investing may also find it difficult to take advantage of technical progress as well.

Without capital accumulation or technical progress, such countries are indeed stuck in the Malthusian trap. As population expands, more labour is added to a fixed land supply and labour productivity falls. Even worse, global warming may adversely affect the land quality too, so that a growing population is having to work with a land supply that is effectively shrinking, making the Malthusian trap spring shut even more quickly.

Some of these countries also have civil wars or corrupt governments that appropriate the country's meagre wealth for the ruling elite. This reminds us that economic success depends on a flourishing civil society, good governance and other attributes that cannot narrowly be explained by economics alone.

The costs of growth

Some people believe that the benefits of economic growth are outweighed by its costs. Pollution, congestion and a hectic lifestyle are too high a price to pay for a rising output of cars, washing machines and video games.

Since GDP is an imperfect measure of the net economic value of output made by the economy, there is no presumption that we should aim to maximize the growth of measured GDP. We discussed issues such as pollution in Chapter 9. Without government intervention, a free market economy is likely to produce too much pollution.

However, zero pollution is also wasteful. Eliminating the last little bit of pollution costs a lot and has only a little benefit. Rather, society should reduce pollution until the marginal benefit of more pollution reduction equals its marginal cost.

This is the most sensible and direct way in which to approach the problem. In contrast, the 'zero-growth' solution tackles the problem only indirectly.

The **zero-growth proposal** argues that, because higher output has adverse side effects such as pollution and congestion, we should therefore aim for zero growth of measured output.

The zero-growth approach does not distinguish between outputs that have adverse side effects and those that do not. It does not provide the right incentives. When society believes that there is too much pollution, congestion, environmental damage or stress, the best solution is to provide incentives that directly reduce these activities. Restricting growth in measured output is a very crude alternative that is distinctly second best.

Some of these difficulties might be removed if economists and statisticians could devise a more comprehensive measure of GDP that included all the 'quality of life' activities (clean air, environmental beauty, serenity) that yield consumption benefits but at present are omitted from measured GDP. Inevitably, voters and commentators assess government performance according to published, measurable statistics. A better measure of GDP might remove some of the conflicts that governments feel between measured output and quality of life.

Case study 10-2   The road to riches

For centuries, growth in income per person was tiny. Most people were near starvation. Now we take growth for granted. After 1750, industrialization changed everything. Capital and knowledge, accumulated by one generation, were inherited and augmented by the next generation.

Why 1750? Partly because mathematical and scientific ideas reached a critical mass, allowing an explosion of practical spin-offs. Yet many pioneers of the industrial revolution were common-sense artisans with little scientific training. Conversely, the ancient Greece of Pythagoras and Archimedes achieved scientific learning but not economic prosperity.

By the start of the fifteenth century, China understood hydraulic engineering, artificial fertilizers and veterinary medicine. It had blast furnaces in 200 BC, 1500 years before Europe. It had paper 1000 years before Europe, and invented printing 400 years before Gutenberg. Yet in 1600 China was overtaken by Western Europe, and by 1800 had been left far behind.

Economic historians continue to debate the root causes of progress, but three ingredients seem crucial: values, politics and economic institutions. Growth entails a willingness to embrace change. China's rulers liked social order, stability and isolation from foreign ideas – fine attitudes when progress was slow and domestic but a disaster when the world experienced a profusion of new technologies and applications.

Powerful Chinese rulers could enforce bans and block change in their huge empire. When individual European rulers did the same, competition between small European states undermined this sovereignty and offered opportunities for growth and change. Economic competition helped separate markets from political control. Rights of merchants led to laws of contract, patent, company law and property. Competition between forms of institution allowed more effective solutions to emerge and evolve. Arbitrary intervention by heads of state was reduced. Opportunities for trade, invention and innovation flourished. The table below lists some milestones in the making of Western Europe.

Year	Income per person (US$, 1990 prices)	Inventions
1000	400	Watermills
1100	430	Padded horse collar
1200	480	Windmills
1300	510	Compass
1400	600	Blast furnace
1500	660	Gutenberg printing press
1600	780	Telescope
1700	880	Pendulum clock, canals
1800	1280	Steam engine, spinning and weaving machines, cast iron, electric battery
1900	3400	Telegraph, telephone, electric light, wireless
2000	17 400	Steel, cars, planes, computers, nuclear energy

Source: *The Economist*, 31 December 1999

 ## Business cycles

In practice, aggregate output does not grow as smoothly as long-run growth theory might suggest. In some years output grows a lot, but in other years it actually falls.

The **business cycle** is short-term fluctuation of output around its trend path.

Is there an actual cycle? We know output fluctuates a lot in the short run, but a cycle also requires a degree of regularity. Can we see it in the data? If so, how do we explain it?

Trend and cycle: statistics or economics?

Figure 10-4 shows a business cycle. The smooth curve is the steady growth in trend output over time. Actual output follows the wavy curve. Point *A* is a *slump*, the bottom of a business cycle. At *B*, the economy enters

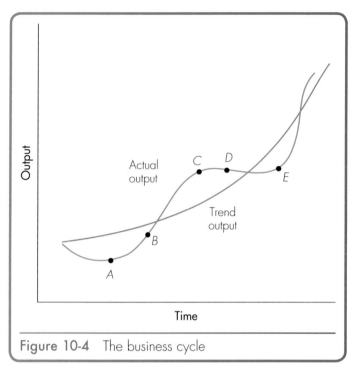

Figure 10-4   The business cycle

the *recovery* phase of the cycle. As recovery proceeds, output climbs above its trend path, reaching *C*, which we call a *boom*. Then it enters a *recession* in which output is growing less quickly than trend output, and may even be falling. Point *E* shows a *slump*, after which the cycle starts again.

Figure 10-5 shows the annual growth of real GDP and of real output per worker in the UK during 1975–2007 up to the eve of the financial crash. Output and productivity grew rapidly in the late 1980s but stagnated in the early 1980s and early 1990s. The figure makes three points. First, short-run cycles *are* important. Second, in the short run there is a close relation between changes in output and changes in labour productivity (output per worker). Third, cycles became less pronounced after the mid-1990s. These are the facts that we need to explain.

Any series of points may be decomposed statistically into a trend and fluctuations around the trend. We begin by assuming that potential output grows smoothly. It follows the trend. Trend growth is what we studied in the previous section.

Political business cycles

Actual output fluctuates because it departs temporarily from the smooth trend path of potential output. But why would this happen? One possibility is a *political business cycle*. Suppose voters have short memories and are heavily influenced by how the economy is doing just before the election. To get re-elected, the government manipulates the economy into a slump, then mops up this spare capacity by using government policy to boost output and income as the election approaches, achieving a temporary period

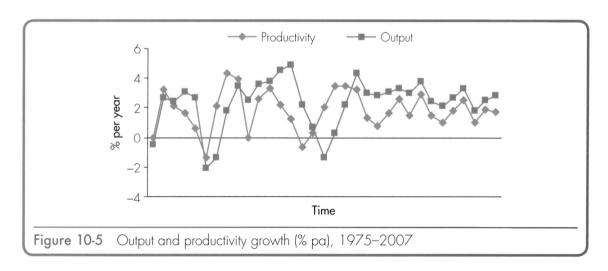

Figure 10-5   Output and productivity growth (% pa), 1975–2007

of impressive-looking growth. The voters think that the government has got things under control and votes it in for another term of office.

A **political business cycle** is caused by cycles in policy between general elections.

The theory contains a grain of truth, but it supposes that voters are pretty naive. In 1997, the Major government lost the UK election even though output was growing strongly. Voters thought Labour could do even better. Moreover, the Bank of England was made independent of political control precisely to take the politics out of monetary policy decisions.

The period between elections is pretty fixed. In the UK it is usually four years, and a maximum of five years. The more that cycles last longer than five years, the less likely it is that politics is the main cause of the business cycle. Indeed, a lengthening of the average duration of the business cycle would be significant evidence that politics was becoming less important as a determinant of cycles.

Ceilings and floors

Cycles are likely when we recognize the limits imposed by supply and demand. The total supply of output provides an output *ceiling* in practice. Although it is possible temporarily to meet higher demand by working overtime and running down stocks of finished goods, output cannot expand indefinitely. In itself this tends to slow down growth as the economy reaches a boom. Having overstretched itself, the economy is likely to bounce back off the ceiling and begin a downturn. Conversely, there is a *floor*, or a limit to the extent to which total demand is likely to fall. Gross investment (including replacement investment) cannot actually become negative unless, for the economy as a whole, machines are being unbolted and sold to foreigners. Although falling investment is an important component of a downswing, investment cannot fall indefinitely, since it cannot fall below zero.

Fluctuations in stock-building

Working capital – partly-finished goods or goods that have been produced but not yet sold – also plays an important role. Consider inventory investment in working capital. Firms hold stocks of goods despite the cost in interest cost forgone on the funds tied up in making goods for which no revenue has yet been received. The corresponding benefit of holding stocks is to avoid temporary changes in production levels, which can be costly. Output expansion entails overtime payments and costs of recruiting new workers. Cutting output involves redundancy payments. Holding stocks lets firms meet short-term fluctuations in demand without incurring the expense of short-run fluctuations in output.

If demand falls, firms initially build up stocks of unsold output. If demand remains low, firms gradually cut output rather than stockpile goods indefinitely. Once demand recovers again, firms are still holding all the extra stocks built up during the recession. Only by increasing output *more slowly* than the rise in aggregate demand can firms eventually sell off these stocks and get back to long-run equilibrium levels of stocks.

Thus, the evolution of stocks helps explain why output adjustment is so sluggish. Output changes more slowly than demand. This helps explain the behaviour of labour productivity in Figure 10-4. Output per worker rises in a boom and falls in a slump. This is because output adjusts more quickly than employment, since changes in employment levels themselves are costly for firms, especially if there is some prospect that these will soon be reversed again.

A fall in demand is met initially both by cutting hours of work and increasing stocks. With a shorter work week, output per worker falls. If the recession intensifies, firms undertake the costlier process of sacking workers and restoring hours to their normal level. Conversely, a boom is the time when output and overtime are high, and productivity per worker peaks.

Real business cycles

Essentially, this explanation implies that cycles in demand are the cause of cycles in actual output around a smooth trend growth path for potential output. However, there is a second possibility. Potential output may itself be subject to fluctuations. This idea is sometimes called a 'real' business cycle, since the causes arise only from changes in the real economy that affect the physical supply of inputs or the technology that affects the output derived from any given quantities of inputs.

Real business cycles are output fluctuations caused by fluctuations in potential output itself.

One source of such cycles might be shocks to technology, which affect potential output by affecting productivity. The age of the train, the car and the microchip have required huge waves of investment, affecting not just aggregate demand but also potential output.

Some economists have been sceptical of this approach for two reasons. First, changes in aggregate supply may occur more slowly than changes in aggregate demand. Second, to provide a theory of cycles, the economy would also need to experience some periods in which productivity *fell* because technology deteriorated. Can we really forget today what we knew how to do yesterday?

Sometimes, we can get new information that causes an important change of opinion about future technology. The end of the Internet boom in 2001 had many features of a real business cycle. It was not that actual productivity fell. Rather, people were unsure about how rapidly the new technologies would increase future productivity. Initially, everyone was optimistic that growth rates would be very high indeed. Investment was very high, anticipating rapid future growth.

As evidence accumulated that that productivity growth was going to be a little slower than first imagined, suddenly everybody realized that there had already been far too much investment in some hi-tech sectors. Share prices collapsed, and further investment dried up. This reflected both a downgrading of ideas about the future level of potential output, and a fall in current aggregate demand since investment then fell.

Research on real business cycles has one vital message for macroeconomic policy. If actual output falls only because of a fall in potential output, there is no longer any gap between actual and potential output that policy should be trying to close. In contrast, if cycles reflect temporary deviations of actual output from potential output, then in an ideal world policy might be trying to stabilize actual output, removing these deviations and allowing output simply to follow its smooth trend path.

Empirical research has found some evidence that technology shocks affect output in the short run; and in 2007–08 the global economy was hit with large adverse supply shocks as the price of energy, minerals and food all soared. But demand shocks are usually more important. The task for stabilization policy – the headache that the Bank of England confronts once a month – is to decide whether visible changes in output have been accompanied by invisible changes in potential output, or whether the gap between actual and potential output has changed. Nobody said the Bank's job was easy.

Box 10-2

Recessions caused by financial crashes

For 60 years after 1945, recessions never lasted long. People complained that their governments were not perfect, but by historical standards economic performance was pretty good. Then we got the financial crash of 2007–08.

The value of assets and debts can be many times the value of annual income. In a financial crash, we downgrade substantially the estimated value of assets without any immediate change in the value of debts. If assets become less valuable than debts, there are only two possible solutions. We can tear up the debts and refuse to pay, thereby achieving an equally rapid fall in debts; however, one person's debt is another person's asset, so this inflicts a further asset value reduction somewhere else in the system. Alternatively, we can tighten our belts and save extra and put this towards rebuilding the value of our assets (or paying down the value of debts).

The problem with the second course is that, if income is small relative to assets, it can take years to save enough to rebuild asset value satisfactorily. During this period of austerity, saving is high and spending low, leading to a very protracted reduction in the demand for goods and services. The normal rules of economic cycles then do not apply. American professors Kenneth Rogoff and Carmen Reinhart have shown that it can take 10–20 years to escape such a trap, which cumulates to an awful lot of lost output.

Britain's National Institute for Economic and Social Research has produced a very interesting chart showing the evolution of major UK recessions since 1900. It shows the recessions of 1930–34 (during the Great Depression of the 1930s), the stagflation recession of 1973–76 (caused by high oil prices), the Thatcher recession of 1979–83 (when the government squeezed demand in order to defeat inflation), the 1990–93 recession (caused initially by raising interest rates to get rid of inflation caused by the Lawson boom, then by entering the precursor to the Eurozone and facing high interest rates necessary to stabilize German inflation after unification with East Germany), and the recession since 2008 caused by the financial crash.

In each case, the chart plots the number of months since output began to fall and the change in the level of output since that date.

The 1990–93 recession (shown in green) was quickly cured by leaving the European monetary system, floating the pound and slashing UK interest rates. Within three years, UK output was higher than its initial level. The recession of the mid-1970s (shown in orange) was also over within three years. The Thatcher recession (in turquoise) took four years to recover the initial level of output. The Great Depression of the 1930s (in blue) was also pretty much over in four years. What is interesting about the post-2008 recession (in purple) is that it is the only one still showing a significant output loss after four years and with no clear sign for optimism about what comes next.

In fact, the chart makes a strong case for renaming the 1930s as the Little Depression. The Great Depression is what we are experiencing now.

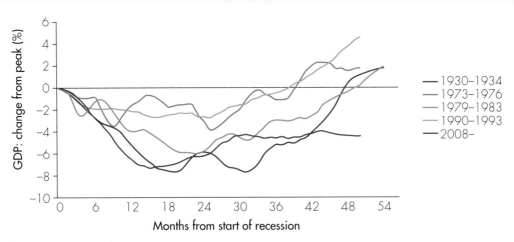

Source: www.niesr.ac.uk

The road ahead

The remaining chapters explain more of the details behind the determination of national income and output. Since macroeconomics is about the system as a whole, it is easy to lose sight of these interactions. For this reason, it is helpful to signpost the chapters to follow:

- *Chapter 11 Short-run fluctuations in income and output.* Why output can deviate from potential output in the short run; demand fluctuations arising from consumption, investment, government fiscal policy and net exports.
- *Chapter 12 Interest rates, money and inflation.* The role of the central bank in managing demand through monetary policy, and its transmission to aggregate demand.
- *Chapter 13 Aggregate supply, inflation and unemployment.* Getting supply back into the story, and the short-run trade-off between inflation and unemployment.
- *Chapter 14 Exchange rates and the balance of payments.* Analysing an economy's relationship with the rest of the world, and the role of macroeconomic policy when international linkages matter.
- *Chapter 15 The global economy.* Moving the analysis on to the world economy as a whole.
- *Chapter 16 European integration.* Understanding the euro.

Recap

- Macroeconomics analyses the economy as a whole.
- Households supply inputs that are used by firms to make output. Households' income from firms is used to buy firms' output. There is a circular flow between households and firms.
- GDP, the value of output made in a country, is measured in three equivalent ways: value added in production, factor incomes including profits, or spending on final output.
- Leakages from the circular flow are household income from firms not then spent on the output of firms. Savings, net taxes and imports are leakages. Injections are revenue for firms not originating with household spending. Investment by firms, government purchases and exports are injections. Total leakages always equal total injections.
- GNP, a country's income, is its GDP plus its net property income from abroad.
- National income deducts depreciation from GNP.
- Nominal GNP is measured at current prices. Real GNP is measured at constant prices.
- In practice, GNP and GDP omit unmarketed activities – 'bads' like pollution, valuable activities like leisure and work in the home – and production unreported by tax evaders. Including these would give a better measure of income and output.
- Economic growth is the percentage annual rise in real GDP or real GDP per head. It is an imperfect measure of the growth in economic well-being.
- Output rises because of larger quantities of inputs of land, labour and capital, or because technical progress raises the output produced by given input quantities.

- Along the long-run equilibrium path, variables grow at the same rate and ratios of these variables are constant. Without technical progress, capital, output and labour grow at the same rate. Whatever its initial level of capital, an economy tends to converge on this steady-state path. With a growing population, this theory can explain output growth but not productivity growth.
- Adding technical progress to this model explains why labour productivity and living standards can grow forever.
- Growth rates should converge because capital deepening is easier when capital per worker is low than when it is high. In practice, some poor countries miss out on growth either because they cannot save or because conflict, corruption and mistrust undermine growth.
- The trend path of output is the long-run path after short-run fluctuations are ironed out. The business cycle describes fluctuations in output around this trend.
- A political business cycle means that the government ensures growth is slow immediately after the election, allowing abnormally rapid growth just before the next election.
- Full capacity and the impossibility of negative gross investment provide ceilings and floors, limiting the extent to which output can fluctuate.
- Fluctuations in stock-building add to the business cycle, and reflect costs of adjusting output.
- Real business cycles assume that cycles reflect fluctuations in potential output. Technology shocks can have this effect.
- Both demand and supply shocks contribute to the business cycle. Policies to stabilize output are appropriate only if cycles reflect demand shocks that create a gap between actual and potential output.

Review questions

To check your answers to these questions, go to pages 387–8.

1 The table shows final sales and purchases of intermediate goods in car production. What is the industry's contribution to GDP?

EASY

	Sales	Intermediate goods bought
Car producer	1000	330
Windscreen producer	200	10
Tyre producer	80	30
Steel producer	50	0

2 GNP is £300. Depreciation is £30 and net property income is −£3. Find the values of GDP and national income.

3 The output of the police is not marketed. GDP statistics use police wages to measure their output. If crime falls, we need fewer police. What happens to measured GDP? Is the country better off? A problem arises because we do not include the negative output of crime in our GDP statistics.

4 Should the following ideally be in GNP? (a) Time spent by students in lectures, (b) the income of muggers, (c) time spent watching football, (d) the salary of traffic wardens, (e) dropping litter.

5 Why are these statements wrong? (a) Unemployment benefit raises national income in years when employment is low. (b) *Trash* earned £1 billion more than *Gone With the Wind* earned 60 years ago. *Trash* is a bigger box office success.

6 'Britain produces too many scientists but too few engineers.' What kind of evidence might help you decide if this is true? Will a free market lead people to choose the career that most benefits society?

7 Name two economic 'bads'. Can they be measured? Are they included in GNP? *Could* they be?

8 'Because we know Malthus got it wrong, we take a more relaxed view about the fact that some minerals are in finite supply.' Is there a connection? Explain.

9 Compare two economies with different rates of population growth. Which has the higher living standards in the long run? Why?

10 If we saved more, would we definitely grow faster?

11 Suppose higher oil prices permanently increase the costs of manufacturers, reducing supply and hence potential output. The government sees a fall in actual output. Should it take action to try to restore the former level of output? Why or why not?

12 Could climate change become the example that finally makes Malthus correct? Explain.

13 Why are these statements wrong? (a) Closer integration of national economies will abolish business cycles. (b) The more we expect cycles, the more we get them.

14 Cycles in export demand could potentially transmit cycles from one country to another. (a) If lower transport costs make the world more integrated, would you expect national cycles to become more or less correlated with one another? (b) If all countries decided to hold their elections on the same day every five years, would this increase or reduce the scope for a political business cycle?

15 Suppose output per person is related to capital per person via the relationship $y = ak$ where a is a positive constant. If population grows at n and the saving rate is s, find the steady-state level of output per person and the steady-state growth rate. In this model, does the steady-state growth rate depend on the saving rate?

16 **Essay question** Imagine we included environmental depreciation in our measure of output. Would this increase or reduce national output? How would it affect incentives for politicians to take the environment more seriously? Why do we not do this already?

17 **Essay question** Do we have to limit the rate of economic growth in order to save the planet?

DIFFICULT

Online Learning Centre

To help you grasp the key concepts of this chapter check out the extra resources posted on the Online Learning Centre at www.mcgraw-hill.co.uk/textbooks/begg.

There are additional case studies, self-test questions, practice exam questions with answers and a graphing tool.

The Solow model of economic growth

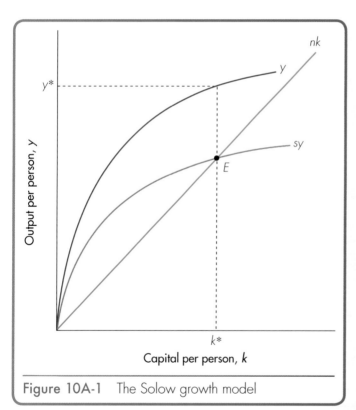

Figure 10A-1 The Solow growth model

Population and labour supply grow at the constant rate n. If each existing worker has an amount of capital k per person, the economy has to invest nk per person to give new workers as much capital as existing workers. If it can save and invest more than this, capital deepening will occur. Figure 10-A1 plots the line nk along which capital per person is constant.

Adding more and more capital per worker k increases output per worker y, but with diminishing returns since labour growth simply remains at n whatever the speed of capital accumulation. Hence the curve y gets flatter as we move to the right and add more capital.

If a constant fraction s of output is saved, sy is saving per person. With leakages equal to injections, saving and investment are equal, hence the curve sy (saving per person) also shows investment per person. In the steady state, the capital per person k is constant. Hence investment per person sy must equal nk, the investment per person needed to keep k constant by making capital grow as fast as labour. k^* is the long-run level of capital per person, and y^* is the long-run level of output per person. Capital and output grow at the same rate n as labour in the long run.

Figure 10-A1 also shows what happens way before the economy reaches this long-run equilibrium path. If capital per worker is low, the economy begins to the left of its eventual position. Per capita saving and investment sy exceeds nk, the per capita investment that makes capital grow in line with labour. Hence, capital per person rises and we move to the right. Conversely, to the right of the steady state, sy lies below nk, capital per person falls, and we move to the left. Figure 10-A1 says that, from whatever k the economy begins, it gradually converges on the (unique) long-run levels of capital per person k and output per person y.

In this long run, labour is growing at the rate n as it always does. Hence capital and output are growing at the rate n, keeping k^* and y^* constant.

A higher saving rate

Suppose people permanently increase the fraction of income saved, from s to s'. Population continues to grow at the rate n. Eventually, *all* variables grow at the rate n. Hence output and capital *must* eventually grow again at n. So what happens to the extra saving? It allows capital deepening, raising capital per worker from its original level k^* to some higher level k^{**}, after which the new steady state is reached, with capital, output and labour all growing at n. As capital per worker increases, the burden of capital widening – providing enough capital for the growing population – becomes harder. When capital per worker has risen enough, all the extra saving and investment are taken up with capital widening. Further capital deepening ceases. Only during the temporary transition from the equilibrium path to the new one has capital (and hence output) grown faster than labour (increasing capital per worker from k^* to k^{**}).

Thus, a rise in the saving rate does not cause a permanent increase in the growth rate, but it does cause a temporary spurt in capital accumulation, while the economy is raising capital per worker to its new equilibrium level. When that is reached, all variables revert to growing at the rate n. The higher saving rate has permanently raised the *level* of capital and output, but not their eventual *rate of growth*.

Growth through technical progress

Now allow for technical progress. Imagine that the creation of new knowledge at the rate t lets each worker do the work of $(1 + t)$ previous workers, increasing the effective labour supply. Effective labour input grows at rate $(t + n)$ because both technical progress and population growth increase the effective labour force. Now, in the long run, capital and output each grow at the same rate $(t + n)$ as the effective labour supply. But actual people continue to grow at the rate n. Hence, capital per worker and output per worker *grow* permanently at the rate t.

With this amendment, our theory of long-run growth now fits all the important facts of the real world. The ration of capital to output is constant in the long run. Both capital and output grow at the rate $(t + n)$, which exceeds the rate n at which population and the labour force grow. Hence capital per worker and output per worker grow steadily in the long run.

Short-run fluctuations in income and output

Learning outcomes

By the end of this chapter, you should be able to:

- Distinguish actual output and potential output
- Analyse aggregate demand and equilibrium output
- Derive the consumption function
- Show the effects of shifts in aggregate demand
- Define and explain the multiplier
- Understand the paradox of thrift
- Show how government spending and taxes affect equilibrium output

- Derive the balanced budget multiplier
- Explain automatic stabilizers
- Discuss limits to active fiscal policy
- Show how foreign trade affects equilibrium output
- Analyse how interest rates affect aggregate demand
- Explain how monetary and fiscal policy interact to determine aggregate demand

In the long run, actual output and potential output cannot diverge indefinitely, so we are essentially analysing the path of potential output. In the short run, the position is very different. A severe recession can cause a period of spare capacity in which output is well below potential output. This chapter analyses what then determines the path of actual output.

 ## 11-1 Output and income in the short run

We now turn from long-run growth of national income and output to movements of income and output in the short run. Since 1960, annual real GDP growth in the UK has averaged 2.4 per cent. But there have been cycles around this trend. In some years, output actually fell, but in other years it grew strongly. What determines national output, and why does it fluctuate? We distinguish *actual* output from *potential* output.

Potential output is national output when all inputs are fully employed. The **output gap** is the difference between actual output and potential output.

Potential output tends to grow smoothly over time as inputs rise and technical progress occurs. Population growth adds to the labour force. Investment in new machinery, education and training increases the quantity not merely of physical capital but also of human capital, the skills embodied in the current workforce. In addition to these increases in the quantity of inputs, technical progress makes any given quantity of inputs more productive. Together, these explain why the UK has grown on average by just over 2.3 per cent a year since 1950, more than quadrupling real GDP over that 60-year period, as shown in Figure 11-1. The figure also shows the sharp fall in UK output in 2009 after the financial crash.

Potential output is not the maximum we could be forced to produce. Rather, it is the output when all markets are in long-run equilibrium. Potential output includes an allowance for 'normal unemployment', probably around 4 or 5 per cent in the UK today. If actual output falls below potential output, workers become unemployed and firms have spare capacity.

Figure 11-2 shows the output gap in the UK during 1997–2012. Initially, the Bank of England succeeded in stabilizing output close to the level of potential output. Output rose above the level of potential output in the years leading up to the financial crash of 2007–08, after which actual output fell dramatically and remained well below the previous level of potential output.

Since we do not observe the level of potential output, we have to make estimates of its likely level. One of the recent controversies has been whether the subsequent recession could have led to a similar reduction in potential output – for example, as factories were permanently closed and some workers gave up the labour market for good – or whether potential output has been largely unaffected by the recession. The answer matters. The Organisation for Economic Co-operation and Development (OECD) believes the latter: hence Figure 11-2 shows a negative output gap and therefore spare capacity that could be mopped

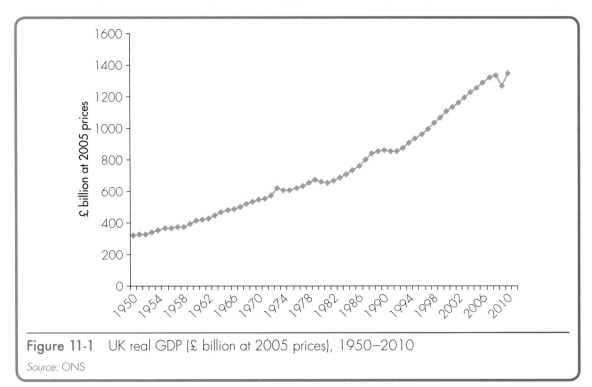

Figure 11-1   UK real GDP (£ billion at 2005 prices), 1950–2010

Source: ONS

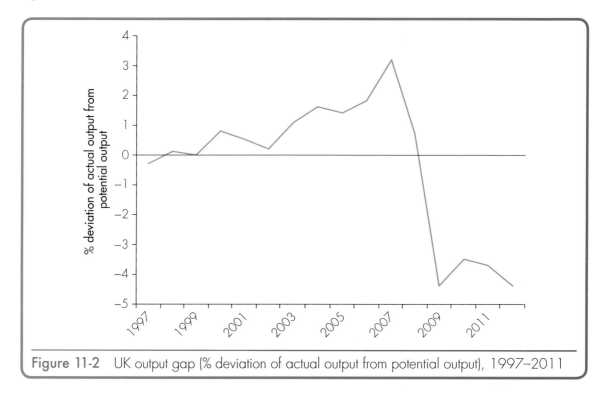

Figure 11-2   UK output gap (% deviation of actual output from potential output), 1997–2011

up if only we could expand the demand for output. If the OECD turns out to be wrong, and potential output has also fallen, then Figure 11-2 is mistaken and there is little spare capacity because the economy's ability to supply has also deteriorated. In the latter case, the effects of the financial crash will be permanent; in the former case, they can eventually be reversed.

This debate reminds us that we need to think carefully about both the demand for output and the supply of output. Both can be hit by shocks. In due course, we will learn to analyse both kinds of shock. Initially, we begin with demand.

To examine how policy affects output, we first need a model of what determines movements in output and causes deviations of output from potential output. To get started, we use the model invented by the great English economist John Maynard Keynes in the 1930s. There are two key assumptions, which we shall later relax. First, all prices and wages are fixed. Second, at these prices and wages, there are workers without a job wanting to work, and firms with spare capacity they want to use. With this excess capacity, any rise in demand is happily supplied. The actual quantity of total output is then *demand-determined*. It depends only on the level of *aggregate demand*.

Aggregate demand

Initially, we ignore the government and the foreign sector. The remaining sources of demand for goods are consumption demand by households, and investment demand by firms. Aggregate demand AD equals $C + I$, the sum of consumption demand and investment demand, but these are determined by different economic groups, and depend on different things.

Consumption demand

Households buy goods and services, from cars and food to holidays and heating. These consumption purchases take about 90 per cent of personal disposable income.

> **Personal disposable income** is household income from firms, plus government transfers, minus taxes. It is household income available to be spent or saved.

Given its disposable income, each household decides how to split this income between spending and saving. A decision about one is a decision about the other. Initially, we assume that consumption demand rises with personal disposable income.

> The **consumption function** relates desired consumption to personal disposable income.

Thus, if Y denotes income and output, and C consumption demand, we can denote the consumption function by

$$C = A + cY \qquad 0 < c < 1$$

where A denotes autonomous consumption demand – all the parts of consumption demand unaffected by income, and c denotes the marginal propensity to consume.

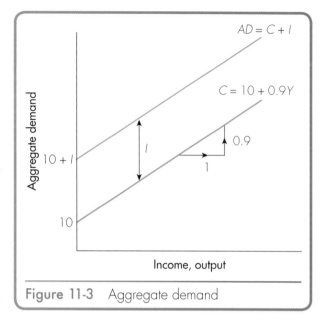

Figure 11-3 Aggregate demand

> The **marginal propensity to consume** is the fraction of each extra pound of income that consumers wish to spend on extra consumption.

Our simple model has no transfer payments, or taxes. Personal disposable income is just national income. Figure 11-3 shows consumption demand C at each level of *national* income.

In this hypothetical example, $C = 10 + 0.9Y$. *Autonomous* consumption demand is unrelated to income. Needing to eat, households want to consume 10 even if income is zero. In Figure 11-3, the consumption function is a straight line with a constant slope. Each extra £1 of income leads to £0.9 of extra desired consumption spending. The slope of the consumption function is the marginal propensity to consume, which is 0.9 in Figure 11-3.

Investment demand

Investment demand for fixed capital (plant and equipment) and working capital (inventories) reflects firms' current guesses about how fast the demand for their output will rise in future. The current *level* of output tells us little about how output will *change*. Sometimes output is high and rising, sometimes it is high and falling. With no close connection between the output level and investment demand, we initially assume that investment demand is *autonomous*. It is independent of current output and income.

Aggregate demand

With only firms and households, aggregate demand is households' consumption demand C plus firms' investment demand I.

> **Aggregate demand** is total desired spending at each level of income.

Figure 11-3 also shows the *aggregate demand schedule*. It adds the constant investment demand I to consumption demand C. The aggregate demand schedule is $AD = [(10 + I) + 0.9Y]$, parallel to the consumption function. The slope of both is the marginal propensity to consume, here 0.9. We now show how aggregate demand determines output and income.

Equilibrium output

When aggregate demand is below potential output, firms cannot sell all they would like. Suppliers are frustrated. But we can at least require that demanders are happy: actual output produced equals the output demanded by households for consumption and by firms for investment.

Short-run equilibrium output is where aggregate demand equals actual output.

Figure 11-4 shows income on the horizontal axis and planned spending on the vertical axis. The 45° line reflects any point on the horizontal axis into the *same* point on the vertical axis. The AD schedule crosses the 45° line only at point E. Equilibrium output and income are Y*. At this income, the AD schedule tells us that the demand for goods is also Y*.

At an output Y_0, less than Y*, the AD schedule is then above the 45° line. Aggregate demand at A exceeds actual output at B. There is excess demand, which firms initially meet by an *unplanned* reduction of inventories. Soon they raise output to meet the excess demand. When output rises to Y*, short-run equilibrium is restored. Aggregate demand again equals actual output.

Conversely, at any output Y_1 above Y*, the AD schedule is below the 45° line, desired spending at J is now below actual output at H, and firms cannot sell all their output. Initially, it piles up as *unplanned* additions to stocks. Then firms reduce their output. Once output is cut to Y*, short-run equilibrium is restored. Aggregate demand again equals actual output.

At the short-run equilibrium output Y*, firms sell all the goods they produce and purchasers buy all the goods they want. But Y* may be *well below* potential output. Suppliers are still frustrated, and cannot sell what they would ideally like to make at the given wages and prices. A lack of aggregate demand prevents expansion of output to potential output. Since firms demand less labour input than at potential output, unemployment exceeds its long-run equilibrium level.

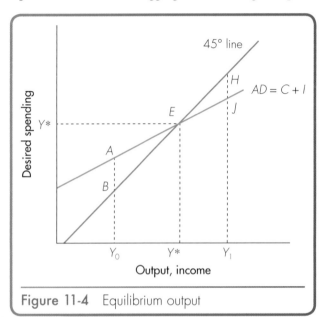

Figure 11-4 Equilibrium output

Movements along the AD schedule versus shifts in the entire AD schedule

The aggregate demand schedule is a straight line whose height reflects total autonomous spending: autonomous consumption demand plus investment demand. Its slope is the MPC.

For a *given level of autonomous demand*, changes in income lead to movements *along a given AD schedule*. Thus, the height of the schedule is determined by the level of autonomous demand. This level of autonomous demand is not permanently fixed, but is independent of income. When autonomous demand is A in Figure 11-5, the schedule AD shows the change in aggregate demand directly induced by changes in income as we move *along* the AD schedule.

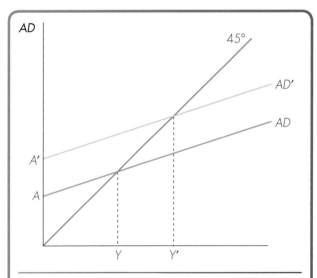

Figure 11-5 Changes in autonomous demand shift the aggregate demand schedule

All other sources of change in aggregate demand – changes in autonomous demand – are shown as *shifts* in the *AD* schedule. For example, if firms decide to invest more, autonomous demand rises from *A* to *A'*, and the aggregate demand is now *AD'*, parallel to, but higher than, the old *AD* schedule. The consequence is a rise in equilibrium output from *Y* to *Y'*.

Planned saving and investment

Equating aggregate demand and actual output is the most intuitive way to understand equilibrium output in the short run. But a second method, which turns out to be equivalent, usually gives the answer even more directly.

> In short-run equilibrium, **planned leakages** must equal **planned injections**.

With no government or foreign sector, equilibrium output Y^* equals aggregate demand, which is planned investment plus planned consumption. However, income Y^* is devoted only to planned consumption or planned saving. Hence, in equilibrium, planned saving equals planned investment. For the moment, we treat planned investment as given. Hence, to understand what happens to output, we need to understand what determines saving.

> The **saving function** shows desired saving at each income level. The **marginal propensity to save MPS** is the fraction of each extra pound of income that households wish to save.

If the consumption function is $C = 10 + 0.9Y$, the saving function must be $S = -10 + 0.1Y$. This ensures that desired $C + S = Y$. Households cannot plan what they cannot afford. For this saving function, the marginal propensity to save is 0.1.

Figure 11-6 shows equilibrium output Y^*, using desired saving and desired investment. The latter is constant, a horizontal line at height I. When income is zero, the saving function implies that saving is -10, the counterpart to autonomous consumption of 10 (since saving is simply the part of income not consumed). Each extra unit of income adds 0.1 to desired saving, so the saving function is an upward-sloping straight line with a constant slope of 0.1. The marginal propensity to save is 0.1. The remaining 0.9 of each extra unit of income is spent on consumption, as the marginal propensity to consume tells us.

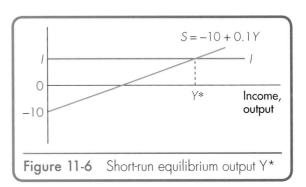

Figure 11-6 Short-run equilibrium output Y^*

Box 11-1

How stable is the saving rate?

In this chapter, to keep things simple, we assume that households save a constant fraction of every extra pound that they earn. A constant marginal propensity to save implies also a constant marginal propensity to consume. This of course is only a simplification to allow us to get started. How realistic is the assumption?

When people are optimistic about the future, they want to spend some of their good fortune today even if their income today has not yet risen. They borrow to go on a binge, whether in retail therapy or foreign holidays. Conversely, when people are pessimistic about the future they know they have

▶

to tighten their belts today, saving more of their current income. We should therefore expect the saving rate to move around depending on people's optimism or pessimism about their future incomes.

We can use this insight to think about the financial crash and its aftermath. In the years leading up to 2007, people felt optimistic. The economy had been growing for a long time. Borrowing was cheap and easy. Why not enjoy today some of the future riches that were bound to come? Saving collapsed as people put very little aside for the future. Then the crash struck and rosy projections about the future went out of the window. Worse, people were left with mountains of debt which had seemed like a good idea but now appeared completely unjustified. There was no alternative to embarking on the long hard slog of saving extra to gradually pay off the excess debt. This logic applied not just to households but to governments themselves. The figure below corroborates this insight – it shows the collapse of the household saving rate (its saving as a percentage of its disposable income) in the years before 2007, and the dramatic adjustment thereafter as people piled on the saving in order to liquidate their large debt burden and feel a bit safer. But with debts having got so large, this requires years of high saving. With people failing to spend on consumption, the economy limps at slower growth rates than usual.

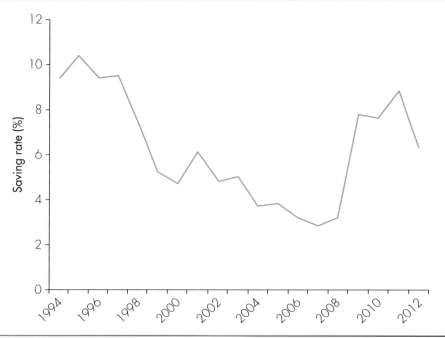

UK household saving rate (household saving as % of disposable income), 1994–2012

Source: Office of National Statistics

It is obviously not true that saving rates remain constant over time. They depend subtly on views about the present relative to the future. For any given view of the future, we can make a useful start by assuming a particular constant marginal propensity to save (or to consume). If the view of the future changes, we can then represent this in our analysis by a change in the marginal propensities to save and to consume. For example, a rise in optimism about the future (or a reduction in inherited debt) will raise the marginal propensity to consume and correspondingly reduce the marginal propensity to save.

Desired saving equals desired investment only at the income Y^*. If income exceeds Y^*, households want to save more than firms want to invest. But saving is the part of income not consumed. Saying that desired saving exceeds desired investment is the same as saying that aggregate demand is below actual output.

Unplanned stocks pile up and firms cut output. Conversely, if income is below Y^*, desired investment exceeds desired saving. Aggregate demand for output is now too high. Firms make unplanned cuts in stocks and raise output. Again, output adjusts towards its equilibrium level Y^*. This is the same level whether we use aggregate demand and actual output in Figure 11-4, or desired investment and desired saving in Figure 11-6.

Desired versus actual

Equilibrium output and income satisfy two equivalent conditions. Aggregate demand equals actual output; and desired investment equals desired saving.[1] By definition, *actual* investment is *always* equal to *actual* saving when there is no government or foreign sector. But out of equilibrium, unplanned changes in inventories always make actual investment equal to actual saving, whatever their desired levels.

A fall in aggregate demand

What alters equilibrium output? After 9/11 and the terrorist attacks on New York, firms became pessimistic about the future demand for their output. Their investment demand fell. How much should that have reduced equilibrium output?

To see the answer directly, we examine desired leakages and injections in Figure 11-7. Suppose the horizontal line showing desired investment shifts down by 20. Equilibrium moves from A to B, achieving a matching vertical fall of 20 in desired saving. Since the saving function has a slope of 0.1, it takes a horizontal leftward move of 200 in output to achieve a vertical fall of 20 in desired saving. Equilibrium output falls by 200 when desired investment falls by 20. Desired saving again equals desired investment.

Until actual output falls by this amount, desired saving exceeds the new lower level of desired investment. But *actual* leakages and injections are *always* equal. When investment demand falls, firms cannot sell their previous output and

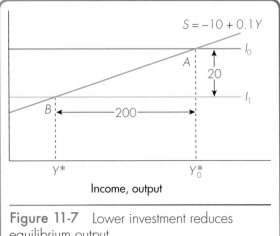

Figure 11-7 Lower investment reduces equilibrium output

unplanned investment in stocks occurs. Firms then cut output. In the final equilibrium, desired investment and saving are again equal.

The multiplier

In this example, investment demand fell by 20 but equilibrium output fell by 200. The multiplier exceeds 1 because it takes a big change in income to alter desired saving by the amount that desired investment has changed.

> The **multiplier** is the ratio of the change in equilibrium output to the change in demand that caused output to change.

---

[1] We use 'desired' and 'planned' interchangeably. Both mean intentions before the fact, rather than outcomes after the fact.

Equilibrium output fell by ten times the original change in investment demand. The multiplier was 10 in this example. Notice that this is simply $[1/(0.1)]$ or $[1/MPS]$. This is indeed the formula for the multiplier for any saving function with a constant marginal propensity to consume. If investment demand falls by 1, eventually desired saving must fall by 1. Each fall in income by 1 reduces desired saving by the smaller amount MPS, so income must fall by $[1/MPS]$ in order to reduce desired saving by 1. In the new equilibrium, desired saving is again equal to desired investment. Hence:

$$\text{Multiplier} = [1/MPS] = 1/[1 - MPC]$$

Since each extra pound of income adds either to desired consumption or desired saving, the marginal propensity to save is simply $[1 - MPC]$, where MPC is the marginal propensity to consume. The larger the marginal propensity to consume, and hence the lower the marginal propensity to save, the larger is the multiplier.

The multiplier makes equilibrium output very sensitive to shocks to aggregate demand (changes in desired investment or desired autonomous consumption). However, if the multiplier were as large as 10 in the real world, the economy would be buffeted by every little shock that hit it. The next section explains why in practice the multiplier is lower than this section suggests.

The paradox of thrift

Suppose people want to save more at each income level, spending less at each income level. This reduces aggregate demand, shifting the AD schedule down because the consumption function shifts down. It also raises desired saving, shifting the saving function up.

Because aggregate demand falls, equilibrium income falls. This reduces equilibrium saving, since saving depends on income. We now have two effects: a desire to save more at each income, but lower equilibrium income, reducing desired saving. Which effect wins?

> The **paradox of thrift** is that a change in the desire to save changes equilibrium output and income, but not equilibrium saving.

Think about desired investment and desired saving. Since nothing happened to desired investment, in the new equilibrium desired saving must be unaffected! A higher desire to save more, and spend less, reduces equilibrium income to the level that leaves desired saving at its original level. If $I = sY$, and I does not change, then any increase in s must be accompanied by a reduction in Y. People save more out of any given income, but income is now lower. Desired total saving stays the same.

Box 11-2

The multiplier–accelerator model of business cycles

Section 10-3 suggested some reasons why business cycles might exist. For the first time, we can now derive a cycle from a particular model. The multiplier–accelerator model distinguishes the causes and effects of a change in investment spending. In the simplest Keynesian model, the effect of higher investment is higher output in the short run. Higher investment adds directly to aggregate demand but the induced rise in income then adds further to consumption demand. We call this process 'the multiplier'.

Up till now, we have treated investment demand as given. What might cause a change in investment demand? Firms invest when their existing capital stock is smaller than the capital stock they would like to hold. The desired capital stock depends partly on the interest rate and hence the opportunity cost of the funds tied up in the capital goods. Changes in expectations about future profits are usually an even more important determinant of investment decisions. If interest rates and wages change only slowly, the main reason to invest in more capital capacity is because demand and output are expected to grow.

The accelerator model of investment assumes that firms guess future output and profits by extrapolating past output growth.

Constant output growth leads to a constant level of investment; it takes accelerating output growth to increase the desired level of investment. The accelerator model is only a simplification. Nevertheless, many empirical studies confirm that it is useful in explaining movements in investment.

Using the table below, we now show how a simple version of the multiplier–accelerator model can lead to a business cycle. The table makes two specific assumptions, although the argument holds much more generally. First, we assume that the multiplier is 2. A unit of extra investment raises income and output by 2 units. Second, we assume that, if last period's income grew by 2 units, firms now increase current investment by 1 unit.

Period t	Change in last period's output $Y_{t-1} - Y_{t-2}$	Investment I_t	Output Y_t
1	0	10	100
2	0	10	120
3	20	20	140
4	20	20	140
5	0	10	120
6	−20	0	100
7	−20	0	100
8	0	10	120
9	20	20	140

The economy begins in equilibrium with output Y_t equal to 100. Since output is constant, last period's output change was zero. Investment I_t is 10, which we can think of as the amount of investment required to offset depreciation and maintain the capital stock intact.

Suppose in period 2 that some component of aggregate demand increases by 20 units. Output increases from 100 to 120. Since we have assumed that a growth of 2 units in the previous period's output leads to a unit increase in current investment, the table shows that in period 3 there is a 10-unit increase in investment in response to the 20-unit output increase during the previous period. Since the assumed value of the multiplier is 2, the 10-unit *increase* in investment in period 3 leads to a further increase of 20 units in output, which increases from 120 to 140.

In period 4, investment remains at 20 since the output growth in the previous period was 20. Thus output in period 4 remains at 140. But in period 5, investment reverts to its original level of 10, since there was no output growth in the previous period. This fall of 10 units in investment leads to a multiplied fall of 20 units in output in period 5. In turn, this induces a further fall of 10 units of

▶

investment in period 6 and a further fall of 20 units in output. But since the rate of output change is not accelerating, investment in period 7 remains at its level of period 6. Hence output is stabilized at the level of 100 in period 7. With no output change in the previous period, investment in period 8 returns to 10 units again and the multiplier implies that output increases to 120. In period 9, the 20-unit increase in output in the previous period increases investment from 10 to 20 units and the cycle begins all over again.

> The **multiplier–accelerator model** explains business cycles by the dynamic interaction of consumption and investment demand.

The insight of the multiplier–accelerator model is that it takes *accelerating* output growth to keep increasing investment. But this does not happen in the table above. Once output growth settles down to a constant level of 20, investment settles down to a constant rate of 20 per period. Then, in the following period, the level of investment must *fall*, since output growth has been reduced. The economy moves into a period of recession, but once the rate of output fall stops accelerating, investment starts to pick up again.

This simple model should not be regarded as the definitive model of the business cycle. If output keeps cycling, surely firms will stop extrapolating past output growth to form assessments of future profits? Firms, like economists, will begin to recognize that there is a business cycle. The less firms' investment decisions respond to the most recent change in past output, the less pronounced will be the cycle. Even so, this simple model drives home a simple result which can be derived in more realistic models. When the economy reacts sluggishly, its behaviour is likely to resemble that of a large oil tanker at sea: it takes a long time to get it moving and a long time to slow it down again. Unless the brakes are applied well before the desired level of the capital stock is reached, it is quite likely that the economy will overshoot its desired position. It will have to turn round and come back again.

Adding the government and other countries

We began our analysis with just two sectors, firms and households. Now we add two other sectors. In modern economies, governments are important and there is extensive trade with other countries. This section examines how the government and foreign countries affect aggregate demand and hence national output.

The government and aggregate demand

Figure 11-8 shows the evolution of government spending and tax revenue in the UK during 1994–2012. The gap between spending and revenue measures the budget deficit. The budget was nearly in balance during 1999–2001.

Figure 11-8 also shows how sharply the Labour government raised government spending after its election victory in 2001, when it committed itself to a substantial increase in spending on health and other public services. Since tax revenue did not increase by the same amount, the government ran a budget deficit. After the crash of 2007–08, government spending was increased to try to prevent output collapsing completely, and the deficit rose sharply. After the 2010 election, the new coalition government began the long task of cutting its spending to reduce the deficit again. However, with output stagnating, tax revenues fell sharply so there was little progress in closing the deficit, as Figure 11-8 confirms.

> **Fiscal policy** is the government's decisions about spending and taxes.

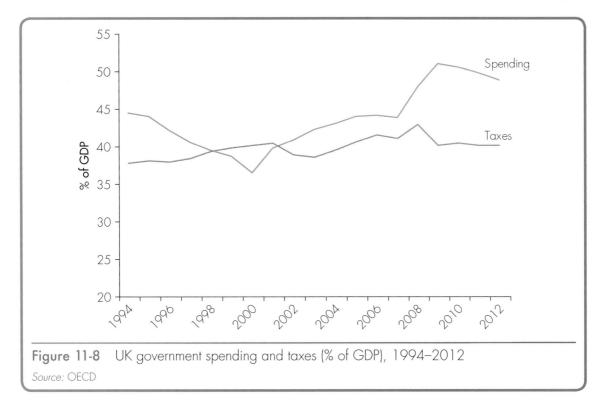

Figure 11-8   UK government spending and taxes (% of GDP), 1994–2012

Source: OECD

We now examine the effects of fiscal policy in more detail. Government purchases G of final output add directly to aggregate demand. Hence, $AD = [C + I + G]$. The level of government demand reflects how many hospitals the government wants to build, how large it wants defence spending to be, and so on. In the short run, these decisions are not affected by changes in actual output. Planned injections also increase to $(I + G)$, which in equilibrium must equal desired leakages. How are desired leakages affected by the government?

The government levies taxes and pays out transfer benefits. At given tax rates and benefit levels, tax revenue and benefit spending both vary with output. To capture this, assume net taxes $NT = tY$, where t is the net tax rate, which in practice is around 0.5. Households' disposable income YD is now $Y(1 - t)$. Households get to keep only about 50p of every £1 of gross income. The other 50p goes to the government in taxes on income and spending because, with higher gross income, people get fewer transfer payments for income support, housing benefit or help in paying council tax.

Suppose households still want to save 10 per cent of each extra pound of *disposable* income. However, with a 50 per cent net tax rate, £1 of gross income adds only 50p to disposable income, and hence only 5p to saving. This is one leakage, but the 50p paid to the government is another leakage not reverting to firms as demand for their output.

In Section 11-1 each extra £1 of national income led only to an extra leakage of £0.10 in extra saving. Now it leads to an extra leakage of £0.55 in extra net tax payments and saving. Whereas each extra £1 of output used to raise consumption demand by £0.90, now it raises it by only £0.45. That is extra desired spending by households on output after adjusting their desired saving and making their tax payments. Changes in income and output now induce much smaller changes in consumption demand. The multiplier is much smaller than in Section 11-1.

It used to be $[1/0.1] = 10$ but is now only $[1/0.55] = 1.82$. Figure 11-9 explains why. Desired injections are now $[I + G]$. Desired leakages, reflecting the need to pay taxes and the desire then to save out of remaining disposable income, are shown by the desired leakage schedule $S + NT$, whose slope is now 0.55.

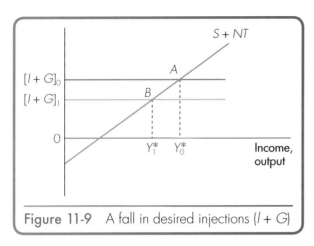

Figure 11-9 A fall in desired injections $(I + G)$

Equilibrium output is initially where the two lines cross at A. A fall in desired injections to $[I + G]_1$ has a smaller effect on equilibrium output the steeper is the desired leakages line. The multiplier is always 1/[marginal propensity to leak]. With a marginal propensity to save of 0.1 and a net tax rate of 0.5, the value of the multiplier is now 1/[0.55] = 1.82.

This value of 1.82 is much smaller than the value of the multiplier earlier in this chapter. Equilibrium output is much less sensitive to shocks to aggregate demand. The net tax rate acts as an automatic stabilizer. When output Y rises, the government gets more tax revenue tY, which helps dampen the expansionary effect of the rise in output. Paying more taxes, households cannot increase consumption demand so much. Conversely, when output falls, tax revenue also falls. By cushioning the disposable income of households, fiscal policy acts as a shock absorber, helping to stabilize aggregate demand and output.

> **Automatic stabilizers** reduce fluctuations in aggregate demand by reducing the multiplier. All leakages act as automatic stabilizers.

Changes in fiscal policy

For a given investment demand, Figure 11-9 shows that lower government demand G cuts planned injections from $[I + G]_0$ to $[I + G]_1$, reducing equilibrium output from Y_0^* to Y_1^*. With less demand for goods, firms must reduce output if they are to produce and sell only the amount that is demanded.

Box 11-3

The limits to active fiscal policy

Why can't shocks to aggregate demand immediately be offset by fiscal policy?

- **Time lags** It takes time to spot that aggregate demand has changed, then time to change tax rates and spending plans; then this policy change takes time to affect private behaviour.

- **Uncertainty** The government does not know for sure the size of the multiplier. It only has estimates from past data. Moreover, since fiscal policy takes time to work, the government must forecast the level that aggregate demand will have reached by the time fiscal policy has had its full effects. Mistakes made in forecasting can frustrate good intentions of policy makers.

- **Induced effects on autonomous demand** Treating investment, exports and autonomous consumption demand as fixed is only a simplification. Fiscal changes may affect private sector confidence, or force the Bank of England to alter interest rates. If the government estimates these induced effects incorrectly, fiscal changes have unforeseen effects. Even if a fiscal expansion raises aggregate demand in a recession, it also adds to the budget deficit. The cure may be worse than the disease if people worry about the consequent rise in government debt or the temptation to print money to finance the budget deficit. Following the financial crash, governments have been reluctant to cut taxes or raise spending for fear of provoking a panic about the solvency of government itself.

On the other hand . . .

In the midst of a financial panic, preventing this panic escalating is an urgent and important objective of policy. Sometimes, the Bank of England can lend money temporarily to banks in order to overcome short-term problems. But if these problems are deeper, and financial institutions are becoming insolvent – their assets have fallen in value to such an extent that their debts now exceed their assets – then an injection of taxpayers' money may be required in order to prevent a domino effect spreading much more widely as the failure of some institutions then causes the failure of related institutions that would otherwise have survived.

Where such bailouts are conducted, the financial cost falls ultimately on the Treasury and taxpayers. Bailouts are therefore a form of emergency fiscal policy. They work not by stimulating the economy but by preventing an implosion that would otherwise have occurred.

Conversely, higher government demand raises short-run equilibrium output because firms must now produce and sell more in order to match aggregate demand. In Figure 11-9, we can view this as an increase in planned injections from $[I + G]_1$ to $[I + G]_0$.

For given government purchases G, a higher net tax rate would make the desired leakages line steeper in Figure 11-9. It must cross a given desired injections line at a *lower* equilibrium output. With higher leakages at any output, output must fall to preserve desired leakages equal to the unchanged desired injections. A higher net tax rate reduces equilibrium output.

Conversely, a tax cut raises equilibrium output. Since the level of injections is unaltered, equilibrium can be attained only if the level of leakages also remains the same. With less tax revenue leaking out of the circular flow at any particular level of output, it requires higher output to restore aggregate leakages to their former level. Equivalently, if consumers are being taxed less heavily, they have more to spend and consumption demand increases, raising aggregate demand and thereby causing a rise in equilibrium output in the short run.

Active or discretionary fiscal policy?

Although automatic stabilizers are always at work, governments may use *active* or *discretionary* fiscal policy to *alter* spending levels or tax rates to try to offset other shocks to aggregate demand. When aggregate demand is low, the government boosts demand by cutting taxes or raising spending. Conversely, when aggregate demand is high, the government raises taxes or reduces spending.

However, it is not always easy to change long-term fiscal plans quickly. Nowadays, much of the burden of stabilizing output falls not on fiscal policy but on monetary policy, the subject of the next chapter.

Foreign trade and output determination

We now complete our model of output determination by adding the role of other countries in aggregate demand. Figure 11-10 shows UK exports X and imports Z since 1950.

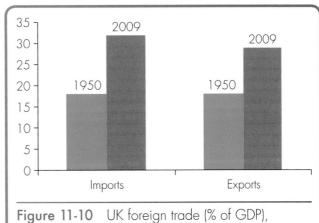

Figure 11-10 UK foreign trade (% of GDP), 1950–2006

Globalization means that both exports and imports have risen substantially. Like other countries, the UK now trades more than ever before. Although exports and imports are large relative to GDP, net exports $X - Z$ are usually small.

The **trade balance** is the value of net exports. When exports exceed imports, the economy has a trade surplus. When imports exceed exports, it has a trade deficit.

When a household spends more than its income, it runs down its assets (bank accounts, stocks and shares) or runs up its debts (overdrafts) to finance this deficit. Similarly, a country with a trade deficit must reduce its net foreign assets to finance this deficit. Net exports $X - Z$ demand adds to aggregate demand, which becomes $AD = C + I + G + X - Z$.

Desired injections are now $[I + G + X]$ and desired leakages $[S + NT + Z]$. Spending on imports is income for foreign producers. It leaks out of the UK circular flow between firms and households.

What determines desired exports and imports? Export demand reflects what is happening in foreign economies, which is largely unrelated to domestic output. Like other injections G and I, initially we treat export demand X as autonomous, or independent of domestic output. Imports from abroad may be raw materials for domestic production or items consumed by UK households, such as a Japanese TV or French wine. Demand for imports rises when domestic income and output rise.

The **marginal propensity to import (MPZ)** is the fraction of each extra pound of national income that domestic residents want to spend on extra imports.

Like the government budget, the trade balance varies with fluctuations in domestic income. Higher output and income raise imports, but leave exports unaffected. Hence, at low output, net exports are positive. There is a trade *surplus* with the rest of the world. At high output, there is a trade *deficit* and net exports are negative.

In Figure 11-11, the horizontal line $I + G + X$ shows desired injections. The upsloping line $S + NT + Z$ is desired leakages. Equilibrium output Y^* makes desired leakages equal to desired injections.

The multiplier in an open economy

With a third leakage through imports Z, an open economy has planned leakages $(S + NT + Z)$ that are even more responsive to output than in our previous discussion. The line for planned leakages in Figure 11-11 is steeper than for planned leakages $(S + NT)$ in Figure 11-9, which in turn is steeper than for planned saving S in Figure 11-6.

The steeper the planned leakages line, the smaller is the effect on equilibrium output of any given upward shift in planned injections. The output multiplier is large in a closed economy with no government and much smaller in an open economy with a government sector.

Even so, a rise in planned injections, from $[I + G + X]_0$ to $[I + G + X]_1$, raises equilibrium output a bit, from to Y_0^* to Y_1^*. This extra output induces extra saving, extra tax revenue and extra imports. Because of all these extra leakages, aggregate output does not increase very much.

Conversely, a higher savings rate, a higher tax rate or a higher marginal propensity to import makes the planned leakages line steeper, reducing equilibrium output. By making leakages higher than before, aggregate demand and equilibrium output are reduced.

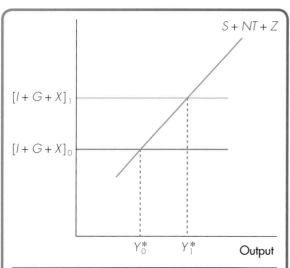

Figure 11-11 Higher desired injections raise equilibrium output

Maths 11-1

Sector balances must offset one another

We measure, and therefore define, national income and output Y to equal $[C + I + G + X - Z]$, and we measure and define saving S residually as the part of income, net of taxes, that is not consumed, so that $S = Y - T - C$. Putting these two together,

$$(G - T) + (X - Z) = (S - I) \tag{1}$$

Equation (1) promises us that the government deficit $G - T$ plus the trade surplus with the foreign sector $X - Z$ must equal the net saving (saving minus investment) of the private sector. For the year ending in September 2011, the UK government's fiscal deficit was 8.8 per cent of GDP; the deficit with foreigners was 2.4 per cent, leaving a private sector surplus of 6.4 per cent. Households were in surplus by a modest 0.9 per cent, so the rest actually came from companies, which had a whopping surplus of 5.5 per cent.

In this book, we tend to focus only on household saving and consumption by households. Normally, companies invest most of what they save. However, when companies are pessimistic about the future, they sharply reduce investment and allow their revenues to pile up in the bank as accumulated saving. This is another consequence of the exceptional circumstances created by the financial crisis and its lingering aftermath.

Paradoxically, at a time of financial fragility among both governments and households, it is companies who are flush with money. Not banks – they still hold plenty of dubious assets that could still prove worthless if the financial crisis returns again – but industrial and commercial companies. Investors looking for a safe place for their funds having been buying corporate debt in the second-hand market, figuring that this is a pretty safe investment.

There are two final implications of the inevitable arithmetic. First, governments around the world are promising to reduce their budget deficits. In the aggregate, foreign surpluses must sum to zero across countries. The planet can only have a trade deficit if it trades with Mars. Hence, success in rebalancing world fiscal positions can come about only if the private sector *reduces* its current net surplus by the same amount as governments reduce their net deficit. Firms and households need to start spending again.

Second, current government deficits are as much the *consequence* of a collapse of private spending as they are of profligacy in the public sector itself. Lower private spending has reduced output and tax revenues, and required higher welfare benefits as unemployment increases.

Import spending and jobs

Do imports steal domestic jobs? Cutting imports raises aggregate demand $[C + I + G + X - Z]$ and creates extra domestic output and jobs, a conclusion confirmed by Figure 11-9. A downward shift in the line for planned leakages would raise equilibrium output.

This view is correct, but dangerous. Other things equal, higher spending on domestic rather than foreign goods *will* raise demand for domestic goods. But import restrictions are dangerous because they may induce retaliation by other countries, which cuts demand for our exports, thereby reducing aggregate demand, planned injections and equilibrium output. In the end, nobody gets more jobs, but world trade shrinks, which hurts everyone.

Case study 11-1   Globalization and international trade

As the global economy becomes more interconnected, to which countries does the UK now export? This figure provides a snapshot for 2011. The numbers in blue show the value of exports to particular countries, and the orange (dark blue) circles show how much higher (lower) this was than in the previous year. £31.7 billion of UK exports still go to the US, but this amount is growing only slowly over time, up just 2.7 per cent from the year before. The Eurozone is now a much more important trading partner, with Germany accounting for £27.5 billion of UK exports, France £18.9 billion, and Netherlands and Belgium together £31.7 billion. When it comes to international trade, countries trade especially strongly with their nearest neighbours. Although trade with emerging market economies is growing much more rapidly, it begins from a much smaller baseline. Hence, in 2011, UK trade with China accounted for only £7 billion of UK exports, and exports to India only £4.6 billion.

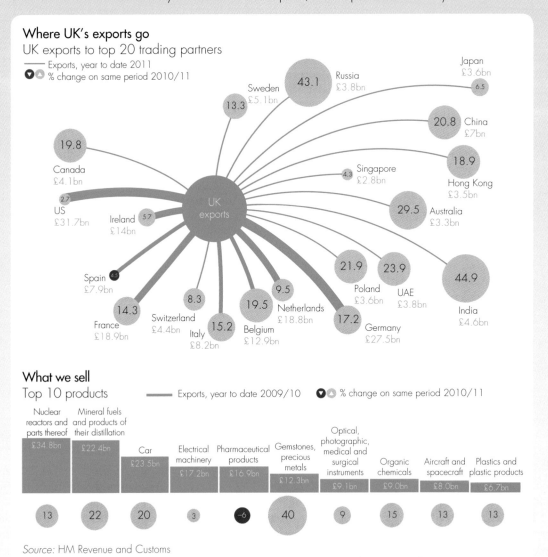

Where UK's exports go
UK exports to top 20 trading partners
— Exports, year to date 2011
⬤⬤ % change on same period 2010/11

Japan £3.6bn — 6.5
Russia £3.8bn
Sweden £5.1bn — 13.3
43.1
China £7bn — 20.8
Canada £4.1bn — 19.8
Singapore £2.8bn — 4.3
Hong Kong £3.5bn — 18.9
US £31.7bn — 2.7
Ireland £14bn — 5.7
UK exports
Australia £3.3bn — 29.5
Spain £7.9bn — 4.3
Poland £3.6bn — 21.9
UAE £3.8bn — 23.9
India £4.6bn — 44.9
France £18.9bn — 14.3
Switzerland £4.4bn — 8.3
Italy £8.2bn — 15.2
Belgium £12.9bn — 19.5
Netherlands £18.8bn — 9.5
Germany £27.5bn — 17.2

What we sell
Top 10 products — Exports, year to date 2009/10   ⬤⬤ % change on same period 2010/11

Nuclear reactors and parts thereof £34.8bn — 13
Mineral fuels and products of their distillation £22.4bn — 22
Car £23.5bn — 20
Electrical machinery £17.2bn — 3
Pharmaceutical products £16.9bn — -6
Gemstones, precious metals £12.3bn — 40
Optical, photographic, medical and surgical instruments £9.1bn — 9
Organic chemicals £9.0bn — 15
Aircraft and spacecraft £8.0bn — 13
Plastics and plastic products £6.7bn — 13

Source: HM Revenue and Customs

In macroeconomic terms, this means that UK aggregate demand depends most strongly on exports to the Eurozone and hence on how well these countries are doing economically. When the Eurozone expands, it imports more goods from everyone, including from the UK; when it contracts, it demands less imports and hence UK exports are likely to suffer. Next most important for UK exporting is the economic performance of the US.

UK aggregate demand depends less directly on what is happening in China, but of course there are also indirect effects. If Chinese economic growth slows, not only does this mean fewer Chinese imports from the UK, it also means fewer from other countries such as the US and the Eurozone. Lower exports to China from the US and the Eurozone lead to lower aggregate demand, as a result of which their demand for imports falls. Hence the UK loses out directly because it exports less to China, but also indirectly because it exports less to the US and the Eurozone. The more interconnected the world, the harder it is to keep track of all these indirect linkages.

We can think about UK imports in exactly the same way. Data from Her Majesty's Revenue and Customs shows that in 2011 the UK imported £41 billion of goods and services from Germany, £25 billion from the US and £24 billion from China. As with exports, the UK's biggest trading bloc for imports is the Eurozone as a whole. Notice that China features much more strongly in UK imports than it does in UK exports. A UK recession will therefore directly reduce aggregate demand most in the Eurozone, the US and China. The full effect will also depend on all the indirect effects, such as the consequence of lower aggregate demand in the Eurozone then feeding back on its import demand from other countries, which in turn will experience lower demand for their exports.

 ## Interest rates, aggregate demand and output

In this chapter, we have explained why short-run equilibrium output can fluctuate, and how fiscal policy can affect the level of output. What about monetary policy?

Monetary policy is the decision by the central bank about what interest rate to set.

In the UK, the central bank is the Bank of England, which acts on behalf of the government.

Figure 11-12 shows the behaviour of actual or nominal interest rates in the UK from the start of the Blair government in 1997 to 2011. However, part of the interest rate is simply to allow lenders to keep pace with inflation. For example, if the nominal interest rate is 10 per cent and inflation is 6 per cent, the real interest rate is only 4 per cent.

The **nominal interest rate** is the actual or monetary cost of borrowing, and reward for lending, during the period. The **real interest rate**, the difference between the nominal interest rate and inflation, is what measures the real cost of borrowing and the real return on lending.

Figure 11-12 shows annual inflation (in orange), nominal interest rates per annum (in turquoise), and hence (in blue) the real interest rate, the difference between the nominal interest rate and the corresponding inflation rate in the same period. During 1997–2007, real interest rates fell not because nominal interest rates were lower but because inflation had risen.

Figure 11-12 also shows the dramatic policy response to the financial crash. Nominal interest rates were slashed to 0.5 per cent in an effort to stave off the worst of the recession and get the economy moving again. At the same time, after a little downward blip, inflation actually rose after 2009 because China and other emerging markets had resumed growth and had a thirst for imports of raw materials, particularly oil and minerals, thereby bidding up the world prices of these commodities.

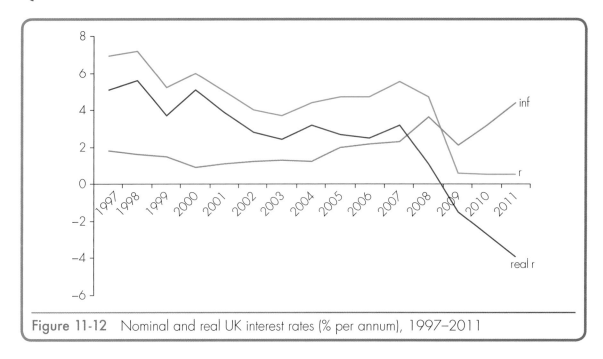

Figure 11-12 Nominal and real UK interest rates (% per annum), 1997–2011

Figure 11-12 shows that the real interest rate became heavily negative after 2009. This meant that borrowing was not just cheap, but that people were actually being paid to borrow. Borrowing at 0.5 per cent and then watching the price of your products rise by 4 per cent yielded a profit on the debt itself. Conversely, the pain for lenders was not merely that the nominal interest rate was 0.5 per cent. Worse, with the cost of living increasing by 4 per cent, it would have taken a nominal interest rate of 4 per cent simply to allow borrowers to break even in real terms. The negative real interest rate meant that lenders were making substantial losses in real terms on their loans. They would have been much better off buying commodities such as gold or copper and enjoying the inflationary increase in the price of these assets.

Central banks, of course, only set the nominal or actual interest rate. They do not set the real interest rate directly. For any given inflation rate, a higher nominal interest rate implies a higher real interest rate. Of course, if the central bank can forecast inflation, any decision about which nominal interest rate to set is implicitly a decision about what real interest rate to create. We now explain why higher real interest rates are likely to reduce aggregate demand.

Interest rates and consumption demand

Changes in interest rates have two effects on household decisions. The *substitution effect* makes everybody want to consume less today because the relative reward for saving has risen. The *income effect* also makes people consume less if initially they were borrowers. Higher interest rates make borrowers poorer, so that they have to consume less. Both effects reduce consumption demand by borrowers.

However, higher interest rates make lenders *richer*. For them, the income effect makes them consume *more* today, whereas the substitution effect – a more attractive return on saving than before – makes them spend *less* today. For lenders, the effect of higher interest rates on consumption demand is ambiguous. Aggregating borrowers and lenders, higher interest rates *reduce* consumption demand. Moreover, the more households have already run up large debts on mortgages and credit cards, the stronger the borrower effect will be, and the more a change in interest rates will affect consumption demand.

Interest rates and investment demand

We began this chapter by treating investment demand as given. Then we introduced the accelerator model, which argues that changes in output growth affect the level of investment demand. But interest rates also matter. Higher real interest rates raise the cost of investment by increasing the opportunity cost of the funds tied up in a new capital good. Other things equal, this reduces investment demand by firms.

At any instant there are many investment projects that a firm *could* undertake. Suppose it ranks these projects, from the most profitable to the least profitable. At a high interest rate, only a few projects earn enough to cover depreciation and the opportunity cost of funds employed. As the interest rate falls, more and more projects are profitable to undertake.

For a given rate of output growth, Figure 11-13 plots the investment demand schedule II showing how a lower interest rate raises investment demand. If the interest rate rises from r_0 to r_1, desired investment falls from I_0 to I_1.

> The **investment demand schedule** shows desired investment at each interest rate.

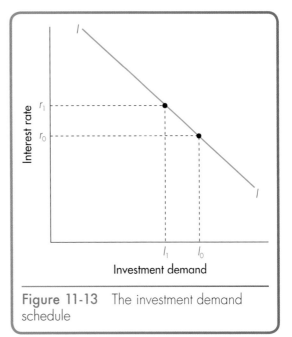

Figure 11-13   The investment demand schedule

The height of schedule II depends on the cost of new capital goods, and the stream of profits to which they give rise. A higher price of new capital goods ties up more money, raising the opportunity cost of the funds employed. Investment demand is lower at any interest rate, shifting the investment demand schedule II downwards. Similarly, more pessimism about future demand reduces the flow of likely profits from new investment, again shifting the entire investment demand schedule downwards.

The slope of the investment demand schedule II depends mainly on the life of the asset. For short-lived capital goods, high rates of depreciation dominate the cost of investment. Changes in interest rates may only have a small effect on investment demand. However, for long-lived capital goods, with low depreciation rates, the interest cost of funds used is the main cost of investment, and investment demand is more sensitive to interest rates.

Hence, the II schedule is flatter for long-lived assets, but could be quite steep for short-lived capital assets. When the dotcom bubble burst, central banks worried that interest rate cuts might not help the sector recover quickly from excess capacity in the computer servers that handle email traffic and data transmission. With high rates of depreciation resulting from rapid technical obsolescence, changes in interest rates and the cost of funds tied up had only a small effect on demand for new computer servers.

Inventory investment

There are two reasons why firms *plan* to hold inventories of raw materials, partly finished goods and finished goods awaiting sale.

First, the firm may be speculating, or betting on future price rises. Second, firms may plan to hold stocks to avoid costly changes in production levels. Suppose demand for the firm's output suddenly rises. A firm would have to pay big overtime payments to meet an upsurge in its order book. It is cheaper to carry some stocks in reserve with which to meet an upswing in demand. Similarly, in a temporary downturn, it is cheaper to maintain production and stockpile unsold goods than to incur redundancy payments, only to re-hire workers in the next upswing.

As with physical capital, the cost of holding inventories is depreciation (and storage costs) plus the opportunity cost of the funds tied up. The investment demand schedule II in Figure 11-13 is thus also relevant to planned investment in stock-building. Other things equal, a higher interest rate raises the cost of holding inventories, and reduces desired investment in inventories.

Thus, higher interest rates reduce all types of investment demand, a move left along the investment demand schedule. A rise (fall) in the cost of capital goods or fall (rise) in expected future profit opportunities shifts this schedule down (up). Since ideas about future profits can change a lot, the investment demand schedule also shifts around quite a lot.

Interest rates and equilibrium output

By cutting interest rates, monetary policy can boost output and income. Suppose the central bank reduces interest rates. With given wages and prices, this is both a reduction in nominal interest rates and in real interest rates. Lower real interest rates raise investment demand and autonomous consumption demand (the part of consumption demand not explained by output and income). Hence, in Figure 11-14(a), aggregate demand rises, raising equilibrium output.

Equivalently, lower interest rates increase desired investment at any output, but also, by raising desired consumption, they reduce the desire to save at any output. Thus desired injections rise and desired leakages fall. In Figure 11-14(b), equilibrium output rises to raise desired leakages by enough to equal the new higher level of desired injections. The vertical rise in desired injections captures the effect on lower interest rates in raising investment demand. The smaller leftward shift in desired leakages captures the effect of lower interest rates on desired saving. For both reasons, output has to rise to move the economy along the desired leakages curve until it intersects the higher level of desired injections.

Demand management and the policy mix

> **Demand management** is the use of monetary and fiscal policy to stabilize output near the level of potential output.

Monetary and fiscal policy are not interchangeable. First, interest rates can be changed frequently, whereas changing tax rates and spending levels is more complicated and is undertaken less frequently. Second, even in the longer run, monetary and fiscal policies affect aggregate demand through different routes and have different implications for the *composition* of aggregate demand.

A given level of aggregate demand can be achieved either by loose or expansionary fiscal policy (high government spending, low tax rates) combined with tight monetary policy (high interest rates); or by

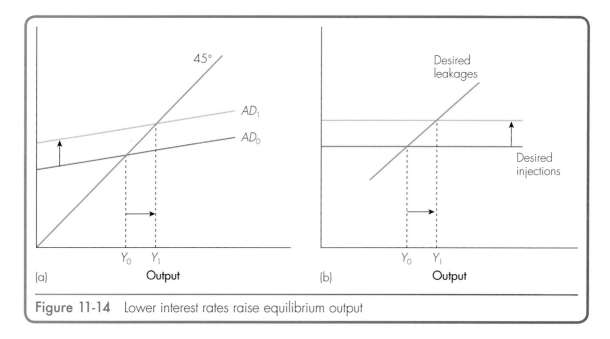

Figure 11-14 Lower interest rates raise equilibrium output

tight or contractionary fiscal policy (low government spending, high tax rates) combined with loose monetary policy (low interest rates).

Loose fiscal policy with easy monetary policy will mean that the public sector is large (high government spending) but the private sector is smaller (high interest rates reduce investment and consumption). Tight fiscal policy plus easy monetary policy will mean that the public sector is smaller but the private sector larger. With low interest rates, the level of investment may also be permanently higher. Thus, different combinations of monetary and fiscal policy affect not only the level of output and spending, but also its composition across sectors.

Box 11-4

Policy conflicts inside the Eurozone

We hear a lot of news about the plight of Greece, Spain, Italy, Portugal and Ireland. Their debts, both government and private sector, are large. Because of previous laxity, their prices and wages have risen to an extent that makes them uncompetitive within the Eurozone at its current exchange rate. Their governments cannot stimulate their economies – government finances are already precarious – nor can they expect much additional demand from exports. Life looks bleak.

Yet for the Eurozone as a whole, their overall debt position is not too bad. Nor does the Eurozone as a whole have a massive trade deficit. The euro exchange rate is not inappropriate for the group as a whole. How can this be?

If the aggregate position is broadly on track, and one subset of members has large deficits, then arithmetically another subset of members must have substantial trade surpluses and a reasonably sound fiscal position. That subset is called Germany (much the largest country in the Eurozone) and its smaller neighbour, the Netherlands.

The countries in trouble would like Germany to create a fiscal stimulus, thereby sucking in imports from Greece, Spain and the others. Moreover, if the overall Eurozone trade balance thereby deteriorated (because some of the extra demand would go on goods from outside the Eurozone), a depreciation of the euro would help all its member states become more competitive.

So why doesn't Germany do what it is being begged to do by its European partners? Germany's vision is that all other countries should adjust to the German model – be austere, acquire competitiveness through hard work and high productivity, and then export. Meeting the others halfway would imply that the overall Eurozone economy converged on a higher inflation rate than Germans would like, and with higher debt levels than Germans would like.

In this tug of war, most of the political power resides with the surplus countries, who are not being forced by markets to adjust, at the expense of deficit countries, who are under enormous market pressure if they fail to make progress.

This chart shows the history of the crisis and the 2012 projections from the OECD in its December 2011 report. Data are for General Government annual deficits as a percentage of GDP. The trends assume that governments manage to stick to promised austerity programmes, which is far from certain. The chart corroborates several aspects of the preceding discussion but also makes some new points.

▶

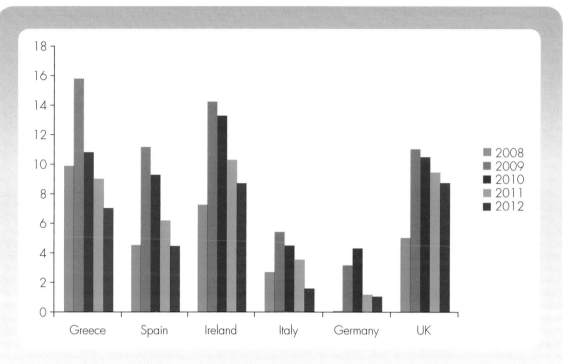

First, Germany, as always, has been extremely responsible and fiscally conservative. Second, Italy and Spain were well behaved up to 2008: they are in trouble now not because their governments had previously spent too much but because the financial crash led to market panic and to output reductions that caused falls in their tax revenue. They were relatively innocent victims of the crash.

Third, by any measure, Greece, Ireland and to some extent the UK were exposed even before the crash took place, having substantial fiscal deficits even in 2008, and very large ones in 2009. All three countries have had to work hard to convince markets that they will take the necessary action to put things right. From its position outside the Eurozone, the UK has not been bound by the policies of others. But it has had to convince speculators to stay away.

Recap

- The government buys some output directly. It also levies taxes and makes transfers.
- Net tax revenue rises with income, reducing the marginal propensity to consume out of national income. This acts as an automatic stabilizer by reducing the value of the multiplier.
- A rise in government purchases raises desired injections, aggregate demand and equilibrium output. A higher tax rate raises desired leakages, reduces aggregate demand and reduces equilibrium output.
- To stabilize aggregate demand and output, the government can set higher net tax rates, thus enhancing automatic stabilizers, or can make discretionary adjustments to government

spending and tax rates to offset other shocks to aggregate demand. Discretionary changes are hard to implement quickly.

- Exports are an injection, adding to demand for domestic output. Imports are a leakage, domestic income spent on foreign output.
- Export demand is autonomous spending unrelated to domestic income. The marginal propensity to import MPZ is the amount an extra unit of national income adds to import demand.
- Imports further reduce the value of the multiplier, and are another automatic stabilizer.
- Higher export demand raises equilibrium output. Higher import demand reduces it.
- The trade surplus (net exports) falls when domestic income rises. Higher export demand raises the trade surplus, but higher import demand reduces it.
- A higher interest rate reduces consumption demand by borrowers but its effect on lenders is ambiguous. In the aggregate, consumption demand falls, especially if consumers have already borrowed a lot.
- The investment demand schedule shows how a higher interest rate reduces investment demand by raising the cost of funds for new capital goods. Higher interest rates move the economy down this schedule. Higher expected future profits, or a lower price of new capital goods, shift the investment demand schedule upwards.
- A lower interest rate raises aggregate demand and equilibrium output.
- A given output can be attained by easy monetary policy and tight fiscal policy or by the converse. In the former case, interest rates are lower and private spending higher.

Review questions

To check your answers to these questions, go to pages 389–90.

1 Consumption demand C is given by $C = 0.7Y$ and investment demand $I = 45$.
(a) Draw a diagram showing the AD schedule. (b) If actual output is 100, what unplanned actions occur? (c) What is equilibrium output? (d) What is the saving function? (e) Draw a diagram showing planned injections and planned leakages. (f) Hence, find equilibrium output. How does your answer compare with your answer to (c)?

2 $I = 150$. If people become thriftier, the consumption function shifts from $C = 0.7Y$ to $C = 0.5Y$. (a) What happens to equilibrium income? (b) What happens to the equilibrium proportion of income saved? (c) Show the change in equilibrium income in a saving investment diagram. (d) Can you show the same change in a diagram using AD and the 45° line?

EASY

3 Which part of actual investment is not included in aggregate demand? Why not?

4   (a) Find equilibrium income when $I = 400$ and $C = 0.8Y$. (b) Would output be higher or lower if the consumption function were $C = 100 + 0.7Y$?

5   Why are these statements wrong? (a) If people save more, investment will rise and hence output will increase. (b) Lower output leads to lower spending and yet lower output. The economy can spiral downwards forever.

6   Equilibrium output in a closed economy is 1000. $C = 800$ and $I = 80$. (a) What level is G? (b) I now rises by 50, and the MPS out of national income is 0.2. What are the new equilibrium levels of C, I, G and Y? (c) Suppose instead G had risen by 50. Would the effect on output have been the same? (d) What level of G makes equilibrium output 1200?

7   In equilibrium, desired savings equal desired investment. True or false? Explain.

8   Why does the government tax people when it can borrow to finance its spending?

9   Suppose $MPZ = 0.4$, $t = 0.2$ and $MPS = 0.2$. Investment demand rises by 136. (a) What happens to the equilibrium level of income and to net exports? (b) Suppose exports, not investment, rise by 100. How does the trade balance change?

10   Why are these statements wrong? (a) The budget raised taxes and spending by equal amounts. It was a neutral budget for output. (b) Countries with a trade deficit during an output boom are irresponsible.

11   Is fiscal policy a good instrument with which to fine-tune aggregate demand, maintaining it at the level of potential output? What prevents the government continuously maintaining aggregate demand at this level?

12   People not previously allowed to borrow get credit cards with a £500 borrowing limit. What happens to the consumption function? Why?

13   Consumers tighten their belts, put in a spurt of saving and pay off many of their credit card debts. How does this affect the effectiveness of monetary policy in future years?

14   Suppose firms expect a huge boom in a couple of years. What happens to investment and output today? How is the Bank of England likely to respond?

15   Recalculate the table in Box 11-3, assuming now that a 1-unit rise in I_t induces a 1-unit rise in Y_t, and a 1-unit rise in $[Y_{t-1} - Y_{t-2}]$ induces a 1-unit rise in I_t. The economy again begins at $Y_t = 100$, and the initial shock is a rise in I_t from 0 to 10.

16   Why are these statements incorrect? (a) Consumer spending cannot rise if disposable income has fallen. (b) Whatever the monetary policy, fiscal policy can always compensate.

17   **Essay question** Following an acute financial crisis in which the Bank of England came under considerable stress, the UK decided to throw in its lot with continental Europe, abolish the pound and adopt the euro. The European Central Bank, which now sets interest rates, then happens to raise interest rates even though UK output is already below potential output. What happens to UK aggregate demand? Ideally, what should UK fiscal policy then do? Would there be any difficulty in doing so?

EASY

DIFFICULT

18 **Essay question** 'Large government deficits were the consequence of the financial crash not the cause of it.' Explain the logic behind this claim, and evaluate the extent to which it is correct. Does the answer depend on whether you are thinking about Greece or Spain?

DIFFICULT

Online Learning Centre

To help you grasp the key concepts of this chapter check out the extra resources posted on the Online Learning Centre at www.mcgraw-hill.co.uk/textbooks/begg.

There are additional case studies, self-test questions, practice exam questions with answers and a graphing tool.

Interest rates, money and inflation

Thirty years ago, the main reason to study money and banking was to understand inflation and interest rates. These are still important, but since 2007 everyone is acutely aware that the world economy has been sent into a deep and protracted period of stagnant output because the banks made mistakes. This chapter explores the role of money and banking in modern economies and the challenges thereby created for policy makers.

 ## Money and banking

In the previous chapter, we simply assumed that the central bank can set whatever interest rate it chooses. How does it do this? This chapter explores the financial system in more detail. In so doing, we explore what is special about a monetary economy, and discover the relation between money, growth and inflation.

In songs and popular language, 'money' is a symbol of success, a source of crime and makes the world go round. Dogs' teeth in the Admiralty Islands, sea shells in parts of Africa, gold in the nineteenth century: all are examples of money. What matters is not the commodity used but the social convention that it is accepted, without question, as a means of payment.

> **Money** is any generally accepted means of payment for delivery of goods or settlement of debt. It is the **medium of exchange**. A **barter economy** has no medium of exchange. Goods are simply swapped for other goods.

In exchanging goods or labour services for money, we accept money not to consume it directly but for its later use in buying what we really want. Imagine an economy without money. In a barter economy, if you want an economics textbook, not only must you find someone wanting rid of one, you must have what that person wants in exchange. People spend a lot of time and effort finding others with whom to swap. Time and effort are scarce resources. Using money makes trading cheaper and more efficient. Society can use the time and effort for better purposes. The World Bank's *1989 World Development Report* gives two nice examples about monetary versus barter economies:

Some years since, Mademoiselle Zelie, a singer, gave a concert in the Society Islands in exchange for a third part of the receipts. When counted, her share was found to consist of 3 pigs, 23 turkeys, 44 chickens, 5000 cocoa nuts, besides considerable quantities of bananas, lemons and oranges . . . as Mademoiselle could not consume any considerable portion of the receipts herself it became necessary in the meantime to feed the pigs and poultry with the fruit.

W. S. Jevons (1898)

In this city of Kanbula [Beijing] is the mint of the Great Khan, who may truly be said to possess the secret of the alchemists, as he has the art of producing money. . . . He causes the bark to be stripped from mulberry trees . . . made into paper . . . cut into pieces of money of different sizes. The act of counterfeiting is punished as a capital offence. This paper currency is circulated in every part of the Great Khan's domain. All his subjects receive it without hesitation because, wherever their business may call them, they can dispose of it again in the purchase of merchandise they may require.

The Travels of Marco Polo, Book II

Other functions of money

British prices are quoted in pounds; American prices are quoted in dollars. However, there are exceptions. During rapid inflation, people may quote prices in foreign currency even if they still take payment in local currency, the medium of exchange.

> The **unit of account** is the unit in which prices are quoted and accounts are kept.

Nobody would accept money as payment for goods today if the money was going to be worthless when they try to spend it later. But money is not the only store of value. Houses, paintings and interest-bearing bank accounts all store value. Storing value is necessary but is not the key feature of money, which is its role as a medium of exchange.

> Money is also a **store of value**, available for future purchases.

Different kinds of money

In prisoner-of-war camps, cigarettes served as money. In the nineteenth century, money was mainly gold and silver coins. These are examples of *commodity money* – ordinary goods with industrial uses (gold) and consumption uses (cigarettes) that also serve as a medium of exchange. But society need not waste valuable commodities by using them as money.

> A **token money** has a value as money that greatly exceeds its cost of production or value in consumption.

A £10 note is worth far more as money than as a 7.5 × 14 cm piece of high-quality paper. By collectively agreeing to use token money, society economizes on the scarce resources required to produce money. A token money survives only if private production is illegal. Society also enforces the use of token money by making it *legal tender*. In law, it must be accepted as a means of payment. Modern economies supplement token money by IOU money.

An **IOU money** is a medium of exchange based on the debt of a private bank.

A bank deposit is IOU money. You pay for goods with a cheque, which the bank must honour when a shopkeeper presents it. Bank deposits are a medium of exchange, a generally accepted means of payment.

Modern banking

When you deposit your coat in the theatre cloakroom, you do not expect the theatre to rent out your coat during the performance. Banks lend out most of the coats in their cloakroom. A theatre would have to get your particular coat back on time, which might be tricky. A bank finds it easier because one piece of money looks just like another.

Bank reserves are cash in the bank to meet possible withdrawals by depositors. The **reserve ratio** is the ratio of reserves to deposits.

Bank assets are mainly loans to firms and households, but also financial securities (promises of future payments), such as bills and bonds, issued by governments and firms. Since many securities are very liquid – easily sellable at a predictable price – banks hold plenty of liquid securities that can be sold quickly if the bank needs money in a hurry. In contrast, many bank loans to firms and households are illiquid: the bank cannot easily get its money back quickly. Yet because there are now so many liquid securities available, modern banks get by with tiny cash reserves in the vault. Why hold cash when it is possible to hold interest-bearing liquid assets instead?

Banks' liabilities are mainly sight and time deposits. Sight deposits mean a depositor can withdraw money 'on sight' with no notice; chequing accounts are sight deposits. Time deposits, which pay higher interest rates, need a period of notice before withdrawing money. Banks have more time to organize the sale of some of their high-interest assets in order to have the cash available to meet these withdrawals. Apart from deposits, the other liabilities of banks are various 'money market instruments', short-term and highly liquid borrowing by banks, often from other banks.

The business of banking

A bank is in business to make profits by lending and borrowing. To get money in, the bank offers favourable terms to potential depositors. UK banks increasingly offer interest on sight deposits, and they offer better interest rates on time deposits. Money from these deposits is then lent by banks, either as advances (overdrafts) to other households and firms, at high interest rates, or by buying securities such as long-term government bonds. Some is more prudently invested in liquid assets, which pay less interest but can be easily sold if necessary. Some is held as cash, the most liquid asset of all.

The bank has a diversified portfolio of investments. Some of this income pays interest to depositors, the rest is for the bank's expenses and profits. Individual depositors have neither the time nor the expertise to decide which of these loans or investments to make.

UK banks' cash reserves are only about 2 per cent of the sight deposits that could be withdrawn at any time. At short notice, banks can cash in *other* liquid assets easily and for a predictable amount. The skill in running a bank is judging how much to hold in liquid assets, including cash, and how much to lend in less liquid assets that earn higher interest rates.

Usually, banks can rely on the dependability of the market for liquid assets, in which assets can be bought and sold easily, cheaply and at predictable prices. But occasionally, things go wrong. And when this happens, banks can get into trouble. This is what happened during the credit crunch that began in 2007.

During a **credit crunch**, traditional sources of lending dry up because potential lenders fear that the borrower may face an acute crisis and then become unable to repay the loan.

Traditionally, one of the most liquid markets was for interbank credit. Banks with surplus funds would lend to banks in need of funds. Huge amounts were traded. Once banks began to wonder if other banks might be in financial trouble, they became nervous of such lending and the market effectively shut down. Putting it differently, assets that had previously been viewed as highly liquid suddenly became highly illiquid. Nobody wanted to trade in them any more.

The UK bank most exposed to this change was Northern Rock, which had borrowed in short-term liquid markets in order to lend aggressively in the long-term loans market for mortgages for residential housing. When its short-term loans ran out and could not be refinanced, the Rock went bust and had to be nationalized by the UK government. It was not until 2012 that the government was able to resell part of this shareholding to Virgin Money.

Before the credit crunch, the gap between the interest rate at which a bank would lend to another bank and the rate which it had to pay to borrow from another bank was around 0.1 per cent. At the height of the credit crunch, this was around 1.45 per cent, nearly 15 times the normal cost. Indeed, when banks had surplus cash, they were not prepared to lend to other banks at a 6 per cent interest rate but happy to lend it to the Bank of England at 4 per cent. This provides some indication of the extent to which banks were worried about the health of their fellow banks.

Case study 12-1   The subprime crisis and its aftermath

Most countries had a house price explosion around 2005–06. Inflation appeared to have been conquered, interest rates were low, and borrowing did not look too risky. Many of those working in the financial sector – whether in banks or in property – were receiving bonuses for doing a large number of deals. There were strong incentives to dream up new products and find new lines of business.

In the US, one of these new products was the subprime mortgage, a housing loan to a low-income high-risk person who had previously been unable to borrow in order to buy a house. Most of these mortgages were at variable interest rates: although initially low and 'affordable', they could subsequently be raised if either general market interest rates rose or if lots of people started to default and it became necessary to build a larger risk premium into the interest rate. It is unclear how much of this was explained to the low-income people being signed up for first-time mortgages.

US house prices peaked in 2006. As they then fell, lenders got scared and began to raise mortgage interest rates, driving many of the poor to default. Suddenly, these subprime mortgages were worth a lot less than had been thought. And the crisis fed upon itself. The more scared people became, the more asset prices fell, validating the initial fears.

If mortgages had simply been issued by a few institutions specializing in loans for house purchases, the damage might have been quarantined. The US government would have had to decide whether to (a) let these particular institutions go bust or (b) inject taxpayers' money to prop them up.

Securitization transformed a local crisis into a global problem. Smart financiers, driven by the prospect of new business and big personal bonuses, had bundled lots of individual subprime mortgages into large bundles and sold them on to new buyers in London, Frankfurt and Mumbai. The market was convinced that this trick was a bit like insurance – although one poor subprime household might go bust, they would not all go bust together. Holding a large bundle made them safer, just as an insurance company pools the risk of individual burglary by having large numbers of clients. This was the alchemy of risk reduction. A recipe for profits and bonuses.

Two things went wrong. First, buyers of securitized mortgages had miscalculated. It was quite likely that circumstances could arise in which all subprime borrowers got into trouble at the same time – a fall in house prices, a fall in confidence, a rise in risk perception – likely to get all subprime borrowers into trouble, especially if they could barely afford the loan in the first place. So smart bankers in London, New York and other financial capitals had mispriced the risk: the securitized bundles were riskier than had been thought.

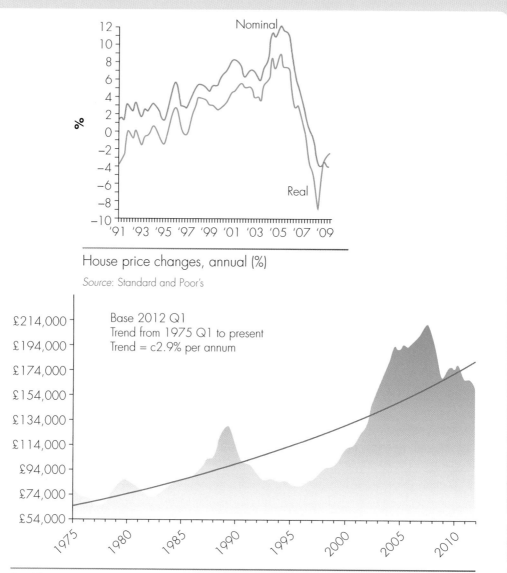

House price changes, annual (%)

Source: Standard and Poor's

Real house prices

Source: http://www.landregistry.gov.uk/houseprices

The charts above show the collapse of real (inflation-adjusted house prices), which began in 2006 in the US and in 2008 in the UK. For the UK, we also show the trend increase in real house prices since 1975, making clear how far above this trend the housing bubble had reached by 2008 and the sharp reductions thereafter.

Second, the perfect storm did indeed arise. As US house prices fell sharply, the chain of events was triggered. Banks found their assets worth much less than they had thought. Worse, the boards of the banks had not even realized the extent to which their bonus-hungry employees had exposed them to such large risks.

As the solvency of banks came into question, people became reluctant to lend to banks, and banks themselves became reluctant to lend to anyone else – aware of the potentially fatal hole in their balance sheet, banks prioritized using resources to rebuild their own reserves. The entire, apparently well-oiled, system of liquidity dried up as banks disappeared from the lending business. One way to see how dramatic this was is to examine interest rate spreads, the difference between the interest rate banks were charging for the few scarce loans they were prepared to make, and the interest rate at which banks could borrow from the Bank of England.

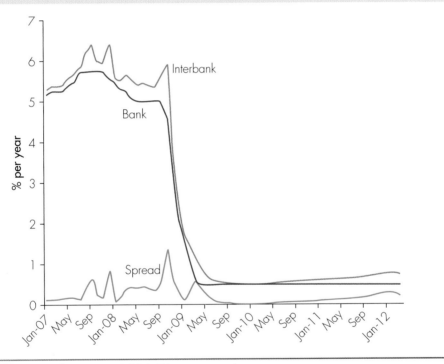

Interest rate spreads, 2007–2012 (% per annum)

Source: Bank of England

The figure above plots in blue the official bank rate, the interest rate at which commercial banks can borrow from the Bank of England, and in orange the interbank rate at which banks lend temporary excess funds to one another. In normal times, competition between banks means that the 'profit margin' between the lending rate and the borrowing rate is very small. Banks charging too much are quickly outcompeted by banks prepared to offer a better deal. This spread between the interbank rate at which banks lend and the bank rate at which they can borrow from the Bank of England is shown in turquoise.

The interest rate spread is a thermometer with which to monitor the health of the banking system. In a healthy system, banks feel confident, competition prevails and spreads are very small. When a crisis breaks out, spreads shoot up, raising the price to ration loans only to the very safest customers. And the volume of bank lending collapses. The figure above shows spreads rising in 2007 and more sharply in 2008–09. Notice that by September 2009 the crisis was largely over, though new concerns (based on possible defaults within the Eurozone) re-emerged in 2011–12.

The chronology of crisis (through UK spectacles)	
2006	US house prices start to fall, the subprime crisis begins, interest spreads edge up around the world, bank lending slows down, liquidity begins to evaporate.
2007	UK bank Northern Rock hits a liquidity crisis in September – not yet because its asset values have fallen (UK house prices still rising) – but because UK credit markets have dried up and the Rock cannot roll over its short-term loans. Borrowing short term to lend long term for housing loans is always a risky business. Crisis temporarily resolved once Bank of England agree to provide liquidity financing to Northern Rock.
2008	February – with UK house prices now having peaked, the market becomes worried not just about Northern Rock's ability to refinance its loans, but also about the value of its underlying assets. A full-blown insolvency crisis. UK government decides to nationalize the Rock.
	March – US investment bank Bear Sterns, which had pioneered the resale of bundles of mortgages and derivative products based on them, suffers an insolvency crisis. Competitor JPMorgan Chase agrees to buy Bear Sterns for a much reduced price. Getting competitors to take over failing banks is often a good way out, since no bankruptcy or severe dislocation ensues.
	September – US Treasury has to bail out Freddie Mac and Fannie Mae, the two largest mortgage lenders in the US.
	September 2008 – US investment bank giant Lehman Brothers is allowed to go bankrupt without US Treasury managing to arrange a satisfactory bail out. Arguably the single event that then triggered financial panic around the world, from which no country was immune.
	October – Royal Bank of Scotland, having overextended itself buying Dutch bank ABM AMRO at a price that subsequently proved much too high, faces a solvency crisis, temporarily resolved by UK Treasury taking 58 per cent stake in RBS.
2009	January – UK government persuades Lloyds bank to buy the potentially insolvent Halifax Bank of Scotland group. Lloyds' shareholders subsequently discover HBOS worth much less than they paid for it. The outcome appears good for the system but bad for Lloyds.
	UK taxpayer eventually has to take an 84 per cent stake in RBS to prevent it going bankrupt.
	Governments around the world gradually admit to the scale of government injections to bail out their banks. Since taxes are not raised to pay for this, the initial consequence is a huge jump in levels of government deficits and government debt.
2010	Where governments have taken large stakes in banks, the key issue will be how much of this money they eventually recover. If the assets are permanently bad, all the injection is needed to restore the banks' solvency. However, if there was an element of liquidity crisis, or if asset prices fell too much in the panic, it is possible that asset values will recover enough to allow substantial repayments by banks (or privatization of those that were nationalized). In the extreme case, governments might even eventually make some profits.
	Future behaviour of banks getting more cautious; changes in the regulation of banks being discussed.

2011	Having split Northern Rock into a 'good bank' and a 'bad bank', UK government agrees sale of good bank, and its associated high street branches, to Virgin Money. Still unable to sell RBS.
	A commission chaired by Sir John Vickers, Oxford economics professor and former chief economist of the Bank of England, recommends tackling the problem of banks being 'too big to fail' and hence holding the government hostage. The report stopped short of recommending that 'boring retail banking' and 'casino investment banking' be undertaken in separate companies, entailing the splitting up of existing banks, but did propose that retail banking and investment banking be separately ring-fenced within the company, and any implicit government guarantee being extended only to the retail banking part which is intrinsic to protection of the payments system.
	Private creditors of Greece are strong-armed into 'volunteering' to take a substantial writedown of the value of their loans.
	Mario Draghi, new governor of the European Central Bank, provides massive medium-term loans to European banks, preventing a lack of liquidity leading to another major crisis. This buys time and is hailed as a success. However, European governments continue to dither in providing a fundamental solution to the solvency problems of banks/governments, the two having become inseparable.

Banks as creators of money

The **money supply** is money in circulation (cash not in bank vaults) plus bank deposits on which cheques can be written.

For simplicity, suppose banks use a reserve ratio of 10 per cent. In Table 12-1, initially citizens have £1000 in cash, which is also the money supply. This cash is then paid into the banks. Banks have assets of £1000 cash and liabilities of £1000 deposits, which is money they owe to depositors. If banks were like cloakrooms, that would be the end of the story. However, since all deposits are not withdrawn daily, banks do not need them to be fully covered by cash in the bank.

In the third row, banks create £9000 of overdrafts. Think of this as loans to customers of £9000, an asset of the banks. But these are loans *of deposits*, against which cheques can be written, and hence also a liability of the banks. Now the banks have £10 000 of total deposits – the original £1000 of cash paid in, plus the £9000 deposits newly lent – and £10 000 of total assets, comprising £9000 to keep track of the loans plus £1000 cash in the vaults. The reserve ratio is now 10 per cent. It does not matter whether this ratio is imposed by law or is merely the profit-maximizing behaviour of banks balancing risk and reward.

Table 12-1 Money creation by the banking system

	Banks				Non-bank private sector			
	Assets		Liabilities		Monetary assets		Liabilities	
Initial		0		0	Cash	1000		0
Intermediate	Cash	1000	Deposits	1000	Deposits	1000		0
Final	Cash	1000	Deposits	10 000	Cash	0	Loans from banks	9000
	Loans	9000			Deposits	10 000		

How did banks create money? Originally, the money supply was £1000 of cash in circulation. When paid into bank vaults, it went out of circulation as money. The public instead got £1000 of bank deposits against which to write cheques. The extra bank reserves were then used to create new loans and deposits, and the public had £10 000 of deposits in chequing accounts. The money supply rose from £1000 to £10 000. Banks created money.

Box 12-1

A beginner's guide to financial markets

A *financial asset* is a piece of paper entitling the owner to a stream of income for a specified period. *Cash* is notes and coins, paying zero interest, but the most liquid asset of all. *Bills* are short-term financial assets paying no interest, but with a known repurchase date and a guaranteed repurchase price of £100. By buying it for less than £100, you earn a capital gain while holding the bill that gives a return similar to other market interest rates. Because bills have a short life, their price is never far below £100, and thus predictable. Bills are highly liquid.

Bank of England
© fazon1

Bonds are longer-term financial assets. A bond listed as Treasury 5% 2008 means that in 2008 the Treasury will buy it back for £100. Until then, the bondholder gets interest of £5 a year. Similarly, 2.5% Consolidated Stock (Consol) is a *perpetuity*, paying £2.5 a year forever. Buying it for £100, you get a return of 2.5 per cent a year. You might happily buy it for £100 if other assets yield 2.5 per cent a year. Suppose other interest rates now rise to 10 per cent. To resell your Consol, you must cut the price to £25. The new buyer then earns £2.5 a year on a £25 investment, matching the 10 per cent yield available on other assets. Bonds are less liquid than bills, not because they are difficult to buy and sell but because their future sale prices are less certain. Generally, the price of longer-term assets is more volatile.

Company shares (*equities*) earn dividends, the part of profits not retained by firms to buy new machinery and buildings. In bad years, dividends may be zero. Hence equities are risky and less liquid because share prices are volatile. Firms may even go bust, making the shares worthless. In contrast, government bonds are *gilt-edged* because the government can always pay.

The monetary base and the money multiplier

Cash is supplied by the *central bank*, which in the UK is the Bank of England. The government controls the issue of token money in a modern economy.

> The **monetary base** is the supply of cash, whether in private circulation or held in bank reserves. The **money multiplier** is the ratio of the money supply to the monetary base.

In our previous example, cash was £1000 and the money supply £10 000, so the money multiplier was 10. Suppose instead that banks operate on a 5 per cent reserve ratio. When £1000 cash is paid into the banks, they now create an extra £19 000 of new loans and deposits. Banks' assets are £1000 cash plus £19 000 loans, and their liabilities are £1000 deposits when the cash was paid in, plus £19 000 deposits as counterparts to new loans. Now a monetary base of £1000 leads to a money supply of £20 000. The money multiplier has risen to 20.

Hence, a lower reserve ratio means that more loans and deposits are created for any given cash in the vaults. The money multiplier is larger. Conversely, the more cash the public keeps under the bed, the less of the monetary base goes into bank vaults, and the lower is the money multiplier for any given reserve ratio. Without cash reserves, banks cannot create additional money.

Measures of money

The money supply is cash in circulation (outside banks) plus bank deposits. It sounds simple, but it is not. Two issues arise: which bank deposits, and why only bank deposits?

There is a spectrum of liquidity. Cash is completely liquid. Sight deposits (chequing accounts) are almost as liquid, and time deposits (savings accounts) only a little less liquid than that. Where people can make automatic transfers between savings and chequing accounts when the latter run low, savings deposits are as liquid as chequing accounts.

Until the 1980s everyone knew what a bank was, and whose deposits counted in the money supply. Financial deregulation has now blurred this distinction. Banks lend for house purchase, building societies (who used to lend only for house purchase) now issue cheque books, and even supermarkets are joining the banking business.

Different measures of money draw different lines in the continuous spectrum of liquidity, and include the deposits of different institutions. The narrowest measure is M0, the *wide monetary base*. M0 measures all cash plus the banks' own deposits with the Bank of England.

Wider measures of money ignore bank reserves but add various deposits to cash in circulation outside the banks. M1 adds sight deposits of banks. M3 also adds other banks' deposits. Adding also the deposits in building societies, we get the M4 measure of broad money.

Since we can no longer distinguish between banks and building societies, routine statistics are now published only for the narrow measure M0, and for the broad measure M4. Once we leave the monetary base, the first sensible place to stop is M4.

London remains a pioneer of financial innovation. Financial regulation has to keep up. In April 2006, the Bank of England decided to change the system of bank reserves. Henceforth, banks and building societies will keep reserves at the Bank of England, and choose a target level of reserves that they wish to hold. If they keep reserves close to the chosen target, the Bank of England will pay interest on these reserves to banks and building societies. Deviations from target will incur penalties.

Hence, in some circumstances the banking system will happily hold large amounts of interest-bearing reserves, which are now more like other assets in their portfolios. It no longer makes sense to publish statistics for M0 that combine non-interest-bearing cash held by the public and interest-bearing reserves held by the banks and building societies. Since 2006, UK monetary statistics refer only to cash in circulation outside the banking system, and to a wider M4 measure that also includes all deposits. Data are shown in Table 12-2.

Table 12-2 Narrow and broad UK money, sterling (£ billion), March 2012

Cash in circulation outside the banks	55
+ retail deposits in banks and building societies	1220
+ wholesale deposits in banks and building societies	782
= money supply M4	2057

Source: Bank of England

Interest rates and monetary policy

Founded in 1694, the Bank of England was not nationalized until 1947. Usually called 'the Bank', it issues banknotes, sets interest rates and is banker to the commercial banks and the government, whose deposits are liabilities of the Bank. The Bank's assets are government securities and loans to commercial banks. Unlike commercial banks, the Bank cannot go bankrupt. It can always print more money to meet any claims upon it.

> A **central bank** is responsible for printing money, setting interest rates and acting as banker to commercial banks and the government.

The Bank and the money supply

The money supply is partly a liability of the Bank (currency in private circulation) and partly a liability of banks (bank deposits). The Bank could affect the money supply through reserve requirements, the discount rate or open market operations.

Reserve requirements

A *required* reserve ratio is a *minimum* ratio of cash reserves to deposits that the central bank requires commercial banks to hold. Banks can hold more than the required cash reserves but not less. If their cash falls below this limit, they must immediately borrow cash, usually from the central bank, to restore their required reserve ratio.

If set above the reserve ratio that prudent banks would anyway have chosen, a reserve requirement reduces the creation of bank deposits by reducing the value of the money multiplier, reducing the money supply for any given monetary base.

The discount rate

The discount rate is the interest rate at which the Bank lends cash to commercial banks. By setting the discount rate at a penalty level above market interest rates, the Bank makes commercial banks hold larger cash reserves to reduce the risk of having to borrow from the Bank. Bank deposits are now a lower multiple of banks' cash reserves. The money multiplier is lower, reducing the money supply for any level of the monetary base.

Maths 12-1

The money multiplier and bank deposit multiplier

Suppose banks wish to hold cash reserves R equal to some fraction c_b of deposits D, and that the private sector holds cash in circulation C equal to a fraction c_p of deposits D.

$$R = c_b D \quad \text{and} \quad C = c_p D$$

The monetary base H is either in circulation or in bank vaults.

$$H = C + R = (c_p + c_b)D$$

Finally, the money supply is circulating currency C plus deposits D.

$$M = C + D = (c_p + 1)D$$

These last two equations give us the money multiplier, the ratio of M to H.

$$M/H = (c_p + 1)/(c_p + c_b) > 1$$

If the public hold cash to the value of 2 per cent of their deposits, $c_p = 0.02$, and if banks hold reserves equal to 1 per cent of deposits, $c_b = 0.02$. Hence the money multiplier would be

$$M/H = 1.02/0.04 = 25.5$$

the ratio of broad money to the monetary base. The ratio M/R, dividing broad money only by bank reserves but not by cash held outside the banks, is called the bank deposit multiplier.

$$M/R = (c_p + 1)/(c_b) = 1.02/0.02 = 51$$

Open market operations

The previous two policies alter the value of the money multiplier. Open market operations alter the monetary base. For a given money multiplier, this alters the money supply.

> An **open market operation** is a central bank purchase or sale of securities in the open market in exchange for cash.

The Bank buys £1 billion of bonds by printing new cash, which adds £1 billion to the monetary base. Some of this ends up in circulation and some in bank reserves. The latter lets banks create new deposits. The broad money supply rises by more than the £1 billion of extra cash.

Box 12-2

The repo market

In American movies, people in arrears on their loans have their cars repossessed by the repo man. In the mid-1990s, London finally established a repo market, catching up with other European financial centres, such as Frankfurt and Milan. Surely central banks are not major players in dubious car loans?

A repo is a sale and repurchase agreement. A bank sells you a long-lived bond with a simultaneous agreement to buy it back soon at a specified price on a particular day. You pay cash to the bank today and get back a predictable amount of cash (plus interest) at a known future date. You effectively made a deposit in the bank, a short-term loan to the bank secured or guaranteed by the bond that you temporarily own. Repos use the stock of long-term assets as backing for secured short-term loans.

Reverse repos work the other way. Now you get a short-term loan from the bank by initially selling bonds to the bank, agreeing to buy them back at a specified date in the near future at a price agreed now. Reverse repos are secured short-term loans from the bank.

Repos and reverse repos augment short-term assets and liquidity. As the cost of lending and borrowing fell, more people made deposits to banks and borrowed from banks. The Bank of England now uses the repo market for most of its open market operations.

Conversely, if the Bank sells £1 billion of bonds in exchange for cash that disappears back into the Bank, the monetary base falls by £1 billion. Bank reserves fall, and commercial banks cut back on lending and deposits. The broad money supply falls by more than £1 billion.

There are three ways for a central bank to change the money supply – by changing reserve requirements, by changing the discount rate or by open market operations. In practice, modern central banks rely almost exclusively on open market operations.

Lender of last resort

Modern money is mainly bank deposits. Since banks have insufficient reserves to meet a simultaneous withdrawal of all their deposits, any hint of large withdrawals may be a self-fulfilling prophecy as people scramble to get their money out before the banks go bust. People still remember the queues of people outside Northern Rock in 2007, scrabbling to get their savings out before the bank went under. The threat of financial panics is reduced if the Bank will act as a lender of last resort.

> The **lender of last resort** lends to banks when financial panic threatens the financial system.

In 2008, the US central bank, the Federal Reserve, acted as lender of last resort on a massive scale, to the tune of several hundred billion dollars, in an attempt to preserve the liquidity of the financial markets and prevent a contagious collapse of even those banks that were probably still sound.

This is useful in helping banks that face a temporary liquidity crisis but whose underlying balance sheet is perfectly sound. When the balance sheet is unsound, that particular bank is usually allowed to go bankrupt, unless the government thinks the repercussions for other banks will generate a massive crisis in confidence. If the problems of a bank look serious, it is the Treasury, on behalf of the taxpayer, that has to authorize any loans. The job of the bank is largely confined to smoothing over liquidity problems, for a single institution or for the banking system as a whole, until confidence is restored.

Of all these functions, the normal role of the central bank is to affect the money supply, and hence set interest rates. To explain the connection, we need to introduce the demand for money.

The demand for money

The UK stock of money M4 was 16 times higher in 2012 than in 1984. Why did UK residents hold so much more money in 2005 than in 1965? Money is a stock, the quantity of money *held* at any given time. Holding money is not the same as *spending* it. We hold money now to spend it later. We focus on three determinants of desired money holdings: interest rates, the price level and real income.

For simplicity, suppose money pays no interest and 'bonds' are all other assets that pay interest. How do people split their assets between money and bonds? Holding money means not earning more interest from holding bonds instead.

> The **cost of holding money** is the interest given up by holding money rather than bonds.

People hold money only if there is a benefit to offset this cost. What is the benefit?

Transactions and precautionary benefits

Holding money economizes on the costs of barter. The size of money holdings to meet this *transactions motive* depends mainly on the scale of our anticipated future spending, which we can proxy by real income Y.

> The **demand for money** is a demand for *real* money balances M/P.

To lubricate a given flow of real transactions, we need a given amount of real money, which is nominal money M, divided by the price level P. If the price level doubles, other things equal, the demand for *nominal* money balances doubles, leaving the demand for *real* money balances unaltered since the anticipated flow of real transactions has not changed.

People want money because of its purchasing power over goods and services. A higher real income raises the benefit of real money M/P, because more transactions occur. Having too little money raises the cost of transacting.

A second reason to hold money is the *precautionary motive*. If you see a bargain in a shop window, you need real money to grab the opportunity. Waiting while you cash in some bonds means that someone else gets the bargain. You hold money to cater for unforeseeable contingencies that require a rapid response. If these situations increase with the scale of economic activity, higher real income also strengthens the precautionary motive for holding money.

The transactions and precautionary motives are the main reasons to hold narrow money. The wider the definition of money, the less important is the role of money as a medium of exchange. We also have to take account of money as a store of value.

The asset motive to hold broad money

Forget the need to transact. Imagine someone deciding in which assets to hold wealth, to be spent at some distant date. A wise portfolio of assets will include some high-earning, but potentially risky, assets, such as company shares, but also some safer assets with a return that is lower on average but also less volatile. Holding some wealth in interest-bearing bank accounts is part of a well-diversified portfolio. Higher income and wealth gives people more to invest, raising the demand for broad money, such as M4.

Equating the marginal cost and benefit of holding money

The transactions, precautionary and asset motives affect the benefits of holding money. The cost is the interest forgone by not holding higher-interest-earning bonds instead. People hold money up to the point at which the marginal benefit of holding more money just equals its marginal cost in interest forgone. Figure 12-1 shows how much money people want to hold.

The horizontal axis plots real money M/P. The horizontal line MC is the marginal cost of holding money, the interest forgone by not holding bonds. MC shifts up if interest rates rise.

The MB schedule is the marginal benefit of holding money, for a given real income and transactions flow. With low real-money holdings, we put lots of time and effort into trading, being quick to invest money coming in, and alert to sell bonds just before every purchase. Also, with little precautionary money, we may miss out on unexpected chances to grab a good deal.

With low real-money holdings, the marginal benefit of money is high. More money lets us put less effort into managing our transactions, and we have more money for unforeseen contingencies. However, for a given real income, the marginal benefit of money falls as we hold more real money. Life gets easier. The marginal benefit of yet more money is lower.

Given our real income and transactions, desired money holdings are L in Figure 12-1. Only at E are the marginal cost and benefit of money equal. How do changes in prices, real income and interest rates affect the quantity of money demanded?

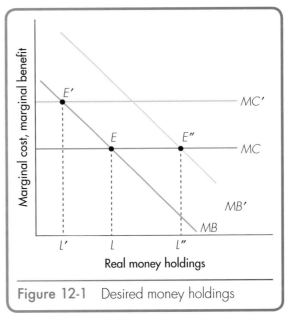

Figure 12-1 Desired money holdings

Higher prices

Suppose all prices and wages double. Since interest rates are unaltered, MC stays the same. With real income unaltered, the MB schedule is unaffected. Hence, the desired holding of *real* money remains L.

People hold twice as much nominal money M when prices P double. Real income and real money M/P are unaffected.

Higher interest rates

If interest rates on bonds rise, the cost of holding money rises. In Figure 12-1, this implies an upward shift in the marginal cost of holding money, from MC to MC'. Desired money holdings are now at point E', so desired real money holdings fall from L to L'. Higher interest rates reduce the quantity of real money demanded.

Higher real income

At each level of real money, higher real income raises the marginal benefit of money. With more transactions and more need of precautionary balances, it takes a greater stock of real money to simplify transacting to the same level as before. At any particular level of money holdings, the marginal benefit of money is higher than before. Hence, the MB schedule shifts up to MB' when real income rises. At the original interest rate and marginal cost MC schedule, desired real-money holdings are now L'. Higher real income raises the quantity of real money demanded.

Broad money

So far we have implicitly been discussing the demand for narrow money M0. To explain the demand for M4, which is mainly bank (and building society) deposits, we re-interpret MC as the average *extra* return from risky assets rather than safer deposits that pay a lower interest rate. MB is the marginal benefit of bank deposits in reducing the risk of the portfolio.

A rise in the average *interest differential* between risky assets and deposits shifts the cost of holding broad money from MC to MC', reducing the quantity of broad money demanded. Higher income and wealth shift the marginal benefit from MB to MB'. More time deposits are demanded.

Table 12-3 summarizes our discussion of the determinants of money demand.

Table 12-3　The demand for money

	Effect of rise in		
Quantity demanded	P	Y	r
Nominal money M	Rises in proportion	Rises	Falls
Real money M/P	Unaffected	Rises	Falls

Case study 12-2　Pushing on a string

Modern monetary policy sets interest rates and then passively supplies the quantity of money needed to make these interest rates compatible with money market equilibrium. When the central bank wishes to cool the economy down, it raises interest rates. This puts a brake on aggregate demand but also reduces the demand for money. To maintain money market equilibrium, the central bank cuts the supply of money in line with the lower money demand.

If the central bank raises interest rates sufficiently, it can make life very tough for the private sector and reduce the demand for consumption and investment. In later chapters, we will see that higher interest rates also lead to an appreciation of the exchange rate that reduces export demand as well. So a tighter monetary policy always works provided the authorities have the nerve to tighten monetary policy. The only reason that monetary policy 'fails' to cool down the economy is that the monetary driver was too scared to put on the brake. If the brake is applied with sufficient force, the economy is bound to slow down.

However, pressing the monetary accelerator is more problematic. When interest rates are 10 per cent, cutting them to 1 per cent will usually stimulate aggregate demand significantly. But when interest rates are low in the first place – say 4 per cent – there is only limited scope to stimulate the economy by further interest rate cuts. The lowest possible interest rate is zero. Because there is a floor on how low interest rates can go (but no corresponding ceiling on how high they can go), significantly looser monetary policy is not always possible.

And things can get even more problematic. What the private sector cares about is the real interest rate – the amount by which the interest rate exceeds the inflation rate. With 10 per cent inflation, an interest rate of 10 per cent inflicts no pain on borrowers and no gain for lenders. They merely keep up with inflation. A 12 per cent interest rate would imply a real interest rate of 2 per cent, the true cost of borrowing and benefit of lending once we adjust for inflation.

So here is the rub. Imagine a serious recession in which monetary policy does everything it can by cutting interest rates to zero. If the recession is bad enough, prices will fall and inflation will be negative. Suppose inflation is –3 per cent. What is the real interest rate? It is (0) – (–3) = +3 per cent! In such circumstances, the cost of borrowing (in real terms) can be high. Monetary policy is powerless to stimulate aggregate demand. In the 1930s, the famous economist John Maynard Keynes compared monetary policy to a string. When you tighten it, you can reliably pull things, but when you push on a string it simply goes limp – you cannot push the object attached to the other end of the string.

In the depression of the 1930s, this concern became a reality. It was fiscal expansion – government spending on the military in the run up to the Second World War – that eventually led economies out of the slump.

Have we seen any postwar examples? The Japanese experience since 1997 is a stark reminder of the danger. Japan, after three decades of postwar success, screwed up in the 1990s. A property crash made banks bankrupt. Instead of admitting this and sorting it out, policy makers ignored the problem. Consumers lost confidence and output fell. The Bank of Japan cut interest rates to zero, but with prices falling, it had no way to reduce real interest rates. The figure shows Japan's ensuing macroeconomic misery. It endured a sustained slump, with a negative output gap (actual output below potential output). Despite cutting interest rates to zero, real interest rates remained around 2 per cent, and monetary policy was unable to stimulate the economy.

This of course is the example that has haunted US and European policy makers since 2008. Avoiding a re-run of the Japanese experience should have been their top priority. Two lessons should be drawn from this example. First, deflation (negative inflation) is really dangerous. Sufficiently high interest rates will always stop inflation if we have the political resolve to administer the medicine; but when prices start falling, monetary policy becomes powerless, like pushing on a string. Second, once interest rates are already low, monetary policy has only limited power to create further boosts to the economy.

Money market equilibrium

The money market is in equilibrium when the quantity of real money demanded equals the quantity supplied. For a given real income, Figure 12-2 shows real money demand *MD*. A higher interest rate raises the cost of holding money and reduces the quantity demanded.

Through open market operations, the central bank can determine the nominal money supply. If the price level is given, this also determines the real money supply. Hence the central bank can set an interest rate r_0 by supplying a quantity of real money L_0. To set an interest rate r_1, the central bank simply raises the money supply to L_1.

Changes in money demand

What would raise the demand for money at each interest rate? Either higher real income, which would raise the marginal benefit of money, or more banking competition, which would raise interest rates paid on deposits, reducing the cost of holding money at any level of interest rates on bonds and other assets.

In Figure 12-3, a rise in money demand shifts *MD* up to *MD'*. With an unchanged real money supply, interest rates rise from *r* to *r'* in order to reduce the quantity of real money demand back to the level of the unchanged real money supply.

However, if the central bank wishes to maintain the interest rate at its original level *r*, it simply undertakes an open market operation to raise the real money supply from *L* to *L'*. When the central bank wants to 'set' interest rates, it therefore passively supplies whatever money is demanded at that interest rate.

Monetary policy

Interest rates are the instrument of monetary policy.

> The **monetary instrument** is the variable over which a central bank exercises day-to-day control.

The *ultimate objective* of monetary policy could be a combination of low inflation, output stabilization, manipulation of the exchange rate and more stable house prices. The Bank of England now has operational independence from government to set interest rates. But the Chancellor has decided the Bank's ultimate objective. It must set interest rates to try to keep inflation close to 2 per cent a year.

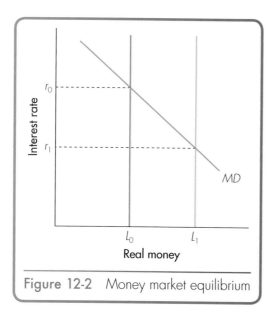

Figure 12-2 Money market equilibrium

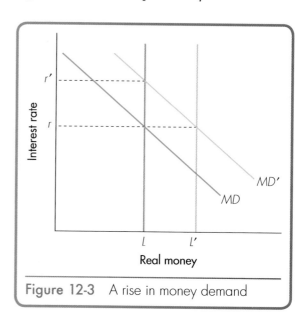

Figure 12-3 A rise in money demand

In making decisions, a central bank tries to get up-to-date forecasts of as many variables as possible. Sometimes, however, it concentrates on one or two key indicators, such as the recent behaviour of prices, the exchange rate or the money supply.

New data on the money supply (largely bank deposits) come out faster than new data on the price level or real output. If the true, but not yet observable, behaviour of output and prices feeds reliably into money demand, then recent data on what happened to the stock of money may be a useful leading indicator of what is happening to the economy.

In the heyday of *monetarism*, central banks responded rapidly to new data on the nominal money stock. When it rose too quickly, the central bank inferred that rises in income or prices had boosted money demand, requiring the passive supply of extra money to maintain the previous interest rate. Given this signal, the central bank then raised interest rates to prevent the economy growing too quickly and bidding up inflation.

Throughout the world, over the past decade there have been two key changes in the design of monetary policy. First, central banks have been told that their ultimate objectives should concentrate more on low inflation control and less on other things. Second, money has become much less reliable as a leading indicator. Rapid changes in the financial services sector keep changing the demand for money. When we see the money stock rising, we no longer know whether this signals imminent growth of prices and output, or whether it reflects a structural change that is making people hold more money even at constant levels of prices and output. Measures of money growth no longer have pride of place in central banks' assessments of whether to change interest rates.

Nowadays, central banks adjust interest rates to keep inflation close to its target level, and passively supply whatever quantity of money is necessary to equate money demand and money supply at the chosen interest rate. Since modern monetary policy is dedicated to the control of inflation, we now study inflation in more detail.

Case study 12-3   Quantitative easing

Banks responded to the financial crisis by prioritizing the rebuilding of their solvency. This had four aspects: (a) holding a much higher percentage of their assets in ultra-safe bank reserves and other very liquid assets; (b) avoiding any new lending that was thought to be risky; (c) raising profit margins throughout the industry in order to build up capital reserves; and where possible (d) issuing new shares in order to attract additional capital from shareholders. Here we focus on the implications of (a) and (b).

This figure documents the collapse of the ratio of UK broad money to UK bank reserves, which fell from 90 in mid-2007 to 14 by 2009. If reserves had remained constant, broad money would have fallen to a sixth of its previous level! The complete drying up of bank lending – to each other and to private firms – transmitted a huge shock to the real economy. House prices fell since new mortgages became very hard to obtain, industrial production fell as firms struggled to find loans to finance work-in-progress until it could be sold, and increasing numbers of bankruptcies were reported.

The Treasury tried to help, by making it a condition of government support for banks such as RBS that these banks continued to lend to the private sector at the same level as in previous years. Unsurprisingly, the banks said they would do so but then did not – why would they wish to lend money to customers they considered, rightly or wrongly, to be very risky? – and there was little that the government could do.

▶

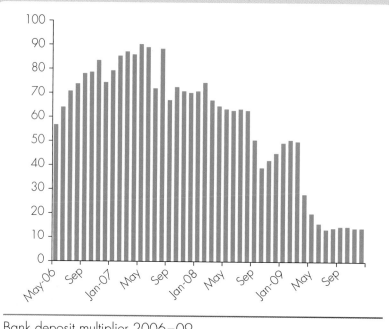

Bank deposit multiplier 2006–09

Source: www.bankofengland.co.uk/statistics

British and American central banks have usually been run by professional bankers not world-class economics professors. At the time of the crisis, the Governor of the Bank of England was Mervyn King, former professor at the London School of Economics, and the Governor of the US Federal Reserve was Ben Bernanke, former economics professor at Princeton University. They understood the problem and adopted a bold solution, quantitative easing.

> **Quantitative easing** is the creation of substantial quantities of bank reserves in order to offset a fall in the bank deposit multiplier and prevent large falls in bank lending and broad money.

The following figures show the aggressive intervention then undertaken by the Bank of England.

In the top chart, the surge in the dark blue area in the middle shows the deliberate creation of bank reserves – not by printing cash but by creation of electronic reserves for the banking system to treat as if they were cash reserves. By 2012 this programme had created an additional £300 billion of bank reserves. To give an idea of scale, in 2012 there was only £55 billion of old-fashioned cash in circulation, so the quantitative easing programme was massive.

The bottom chart provides details of the assets purchased by the Bank in order to get this extra 'money' into the system. Principally, the Bank bought 'safe' bonds from the UK government in exchange for money, and this money gradually worked its way around the economy.

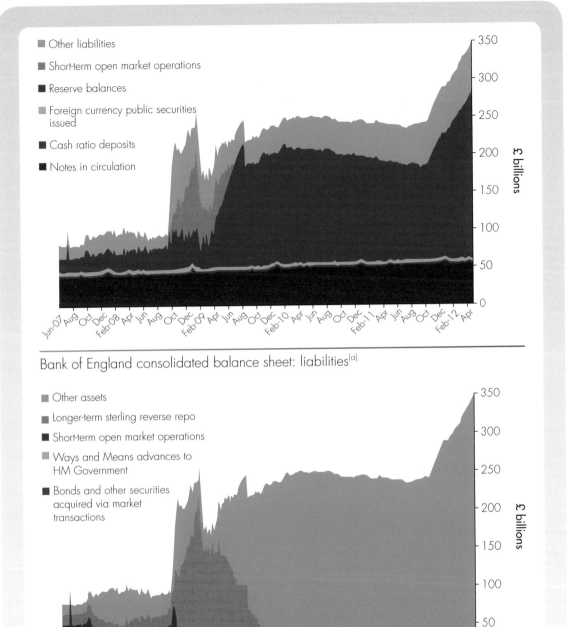

- Other liabilities
- Short-term open market operations
- Reserve balances
- Foreign currency public securities issued
- Cash ratio deposits
- Notes in circulation

£ billions

Bank of England consolidated balance sheet: liabilities[a]

- Other assets
- Longer-term sterling reverse repo
- Short-term open market operations
- Ways and Means advances to HM Government
- Bonds and other securities acquired via market transactions

£ billions

Bank of England consolidated balance sheet: assets[a]

(a) Excludes loans and associated deposits in course of settlement

Source: www.bankofengland.co.uk/monetary policy

▶

Critics of the programme say such a huge increase in narrow money is bound to be inflationary. What actually happened to broad money M4 when bank reserves increased around seven-fold? The figure below provides the answer.

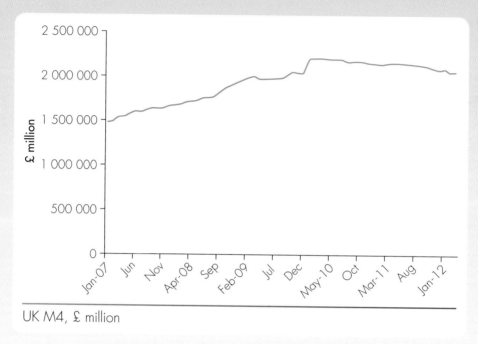

UK M4, £ million

During 2007–12, broad money increased by around 35 per cent, or about 5.5 per cent a year, only a little above the rate of inflation and quite in line with historical trends. The data speak clearly: the consequence of the dramatic policy intervention was to keep broad money growth on track, not to drive it wildly off track. The intervention was required because the collapse of banks' confidence in their ability to lend profitably would otherwise have led to an implosion of money and credit.

Inflation

Persistent inflation is quite a recent phenomenon. The UK price level was *the same* in 1950 as in 1920. Figure 12-4 confirms that UK inflation was negative in some of the interwar years. Yet since 1945 annual UK inflation has never been negative. During 1945–2012 the price level rose 32-fold, more than its rise in the previous 300 years. A similar story applies in most advanced economies.

Inflation and money growth

People care about real variables – the size of their house, the quantity of holidays, the number of raspberries. Hence, we view the demand for money as a demand for real money M/P. It rises with real income Y, but falls with the nominal interest rate r.[1] The real money supply M/P shows the quantity of goods that money

---

[1] Inflation at the rate p reduces the purchasing power of money. The cost of holding money, the real interest rate $(r - p)$ on bonds minus the real interest rate $(-p)$ on money, is thus the nominal interest rate r.

will buy. If nothing in the real economy alters, real money demand is constant. Thus, nominal money M and prices P must be growing at the *same* rate as each other to keep the real money supply M/P constant. This is the quantity theory of money. It is believed to date back at least to Confucius.

> The **quantity theory of money** says that changes in the quantity of nominal money M lead to equivalent changes in prices P, but have no effect on real output.

As a matter of logic, this has to be correct. If nothing real changes, and if the initial cause arises with a change in the nominal money supply M, then the consequence is an equivalent change in prices P. However, the quantity theory needs interpreting with care. First, nowadays, central banks set interest rates in pursuit of inflation targets and then

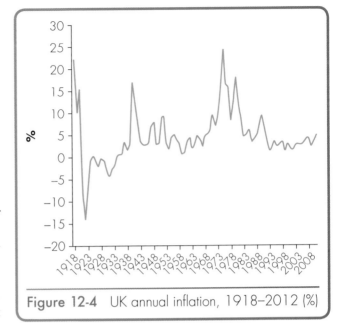

Figure 12-4   UK annual inflation, 1918–2012 (%)

passively supply whatever money is demanded at that interest rate. Causation thus runs from prices to money, not the other way round. It is the rate of change of prices that determines the rate at which central banks are driven to create money.

Second, real money demand is not necessarily constant. It can change either because of short-run changes in real income, or because monetary policy has changed nominal interest rates. When real money demand changes, nominal money and prices must behave *differently* in order to *alter* the real money supply in line with the change in real money demand.

In the long run, the correlation of money and prices is stronger. Eventually, output is fixed at potential output, which changes only slowly. If inflation is permanently high, nominal money must grow at a similar rate. Otherwise, the real money stock is permanently changing, which is incompatible with long-run equilibrium. Eventually we would expect real money to grow at about the same rate as real income, in other words at about 2 or 3 per cent a year.

In this sense, long-run inflation is *always* a monetary phenomenon. Take away the monetary oxygen and the inflationary fire goes out. Central banks with high inflation targets have to print lots of money to maintain the real money stock in line with real money demand. Those with low inflation targets need to print less money. If a central bank stops printing money, so that the nominal money supply is then constant, inflation eventually has to stop. Otherwise, the implication would be that ever higher prices P gradually reduce the real money stock M/P to zero. But from section 12-1 we know that such a cut in the real money supply would cause a massive rise in equilibrium interest rates that would cause a huge slump and kill the inflation stone dead.

Hyperinflation

Ukraine's annual inflation reached 10 000 per cent in 1993, which is nothing compared to Zimbabwe's inflation of over 11 million per cent in 2008.

> **Hyperinflation** is high inflation, above 50 per cent *per month*.

Another famous example is Germany during 1922–23. After the First World War the German government had a big deficit, financed largely by printing money. Eventually, the government had to buy faster printing presses. In the later stages of the hyperinflation they took in old notes, stamped on another zero, and reissued them as larger-denomination notes in the morning. By October 1923, it took 192 million marks to buy a drink that had cost 1 mark in January 1922. People shopped by carrying money around in wheelbarrows. Muggers took the barrows but left the near-worthless money behind!

During hyperinflation, people try to get by with low real-cash balances to avoid their nominal cash balances being eroded by inflation. In 1923, Germans were paid twice a day so they could shop at lunchtime before the real value of their cash depreciated. Any unspent cash was quickly deposited in a bank where it could earn interest. People spent a lot of time at the bank.

Hyperinflations arise because governments can no longer raise enough taxes to finance their spending commitments, including interest on accumulated government debts. They try to print more and more money to cover the growing budget deficit. The additional money causes more and more inflation. The 'solution' often involves defaulting on the old debt, which dramatically reduces government spending, thereby removing the need to print money to finance the budget deficit.

In a modern economy, there are two ways to ensure that hyperinflations, or even moderate inflations, never arise. The first is to make the central bank independent of political control, so that it can no longer be ordered to print money to finance a budget deficit. The second is to restrict the ability of governments to run deficits in the first place. Before examining how different countries have implemented these solutions, it is important to understand why inflation should be public enemy number one as far as policy design is concerned.

The costs of inflation

Inflation illusion

Voters may suffer from inflation illusion, confusing nominal and real changes. It is wrong to say that inflation is bad *because* it makes goods more expensive. If *all* nominal variables rise together, people have larger nominal incomes and can buy the same physical quantity of goods as before. Nothing real has changed. However, if people fail to understand what is going on, they may make incorrect decisions by confusing nominal and real changes. If so, this may be a serious cost of inflation.

Assessment costs

You buy bread every day, and probably have a good idea of what is happening to bread prices in comparison to incomes and the prices of other goods. But what about some good, such as a washing machine, that a household typically purchases only every five or ten years? When inflation is significant, how do you decide what has happened to the real price of washing machines since you last bought one? Even if you remember what you paid five years ago, you have some complicated arithmetic to do in order to check whether or not the real price has risen or fallen. Wasting time on thinking and arithmetic is an important cost of inflation. When prices are stable, these calculations become trivially easy. People who avoid the costs of thinking and doing arithmetic simply by making a wild guess are likely to make mistakes and take decisions that are not in fact in their best interests. That is another way of viewing this cost of inflation.

Even if there were no assessment costs, there may be other costs. How large they are depends on whether inflation was expected and whether or not economic institutions can adapt to it.

Adaptation plus anticipation

If everyone sees inflation coming, and can adapt fully, all nominal variables should adjust in advance to restore real variables to their former levels. Nominal wages and nominal interest rates are set at appropriate levels. In that case, with unchanged real wages and real interest rates, workers and savers are protected from expected inflation. Nominal taxes and nominal government spending are adjusted regularly to maintain the real level of taxes and welfare benefits. Does inflation hurt anyone?

Cash cannot be protected from inflation since its zero interest rate cannot be adjusted. Higher inflation makes people hold less real cash, thus raising the time and effort needed for transacting.

Shoe-leather costs of inflation are shorthand for the extra time and effort in transacting when inflation reduces desired real-cash holdings.

Hyperinflation is a spectacular example of when shoe-leather costs become huge.

A second unavoidable cost arises because of the need to keep changing price labels and to keep reprinting catalogues to reflect the ever-changing price information. Higher inflation means these costs are incurred more frequently.

Menu costs of inflation are the physical resources used in changing price tags, reprinting catalogues and changing vending machines.

Even with complete adaptation and full anticipation, we cannot avoid shoe-leather and menu costs of inflation. These are big if inflation is high, but are probably small when inflation is low.

Anticipation without adaptation

Sometimes, our institutions are not inflation-neutral. This stops full adjustment to foreseen inflation, raising the distortions that inflation creates. For example, if nominal tax allowances do not rise with prices, people are driven into higher real-tax payments. If the government taxes all interest income (only the real interest rate is a genuine profit on lending, the rest is just for keeping up with inflation), or taxes all capital gains (only the gain in excess of inflation is real profit), then higher inflation raises effective tax rates. The government gains from the failure to use proper inflation accounting, but the private sector changes its behaviour as a result. These institutional imperfections imply that even anticipated inflation has costs for society.

Unexpected inflation

Surprise inflation alters the real value of nominal contracts. Lenders lose out, having failed to charge an adequate nominal interest rate. Workers lose out, having failed to settle for an adequate nominal wage. Conversely, borrowers and firms benefit. One person's gain is another person's loss. In the aggregate, these cancel out. But unexpected inflation redistributes income and wealth – for example, from lenders to borrowers. We might think this is also costly.

Uncertain inflation

Uncertainty about future inflation makes long-term planning harder. People also dislike risk itself. The extra benefits of the champagne years are poor compensation for the years of starvation. People would rather average out these extremes and live comfortably all the time. Uncertain inflation makes the real value of the contract less certain. This is a significant cost of inflation. There is some empirical evidence that inflation that is high on average also tends to be more volatile and harder to predict. One benefit of low inflation is that the institutional changes necessary to deliver it also tend to make it more predictable.

Together, these costs of inflation are significant. There is one final argument to consider. Whatever the costs of inflation itself, inflation arises usually as the symptom of some deeper problem, such as the inability of the government to run a prudent budget policy. Hence, the benefits of curing inflation may be not merely avoidance of the damage that inflation does but also benefits that arise from curing the underlying problem that was giving rise to the need to print money and create inflation. Modern governments are tough on inflation and tough on the causes of inflation.

Committing to low inflation

Central bank independence has been a useful commitment to tight monetary policy and low inflation. During 1995–2007, this institutional commitment succeeded in country after country in keeping inflation low.

Case study 12-4   The secret of inflation control?

Defeating inflation was achieved by designing better policies, and this lesson has now been learned in over 50 countries during the last two decades. As a controlled experiment, this is as good as it gets in economics. Policy was changed, and the expected result ensued. Inflation came tumbling down permanently without causing permanent falls in output or permanent rises in unemployment. The key lay in recognizing that politicians were the problem not the solution. Reducing the scope for political control (interference?) allowed the pursuit of better policies.

UK policy, 1992–97

In 1992, the UK abandoned its policy of pegging its exchange rate to European currencies, for which it had been necessary to set a similar monetary policy to that in European economies. Free to set UK monetary policy, the government first moved towards using inflation as a target for choosing interest rate policy. Although happy to receive advice from the Bank of England, the Chancellor of the Exchequer still had the final say in setting interest rates. Even so, these arrangements partially committed the government to low inflation. Minutes of the monthly meeting between the Chancellor and the Governor of the Bank of England were published a few weeks later, so any objections by the Bank were highly publicized. Moreover, the Bank was told to publish a quarterly *Inflation Report*, completely free from Treasury control. This report soon became very influential, because it was transparent and used good economic analysis.

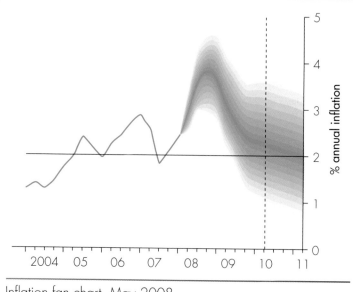

Inflation fan chart, May 2008

Source: Bank of England

The *Inflation Report* includes the famous *fan chart* for inflation. A fan chart shows not just the most likely future outcome, but also indicates the probability of different outcomes. The darker is the projected line, the more likely the outcome. Thus, in May 2008 the Bank was expecting UK inflation to average around 3.5 per cent in 2008, but, looking forward to 2010, the range of possible outcomes had widened to between 1 per cent and 4 per cent. The figure shows how quickly uncertainty increases as we look into the future. Notice that the Bank is also uncertain about the recent past, and has to go quite a long way back before it can be confident that the data are reliable.

UK policy, 1997–2007

In May 1997, the new Chancellor, Gordon Brown, gave the Bank of England 'operational independence' to set interest rates in pursuit of the inflation target that he laid down. Any change in the target will be politically difficult, except in truly exceptional circumstances. Operational central bank independence is a commitment to low inflation.

UK monetary policy is now set by the Bank of England's Monetary Policy Committee, meeting monthly to set interest rates to try to hit the inflation target. Initially, the inflation data were based on the growth of the Retail Price Index, and the annual inflation target was set at 2.5 per cent, plus or minus 1 per cent. However, in December 2003 the Chancellor decided to switch to an inflation measure based on the growth of the Consumer Price Index, a slightly different measure of inflation. Because CPI inflation is usually less than RPI inflation, the inflation target was cut to 2 per cent, still plus or minus 1 per cent.[2]

Most people gave the Monetary Policy Committee high marks for its performance up to 2007. It was prepared to change interest rates even when this was unpopular, and inflation stayed close to target as a result. With low expected inflation, nominal interest rates were lower than for decades.

Policy since 2007

The early years of central bank independence had enjoyed a benign environment. Oil prices were low and cheap imports from China helped to hold down prices in Europe and America. Two things changed after 2007.

First, the influence of China was felt not merely through its supply of manufactures but also increasingly through its demand for raw materials. This led to a rise in global commodity prices. For the rich countries, this was an unwelcome, adverse supply shock that put upward pressure on inflation. Second, the credit crunch, initially in the US but quickly spreading around the globe, led to a collapse in lending, confidence and demand.

Faced only with the credit crunch, monetary policy would have cut interest rates substantially to offset the shock to demand. Because the Bank could not cut interest rates below zero, it resorted to quantitative easing, provided liquidity and helped keep interest rates at minimal levels.

Facing simultaneously the inflationary pressure of higher commodity prices, central banks were between a rock and a hard place. With interest rates so low, they had no ammunition with which to fight rising oil prices caused by supply shocks in the Middle East and by booming demand in China and India.

Central bank independence can help prevent government being the source of shocks but it is not a panacea in all situations: when confronted with two global shocks requiring opposite policy responses, the institutional design of the central bank cannot dispel the policy dilemma on how to respond.

---

[2] Alert readers may have noticed the discrepancy between UK inflation in Figure 12-4 and the inflation shown in the fan chart above. The former is RPI inflation, the latter CPI inflation. Each index measures a slightly different basket of goods. Typically, RPI inflation has exceeded CPI inflation by around 1 per cent.

Recap

- Money is the medium of exchange, for which it must be a store of value. It is usually also the unit of account.
- Bartering takes huge time and effort. Money reduces the resources used in trading. A token money's value as a money greatly exceeds its commodity value in other uses.
- Token money is used by social convention or because it is legal tender. The government has a monopoly on its supply.
- Modern banks attract deposits by offering interest and cheque-book facilities, but lend out funds at higher interest rates. If reserve ratios are below 100 per cent, banks create money by using their cash reserves to create extra loans and deposits.
- During a credit crunch, traditional sources of loans dry up because lenders fear that borrowers' creditworthiness has become abnormally low and the loan may not be repaid.
- The money supply is currency in circulation plus relevant deposits. The monetary base M0 is currency in circulation and in banks. Broad money M4 is currency in circulation plus deposits at banks and building societies.
- The money multiplier is the ratio of the money supply to the monetary base. For M4 it is currently about 28. The money multiplier is larger (a) the smaller the reserve ratio and (b) the less of the monetary base is held outside banks and building societies.
- The Bank of England is the UK central bank acting as banker to the banks and to the government. Since it can print money, it can never go bust. It acts as lender of last resort to the banks.
- The Bank mainly controls the monetary base through open market operations, by buying and selling government securities. It could also change the money multiplier by imposing reserve requirements on the banks, or setting the discount rate at a penalty level.
- The demand for money is a demand for real balances. It rises if real income rises, but falls if the interest rate rises.
- To set the interest rate, the central bank passively adjusts the money supply to the level of money demand at that interest rate.
- Interest rates are the instrument of monetary policy. Nominal money is now less reliable as a leading indicator of future price and output data. Modern central banks adjust interest rates to keep inflation close to its target level.
- In the short run, there is a close correlation between nominal money and prices only if real-money demand happens to remain constant. In the long run, the correlation is closer since eventually real-money demand tends to grow slowly in line with potential output. Without rapid change in real money, any rapid growth in nominal money must be reflected in rapid growth in prices.

- Some 'costs' of inflation are illusory, but illusion can also cause costly mistakes in decision making. Assessment costs, shoe-leather costs and menu costs are also unavoidable. Other costs of inflation depend on whether it was anticipated, and on whether an economy's institutions are inflation neutral. Uncertainty about inflation is also costly. Uncertainty may be greater if inflation is already high.
- Operational independence of central banks removes the temptation faced by politicians to boost the economy too much or to fund budget deficits by printing money.

Review questions

To check your answers to these questions, go to pages 391–2.

1 (a) Is a car taken in 'part exchange' for a new car a medium of exchange? (b) Could you tell, by watching someone buying mints (white discs) with coins (silver discs), which is money?

2 How do commercial banks create money? What happens if their reserve ratio is 100 per cent?

3 Are (a) travellers' cheques, (b) season tickets or (c) credit cards money?

4 Sight deposits = 30, time deposits = 60, banks' cash reserves = 2, currency in circulation = 12, building society deposits = 20. Calculate M0 and M4.

5 Why are these statements wrong? (a) Since their liabilities equal their assets, banks do not create anything. (b) Tax evasion raises the money supply since people keep more cash under the bed.

6 If commercial banks hold 100 per cent cash reserves against deposits, and the public hold no cash, what is the value of the money multiplier?

7 How do credit cards affect the precautionary demand for money?

8 Suppose banks raise interest rates on time deposits whenever interest rates on other assets rise. How much does a general rise in interest rates affect the demand for M4?

9 What are the desirable properties of a good leading indicator?

10 Why are these statements wrong? (a) Since higher interest rates on bank deposits make people hold less cash, they reduce the money supply. (b) Cash can never pay a decent rate of return.

11 Name three groups who lose out during inflation. Does it matter whether this inflation was anticipated?

EASY

12 Suppose confidence returns to the banking system, and bank lending and bank deposits revert to more normal levels. What will happen to M4 if no offsetting action is taking by monetary policy? What would be the effect on inflation? What would you expect the Bank of England to do in these circumstances?

13 Why are these statements wrong? (a) Inflation stops people saving. (b) Inflation stops people investing. (c) Foreseen inflation is costless.

14 (a) Your real annual income is constant. You borrow £200 000 for 20 years to buy a house, paying interest annually and repaying the £200 000 in a final payment at the end. In one scenario, inflation is 0 per cent and the nominal interest rate is 2 per cent a year. In a second scenario, annual inflation is 100 per cent and the nominal interest rate is 102 per cent. Are the two scenarios the same in real terms?

15 Suppose the Bank of England's inflation target had been 6 per cent not 2 per cent. Roughly what would nominal interest rates have been? How would the Bank have reacted to the recession? Would quantitative easing have been necessary?

16 **Essay question** 'The role of politicians is to make political decisions.' What do you think are the advantages and disadvantages of delegating economic policy to independent officials who are unelected? Would your answer change during wartime? Why or why not?

17 **Essay question** Monetarists believe that there is a strong link between the total quantity of money and the level of prices, so that excess money creation leads inflation. Other things equal, is this correct? What other things are not usually constant? How reliable are monetary indicators as predictors of inflation?

Online Learning Centre

To help you grasp the key concepts of this chapter check out the extra resources posted on the Online Learning Centre at www.mcgraw-hill.co.uk/textbooks/begg.

There are additional case studies, self-test questions, practice exam questions with answers and a graphing tool.

CHAPTER 13

Aggregate supply, inflation and unemployment

Learning outcomes

By the end of this chapter, you should be able to:

- Explain the classical model of output and inflation
- Show how inflation affects aggregate demand
- Derive the equilibrium inflation rate
- Explain why wage adjustment is sluggish in the short run
- Show how temporary output gaps emerge
- Describe how the economy eventually returns to potential output
- Distinguish classical, frictional and structural unemployment

- Explain voluntary and involuntary unemployment
- Assess determinants of UK unemployment
- Distinguish private and social costs of unemployment
- Analyse the short-run Phillips curve
- Analyse the long-run Phillips curve
- Evaluate the short-run correlation of inflation and unemployment
- Discuss the long-run independence of inflation and unemployment

Our discussion of macroeconomic fluctuations has so far been all about aggregate demand. Provided there is spare capacity, we can ignore aggregate supply completely. This was just a simplication to get us started. Now we have to rectify it.

This chapter introduces aggregate supply, which will eventually allow us to discuss how output is affected in the short run not just by shocks to aggregate demand but also by shocks to aggregate supply. This also provides a framework for exploring temporary but not permanent deviations of output from potential output. The chapter also makes explicit the connection between output supply, demand for workers, and hence what is going on simultaneously in the labour market.

Finally, this framework allows us to investigate inflation effects, and is affected by, the output and labour markets.

 # Aggregate supply and equilibrium inflation

Chapter 10 introduced key macroeconomic concepts and discussed the long-run growth of an economy's national output. In the long run, output increases because aggregate supply increases. The economy has a greater capacity to produce. Next, in the previous three chapters, we examined how fluctuations in aggregate demand can move the economy away from potential output in the short run, and the role of macroeconomic economic policy in stabilizing aggregate demand by the use of monetary and fiscal policy.

Initially, we analysed how aggregate demand affects output, and hence how monetary and fiscal policy can be used to change equilibrium output in the short run. But we have also seen that monetary policy nowadays is principally concerned with stabilizing inflation rather than output. Are the two connected? If so, how?

This chapter provides an answer. To do so properly, we need to analyse supply as well as demand. In so doing, we discard the simplifying assumption that the economy has spare capacity and that output is demand determined in the short run. By simultaneously analysing supply and demand, we have a better model. One benefit of this is that the relationship between inflation and output can be seen more easily. Having undertaken this analysis for output, we complete the chapter by showing what is simultaneously happening in the market for labour.

Previously, our model of output determination treated prices and wages as given. Yet, in practice there has often been inflation, a rise in the general level of prices. Figure 13-1 shows again the UK annual inflation rate since 1918. Inflation is lower than it used to be. As explained in Chapter 12, politicians have seen the wisdom of better discipline in monetary and fiscal policy.

Once we start to discuss inflation we have to abandon our previous assumption that prices are given. Once we stop treating prices as given, it no longer makes sense to simplify by treating output as demand determined. Higher aggregate demand does not always raise output: with finite resources, the economy cannot expand output indefinitely. We now introduce aggregate supply – firms' willingness and ability to produce – and show how demand and supply *together* determine output. And the balance of supply and demand affects what is happening to inflation.

Initially, we swap the Keynesian extreme, with fixed wages and prices, for the opposite extreme, full wage and price flexibility.

The **classical model** of macroeconomics assumes wages and prices are completely flexible.

In the classical model, the economy is *always* at potential output. Any deviation of output causes instant changes in inflation to restore output to potential output. In the short run, before prices and inflation adjust, the Keynesian model is relevant. In the long run, after all adjustment is complete, the classical model is relevant. We examine how the economy evolves from the Keynesian short run to the classical long run.

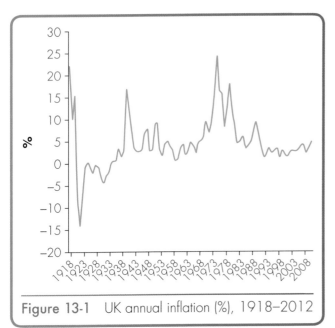

Figure 13-1   UK annual inflation (%), 1918–2012

Aggregate supply

The **aggregate supply schedule** shows the output firms wish to supply at each inflation rate.

With complete flexibility, output has always adjusted back to potential output. All inputs are fully employed. This is the long-run equilibrium output of the economy. Potential output reflects technology, the quantities of available inputs in long-run equilibrium, and the efficiency with which resources and technology are exploited. Chapter 10 studied how potential output grows in the long run. In the short run, we treat potential output as given.

How does more rapid growth of prices and nominal wages affect the incentive of firms to supply goods and services? We assume that people do not suffer from inflation illusion. If wages and prices both double, real wages are unaffected. Neither firms nor workers change their behaviour. Aggregate supply is unaffected by *pure* inflation, as shown in Figure 13-2.

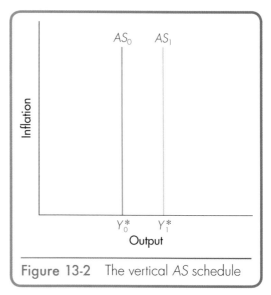

Figure 13-2   The vertical *AS* schedule

In the classical model, the **aggregate supply schedule** is vertical at potential output.

Equilibrium output is *independent* of inflation. Since nobody has inflation illusion, people adjust nominal variables to keep pace with inflation. Nothing real changes, and output is constant. If potential output increases, the aggregate supply schedule shifts from AS_0 to AS_1 in Figure 13-2.

Box 13-1

Price level or inflation rate?

Since last period's price level is already known this period, once we know this period's price level we also know the inflation rate between last period and this period. Conversely, if we know the inflation rate and last period's price level, we can deduce this period's price level. Knowing one, we always know the other.

In this chapter, we show the inflation rate on the vertical axis when discussing the aggregate price level. We could instead have shown the price level on the vertical axis in Figure 13-2 and all the ensuing diagrams in this chapter. The analysis still works.

Textbooks used to focus on the price level, but, like us, most authors of modern textbooks now focus on the inflation rate instead. One obvious reason to switch is that modern monetary policy is geared to the pursuit of inflation targets not targets for price level. You probably know roughly what the UK inflation rate is at present, but you would be hard pressed to describe what the current value of the UK price level is.

A second reason is that the Phillips curve, discussed later in the chapter, uses inflation on its vertical axis. Doing the same for aggregate supply allows a direct integration of demand, supply and the Phillips curve. Focusing on prices for supply, but inflation for the Phillips curve, merely confuses the issue.

Nothing in the theory hinges on which we use, but it is much more attractive to use the inflation rate in our analysis. As an exercise, you could try reworking the argument of the chapter using the price level instead. Either way the central point is that producers should care about real variables not nominal ones.

Inflation and aggregate demand

In the classical model, inflation does not affect aggregate supply but it does affect aggregate demand. If the central bank is pursuing a given inflation target, any increase in inflation above target induces the central bank to raise *real* interest rates in order to reduce aggregate demand and make firms less eager to raise prices.

Since the real interest rate is the nominal rate r minus the inflation rate π, in order to raise *real* interest rates the central bank has to raise the *nominal* interest rate r by *more* than the increase in inflation π so that the real interest rate $(r - \pi)$ increases, thereby exerting contractionary pressure on the economy by reducing aggregate demand.

> Following an **inflation target**, a central bank raises the real interest rate if it expects inflation to be too high, and cuts the real interest rate if it expects inflation to be too low.

Figure 13-3 illustrates how inflation affects aggregate demand. When inflation is high, the central bank implements its monetary policy by raising real interest rates, reducing aggregate demand and equilibrium output. The *AD* schedule slopes downwards, showing that lower inflation induces a cut in real interest rates and hence an expansion in aggregate demand.

Movements *along* the *AD* schedule reflect interest rate changes in pursuit of a given inflation target. Interest rate changes take time to affect output and inflation, so the central bank cannot keep inflation perfectly on track, though it hopes to be moving in the right direction. In contrast, *shifts* in *AD* reflect a switch to a *different* monetary policy with a *different* inflation target. If monetary policy is less tight, the central bank is prepared to accept a higher inflation target, and the *AD* schedule shifts upwards. Conversely, a tighter monetary policy corresponds to a downward shift in the *AD* schedule.

The equilibrium inflation rate

The equilibrium inflation rate π^* reflects the positions of the *AD* and *AS* schedules. See Figure 13-4.

With aggregate supply AS_0 and aggregate demand AD_0, inflation is π_0^* and output is Y_0^*. Equilibrium is at *A*. Output is at potential output, and the inflation target is being achieved.

A permanent supply shock

Supply shocks may be beneficial, such as technical progress, or may be adverse, such as higher real oil prices or loss of capacity after an earthquake. Suppose potential output rises. In Figure 13-5, the *AS* schedule

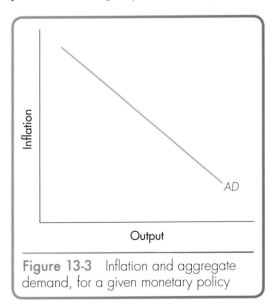

Figure 13-3 Inflation and aggregate demand, for a given monetary policy

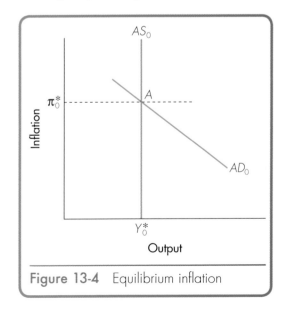

Figure 13-4 Equilibrium inflation

shifts to the right, from AS_0 to AS_1. To maintain the target inflation rate π_0^*, the central bank *loosens* monetary policy, setting a lower interest rate than before at any level of actual inflation. This raises demand, shifting AD_0 to AD_1, meeting the original inflation target π_0^* in long-run equilibrium at C not D.

> Monetary policy **accommodates** a permanent supply change by changing the average level of real interest rates, thereby permanently altering aggregate demand in line with permanently altered aggregate supply.

A demand shock

For a given aggregate supply AS_0, suppose a rise in export demand raises aggregate demand from AD_0 to AD_1, which would take the economy from A to B. Inflation π_1^* now exceeds the long-run inflation target at π_0^*. The central bank

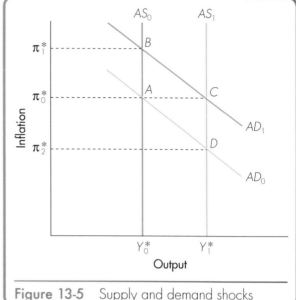

Figure 13-5   Supply and demand shocks

has to *tighten* monetary policy, setting a higher real interest rate at *each* possible output level. This shifts AD_1 back to AD_0 and restores equilibrium at A, letting the central bank continue to meet its inflation target.

Similarly, if the initial cause of the upward shift in demand was not a rise in export demand but a rise in government spending, there is a consequent tightening of monetary policy until private expenditure has been reduced by the same amount as government expenditure had increased. Only then is total aggregate demand restored to the level of potential output, which by assumption has not changed.

> In the classical model, there is **complete crowding out**. Higher government spending causes an equivalent reduction in private spending, since total output can't change.

In other words, to keep hitting its inflation target, the central bank must raise real interest rates enough to depress consumption and investment demand so that aggregate demand remains at potential output despite higher government spending.

If government spending falls, we can use Figure 13-5 in reverse. Beginning at A, tighter fiscal policy shifts AD_1 down to AD_0. To prevent inflation falling below the target π_0^*, the central bank must loosen monetary policy, which shifts demand back up to AD_1. Lower government spending then *crowds in* an equal amount of private spending because of lower real interest rates.

A rise in the inflation target

Suppose the inflation target is raised from π_0^* to π_1^*. The central bank no longer needs such high interest rates at any particular level of inflation. Real interest rates fall and the macroeconomic demand schedule shifts up from AD_0 to AD_1. With an unchanged AS schedule, equilibrium moves from A to B in Figure 13-5.

Inflation is higher but real output is unaltered. Since this is a full equilibrium, all real variables, including real money M/P, are then constant. Hence, money and prices are growing *at the same rate*. In the classical model, higher inflation is accompanied by faster growth of nominal money. The idea that nominal money growth is associated with inflation, but not higher output, is the central tenet of *monetarists*. Figure 13-5 confirms that this is correct in the classical model with full wage and price flexibility.

Sluggish adjustment in the short run

In practice, prices and wages do not instantly respond to excess supply and demand. Output can deviate from potential output in the short run. Some firms, in long-run relationships with their customers, prefer not to vary prices with short-run market conditions. It takes time and effort to decide how to react, to inform people of changes and to alter catalogues.

Wages are even slower to adjust than prices. Since wages are the main part of costs, which in turn affect prices, sluggish wage adjustment also helps explain sluggish price adjustment. Long-run relationships matter a lot in the labour market. Teambuilding, trust and the acquisition of firm-specific skills take time to develop. It makes more sense for workers' pay to reflect longer-term considerations. Nor can a firm and its workforce continuously negotiate how wages should next be changed. Too much time negotiating means too little time producing. Costly negotiations are only undertaken at intervals, often once a year.

Short-run aggregate supply

In Figure 13-6, the economy is at potential output A. In the short run, the firm inherits a given rate of nominal wage growth (not shown) that had anticipated staying at A with inflation π_0. By keeping up with inflation, nominal wage growth is expected to maintain the correct real wage for labour market equilibrium.

If inflation exceeds the expected inflation rate π_0, firms have higher prices but nominal wages have risen less than they should. Firms take advantage of their good luck by supplying a lot more output. They pay overtime to buy workforce co-operation, and may also hire temporary extra staff.

Conversely, if inflation is below π_0, the real wage is now higher than anticipated when the nominal wage was agreed. Since labour is now costly, firms cut back output a lot. In Figure 13-6, they move along the short-run supply schedule SAS in the short run.

Figure 13-6 Short-run aggregate supply

The **short-run supply curve SAS** shows how desired output varies with inflation, for a given inherited growth of nominal wages.

Suppose the economy begins at A, but then the central bank adopts a lower inflation target, shifting macroeconomic demand down from AD to AD'. After full wage and price adjustment, the final equilibrium is at E. Inflation is lower, but output is unchanged since nothing has happened to aggregate supply and potential output.

In the short run, firms inherit particular nominal wage settlements that were based on inflation expectations that were higher than the lower inflation that is now going to transpire. This means that real wages have actually risen, not because of what has happened to nominal wages W but because, with lower inflation, prices P are lower than would have been the case and hence the real wage W/P has gone up. Firms respond to more expensive labour by choosing to produce less. They move down their short-run supply curve for output to point B. Output is now below potential output, just as in the simple Keynesian model. Instead of *assuming* output is entirely demand determined, our model now has output jointly determined by demand and short-run supply. At B, output is below potential output. There is an output gap.

The **output gap** is actual output minus potential output.

Lower output and employment gradually bid down wages, reducing firms' production costs and shifting the short-run supply schedule down to *SAS'*. Eventual equilibrium at *E* is a point on the new demand schedule *AD'*, but also on both the supply schedules *SAS'* and *AS*. Shifts in short-run supply reconcile it eventually with long-run supply at potential output. The output gap disappears.

Figure 13-6 can be used to examine not just a temporary slump but also a temporary boom. Beginning at *E*, suppose the central bank loosens monetary policy and raises the inflation target. Aggregate demand rises from *AD'* to *AD*. Given the inherited wage settlements, a higher level of output prices is needed to induce firms to produce extra output, taking the economy initially to point *D*. Gradually, however, workers catch on to the fact that inflation is higher, and raise wage demands. The supply curve shifts up from *SAS'* to *SAS* and long-run equilibrium is restored at point *A*. Inflation has risen (because the inflation target was raised, and a suitable monetary policy was adopted), but output has reverted to long-run aggregate supply.

How long it takes to make the transition from short run to long run is a key issue in macroeconomics. Some economists think it is rapid, so that the insights of the classical model quickly become relevant. Others think the Keynesian model of the previous chapter remains relevant for a long time. The mainstream view is somewhere in the middle. Within a year price adjustment has begun, but it takes probably between two and four years to get to the new long-run equilibrium.

In practice, many of the shocks that an economy experiences in the short run are demand shocks. As the aggregate demand schedule shifts, it moves the economy along the short-run supply schedule in a figure such as Figure 13-6. Since suppliers need higher prices to produce more output, this means that, in the short run, higher inflation is usually correlated with higher output. One implication of this is that stabilizing inflation will also stabilize output, provided the economy is mainly subject to demand shocks.

However, an adverse supply shock leaves the central bank with no easy option. Higher oil prices not only add to inflationary pressures today, they also reduce the level of potential output. If the central bank takes care of the inflation problem by raising interest rates a lot, aggregate demand may fall substantially. The economy then experiences stagflation – high inflation and output stagnation (or outright recession) – until tighter monetary policy has got inflation back under control again.

If the fall in potential output is expected to be permanent, the central bank has to be prepared to see aggregate demand fall, even if this causes difficulties while the economy adjusts. If the fall in potential output is expected to be temporary, the central bank is likely to go more gently, raising interest rates by less, since it will be anxious to avoid an unnecessary collapse of output that is not required in the long run. Nevertheless, interest rates do have to go up, and by more than the amount inflation has risen – only then will real interest rates rise and the process of fighting inflation begin.

Case study 13-1   UK economic history through output gap spectacles

The output gap shows the percentage deviation of actual output from potential output. An output gap of +1 per cent thus means output is 1 per cent above potential output, which is unsustainable in the long run. People are working overtime, and firms are working machinery abnormally hard, perhaps by skipping maintenance activities for a while. Conversely, an output gap of −1 per cent means that output is below potential output and the economy has spare capacity that in the long run will be taken up as the economy reverts to full capacity. The OECD produces data on the evolution of the output gap in each of the leading economies. Looking at output gaps is a good way to get a picture of the shocks that an economy is experiencing.

▶

The following figure shows UK data since 1994. During 1990–92 the UK had been a member of the European Exchange Rate Mechanism and subject to the high interest rates needed to control inflation during German unification. The UK abandoned the experiment in 1992, slashed interest rates and allowed sterling to depreciate, gradually leading to a recovery. The figure shows that output had still not returned to potential output by 1994 but did so by 1997.

The Blair government inherited an improving economy and output grew strongly until 2007 by which time, with a housing price bubble, easy credit, low interest rates and a false confidence that things could never go wrong, the UK economy was seriously overheating, and actual output was about 3 per cent above potential output, which would have been unsustainable even without the impending financial crisis.

In 2007, setting monetary policy became considerably more difficult. Not only did the credit crunch create a large adverse demand shock, pressure from global price rises in oil, food and commodities created a large inflationary shock in most Western economies. The result was a significant fall in output and the emergence of a large negative output gap. The speed at which it appeared is testimony to the sharp, almost unprecedented, fall in output during 2009.

The OECD continues to take the view that potential output has been affected only to a small degree by the big recession. The figure implies that, if only we could find a way to boost demand, despite having near-zero interest rates and little room for further fiscal expansion, output would surge upwards because there is currently so much spare capacity.

Not everyone takes this view. Professors Rogoff and Reinhart, the gurus of financial market crashes and their aftermath having studied previous such crashes over eight centuries in their book *This Time is Different* (2009), argue that the recovery will be prolonged and that a good portion of previous aggregate supply will disappear in the meantime as firms scrap factories, unemployed workers lose heart and firms fail to invest at the rate that would have occurred in normal times.

According to such a view, both actual output and potential output have fallen and the output gap is much smaller than implied by the OECD chart. If Rogoff and Reinhart are correct, subsequent attempts to boost demand will quickly lead to inflation because there will be little spare capacity in the first place.

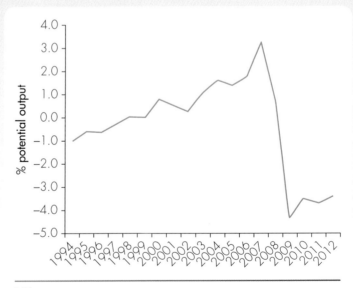

UK output gap

Source: OECD Economic Outlook

13-2 Unemployment

In the early 1930s over a quarter of the UK labour force was unemployed, which was both a waste of output and the cause of misery, social unrest and hopelessness. Postwar policy was geared to avoiding a rerun of the 1930s. Figure 13-7 shows that it succeeded. Figure 13-7(a) shows a sustained period of much lower unemployment during 1945–75.

This was followed by a difficult decade as OPEC-induced high oil prices caused stagnation and high inflation; nor could governments spend their way out of it by boosting demand. The higher price of oil had undermined aggregate supply. By the early 1980s, governments understood the need to get a grip on inflation – which temporarily made unemployment even worse – before then allowing steady recovery.

After 1992 things improved steadily, both because the period of tight demand was over now that inflation had been defeated, and because governments increasingly adopted supply-friendly policies, including labour market reform and greater competition in output markets.

Figure 13-7(b) provides more recent details, illustrating a steady increase in UK unemployment since 2004, with a particularly sharp increase in 2008–09 when output collapsed.

Is there a fixed amount of work to be shared out, or can an economy absorb a growing labour force? Those with no economics training often think there is an easy way to cut unemployment: shorten the working week, so that the same amount of total work is shared between more workers, leaving fewer people unemployed.

But a shorter work week is a very weak idea. The demand for labour (in person-hours) depends on the cost of hiring workers. Shortening the working week, without cutting wages, raises the cost of labour, so firms hire fewer workers. A daily eight-hour shift probably has an hour of dead time (coffee breaks, tidying the desk, chatting to colleagues, sneaking out to the shops). With a six-hour shift, dead time rises from one-eighth to one-sixth, making labour more expensive.

The **labour force** is everyone who has a job or wants one. The **unemployment rate** is the fraction of the labour force without a job.

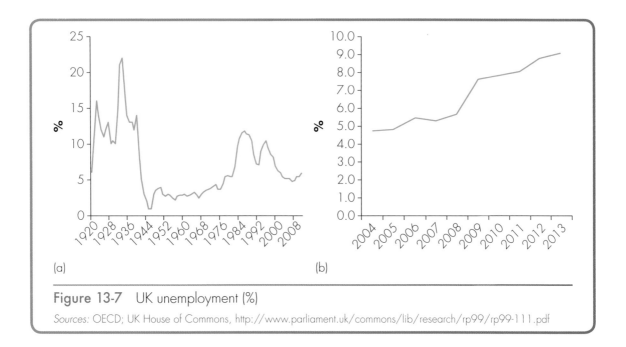

(a) (b)

Figure 13-7 UK unemployment (%)

Sources: OECD; UK House of Commons, http://www.parliament.uk/commons/lib/research/rp99/rp99-111.pdf

Since the labour force is much larger than 100 years ago, it cannot be the case in the long run that increases in the labour force lead to ever higher levels of unemployment – otherwise, unemployment would be at an all-time high. Eventually, supply and demand come to the rescue. With too much supply, the price of labour falls until the quantity demanded increases. Remember also, from our discussion of economic growth in Chapter 10, that capital accumulation and technical progress are raising labour productivity, thereby steadily increasing the demand for labour at any given wage.

In the short run, it is a slightly different story. A surge in the supply of a particular type of labour may lead temporarily to higher unemployment of that type of labour until the market can adjust. If Polish builders move permanently to the UK, some UK builders may find it hard to get the work they used to get. There are then three possible outcomes: (a) builders cut the wage for which they are prepared to work in order to safeguard their old jobs, (b) builders refuse to cut wages and experience unemployment, or (c) some builders leave the industry and become taxi drivers or security workers in the nightclub industry.

Stocks and flows

Unemployment is a stock, measured at a point in time. Like a pool of water, it rises when inflows (the newly unemployed) exceed outflows (people getting new jobs or quitting the labour force entirely). Table 13-1 shows that the pool of unemployment is not stagnant. Even with 1.7 million unemployed, many more than this number of people enter and leave the pool *every* year. Most people escape quickly, though those with few skills may visit the pool many times in their working lifetime. However, some people get stuck in the pool, lose confidence and get stigmatized as a poor bet for an employer. Sometimes this is because the labour market has identified a worker who is genuinely less willing or able, but sometimes it just reflects bad luck that then becomes self-reinforcing.

Table 13-1   UK unemployment (millions), 2006

Inflow to unemployment	2.6
Outflow from unemployment	2.5
Stock of unemployed	1.7

Source: ONS, *Labour Market Trends*

Types of unemployment

Unemployment can be frictional, structural, demand-deficient or classical.

Frictional unemployment is the irreducible minimum unemployment in a dynamic society.

It includes some people with disabilities that make them hard to employ, but also includes people spending short spells in unemployment as they hop between jobs in an economy where both the labour force and the jobs on offer are continually changing.

Structural unemployment reflects a mismatch of skills and job opportunities when the pattern of employment is changing.

Frictional unemployment arises from temporary impediments; structural unemployment reflects medium-run forces. A skilled welder made redundant at 50 in the north of England may have to retrain or move south to find work. Firms are reluctant to take on and train older workers, and housing in richer areas may be too dear. Such workers are victims of structural unemployment.

Demand-deficient unemployment occurs when output is below full capacity.

Until wages and prices adjust to their new long-run equilibrium level, a fall in aggregate demand reduces output and employment. Some workers want to work at the going real-wage rate but cannot find jobs.

Classical unemployment arises when the wage is kept above its long-run equilibrium level.

This may reflect trade union power or minimum wage legislation. If wages cannot adjust, the labour market can restore low unemployment in long-run equilibrium.

The modern analysis of unemployment takes the same types of unemployment but classifies them differently, distinguishing between *voluntary* and *involuntary* unemployment.

Equilibrium unemployment

Figure 13-8 shows the market for labour. The labour demand schedule LD slopes downwards, since firms hire more workers at a lower real wage. The schedule LF shows how many people join the labour force at each real wage. A higher real wage makes (a few) more people want to work. The schedule AJ shows how many people accept a job at each real wage. It must lie left of the LF schedule, since the labour force is the employed plus the unemployed. The horizontal gap between AJ and LF shows voluntary unemployment at each real wage.

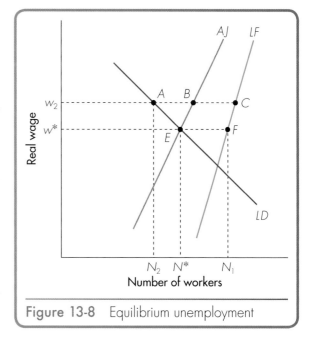

Figure 13-8   Equilibrium unemployment

Voluntary unemployment is people looking for work who will not yet take a job at that real wage.

People house hunting do not take the first house they see. Similarly, some people invest in searching a bit longer for a more suitable job. At high real wages, people grab job offers quickly and the AJ and LF schedules are close together. At low real wages, people are more selective about accepting offers, especially if the offer is little above the benefits available to those out of work. Hence, the AJ and LF schedules are further apart at low real wages. Labour market equilibrium is at E. Employment is N^* and unemployment is the distance EF.

Equilibrium unemployment is unemployment when the labour market is in equilibrium.

Since it is the gap between the desire to accept jobs and the desire to be in the labour force, this unemployment is entirely voluntary. At the equilibrium real wage w^*, N_1 people want to be in the labour force but only N^* want to accept job offers; the remainder do not want to work at the equilibrium real wage.

Equilibrium unemployment includes frictional and structural unemployment. What about classical unemployment: for example, if unions keep wages at w_2, above w^*? Total unemployment is now AC, which exceeds EF. At the wage w_2, BC workers are voluntarily unemployed, but AB workers are now involuntarily unemployed. Firms hire at point A, but individual workers want to be at point B.

Involuntary unemployment means the unemployed would take a job offer at the existing wage.

However, through their unions, workers collectively have chosen a wage of w_2 in excess of w^*, thus reducing employment. For workers as a whole, this extra unemployment is voluntary. It has raised equilibrium unemployment from EF to AC.

Keynesian or demand-deficient unemployment is entirely involuntary, and arises when wages have not yet adjusted to restore labour market equilibrium. Suppose in Figure 13-8 that the original labour demand schedule goes through points E and F. Equilibrium employment is at B, and equilibrium unemployment is BC. Now labour demand falls to LD. Until wages adjust, BC remains voluntary unemployment but AB is involuntary unemployment, pure spare capacity. Boosting labour demand again could move the economy from *A* back to *B*. Without such a boost to demand, involuntary unemployment will slowly bid wages down, moving the economy from *A* down to *E*. If this takes a long time, policies to boost demand may be preferable.

Thus, total unemployment is equilibrium unemployment plus demand-deficient unemployment. Only the latter is spare capacity that could be mopped up by shifting demand upwards. When the labour market is already in equilibrium, shifting demand up makes hardly any difference to the gap between the nearly parallel *AJ* and *LF* schedules. We then need *supply-side policies* that can close the gap between these two schedules that together reflect labour supply to the economy.

Why was unemployment so high?

Did high unemployment reflect inadequate demand or a rise in equilibrium unemployment?

Figure 13-9 shows the average unemployment rate during ten periods, from 1956–59 through to 2008–12. It shows how actual unemployment rose dramatically in the 1980s, fell back, and has renewed impetus since the financial crash. The figure also shows an estimate of what was happening to equilibrium unemployment. Clearly, most of the rise and fall of actual unemployment was accompanied by a rise and fall of *equilibrium* unemployment, which had many causes.

Unions became more powerful after the 1960s, but were then undermined by globalization, privatization and legislation aimed at diminishing their power. Mismatches of jobs, and hence structural unemployment, arose in regions and skills in which manufacturing decline had severe effects. More generous welfare benefits undermined work incentives at the lower end of the wage scale and disconnected people from the labour market.

Recent policy also emphasized encouraging people back into work by trying to reduce disincentives for poorer workers. People out of work but receiving income support, housing benefit and council tax assistance lose benefits rapidly as they begin to earn income. The interaction of different policies used to impose effective tax rates of over 90 per cent on initial income work. Reforms during 1997–2007 reduced this to below 70 per cent, and help explain why equilibrium unemployment fell.

Governments need revenue to provide benefits for the very poor, including those out of work. But why do we tax the nearly poor so very heavily? We long ago abandoned 70 per cent income tax rates on the rich, who now pay 40 per cent. In practice, middle-class voters are more likely to be the swinging voters who decide the outcomes of elections. Hence, they have significant political power. In contrast, the poor-in-work are unlikely to vote for parties associated with support for the well-off, and hence have less political influence.

Figure 13-9 also shows a few periods when demand-deficient unemployment was important, particularly in the early 1980s, when the Thatcher government first adopted tough policies to defeat inflation, in the early 1990s, when monetary and fiscal policy were tightened to conquer inflation that had emerged in the late 1980s, and of course since 2008. During these recessions, Keynesian unemployment existed.

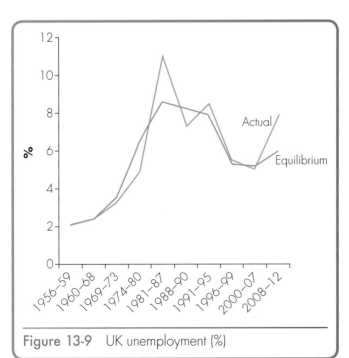

Figure 13-9 UK unemployment (%)

Conversely, in the 1970s, despite the rise in unemployment, the economy was actually overheating and unemployment was less than its equilibrium level. Policy makers, assuming that rising unemployment had been caused by deficient demand, boosted demand to mop up the slack. Since there was no slack, this merely added to inflation. Similarly, Figure 13-9 shows the Lawson boom at the end of the 1980s, another period of overheating, which is why the brakes had to go on in the early 1990s.

Figure 13-9 confirms again the message that policy was much more successful after 1992. The switch to central bank independence and inflation targeting took the politics out of monetary policy and provided macroeconomic stability. During 1995–2005, unemployment remained quite close to its equilibrium level. The other reason is that governments gradually learned about the importance of supply-side policies to reduce equilibrium unemployment itself. None of this will insulate the UK economy from severe global shocks from the credit crunch and higher commodity prices, but at least there have been fewer own goals caused by domestic policy.

Keynesians believe that the economy can deviate from full employment for quite a long time, certainly for a period of several years. Monetarists believe that the classical full-employment model is relevant much more quickly. Both agree that the long-run performance of the economy depends on aggregate supply, and thus what happens to potential output and equilibrium unemployment.

Case study 13-2 How bad could unemployment become?

The OECD is a club of the most advanced economic nations in the world – living standards and per capita income count more than absolute size. Newer members include Turkey, Mexico and Hungary. China and India are not yet members despite their vast populations. Currently the OECD has 30 members.

The 2009 OECD *Employment Outlook* discusses prospects for unemployment and possible policy responses. The evolution of unemployment depends on (a) the size of the shock, (b) the flexibility of the economy to respond, and (c) the extent of support by government. In the worst previous postwar recession of 1973–76, OECD unemployment increased by half. By 2009, the OECD reckoned that unemployment would rise by 80 per cent – from 5.5 to 10 per cent of the labour force – during 2007–10. And they turned out to be correct.

This analysis reflected the magnitude of the initial shock. Clearly, this would affect different countries differently. One way in which to assess which economies were most vulnerable is to estimate their capacity to absorb shocks through flexible labour markets that match potential workers and job opportunities more quickly. This is likely to depend on wage flexibility, labour market mobility, attitudes of trade unions and the extent of labour market regulation.

The following figure shows a measure of labour market flexibility based on labour market history during 2000–05. It plots the annual fraction of workers hired to new jobs or leaving existing jobs (by choice or dismissal) during the year. In Turkey, Denmark and the US, half of all workers are changing jobs annually. In contrast, the countries with the lowest labour market mobility are Greece, Italy and Austria.

Countries with greater job stability are probably slower to experience initial unemployment but, when unemployment does increase, they are also less successful at helping people out of unemployment back into work. Since there is considerable cross-country evidence that those in longer-term unemployment find it ever more difficult to reconnect with the labour market, in the medium run

▶

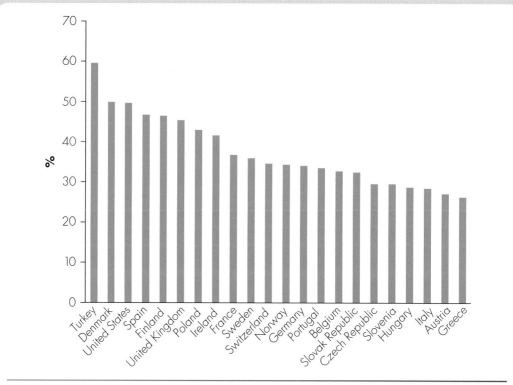

Annual fraction of workers hired or fired (%)

Source: OECD, *Employment Outlook*, 2009

this fiscal burden of unemployment benefits is likely to be greater in countries with less flexible labour markets.

Governments provide two kinds of support. The first is measurable by the generosity of unemployment benefit, which has two dimensions – the *replacement rate* (the ratio of benefit to previous wages in work) and the *number of years* for which benefit is available. The table below documents considerable differences across countries.

In Norway and Belgium, with strong traditions of social democracy, unemployment benefit is generous both because it is high relative to wages in work and because it continues for at least five years after a spell of unemployment begins. French unemployment benefit is initially as generous but less so after year 2. The UK is considerably less generous in replacement rate, but entitlement continues undiminished over the five-year period. In countries such as Japan, Greece and the US, unemployment benefit is almost worthless after the first year in unemployment.

The second aspect of state support for the unemployed is through active labour market policies that enhance incentives, confidence, and the ability of the unemployed to look for jobs. Even if the post-crash recession reflected a sharp fall in demand – for output and then for labour – it is important not to neglect supply-side policies that maintain the maximum labour market flexibility.

Duration of unemployment	Year 1	Year 2	Year 5
	Replacement rate (%)		
Norway	72	72	72
Belgium	65	63	63
France	67	64	31
UK	28	28	28
Japan	45	3	3
Greece	33	5	1
US	28	0	0

Source: OECD, Employment Outlook, 2009

Tax cuts

Would lower tax rates improve work incentives and labour supply? Figure 13-10 again shows labour demand LD, the labour force schedule LF and the job acceptances schedule AJ. As in Figure 13-8, the horizontal distance between AJ and LF shows voluntary unemployment, which decreases as the real wage rises relative to the given level of welfare benefits.

Now imagine an income tax equal to the vertical distance AB. Equilibrium employment is now N_1, which is both the number of workers that firms want to hire at the gross wage w_1 and the number of workers wanting to take jobs at the corresponding after-tax wage w_3. The horizontal distance BC is now equilibrium unemployment – people in the labour force, but not taking a job at the going rate of take-home pay.

If income tax is abolished, the gross wage to the firm now coincides with the take-home pay of a worker, and labour market equilibrium is at E. Equilibrium employment has risen, and equilibrium unemployment falls from BC to EF. Higher take-home pay, relative to unemployment benefit, reduces voluntary unemployment.

Trade unions

By restricting job acceptances and making labour more scarce, trade unions shift the AJ schedule to the left, widening the gap between AJ and LF. Imagine a new AJ' schedule through point B in Figure 13-10. Point B is now labour market equilibrium. Since labour is scarcer, the real wage has risen, but equilibrium has increased from EF to BC. Conversely, equilibrium unemployment falls if union power is weakened. Unions are less successful in restricting labour supply and forcing up wages.

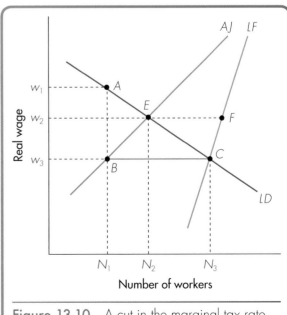

Figure 13-10   A cut in the marginal tax rate

Welfare to work

Recent UK policies have tried to reconnect unemployment to the labour market, both by offering assistance and by removing the option to be in permanent receipt of unemployment benefit without making an effort to look for work. In effect, this shifts the *AJ* schedule to the right, by inducing or forcing more of the labour force to take jobs.

Maths 13-1

Voluntary and involuntary unemployment

Suppose the labour force is given by $L = 2a + bw$, where w is the take-home wage. The number of people wishing to accept a job offer is given by $N = 2bw$. The demand for workers by firms is given by $N = 3a - bw$, where a and b are positive constants.

In labour market equilibrium, job acceptances equals job offers, whence $3a - bw = 2bw$. Hence $w^* = a/b$, and equilibrium employment $N^* = 2a$. Facing the wage w^*, the number of people wishing to join the labour force is $L^* = 2a + a = 3a$. Equilibrium unemployment is therefore $L^* - N^* = a$.

Now suppose w continues to be the take-home wage, but employers have to pay national insurance at the rate t per worker. Labour demand becomes $N = 3a - b(w + t)$. Equilibrium employment occurs when $N = 2bw = 3a - b(w + t)$, which implies $w^* = (a/b) - (t/3)$ and $N^* = (2a) - (2bt/3)$. This is less than 2a, so any positive tax reduces equilibrium employment.

Equilibrium unemployment is $[2a + bw^*] - [2bw^*] = 2a - bw^* = 2a - (b)[(a/b) - (t/3)] = a + (bt/3)$. So the higher the tax rate on labour, the higher is equilibrium unemployment.

This does not mean that labour taxes should be zero. Almost all taxes distort and create an economic distortion, but the government needs tax revenue for many good purposes, from providing public goods to financing welfare payment. A well-designed tax system spreads these distortions around so that no individual distortion becomes too large.

Costs of unemployment

The private cost of unemployment

Voluntary unemployment has a private cost to those unemployed, the sacrifice of the wage they would get by taking a job. The private benefit is that they may find a better job offer by looking longer; they also get some state benefits in the meantime. Whereas the voluntarily unemployed prefer not to take a job just yet, those involuntarily out of work would prefer immediate employment and may be much worse off in unemployment. When unemployment is involuntary, people are suffering more.

The social cost of unemployment

This also varies with the nature of unemployment. Voluntary unemployment, by definition, is preferred by the individual, but should society value it too? Whereas these individuals count their benefit cheque as part of the gain from unemployment, socially this transfer payment does not contribute to national output or income.

Even so, society should not eliminate voluntary unemployment completely. First, transfer benefits may compensate for *other* market failures, such as difficulties in borrowing to acquire proper training. Second, society benefits directly from some voluntary unemployment. A changing economy needs to match up the right people to the right jobs, thus raising productivity and total output. The flow through the pool of unemployment is one way in which this is done.

Involuntary or Keynesian unemployment has a higher social cost. An economy producing below full capacity is wasting resources, which adds to the social cost of unemployment.

 ## Inflation and unemployment: the Phillips curve

In 1958, using UK data on inflation and unemployment, Professor A. W. Phillips of the London School of Economics discovered an empirical relationship that became famous, since it seemed also to work for other countries.

> The **Phillips curve** shows that higher inflation is accompanied by lower unemployment.

The Phillips curve in Figure 13-11 shows the trade-off that people thought they faced in the 1960s. It suggested that UK inflation would fall to zero if only people would tolerate unemployment as high as 2.5 per cent. If only! Since then, we have had years when *both* inflation and unemployment exceeded 10 per cent. The simple Phillips curve ceased to fit the facts.

We now realize that this Phillips curve is simply the mirror image of the aggregate supply curve. The latter relates inflation to output; the former relates inflation to unemployment.

The two are connected because high output goes with low unemployment.

> **Equilibrium unemployment** U^* is the level of unemployment in long-run equilibrium.

The previous section explained why equilibrium unemployment is above zero. Once all variables can adjust, the market returns to equilibrium unemployment. There is no *long-run* trade-off

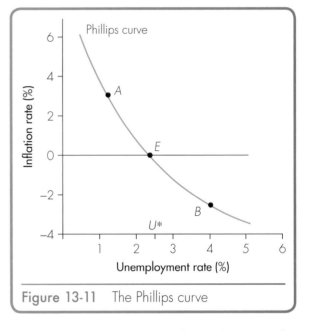

Figure 13-11 The Phillips curve

between inflation and unemployment. Just as the long-run aggregate supply curve for goods is vertical at potential output, the long-run Phillips curve is vertical at equilibrium unemployment U^* in Figure 13-11. An increase in equilibrium unemployment shifts the long-run Phillips curve to the right.

> The **long-run Phillips curve** is vertical at equilibrium unemployment.

The height of a *short-run* aggregate supply curve reflects the inflation expectations already built into nominal wages. The same holds in the labour market.

> Each **short-run Phillips curve** is a negative relation between inflation and unemployment, given the inflation expectations already built into nominal wages.

In Figure 13-12, inflation expectations π_1 are already embodied in nominal wages and the short-run Phillips curve is PC_1. Suppose the central bank adopts a lower inflation target. Initially, this is below the previous level of expected inflation. The central bank raises interest rates and tightens monetary policy. The economy moves from E to A along the short-run Phillips curve.

Notice that two things are going on. First, with lower aggregate demand, caused by tighter monetary policy, output and employment have fallen and unemployment has risen. Second, to the extent that wage settlements have not yet had a chance to adjust to the new monetary policy, wage growth corresponding

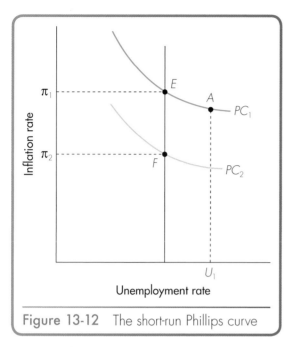

Figure 13-12 The short-run Phillips curve

to the inflation level expected at point E has turned out to be higher than price growth, corresponding to inflation at point A. Since wages have grown more quickly than prices, real wages have risen. So not only has aggregate demand fallen, aggregate supply has fallen in the short run too: with more expensive labour, firms are less keen to produce output.

If people expect lower inflation to be sustained, new wage settlements eventually embody lower inflation expectations, the Phillips curve shifts down to PC_2, and the eventual equilibrium is at F. Unemployment and output are back in long-run equilibrium, and inflation expectations have adjusted to the new policy. Since F is vertically below E, in the long run there is no trade-off between inflation and unemployment.

What about interest rates? The equilibrium level of output in the long run is consistent with a particular real interest rate. Once the economy has made the transition from point E to point F, all that has changed is that inflation is lower. Hence nominal interest rates eventually are lower by the same amount, so that real interest rates revert to their previous long-run level.

The original Phillips curve of Figure 13-11 was not a *permanent* trade-off between inflation and unemployment. It showed a temporary trade-off, for a given level of inherited inflation expectations and nominal wage growth. During the long historical period examined by Phillips, expected inflation happened to be low. In the second half of the twentieth century, inflation was higher on average and more variable. Hence, the short-run Phillips curve shifted up and down as inflation expectations changed.

Inflation got out of control because monetary growth was no longer tied to growth in the stock of gold, as it had been in the nineteenth century. Governments could print money. Workers, perceiving that governments were fearful of unemployment, kept raising nominal wages. Frightened to put on the monetary brakes and raise real interest rates, governments instructed their central banks to print money and accommodate nominal wage increases. The expectation of this behaviour became a self-fulfilling prophecy.

This example shows the crucial role of expectations, and explains why governments now go to such lengths to try to convince the public of their good intentions. The good years 1995–2007 were a period in which people had become convinced that inflation would be low, hence they could afford to settle for low rates of nominal wage growth. Nominal interest rates were also low because people were expecting low inflation.

- Higher inflation reduces aggregate demand because the central bank raises real interest rates to get inflation back on target. The height of the aggregate demand schedule reflects the inflation target.

- In the classical model with complete wage and price flexibility, output is always potential output and the vertical long-run supply curve is valid immediately.

- The equilibrium inflation rate thus occurs at the inflation target. A rise in demand caused by fiscal expansion or private optimism induces a rise in real interest rates to reduce aggregate demand back to the level of potential output.

- The short-run supply curve shows how higher inflation temporarily raises output because inherited nominal wages have not yet had time to adjust. Over time, shifts in the short-run supply curve restore long-run equilibrium at potential output and the inflation target.

- How quickly actual output returns to potential output is a key issue in macroeconomics. If this is rapid, demand management is unnecessary. If it is slow, demand management is essential.

- Permanent supply shocks change potential output. To preserve the target inflation rate, monetary policy must accommodate the shock, thus providing the required change in aggregate demand.

- People are either employed, unemployed or out of the labour force. Unemployment rises when inflows to the pool of the unemployed exceed outflows. Inflows and outflows are large relative to the pool of unemployment.

- Unemployment may be frictional, structural, classical or demand-deficient. The first three types are voluntary unemployment; the last is involuntary, or Keynesian, unemployment. Equilibrium unemployment is voluntary unemployment in long-run equilibrium.

- In the long run, a sustained rise in unemployment must reflect higher equilibrium unemployment. In temporary recessions, Keynesian unemployment also matters.

- Supply-side economics aims to raise potential output, and reduce equilibrium unemployment, by improving microeconomic incentives.

- Some unemployment allows a better match of people and jobs, especially if inflows and outflows to the unemployment pool are large.

- Keynesian unemployment is involuntary, and represents wasted output. Society may also care about the human misery inflicted by involuntary unemployment.

- The Phillips curve shows the relation between inflation and unemployment. In the long run, the Phillips curve is vertical at equilibrium unemployment. There is no correlation between long-run inflation and long-run unemployment.

- The short-run Phillips curve is a negative relation between inflation and output. Given the nominal wages that firms have agreed, higher output prices induce higher output and lower unemployment. This curve shows in the labour market what the short-run supply curve shows in the output market.

- The height of the short-run Phillips curve, like the height of the short-run supply curve for output, depends on the inflation expectations that have been determined by recent nominal wage agreements.

Review questions

To check your answers to these questions, go to pages 392–3.

1 Suppose easier migration within the European Union allows large numbers of extra people to join the UK labour force. Using the framework of aggregate demand and aggregate supply, discuss the effects on output and inflation, in the short run and in the long run.

2 Suppose the Bank of England wants to keep inflation constant during this transition. How should interest rates be adjusted?

3 'Supply shocks change output; demand shocks change inflation.' Is this statement correct, in either the short run or the long run? Does the answer depend on what kind of demand shock it is?

4 Discuss the effect of a rise in export demand when wage adjustment is sluggish. What happens to (a) interest rates, (b) investment and (c) tax revenue?

5 Why are these statements wrong? (a) Higher inflation reduces output by making it more expensive for firms to produce. (b) Higher inflation reduces output because consumers demand fewer goods when prices are higher.

6 World oil prices increase permanently because of an earthquake in the Middle East that destroys oil wells. You are in charge of setting interest rates in pursuit of an inflation target of 2 per cent. What do you do? What happens to output?

7 'The microchip has caused a permanent rise in unemployment.' Discuss this assertion, showing its effects on labour demand, the labour force and job acceptances.

8 How is high unemployment explained by: (a) a Keynesian economist and (b) a classical economist?

9 How do lower taxes affect unemployment: (a) when the economy begins at equilibrium unemployment, and (b) when initially it also has Keynesian unemployment?

10 Why is unemployment among school-leavers higher than that among adults?

11 Why are these statements wrong? (a) So long as there is unemployment, there is pressure on wages to fall. (b) Unemployment arises only because greedy workers are pricing themselves out of a job.

12 Is the claim that the long-run Phillips curve is vertical consistent with the claim that inflation is very damaging?

13 Imagine that UK annual output growth averages 1 per cent over the next decade. (a) How quickly do you think potential output normally grows? Why? (b) What is likely to happen to UK unemployment in this scenario? (c) Is potential output likely to grow more quickly or more slowly than its historical average rate? Why?

14 Suppose you became the next prime minister of Greece with a mandate to reform its labour market and reduce its unemployment. What measures would you introduce?

15 Would Professor Phillips have found a reliable statistical relationship between inflation and unemployment if he had happened to examine a period in which: (a) equilibrium unemployment was constant and inflation expectations were high but constant, (b) equilibrium unemployment kept changing and (c) inflation expectations kept changing? Explain.

16 A newly elected government announces that it intends to run a large budget deficit, print money to pay for this, and impose laws to prevent wages and prices from being raised. (a) What do you predict will happen? Why? (b) If this government loses the next election, what policy advice would you give to the next government?

DIFFICULT

17 **Essay question** 'Fifteen years of low inflation after 1992 was caused neither by insulating monetary policy from government meddling nor by policies to diminish the power of trade unions, but rather by cheap imports from China. Once China became an economic superpower, its demand for raw materials bid up world commodity prices, creating a new inflation that neither central bank independence nor the weakening of trade unions was able to prevent.' Discuss.

18 **Essay question** Should the government extend or abolish a compulsory retirement age because people are living longer? Discuss the possible consequences of such a change.

Online Learning Centre

To help you grasp the key concepts of this chapter check out the extra resources posted on the Online Learning Centre at www.mcgraw-hill.co.uk/textbooks/begg.

There are additional case studies, self-test questions, practice exam questions with answers and a graphing tool.

CHAPTER 14

Exchange rates and the balance of payments

Learning outcomes

By the end of this chapter, you should be able to:

- Explain the forex market
- Discuss balance of payments accounting
- Compare internal and external balance

- Analyse monetary policy with fixed exchange rates
- Show the impact of devaluation
- Analyse monetary policy with floating exchange rates

Although our macroeconomic analysis has recognized exports to, and imports from, the rest of the world, to date we have examined only how trade is affected by fluctuations in national income. It also depends importantly on competitiveness. To make sense of this, we first need to understand how exchange rate markets work.

Second, we need to understand how external surpluses and deficits lead to changes in a country's stock of foreign debts or assets. Governments who owe their own citizens money usually have less to fear than governments with foreign creditors who eventually may be less sympathetic.

 ## Exchange rates and the balance of payments

Exports and imports are each about 15 per cent of GDP in the US, about 30 per cent in the UK, over 40 per cent in Germany, but only 11 per cent in Japan (Figure 14-1). As transport costs fall and communications improve, the world economy is becoming more integrated and international trade is increasing. To compete within this global economy, everyone has to specialize in what they are good at. Small countries tend to export a larger fraction of their national output: once they specialize and produce on a world scale,

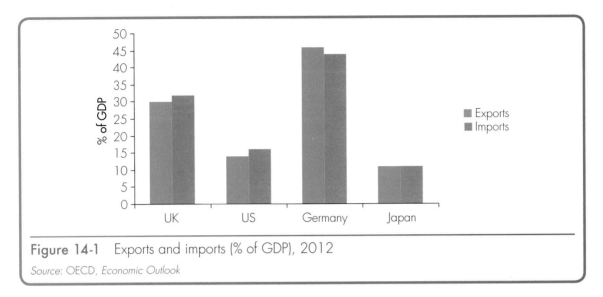

Figure 14-1 Exganeous Exports and imports (% of GDP), 2012

Source: OECD, Economic Outlook

they are making much more of particular commodities than they will ever wish to consume at home. Instead, they export a lot, and acquire most of their consumption needs by spending this income on imports.

When an economy is very open to foreign trade, the exchange rate, international competitiveness and the trade balance with foreigners become major policy issues. We show how openness to trade and financial flows affects the domestic economy.

The foreign exchange market

The **foreign exchange (forex) market** exchanges one national currency for another.
The **exchange rate** is the price at which two currencies exchange.

An exchange rate of $1.50/£ measures the international value of sterling: how much foreign currency ($) a unit of the domestic currency (£) is worth.

Who supplies $ to the forex market, wanting £ in exchange? This demand for £ arises from UK exporters wanting to convert $ back into £, and from US residents wanting to buy UK assets for which they must pay in £. Conversely, a supply of £ to the forex market reflects UK importers wanting $ to buy US goods, and UK residents wishing to buy US $ assets.

Figure 14-2 shows the resulting supply *SS* and demand *DD* for £. The equilibrium exchange rate e_1 equates the quantity of £ supplied and demanded. If the US demand for UK goods or assets rises, the demand for £ shifts right to DD_1, and the equilibrium $/£ exchange rate rises. A higher $/£ exchange rate means the £ has *appreciated*, because its international value has risen. The $ has simultaneously *depreciated*, since its international value is lower. A fall in the $/£ exchange rate has the opposite effect.

Exchange rate regimes

An exchange rate regime describes the rules under which governments allow exchange rates to be determined.

A **fixed exchange rate** means that governments, acting through their central banks, will buy or sell as much of the currency as people want to exchange at the fixed rate.

In Figure 14-2, a fixed exchange rate e_1 is the free market equilibrium rate if the supply and demand for £ are *SS* and *DD*. The market clears unaided. Suppose the demand for £ now shifts up to DD_1. Americans, hooked on whisky, need more £ to import from the UK. In a free market, the equilibrium is now at *B* and the £ appreciates against the $.

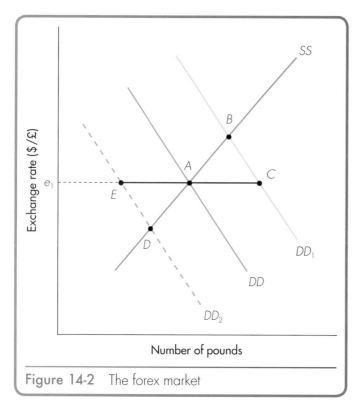

Figure 14-2 The forex market

At the fixed exchange rate e_1, there is an excess demand AC for £. To meet this, the Bank of England prints AC extra £ and sells them in exchange for $[e_1 \times AC]$ of $, which are added to the UK foreign exchange reserves.

The **foreign exchange reserves** are the foreign currency holdings of the domestic central bank.

Conversely, if the demand for £ shifts down to DD_2, few foreigners now want British goods or assets. The free market equilibrium exchange rate is below e_1 unless the central bank intervenes. To defend the fixed exchange rate e_1, at which there would be an excess supply EA of £, the central bank demands EA in £, paid for by selling $(EA \times e_1)$ of $ from the foreign exchange reserves. When the central bank is forced to buy or sell £ to support the fixed exchange rate, it *intervenes* in the forex market.

If the demand for £ on average is DD_2, the Bank on average is reducing the UK forex reserves to support the £ at e_1. The £ is overvalued. As reserves run out, the government may try to borrow foreign exchange reserves from the International Monetary Fund (IMF), an international body that lends to governments in short-term difficulties. At best, this is a temporary solution. Unless the demand for £ rises in the long run, it will be necessary to *devalue* the pound.

A **devaluation (revaluation)** is a fall (rise) in the fixed exchange rate.

In November 1967, the UK government, after consultations with other governments, devalued the pound from $2.80/£ to $2.40/£. However, the UK has not always pursued a fixed exchange rate.

In a **floating exchange rate** regime, the exchange rate is allowed to find its free market equilibrium without any intervention using the foreign exchange reserves.

Thus, in Figure 14-2 the demand schedule shifts from DD_2 to DD to DD_1 would be allowed to move the equilibrium point from D to A to B.

Of course, it is not necessary to adopt the extreme regimes of pure floating or perfectly fixed exchange rates. *Dirty floating* means some intervention in the short run but allowing the exchange rate to find its equilibrium level in the longer run. By understanding the two polar cases – completely fixed and freely floating – we can see how the intermediate regimes would work.

Next, we explain balance of payments accounting, and its connection to exchange rate regimes.

Box 14-1

Effective exchange rates

Each currency has a bilateral exchange rate against each other currency. For example, for sterling we can measure the dollar/sterling exchange rate $/£ or euro/sterling exchange rate €/£. Sometimes it is useful to examine the average exchange rate against all countries.

> The **effective exchange rate (eer)** is a weighted average of individual bilateral exchange rates.

Usually, we use the share of trade with each country to decide the weights. Important trading partners get more weight in the effective exchange rate index. Thus, for the UK, the dollar/sterling exchange rate has a larger weight than the yen/sterling exchange rate because the UK trades more with the US than with Japan.

The figure below shows the *actual* bilateral exchange rates of sterling against the UK's two main trading partners, the US and the Eurozone. The £ has fluctuated against both. During the first part of the decade, sterling appreciated strongly against the dollar. Then, after the financial crash, to which the UK was particularly exposed because of the size of its financial sector, sterling depreciated substantially in 2009. Against the euro, sterling has been depreciating much more steadily. The strength of German exports has helped maintain a strong overall exchange rate for the euro (a key

Bilateral and effective exchange rates

Source: Bank of England

reason why Greece and Spain have become so uncompetitive; unlike sterling, they were not able to achieve a rapid depreciation to raise competitiveness when their economies got into trouble).

The third exchange rate shown in the figure is sterling's effective exchange rate against all currencies. Since the dollar and the euro are much the most important, is unsurprising that the effective exchange rate is largely an average of what was happening to the two main bilateral exchange rates. The effective exchange rate is an artificial construction, and we can set the initial value of the index at any level we like. Its purpose is to measure changes thereafter. In the figure below we set the index at an intermediate level between the $/£ exchange rate and €/£ exchange rate on 1 January 2000.

The figure makes two important points. First, the effective exchange rate, being an average, fluctuates less than its component parts. The turquoise line displays less volatility than the orange line or blue line, and always lies between them. Second, since UK trade with the Eurozone greatly exceeds trade with the US, the overall average is closer to the €/£ than to the $/£.

The balance of payments

The **balance of payments** records all transactions between a country and the rest of the world.

All international transactions giving rise to an inflow of £ to the UK are credits in the UK balance of payments accounts. Outflows of £ are debits, entered with a minus sign. Table 14-1 shows the actual UK balance of payments accounts in 2011.

The **current account** of the balance of payments records international flows of goods, services and transfer payments.

Visible trade is exports and imports of goods (cars, food, steel). *Invisible trade* is exports and imports of services (banking, shipping, tourism). Together, these make up the trade balance or net exports of goods and services. To get the current account, we take the trade balance and add *net* transfer payments from abroad. These comprise interest income on net foreign assets, and other international transfer payments

Table 14-1	UK balance of payments (£bn), 2011		
(1)	Current account, of which		−29
	Trade in goods	−100	
	Trade in services	+72	
	Current transfers and other income	−1	
(2)	Capital account		+4
(3)	Financial account		+28
(4)	Balancing item		−3
(5)	UK balance of payments (1 + 2 + 3 + 4)		0
(6)	Official financing (= −4)		0

Source: www.ons.gov.uk/ons/rel/bop

(for example, net aid to foreign countries, which is an outflow). The UK current account was £29 billion in deficit in 2011.

> The **capital account** of the balance of payments shows international flows of transfer payments relating to capital items.

This covers payments received from the EU for investment in regional infrastructure projects, the transfer of capital into or out of the UK by migrants and UK forgiveness of foreign debt. Typically, capital transfer payments are small.

> The **financial account** of the balance of payments records international purchases and sales of financial assets.

Table 14-1 shows a net financial inflow of £28 billion in 2011. The inflow of money to the UK as foreigners bought UK physical and financial assets exceeded the inflow of money from the UK as residents bought assets abroad.[1]

The balancing item is a statistical adjustment, which would be zero if all previous items had been correctly measured. It reflects a failure to record all transactions in the official statistics. Adding together the (1) current account, (2) capital account, (3) financial account and (4) balancing item yields the UK *balance of payments* in 2011. As it happens, it was just in balance.

> The **balance of payments** records the net monetary inflow from abroad when households, firms and the government make their desired transactions.

The final entry in Table 14-1 is *official financing*. This is always of equal magnitude and opposite sign to the balance of payments in the line above, so that the sum of all the entries is *always* zero. Official financing measures the international transactions that the government must take to *accommodate* all the other transactions in the balance of payments accounts.

Floating exchange rates

If the exchange rate is freely floating, with no central bank intervention, the forex reserves are constant, and the exchange rate equates the supply and demand for £.

The supply of £, by people needing $ to buy imports or foreign assets, measures outflows or minus items in the UK balance of payments. The demand for £, by people selling $ earned from exports and sales of assets to foreigners, measures inflows or plus items in the UK balance of payments. A freely floating exchange rate equates the quantities of £ supplied and demanded. Hence inflows equal outflows and the balance of payments is *exactly* zero. There is no intervention in the forex market, and thus no official financing.

With a zero balance of payments, under floating exchange rates a current account surplus is exactly matched by a deficit of the same size on combined capital and financial accounts, or vice versa. A current account surplus (deficit) means a country underspends (overspends) its international income. This saving (dissaving) adds to (subtracts from) its net international assets. That is precisely what the capital and financial accounts record. Since transfers on the capital account are tiny, henceforth we assume that they are zero.

Hence, under floating exchange rates, a current account surplus is exactly matched by a financial account deficit. Conversely, a current account deficit is exactly matched by a financial account surplus. The balance of payments is always in balance.

Fixed exchange rates

With a fixed exchange rate, the balance of payments need not be zero. A payments deficit means that total outflows exceed total inflows on the combined current and capital accounts. The supply of £ to the

---

[1] UK statistics now follow modern international practice in distinguishing the capital and financial account. Previously, rows (2) and (3) were amalgamated and simply called the 'capital account' even though all the large items were financial flows. References to international capital flows nearly always mean financial flows.

forex market, from UK imports or purchases of foreign assets, exceeds the demand for £, from UK exports or sales of assets to foreigners. The balance of payments deficit is precisely the excess supply of £ in the forex market.

To peg the exchange rate, the Bank of England must demand this excess supply of £, reducing UK forex reserves by selling $ to buy £. This is 'official financing' in the balance of payments. Hence, with a balance of payments deficit (surplus), forex reserves must be sold (bought).

The current account

UK imports depend in part on the level of UK income. Hence, UK exports, which are someone else's imports, depend partly on income in the rest of the world. The second key determinant of net exports is international competitiveness. However, we must distinguish nominal and real variables. International competitiveness depends on the real exchange rate.

> The **real exchange rate** is the relative price of domestic and foreign goods, when measured in a common currency.

A higher real exchange rate, raising the price of UK goods relative to US goods measured in the same currency, makes the UK less competitive relative to the US. A fall in the UK's real exchange rate makes the UK more competitive in international markets.

The real exchange rate can thus depreciate for three different reasons: a fall in the actual or nominal $/£ exchange rate; a rise in the price of US goods; or a fall in the price of UK goods. The arithmetic does not care which it is.

Thus, if UK annual inflation is 10 per cent and US inflation is zero, the UK's real exchange rate depreciates by 10 per cent a year if the nominal exchange rate is fixed. However, the real exchange rate would appreciate if the nominal exchange rate fell by more than 10 per cent a year.

In summary, higher UK output raises UK imports, reducing UK net exports. Higher output abroad raises demand for UK exports, raising UK net exports. A depreciation of the UK real exchange rate makes the UK more competitive, raising UK net exports.

Other items on the current account include net government transfers to foreigners, which we treat as given. However, a country with large foreign assets has a large net inflow of property income, boosting its current account. Conversely, a country with large foreign debts has a large outflow of net property income, making its current account balance smaller than its trade balance.

Box 14-2

Calculating real exchange rates

Each row in the following table shows a different combination of the nominal exchange rate, the price of domestic goods and the price of foreign goods. In the first row, UK shirts cost £6 and US shirts $10. At a nominal exchange rate of $2/£, a UK shirt costs $12 and is 1.2 times as expensive as a US shirt when measured in $. Since a $10 US shirt costs £5 at an exchange rate of $2/£, £6 UK shirts are also 1.2 times as expensive as US shirts if we measure them both in £. It never matters which currency we use for the comparison, but we must use the same currency for both.

In the second row, the nominal exchange rate falls by 25 per cent from $2/£ to $1.5/£, and the table shows that, other things equal, the real exchange rate also falls by 25 per cent. Nominal devaluation of the $/£ has made the UK more competitive and the US less competitive.

The third and fourth rows show that the same change in the real exchange rate can be achieved by a fall in UK prices, or a rise in US prices, without any change in the nominal exchange rate. Real exchange rates can therefore change in a monetary union even though nominal exchange rates are fixed forever.

Nominal exchange rate ($/£)	UK shirt price (£)	UK shirt price ($)	US shirt price ($)	Real exchange rate
2.0	6	12	10	1.2
1.5	6	9	10	0.9
2.0	4.5	9	10	0.9
2.0	6	12	13.3	0.9

Instead of beginning with the path of the nominal exchange rates and using the evolution of prices, at home and abroad, to calculate the consequent path of the real exchange rate, we can also undertake the same calculation in reverse. Given the evolution of prices at home and abroad, what path would the nominal exchange rate have to follow in order to keep the real exchange rate constant?

> The **purchasing power parity (PPP)** path of the nominal exchange rate is the hypothetical path that it would have to follow in order to maintain the real exchange rate at its initial level.

Thus, for example, if we know the real exchange rate that is appropriate in long-run equilibrium, we can use this as a baseline. By keeping track of what happens to prices at home and abroad, we can calculate the PPP level of the nominal exchange rate at any point in time. Comparing this with the actual nominal exchange rate lets us know how much the nominal exchange rate would have to change to get back to the level that would generate the appropriate real exchange rate.

To check you have understood, here are two simple examples. In the first case, the initial exchange rate is $2/£, and the UK and US economies appear to be in long-run equilibrium. Five years later, UK prices have doubled but US prices are unaltered. What is the new PPP value of the nominal exchange rate? The doubling of UK prices has halved the level of UK competitiveness. To restore it to its initial level, it requires a 50 per cent depreciation of the nominal exchange rate to restore the initial real exchange rate. Hence, after five years, the PPP exchange rate has fallen from $2/£ to $1/£.

Here is a second example. UK inflation is 5 per cent and US inflation is 3 per cent a year. What is happening to the PPP nominal exchange rate path? Every year, sterling must depreciate by 2 per cent against the dollar to maintain purchasing power parity.

PPP exchange rates provide a useful compass against which to assess the evolution of economies and the extent to which their actual nominal exchange rates will need to change in the long run if full equilibrium is eventually to be restored.

In the short run, if real exchange rates and competitiveness have been bid by market forces to levels well away from the long-run equilibrium level, what is the short-run symptom of this imbalance? The answer is the current account of the balance of payments. Countries that are abnormally uncompetitive will be running substantial current account deficits, whereas countries that are abnormally competitive will be running substantial current account surpluses. Neither situation will persist forever.

Although we continue to ignore the capital account, because capital transfers are usually so small, we cannot ignore the financial account.

The financial account

Purchases and sales of foreign assets are increasingly important. Computers and telecommunications make it as easy for a UK resident to transact in the financial markets of New York, and Tokyo, as in London. Moreover, the elaborate system of controls, restricting flows of financial capital, has gradually been dismantled. There is now a global financial market in which footloose funds flow freely from one country to another in search of the highest expected return.

Huge one-way financial account flows would swamp the typical flows of imports and exports on the current account. Forex market equilibrium requires that expected returns adjust until assets in different currencies offer the *same* expected return, *removing* the incentive for vast, one-way flows of financial capital.

The return on any asset is the interest rate plus the capital gain you make while the asset is held. Exchange rate changes lead to capital gains or losses while you temporarily hold assets abroad. You have £100 to invest for a year. UK interest rates are 10 per cent, but US interest rates are zero. Keeping your funds in £, you have £110 by the end of the year. What if you lend abroad for a year?

With an initial exchange rate of $2/£, your £100 buys $200. At a zero interest rate, you have $200 at the end of the year. But if the £ falls 10 per cent in the year to $1.80/£, your $200 converts back to £110. You made 10 per cent less interest in $ but earned an extra 10 per cent capital gain while the $ rose against the £ and the £ fell against the $.

If the $/£ exchange rate falls by more than 10 per cent during the year, you do better by lending in $, since the capital gain outweighs the interest forgone. When international financial capital mobility is high,[2] massive flows are avoided only if the interest parity condition holds.

> **Perfect capital mobility** means expected total returns on assets in different currencies must be equal if huge capital flows are to be avoided. A positive interest differential must be offset by an expected exchange rate fall of equal magnitude. This is the **interest parity condition**.

Internal and external balance

> **Internal balance** means aggregate demand equals potential output. **External balance** means that the current account of the balance of payments is zero. Long-run equilibrium requires both.

Chapter 11 explained how a closed economy eventually returns to potential output and internal balance. External balance must also hold in the long run. The current account shows a country's flow of income from abroad minus its flow of spending on foreign goods, services and transfer payments. With a permanent current account deficit, a country goes bankrupt by overspending its foreign income indefinitely. With a permanent current account surplus, the country is saving and adding to net foreign assets forever. This makes no sense since the country could afford to import more foreign goods.

We can use internal and external balance to analyse a country's equilibrium real exchange rate in the long run. Internal balance means each country's output is at potential output. Taking this as given, the main determinant of the current account is the real exchange rate. A higher real exchange rate makes the country less competitive, reducing its net exports.

In Figure 14-3, the current account schedule *CA* shows how a higher real exchange rate reduces the current account balance by making the country less competitive. Only the real exchange rate *R* will achieve external balance in the long run. With a higher real exchange rate, competitiveness would be lower and there would be a current account deficit. A real exchange rate below *R* makes the country too competitive and it would have a permanent current account surplus.

---

[2] Because economists used to use the term 'capital account' to describe what we now call the 'financial account', the term 'perfect capital mobility' always referred to movements of *financial* capital. We still use the shorthand 'capital mobility' to refer to financial flows.

Suppose the UK discovers North Sea oil. It now has a larger current account surplus at any real exchange rate since it no longer has to import oil. The current account schedule shifts right from CA to CA_1. Only an appreciation of the real exchange rate to R_1 can restore external balance. Manufacturers complain that they are doing badly at the less-competitive exchange rate, but the brutal reality is that, if the UK exports more oil, it must export less of something else.

Forget North Sea oil; now think net foreign assets. A country that has previously stockpiled a lot of foreign assets now has a big current account inflow from interest, profit and dividends. Again, its CA schedule shifts right to CA_1. Again, this induces a rise in the long-run real exchange rate.

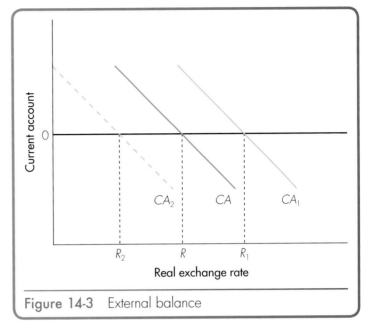

Figure 14-3 External balance

With more current account inflows from net asset income, net exports must fall if the overall current account is to remain in balance. Getting uncompetitive is what makes this happen.

Thus, countries with large foreign debts, on which they pay flows of interest on the current account, face schedule CA_2 in Figure 14-3. However, a suitably low real exchange rate makes them competitive enough to have net export surpluses large enough to finance the outflow of interest payments on the current account.

Box 14-3

Soaring Aussie dollar inflicts pain on Australian wine exports

Figure 14-3 showed that discovery of a natural resource is likely to lead to an appreciation of the real exchange rate. If a country has more of one commodity to export, it eventually must export less of other commodities. Becoming less competitive is the market mechanism that brings this about. Economists call this Dutch disease because it was first noted when the Netherlands discovered natural gas in the North Sea in the 1960s. Subsequently, both the UK and Norway have experienced periods of a strong currency while they enjoyed the benefits of oil deposits in the North Sea.

A more recent example is Australia. For years, Australia was remote from the world's powerhouse economies in the US and Europe. Then along came China. During three decades of annual growth approaching 10 per cent each year, China has had a thirst for raw materials, including oil, coal, iron ore, copper, nickel, gold and silver. Australian resources companies, whether Australian-owned or foreign multinationals – have become global superstars – BHP Billiton, Rio Tinto, Xstrata and Alcoa, to name but a few. Resources companies now comprise 20 per cent of the Australian stock market by value. Australia is now the world's largest coal exporter.

▶

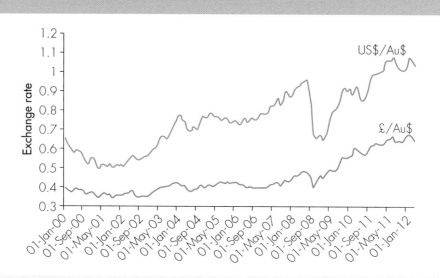

You can guess what all this has done to Australia's exchange rate. Booming exports have bid up the value of the Aussie dollar. This chart shows by just how much.

In May 2001, an Aussie dollar bought only 50 cents; by 2012 an Aussie dollar was worth a full US dollar, a dramatic appreciation of the Aussie dollar. Since sterling depreciated against the US dollar during the period, the Au$ appreciation against sterling was not quite so strong, but there was still a 50 per cent appreciation between September 2008 and early 2012.

During the entire period, the UK, the US and Australia were all pursuing inflation targeting, so there were only relatively minor differences in national inflation rates. Hence, most of the change in the nominal exchange rates translated into a similar change in real exchange rates. As a consequence, Australian industry became much less competitive after the real exchange rate appreciation.

For resources companies, this did not matter – it was precisely the strength of demand for their output that was inducing the exchange rate changes in the first place. But for other Australian industries in the traded goods sector, the loss of competitiveness was crippling. The domestic car industry now had to face much cheaper imported cars, and the Australian wine industry, which had been caus-ing the French wine industry real grief, was now being priced out of many key export markets.

These changes had many other consequences. Since resources companies are mainly located in Western Australia, property prices soared in Perth, its capital. In contrast, with wineries in South Australia's Barossa valley beginning to struggle, house prices in nearby Adelaide did much less well than in Perth. By 2011 Sydney's salubrious Vaucluse area still had a high median rent at Au$2300 a week, but you needed a similar amount to lease an unremarkable house in Western Australia's mining towns of Port Hedland, Pegs Creek, Nickol and Baynton.

Nor should we forget about monetary policy. Whilst the US and Europe were slashing interest rates to try to prevent outright depression after the financial crash, the Reserve Bank of Australia was struggling to prevent Australia's export boom causing too much inflation. Australian interest rates were therefore much higher than in Europe and the US. In themselves, high interest rates caused falls in house prices in much of Australia, even in Perth after 2011.

Monetary policy in open economies

Having introduced the key features of an open economy, we now ask how our previous analysis of monetary and fiscal policy must be amended once we recognize that an economy is open to international trade and financial flows. The answer is very different, depending on whether the economy has fixed or floating exchange rates, so we need to examine the two cases separately.

Fixed exchange rates

Perfect capital mobility means international lenders must get the same expected return in all currencies. Pegging the exchange rate prevents capital gains or losses on the exchange rate while holding foreign assets. Capital mobility and pegged exchange rates can be reconciled only by setting the *same* interest rate in both countries. Only then will investors expect the same return in both countries. For at least one country, this represents a loss of monetary sovereignty. It can no longer set the interest rates that it wants. Fixed exchange rates take away monetary independence.

Suppose the UK wished to peg its exchange rate against the US dollar. One possibility is that the US would meekly accept whatever interest rate the Bank of England wished to set. But this is not very likely! Given the relative size and power of the two countries, it is more likely that the Bank of England would have to match whatever interest rate the US central bank wished to set.

Suppose the UK housing market was booming and the Bank tried to raise UK interest rates above those in the US. What would happen? With a pegged exchange rate, there would be a massive inflow of financial capital to take advantage of the high interest rate. This balance of payments surplus and excess demand for pounds forces the Bank to print more pounds, with which it buys foreign exchange reserves. However, the rise in the UK money supply, or stock of circulating pounds, bids down UK interest rates. The attempt to raise interest rates is thwarted by the capital inflow then induced.

Adjusting to shocks

What happens if export demand falls? Interest rates cannot respond since they have to continue to match those in the partner country. Suppose fiscal policy is also unchanged. Hence, the fall in aggregate demand causes a fall in output and a rise in unemployment. Eventually, this bids down wages and prices. With a given nominal exchange rate, the real exchange rate falls and the country gets more competitive, not because its nominal exchange rate has changed but because the domestic price of its goods has fallen. This eventually restores net exports to their former level. Internal and external balance are then restored.

This confirms that market forces can adjust to shocks, even under a fixed exchange rate system. A monetary union is simply a permanent commitment to fixed exchange rates. Most of the European Union would not have embarked on a monetary union unless there was some default mechanism to restore internal and external balance. That safety valve is the response of domestic wages and prices to booms and slumps, and the consequent effect on competitiveness.

Devaluation

Countries such as Germany, France and Italy have traditions of strong trade unions, and substantial employment protection. This tends to make wage and price adjustment slow. It may therefore take a protracted recession to achieve the required fall in domestic wages and prices when such a country becomes uncompetitive. Some people have argued this is one reason that the Eurozone countries have not grown more quickly during the past five years.[3]

---

[3] You should not always take such arguments at face value. Recall from Chapter 10 that long-run growth is achieved by enhancing aggregate supply and potential output. The longer Eurozone stagnation continues, the more likely it is that this is because of permanently slow growth in potential output rather than because output is temporarily below potential output. Moreover, in 2005 Germany announced a record trade surplus, hardly evidence of stagnation caused by lack of competitiveness. As you master the foundations of economics, you will spot more and more fallacies in the public debate!

For a country not committed to a permanently fixed exchange rate, devaluation immediately raises competitiveness, achieving overnight what might have taken years of domestic recession to accomplish. When a country devalues its nominal exchange rate, adopting a lower exchange rate peg, the real exchange rate changes because the nominal exchange rate has changed. Resources are drawn into export industries and into domestic industries that compete with imports. However, there are two points to note.

First, the initial *quantity* response may be quite slow. Demand may change slowly if there were some long-term contracts made at the old exchange rate. Supply may change slowly if it takes time to expand new production. Devaluation may not improve the trade balance in the short run. The trade balance refers to value not volume. With low initial quantity responses, cutting the $ price of UK goods may initially yield less revenue, not more. The same quantity of goods is being sold for a lower dollar price than before. However, in the longer run, quantities are more responsive and net trade revenues increase.[4]

In the medium run, the country will regain internal balance at which potential output equals aggregate demand $\{[C + I + G] + [X - Z]\}$. For a given level of potential output, net exports can respond more to devaluation the lower is the level of domestic absorption $[C + I + G]$.

If the economy returns to internal balance before net exports have increased by the desired amount, further increases in net exports raise aggregate demand above potential output. This causes inflation, reducing competitiveness at the fixed nominal exchange rate, and undoing all the good work that devaluation has accomplished. Sometimes, it is necessary to tighten *fiscal* policy, thereby reducing domestic absorption, to make sure that there are enough spare resources to produce the extra net exports required.

Taking an even longer view, in the very long run real variables determine other real variables. Changing the nominal exchange rate will not accomplish anything that adjustments of domestic wages and prices could also have accomplished. The case for devaluation is that it may speed up the process when wage and price adjustment is sluggish.

Case study 14-1 International flows of financial capital

Flows on the financial account of the balance of payments may be short term, such as putting money in a foreign bank account, or long term, such as taking a permanent stake in a foreign company.

Foreign direct investment (FDI) is the purchase of foreign firms or the establishment of foreign subsidiaries.

Surely globalization has made capital flows more important recently? The following figure shows average annual capital flows, relative to GDP, for 12 OECD economies in peacetime years during 1870–1996. Capital flows dried up in the 1930s, during the Great Depression, but today we tend to forget that the late nineteenth century was also a great period of foreign investment.

Whereas this 100-year view shows no sign of an upward trend, focusing more recently reveals that financial globalization is indeed a new phenomenon, as the second figure illustrates. After 1995 there was a quadrupling of gross financial flows relative to world GDP, which itself was growing quickly. We now live in a world of highly mobile financial capital.

You might have expected this to be one-way traffic: rich, advanced countries investing in emerging markets, such as China, India and the Gulf states. But this was not always the case. China has used its export surpluses to buy debt issued by Western governments, and also to lend to their private sectors; 'sovereign wealth funds' from the oil-rich states of Abu Dhabi, Qatar, Kuwait and Bahrain have done the same. Without capital inflows on this scale, the pre-crash credit binge in Western countries would not have been as extensive.

This figure of gross international capital flows also confirms that international capital flows are increasingly volatile. This leads to two questions. First, when countries borrow from foreigners can they rely on this inflow

---

4 Since devaluation causes an initial fall in the value of net exports but then a subsequent rise in export values, this response is called a J-curve. As time elapses, the current account falls down to the bottom of the J but then rises to above its initial position.

being stable, or do they have to worry about possible outflows again? Second, if international capital is so mobile, would it be feasible and desirable to regulate it to reduce its mobility? These questions lie at the heart of international macroeconomics. We return to them in more detail in subsequent chapters.

These two figures need to be interpreted with care. They refer to gross flows – total inflows, total outflows, or the sum of the two. This is not the same as net inflows or outflows. Since official financing is usually small, our balance of payments arithmetic guarantees that the sum of the current and financial accounts must be near zero, especially when averaged over many years. If countries cannot run large current account deficits, they cannot have large net capital inflows either. In equilibrium the size of the net flow must be of the same order of magnitude as the size of the current account. Since current account balances are rarely in excess of 10 per cent of GDP, we need to understand the market forces or policy responses that ensure that net capital flows are similar in size.

Looking at the *size* of capital flows does not itself tell us about capital mobility, which relates to the *sensitivity* of capital flows to perceived profit opportunities. If exchange rates adjust to *prevent* massive capital flows, we will never see large flows in the data whatever the degree of capital mobility.

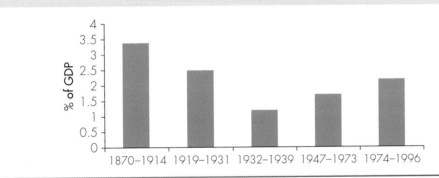

The scale of capital flows (% of GDP) since 1870

Source: M. Obstfeld, 'The global capital market: benefactor or menace?', *Journal of Economic Perspectives*, 1988

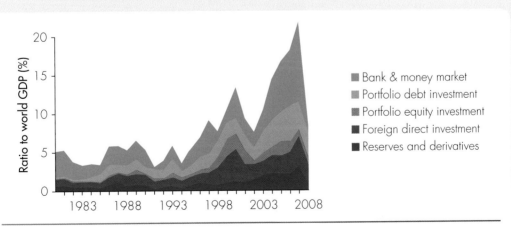

Gross international capital flows, 1983–2008

Source: C. Becker and C. Noone, 'Volatility in international capital movements', Reserve Bank of Australia, 2009

Putting this differently, devaluation, which raises the cost of imports, is eventually passed on into higher wages and prices, making no real difference. Most empirical models of the UK economy, based on past data, conclude that the effects of a nominal devaluation are offset by a rise in domestic prices and wages by the end of five years.

Having studied how macroeconomic policy works under fixed exchange rates, we now examine the same issues when a country decides to float its exchange rate.

Floating exchange rates

With a floating exchange rate, domestic monetary policy can set any interest rate that it wishes. Monetary sovereignty is restored, and may use an inflation target to decide how to set interest rates.

The long-run *real* exchange rate must be consistent with internal balance (aggregate demand equals potential output) and external balance (current account equals zero). If the nominal exchange rate is fixed, domestic prices and wages must eventually adjust to get the appropriate real exchange rate. Under a *floating* exchange rate, knowing the inflation targets at home and abroad, people can work out what path the nominal exchange rate must eventually reach to deliver the appropriate equilibrium real exchange rate in the long run. The higher a country's price level has become, relative to its competitors, the lower must be its nominal exchange rate to achieve the correct real exchange rate. Hence, in the long run, the inflation targets at home and abroad essentially determine the paths of domestic and foreign prices, from which we can deduce the path that the nominal exchange rate will have to follow to achieve the correct real exchange rate and current account balance.

Countries cannot depart from external balance in the long run, and the current account is all-important. However, in the short run the role of the current account is dwarfed by the *threat* of massive financial capital movements. The forex market cannot cope with massive one-way capital flows, and must keep adjusting the exchange rate to prevent them. This implies setting the exchange rate at a level from which interest parity is expected to hold *from now on*. In the short run, the financial account can drive the exchange rate a long way away from the path that balances the current account.

In the long run, countries with high inflation rates also have higher nominal interest rates (so that their real interest rates can remain appropriate). Their long-run equilibrium exchange rate is falling steadily to preserve the right real exchange rate. This does not stimulate big capital flows because the capital losses on the depreciating exchange rate are just offsetting the high nominal interest rates earned by lending in that currency.

However, when a country has higher interest rates in the short run than it is expected to have in the long run, the currency looks temporarily attractive to financial investors. To stop them all piling in, the currency must appreciate rapidly and significantly to such a level that from now on the only way is down. The prospect of capital losses from holding the currency from now on is what offsets the attraction of high interest rates in the short run.

The upward jump in the exchange rate takes the market by surprise. Had it been foreseen, market participants would already have piled into the currency to get the capital gain. The exchange rate jumps up to make it credible that the foreseeable direction will be down from now on. Conversely, a temporary cut in domestic interest rates makes the exchange rate jump down, so that from now on it can offer capital gains to offset the low interest rate.

Monetary policy under floating exchange rates

Under fixed exchange rates, domestic monetary policy was powerless; under floating exchange rates, the converse is true.

A given rise in domestic interest rates does not merely depress domestic demand, it also makes the exchange rate jump up, which reduces net export demand substantially if wages and prices are sluggish and cannot respond quickly. Hence, monetary policy has a strong effect in the short run under floating exchange rates. The domestic demand effect is reinforced by the exchange rate effect on competitiveness.

Maths 14-1

Interest parity conditions

Let r denote the domestic interest rate, r^* the foreign interest rate, s the nominal exchange rate (international value of the domestic currency) and ds/dt the instantaneous rate of change of the exchange rate. $(1/s)ds/dt$ is then the instantaneous percentage capital gain that a domestic investor makes by holding the foreign currency for an instant before repatriating the money, and, under perfect certainty, the interest parity condition implies

$$r^* + (1/s)ds/dt = r \tag{1}$$

The real exchange rate v is given by

$$v = sp/p^* \tag{2}$$

where p is the domestic price level and p^* the foreign price level. The instantaneous change in the real exchange rate obeys

$$(1/v)dv/dt = (1/s)ds/dt + (1/p)dp/dt - (1/p^*)dp^*/dt = (1/s)ds/dt + \pi - \pi^* \tag{3}$$

where π denotes the rate of inflation. Real exchange rate appreciation reflects nominal exchange rate appreciation, domestic inflation or foreign deflation.

Combining equations (1) and (3),

$$r^* - \pi^* = r - \pi + (1/s)ds/dt + \pi - \pi^*, \text{ so that}$$

$$[r^* - \pi^*] = [r - \pi] + [(1/v)dv/dt] \tag{4}$$

Thus, the interest parity condition expressed in nominal terms in equation (1) – nominal interest differentials must be offset by appropriate capital gains or losses in nominal exchange rates to preserve the equality of return in different currencies under perfect international capital mobility – implies a similar statement in terms of real interest rate differentials being offset by capital gains or losses on the real exchange rate.

Although derived for an instantaneous decision, we can always view a longer horizon as a series of instant decisions. Hence, interest parity conditions also hold over longer horizons, provided the duration of the interest rates matches the period over which exchange rate changes are assessed.

Finally, once uncertainty exists, we have to replace actual exchange rate changes by those expected at the outset of the period. An investor contemplating lending abroad for a year can always obtain a one-year foreign bond with known interest rate today, but will have to take a view on the likely change in the exchange rate over the year.

Recap

- The exchange rate is the relative price of two currencies in the forex market.
- The demand for domestic currency arises from exports, and from sales of domestic assets to foreigners; the supply of domestic currency arises from imports and purchases of foreign assets. Floating exchange rates equate supply and demand when there is no government intervention in the forex market.
- Under fixed exchange rates, the Bank of England intervenes to buy any excess supply of £, thus reducing its forex reserves. The Bank creates and supplies £ to meet any excess demand for £, thus raising its forex reserves.
- The balance of payments records monetary inflows as credits and monetary outflows as debits. The current account is the trade balance plus net transfer payments from abroad, which mainly reflect income on net foreign assets. The capital account shows capital transfers. The financial account shows net sales of foreign assets. The balance of payments is the sum of the current, capital and financial account balances (plus any balancing item to correct for mismeasurement).
- Under floating exchange rates, the balance of payments is zero. Under fixed exchange rates, a payments surplus (deficit) is offset by official financing, raising (lowering) the domestic money supply.
- The real exchange rate adjusts the nominal exchange rate for prices at home and abroad. It is the relative price of domestic to foreign goods, when measured in a common currency. A higher real exchange rate reduces competitiveness.
- The purchasing parity path of the nominal exchange rate is the path that offsets differential price changes at home and abroad, thereby maintaining the real exchange rate at its initial level.
- Higher domestic (foreign) income raises the demand for imports (exports). A higher real exchange rate reduces the demand for net exports.
- Perfect international capital mobility implies a vast financial capital flow on the financial account if the expected return differs across countries. To prevent this, any interest differential between domestic and foreign assets must be offset by a matching expected capital gain or loss on the exchange rate while temporarily holding foreign assets.
- At internal balance, aggregate demand equals potential output. At external balance, the current account is zero. Both are needed for long-run equilibrium.
- Discovery of a natural resource, or higher net foreign assets, raises the long-run equilibrium real exchange rate.
- With perfect capital mobility, monetary policy is powerless under pegged exchange rates. Domestic interest rates must match foreign interest rates. However, fiscal expansion no longer bids up domestic interest rates.

- A devaluation lowers the fixed exchange rate. With sluggish price adjustment, it raises competitiveness and aggregate demand. With spare resources, output increases. Without spare resources, higher demand bids up prices, reducing competitiveness again.
- In the long run, devaluing the nominal exchange rate has little real effect. But it adjusts competitiveness quickly in the short run.
- Under floating exchange rates, domestic and foreign monetary policies determine domestic and foreign prices. Together with the real exchange rate required for external balance, this determines the eventual nominal exchange. However, in the short run the exchange rate moves around to prevent massive one-way financial capital flows. Temporarily, the exchange rate can deviate a lot from the level that achieves current account balance.
- Floating exchange rates magnify the effect of interest rate changes on aggregate demand, by inducing short-run changes in the exchange rate and competitiveness.

Review questions

To check your answers to these questions, go to pages 393–4.

1 A country has a current account surplus of £6 billion but a financial account deficit of £4 billion. (a) Is its balance of payments in deficit or surplus? (b) Are the country's foreign exchange reserves rising or falling? (c) Is the central bank buying or selling domestic currency?

2 For over 20 years, Japan has run a current account surplus. (a) How is this compatible with the statement that countries must eventually get back to external balance? (b) Would it be so easy to run a persistent current account deficit?

3 Which of these increase a country's competitiveness: (a) a fall in domestic wages, (b) a fall in foreign wages, (c) a fall in the foreign country's exchange rate, (d) a fall in the domestic country's wage rate, (e) a productivity increase in the domestic country?

4 In each answer to question 3 above, say whether the domestic country's real exchange rate appreciates or depreciates.

5 'The exchange rate depreciated.' 'The exchange rate was devalued.' Do these statements mean the same thing? If not, why not?

6 You are running the German economy the day after unification of East and West Germany. You know East Germans will need large government subsidies to get them on their feet. (a) What happens to German fiscal policy? (b) As a result, is German aggregate demand above or below potential output? (c) If you run German monetary policy, how do you ensure your inflation target is still achieved? (d) What would have happened if Germany had revalued its exchange rate upwards?

EASY

7   Rank the following according to the ability of monetary policy to affect real output in the short run: (a) a closed economy, (b) an open economy with fixed exchange rates, (c) an open economy with floating exchange rates. Explain.

8   Newsreaders say that 'the pound had a good day' if the UK exchange rate rises. (a) When is an appreciation of the exchange rate desirable? (b) When is it undesirable?

9   Kuwait has a large stock of foreign assets. (a) What does this imply about its previous current account balances? (b) If Kuwait is now in external balance, is it likely to have a trade surplus or a trade deficit?

10 Suppose there is a binding and effective world agreement to abolish the cocaine trade. What happens to exports of Colombia? What happens to its real exchange rate? Is this good news or bad news for flower exporters in Colombia? What about for Colombian importers of US cars?

11 Victorian Britain was the workshop of the world in the early nineteenth century because of its lead in the industrial revolution. (a) Do you think Britain had a current account surplus or deficit during these years? (b) By the late nineteenth century, what do you think Britain's net foreign asset position was? (c) What would this imply about its net interest income from abroad on the current account of its balance of payments?

12 (a) If Britain was in external balance in the late nineteenth century, would it have a large trade surplus or large trade deficit? (b) What has to happen to competitiveness and Britain's real exchange rate to bring this about? (c) Do you think it surprising that late Victorians worried about whether success and moral decay had undermined Britain's ability to compete? (d) Was their diagnosis correct?

13 Why are these statements wrong? (a) If global speculators have more money than central banks, central banks can no longer defend fixed exchange rates. (b) Floating exchange rates are volatile because imports and exports fluctuate a lot.

14 **Essay question** Why does a floating exchange rate have to adjust continuously to prevent large one-way financial flows between one country and another? What would happen if these one-way flows were allowed to occur? Can they occur under fixed exchange rates?

15 **Essay question** 'Small countries should not join a monetary union since there is then no mechanism for them to adjust their international competitiveness.' Discuss.

Online Learning Centre

To help you grasp the key concepts of this chapter check out the extra resources posted on the Online Learning Centre at www.mcgraw-hill.co.uk/textbooks/begg.

There are additional case studies, self-test questions, practice exam questions with answers and a graphing tool.

CHAPTER 15

The global economy

Learning outcomes

By the end of this chapter, you should be able to:

- Describe patterns of international trade
- Explain comparative advantage
- Discuss why we observe two-way trade in the same product
- Analyse the gains from trade
- Show when trade restrictions are beneficial
- Explain the handicaps with which poor countries begin
- Discuss whether comparative advantage is a secure route to prosperity

- Describe industrialization and the export of manufactures
- Analyse the international debt crisis
- Assess the importance of aid from rich countries
- Describe what globalization means
- Explain why globalization is occurring
- Evaluate opportunities and threats to which globalization gives rise

This chapter looks at the world economy, a group of economies increasingly integrated by globalization. We explore the extent of trade and the motives for trade. We examine why some countries have been left behind and others are rapidly emerging. Finally, we evaluate the threats and opportunities posed by globalization itself.

 ## International trade

This chapter looks at the global economy as a trading system. Why does international trade occur? Why have some countries been left behind while others prosper as never before? And what can we say about globalization, so frequently a source of fear and concern in the public debate? Is globalization a threat or an opportunity?

International trade is part of daily life. Britons drink French wine, Americans drive Japanese cars and Russians eat American wheat. Through *exchange* and *specialization*, countries supply the world economy with things that they produce relatively cheaply, receiving in exchange things made relatively more cheaply elsewhere.

These gains from trade are reinforced by scale economies in production. Instead of each country having many small producers, different countries specialize in different things so that all countries benefit from the cost reductions that ensue. Because foreign competition may make life difficult for some voters, governments are often under pressure to restrict imports. We end the section by discussing trade policy and whether it is ever a good idea to restrict imports.

World exports are now over 20 per cent of world GDP. World trade has grown by over 7 per cent a year since 1950, as transport costs and other barriers to trade keep falling. Countries are becoming steadily more open to trade, as Figure 15-1 confirms. Events in other countries affect our daily lives much more than they did 20 years ago. Smaller countries are of course more open; when New York trades with California it does not count as *international* trade.

Table 15-1 shows that, by 2009, half of world trade was trade between the rich industrial countries. Only 19 per cent of trade did not involve these countries at all. World trade and world income are organized around the rich industrial countries.

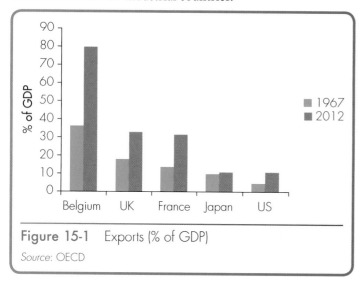

Figure 15-1   Exports (% of GDP)

Source: OECD

Services are over 70 per cent of GDP in rich countries, but a much smaller share of their trade. Trade in goods (merchandise trade) remains important because many countries import goods, add a little value and then re-export them. The value added makes a small contribution to GDP but gross flows of imports and exports of goods are large.

Table 15-2 distinguishes between *primary products* (agricultural commodities, minerals and fuels) and manufactured commodities. Although the EU is chiefly an exporter of manufactures, primary commodities account for one-fifth of exports.

Table 15-1   Trade patterns, 2009 (% of world exports)

Origin of exports	Destination of exports			
	1980		2009	
	Developed	Other	Developed	Other
Developed countries	50	21	41	16
Other	21	8	24	19

Source: UNCTAD, Handbook of Statistics

Table 15-2   Merchandise trade patterns, 2009 (% of region's exports)

	Agriculture	Fuels, minerals	Manufactures
World	9	23	66
North America	11	17	68
Europe	9	12	77
Former Soviet Union	7	67	25
Africa	7	71	18
Middle East	2	74	21
Asia	6	12	79

Source: WTO, International Trade Statistics

Having discussed trade patterns, we now examine the reasons why trade takes place at all.

Gains from trade

Comparative advantage

Trade is mutually beneficial when there are cross-country differences in the *relative* cost of making goods.

> The **law of comparative advantage** says that countries specialize in producing and exporting the goods that they produce at a lower *relative* cost than other countries.

One reason why relative costs may differ is differences in technology across countries. Suppose labour is the only factor of production and there are constant returns to scale. Table 15-3 assumes that it takes 30 hours of American labour to make a car and 5 hours to make a shirt. UK labour is less productive. It takes 60 hours of UK labour to make a car and 6 hours to make a shirt.

Suppose US workers earn $6 an hour, and British workers £2 an hour. Table 15-3 shows the *unit labour requirement* (ULR) or hours of work to make a unit of each good. US labour is *absolutely* more productive than UK labour in making either good. However, US labour is *relatively* more productive in cars than in shirts. UK labour takes twice as long to make a car, but only sixth-fifths as long as US labour to make a shirt. Different relative productivity makes trade mutually beneficial.

Table 15-3   Relative costs and comparative advantage

		ULR (hours)	Hourly wage	ULC (cost)	OC (sacrifice)
US	Cars	30	$6	$180	6 shirts
	Shirts	5	$6	$30	$1/6$ car
UK	Cars	60	£2	£120	10 shirts
	Shirts	6	£2	£12	$1/10$ car

The *opportunity cost* (OC) of making a unit of one good is the quantity of the other good that must be given up to create the extra production resources. Table 15-3 shows these opportunity costs OC in each country prior to trade. Because of different relative productivity, the opportunity cost of a car is 6 shirts in the US but 10 shirts in the UK, whereas the opportunity cost of a shirt is one-sixth of a car in the US but only one-tenth of a car in the UK.

If the UK makes 60 more shirts, giving up 6 cars, the US makes these 6 cars for the loss of only 36 shirts. International trade and specialization let the world economy have 24 more shirts with no loss of cars. Similarly, if the US makes 10 more cars, giving up 60 shirts, the UK makes these extra shirts for the loss of only 6 cars, giving the world 4 more cars but no fewer shirts.

The **gains from trade** are additional output of some goods with no loss of other goods.

The market also gets the world economy to the right answer. Table 15-3 also shows the *unit labour cost* (ULC) of making each good. We assume that the hourly wage is $6 in the US and £2 in the UK. If labour is the only input, the unit labour cost is the average total cost of a good, and the price for which it is sold in a competitive market.

Since the US and UK use different currencies, a foreign exchange market is set up and an equilibrium exchange rate established. Suppose the $/£ is high. This makes all UK goods, initially produced in pounds, cost a lot of dollars. The UK is uncompetitive in both goods. Now consider lower and lower values of $/£. When the exchange rate is low enough, the UK can compete by exporting one good. Which one? The one it is relatively better at making.

For example, in Table 15-3 if the exchange rate is $2/£, then UK cars can be sold for $240 and UK shirts for £24. The UK can undercut the US in shirts but not in cars. Similarly, US cars sell for £90 and US shirts for £15. Again, the UK is competitive in shirts but not in cars.

This is why absolute advantage is unimportant. The single exchange rate can adjust to make any country's goods competitive *on average*; but which goods it then imports, and which it then exports, depends on which it makes relatively better or worse than average, which is precisely what the law of comparative advantage promises us.

The law has many applications in everyday life. Suppose two students share a flat. One is faster both at making the dinner and at vacuuming the carpet. If tasks are allocated according to absolute advantage, one student does nothing. The jobs get done faster if each student does the task at which he or she is *relatively* faster.

Relative factor abundance

One country can eventually learn another country's technology. Technology differences are probably not the main explanation for comparative advantage. The main reason that a country has a relatively low price for a particular output is that it has a relatively low price for the inputs which that output uses. In turn, relatively low input prices are largely explained by having relatively abundant quantities of those inputs available.

If the UK is relatively generously supplied with human capital, it should export university places to foreign students from the Caribbean. If the Caribbean is relatively well endowed with tropical land, it exports bananas and nutmeg to the UK. Differences in relative factor supply are a vital reason for comparative advantage and the pattern of international trade.

Figure 15-2 displays evidence confirming this analysis. Countries with scarce land but abundant skills have high shares of manufactures in their exports; countries with lots of land but few skills typically export raw materials. As well as dots for individual countries, the figure also shows that the explanation works for groups of countries, represented by diamond shapes.

Thus, comparative advantage reflects initial differences in relative production costs, arising from differences in technology or in relative factor abundance.

Two-way trade

Different relative factor abundance explains why OPEC exports oil, and China exports labour-intensive goods from toys to trainers. However, this approach cannot explain why the UK exports cars (Aston

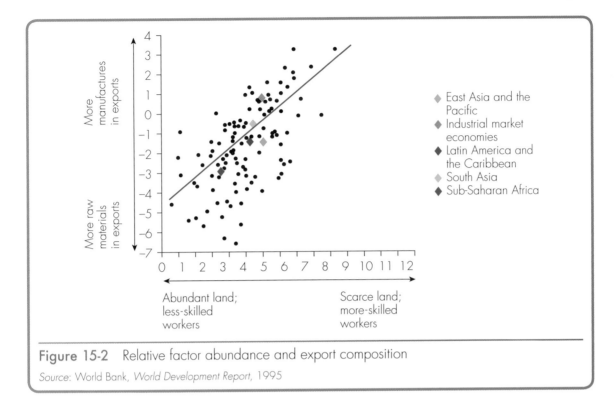

Figure 15-2 Relative factor abundance and export composition

Source: World Bank, *World Development Report, 1995*

Martin, Jaguar) to Germany but also imports cars (Mercedes, BMW, VW) from Germany. The UK cannot simultaneously be scarce and abundant in the inputs used to make cars.

Intra-industry trade is two-way trade in goods made by the same industry.

Two-way trade *within* the same industry occurs where consumers like a wide choice of brands that are similar but not identical. A Jaguar is not quite a Mercedes, nor is Danish Carlsberg identical to Belgian Stella. Consumers like variety.

However, we also need economies of scale. Instead of each country trying to make small quantities of each brand in each industry, the UK makes Jaguars, Germany makes Mercedes and Sweden makes Volvos, then we swap them around through international trade. We all benefit from low cost and greater variety.

Figure 15-3 summarizes the two principal reasons for international trade, and illustrates how these apply to different industries.

Winners and losers

Table 15-3 confirms that exploiting initial differences in relative costs allows gains from trade. The world gets more output from any given inputs. Similarly, intra-industry trade offers variety and cost reduction through scale economies. But this does not imply that *everybody* gains. Here are two examples of how some people can lose.

Refrigeration

The invention of refrigeration let Argentina supply frozen meat to the world market. Its meat exports, non-existent in 1900, were 400 000 tons a year by 1913. The US, with exports of 150 000 tons in 1900, had virtually stopped exporting beef by 1913.

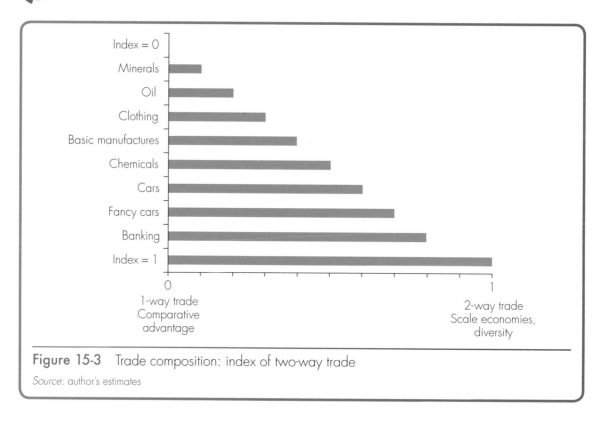

Figure 15-3 Trade composition: index of two-way trade

Source: author's estimates

Who gained and who lost? Argentinian cattle grazers and meat exporters attracted resources. Owners of cattle and land gained; other land users lost out because, with higher demand, land rents increased. Argentine consumers found their steaks became dearer as meat was shipped abroad. Argentina's GNP rose a lot, but the benefits of trade were not equally distributed. Some people in Argentina were worse off. In Europe and the US, cheaper beef made consumers better off. But beef producers lost out because beef prices fell.

As a whole, the world gained. In principle, the gainers could have compensated the losers and still had something left over. In practice, gainers rarely compensate losers. Some people lost out.

The UK car industry

As recently as 1971, UK imports of cars were only 15 per cent of the domestic UK market. Imports are now over 60 per cent of the UK market. However, car exports have expanded as Nissan, Honda and Toyota established UK plants to produce for the EU market; Ford, and then Tata, invested in turning round the Jaguar Land Rover business which is now exporting to both the US and China; BMW took over the Mini and Rolls Royce brands; and VW-Audi bought Bentley. In all these cases, the UK car industry, starved of investment for years, finally received long-term investment as well as foreign technology and HR know-how.

Both UK car buyers – whether households or corporate fleets of company cars – and foreign producers – such as Fiat, Peugeot and VW – benefited from the rise in UK imports of cheaper foreign cars. But a traditional UK car producer like Rover had a tough time, and eventually was sold off to the Chinese. UK governments faced repeated pressure to protect UK car producers from foreign competition. Restricting imports would help domestic producers but hurt domestic consumers by raising prices to UK car buyers.

Should the government please producers or consumers? More generally, how should we decide whether to restrict imports or have free trade in all goods? In analysing the costs and benefits of tariffs or other trade restrictions, we move from *positive economics*, why trade exists and what form it takes, to *normative economics*, what trade policy the government should adopt.

Trade policy operates through import tariffs, export subsidies and direct quotas on imports and exports.

The economics of tariffs

An **import tariff** is a tax on imports.

If t is the tariff, the domestic price of imported goods is $(1 + t)$ times the world price of the imported good. By raising the domestic price of imports, a tariff helps domestic producers but hurts domestic consumers.

Figure 15-4 shows the domestic market for cars. Suppose the UK faces a given world price, £10 000 per car, shown by the solid horizontal line. Schedules *DD* and *SS* are the domestic demand for cars and supply of cars. Suppose brands do not matter. Domestic and foreign cars are then perfect substitutes.

At a price of £10 000, UK consumers wish to purchase Q_d cars, at point *G* on their demand curve. Domestic firms want to make Q_s cars at this price. *CG* shows imports, the gap between domestic supply Q_s and domestic demand Q_d.

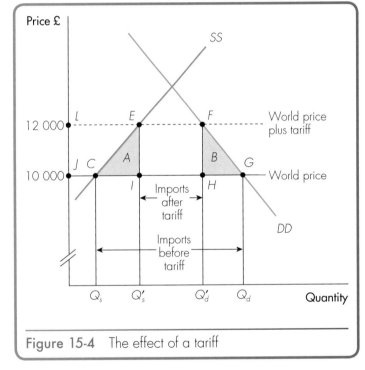

The effect of a tariff

With a 20 per cent tariff on imported cars, car importers must charge £12 000 to cover their costs inclusive of the tariff. The broken horizontal line at this price shows that importers are willing to

Figure 15-4   The effect of a tariff

sell any number of cars in the domestic market at a price of £12 000. The tariff raises the domestic tariff-inclusive price above the world price.

By raising domestic car prices, the tariff boosts domestic car production from Q_s to Q'_s and offers some protection to domestic producers. In moving up the supply curve from *C* to *E*, domestic producers with marginal costs between £10 000 and £12 000 can now survive because the domestic price of imports has been raised by the tariff.

The higher price also moves consumers up their demand curve, from *G* to *F*. The quantity of cars demanded falls from Q_d to Q'_d. From the consumers' viewpoint, the tariff is like a tax. Consumers pay more for cars.

Imports fall from *CG* to *EF* both because domestic production rises *and* because domestic consumption falls. The flatter the domestic supply and demand schedules, the more a given tariff reduces imports. If both schedules are steep, the tariff-induced rise in the domestic price has much less effect on the quantity of imports.

Costs and benefits of a tariff

We need to distinguish *net costs to society* from *transfers* between one part of the economy and another. After the tariff, consumers buy Q'_d, which costs them $(£2000 \times Q'_d)$ *more* than buying this quantity at the world price. Who gets these extra payments, the area *LFHJ* in Figure 15-4?

Some goes to the government, whose revenue from the tariff is the rectangle *EIHF*, the tariff of £2000 times $(Q'_d - Q'_s)$ imported cars. This transfer *EFHI* from consumers to the government is *not* a net cost to society. The government may use the tariff revenue to reduce income tax rates.

Some of the higher consumer payments go to firms as extra profits. The supply curve shows how much firms need to cover production costs. Hence the area *ECJL* is the rise in firms' profits, extra revenue from higher prices over and above extra production costs. Thus *ECJL* is transfer from consumers to the profits of firms, but not a net cost to society as a whole.

The shaded area A is part of the extra consumer payments *LFHJ* going neither to firms as extra profit nor to government as tariff revenue. It is a net cost to society: the cost of supporting inefficient domestic firms.

Society *could* import cars from the rest of the world in unlimited quantities at the world price £10 000, which is the true marginal cost of cars to the domestic economy. Triangle A is the resources society wastes by producing $(Q'_s - Q_s)$ domestically when it could have been imported at a lower cost. The resources drawn into domestic car production could be used more efficiently elsewhere in the economy, including its export sectors.

There is another net loss to society, triangle B. If the tariff was abolished, the quantity of cars demanded would rise to Q_d. Triangle B is the excess of consumer benefits, as measured by the height of the demand curve showing how much consumers want the last unit demanded, over the marginal costs of expanding from Q'_d to Q_d, the world price at which imports could be purchased. Triangle B shows the net benefit society has lost by consuming too few cars.

To sum up, a tariff leads to a rise in the domestic price, inducing both transfers and pure waste. Money is transferred from consumers to the government and to producers. As a first approximation, the net cost of these transfers to society as a whole is zero, though there are distributional implications. Some individuals win while others lose.

In addition, a tariff involves pure waste, since post-tariff prices exceed the true marginal cost of cars to society, which remains the world price. Hence, consumers buy too few cars, and domestic producers make too many cars. Since zero tariffs avoid this waste, this is the *case for free trade*.

Should a tariff ever be adopted? Table 15-4 lists some common arguments for tariffs. The *first-best* argument is a case where a tariff is the best way to achieve a given objective. *Second-best* arguments are cases where the policy is beneficial but another policy exists that would be even better. Non-arguments are partly or completely fallacious.

The optimal tariff: the first-best argument

The case for free trade requires that an economy's imports have no effect on the world price. For a small economy, this is correct. However, a large country may affect the world price of its imports. For society, the marginal cost of the last unit of imports then exceeds the world price. Another import bids up the

Table 15-4 Arguments for tariffs

	Example
First-best	Imports bid up world prices
Second-best	Ways of life, Anti-luxury, Infant industry, Defence, Revenue
Fallacious	Cheap foreign labour

world price that all other importers must pay, but each small importer in the big country ignores any effect of their actions on world prices. Under free trade, the country imports too much.

For the country as a whole, the marginal cost of imports exceeds the price paid by individual importers. A tariff puts this effect back into the price, inducing individual importers to act in the way that is best for society.

When a country affects the price of its imports, the **optimal tariff** makes individual importers take account of their effect on the price that other importers must pay.

Second-best arguments for tariffs

The **principle of targeting** says that the best way to meet an aim is to use a policy that affects the activity directly. Policies with side effects are second best because they distort other activities.

The optimal tariff is an application of the principle of targeting. When the problem lies in the market for imports, a tariff on imports is the most efficient solution. Now we turn to second-best arguments for tariffs where the original problem is not directly to do with trade. The principle of targeting tells us that there are other ways to solve these problems at a lower net social cost.

Suppose society wishes to help inefficient farmers or craft industries to *preserve the old way of life*. Tariffs protect these producers from foreign competition but also hurt domestic consumers through higher prices. A *production subsidy* would still keep farmers in business but, by tackling the problem directly, would not hurt consumers. In Figure 15-4, the cost of triangle A must be incurred to prop up domestic producers so they can make Q'_s not Q_s. But a tariff unnecessarily incurs the cost of triangle B as well.

Some poor countries dislike their few rich citizens enjoying luxury yachts when society needs its resources to stop people starving. To *suppress luxury consumption*, a *consumption tax* is best. Of course, it incurs triangle B in Figure 15-4 since domestic prices for consumers rise, but it avoids triangle A. A tariff on yachts also reduces consumption, but higher domestic prices then provide an incentive for inefficient domestic firms to make yachts, incurring triangle A as well.

In case there is a future war, some countries want to preserve their *defence capability* by protecting domestic industries making food or jet fighters. Again, a production subsidy rather than an import tariff is the best way to meet this objective.

A common argument for tariffs is to let *infant industries* get started. With initial protection, they learn the business and can eventually meet foreign competitors on equal terms. If the industry is such a good idea in the long run, why however can private firms not borrow the money to see them through the early period until they can compete? If the problem lies in bank lending to small firms, the principle of targeting says that a better policy is to solve the banking problem directly. Failing this, a production subsidy in the early years is still better than a tariff, which also penalizes consumers. The worst outcome is the imposition of a *permanent* tariff, which lets the industry remain inefficient long after it is supposed to have mastered its trade.

In the eighteenth century, most *tax revenue* came from tariffs, which were administratively easy to collect. This remains in some developing countries. But modern economies can raise taxes through many channels. Administrative simplicity is no longer a pressing concern.

Fallacious arguments for tariffs

Domestic firms often complain about *cheap foreign labour*. However, the whole point of trade is to exploit international differences in the relative prices of different goods. If the domestic economy is relatively well-endowed with capital, it benefits from trade because its exports of capital-intensive goods let it buy labour-intensive goods more cheaply from abroad than it could make them at home.

Over time, countries' comparative advantage evolves. Nineteenth-century Britain exported Lancashire textiles all over the world. But textile production is labour-intensive. Once Southeast Asia had the technology, their relatively abundant labour endowment gave them a comparative advantage in making textiles. The domestic producers who have lost their comparative advantage then complain about competition from imports using cheap foreign labour.

In the long run, the country as a whole benefits by facing facts, recognizing that its comparative advantage has changed, and transferring production to the industries in which its comparative advantage now lies. Our analysis of comparative advantage promises us that there *must* be some industry in which each country has a comparative advantage. In the long run, trying to use tariffs to prop up industries that have lost their comparative advantage is both futile and expensive.

In the short run, the adjustment may be painful and costly. Workers lose their jobs and must start afresh in industries where they do not have years of experience and acquired skills, but the principle of targeting tells us that, if society wants to smooth this transition, some kind of retraining or relocation subsidy is more efficient than a tariff.

Even though anti-capitalist protesters may sympathize with domestic workers who are losing their jobs and having to adjust, freezing the previous structure of employment is not merely undesirable but probably impossible. We no longer have decorators of cave dwellings or handloom weavers.

Maths 15-1

The algebra of tariffs

A country's supply curve, aggregating perfectly competitive individual firms, is $q = a + bp$ and its demand curve is $q = c - dp$, where a, b, c and d are all positive constants, and $c > a$. Without any government intervention, in a closed economy the equilibrium price is therefore $p = (c - a)/(b + d)$ and the corresponding equilibrium quantity is $(ad + bc)/(b + d)$. Suppose the world price is p^*. If this lies below the closed economy equilibrium price $(c - a)/(b + d)$, the country will import the good if it can, whereas it will export the good if p^* is higher than $(c - a)/(b + d)$. At this fixed price p^*, in an open economy consumers will demand $q_d = c - dp^*$ and producers will produce $q_p = a + bp^*$. Hence total imports are given by $q_d - q_p = (c - a) - (b + d)p^* > 0$.

Suppose p^* is low, and the tariff on imports is t per unit. Consumers now face the price $(p^* + t)$ and demand the quantity $q_d = c - d(p^* + t)$. Domestic producers expand, moving upwards along their supply curve until they too reach this price, at which point $q_p = a + b(p^* + t)$. Now total imports are $q_d - q_p = (c - a) - (b + d)(p^* + t)$. Comparing this with the zero-tariff case, the consequence of the positive tariff t is therefore to reduce the quantity of imports, which are lower by $(b + d)t$.

The World Trade Organization

In the nineteenth century, world trade grew rapidly. The leading country, the UK, pursued a vigorous policy of free trade. Early US tariffs averaged about 50 per cent, but had fallen to around 30 per cent by the early 1920s. As the industrial economies went into the Great Depression of the late 1920s and 1930s, there was increasing pressure to protect domestic jobs by keeping out imports. Tariffs in the US returned to around 50 per cent, and the UK abandoned the policy of free trade it had pursued for nearly a century. The combination of world recession and increasing tariffs led to a disastrous slump in the volume of world trade. Figure 15-5 shows that it took a long time for world trade to recover.

After the Second World War, there was a collective determination to restore world trade. The International Monetary Fund and the World Bank were set up, and many countries signed the General Agreement on Tariffs and Trade (GATT), a commitment to reduce tariffs successively and dismantle trade restrictions.

Under successive rounds of GATT, tariffs fell steadily. By 1960, US tariffs were only about one-fifth of their level in 1939. By 2000, Europe had completely abolished tariffs and other trade barriers for trade within the European Union, and the US and China had reached agreement to allow Chinese membership of the WTO. Thus, tariff levels throughout the world are probably as low as they have ever been, and world trade has seen six decades of rapid growth, arising at least in part from tariff reduction.

Non-tariff barriers to trade

Domestic firms can be protected by their governments in many subtle ways. Build a railway with a different width, favour domestic firms in defence procurement, drive on the other side of the road, create paperwork to ensure major delays at the border. One reason that the European Union is keen to harmonize standards is to reduce segmentation of the European market, which shelters inefficient national firms.

A more direct form of protection is a quota on imports.

A **quota** is a ceiling on import quantities.

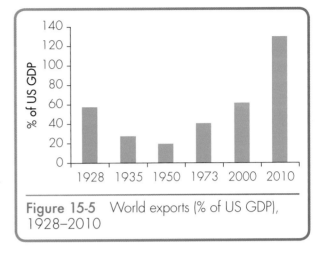

Figure 15-5   World exports (% of US GDP), 1928–2010

Although quotas restrict the *quantity* of imports, this does not mean they have no effect on domestic prices of the restricted goods. With a lower supply, the equilibrium domestic price is higher than under free trade.

Thus quotas are rather like tariffs. The domestic price to the consumer is increased, and it is this higher price that allows inefficient domestic producers to produce a higher output than under free trade. Quotas lead to social waste for exactly the same reasons as tariffs.

Because quotas raise the domestic price of the restricted good, the lucky foreign suppliers who manage to sell goods make large profits on these sales. In terms of Figure 15-4, the rectangle *EFHI*, which would have been tariff revenue for the government, now goes in profits to foreign suppliers. It is the difference between domestic and world prices of the goods imported, multiplied by the quantity of imports allowed.

If these profits accrue to foreigners it means the social cost of quotas is much bigger than the social cost of the equivalent tariff. Sometimes, however, the government can auction licences to import and thus recoup this revenue. Private importers or foreign suppliers will bid up to this amount to get their hands on a valuable important licence.

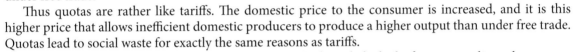

Case study 15-1   Changes in equilibrium real exchange rates

Paul Samuelson, one of the fathers of modern economics, won the Nobel Prize for his work on many aspects of economics, including international trade. Empirical research confirms a relation first noticed by Bala Balassa and Paul Samuelson: countries with higher per capita real incomes have a higher real exchange rate.

Typically, there is more technical progress in industries making goods for trade (computers, cars, telecommunications) than in industries making services for the home economy (haircuts, laundry, crèches). Similarly, productivity-enhancing capital accumulation occurs mainly in the traded goods sector. The main difference between a rich country and a poor country is not that hairdressers or childminders are more productive in rich countries, but that industries making exports and competing with imports are more productive.

Countries with high per capita incomes therefore have high real exchange rates because their traded goods sector is more productive. Without real exchange rate appreciation such countries would be too competitive. Why does the Belassa–Samuelson effect matter? Here are some examples.

▶

At what exchange rate should Eurozone members be admitted?

Suppose, just suppose, the Eurozone is flourishing and decides to allow Turkey to join its fixed exchange rate club. A country outside the Eurozone will typically have a floating exchange rate which will move around a bit. How do negotiators decide what a sensible exchange rate would be to permanently fix to the currency of a new entrant?

They might look at past data, hoping to find a period of internal and external balance in that country. This would be a starting point for calculating a sensible real exchange rate that would provide just the right amount of competitiveness.

So, from the base date, they would calculate how much relative prices of Turkey and the Eurozone had changed up to the date of Turkish entry, and adjust the original nominal exchange rate by this amount to restore the real exchange rate to the level at which it had last appeared correct. This would determine the nominal exchange rate at which Turkey was admitted to the common currency.

Without knowing about the Belassa–Samuelson effect, negotiators might make a mistake in assuming that the past was the perfect guide to the future. More sophisticated negotiators might take the above as a starting point but then ask whether Turkey was still an emerging economy, in relation to the more mature Eurozone economies, and therefore make an estimate of whether the further real appreciation of the Turkish currency might be compatible in the longer run with achieving a sustainable real exchange rate. This would lead to a different estimate of a suitable initial exchange rate for Turkish entry.

Overcompetitive China

Perhaps the most obvious example in the current global economy is the Chinese exchange rate. For years, China chose to fix its exchange rate to the US dollar, and to maintain this peg at a level that kept the Chinese economy supercompetitive. This explains why China had massive current account surpluses (and an outflow of capital as it invests these abroad again). In February 2010 the *Financial Times* reported an estimate by the US Petersen Institute that the Chinese exchange rate was undervalued by 41 per cent relative to the level consistent with internal and external balance (Geoff Dyer, *Financial Times*, 23 February 2010).

Policy makers, from Washington to Paris, complain that China's exchange rate policy is bankrupting their economies, leading to an export of jobs from the West to Asia, and leaving Western economies exposed to the inflows of financial capital from China that might, at some future date, decide to become outflows.

An upward adjustment of China's nominal exchange rate peg would reduce this problem overnight. But it is not the only adjustment mechanism. As China prints domestic money to fuel its incredible economic expansion, it is possible that Chinese domestic prices will rise sufficiently more quickly than those in the West and that its real appreciation – or loss of competitiveness – will be achieved not by a nominal exchange rate change but by a change in relative price levels in China and the West.

For the optimists who think such market forces may be an adequate substitute for a proactive change in the nominal exchange rate peg, the Belassa–Samuelson effect comes as bad news. As Chinese economic development continues, rapid productivity growth in its traded goods sector will allow it to cope with some degree of real appreciation without losing competitiveness. So, at a fixed nominal exchange rate, its supercompetitiveness will be reduced only if its domestic inflation (relative to competitors) exceeds its productivity growth (relative to competitors). A big inflation would have that effect; a small inflation probably will not.

15-2 Less-developed countries

In Europe or the US a drought is bad for the garden; in poor countries it kills people.

Less-developed countries (LDCs) have low levels of per capita output. We use the term **emerging market economies** for those middle-income countries that have embraced open markets and made considerable recent progress. Some poorer countries remain adrift of the general rise in world living standards.

Many LDCs feel that the world economy is arranged to benefit the industrial countries and to exploit poor countries. Altogether, 21 per cent of the world's people live in poor countries, with an average annual income of about $524 per person. In the rich countries, average annual income is over $39 000 per person. *Most of the world's people live in poverty beyond the imagination of people in rich Western countries.* Table 15-5 shows data on per capita income, life expectancy at birth and adult illiteracy. The low-income countries are badly off on every measure.

Nevertheless, the situation of low-income countries has improved. There has been a marked increase in life expectancy in low-income countries, an indication that the quality of life has improved. Per capita income grew in all groups of countries, yet, in absolute terms, poor countries fell even further behind the rest of the world.

To be so poor, these countries must have grown slowly for a long time. What special problems do they face?

Handicaps faced by poorer countries

Population growth

In rich countries birth control is widespread; in poor countries much less so. Without state pensions and other benefits, having children is one way people try to provide security against their old age when they can no longer work. With faster population growth, merely to maintain living standards poor countries grow more quickly than rich countries. However, poor countries cannot expand supplies of land, capital and natural resources at the same rate as the labour force. Decreasing returns to labour set in: the Malthusian trap.

Resource scarcity

Abu Dhabi, generously endowed with oil, has a per capita income above that of the US or Germany. Many poor countries have not been blessed with natural resources that can profitably be exploited. And having resource deposits is not enough: it takes scarce capital resources to extract mineral deposits. Allowing foreign investors to do the job seems to let them keep most of the income too.

Table 15-5 World welfare indicators, 2007–08

Country group	Poor	Middle-income	Rich
Per capita GNP ($)	524	3260	39 686
Life expectancy at birth (years)	58	69	80
Adult illiteracy (%)	36	17	1

Source: World Bank, *World Development Report,* 2010

Capital

Rich countries have built up large stocks of physical capital, which make their workers productive. Poor countries have few spare domestic resources to devote to physical investment. Financial loans and aid let poor countries buy foreign machinery and pay foreign construction firms. However, poor countries frequently complain that financial assistance is inadequate.[1]

Human capital

Without resources to devote to investment in health, education and industrial training, workers in poor countries are less productive than workers using the same technology in rich countries. Yet, without higher productivity, it is hard to generate enough output (surplus to consumption requirements) to raise investment in people as well as in machinery.

Lack of human capital also makes it more difficult to regulate domestic markets to offset market failures such as monopoly or environmental pollution, and to achieve reliable enforcement of contracts through a transparent legal system.

Social investment in infrastructure

Developed countries achieve economies of scale and high productivity through specialization, assisted by sophisticated transport and communications. Without investment in power generation, roads, telephones and urban housing, poor countries must operate in smaller communities, unable to exploit scale economies and specialization.

Conflict

Some of the poorest regions have been those where colonially imposed boundaries made little sense and where the end of empire left governments without wide domestic support. Both internal and international conflict have followed. Recent research also suggests conflict is more likely in poor countries that are well-endowed with mineral resources. Competing interests then fight to control the spoils.

How can the world economy help? Our discussion examines all countries classified as LDCs, from the newly-industrialized nearly-rich to the very poorest countries lagging far behind.

Development through exports of primary products

Section 15-1 analysed the gains from trade when countries specialize in the commodities in which they have a comparative advantage. Relative factor abundance is an important determinant of comparative advantage. In many LDCs the relatively abundant input is land. This suggests that LDCs can best use the world economy by exporting goods using land relatively intensively.

> **Primary products** are agricultural goods and minerals, the output of both of which relies heavily on the input of land.

These include 'soft' commodities, such as coffee, cotton and sugar, and 'hard' commodities or minerals, such as copper or aluminium. As late as 1960, exports of primary commodities were 84 per cent of all LDC exports. Many countries are now sceptical of development through specialization in production of primary products. Today, less than half of all LDC exports are primary products. Figure 15-6 shows that on average the real price of most commodities fell steadily during 1940–2010. This reflected both greater supply and lower demand. Technical advances, such as artificial rubber and plastics, reduced the demand for many primary products. Greater supply reflected the success of LDCs in increasing productivity and

---

[1]   At the 1996 Food Summit, Jacques Diouf, Director of the Food and Agriculture Organization, said his annual budget was 'less than what nine developed countries spend on dog and cat food in six days, and less than 5 per cent of what inhabitants of just one developed country spend on slimming products every year' (*The Times*, 14 November 1996).

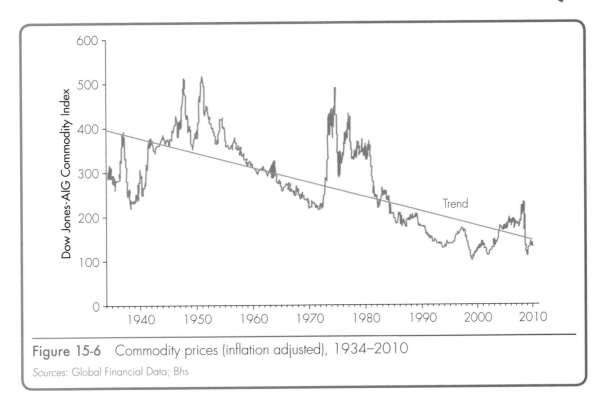

Figure 15-6 Commodity prices (inflation adjusted), 1934–2010

Sources: Global Financial Data; Bhs

output. With better drainage and irrigation, better seeds and more fertilizer, agriculture was transformed by the 'green revolution'. Similarly, mineral producers, often with foreign help, developed more capital-intensive mining methods. Even where each individual LDC was small, their collective effort to raise exports induced a fall in the real price of their export commodities.

This effect was exacerbated by extensive protection of farmers in rich countries such as the US and those in the EU. Deprived of access to these large markets, LDCs have had to sell their larger supply in smaller markets, thus depressing the price much further than would otherwise have been the case.

Allowing LDC agricultural goods into the markets of the rich countries is probably the policy change that would have the greatest benefit for LDCs as a whole. Their income from exports of primary products would soar, providing a surplus to invest in physical and human capital. Consumers in rich countries would also benefit. A rise in the supply of food would reduce the price of food in London and New York.

Figure 15-6 shows that during 2000–08 there was a sharp increase in world commodity prices. In principle, this should have started to help poor countries that export primary products. In practice, the gains have not been equally enjoyed. Oil-producing countries were back in the boom days of the early 1980s. Metals producers have also enjoyed great prosperity.

Just when poor countries were starting to believe the world economy had come to their rescue, the financial crash, and collapse of output, led to a sharp drop in commodity prices. However, by 2010 commodity prices had clearly started to recover again. A key issue therefore is whether economic recovery can be sustained, in which the demands of India, China and others will continue to put upward pressure on commodity prices, or whether there is a further setback to recovery from the financial crisis.

The experience of food producers has been more mixed. In the poorest countries, the gain from higher prices for their output has been largely offset by the higher prices they pay for their inputs – seeds to plant, and fuel with which to harvest and transport their goods. The rise in food prices has not yet made the poor producers rich.

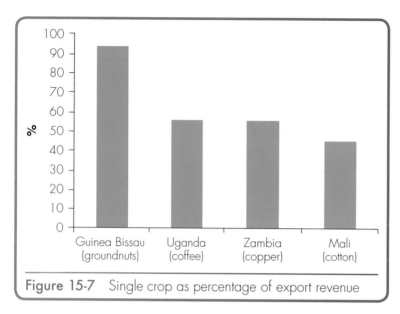

Figure 15-7 Single crop as percentage of export revenue

A second disadvantage of concentrating on the production of primary products has been the volatility of their real prices. Both supply and demand are price-inelastic in the short run. On the demand side, people need food and industrial raw materials. On the supply side, crops have already been planted and perishable output has to be marketed whatever the price. When both supply and demand curves are very steep, a small shift in one curve leads to a big change in the equilibrium price.

Declining prices and price volatility are especially important when exports of a single crop are a large share of total export revenue. As shown in Figure 15-7, some LDCs are very vulnerable because they depend so heavily on a single export crop.

Development through industrialization

Many countries have concluded that the route to development lies not through increased specialization in making primary products but in the expansion of manufacturing industry. This has taken two very different forms.

Import substitution

When world trade collapsed in the 1930s, many LDCs found their export revenues cut in half. Many LDCs resolved never again to be so dependent on the world economy. After the Second World War, they began a policy of import substitution.

> **Import substitution** replaces imports by domestic production under the protection of high tariffs or import quotas.

Import substitution reduces world trade and suppresses the principle of comparative advantage. LDCs used tariffs and quotas to direct domestic resources away from the primary products into industrial manufacturing, where initially they had a comparative disadvantage.

International trade theory suggests that this policy is likely to be wasteful. For example, by closing itself off from the world economy, the communist bloc pursued import substitution on a grand scale, but without eventual success. Import substitution has one great danger and one possible merit.

The danger is that import substitution may be a dead end. Although domestic industry may expand quite rapidly behind tariff barriers while imports are being replaced, once import substitution has been completed economic growth may come to a halt. The country is then specialized in industries in which it has a comparative *disadvantage*, and further expansion can come only from expanding *domestic* demand.

The possible merit is that comparative advantage is dynamic not static. A tariff may help an infant industry, even though production subsidies would achieve the same outcome at lower social cost. By developing an industrial sector and learning to use the technology, LDCs may eventually acquire a comparative advantage in some industrial products. Thus, import substitution may not be an end in itself, but a prelude to export-led growth.

Table 15-6   The Asian tigers

	Annual real growth of per capita GDP (%)		Percentage of manufactures in total exports	
	1965–80	1980–2010	1965	2010
Indonesia	9	5	2	42
Malaysia	7	4	6	71
Singapore	10	5	34	76
South Korea	10	6	59	89
Thailand	7	5	4	76
China	4	8	47	93

Source: World Bank, World Development Report (various issues)

Export-led growth stresses output and income growth via exports, rather than by displacing imports.

Exports of manufactures

The real success story of the past three decades is the group of countries that have turned the world economy to their advantage by exporting manufactures using their relatively cheap labour. Many of these countries are in Southeast Asia. Table 15-6 shows how successful they have been. The booming industries of a middle-income country are often the declining industries of the rich countries, where a further loss of market share causes problems as workers have to be reallocated elsewhere. Although the evolution of comparative advantage says that this is efficient, politicians still have to respond to the short-run difficulties, and may be tempted to try to postpone adjustment for a little longer.

It is also now common to focus on the BRICs – Brazil, Russia, India and China – because these four economies are the largest of the emerging markets. Russia is principally an energy exporter of oil and gas – currently only 17 per cent of its exports are manufactures. Although 47 per cent of Brazil's exports are manufactures, it is also, like Australia, a huge exporter of mineral resources to feed the thirst of the rapidly growing East Asian economies, including, but not confined to, China.

Development through borrowing

A third route to economic development is by external borrowing, and a third complaint of poor countries about the way the world economy works is that borrowing terms are too tough. Poorer countries have traditionally borrowed in world markets to finance imports of capital goods. Recall the balance of payments arithmetic:

$$\text{Current account deficit} = \text{trade deficit} + \text{debt interest}$$
$$= \text{increase in net foreign debt}$$

The first line shows the sources of the current account deficit; the second reminds us that it has to be financed by selling domestic assets to foreigners or by new foreign borrowing.

Table 15-7 shows debt/GNP ratios by region. During 1980–2007, every region became considerably more indebted in relation to its income and ability to pay. However, since 2007 programmes to reduce the external

Table 15-7   LDC debt (percentage of GNP), 1980–2010

	1980	2007	2010
Sub-Saharan Africa	29	41	20
Eastern Europe, Central Asia	24	42	42
Latin America, Caribbean	35	62	22
East Asia, Pacific	17	117	14
Middle East, North Africa	31	31	14
South Asia	17	69	19

Source: World Bank, *World Development Report*, various issues

debt burden have succeeded in substantially shrinking the debt/GNP ratios in all regions. The *burden* of the debt reflects not just the amount of debt but also the interest rate that creditors demand. When rates are high, the burden is larger. As interest rates have fallen, this has also reduced the debt burden.

We also have to keep track of how the money was spent. Loans that are spent on consumption do little to enhance future ability to repay. Loans successfully invested in productive projects can generate output sufficiently large to meet the interest payments with ease. One problem is that during 1980–95 the rate of return on large investment projects was often disappointing, leaving countries with the cost of the debt without a corresponding benefit. Conversely, the boom in many emerging market economies during the last 15 years has included many successful projects that will enhance future ability to pay.

Aid

Aid is an international transfer payment from rich countries to poor countries.

Poor countries often argue that they should get more aid from rich countries. Many of the rich countries are also failing to honour their previous promises about the amount of aid that they will give.

Box 15-1

Debt forgiveness for highly indebted poor countries

Bob Geldof and other famous personalities have long been campaigning for rich countries to write off the debts of the world's poorest nations. It is a laudable aim, but we have to do it correctly.

Once a country cannot pay its debts, why not recognize reality, let them off, and make a fresh start? One problem for creditors is how to do so without encouraging the belief that all future debtors will be bailed out, in which case no debtor will struggle much in order to repay debts.

Another problem is that the big winners could be Western banks rather than impoverished borrowers. Suppose a country owes £100 million a year but can only pay £50 million a year. Every creditor is only getting half what they should get.

Now, suppose benevolent European governments write off £50 million of the debts owed to them. They raise money from their taxpayers and give it to their own banks in exchange for a bonfire of £50 million of outstanding debts from poor countries. After this, the debtor countries, instead of being able to pay £50 million on £100 million, now are able to pay £50 million on the outstanding £50 million still owed to banks in London and Frankfurt. Since the debtors can afford to pay £50 million, these banks will continue to demand to be paid. The country gets no relief as a result of the debt forgiveness. If the assistance did not benefit the country, where did it go? It helped the creditors whose outstanding debt is now more valuable since it is being paid in full. The entire operation was a transfer from Western taxpayers to Western banks.

Helping rich banks was not the intention. The message? Debt forgiveness must write off *more than* the amount the borrower was *failing* to pay. Remaining creditors are paid in full, but there is some left over to reduce total payments by the borrower. That is one reason why rich countries often focus their debt relief on the poorest countries. Not only are the poorest countries more deserving but also spreading a given amount of debt forgiveness across too many countries would fail to meet the criterion that forgiveness must exceed the debt shortfall. By concentrating their aid on fewer countries, Western leaders try to make sure that some of the benefit of this relief is felt in the countries intended to be helped.

> *The Joint IMF–World Bank comprehensive approach to debt reduction is designed to ensure that no poor country faces a debt burden it cannot manage. To date, debt reduction packages under the HIPC Initiative have been approved for 36 countries, 30 of them in Africa, providing US$76 billion in debt-service relief over time. Three additional countries are eligible for HIPC Initiative assistance.*
>
> IMF, Debt Relief Under the Heavily Indebted Poor Countries (HIPC) Initiative

The HIPC Initiative was launched in 1996 by the IMF and World Bank, to try to ensure no poor country faced a debt burden it could not manage. Since then, the international financial community, including multilateral organizations and governments, have worked together to reduce to sustainable levels the external debt burdens of the most heavily indebted poor countries.

In 2005, to help accelerate progress toward the United Nations Millennium Development Goals (MDGs), the HIPC Initiative was supplemented by the Multilateral Debt Relief Initiative (MDRI), which allows for 100 per cent relief on eligible debts by three multilateral institutions – the IMF, the World Bank and the African Development Fund (AfDF) – for countries completing the HIPC Initiative process. In 2007, the Inter-American Development Bank (IaDB) also decided to provide additional debt relief to the five HIPCs in the Western Hemisphere.

Countries must meet certain criteria, commit to poverty reduction through policy changes and demonstrate a good track record over time. The Fund and Bank provide interim debt relief in the initial stage and, when a country meets its commitments, full debt relief is provided. To be considered for HIPC Initiative assistance, a country must fulfil four conditions, which broadly mean it is co-operating with the IMF and World Bank and has a track record of trying to pursue sensible policies. Thereafter, it is assessed by the IMF and World Bank for debt relief, and the international community commits to reducing debt to a level that is considered sustainable. To obtain subsequently the full amount of debt relief, it must continue to demonstrate a track record of sound economic policies.

Since the scheme was established, 35 countries are receiving full debt relief from the IMF and other creditors. By 2013, an additional four countries had been identified for help or already received some kind of interim debt relief. These countries include:

▶

Afghanistan	Ethiopia	Mozambique
Benin	The Gambia	Nicaragua
Bolivia	Ghana	Niger
Burkina Faso	Guinea	Rwanda
Burundi	Guinea-Bissau	São Tomé and Príncipe
Cameroon	Guyana	Senegal
Central African Republic	Haiti	Sierra Leone
Chad*	Honduras	Somalia*
Comoros	Liberia	Sudan*
Republic of the Congo	Madagascar	Tanzania
Democratic Republic of the Congo	Malawi	Togo
Côte d'Ivoire	Mali	Uganda
Eritrea*	Mauritania	Zambia

Countries in pre-decision or between decision and completion point

Aid can take many forms: subsidized loans, gifts of food or machinery, or technical help and free advice. How much aid rich countries should give is of course a moral or value judgement. However, many of the poorest countries feel that Northern prosperity was built during a colonial period when the resources of the South were exploited. Aid seems at least partial compensation. The Northern countries do not share this interpretation of history.

As we indicated earlier, many poor countries and emerging market economies believe the best contribution rich countries can make is to be allowed free access to markets in the developed countries. 'Trade, not aid' is the slogan. Just as it is better for the government to retrain a domestic worker who has become unemployed than to provide a lifetime of welfare support, useful market access is better than a culture of dependency on aid handouts from rich countries.

The quickest way to equalize world income distribution would be to permit free migration between countries. Residents of poor countries could go elsewhere in search of higher incomes and, in emigrating, they would increase capital and land per worker for those who stayed behind.

The massive movements of population from Europe to the Americas and the colonies in the nineteenth and early twentieth centuries were an income-equalizing movement of this sort. Since 1945, migrations have been much smaller. If the gap between rich and poor widens further, rich countries may find it harder and harder to keep out economic migrants.

In this respect, one trend will eventually operate in favour of poorer countries and emerging market economies. The richest countries are getting top-heavy with old people, and have fewer and fewer young workers to pay the taxes and finance the pensions. Eventually, young labour will be in high demand, and it may have to be imported. At some future date, immigrants may be shown the red carpet, not the cold shoulder.

15-3 Globalization

Global brands, such as Coca-Cola and McDonald's, are highly visible symbols of the increasing integration of world markets. Lower transport costs, better communications, new information technology and deliberate policies to reduce trade barriers have all enhanced the size of the relevant economic market.

This starts to erode the sovereignty of national governments, by undermining the ability of an individual government to raise taxes, constrain firms and regulate markets. Too much intervention and business migrates to an easier location elsewhere. In turn, perceiving the erosion of the power of their national governments to influence events, voters become apathetic and lose interest in national politics. Multinational corporations (MNCs) sometimes seem to have become more powerful than governments.

Globalization is the increase in cross-border trade and influence on the economic and social behaviour of nation states.

Section 15-1 discussed how international trade can benefit everyone, but may also create losers if the winners claim all the spoils for themselves. Section 15-2 identified the disadvantages with which poor countries begin, and why some countries have yet to share in world prosperity.

Have the benefits of globalization been outweighed by its costs? Should globalization now be resisted? The next time a hamburger outlet is being trashed by anti-globalization protesters, should you be leading the charge or explaining that there is a better way to meet their concerns? To help you make up your mind, we now discuss some of the most frequent criticisms of globalization.

Globalization is a new phenomenon, requiring a new policy response

Actually, since communications and transport have been steadily increasing for centuries, globalization is also centuries old. By many measures of trade, migration and capital flows across borders, the period 1870–1913 was comparable to the globalization of the past few decades.

Globalization is thus neither new nor irreversible. Globalization during 1870–1913 created many winners but also some powerful losers. Cheaper grain from the US drove down grain prices and land rents in Europe, prompting agricultural protection in the 1920s. Massive migration to the US drove down wages there, leading to the introduction of immigration controls; it also helped reduce the excess supply of labour in Europe in the interwar period.

When the pace of globalization accelerates, there can be large changes in patterns of demand and supply, and hence in equilibrium prices. History warns us that sustaining the momentum for globalization requires sufficient redistribution to ensure that powerful groups of losers do not emerge to create a backlash.

Consider for example the spectacular increases in commodity prices – energy, minerals, food – so vividly illustrated in Figure 15-6. In oil-exporting countries, such as in the Gulf, incomes rise and citizens become ever wealthier. In oil-importing countries, including those in Europe, standards of living fall. Heating bills rise, lorry drivers protest about fuel costs and livestock farmers are squeezed by higher prices for grains for animal feed.

If all this was going on within a single country, the government could, if it so wished, tax those who had got richer and use the money to subsidize those who had got poorer. But this is not much of an option within most nation-states. In countries such as the UK, a net loser from higher commodity prices, most people have got poorer and there are few who have got richer. If the government wants to provide relief for the poor, it has to tax the well-off more, despite the fact they themselves may be hurting from higher commodity prices. Conversely, in Saudi Arabia, there are lots of winners and few losers in need of support.

Logically, global problems require global solutions. A global government could address this particular problem more effectively. So why don't we have a global government? A significant part of the answer is that the common citizen-electors have to feel some identity with one another. National rivalries, and ignorance of other cultures, make it difficult to extend sovereignty too widely. In particular, those being taxed start to resent subsidizing people they regard as distant strangers with whom they have no affinity. Even within the small, integrated and relatively similar states of Western Europe, closer integration has not been easy.

Globalization may not be new, but it is extensive and ever more so. We see its consequences not just in economics but in issues such as climate change and migration, and we will eventually see serious disputes about ownership of water resources. For now, global government is not on the cards. If these problems become sufficiently acute, people may have to rethink their political views about the nation-state.

Table 15-8   World welfare indicators, 1820–1992

	1820	1910	1950	1992
Average income/person (1990 $000's)	0.7	1.5	2.1	5.0
World population (billion)	1.1	1.7	2.5	5.5
Income share: richest 10% of people	43	51	51	53
poorest 10% of people	5	4	2	2
People earning <$1/day (billion)	0.9	1.1	1.4	1.3

Source: Centre for Economic Policy Research, *Making Sense of Globalization*, London, 2002

Globalization increases inequality in the global economy

A few facts are helpful. Table 15-8 summarizes the last 200 years. Globalization *did* cause a big increase in inequality during 1820–1950, when the income share of the richest 10 per cent of the world's population rose from 43 per cent to 51 per cent while the income share of the poorest 10 per cent of people fell from 5 per cent to 2 per cent. However, since 1950 it is *not* true that the income share of the poor has kept falling, nor has the income share of the rich risen much. You only have to realize that many of the poor used to live in China; three decades of per capita income growth at 9 per cent per annum have substantially reduced the number of very poor people in China, even making allowance for the fact that most of the prosperity has occurred in cities.

Global inequality is acute, but not getting worse. Inequality is about relative incomes. We can also ask what is happening to the absolute incomes of the poor. Table 15-8 shows that the number of people earning less than a dollar a day (inflation adjusted, at 1990 prices) has fallen since 1950, *despite* the doubling of world population in the same period. Most of us would feel happier if the conditions of the poor were improving more rapidly. But they are improving slowly, whether measured by income, as in Table 15-8, or by life expectancy or literacy.

Globalization has lifted a large number of people out of poverty by fostering economic growth in large previously poor countries. Figure 15-8 shows the steady progress during 1980–2008.

Why, then, do people make the connection between globalization and poverty? Nowadays, we see it on the news, on documentaries and on charity appeals. Previously, it was there, and was worse, but we were less aware of it. Similarly, people living in poor countries are much better informed about how rich the rich countries have become. Globalization of information has increased dissatisfaction

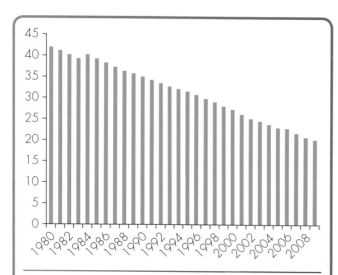

Figure 15-8   Percentage of world population in extreme poverty (1980–2009)

Source: World Bank

about what has always existed. In so doing, it may encourage more people to get involved in trying to make the world a better place.

Multinational corporations exploit workers and play off poor governments against one another

Local workers employed by MNCs, whether mining minerals or producing clothes and trainers, seem to us to work for pitifully low wages and in conditions that workers in rich countries would not tolerate. However, their wages are usually higher than those earned by their compatriots in domestic industries, and working conditions in MNCs are often better than those in domestic factories, not least because MNCs care about their global image.

If workers in poor countries began with much larger quantities of physical and human capital, they would be richer and more productive. In principle, rich countries could vote for a massive transfer of aid to purchase these valuable inputs for poor countries. But they never have, and the reality is that they probably never will. Without these advantages, the equilibrium wage of the disadvantaged is low. Allowing them access to the world economy lets them gradually accumulate more of the valuable inputs that eventually enhance their own prosperity.

Well-meaning attempts to force 'improvements' in their wages and working conditions simply price them out of world markets and reduce their eventual prosperity. For an example closer to home, think of German unification in 1990. West German trade unions raised wages in East Germany, but East Germans were not initially as productive as West Germans. The result was a decade of high unemployment and discontent in East Germany. So who gained? West German workers, protected from competition from cheap labour in East Germany!

What poor countries need is not less globalization but more. Here, rich countries can help a lot, principally by opening up their market in agriculture and textiles, industries in which poor countries have a natural comparative advantage. Removing tariffs would reduce prices in the rich countries but raise prices received by exporters in emerging market economies. Current estimates are that a 40 per cent reduction in agricultural tariffs would generate gains of $70 billion a year. Incidentally, it would also reduce the food bill of each EU citizen by £200 a year. Since the losers would be farmers in rich countries, the challenge for policy makers is to find a way to buy off these losers sufficiently.

If you are reading this book, the chances are that you are below the age of 25. You may well be outraged about the mess that previous generations have created on our planet. You can campaign against climate change, protest about conflict and even trash the odd fast-food restaurant. If you want to make the largest and fastest difference to living standards of the poor in the developing world, however, you should probably campaign to reduce agricultural protection in the West. A few rich farmers will suffer, but Western consumers would benefit from lower food prices and the economies of poor countries would simply be transformed.

What about the claim that MNCs play off poor countries against one another? The trainers that you wear may have an American logo, but they were probably made in China, the Dominican Republic or Vietnam. MNCs effectively get each country to bid for hosting inward investment in a new factory. Does competition between countries ensure that the investment goes to the country with the lowest wages and lightest regulation?

Actually, it does not. MNCs like low wages, but they also like workers with education and skills, good transport infrastructure and predictable legal environments. Foreign investment has flooded into Singapore not Somalia.

Moreover, competition between countries is one disciplining force on corruption in national bureaucracies that would otherwise be sheltered monopolies. The price of abuse is the failure to attract valuable inward investment. Globalization on balance is probably a force that fosters democracy, transparency and good governance. One problem with sub-Saharan Africa is that it has been too little exposed to the global economy rather than too much.

Globalization destroys the environment

Rainforests are cut down to rear beef cows for hamburgers, oil production wipes out wildlife and mining scars the landscape. All true. And all exacerbated by globalization. However, we need to remember the principle of targeting.

If the environment is wrongly priced – encouraging overexploitation because producers do not pay the full social cost of what they do – the best solution is to encourage better pricing of the environment. Trying to suppress trade is a second-best solution.

Though logically correct, this is a counsel of perfection. Even countries rich in human capital have yet to implement sophisticated schemes that price and regulate use of the environment adequately. It is unrealistic to imagine that countries with fewer enforcement resources will do better in pricing their environments.

Global measures, such as a carbon tax that applies everywhere, may be a reasonable compromise. Not only could this protect the environment, it would be a useful source of tax revenue for poor countries. However, the failure to date of the US to commit convincingly to global accords on climate change mitigation indicates a current unwillingness on the part of the US to play much of a role in such agreements.

History suggests that it is wrong for the winners to believe that there is no need to heed the grievances of the losers, as the collapse of globalization in the interwar period attests (see again Figure 15-5, which shows the dramatic collapse of world trade once protection broke out). If globalization is not harnessed through better political management of the process, it may eventually be undone by conflict.

Case study 15-2 The *Fortune Global 500*

In early 2012, Apple became the most valuable company in the world on the stock market, valued at $600 billion. Much of this of course was based on extrapolating its extraordinary revenue growth and estimating the value of these future revenues; its current revenues are much smaller. The *Fortune Global 500*, computed annually by the business magazine *Fortune*, is based on revenues and profits during the *current year* alone.

The top 500 used to be almost exclusively American companies. Even as recently as 2005, over one-third of the companies in the top 500 were American. By 2012 it was only one-quarter. Globalization is creating large new companies, many of them in the BRICs. Even in 2005, China had 16 companies in the top 500, by 2012 it had 61. The other BRIC countries have also more than doubled their representation since 2005. It will not be many years before the BRICs collectively overtake the US in this ranking.

Often the giants are in the energy sector. Currently Sinopec (China) ranks 5th, Petrobras (Brazil) 34th, Gazprom (Russia) 35th and Indian Oil 98th. Indian conglomerate Tata has bought Jaguar Land Rover and most of the UK steel industry. Australian mining conglomerate Rio Tinto now has substantial Chinese ownership. Sovereign-wealth funds (state-owned investment funds) of various Arab kingdoms have taken large stakes in banks around the world, including Barclays.

Lenovo, a Chinese computer-maker, became a global brand in 2005, paying around £1 billion for IBM's computer manufacturing business, from mainframes to ThinkPad laptops. Within two years, Lenovo no longer felt the need to use the IBM brand name, so strong was its own brand. One reason for Lenovo's confidence was its key position in the booming Chinese market. After 30 years with an annual growth rate of 10 per cent, China now has millions of citizens who can afford laptops and cars. 'It took 25 years for the world to sell 1 billion personal computers, but with China [and India, Russia and Brazil] booming, it may take only seven years to reach the next billion consumers,' according to Bill Amelio, Lenovo's chief executive. Globalization is therefore creating spectacular opportunities (and pitfalls) for large companies wherever their home base.

Phase 1 of globalization often involved the export of cheap raw materials and cheap manufactures from developing economies to advanced countries, in return for imports of high-tech goods from these knowledge-based economies. But globalization is now entering Phase 2, in which emerging market economies are enjoying rapid increases in their standard of living, and are themselves demanding fuel and raw materials, producing increasingly sophisticated goods, and competing in the knowledge economy itself. Local BRIC producers may also market more effectively to BRIC consumers, freezing out some Western multinationals. For example, they may produce products with a quality and price more suited to their medium-rich markets. Established giants are of course trying to fight back. For example, American companies such as Hewlett-Packard and Dell are making a big effort to crack the emerging computer market in countries such as China.

Nor is this confined to the four BRIC countries. South Korea tops the world ranking of criteria, such as education attainment, supportive of future economic growth, and it contains many companies doing extremely well in the global economy – Hyundai and Kia and two of the three fastest-growing car manufacturers in Europe at present; Samsung has left Nokia for dead and even overtaken Apple's iPhone in the number of mobile devices sold in 2012.

The 2012 top ten in the Global 500 were Walmart (supermarkets, US), Royal Dutch Shell (energy, UK and Netherlands), Exxon Mobile (energy, US), BP (energy, UK), Sinopec (energy, China), China National Petroleum (energy, China), State Grid (electricity, China), Toyota (cars, Japan), Japan Post (postal, Japan) and Chevron (energy, US). In contrast, the top Internet service provider is Amazon, at number 270. Just watch how quickly the Internet companies catch up over the next decade.

The financial crisis and subsequent recession, largely escaped by the BRICs, has obviously affected the speed at which the mature Western companies are being caught up and overtaken. Recession also tends to increase the pressure for protection from import competition – higher tariffs, greater restrictions on takeovers of domestic companies by foreign investors and barriers to foreign workers. The crash of 1929 gave rise to a huge wave of protection in the 1930s that it took four decades to undo. Globalization could still go into reverse.

In their 2007 book *Good Capitalism, Bad Capitalism and the Economics of Prosperity and Growth*, William Baumol, Robert Litan and Carl Schramm distinguish four models of capitalism: entrepreneurial, big-firm, oligarchic and state-led. The best economies, say the authors, blend big-firm and entrepreneurial capitalism; the worst combination is oligarchic and state-led capitalism, both prevalent in many emerging markets. Yet the combination of takeovers by foreign firms and investment by sovereign-wealth funds is tipping world capitalism away from democracies towards oligarchic and state-led models.

It is too soon to tell whether the US has safely recovered from the financial crisis; hence we cannot yet revise our view that capitalism thrives best in democracies that foster entrepreneurial, big-firm capitalism. Nor can we take it for granted that state-led capitalism is always a failure. China has just delivered 30 years of 10 per cent annual growth without any population explosion. With a one-child-per-family policy, output per person grew annually by 8 per cent for the last 30 years, a truly unprecedented achievement, albeit that some of this was merely the reversal of Mao's great leap backwards.

The growing role of states with few democratic credentials may create a sense that competition from emerging-economy champions and investors is unfair. Rich-country firms are losing out to less well-run competitors that enjoy various favours from their governments, not least in extractive industries where the granting of exploration licences is highly political.

Will 'bad capitalism' drive out 'good capitalism'? Maybe, or perhaps the world will be grateful that these new frontiers provide not merely an underpinning to raise living standards of vast numbers of poor people in the world but also a flywheel to keep the world economy spinning until the advanced countries, particularly in Europe, get their act together again after the giant mess created when banks went bust and then governments took over their debts.

Recap

- World trade has grown rapidly in the past 50 years, and is dominated by developed industrial countries. Primary commodities are a quarter of world trade; the rest is trade in manufactures.
- Countries trade if they can buy goods more cheaply from abroad. Cross-country differences in costs arise from differences in technology and input endowments. Economies of scale also lead to international specialization.
- Countries export the goods in which they have a comparative advantage, or make relatively cheaply. The equilibrium exchange rate offsets average differences in absolute advantage. Every country has a comparative advantage in something.
- By exploiting international differences in opportunity costs, trade leads to a pure gain. Since people share differently in the gain, some may actually lose.
- Intra-industry trade reflects scale economies plus consumer demand for variety.
- By raising the domestic price, a tariff reduces domestic consumption but raises domestic production. Hence imports fall.
- A tariff has two social costs: overproduction by domestic firms whose marginal cost exceeds the world price and underconsumption by consumers whose marginal benefit exceeds the world price.
- When a country collectively affects the price of its imports, the optimal tariff induces individual importers to take account of their adverse effect on other importers for whom the import price is bid up.
- Other arguments for tariffs are either second-best solutions – a production subsidy or consumption tax would meet the objective at lower social cost – or are fallacious.
- Tariffs fell sharply after 1945, partly in response to the damage done by high tariffs in the 1930s. The World Trade Organization tries to negotiate further reductions and regulate existing agreements.
- World income and wealth are very unequally divided. LDCs complain that they are denied access to rich markets, that borrowing is too expensive, that past debt should be forgiven and that aid is insufficient.
- In the poorest countries, population and labour are growing faster than other production inputs, driving down living standards and removing surplus resources to invest in sustainable growth.
- Falling real prices, price volatility and concentration in a single commodity have made LDCs reluctant to pursue development by exporting primary products.
- LDC exports of labour-intensive manufactures are growing rapidly. Rich countries should not respond by protecting their manufacturers.
- Many LDCs have large external debts without the corresponding fruits of these investments. Token debt relief benefits Western creditors not LDC borrowers. To be successful, debt relief has to be substantial.

- Market access and trade may help the LDCs more effectively than aid, though more aid would also help. Migration would also reduce income disparities.
- Globalization is neither new nor irreversible. It is caused by cheaper transport, better communications and policies to reduce trade protection. In the absence of other distortions, this yields gains from trade and net benefits for the global economy. However, some groups may lose out.
- In the past half-century, global inequality has diminished and the number of people in absolute poverty has fallen, despite rapid population growth. Trade is usually the route to prosperity. No country ever got rich without international trade. However, better global information has made everyone aware of the extent of poverty that still exists in the world.
- Liberalizing agriculture and textile markets in rich countries would hugely benefit not only their own citizens but also potential exporters in poor countries. The gains would easily allow the losers (rich farmers and textile producers) to be bought off.
- Globalization exacerbates existing distortions, for example the overexploitation of the environment or inadequate financial regulation in poor countries. The ideal solution is to improve these by domestic policy reform, not to curtail trade. Foreign aid could usefully be channelled into these areas.
- Taxing pollution and environmental depreciation would also generate useful tax revenue, in both poor and rich countries.
- Allowing powerful groups of uncompensated losers to proliferate is the most likely way in which globalization may eventually be arrested or even reversed. Deliberate redistribution is required to sustain the benefits of globalization. In that case, rich and poor will benefit. Aid alone will never be enough to raise the poor out of poverty.

Review questions

To check your answers to these questions, go to pages 395–6.

1 'A country with uniformly low productivity must be hurt by allowing foreign competition.' Is this true? Can you provide a counter-example?

2 'Large countries gain less from world trade than small countries.' True or false? Why?

3 Cars, wine, steel: which of these do you think have high intra-industry trade? Why?

4 To preserve its national heritage, society bans exports of works of art. (a) Is this better than an export tax? (b) Who gains and who loses from the export ban? (c) Will this measure encourage young domestic artists?

5 Why are these statements wrong? (a) British producers are becoming uncompetitive in everything. (b) Free trade is always best. (c) Buy British to help Britain.

EASY

6 Discuss two forces tending to reduce the real price of food in the long run.

7 Why were LDCs so successful in exporting textiles, clothing and leather footwear?

8 A country pays 8 per cent interest on its foreign debt, but its GDP grows by 8 per cent a year. What happens to its debt/GDP ratio if it meets all existing interest payments by new borrowing? What happens if its output growth then slows?

9 Prior to full membership of the EU, countries in Eastern Europe were allowed free trade with the EU in many products but with some notable exceptions. (a) On which products do you think the EU still applied big tariffs? (b) Were these likely to be goods in which Eastern Europe had a comparative advantage?

10 Why are these statements wrong? (a) Aid is all the help LDCs need. (b) Europe needs tariffs to protect it from cheap labour in the LDCs.

11 Could protecting the local film industry from 'cultural imperialism' from Hollywood be justified? If so, what would be the best way in which to do this?

12 Absolute poverty refers to the real amount of income or consumption that a person enjoys. Relative poverty refers to their income relative to the national or global average. (a) Can relative poverty ever be eliminated? (b) What would increase the amount of relative poverty?

13 Countries mainly interact with their near neighbours. There is a lot of evidence that physical distance reduces trade flows, and thus acts as a protective barrier. Do you expect New Zealand or Austria to have more scope for independent national decisions in economic policy? Explain.

14 Why are these statements wrong? (a) Globalization has now led to cross-border migration on an unprecedented scale. (b) Globalization has made the poor poorer.

15 China is investing heavily in Africa. What is its motive? Is this likely to be good or bad for Africa? For other regions of the world?

16 Drug companies say that most R&D leads to failure; only the prospect of large profits on the occasional success keeps them in the industry. Poor countries in sub-Saharan Africa say it is unfair that they have to pay high prices for drugs that combat AIDS. Can an economist offer any advice?

17 'GDP data says that companies in the services sector account for three-quarters of the economy, yet data from international trade still relates mainly to merchandise trade in good not services, and the *Fortune 500* is led by companies making goods not services.' Is this claim accurate? Is there any 'problem' to explain? If there is, how would you explain it?

18 **Essay question** Suppose China keeps growing at 10 per cent a year for another 30 years and gradually becomes a large share of the world economy. Is this likely to make solutions to global problems easier or harder?

19 **Essay question** Would internationally traded carbon emissions permits be an efficient way in which to mitigate global warming? Why is the market proving difficult to establish?

Online Learning Centre

To help you grasp the key concepts of this chapter check out the extra resources posted on the Online Learning Centre at www.mcgraw-hill.co.uk/textbooks/begg.

There are additional case studies, self-test questions, practice exam questions with answers and a graphing tool.

CHAPTER 16

European integration

Learning outcomes

By the end of this chapter, you should be able to:

- Identify the forces that led to closer integration of the EU single market
- Explain why many EU countries formed a monetary union
- Analyse the macroeconomics of the Eurozone
- Evaluate the causes of the current Eurozone crisis

The European economy of 2012 was very different from the Europe of 60 years earlier. Some developments were political, but many were economic. The economics you have learned in this book helps make sense of them. We now analyse the forces at work, and set out a checklist of what to watch for as the future unfolds.

This chapter is about two things. First, the Single European Act of 1986 committed members of the EC to a single market in goods, services, assets and people by 1992. Did it work? Second, the Eurozone (EZ) began in January 1999. Why did the EZ happen, how does it work and will it survive?

 ## The EU single market

The European Community was founded in 1957. It was a free trade area, with some EC-wide programmes financed by (small) fiscal contributions from Member States. Its largest programmes were the Common Agricultural Policy (CAP), a system of administered high prices for agricultural commodities that created excess supply and led to wine lakes and butter mountains; and the Structural Funds, providing subsidies for social infrastructure within poorer areas of the EC.

Over the next 55 years, the EC was enlarged. The original six – West Germany, France, Italy, the Netherlands, Belgium and Luxembourg – were joined by Denmark, Ireland and the UK in the 1970s, by Spain, Portugal and Greece in the 1980s, and by Austria, Finland and Sweden in the 1990s. The European

Community (EC) became the European Union (EU). In 2004, the EU admitted the Baltic republics (Estonia, Latvia and Lithuania), the countries of Central Europe (Hungary, Poland, the Czech Republic, Slovakia and Slovenia) and the Mediterranean islands of Malta and the Greek part of Cyprus. Bulgaria and Romania were admitted in 2007. Croatia is scheduled to join in 2013. Iceland, the Former Yugoslav Republic of Macedonia, Montenegro, Serbia and Turkey are exploring whether at some future stage they might join.

Interestingly, the two European countries with the highest per capita income – Switzerland and Norway – have been careful not to join. Redistributive taxation within the EU makes them likely contributors to taxation without corresponding benefits. They have been content to remain outside the EU but part of a wider European Economic Area that enjoys the free-trade benefits of EU membership.

EU enlargement was not initially accompanied by any change in its fundamental structure. Member Sates still set national policies. Closer integration, for example the harmonization of industrial standards or national tax rates, was usually thwarted for two reasons. First, since each country did things differently, it was hard to find a single set of regulations for all Member States. Second, it was political dynamite. No country wanted to adopt the policies of others.

The mid-1980s saw a breakthrough. Instead of trying to agree a single set of detailed rules, Member States agreed some broad outlines for harmonizing policy. Each country then decided how to implement them. And each country recognized the validity of the regulations imposed by other Member States. For example, a bank registered in the UK under UK law did not previously comply with standards laid down for banks in France, Germany or Italy. Banks in one country could not compete in other countries. National markets were segmented. Since there are economies of scale in banking, each small national market had only a few high-cost banks enjoying significant market power.

Instead, Member States agreed on some general principles governing the regulation of banks – minimum standards for capital adequacy (the amount of financial backing needed to undertake particular types of risky business), for external monitoring (to check that managers are doing their job properly), and so on. Then each government decided how to apply these general criteria and to license banks in its country. Finally, and crucially, a bank registered in Germany under German law was allowed to operate throughout the EU.

Countries adopting good regulatory structures found their firms getting a bigger share of EU trade. Countries with poor systems (which might have too much regulation but might have too little: business hates anarchy, legal ambiguity and possible fraud) lost business. Thus, *competition between forms of regulation* took place.

The new approach broke the log jam. The EC ratified the Single European Act, setting 1992 as the deadline to complete the internal EU market by harmonizing regulations. Among its main objectives were: (a) abolition of remaining controls on capital flows; (b) removal of all non-tariff barriers to trade in the EU (different trademarks, patent laws and safety standards); (c) ending the bias in public sector purchasing to favour domestic producers; (d) removal of frontier controls (delays); and (e) progress in harmonizing tax rates.

A **single market** is not segmented by national regulations, taxes or informal practices.

Benefits of the single market

Completion of the single market created an economic area larger than the US or Japan, even before the accession of countries from Central and Eastern Europe. The potential gains for Member States fall into three categories: more efficient resource allocation, more scale economies and more competition.

In Chapter 15 we explained how trade allows each country to specialize in the commodities that it makes *relatively* cheaply, thereby raising joint output. Although the EC was always a free-trade zone, with no internal tariffs, until 1992 a set of non-tariff barriers segmented national markets.

Non-tariff barriers are different national regulations or practices that prevent free movement of goods, services and factors across countries.

By removing non-tariff barriers, the single market aimed to allow countries to exploit their comparative advantage more fully.

A second inefficiency in small and segmented national markets is that firms cannot fully exploit economies of scale. As barriers came down, firms got larger and costs fell. Two-way trade in the same industry increased, not just in goods but also in services such as banking.

Third, the single market intensified competition in two ways. (a) Competition between forms of regulation led to lower levels of regulation. For many continental countries, the single market led to substantial deregulation from high initial levels. (b) A larger market enabled large firms to enjoy scale economies *without* the high market share and potential monopoly power that this would have meant in small, segmented economies.

Box 16-1

EU reduces roaming rip off (again)

People taking foreign holidays are often staggered by their mobile phone bill when they get home – if they haven't already been cut off during the holiday itself! 'The cost of using smartphones and tablet computers while travelling in Europe will drop in time for the summer holidays as part of the EU's annual cut to roaming charges,' reported *The Telegraph* in March 2012.

@ Adam Radosavljevic

Every year since 2007, the EU reduced the maximum cap on the high prices charged by network providers to mobile users travelling abroad within the EU. The cost of mobile data roaming, using the Internet, will fall to 59p for a one-megabyte download in July 2012 and to 34p by July 2014. The agreement will also let mobile, smartphone or tablet users sign on for a separate roaming contract by July 2014 if another network offers a better deal. From July 2012, EU residents visiting another EU country will pay a maximum of 24p for a phone call, 7p to receive one, and 8p to send a text message. These price ceilings will fall again in 2014. 'Consumers are fed up being ripped off by high roaming charges,' said Neelie Kroes, the EU's commissioner for digital services.

Why did such high charges exist in the first place? First, holidaymakers and business people on a foreign trip have a relatively inelastic demand for mobile services. Sometimes they simply have to know the football score or stock market movement. Providers can exploit this to charge higher prices to such desperate customers. Second, if French providers benefit from exploiting German tourists, and vice versa, there may be only limited market competition to eliminate high roaming fees.

This example illustrates how achieving the benefits of the single market sometimes requires regulation at the EU level. National competition regulators can consider whether mobile phone fees inside the country are appropriate, but roaming applies to the use in one country of a mobile phone whose contract is with an operator in another country. As more and more technologies become truly international, inevitably the effectiveness of national regulators will decline, and the need for pan-national regulators will increase.

To take a different example, European banking would probably have been more effectively regulated if there had only been one European regulator and no national regulators at all. Too many issues fell between the responsibilities of different national banking regulators.

Adapted from: B. Waterfield, 'EU to cut cost of data roaming in time for summer holidays', *The Telegraph*, 28 March 2012.

Quantifying the gains

In general, small countries gained more than large countries, but gains also reflected the trade pattern. The largest gains came as the most protected activities were opened up. Not only was the single market good for the EU, it turned out to boost trade with the outside world. Fears of fortress Europe were unfounded.

In January 2007, the DTI, together with HM Treasury, issued a report, *The Single Market: A vision for the 21st century*, outlining the challenges that the single market faces – globalization, climate change, demographic change – and the principles needed to ensure that the single market continues to deliver for Europe's consumers and businesses.

The free movement of goods, persons, services and capital is a fundamental principle of the European Union. It is these four freedoms, as set out in the EC Treaty, which form the basis of the single market. The government believes that the single European market benefits the economy of each Member State, and that the removal of trade barriers leads to a reduction in business costs as well as increasing competition and stimulating efficiency, benefiting consumers and encouraging the creation of jobs and wealth.

The single market is a *wider market* for UK goods, comprising nearly 380 million consumers and making up almost 40 per cent of world trade. Such a huge market gives consumers greater choice.

The greater *competition* and *liberalization* the single market has helped bring about have led to *lower prices*. Take air fares, for example: cheap airlines such as easyJet would not have been possible without the single market. Airlines can now fly where they want, without national restrictions. BA has become the second-largest domestic airline in France.

The single market provides for better *consumer protection*; for example, the Toy Directive means that all toys sold in the EU must be safe for children. Another example is the Motor Insurance Directives that makes it easier for those involved in motor accidents in other Member States to make an insurance claim when returning to their state of residence.

The single market principle of mutual recognition of standards means British manufacturers can sell their products all over Europe without expensive re-testing in every country. For business, there has been a significant reduction in export bureaucracy. The single market is in effect a domestic market for European business.

UK citizens have the *right to work*, *study* or *retire* in all the other Member States – there are around three-quarters of a million Britons living in other EU countries. Conversely, of course, EU workers from Poland to the Balkans have been allowed to live and work as plumbers in the UK. Generally, this has been good for UK households, if it has meant cheaper and better plumbing, but bad for those UK plumbers who have been outcompeted by foreign workers.

Nor should we assume that all effects were automatically beneficial. The single market in banking enhanced competition but also created a lot of cross-border business that has proved messy to unscramble after the financial crisis. When a bank gets into trouble, whose taxpayers should bail it out? What is the answer for a bank headquartered in Belgium but doing lots of business in the Netherlands and France?

In practice, in the absence of more explicit international co-operation the answer has been that taxpayers in the country in which the bank is headquartered and registered have largely picked up the cost of any bank rescue. Nor should an economist object to this outcome. If the Single Market works by allowing firms registered in one EU Member State to trade in other Member States, then holding the registering country ultimately responsible for failure provides appropriate incentives to conduct registration and supervision properly in the first place.

The real problem is that effective supervision requires detailed local knowledge of how the bank is doing. Once banks trade in multiple countries, the entire business of supervision becomes harder, whoever is conducting the task.

Box 16-2

Recent estimates of the gains from the Single Market

This box, summarizing the conventional wisdom in 2010, is adapted from the UK National Archives displayed on the website of the UK Department of Business Innovation and Skills.

The Single Market provided sizeable benefits for the EU economy as a whole. During the first 15 years, from 1992 to 2006, the Single Market:

- Caused EU GDP by 2006 to be 2.2 per cent higher than it would have been without the Single Market – an average increase in benefits to consumers of €518 per person.

- Created an additional 2.75 million jobs across Europe.

Increased levels of competition have benefited both businesses and consumers alike; increased levels of innovation led to higher productivity, lower costs and prices, and a greater choice for consumers with a wider diversity of higher quality products now available.

The Single Market – population almost 500 million – allowed larger businesses to benefit from economies of scale. Easier cross-border trade within the EU means that small- and medium-sized enterprises now have access to new export markets, which previously were not an option because of the cost and hassle that was involved with border bureaucracy.

It became easier to start or buy a business – the average cost for setting up a new company in the former EU-15 fell from €813 in 2002 to €554 in 2007, and the time needed to cope with the administrative procedures to register a company fell from 24 days in 2002 to 12 days in 2007.

The Community Trade Mark and the Community Design enabled UK companies to protect their trade marks and designs throughout the EU by making a single application for EU-wide registration. This cuts down bureaucracy – avoiding the need for trade marks or designs to be examined in 25 different jurisdictions each with its own rules.

The free movement of goods and services means that consumers now have a much wider choice of high quality products to choose from. Three out of four European citizens think that the possibility to market products from other Member States under the same conditions as domestic products has had a positive impact, while 73 per cent consider that the Single Market has contributed positively to the range of products and services on offer. The opening up of national markets has resulted in lower prices for goods and services in many cases. Telephone prices charged by the former monopolies for national and international calls fell by more than 40 per cent on average between 2000 and 2006.

Consumers now enjoy far greater protection thanks to the Single Market. Over half of citizens consider that internal market rules have increased consumer protection within the EU. Single Market laws require that degradable products, such as food and medicines, are labelled with 'best before' dates, and carry a list of ingredients, colourings and additives. EU enforcement agencies have acted against rogue traders operating across borders.

There are many examples of situations in which the European Commission has worked to eliminate anti-competitive practices, an area in which individual countries such as the UK could not have acted effectively alone. For example, in February 2008 the European Commission fined Microsoft €899 million for failing to comply with sanctions imposed on it for anti-competitive behaviour. An investigation in 2004 had concluded that Microsoft was guilty of freezing out its rivals in products like media players while at the same time linking its Internet browser to its Windows operating system.

The Single Market means that individuals have a right to live, work or study in another EU country. Fifteen million EU citizens have moved to other EU countries to work or to enjoy their retirement, benefiting from the transferability of social benefit, while 1.5 million young people have completed part of their studies in another Member State with the help of the Erasmus programme. The possibility to study abroad is considered positive by 84 per cent of EU citizens. Employees' rights have been greatly strengthened because of EU regulations.

This provides a useful checklist of possible benefits of market enlargement, to which one should add that greater competition reduces the need for national governments to get involved in regulating market power.

The catalogue of consequences of the Single Market would have been more compelling if it had contained an equally assiduous examination of the possible detrimental effects of enlarging the market. Next time a comprehensive EU study is conducted, it will have to consider more carefully the causes of the financial crash and the extent to which EU regulation and supervision of the financial sector was helped or hindered by the Single Market.

Source: Department for Business Innovation and Skills, 'The Benefits and Achievements of EU Single Market', http://webarchive.nationalarchives.gov.uk/+/bis.gov.uk/policies/europe/benefits-of-eu-membership

Creating the Eurozone

The single market was not easily reconciled with volatile floating exchange rates that could lead to rapid changes in competitiveness among countries that traded a lot with one another. For this reason, the EU countries had endeavoured to peg exchange rates most of the time and devalue or revalue these central parities from time to time. This arrangement was called the Exchange Rate Mechanism (ERM).

Before the Single Market, speculation against bilateral exchange rates of Member States was impeded by controls prohibiting short-term capital flows. These controls had to be abandoned if a Single Market was to be created. Once the speculators were allowed in, it was only a matter of time before they attacked the pegged exchange rates of the ERM. One solution was to go forward rapidly to completely fixed exchange rates.

A **monetary union** has permanently fixed exchange rates within the union, an integrated financial market, and a single central bank setting the single interest rate for the union.

A monetary union usually has, but need not have, a single currency. English and Scottish currencies circulate side by side in Edinburgh. What matters is that the exchange rate is certain, forever, and that a single authority (the Bank of England) sets the single interest rate for both currencies.

The Treaty of Maastricht in 1991 set out the path to monetary union. Any remaining capital controls were abolished, and the UK was encouraged to join the ERM (it joined in 1990). By 1994, realignments of the fixed exchange rates became even harder to obtain, and excessive budget deficits were to be discouraged but not outlawed.

Stage 3, in which exchange rates were irreversibly fixed and the single monetary policy began, was to start in 1997 if a majority of potential entrants fulfilled the 'Maastricht criteria' (in the event they did not). Otherwise, EMU was to begin in January 1999 with whatever number of countries then met the criteria. Monetary policy in EMU was to be set by an independent central bank, mandated to achieve price stability as its principal goal.

The **Maastricht criteria** for joining the EMU said that a country must already have achieved low inflation and sound fiscal policy.

The fiscal criteria said budget deficits must not be excessive, interpreted to mean that budget deficits should be less than 3 per cent of GDP; and that the debt/GDP ratio should not be over 60 per cent. Tight fiscal policy would mean there was little pressure on the central bank to print money to bail out fiscal authorities.

Sterling and UK membership

The UK was reluctant to join both the ERM and then the Eurozone (EZ). Whereas the core countries of Europe are now very integrated with one another, offshore UK is less integrated with the rest of Europe. A common policy is less suitable. Table 16-1 shows the composition of UK trade and how it has changed since the UK joined the EU. The trend is clear. The UK is becoming more integrated with continental Europe all the time, even if from a lower baseline than some other European countries. Eventually, it may be in the UK's interest to join the EZ.

Black Wednesday (16 September 1992) made it hard for UK politicians to enthuse about the EZ. While Chancellor of the Exchequer, John Major took the UK into the ERM in 1990 to combat rising inflation at the end of the Lawson boom. Unfortunately, this coincided with German reunification. Big subsidies to East Germany caused the German economy to overheat. The Bundesbank raised interest rates to cool

Table 16-1   UK trade patterns (%), 1970–2011

	EU	North America	Rest of world
1970	34	17	49
2011	56	14	30

Sources: UN, *International Trade Statistics*; www.statistics.gov.uk

down the German economy. Interest rates high enough to do this job were far too high for Germany's partners in the ERM. This provoked the crisis of 1992–93. The UK and Italy left the ERM, slashed interest rates and depreciated their currencies. Other countries struggled on inside the ERM until the EZ was launched in 1999.

Remaining outside the EZ gives the UK both the freedom to set its own interest rate and to print its own money. Until the financial crisis, the principal benefit appeared to be that, relative to the single interest rate prevailing in the EZ, UK interest rates could be slightly more fine-tuned to the needs of the UK economy. Leaving aside the unique episode of German reunification, this benefit can perhaps be overstated. UK and EZ interest rates have rarely been more than 1 percentage point apart.

Rather the benefit arises from the knowledge that, in extremis, the UK *could* take more drastic interest rate action if necessary. This argument applies even more strongly to the ability to print money. The Bank of England has an inflation target very similar to that of the European Central Bank. But, if the UK government was having trouble meeting its budget deficit, *in extremis* it could print money to cover the budget deficit. For countries such as Greece and Spain, who no longer have this power, the only alternative is outright default on their debts. Since 2008, the financial markets appear to have rewarded the UK (by not demanding a high interest rate in exchange for continued lending) both because (a) the UK government has looked tough on austerity and deficit reduction and (b) the danger of outright default was much lower than for individual EZ members.

The economics of the EZ

In 1999, Professor Robert Mundell won the Nobel Prize for Economics in part for his pioneering work on optimal currency areas.

> An **optimal currency area** is a group of countries better off with a common currency than keeping separate national currencies.

Mundell, and the economists who came after him, identified three attributes that might make countries suitable for a currency area. First, countries that trade a lot with each other may have little ability to affect their equilibrium real exchange rate against their partners in the long run; but they may face temptations to devalue to gain a temporary advantage. A fixed exchange rate rules out such behaviour and allows gains from trade to be enjoyed.

Second, the more similar the economic and industrial structure of potential partners, the more likely it is they face common shocks, which can be dealt with by a common monetary policy. It is country-specific shocks that pose difficulties for a single monetary policy.

Third, the more flexible are the labour markets within the currency area, the more easily any necessary changes in competitiveness and real exchange rates can be accomplished by (different) changes in the price level in different member countries.

Conversely, countries gain most by keeping their monetary sovereignty when they are not that integrated with potential partners, have a different structure, and hence are likely to face different shocks, and cannot rely on domestic wage and price flexibility as a substitute for exchange rate changes.

To these purely economic arguments, we should add an important political argument. Currency areas are more likely to work when countries within the area are prepared to make at least some fiscal transfers to partner countries. In practice, this cultural and political identity may be at least as important as any narrow economic criteria for success.

Case study 16-1 Competitiveness within the EZ

Irish unions agree to link pay rises to efficiency, reported John Murray Brown in the *Financial Times* (30 March 2010), following a deal between the government and public sector trade unions. In exchange for the avoidance of compulsory redundancies, unions agreed to flexible work practices and to pay cuts as well.

The objective of the policy was two-fold. The direct effect was to tighten fiscal policy by shrinking public spending. During 2008–10, Irish fiscal policy was tightened by 6 per cent of GDP. Ireland aimed to have reduced its budget deficit from 12 per cent in 2008 back to the Stability Pact target of 3 per cent of GDP by 2014.

The second effect of the policy was to reduce the price level in Ireland. If nominal wages were reduced, and prices then fell, Ireland's competitiveness would increase even within the Eurozone. Domestic wage and price reduction was a substitute for nominal exchange rate depreciation.

In the December 2009 budget, public sector workers took *pay cuts* from 5 per cent for people earning below €30 000 to 10 per cent for those on higher incomes. This was on top of a pension levy in February 2009 that reduced take-home pay by 5 per cent.

Suppose Irish prices and wages each fall by 10 per cent. How much poorer have Irish people become? The answer depends on the openness of the Irish economy. If imports were only 10 per cent of the size of GDP, real wages would be reduced only a little since most goods are produced domestically and their prices have fallen by the same percentage as nominal wages. Conversely, if imports are 90 per cent of the size of GDP, then the nominal wage cut is matched by a price cut on only the 10 per cent of goods produced and consumed in Ireland, and Irish residents are worse off by around 9 per cent in real terms. For exactly the same reason, Irish competitiveness has increased substantially.

Since we know Ireland is a small open economy, the answer in practice is closer to the latter example than the former. Annual consumer price deflation bottomed out in Ireland at −6.4 per cent in October 2009, but was still −4 per cent as late as January 2010, reaching only 1 per cent for 2010 as a whole. Because Ireland had less inflation than the EZ average, it was able to gain competitiveness while remaining inside the EZ.

This chart is really important. It compares relative unit labour costs, converted to the same currency (any currency will do). When this index rises, a country becomes less competitive.

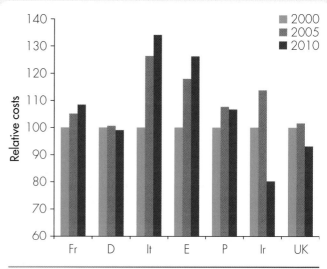

Relative unit labour costs, 2000–2010

Source: OECD

German competitiveness has remained constant throughout the decade 2000–10. France has lost only a little competitiveness. Ireland, Spain and Portugal (and Greece if we showed it) have lost a huge amount of competitiveness. When they joined the EZ, and shared a currency with Germany, they wanted German wage levels and German beer prices even though they did not have German productivity levels – big mistake.

The UK, which retained the ability to float its exchange rate, has essentially maintained constant competitiveness too. The 20 per cent depreciation of sterling after the financial crash has partly been unwound and been somewhat offset by higher import prices and slightly higher wages; even so, the UK was nearly 10 per cent more competitive in 2010 than it had been in 2005. This in itself was useful for UK economic growth. Unfortunately, since over half of UK exports are to the EU, recession in the EZ offset the benefit that greater UK competitiveness would otherwise have achieved for export growth.

The case that is really interesting, however, is Ireland. Having suffered a 13 per cent deterioration in its competitiveness during 2000–05, Irish self-discipline and wage restraint then achieved a massive 30 per cent improvement in competitiveness during 2005–10, and by more than was managed by the UK with its floating exchange rate.

Ireland is the textbook example of how a monetary union is supposed to work. The EZ is in trouble not because its economic design is irretrievably flawed but because the political and labour market institutions of Greece, Spain, Portugal and possibly Italy were not up to the task. When the going got tough, they flunked the test. Too reliant on the state sector, and with powerful trade unions but electorates unprepared to take tough medicine, they failed to address their competitiveness problems or their debt problems. The chart above shows that, even if their debt was written off entirely, they would still be in trouble because they have become so uncompetitive.

This diagnosis explains one problem but raises another. If this is the case, why doesn't the external value of the euro depreciate, making the entire EZ more competitive? To understand the answer, it is necessary to appreciate asymmetries within the EZ. Although the periphery is struggling, the inner core is doing rather well. In particular, Germany is enjoying an export-led boom. With constant competitiveness, it has been able to take advantage of rapid growth in emerging markets – not only the BRICs but also South Korea and the other Asian Tigers – and a partial recovery in the US.

The external value of the euro reflects the trade performance of the EZ as a whole. With German export surpluses offsetting the external deficits of peripheral EZ countries, the financial markets perceived no need to reduce the external value of the euro, at least until the Greek election stalemate of 2012 finally sparked a panic.

This example is merely a special case of a general proposition. When Member States are in different situations and need to converge, they can either meet in the middle or one group of economies can do all the adjustment. Germany refuses to meet in the middle. It has low inflation, low debt and a strong external position. To date it has been unwilling to jeopardize any of these. It is trying to avoid either a depreciation of the euro or a fiscal expansion in Germany, the two measures that would most quickly take the pressure off suffering EZ members. Germany is trying to insist that the deficit countries take all the pain, and adjust all the way to German behaviour. It remains to be seen whether this will happen.

Is Europe an optimal currency area?

Those who have studied the structure of national economies, and the correlation of shocks across countries, generally reach the following conclusions. First, Europe is quite, but not very, integrated. Second, there is a clear inner core of countries – the usual suspects – more closely integrated than the rest. Those on the periphery – Ireland, Greece, Spain, Portugal and maybe Italy – have economies that are slightly more semi-detached. In many cases they also have relatively weak political systems that find it difficult to take tough and unpopular economic measures.

The act of joining the EMU is likely to change the degree of integration, possibly quite substantially. A common currency, by eliminating a source of segmentation into national markets, will increase integration. Moreover, there is evidence that countries that trade a lot have more correlated business cycles. And countries which belong to currency unions tend historically to trade much more with each other than can be explained simply by the fact that their exchange rates are fixed.

These bits of evidence imply that it may be possible to start a currency union before the microeconomic preconditions are fully in place. The act of starting speeds up the process.

The Stability Pact

The Stability Pact, ratified by the Treaty of Amsterdam in 1997, confirmed that the Maastricht fiscal criteria would not merely be EZ entry conditions but would continue to apply after countries joined the EZ. Some members had debt/GDP ratios of close to 100 per cent. Reducing these towards 60 per cent would have taken decades even if the financial crisis had not then erupted. In practice the initial focus was on the other limit, the 3 per cent ceiling for budget deficits.

In principle, countries exceeding the limit may have to pay fines unless their economy is in evident recession. Thus countries have to wait for output to fall before they are allowed to expand fiscal policy by having deficits above the ceiling of 3 per cent of GDP.

The pact does not preclude countries from using fiscal policies more vigorously. But to do so, they need to aim for something more like budget balance in normal times. Then they still have room to increase deficits in times of trouble without exceeding the 3 per cent ceiling.

You never know how binding a limit is until it is reached. In practice, Germany was the first major country to breach the 3 per cent limit in 2003, and did so with impunity. Even if it had been a good idea to set fiscal guidelines, countries subsequently got the idea that these fiscal rules were not that binding. This led to a general climate in which, in the years running up to the fiscal crisis, countries had relatively lax fiscal policies, leaving them poorly prepared for the crisis when it hit them.

Maths 16-1

Interest parity and competitiveness

Let r denote the domestic interest rate, r^* the foreign interest rate, s the nominal exchange rate (international value of the domestic currency) and ds/dt the instantaneous rate of change of the exchange rate. $(1/s)ds/dt$ is then the instantaneous percentage capital gain that a foreign investor makes by holding the domestic currency for an instant before repatriating the money, and, under perfect certainty, the interest parity condition implies

$$r^* + (1/s)ds/dt = r \tag{1}$$

The real exchange rate v is given by

$$v = sp/p^* \tag{2}$$

where p is the domestic price level and p^* the foreign price level. The instantaneous change in the real exchange rate obeys

$$(1/v)dv/dt = (1/s)ds/dt + (1/p)dp/dt - (1/p^*)dp^*/dt = (1/s) = ds/dt + (\pi - \pi^*) \tag{3}$$

where π denotes inflation, the rate of change of p.

Real exchange rate appreciation reflects nominal exchange rate appreciation, domestic inflation or foreign deflation. Combining equations (1) and (3)

$$r^* - \pi^* = r - \pi + (1/s)ds/dt + \pi - \pi^*, \text{ so that}$$

$$[r^* - \pi^*] = [r - \pi] + (1/v)dv/dt \tag{4}$$

Thus, the interest parity condition expressed in nominal terms in equation (1) – nominal interest differentials must be offset by appropriate capital gains or losses in nominal exchange rates to preserve the equality of return in different currencies under perfect international capital mobility – implies a similar statement in terms of real interest rate differentials being offset by capital gains or losses on the real exchange rate.

Although derived for an instantaneous decision, we can always view a longer horizon as a series of instant decisions. Hence, interest parity conditions also hold over longer horizons, provided the duration of the interest rates matches the period over which exchange rate changes are assessed.

Equation (4) can also be used to compare the evolution of competitiveness of one EZ partner against another. If $r = r^*$, then differential inflation $\pi - \pi^*$ is the principal source of changes in the relative competitiveness of different EZ countries.

The European Central Bank

The single monetary policy is now set in Frankfurt by the European Central Bank (ECB). National central banks have not been abolished, but the board of the ECB sets the interest rate on the euro.

The ECB mandate says its first duty is to ensure price stability, but it can take other aims into account provided price stability is not in doubt. In press conferences, the ECB emphasizes that its interest rate decisions largely reflect the pursuit of price stability. Neither the financial markets nor academic economists are entirely convinced. ECB behaviour looks as if it pays some attention to output gaps as well as inflation.

Controversially, the ECB has adopted not one but two intermediate targets, the so-called 'twin pillars' of its monetary strategy. The first pillar is a monetary target, the growth rate of the M3 measure of nominal money. The second pillar is expected inflation. The ECB insists that it takes both pillars into account in setting interest rates in the euro area.

Figure 16-1 shows the interest rate decisions of the ECB, the evolution of inflation (in the harmonized index of consumer prices, HICP) and the rate of nominal money growth. It is easy to see how the rise and fall of actual and expected inflation led to the rise and fall of interest rates in the Eurozone. It is very hard to detect any role for nominal money growth. The reason is straightforward. Money demand fluctuates, and money supply growth is not a reliable guide to future inflation.

For example, after the terrorist attacks of 11 September 2001, people sold stocks and shares and put money into bank accounts. These accounts were part of the M3 measure of money. The sharp rise in the money stock reflected a rise in money demand. Money supply could safely be allowed to increase since

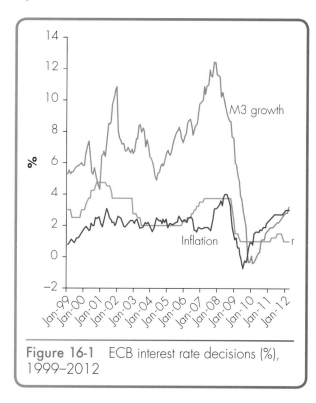

Figure 16-1 ECB interest rate decisions (%), 1999–2012

people wanted to hold the extra money not spend it. In fact, the fall in aggregate demand for goods after 11 September meant that all central banks sensibly cut interest rates to boost aggregate demand. Figure 16-1 confirms that interest rates fell *despite* the rise in the nominal money stock.

Conversely, after the financial crash banks stopped lending, so that overdrafts and corresponding deposits collapsed. In Case study 12-2 we showed how the Bank of England successfully used quantitative easing to offset the collapse of the bank deposit multiplier and sustain the growth of the money supply to support the economy at a time of weakness. Figure 16-1 shows that the European Central Bank did not follow suit. Growth of broad money, as measured by M3, fell rapidly in 2009, adding to the credit crunch.

Swings in both money demand and the confidence of the banking system make monetary aggregates difficult to interpret as a leading indicator for monetary policy. That is why most central banks abandoned monetary targeting in favour of flexible inflation targets. The ECB continued to insist that monetary targets have an important role because it wanted to emphasize continuity with the respected German Bundesbank, which had used monetary targets. But it is paying a price for continuing the tradition.

Fiscal federalism?

One reason for the survival of the monetary union that we call the US is its federal fiscal structure. When a particular state has a slump, it pays less income tax revenue to Washington, and gets more social security money from Washington, without any decisions having to be taken. Automatic stabilizers are at work, courtesy of federal tax rates and federal rates of social security payments. Conversely, a booming state pays more tax revenue to Washington, and gets less social security money back.

> A **federal fiscal system** has a central government setting taxes and expenditure rules that apply in its constituent states or countries.

When state income rises $1, the state pays an extra 30 cents in income tax and gets 10 cents less in social security. Conversely, when state income falls $1, the state pays 30 cents less in federal taxes and gets an extra 10 cents in social security. Originally, economists thought that this meant each state was effectively insured up to about 40 cents in the dollar. The Eurozone has no federal fiscal structure on anything like this scale. Before the crash, the pessimists concluded that the EZ would come under pressure from country-specific shocks; and since the crash it has become commonplace to say that the EZ can survive only if it makes rapid progress towards fiscal union.

The original US calculations are relevant to a world in which state incomes are uncorrelated with each other. Then the joint club provides helpful insurance to all members. When one is doing well, another is doing badly. But in practice, there is usually a positive correlation. Hence, when one state slumps and gets help from Washington, many other states are slumping and also getting help. But this increases US government debt and means *every* state has to pay higher future taxes.

But an individual state could have done that on its own, without membership of the federal 'mutual insurance' club. It could have borrowed in the slump to boost its own fiscal spending, and paid it back later when times were better. Making allowance for this, US states are probably insured by nearer to 10 cents in the dollar than 40 cents.

Hence, fiscal union, if it is to work, must act not as a mutual insurance club but as a permanent transfer mechanism, in which the rich are always paying for the poor. For this to be a robust solution, the rich must identify sufficiently with the poor that they are happy to keep paying for them. Nation-states provide many examples of the tensions that then arise. In Italy, the Northern League protest about rich Milan and Turin paying year after year for the depressed South of Italy. In Spain it is prosperous Barcelona and Madrid that have to keep paying for impoverished Andalusia in the South. In the UK, people keep doing the sums as to whether Scotland gains or loses by being part of the United Kingdom.

Hence it cannot be taken for granted that fiscal union alone will solve the problems of monetary union. Recall that rich Norway and Switzerland have not even joined the EU because they could foresee perfectly well the one-way fiscal traffic that would then ensue.

Macroeconomic policy in an EZ member

Figure 16-2 shows what life is like for an EZ member. Interest rates are set by the ECB in Frankfurt. From an individual country's viewpoint, it is as if the LM curve is horizontal at r_0, and the smaller the country, the less influence it has over at what level the EZ has set this interest rate. Suppose the initial level of the IS curve allows equilibrium at A. Aggregate demand equals potential output.

Now the country faces a shock that shifts the IS curve down to IS_1. With full monetary sovereignty, the country might have cut its interest rate to restore full employment output at C. This might still happen in the EZ if the country is highly correlated with other EZ countries. The ECB will react to what is happening throughout Euroland and cut interest rates for everybody.

However, if no other countries face the IS curve shock and the country is too small to influence Eurozone data to which the ECB reacts, interest rates will remain at r_0.

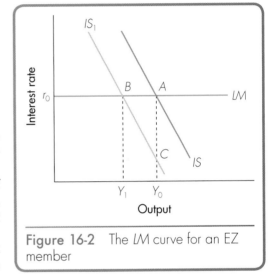

Figure 16-2 The LM curve for an EZ member

The country now faces two choices. Provided it does not infringe the Stability Pact, it can use fiscal policy to shift IS_1 to the right, or it can wait for its labour market to do the same thing.

How does this work? At B, the country is facing a slump. This gradually reduces inflation. At the fixed nominal exchange rate against its partners, this makes the country more competitive. Higher exports and lower imports shift the IS_1 curve to the right. If wage and price flexibility are high enough, there may be no need for fiscal policy. However, many European labour markets are quite sluggish. Sensible use of fiscal policy may speed up the process, provided there is any room for fiscal manoeuvre in the first place.

For both reasons, the limits on fiscal policy and the sluggishness of wage and price adjustment, the EZ framework raises the burden on monetary policy to react to shocks even before they have fed fully through into output and inflation.

Box 16-3

The EZ debt crisis

When the financial crisis hit, the UK was the country in Europe most exposed because London was Europe's financial capital and the UK economy relied disproportionately on financial services. Life in the UK was far from easy. Its banks got into trouble and several needed help from the government. As elsewhere, this largely transferred private bank debt to government debt. At the time, there was probably little alternative. Governments have deeper pockets and more borrowing opportunities than private companies. They have broader shoulders with which to bear the pain.

What happened next depended on several things. First, were measures taken to sort out the solvency of banks or, relieved of their worst debts, did they keep staggering along only just afloat? This matters, both for confidence in the banking system and for whether future governments may need to bail out the banks all over again. Broadly speaking, the US was more aggressive than Europe in sorting out its banks. In 2012 the world's most successful investor over the last 40 years, Warren Buffet, pronounced US banks healthy whereas European banks had yet to be remedied.

> *Billionaire Warren Buffett says American banks are in much better financial shape than European counterparts because of measures taken during the financial crisis. The leader of the conglomerate Berkshire Hathaway Inc. said during a CNBC interview on Monday that the United States already injected more capital into its banks and forced them to clean up their balance sheets. Buffett says the United States did a better job imposing austerity measures and improving its fiscal situation after the financial crisis of 2008.*
>
> The Associated Press, 2012

Second, to what extent were governments able to remedy the solvency problem with which they had been afflicted when rescuing the banks? Greece apart, it is important to remember that government fiscal troubles are largely the consequence of their doing the right thing at the height of this financial storm. Letting just one bank – Lehman Brothers – go bankrupt in 2008 had caused havoc. If governments had not intervened to rescue banks in general, think how much worse things would have been. Limping recovery and double-dip recessions represent success not failure; it could have been so much worse.

Third, can economies now grow their way out of trouble without risking a new fiscal crisis? The economics you have learned in earlier chapters suggests that fiscal contraction is likely to be bad for output, and therefore growth, at least in the short run. The following chart, based on calculations by Martin Wolf, chief economics correspondent of the *Financial Times*, confirms that on average the countries undertaking the largest fiscal contraction within the EZ have experienced the slowest growth during 2008–12. Thus, austerity-based attempts to shrink the numerator of the debt/GDP ratio are at least partly offset by induced reductions in the denominator. This does not always make such policies inappropriate, especially in heavily indebted countries, but it does mean that austerity always generates its own headwinds.

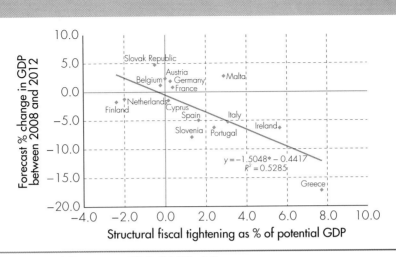

Fiscal tightening and Eurozone GDP, 2008–12

Source: Financial Times, 27 April 2012 (based on OECD data)

The chart below shows the history of the UK debt/GDP ratio, which rose to around 250 per cent after both the Napoleonic War and the Second World War. In both cases, the UK economy boomed thereafter and grew its way out of the problem, more by increasing the numerator of the debt/GDP ratio than by shrinking the numerator.

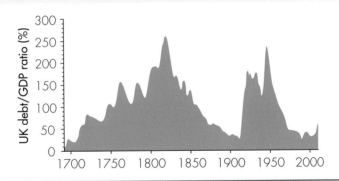

Public net debt, UK from FY 1692 to FY 2011

Source: ukpublicspending.co.uk

The problem of course is how to stimulate growth. One possibility is to stimulate supply by deregulating labour markets, abandoning planning laws and reducing red tape. Stimulating supply is important if an economy is already at full capacity, but much less important if there is already considerable spare capacity.

To the extent that spare capacity exists, it is demand stimulation that it is imperative. In the UK and the US, monetary policy has interest rates jammed pretty much as low as they will go. The European Central Bank still has room to reduce interest rates further, but has refrained from doing so partly because inflation, as elsewhere, is stubbornly high because of imported inflation via commodity prices that are being bid up by prosperity in the BRICs and elsewhere.

A second possibility is to ease fiscal policy precisely to stimulate growth but at the cost of increasing the debt and deficit. This may be a good idea to 'kick start' an economy that has lost confidence, but a sustained period of fiscal laxity adds to the numerator of the debt/GDP ratio as well as adding to its denominator by boosting demand and mopping up spare capacity.

External currency depreciation offers a different possible source of extra demand. But all countries cannot simultaneously depreciate. Case study 16-1 explained why Germany, the EZ paymaster, has been reluctant to encourage a depreciation of the euro. The case study also points to a different solution – reducing domestic wages and prices – and explains why Ireland succeeded but Southern Europe failed to do so.

A final possibility is to default on the debt, thereby escaping the burden of debt interest, and using this leeway to boost government spending to stimulate growth. This gives rise to several issues.

These charts allow us to explore which countries got into trouble and why.

The top chart shows bond yields on 8 May 2012, just after the Greek elections rejected the parties pursuing austerity. Greek interest rates had risen to 23 per cent as the market prepared for default. Portuguese interest rates were over 10 per cent, and those in Spain and Italy around 6 per cent. All these rates spell danger since high interest payments mean that the debt escalates quickly.

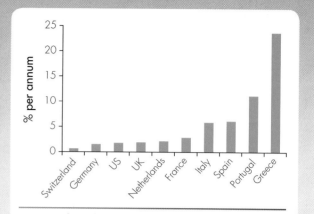

10-year bond yield, May 2012

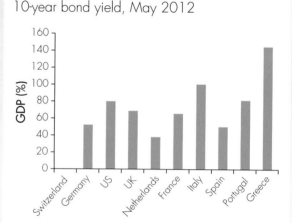

Net debt, 2011

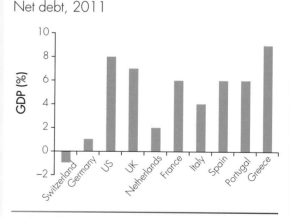

Budget deficit, 2011

What were markets worried about? The middle chart shows the extent of government net debt. Greek debt is 145 per cent of GDP, so Greece was paying huge interest rates on a high debt. But

Spanish debt was only 50 per cent of GDP, well below the UK or US. Why were markets so worried about Spain? The bottom chart shows budget deficit data. Now Spain and Portugal appear more worrying, though Italy appears less so.

What these charts still miss is government liabilities that have not yet shown up. In particular, markets worried about housing bubbles, particularly in Spain, where the subsequent collapse of house prices was going to create a lot of bad debts for the banks, that in turn would require bailouts from their governments. Together with the other charts, this helps explain differences in bond yields and market confidence.

The final factor of course is the determination of government to take future actions not yet captured in the data. The Greek election spooked markets and led to sharp increases in bond yields precisely because it signalled a reduction in the probability that Greek governments would attempt to honour their debts.

Defaulting on debt is heavily penalized by financial markets, which usually refuse to lend any money for years to come. It does not of itself imply exit from the EZ – New York was on the verge of default in 1975 when bailed out by President Ford – and eight US states actually defaulted in 1841. In neither case did the city or state have to leave the dollarzone.

The benefit to default is larger (a) the larger the debt, (b) the larger the interest rate now being charged by the market, (c) the more off-balance-sheet liabilities (such as future bank bailouts) have still to be recognized, and (d) the larger the current recession and the more urgent the need for output stimulus.

In the current financial crisis, people sometimes cite the example of Argentina, which faced a similar crisis. In 2002, it defaulted on its debt, allowed its exchange rate to plummet, thereby slashing living standards but enhancing competitiveness, and within a year was on the road to recovery, as shown by the following chart.

Although a correct description of what happened, the comparison is somewhat misleading. Whereas, having devalued, Argentina was then able to export into a booming world economy, today Western Europe and Japan are struggling, the US is growing but only slowly, and there are signs that rapid growth in China and India is beginning to slow. We cannot guarantee that the same medicine will have the same effect, though it cannot be denied that an improvement in competitiveness is a key part of the solution for the peripheral EZ countries in trouble.

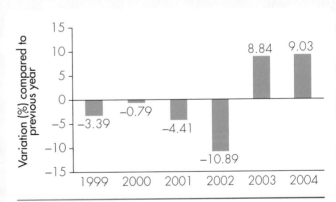

Argentine GNP, 1999–2004

Source: http://en.wikipedia.org/wiki/File:Evolution_of_the_Argentine_GNP,_1999-2004.png

It remains the case that growing out of the problem is more attractive than endeavouring to solve it through austerity alone.

Recap

- The Single European Act committed EU governments to a single market by 1992. The principles were common, broad outlines for regulation; national implementation; and mutual recognition of firms licensed by other Member States.

- For many countries, this meant substantial deregulation. Together with enlarged market size, this increased competition.

- The main winners were the small Southern countries of the EU, which had relatively cheap labour and scope for scale economies. However, even the large, rich EU countries benefited.

- A monetary union means permanently fixed exchange rates, free capital movements and a single interest rate.

- In abolishing capital controls before 1992, the ERM had already harmonized monetary policy, under German leadership. The UK became an ERM member in 1990, but left in 1992.

- The Maastricht criteria say that EZ entrants, including future ones, must have shown low inflation, low interest rates and stable nominal exchange rates before entry; and must have budget deficits and government debt under control.

- EZ members must continue to obey the Stability Pact, which fines countries for excessive budget deficits, except if they are in recession.

- In the EZ, a country's competitiveness can change through the slow process of domestic wage and price adjustment. Without a federal fiscal system, individual Member States may want to keep control of fiscal policy to deal with crises.

Review questions

To check your answers to these questions, go to pages 396–7.

1 Name three EU countries that you think have a comparative advantage in goods that use human capital intensively. Name three countries for which this is not the case.

2 Two countries belong to a monetary union, and face a single interest rate on bank deposits. However, one government has large debts and has trouble raising taxes or cutting spending. (a) Will government bonds in the two countries pay the same interest rate? (b) Will there be large capital flows between the countries? (c) Is this a monetary union? If not, why not?

EASY

3 The Stability Pact forces EZ members to maintain low budget deficits. What is the rationale for this policy? Why is it needed if the European Central Bank is independent and committed to low inflation?

4 Which of these characteristics may make countries more likely to benefit from a monetary union? (a) They are small open economies. (b) They trade a lot with their potential partners. (c) They have a different industrial structure from their potential partners. (d) They have inflexible labour markets.

5 Explain the problems in regulating banks that operate in many countries simultaneously. Should France take a similar view of a Belgian bank and an American bank operating in France?

6 How has Ireland, an EZ member, managed since 2005 to gain more competitiveness than the UK, despite the fact that Britain had a floating exchange rate which depreciated by over 20 per cent during the period?

7 'Workers have power in the labour market only because their own firms have power in the goods market. In a perfectly competitive firm, attempts to raise wages just drive the firm out of business.' Is this statement correct? If 1992 increased competition in product markets, what was the effect on EU labour markets?

8 Why are these statements wrong? (a) The EU was always a free trade zone, and must always have had a single market. (b) Monetary union involves as big a loss of monetary sovereignty for Germany as for Luxembourg. (c) The European Central Bank must guarantee price stability but be under democratic political control.

9 **Essay question** What determines the interest rate that markets charge governments in the bond market?

10 **Essay question** Suppose Greece defaults on its debt and withdraws from the EZ. Discuss what happens next. Be sure to mention (a) the exchange rate, (b) speculative pressure during the run up to EZ exit, and (c) who gains and loses from default itself.

Online Learning Centre

To help you grasp the key concepts of this chapter check out the extra resources posted on the Online Learning Centre at www.mcgraw-hill.co.uk/textbooks/begg.

There are additional case studies, self-test questions, practice exam questions with answers and a graphing tool.

Glossary

The **accelerator** model of investment assumes that firms guess future output and profits by extrapolating past output growth.

Monetary policy **accommodates** a permanent supply change by changing the average level of real interest rates, thereby permanently altering aggregate demand in line with permanently altered aggregate supply.

Adverse selection means individuals use their inside information to accept or reject a contract. Those accepting are no longer an average sample of the population.

Aggregate demand is total desired spending at each level of income.

The **aggregate supply schedule** shows the output firms wish to supply at each inflation rate.

In the classical model, the **aggregate supply schedule** is vertical at potential output.

Aid is an international transfer payment from rich countries to poor countries.

The **asset price** is the sum for which the stock can be bought, entitling its owner to the future stream of capital services from that asset.

Assets are what the firm owns.

Automatic stabilizers reduce fluctuations in aggregate demand by reducing the multiplier. All leakages act as automatic stabilizers.

Average cost is the total cost divided by output.

Average revenue is total revenue divided by output. But revenue is just output multiplied by price. So average revenue *is* the price the firm receives for its output.

If T is the amount paid in tax, and Y is income, then T/Y is the **average tax rate**.

The **balance of payments** records all transactions between a country and the rest of the world.

Bank reserves are cash in the bank to meet possible withdrawals by depositors.

A **barter economy** has no medium of exchange. Goods are simply swapped for other goods.

The **budget share** of a good is the spending on that good as a fraction of total consumer spending.

The **business cycle** is short-term fluctuation of output around its trend path.

Capital is the input that exists because of a previous production process, and still exists at the end of the production process.

The **capital account** of the balance of payments shows international flows of transfer payments relating to capital items.

Capital deepening raises capital per worker for all workers.

In a growing economy, capital widening gives each new worker as much capital as that used by existing workers.

Cash flow is the net amount of money received by a firm during a given period.

A central bank is responsible for printing money, setting interest rates and acting as banker to commercial banks and the government.

The circular flow is the flow of inputs, outputs and payments between firms and households.

The classical model of macroeconomics assumes wages and prices are completely flexible.

Classical unemployment arises when the wage is kept above its long-run equilibrium level.

A closed shop means that all a firm's workers must be members of a trade union.

Collusion is an explicit or implicit agreement between existing firms to avoid competition.

In a command economy government planners decide what, how, and for whom goods and services are made. Households, firms and workers are then told what to do.

A commitment is an arrangement, entered into voluntarily, that restricts one's future actions.

The Competition Commission examines whether a monopoly, or potential monopoly, is against the public interest.

Competition policy tries to promote efficiency through competition between firms.

A rise in the price of one good raises the demand for substitutes for this good, but reduces the demand for complements to the good.

In the classical model, there is complete crowding out. Higher government spending causes an equivalent reduction in private spending, since total output cannot change.

There are constant returns to scale if *LAC* is constant as output rises.

The consumption function relates desired consumption to personal disposable income.

A contestable market has free entry and free exit.

The convergence hypothesis says poor countries should grow quickly but rich countries should grow slowly.

The cost of holding money is the interest given up by holding money rather than bonds.

A firm's costs are expenses incurred in production and sales during the period.

A credible threat is one that, after the fact, it is still optimal to carry out.

During a credit crunch, traditional sources of lending dry up because potential lenders fear that the borrower may face an acute crisis and then become unable to repay the loan.

The current account of the balance of payments records international flows of goods, services and transfer payments.

Data are pieces of evidence about economic behaviour.

Demand is the quantity buyers wish to purchase at each conceivable price.

A demand curve shows the quantity demanded at each possible price, other things equal.

Demand-deficient unemployment occurs when output is below full capacity.

The demand for money is a demand for *real* money balances M/P.

Demand management is the use of monetary and fiscal policy to stabilize output near the level of potential output.

Depreciation is the cost of using capital during the period.

Depreciation is the fall in value of the capital stock during the period through use and obsolescence.

A devaluation is a fall in the fixed exchange rate.

Tastes display **diminishing marginal utility** from a good if each extra unit adds successively less to total utility when consumption of other goods remains constant.

Direct taxes are taxes on income.

A **discriminating monopoly** charges different prices to different buyers.

There are **diseconomies of scale** (or decreasing returns to scale) if *LAC* rises as output rises.

A **distortion** or **market failure** exists if society's marginal cost of making a good does not equal society's marginal benefit from consuming that good.

Economic growth is the rate of change of real income or real output.

Economic losses mean that the resources could earn more elsewhere.

Economic (supernormal) profits in excess of normal profit are a signal to switch resources into the industry.

Economics is the study of how society decides what, how and for whom to produce.

There are **economies of scale** (or increasing returns to scale) if long-run average cost *LAC* falls as output rises.

The **effective exchange rate (eer)** is a weighted average of individual bilateral exchange rates.

For given tastes, inputs and technology, an allocation is **efficient** if no one can then be made better off without making at least one other person worse off.

The **elasticity of supply** measures the *responsiveness* of quantity supplied to the price that suppliers receive.

Entry is when new firms join an industry.

The **equilibrium price** clears the market. It is the price at which the quantity supplied equals the quantity demanded.

Equilibrium unemployment is unemployment when the labour market is in equilibrium.

Equilibrium unemployment U^* is the level of unemployment in long-run equilibrium.

The **exchange rate** is the price at which two currencies exchange.

Exit is when existing firms leave an industry.

Export-led growth stresses output and income growth via exports, rather than by displacing imports.

Exports X are made at home but sold abroad.

External balance means that the current account of the balance of payments is zero.

An **externality** arises if a production or consumption decision affects the physical production or consumption possibilities of other people.

A **federal fiscal system** has a central government setting taxes and expenditure rules that apply in its constituent states or countries.

The **financial account** of the balance of payments records international purchases and sales of financial assets.

Fiscal policy is the government's decisions about spending and taxes.

Fixed costs do not vary with output levels.

A **fixed exchange rate** means that governments, acting through their central banks, will buy or sell as much of the currency as people want to exchange at the fixed rate.

A **fixed input** cannot be varied in the short run.

In a **floating exchange rate** regime, the exchange rate is allowed to find its free market equilibrium without any intervention using the foreign exchange reserves.

A **flow** is the stream of services that an asset provides in a given period.

Foreign direct investment (FDI) is the purchase of foreign firms or the establishment of foreign subsidiaries.

The **foreign exchange (forex) market** exchanges one national currency for another.

The **foreign exchange reserves** are the foreign currency holdings of the domestic central bank.

In a **free market economy**, prices adjust to reconcile desires and scarcity.

A **free rider**, knowing he cannot be excluded from consuming a good, has no incentive to buy it.

Frictional unemployment is the irreducible minimum unemployment in a dynamic society.

The **functional income distribution** is the division of national income between the different production inputs.

The **gains from trade** are additional output of some goods with no loss of other goods.

A **game** is a situation in which intelligent decisions are necessarily interdependent. The *players* in the game try to maximize their own *pay-offs*. In an oligopoly, the firms are the players and their pay-offs are their profits in the long run. Each player must choose a strategy.

Globalization is the increase in cross-border trade and influence on the economic and social behaviour of nation-states.

Gross domestic product (GDP) measures an economy's output.

Gross investment is the production of new capital goods and the improvement of existing capital goods.

Gross national product (GNP) is the total income of citizens wherever it is earned. It is GDP plus net property income from abroad.

Horizontal equity is the identical treatment of identical people.

Human capital is the stock of accumulated expertise that raises a worker's productivity.

Hyperinflation is high inflation, above 50 per cent *per month*.

An **imperfectly competitive** firm recognizes that its demand curve slopes down.

Imports Z are made abroad but bought at home.

Import substitution replaces imports by domestic production under the protection of high tariffs or import quotas.

An **import tariff** is a tax on imports.

The **income effect** says, for a given nominal income, a fall in the price of a good raises real income, affecting the demand for all goods.

The **income elasticity of demand** measures the percentage increase in quantity demanded when income rises by 1 per cent, other things equal. It is positive for a **normal** good, but negative for an **inferior** good.

An **index number** expresses data relative to a given base value.

Indirect taxes are taxes on spending.

An **industry** is the set of all firms making the same product.

For an **inferior good**, demand falls when income rises.

Following an **inflation target**, a central bank raises the real interest rate if it expects inflation to be too high, and cuts the real interest rate if it expects inflation to be too low.

Investment I is firms' purchases of new capital goods made by other firms; it is an **injection** to the circular flow, money earned by firms but *not* from sales to households.

An **innocent entry barrier** is one made by nature.

An **input** (sometimes called a *factor of production*) is any good or service used to make output.

Internal balance means aggregate demand equals potential output.

Intra-industry trade is two-way trade in goods made by the same industry.

The **investment demand schedule** shows desired investment at each interest rate.

Involuntary unemployment means the unemployed would take a job offer at the existing wage.

An **IOU money** is a medium of exchange based on the debt of a private bank.

Labour is the production input supplied by workers.

Labour-augmenting technical progress increases the effective labour supply.

The **labour force** is everyone in work or seeking a job.

Land is the input supplied by nature.

The **law of comparative advantage** says that countries specialize in producing and exporting the goods that they produce at a lower *relative* cost than other countries.

Holding all factors constant except one, the **law of diminishing returns** says that, beyond some level of the variable input, further rises in the variable input steadily reduce the marginal product of that input.

Saving is a **leakage** from the circular flow, money paid to households but *not* returned to firms as spending. Leakages always equal injections, as a matter of definition.

The **lender of last resort** lends to banks when financial panic threatens the financial system.

Less-developed countries (LDCs) have low levels of per capita output.

Liabilities are what a firm owes.

Long-run average cost LAC is LTC divided by the level of output Q.

Along the **long-run equilibrium path**, output, capital and labour grow at the same rate. Hence output per worker, y, and capital per worker, k, are constant.

Long-run marginal cost LMC is the rise in total cost if output permanently rises by one unit.

The **long-run Phillips curve** is vertical at equilibrium unemployment.

A competitive firm's **long-run supply curve** is that part of its long-run marginal cost *above* minimum average cost. At any price below P_3, the firm leaves the industry. At price P_3, the firm makes Q_3 and just breaks even after paying all its economic costs.

Long-run total cost LTC is the total cost of making each output level when a firm has plenty of time to adjust fully and produce this output level by the cheapest possible means.

A **luxury good** has an income elasticity above 1.

The **Maastricht criteria** for joining the EMU said that a country must already have achieved low inflation and sound fiscal policy.

Macroeconomics analyses interactions in the economy as a whole.

Marginal cost is the change in total cost as a result of producing the last unit.

The **marginal principle** says that, if the slope is not zero, moving in one direction must make things better, moving the other way makes things worse. Only at a maximum (or a minimum) is the slope temporarily zero.

The **marginal product** of a variable input (labour) is the *extra* output from *adding* 1 unit of the variable input, holding constant the quantity of all other inputs (capital, land, energy) in the short run.

The **marginal product of labour MPL** is the extra physical output when a worker is added, holding other inputs constant.

The **marginal propensity to consume MPC** is the fraction of each extra pound of disposable income that households wish to consume.

The **marginal propensity to import MPZ** is the fraction of each extra pound of national income that domestic residents want to spend on extra imports.

The **marginal propensity to save MPS** is the fraction of each extra pound of income that households wish to save.

Marginal revenue is the change in total revenue as a result of making and selling the last unit.

The **marginal revenue product of capital** *MRPK* is the extra revenue from selling the extra output that an extra unit of capital allows, holding constant all other inputs.

The **marginal revenue product of labour** *MRPL* is the change in sales revenue when an extra worker's output is sold, holding other inputs constant.

The **marginal tax rate** shows how total tax T increases as income Y increases.

The **marginal utility** of a good is the *extra* utility from consuming one more unit of the good, holding constant the quantity of other goods consumed.

A **market** uses prices to reconcile decisions about consumption and production.

The **market demand curve** is the horizontal sum of individual demand curves in that market.

Menu costs of inflation are the physical resources used in changing price tags, reprinting catalogues and changing vending machines.

A **merger** is the union of two companies where they think they will do better by amalgamating.

Microeconomics makes a detailed study of individual decisions about particular commodities.

The lowest output at which all scale economies are achieved is called **minimum efficient scale**.

In a **mixed economy**, the government and private sector interact in solving economic problems.

A **model** or **theory** makes assumptions from which it deduces how people behave. It deliberately simplifies reality.

The **monetary base** is the supply of cash, whether in private circulation or held in bank reserves.

The **monetary instrument** is the variable over which a central bank exercises day-to-day control.

Monetary policy is the decision by the central bank about what interest rate to set.

A **monetary union** has permanently fixed exchange rates within the union, an integrated financial market, and a single central bank setting the single interest rate for the union.

Money is any generally accepted means of payment for delivery of goods or settlement of debt. It is the **medium of exchange**.

The **money multiplier** is the ratio of the money supply to the monetary base.

The **money supply** is money in circulation (cash not in bank vaults) plus bank deposits on which cheques can be written.

A **monopolist** is the sole supplier or potential supplier of the industry's output.

An industry with **monopolistic competition** has many sellers making products that are close but not perfect substitutes for one another. Each firm then has a limited ability to affect its output price.

Monopoly power is measured by price *minus* marginal cost at any output level.

A **monopsonist** must raise the wage to attract extra labour.

Moral hazard exploits inside information to take advantage of the other party to the contract.

The **multiplier** is the ratio of the change in equilibrium output to the change in demand that caused output to change.

The **multiplier–accelerator model** explains business cycles by the dynamic interaction of consumption and investment demand.

In **Nash equilibrium**, each player chooses his best strategy, *given* the strategies chosen by other players.

National income is GNP minus depreciation during the period.

A **natural monopoly**, having vast scale economies, does not fear entry by smaller competitors.

A **necessity** an income elasticity below 1.

Net investment is gross investment minus the depreciation of the existing capital stock.

Net worth is a firm's assets minus liabilities.

Nominal GNP is measured at the prices when income was earned.

Nominal values measure prices at the time of measurement.

Non-tariff barriers are different national regulations or practices that prevent free movement of goods, services and factors across countries.

For a **normal good**, demand rises when income rises.

Normal profit is the accounting profit to break even after all economic costs are paid.

Normative economics offers recommendations based on personal value judgements.

The **Office of Fair Trading** is responsible for making markets work well for consumers, by protecting and promoting consumer interests while ensuring that businesses are fair and competitive.

An **oligopoly** is an industry with only a few, interdependent producers.

An **open market operation** is a central bank purchase or sale of securities in the open market in exchange for cash.

Opportunity cost is the amount lost by not using resources in their best alternative use.

The **opportunity cost** of a good is the quantity of *other* goods sacrificed to get another unit of *this* good.

An **optimal currency area** is a group of countries better off with a common currency than keeping separate national currencies.

When a country affects the price of its imports, the **optimal tariff** makes individual importers take account of their effect on the price that other importers must pay.

Other things equal is a device for looking at the relation between two variables, but remembering other variables also matter.

The **output gap** is actual output minus potential output.

The **paradox of thrift** is that a change in the desire to save changes equilibrium output and income, but not equilibrium saving.

The **participation rate** is the fraction of people of working age who join the labour force.

Perfect capital mobility means expected total returns on assets in different currencies must be equal if huge capital flows are to be avoided. A positive interest differential must be offset by an expected exchange rate fall of equal magnitude. This is the **interest parity condition**.

In **perfect competition**, actions of individual buyers and sellers have no effect on the market price.

Personal disposable income is household income from firms, plus government transfers, minus taxes. It is household income available to be spent or saved.

The **personal income distribution** shows how national income is divided between people, regardless of the inputs from which these people earn their income.

The **Phillips curve** shows that higher inflation is accompanied by lower unemployment.

Physical capital is any input to production not used up within the production period. Examples include machinery, equipment and buildings. *Investment* is additions to physical capital.

Physical capital is the stock of produced goods used to make other goods and services.

In short-run equilibrium, **planned leakages** must equal **planned injections**.

A **political business cycle** is caused by cycles in policy between general elections.

Positive economics deals with scientific explanation of how the economy works.

Potential output is national output when all inputs are fully employed.

Potential output is the level of GDP when all markets are in equilibrium.

The **poverty trap** means that getting a job makes a person worse off than staying at home.

A **price control** is a government regulation to fix the price.

The **price elasticity of demand (ped)** measures the *responsiveness* of quantity demanded to changes in the price of that good or service.

The **price of an asset** is the sum for which the asset can be purchased outright. The owner of a capital asset gets the future stream of capital services from this asset.

Primary products are agricultural goods and minerals, whose output relies heavily on the input of land.

The **principle of targeting** says that the best way to meet an aim is to use a policy that affects the activity directly. Policies with side effects are second best because they distort other activities.

A firm's **profits** are the excess of revenue over costs.

A **production technique** is a particular way of using inputs to make output.

A **public good** is necessarily consumed in equal amounts by everyone.

The **purchasing power parity (PPP)** path of the nominal exchange rate is the hypothetical path that it would have to follow in order to maintain the real exchange rate at its initial level.

For a **pure monopoly**, the demand curve for the firm is the industry demand curve itself. There is only one firm in the industry and it has no fear of entry by others.

The **quantity theory of money** says that changes in the quantity of nominal money M lead to equivalent changes in prices P, but have no effect on real output.

A **quota** is a ceiling on import quantities.

Raw materials are the physical inputs used up during the production process.

Real business cycles are output fluctuations caused by fluctuations in potential output itself.

The **real exchange rate** is the relative price of domestic and foreign goods, when measured in a common currency.

Real GNP adjusts for inflation by valuing GNP in different years at the prices prevailing at a particular date.

The **real interest rate**, the difference between the nominal interest rate and inflation, is what measures the real cost of borrowing and the real return on lending.

Real values adjust nominal values for changes in the general price level.

The cost of using capital services is the **rental rate** for capital services.

The **required rental** is the income per period that lets a buyer of a capital asset break even.

The **reserve ratio** is the ratio of reserves to deposits.

A firm's **revenue** is income from sales during the period.

A **revaluation** is a rise in the fixed exchange rate.

Saving S is the part of income not spent buying output.

The **saving function** shows desired saving at each income level.

For a **scarce resource**, the quantity demanded at a zero price would exceed the available supply.

A **scatter diagram** plots pairs of values simultaneously observed for two different variables.

Shoe-leather costs of inflation are shorthand for the extra time and effort in transacting when inflation reduces desired real cash holdings.

Short-run average fixed cost is short-run fixed cost divided by output.

Short-run average total cost is short-run total cost divided by output.

Short-run average variable cost is short-run variable cost divided by output.

Short-run equilibrium output is where aggregate demand equals actual output.

Short-run marginal cost *SMC* is the extra cost of making one more unit of output in the short run while some inputs are fixed.

Each **short-run Phillips curve** is a negative relation between inflation and unemployment, given the inflation expectations already built into nominal wages.

The **short-run supply curve** *SAS* shows how desired output varies with inflation, for a given inherited growth of nominal wages.

A competitive firm's **short-run supply curve** is that part of its short-run marginal cost curve above its shutdown price.

A firm's **short-run supply decision** is to make Q_1, the output at which $MR = SMC$, provided the price covers short-run average variable cost $SAVC_1$ at this output. If the price is less than $SAVC_1$, the firm produces zero.

A **single market** is not segmented by national regulations, taxes or informal practices.

There are two **social costs of monopoly power**. The first is too little output, the second is wastefully high cost curves.

A **stock** is the quantity of an asset at a point in time (e.g. 100 machines on 1/1/06).

Stocks are measured at a point in time; **flows** are corresponding measures over a period of time.

Money is also a **store of value**, available for future purchases.

Strategic entry deterrence is behaviour by incumbent firms to make entry less likely.

Your **strategic move** influences the other player's decision, in a manner helpful to you, by affecting the other person's expectations of how you will behave.

A **strategy** is a game plan describing how the player will act or *move* in each situation.

Structural unemployment reflects a mismatch of skills and job opportunities when the pattern of employment is changing.

A rise in the price of one good raises the demand for **substitutes** for this good, but reduces the demand for **complements** to the good.

The **substitution effect** says that, when the relative price of a good falls, quantity demanded rises.

Supply is the quantity producers wish to offer for sale at each conceivable price.

A **supply curve** shows the quantity supplied at each possible price, other things equal.

Tastes describe the utility a consumer gets from the goods consumed. Utility is happiness or satisfaction.

Tax incidence is the final tax burden once we allow for all the induced effects of the tax.

The **tax wedge** is the gap between the price paid by the buyer and the price received by the seller.

A technique is said to have **technical efficiency** if no other technique could make the same output with fewer inputs.

Technical progress is the discovery of a new technique that is more efficient than existing ones, making a given output with fewer inputs than before. It needs both **invention**, the discovery of new ideas, and **innovation** to incorporate them into actual production techniques.

Technology is the current stock of ideas and techniques about how to make output.

A **token money** has a value as money that greatly exceeds its cost of production or value in consumption.

The **total cost curve** shows the lowest-cost way to make each output level. Total cost rises as output rises.

Total costs are total fixed costs plus total variable costs.

Total revenue is the output price times the quantity made and sold.

The trade balance is the value of net exports. When exports exceed imports, the economy has a trade surplus. When imports exceed exports, it has a trade deficit.

Trade policy operates through import tariffs, export subsidies, and direct quotas on imports and exports.

Transition economies are making the adjustment from central planning to a market economy.

The unemployment rate is the fraction of the labour force without a job.

The unit of account is the unit in which prices are quoted and accounts are kept.

Value added is net output, after deducting goods used up during the production process.

Variable costs change with output.

A variable input can be adjusted, even in the short run.

Vertical equity is the different treatment of different people in order to reduce the consequences of these innate differences.

Voluntary unemployment is people looking for work who won't yet take a job at that real wage.

The zero-growth proposal argues that, because higher output has adverse side effects such as pollution and congestion, we should therefore aim for zero growth of measured output.

Answers

Chapter 1

1. Sometimes by hierarchy or command (no, you can't have the car tonight!), sometimes by negotiation (I'll do the dishes if you let me go to the cinema), and sometimes using money and prices (you may get pocket money or an allowance, and have some discretion about what you spend it on).

2. All scarce except (b).

3. (a) 20 cakes. (b) 15 shirts. (c) 1.33 cakes.

4. (a), (c) and (e) are positive; (b) and (d) are normative.

5. Buying and selling take time, which soldiers do not have in an emergency. Certainty is also important in extreme circumstances.

6. Wages fall in jobs that students then want to do (beer tasting, modelling, sports commentating!). With lower wages, firms in these industries can cut their prices, raising the quantity sold and hence the demand for workers doing these jobs.

7. Europeans have accumulated more human and physical capital, have longer-established democracies that provide stability and continuity, and have access to world markets of the rich countries. Allowing poor farmers access to rich markets is probably the most significant policy change that rich countries could make.

8. An upward-sloping line: each extra £1000 of income is associated on average with an extra seven club visits. Higher income is probably the cause of a higher demand for club visits. But if you go clubbing to network, and end up with a better job, it is just possible that more club visits also cause higher income. Of course, if you feel terrible the next day, they could also reduce income!

9. (a) Cross-section data (e.g. by county) for crime and unemployment. (b) Collect other data to control for income, police resources, and whether urban or rural. Sort counties by these other attributes. Comparing similar counties, examine whether there is a link between more crime and more unemployment. Even if there is, discuss which causes which.

10. Many sciences (e.g. astronomy) cannot conduct laboratory experiments. What matters is the formulation of testable hypotheses and careful examination of whatever relevant data can be collected.

11. Upsloping line. Rise in RPI associated with rise in house prices; time series.

12 (a) Because demand is high and the size of arena (supply of seats) is limited. (b) No. Other things equal, higher prices reduce the quantity demanded.

13 (a) Theory organizes facts by providing a simple framework in which to interpret them. (b) Molecules are individually random but collectively predictable. People's individual whims cancel out in larger groups.

14 Equilibrium price £16; quantity 7.

15 (a) Excess demand = 5, and price rises. (b) Excess supply = 3, and price falls. (c) Long queue when excess demand.

16 (a) Fall in quantity of labour demanded, so employment falls. (b) Unions might support if they think their members will not be the ones to be priced out of a job. (c) No.

17 (a) A low enough price can fill any stadium. (b) It shows the effect of a price floor for farm goods that creates excess supply.

18 (a) No help to Greece. It will now be asked to pay £3 billion of the £5 billion it owes, and still have to contribute £2 billion of its own resources. (b) Just the same as in (a) – now foreign creditors get £2 billion from Greece and £1 billion from the bailout.

19 If nobody else pays, your small contribution won't create much safety. If everyone else pays, you get safe streets anyway. So there is no reason for you to offer to pay. Everyone else reasons similarly, and so nobody pays, and no safe streets are created through market means. That is why we have politics and elections.

20 (a) Would be close to $80/barrel. (b) Yes. (c) Increase.

21 In the long run, speculation is profitable only if it is stabilizing. However, in the short run, nobody is quite sure what the equilibrium price is – that is why armies of bright economics graduates are employed in financial services to try to use the latest information to outguess their rivals. Since nobody is quite sure what everyone else knows, this often leads to herding, where everyone copies everyone else in case they have superior information. This leads to bandwagons that induce significant and sustained departures from the equilibrium price until everyone comes to their senses and there is a sharp adjustment of prices.

22 (a) Supply rises, price falls. (b) Demand and price fall. (c) Unless all these additions raise the attractiveness of the area for potential country house owners by more than they think, the expansion of other housing reduces rural amenities.

23 Free could mean 'free of regulation' or 'free of price'. Some minimal regulations are usually needed to make activities sustainable – thus racism, incitement to commit crimes, and deliberate lying are usually prohibited. If all Internet activities are supplied without any charge, we are eventually back in the world of Question 19. If no revenues can be earned, people will cease many of the activities sooner or later, especially the business ones. Advertising revenue may be an alternative to charging. Similar issues arise in 'free banking' where depositors are not explicitly charged the cost of banking services, but banks find indirect ways to cover their costs, for example by offering lower interest rates on deposits than they otherwise would have done.

Chapter 2

1 (a) To sell 10 per cent fewer peaches, raise the price by 20 per cent to £1.20. (b) Vertical supply curve, now at 90 peaches. (c) Now earn £108, which is more than before despite the lower volume of sales.

2 (a) Moves people upwards along given demand curve. (b) Shifts demand curve to the left.

3 Vegetables: inelastic, necessity. Catering: elastic, luxury.

4   These data are for nominal not real spending on bread. In fact, real spending on bread (excluding ciabatta and the fancy foreign stuff) fell as real income rose, suggesting it is an inferior good.

5   (a) At high enough prices, demand may be price elastic, even for tobacco. If so, raising taxes and the price of cigarettes may so reduce the quantity demanded that tax revenue then falls. When we talk about demand for particular goods being elastic or inelastic, we mean 'in the range of prices normally experienced'. Outside this range, things could be different. Necessity refers to the effect of income changes not the effect of price changes. (b) If bad weather hits all farmers, it raises prices and helps incomes: 'good' weather needs insurance! (c) Since only one farmer is affected, there will not be a significant change in total supply or equilibrium price. Hence this farmer needs insurance when that farmer's quantity falls.

6   Not for producers of inferior goods, for which demand falls as income rises.

7   First statement is substitution effect; second is income effect. Since they go in opposite directions, either outcome is possible when both effects operate together.

8   (a) Both income and substitution effects reduce demand: consumer feels poorer and buys less, and trips are relatively more expensive. (b) Demand curve shifts down: equilibrium price and quantity fall.

9   (a) Utility is the satisfaction from consuming a particular bundle of goods and services. (b) Marginal utility is extra satisfaction gained by consuming one more unit of one good, holding constant consumption of all other goods. (c) Diminishing marginal utility means that successive additions of one extra good yield less and less extra satisfaction, other things equal.

10   Alcohol, double cream, economics revision!

11   It could be true where the consumer needs a group of things to get much satisfaction. For a nicotine addict, a single puff of a cigarette might be worse than no puff at all; for a keen gardener, a clump of roses might be much better than a single solitary rose. In most cases, this pleasure from a minimum critical mass occurs at pretty low quantities, thereafter diminishing marginal utility sets in reliably. For an individual, the implication is that the demand curve might slope up at its very left-hand end in a few rare cases, before then sloping down over the rest of its range. In the aggregate, since different individuals have different minimum thresholds, it is likely that the demand curve will slope down throughout its range.

12   For an individual, the consumer benefit is the area under the individual demand curve, and consumer surplus the triangle created by the excess of this area over the rectangle showing quantity times price actually paid. Total consumer surplus is the same, applied to the aggregate demand curve. These rectangles exist only because of the assumption of uniform pricing, that all units are sold for the same price. For all units below the equilibrium quantity, the good was more valuable to the consumer than the price actually charged in order to sell that last unit. If a supplier can price discriminate perfectly, charging a different price for each and every unit, then the supplier can capture as revenue the entire area under the demand curve. There is then no surplus for the consumer, who has to pay, unit by unit, the exact value of the benefit received.

13   (a) US and Australia – rich countries with arid climates and hot summers. (b) Rises, rises, rises. (c) Unchecked, eventually global warming would have adverse effects on income and living standards; feeling poorer, people might then demand fewer air conditioners, other things equal. In practice, governments are likely to take action before then (higher taxes on air conditioners, dearer electricity and other measures).

14   (a) Since both nominal income and prices rise, the previous quantities of goods are still affordable and still best of the affordable bundles. (b) There is also an income effect – since the return on saving is no higher, people are richer and do not have to save so much to get any particular level of future income. This income effect makes them save less. The substitution effect – saving is now relatively better rewarded than before – makes them save more. Empirically, the two effects largely cancel out.

15 An economist would probably say that, if the two situations were truly identical, the person really would behave the same way in both, and therefore that we have failed to spot something about the two situations that in fact makes them different. Theories and models of course are a deliberate simplification. Tossing a coin appears to get different answers in different particular coin tosses. But that is because our theory – equal chance of head or tail – is only a simplification. Measuring nerve impulses, wind speeds, humidity and 100 other things, we could probably be more accurate in our predictions by differentiating apparently similar situations that turn out on closer inspection to be different from one another.

16 If consumers pay different prices from one another, they may set up a second-hand market; selling to one another undermines the producer's attempt to charge different prices. Since services have to be consumed in the place and time they are produced, resale is much easier for goods than for services. We therefore expect more price discrimination in services.

Chapter 3

1 (a)–(c) all increase supply. (d) is the result of higher demand, and the higher equilibrium price moves suppliers upwards along a given supply curve.

2 Drought, sheep disease, higher wages for shepherds. Change in price of wool moves farmer along given supply curve but does not shift supply curve.

3 (a) $p = 2$, $1 = 6$. (b) $p = 2$, $q = 6$. (c) $S'S'$ is more inelastic since given price increase leads to less extra quantity supplied than on SS. (d) $p = 3$, $q = 8$; $p = 4$, $q = 7$. (e) SS.

4 Knowing that partners can lose all their personal wealth may encourage trust in the activities of the firm.

5 Shareholders care about share price, which mainly depends on long-run profits. Persistently achieving good short-run profits should be good for long-run profits too, but there may be some conflicts. Investing for the long run will diminish profits in the short run. Conversely, when borrowing becomes difficult, as in a financial crisis, it may be important to do well in the short run, for example by selling off assets not core to the business, even if this slightly reduces long-run profits.

6 Expand output a bit and see if this is still true. Reduce output a bit and see if this is still true.

7 Only the factory is a stock, the rest are all flows.

8 $q = 3$, at which output $MC = MR$.

9 Setting $MC = MR$ leads to the optimal output choice of 3 units. The table below shows that 3 units yield a profit of 2, at least as good as any other output. With discrete integers, it turns out that 2 units also yield a profit of 2. This arises because costs and revenues are discrete rather than continuous. Beginning from an output of 2, the marginal cost and marginal revenue of an extra unit are both 6, so no profit is gained or lost by raising output to 3. And beginning at an output of 3, no profit is gained or lost by cutting output to 2. With smooth cost and revenue curves, whose slope is changing continuously, setting $MC = MR$ generally yields a unique output choice.

Output (units)	0	1	2	3	4	5	6
Total cost TC	5	9	13	19	26	34	43
Total revenue TR	0	8	15	21	26	30	33
Total profits = $TR - TC$	−5	−1	2	2	0	−4	−10

10 When demand is price inelastic, producing and selling a higher quantity will reduce revenue and income. Since the marginal cost of this extra output is positive, profits are definitely reduced. Reducing output would increase revenue, reduce costs and increase profits.

11 At the top of each hill, the slope is zero. Yes, if the hill has only one peak. A firm will maximize profit by choosing an output at which a marginal change in output has no effect on profit (otherwise it could change output to do better), which implies that marginal cost equals marginal revenue. This is the top of one hill. The other hill that it must check out is the hill corresponding to zero output.

12 (a) An accounting profit may not cover the opportunity cost of the time and money tied up in the business. (b) A managerial genius may get to the right answer intuitively, but the laws of arithmetic guarantee that marginal cost will equal marginal revenue if profit maximization is achieved. (c) Sales revenue is maximized when marginal revenue is zero. Since marginal cost is usually above zero, maximizing sales revenue means output is too high to maximize profits.

13 (a) No change. (b) No change. (c) By reducing future total profits, a future tax reduces the payoff to investing in costly measures today in order to shift cost curves down in the future. If cost curves are different from what they would have been, profit-maximizing output is likely to be affected in the future.

14 The venture capital industry specializes in funding young businesses before they can eventually float on the stock market if they survive. Interestingly, most funding of businesses is organic, ploughing back the profits that business itself has made. Why should this be the commonest form of business financing whatever the size of the firm? It is because people running the firm have more information about its true prospects than the information easily available to potential outside creditors. Insiders typically think that outsiders are charging too high an interest rate to cover risks that really don't exist. But this does not reassure outsiders, who have no easy way to verify what insiders really know.

15 Tying bonuses to long-term profits is likely to make managers behave in ways that are good for shareholders. Paying bonuses against criteria that managers can manipulate in the short run is not sensible; for example, it may encourage too much risk-taking by managers. One problem for shareholders is the problem of collective action. If there are many shareholders, it is costly to organize them to act in a united way. If each expects the others not to bother, it may be individually rational not to bother since an individual will make little difference. Things are very different when shareholding is concentrated in a few shareholders, who then find it easy to take the trouble to be good shareholders, monitor management effectively, and provide appropriate incentives.

Chapter 4

1 Demand is more elastic in the long run because people have more time to adjust their behaviour to the change in price. They can get out of existing contracts, look for more suitable alternatives, and even break patterns of addiction. If all other things are held constant, this is probably always the case. Of course, something else might change in the long run (for example, tastes) so that elasticities appear to become smaller, but this would not be the pure effect of a price change.

2 (a), (c) and (d) refer to income elasticity; (b) and (e) to price elasticity of demand.

3 The substitution effect must reduce quantity demanded. Only if the service is inferior can quantity demanded increase.

4 (a) False. (b) True. (c) True. (d) False.

5   (a) Negative – more expensive shoes reduce the demand for shoelaces. (b) Positive – more expensive coffee increases the demand for tea. (c) Hence, complements tend to have negative cross-price elasticities, substitutes tend to have positive cross-price elasticities. To be completely correct, these statements apply to the direction of the substitution effect alone. Income effects can sometimes overturn the total effect on quantity demanded.

6   Since supply curves slope upwards, price and quantity always change in the same direction (unlike demand, where they change in opposite directions). Unit elastic demand is the special case in which these offsetting changes just cancel out. For supply, there is no such conflict and hence no particular reason to focus on a unit elasticity of supply. Revenue of sellers always rises when price increases, other things equal.

7   You have to sell them before they become rotten. At the start of the day, you may be prepared to hold out for high prices and your supply curve is upward sloping – you are more willing to supply your strawberries at the high price you are offered. As the day wears on, you become desperate to sell – your supply curve becomes steeper and steeper. By the end of the day, it is vertical. You will sell at any price that you are offered.

8   All three justifications correct. Note that price discrimination is possible only because transport is a service.

9   High quality producers have made a long-term investment in their brand image. Even if they knew how to compete in production of cheap variants, which itself might take some time to master, it would confuse consumers and eventually undermine their ability to charge high prices for high quality products. In this example, the pursuit of long-run profits explains why it may be necessary to sacrifice short-run profits.

10 (a) Quantity supplied falls. (b) Falls even more in the long run as landlords have more time to adjust to the lower price. (c) More elastic in the long run.

11 (a) Above some tax rate (and therefore price of cigarettes), the quantity demanded is likely to fall a lot. Above some tax rate, further tax rises reduce tax revenue because they reduce quantity by more than they increase the tax rate per unit. (b) At this point, demand is unit elastic. If demand is inelastic, raise taxes and the price even more; if it is elastic, you have already raised the tax rate too much. (c) Set a higher price than that which maximizes tax revenue because the higher price also reduces quantity of cigarettes demanded and makes people healthier.

12 Sharp increase in food prices initially; smaller increase in the long run. To the extent that the UK can import food, supply of food falls by less and prices rise by less. Consumers may also be able to adjust more in the long run. If demand is more elastic in the long run than in the short run, more of the fall in food supply will be reflected in a lower quantity of food demanded and less of it in a higher equilibrium price of food.

13 The conflicting aims are maximization of revenue and diversity of access. The latter is definitely the 'for whom' question. However many tickets are set aside for this purpose, you probably then want to maximize income from the remainder. This certainly entails price discrimination where possible, for example by having corporate sponsorship packages at high prices, while selling others to (reasonably well off) retail customers.

Chapter 5

1   (a) Production function relates output to minimum quantities of inputs required. (b) You still need to know input prices and demand curve for output to calculate profit-maximizing output.

2   (a) Scale economies reflect opportunities to spread fixed costs in the short run and to adopt large-scale production methods in the long run. (b) Choose methods 1, 3 and 5 rather than 2, 4 and 6

(see table below). Average cost thus falls from 8.25 to 8 to 7.25 as output expands. (c) Scale economies are present.

Units of	Method 1	Method 2	Method 3
Labour input	5	6	10
Capital input	4	2	7
Output	4	4	8
Total cost	33	34	64
Average cost	8.25	8.5	8

Units of	Method 4	Method 5	Method 6
Labour input	12	15	16
Capital input	4	11	8
Output	8	12	12
Total cost	68	87	96
Average cost	8.5	7.25	8

3 (a) Methods 1 and 3 still dominate methods 2 and 4, but now method 5 has total cost of 96 and method 6 has total cost of 94, so if demand conditions make firm want to produce 12 units, will now use method 6 not 5. (b) However, total cost (and average cost) is higher at each output when any input price is higher.

4

Output	0	1	2	3	4
Total cost	12	25	40	51	60
Marginal cost		13	15	11	9
Average cost		25	20	17	15

Output	5	6	7	8
Total cost	70	84	105	128
Marginal cost	10	14	21	23
Average cost	14	14	15	16

These are short-run costs. In the long run, a firm with positive costs at zero output is losing money and should leave the industry. Hence, this must be a short-run cost curve.

5 If $MC < AC$, another unit can be produced more cheaply than the average for existing units, dragging down the average. Hence, to the left of minimum average cost, MC is below AC but AC is falling. Conversely, if $MC > AC$, making another unit increases average costs since the extra unit

costs more than the existing average cost. Now *MC* lies above *AC* and *AC* is rising. Hence *MC* must cross *AC* at the point of minimum average cost.

6   (a) Given time to adjust, it may be possible to reduce costs sufficiently to stop losing money. (b) If diseconomies of scale exist, larger output raises average cost, and big firms are undercut by smaller firms. (c) If scale economies exist, a firm can reduce average cost by expanding output, thus undercutting its smaller competitors.

7   Yes, because the firm must take the price as given. The fact that a firm cannot affect the price of its output, and hence its marginal revenue is simply the price it receives, is the key feature of perfect competition.

8   In the short run, the cost curves of each firm shift down. By shifting their marginal cost curves lower, this shifts their supply curves downwards too. Industry output rises and the price falls a bit, but by less than the downward shift in supply. Existing firms are making profits. In the long run, more firms enter until economic profit is driven down to zero. Hence, the price falls further and quantity expands further.

9   When the market is not in equilibrium, either buyers or sellers are frustrated. This creates temporary market power to change the price. For example, with excess demand, a firm raising its price will not lose all its market share to competitors, who do not have the capacity to take advantage of their relatively lower price.

10   Although each firm in both industries has a U-shaped average cost curve, it is much easier in the long run to expand the supply of new hairdressing firms than to discover new coalfields. Hairdressing has more elastic long-run supply.

11   The average cost is falling throughout the entire range. Since marginal cost intersects from below the lowest point of average cost, marginal cost is below average cost throughout the entire range. Any particular firm producing more than its rivals enjoys lower average cost and can undercut all its rivals, gaining the entire industry for itself.

12   Demand curve shifted left, and short-run supply curve was fairly inelastic, generating large price fall and small quantity fall. Once suppliers had more time to adjust, supply curve shifted left, helping to restore the price but reducing output further.

13   Ford cars and Vauxhall cars are subtly different and thus not perfect substitutes for one another. Each firm has some scope to vary its price without losing all its market share to the other. Moreover, since each firm is large, each will try to anticipate the effect of its actions on the other firm. They are not price takers and not perfectly competitive.

14   (a) Opportunity cost of everything is being covered when a firm makes only normal profits, so all resources employed are earning the return they need. (b) Each firm's supply curves shift up, and the induced shift in industry supply changes the equilibrium price and quantity.

15   Perfect competition requires that each firm is a price taker. Since globalization is increasing competition between countries, each firm faces a more elastic demand curve – if it tries to raise the price of goods at home, it is more likely to induce a flood of imports and face a large reduction in the quantity of its goods demanded. However, there remain important limitations to the ability of imports to be perfect substitutes for domestic products – for example, transport costs, local information and culture. Sometimes, globalization also allows giant firms to emerge to exploit huge opportunities for scale economies – just think of Boeing and Airbus.

16   A firm whose R&D is successful has a temporary monopoly in the new product, at least until other firms can copy it successfully and legally. These temporary profits are the incentive to invest in R&D even if, in the long run, all excess profits are competed away by entry of new firms.

Chapter 6

1

P	8	7	6	5	4	3
Q	1	2	3	4	5	6
TR	8	14	18	20	20	18
MR	8	6	4	2	0	-2

Monopolist has $Q = 2$, $P = 7$. Competitive industry has $Q = 4$, $P = 5$. Monopolist's output is lower because marginal revenue is below price. With lower output, it takes a higher price to equate supply and demand.

2 No effect. MC and MR are unaltered, and profits are lower but still positive.

3 (a) No effect on profit-maximizing output. Maximizing pre-tax profit is still the best way to maximize post-tax profits. (b) Marginal profit is zero on the last unit produced since $MC = MR$. (c) This is why decision about last unit is independent of the rate of profits tax. With zero profit on the last unit, the tax rate is irrelevant at that point.

4 The golf club faces two separate demand curves, from peak users who really want to play at peak times and don't mind paying for it, and off-peak users who can more easily decide when to play. The golf club wants to equate marginal revenue across the two groups (otherwise it can make more by having more of one group and less of the other). The more inelastic the demand curve, the more price exceeds marginal revenue. Hence the group with the more inelastic demand curve (peak users) pays more.

5 Monopolist has greater incentive to innovate than a competitive firm because the latter knows that eventually new entrants will compete away excess profits, whereas monopolist knows these can be enjoyed forever. Conversely, those running a monopoly might decide to have an easy life and forget about maximizing profits. Competitive firms that do not stay on their toes will be outcompeted by other firms and go out of business.

6 (a) If scale economies are large, breaking up a large firm into smaller units means that each firm then produces at higher cost. This disadvantage could outweigh the benefits of more competition between the firms. (b) Raising its price above marginal cost might lead to new entry, either from new firms or in the form of competition from imports. If the threat of competition prevents a single producer raising prices, that firm is not a monopolist.

7 (a) Certification by a reputable agency saves customers the cost of checking themselves. For mechanics, after a bad experience, you can go elsewhere. Reputation helps solve the information problem. (b) For doctors, you might be dead after a bad experience. Hence regulation of doctors even more important than of car repairers.

8 (a) $Q = 4$, $P = 7$. (b) Same again. (c) Because each firm has $MC = 3$, but will face $MR > 3$ if it alone expands: price won't fall so much since other firm is not expanding too.

9 Small shops have room for only one freezer cabinet. If one supplier controls the cabinet, it can manipulate which firms' ice creams are sold in it, preventing competition by competitors. Eventually, this practice was outlawed by the UK Competition Commission, claiming that greater competition would reduce the average price of ice creams.

10 There are many fewer books produced than before, though some remain as collectors' items. Wikipedia freely provides large amounts of wonderful information, but since anyone can

volunteer to write, it is difficult to be sure of the quality of the information. Since Google is a for-profit company, it has more to lose if it provides misleading information, and therefore has a larger incentive to check the accuracy of the material it provides.

11

Q	1	2	3	4	5	6	7
P	8	7	6	5	4	3	2
TR	8	14	18	20	20	18	14
MR	8	6	4	2	0	-2	-4

With A producing 2, Z faces the 'residual demand curve' shown in the table. With $MC = 3$, it therefore produces an output of 3.

12 (a) Can't police cheating on the collective agreement. Also, each competitive firm has a negligible impact on price by cutting back its own output. More importantly, new firms then enter, raising output and driving the price down again. (b) Firms might also advertise to deter entry of other firms.

13 One device is to invest in building a reputation. Much as the parent dislikes punishing the child the first time, the cost of not punishing is a loss of credibility that makes the future tougher for the parent. Recognizing this, the parent is more likely to do what was promised. Another device is to reach agreement on parenting with the other parent or with grandparents. Then the cost to the parent of not honouring commitments is loss of reputation with several people. Third, do not promise what you know you won't be able subsequently to deliver.

14 There are two possible explanations. First, discounts and vouchers can easily be withdrawn again when demand is stronger; a firm may suffer more adverse consumer reaction to an explicit price increase. Second, if a firm uses a high price to signal that the quality of its product is good, then explicitly cutting the price may lead some consumers to wonder if the quality has been reduced.

Chapter 7

1 The firm simultaneously chooses what output to supply and what inputs therefore to demand. The only purpose of hiring inputs is to use them to make output.

2 (a) Other inputs by assumption are fixed, so eventually adding more workers means that each worker is handicapped by having fewer other inputs with which to work. This may not happen initially if there are too many other inputs for a few workers to use effectively. (b) The downward-sloping labour demand curve shifts up. Vertical axis shows the real wage; horizontal axis shows the level of employment.

3 (a) Substitution effect means work more, but income effect means work less since leisure is a normal good. (b) More people join labour force and extra bodies may compensate for fewer hours per person.

4 The only reason that film studios pay high salaries is because there is high demand for film output in which these stars appear.

5 When the industry is small relative to the whole economy and is a price taker for workers whose wages are set by national labour market.

6 (a) Demand is high; and nobody else can supply it. (b) Only via the substitution effect. The income effect makes people want more leisure (less work) since they are richer.

7 Screening lets you get a better-paid job on leaving university since firms believe they have discovered a talented worker. It would not matter what you study if all degrees are equally difficult. If economics graduates earn more this means (i) that the degree is tougher than others and screens more effectively, or (ii) that human capital from an economics training is a valuable asset.

8 Cost of training is £60 000 lost income and £21 000 fees, so £81 000. Thirty-seven years of working life then remain, so an extra salary of around £2200 per annum would pay back the loan by the end of your working life.

9 With fewer economists, their scarcity would raise wages by restricting supply. To restrict entry into economics, have tough exams and compulsory early morning lectures. Destroy all copies of *Foundations of Economics*, making study harder.

10 It is correct that youth unemployment is much higher than the national average, and also the case that people who avoid early unemployment have better labour market careers. These facts both argue for a differential minimum wage, lower for young people than older people, because the productivity and skills of young people are lower. However, reducing the cost of young labour is only part of the solution. Proactive training to raise their skills also matters. Germany is famous for its apprenticeship system that combines paid work, on the job training, and continuation of formal education.

11 One solution is to announce a pay schedule that starts with low wages and has wages increasing strongly with age during the age range in which the firm is worried about losing female workers. This schedule can be offered both men and women. Only those intending to stay for a long time will find it initially attractive. This solves the firm's problem, but does nothing to solve society's problem about encouraging people to have children and then re-enter the labour force. Wider social measures are needed to solve that problem.

12 Unions raising wages in a single competitive firm force it out of business. In a monopoly, unions that raise wages reduce the firm's profit. Although unions could organize the whole of a competitive industry, free entry makes this extremely difficult. So does globalization and competition from foreign firms. Hence union power is likely to decline further.

13 (a) Neglects the opportunity cost of wages forgone while in education. (b) Not if the unskilled are disproportionately represented in unions in the first place. They might have got even lower wages if unions did not exist.

14 If this screens out the good doctors of the future, maybe currently irate doctors should recognize that they will get big future salaries as compensation. Second explanation is that young doctors are implicitly paying for their training, a valuable investment in human capital from which they recoup high future incomes. Third explanation is that it acts as an entry deterrent, ensuring scarcity of future consultants and keeping their incomes high.

15 American economists often contrast the European 'social model' with the US 'competitive model'. In Europe, social norms and active trade unions ensure a reasonable minimum wage. Firms only employ workers with good productivity. Workers without such skills and attitudes then find it hard to find and keep a job. In the US, not only is the power of unions much weaker, there has been a border with Mexico that was hard to police, leading to a stream of immigrants that kept equilibrium wages low. So the US model has lower wages, and higher employment. There is also much less generosity in the welfare system, so people have to take work even at low wages in order to support themselves and their families.

Chapter 8

1 Only (b) is a flow; the rest are stocks.

2 Demand for capital input depends on demand for the firm's output, on quantities of other inputs with which capital co-operates, and on technology. Higher tax on output reduces the demand for all inputs, including capital. Demand curve for capital shifts down for both firm and industry.

3 Overnight, the demand for, and supply of, capital services is unaffected. However, the lower interest rate means that the required rental on capital falls. Since actual rentals now exceed required rental, firms start investing in additional capital stock, which adds to the supply of capital services. When this bids the rental on capital down to the level of the required rental, further additions to the capital stock cease.

4 Office buildings have a much longer life than cars. Since present values are more sensitive to the interest rate the further into the future we look, the price of office buildings is affected by more than the price of cars. Since office buildings are now more valuable than before, the construction of office buildings increases. Additional supply reduces the rental on office buildings (and the price of the stock of buildings) and this process continues until rentals have fallen to the new (lower) required rental. Equivalently, the price of office buildings has fallen back to the price for which they can be produced.

5 The demand for land is a derived demand. If supply is fixed, only a rise in demand for land can bid up land prices. Tenant farmers face higher rentals but extra income from their crops is what started the process. However, farmers lose out if land prices and rentals are bid up by higher demand for housing.

6 (a) Can affect land supply via fertilizers, reclaiming it from the sea, altering the level of land pollution, and many other channels. Nevertheless, the total supply of land is much harder to change than the supply of capital or labour. (b) However, if land can be switched between individual users, the supply of land to the individual firm is not fixed at all.

7 With a vertical supply curve for land, upward shifts in the demand for land raise land prices and land rentals. Since richer countries have a demand for land, there is no reason why land rentals should not keep pace with the other incomes. In most advanced countries, land has been a profitable investment over many decades precisely because of this upward pressure on land prices.

8 Income tax, VAT on luxury goods, excise duties on luxury goods. Taxes on tobacco are regressive since smoking (at least of tobacco) is disproportionately an activity of poorer people.

9 Greater dispersion in educational opportunities means that there are many workers earning low wages, whereas in European countries education is more equally distributed. Nor does Brazil have high inheritance taxes, as does Europe, so concentrated wealth is passed down the generations. And Brazil's welfare state provision is less generous than in Europe.

10 Global competition between nation-states makes it more costly to raise taxation (the tax base is tempted to flee abroad) and more costly to provide generous welfare benefits (foreigners come in to take advantage). Hence nation-states respond with less taxation and less welfare benefits, both of which help the rich and hurt the poor. If far-right parties principally represent the unskilled indigenous population who are steadily losing out, they will tend to oppose globalization.

11 The share price should reflect the (present value of the) stream of future dividends that shareholders expect to earn, which is closely linked to estimates of the stream of future profits. There are two circumstances in which the statement could be true: (a) if the market had been expecting an even larger rise in the profits than was announced, and is therefore disappointed; (b) if there is some reason to believe that, despite the rise in current profits, the market has just got wind of the fact that future profits will be much lower.

12 (a) It also makes future nominal income rise, raising labour demand. (b) Competition between users is what bids up the price to ration the scarce land supply.

13 (a) Use Figure 8-1 in reverse. Begin at point C with the demand curve $D'D'$, which then shifts up to DD. (b) The immediate effect is a move vertically upwards and a sharp rise in the rental price of capital services. (c) This provides the signal to start building new power stations. As they come on stream, the supply of capital services rises and the rental falls back to the required rental, at which

point the stock of capital stops increasing. From then on, physical investment is just sufficient to offset depreciation and keep the capital stock constant.

14 Generally, by fostering trade and demand, the derived demand for land will rise, implying an increase in the price of land and other commodities (e.g. metal ores, oil) in relatively fixed supply. However, there are also losers from globalization. Suppose Chinese textiles, based on cheap labour in China, displace European textile production from regions such as Lancashire. Other things equal, the demand for Lancashire land, and hence its price, falls.

15 One could try to make the case for the reduction from 50 to 45 per cent by arguing: (a) that people might be more inclined to pay the tax and spend less time on tax avoidance; (b) that they would be less inclined to move abroad to find a lower tax regime in which to live and work. Both arguments contain some truth but are unlikely to be large effects. To make the case against the cut, one could argue: (a) that it is unfair; (b) that it will not have important incentive effects on work or saving, since income and substitution effects go in opposite directions.

Chapter 9

1 (a) Efficient, not equitable. (b) Neither efficient nor equitable. (c) Both efficient and equitable. (d) Not efficient nor very equitable. (e) Efficient, not equitable. Equitable asks: 'How fair is distribution?'

2 Yes. Taxing (charging) for rush-hour road use would make drivers pay the true social cost. Since rural roads are not congested, nor are urban roads at 5 a.m., a fuel tax is a blunt instrument – it may reduce rush-hour traffic, but it also wrongly reduces other valuable road usage.

3 Probably, since in deciding whether to fasten your seatbelt you ignore several spillovers onto others. In the event of an accident, you may not pay the full cost of treatment. You may also cause psychological damage to others if you are killed in an accident that need not have been fatal.

4 First two are public goods, since either everybody enjoys them or nobody does. Post office network has public good aspects, though individual transactions are private goods.

5 (a) For further pollution reduction, marginal cost exceeds marginal benefit once pollution is already low. (b) Same applies to achieving the last little bit of safety; 100 per cent safe is too safe. (c) Monopoly, externalities, etc. are important market failures.

6 All except (d).

7 All progressive except tax on beer, which is a larger share of poor people's income.

8 18, 24, 28.8 per cent. It is progressive, and more so the higher the exemption level. With an exemption of £1 million, the tax would only hit the rich!

9 (a) No change in labour supplied, so no distortion triangle. (b) Big triangle, and firms now bear most of the tax. Draw a supply curve and two demand curves of different slope. For a given vertical tax wedge, the gross-of-tax wage rises more when labour demand is steeper.

10 (a) Some taxes offset externalities. (b) Existence of marginal taxes still induces people to change the quantities that they supply and demand.

11 Competitive price is £5. Under monopoly, the social cost triangle has height of £3 (the amount by which price exceeds £5), and length of 200 000 (the output fall). Hence cost is £300 000.

12 The triangle now has height £1 and length less than 200 000 since quantity demanded will lie between 800 000 and 1 million. So social cost is less than £200 000. A price ceiling of £5 will achieve the efficient outcome, since the monopolist will regard £5 as marginal revenue and produce as under perfect competition.

13   From a national viewpoint, Australia should set the tax at the level of the marginal social damage that its pollution causes to itself. Since the earth's atmosphere affects all countries, not just Australia, the damage to Australia is much smaller than the damage to the planet. From a planetary viewpoint, the carbon tax rate should be higher. Setting a tax leads to uncertain implications for quantity if we are unsure of the behavioural response. A tradable quota would be less risky.

14   It is correct that the reduction of activities of which we are already doing too much is a good thing not a bad thing, a point not well understood by those arguing that such taxes are bad for the economy. If the government is worried about recession, it can always use the revenue from carbon tax to finance a reduction in VAT, thereby ensuring that fiscal policy does not reduce overall demand, merely switching it from carbon-intensive activities to other activities.

15   MC lies below AC while AC is still falling. Although efficient point is where MC crosses demand curve, setting that price as a price ceiling would entail losses since $MC < AC$. Private monopolist would rather quit.

16   (a) Profit may just reflect monopoly power. (b) Private benefits of mergers may include monopoly profits, which are a social cost.

17   Key points to be made: generally, the need for merger control is less when the market is larger. However, creation of a global monopoly would be worrying, for example if Boeing merged with Airbus, or if all the mobile phone companies merged. Hence the extent of competition depends on the size of actual and potential firms relative to the size of the relevant market. The potential cost of monopoly power also depends on the effectiveness of the regulatory structure in place to restrain the abuse of monopoly power even when that power potentially exists.

18   If different countries have different national regulations, international banks will exploit these differences. Moreover, when a bank gets into trouble, it is usually a nation's taxpayers who have to bail it out. Since banking has become the cross-border activity that trumps all others, this increases the case for: (a) a multi-country deposit insurance scheme to prevent panics; and (b) clear cross-national rules on the regulation of banks and on the way in which the burden of failure will be shared across countries.

Chapter 10

1   Adding the value-addeds: 670 + 190 + 50 + 50 = 960.

2   GDP = 303; national income = 267.

3   GDP falls initially but the country is potentially better off since labour can now be diverted to making other things.

4   (a) Leisure is lost but investment in human capital occurs. (b) No – just a transfer payment. (c) Yes. (d) Yes. (e) Pollution should ideally be subtracted from GNP.

5   (a) Just a transfer payment, not real output. (b) Only because people compare nominal receipts. In real terms, *Gone With the Wind* wins by a mile!

6   Compare with other countries to see if it is factually true that we are different. For different countries, correlate long-run growth with usual explanations (labour input, capital input, etc.) and see if there is an extra role for the fraction of population who are scientists or engineers. Private and social benefits differ if there are externalities (some skills make it easier for people with other skills). Subsidies to education also imply discrepancy between private and social cost.

7   Pollution and congestion. Can quantify and value some (e.g. how much house prices are lower under an airport flight path). As information technology lets us record data better, it will get easier to include these in GNP.

8   Despite difficulties in increasing land input, there have not been diminishing returns to increased labour input. We accumulated other factors (human and physical capital) as substitutes for land, and technical progress invented ways to economize on land. Same is already happening for other scarce inputs.

9   The economy with faster population growth is having to devote more resources to providing new workers with the same amount of capital as existing workers enjoy. Like a swimmer swimming against a stronger current, this leaves less left over to enjoy. Living standards are lower.

10 In the long run the growth rate is determined by population growth and technical progress and is therefore unaffected unless either of these is affected. The higher saving rate allows higher gross investment per person, but eventually this goes entirely into sustaining a higher capital stock per person, and providing this more onerous burden to the ever-growing population. Living standards are higher than they would have been, but the growth rate eventually reverts to the same old rate.

11 With aggregate supply permanently lower, aggregate demand must eventually fall too. Government may wish to smooth this fall a little, but should not seek to prevent it.

12 The central point of Malthus was that ever-more population, combined with finite land, would eventually generate starvation that would reduce population growth again. Reinterpret land as the sustainable capacity of the planet, and replace population growth with economic growth. Economic growth will eventually destroy the finite sustainable capacity of the planet, reversing growth itself. This will be true only if we (a) fail to change our carbon usage and pollution and (b) fail to devise new technologies to mitigate the effects of our behaviour.

13 (a) Countries are more likely to cycle together but still cycle.
    (b) If a cycle is expected, people would take actions that are then likely to dampen the cycle.

14 (a) Since even a single country has a business cycle, even a single global economy would too. (b) If firms in a slump could already foresee the next boom, they would be less pessimistic and investment demand would not have fallen so much in the first place. Conversely, in a boom, foreseeing a subsequent slump, firms would be less keen to invest a lot, thereby dampening the initial boom.

15 Gross saving per person is sy, which equals sAk. Gross investment per person is $(g + n)k$, where gk is the rate of capital deepening and nk is the capital widening needed to give the new population the same level of capital as existing people. Hence, $g = sA − n$, and for sufficiently high saving the economy can have permanent capital deepening. Moreover, this rate of capital deepening depends on the saving rate s, in contrast to the neoclassical model in which classical deepening depends only on the rate of technical progress.

16 First, we need to specify the economic growth of what? How is net economic activity measured? If it includes environmental depreciation, then the rapid growth of activities that cause environmental damage may already be reducing the growth of net activity properly measured. Second, even if net activity is well measured, constraining its aggregate growth is an inefficient way to mitigate environmental depreciation. Other policies (including pricing of the relevant goods and bads) may do the job more effectively. Engineering a switch out of activities that are socially costly may allow overall economic growth to proceed without threatening the planet. We are, however, some way away from achieving that desirable objective.

17 First, it would be nice to measure economic growth properly, taking account of environmental depreciation. When this is ignored, as in our present accounts, we get a false sense of what economic growth rates are. Second, we may be able to make continuing technical breakthroughs, such as carbon sequestration that captures emissions and stores them underground in old oilfields, preventing them contaminating the atmosphere. Third, we may be able to switch to more sustainable energy sources and tax emissions throughout the world in an effective way. Only if all these fail will we have to reduce or abandon growth. But we have little time left – the icecaps are melting and methane is now seeping out of the tundra as it warms up.

Chapter 11

1   Upsloping line, slope 0.7 and intercept 45. At $Y = 100$, $AD = 70 + 45 = 115$. Excess demand and unplanned destocking. Output then rises. Equilibrium output $= I/[1 - c] = 45/0.3 = 450/3 = 150$.

2   (a) Falls from 500 to 300. (b) The level of saving is still 150 but rises as a fraction of output. (c) The horizontal injections line remains unaltered; the up-sloping leakages line is now steeper; the two intersect at lower output. (d) AD schedule becomes steeper and intersects the 45° line at lower output.

3   Unplanned inventory investment (whether positive or negative). Aggregate demand refers to plans, not outcomes after the fact.

4   (a) Equilibrium $Y = 400/0.2 = 2000$. (b) Equilibrium $Y = [400 + 100]/[0.3] = 1667$.

5   (a) There is no causal link between rise in desire to save and change in desired investment. (b) Since the marginal propensity to consume is smaller than 1, each fall in output induces a smaller fall in AD, so AD and Y converge to new lower level, as multiplier formula promises.

6   (a) $Y = 1000$, $C = 800$, $I = 80$, so $G = 120$. (b) When I rises by 50, equilibrium output must rise by 250, so C rises by 200. (c) Yes. (d) $C = 0.8 \times 1200 = 960$, $I = 80$. Hence $G = 160$.

7   Desired injections must equal desired leakages in equilibrium. Desired saving and investment are equal only if the other parts of desired leakages and injections equal one another.

8   Debt would spiral, implying very high future tax payments and perhaps even bankruptcy. Long before this, people would choose to stop lending to the government.

9   (a) Multiplier $= 1/[1 + MPZ - (1 - t)MPS] = 1/[1 + 0.4 - 0.04] = 1/[1.36]$. Hence, when investment demand rises by 136, equilibrium output rises by 100. (b) Again, rises by 100. Hence, desired imports rise by 40. Since exports rise by 136, trade balance improves by 96.

10   (a) Aggregate demand will rise. Higher spending by 1 adds 1 to $[C + I + G + X - Z]$. Adding 1 to taxes reduces disposable income by 1 but only reduces consumption by c. Since the marginal propensity to consume is less than 1, the fall in consumption demand is less than the rise in government demand, so aggregate demand rises. (b) When domestic output falls, import demand will fall and the trade balance will improve.

11   Government spending is difficult to change quickly without disrupting planning in the public sector; frequent changes in tax rates are costly. And even when the need for change has been diagnosed, and changes in fiscal policy implemented, these still take time to affect aggregate demand. Changing interest rates is quicker and easier in the short run, but also takes time to have its full effect on aggregate demand – anything up to two years.

12   Initially, the consumption function shifts up (and desired saving falls) since people want to spend more at any income level. Eventually, since people have to pay interest on this new debt, income available for buying goods and services falls and the consumption function shifts down.

13   It makes consumption demand less sensitive to changes in interest rates.

14   Investment rises in advance to get new capacity in place. This raises current output, forcing monetary policy to raise interest rates in order to keep inflation on track. Higher interest rates have most effect on long-term investment. Moreover, since the Bank realized that it takes up to two years for a change in interest rates to have its full effect, it will begin raising interest rates as soon as it recognizes that a future boom is on the way.

15 Beginning with output of 100, a rise in investment from 0 to 10 has the following effects:

Period	Change in last period's output $Y_{t-1} - Y_{t-2}$	Investment I_t	Output Y_t
$t + 1$	0	10	100
$t + 2$	0	10	120
$t + 3$	20	20	140
$t + 4$	20	20	140
$t + 5$	0	10	120
$t + 6$	220	0	100
$t + 7$	220	0	100
$t + 8$	0	10	120
$t + 9$	20	20	140

16 (a) It could be rational if either (i) interest rates have fallen or (ii) people have raised their estimates of expected future income. (b) Fiscal policy is harder to change quickly. Moreover, monetary and fiscal policy affect different components of aggregate demand. Even if fiscal policy could achieve the same level of aggregate demand, it could not also achieve the same composition of demand as monetary policy.

17 Without any further policy changes, this will reduce UK aggregate demand, which will therefore fall even further below UK potential output. In principle, UK fiscal policy can be loosened to provide an offsetting boost to aggregate demand, though this is likely to take time to take effect. Fiscal rules within the Eurozone may restrict the ability of member states to expand fiscal policy if that state already has excessive budget deficits or a high level of national debt. Even without such restrictions, the UK might choose not to expand fiscal policy – had it been willing to do so it might not have had to join the euro in the first place. Finally, failing all else, aggregate demand will be low, a recession will ensue, and the induced fall in inflation will eventually stimulate aggregate demand for reasons that we explore in later chapters.

18 We know from national income accounting, and the equality of leakages and injections, that $(G - T) = (S - I) + (Z - X)$. If foreign surpluses and deficits never get huge, then any government deficit $G - T$ is essentially offset by a private sector surplus $S - I$. These are simultaneously determined and which causes which is far from clear. In a country such as Spain that did not begin with a large government deficit, it was the collapse of the property market and the desperate efforts of private Spaniards to save in order to get back to financial safety that induced the government deficit. In Greece, this was also partly true, but it is also true that the government itself was causing a large deficit. Conversely, the dramatic shrinking of the Greek budget deficit during 2010–12 was partly caused by government cutbacks and partly by a reduction in Greek private saving as their citizens hit the poverty line.

Chapter 12

1   (a) No. Cannot be used directly to finance subsequent transactions. (b) Watch which one is then retraded and not swallowed.

2   By simultaneously creating loans and deposits to match, without requiring a new deposit as part of the transaction. If the reserve requirement is 100 per cent, banks are unable to do this, and can no longer create money.

3   (a) They have a one-off use as money but are not subsequently retraded repeatedly. (b) No. (c) They reduce your demand for money, but do not affect supply: credit card stubs cannot be reused to purchase other goods.

4   M0 = 12 + 2 = 14; M4 = 12 + 30 + 60 + 20 = 122.

5   (a) Most of the money supply is bank deposits, a liability of banks. By simultaneously expanding both sides of their balance sheet, banks increase the money supply. (b) If people put less cash in banks, banks will be less able to multiply up reserves into deposits.

6   The money multiplier = 1.

7   Need less money for precautionary purposes.

8   Opportunity cost of holding money is unaffected by change in interest rates.

9   Data must come out before the data on the variable one is really interested in, and must be reliably correlated with those subsequent data.

10   (a) With more cash in the banks and less with the public, banks can multiply up into more bank deposits. (b) If inflation is negative, the real value of cash is rising at the same rate as that at which prices are falling.

11   Surprise inflation hits people with fixed nominal incomes (lenders, holders of cash, pensioners). Bonds and pensions could have adjusted their nominal payout had inflation been correctly foreseen, but the zero nominal return on cash cannot be adjusted even when inflation is foreseen.

12   Large increase in M4 as the bank deposit multiplier increases, and large inflation because so much extra money without many extra goods. In those circumstances, the Bank would then reverse quantitative easing, reducing the monetary base by selling government bonds that it holds, until M4 was back to a sensible level again.

13   (a) Not if nominal interest rates have risen to protect real interest rates. (b) Firms' revenues will also rise in nominal terms. (c) Menu and shoe-leather costs cannot be avoided.

14   We say that the real interest rate is 2 per cent in both cases. Although on average they are the same over the life of the contract, the two scenarios are not identical. With zero inflation, your real income and real interest payments are the same year after year. Because lenders (stupidly) insist on constant annual payments even during inflation, when inflation is 100 per cent the initial payments are very high in real terms, but after a few years this constant nominal repayment has shrunk in real terms to a tiny value. If lenders wanted to make you pay a constant annual stream of payments in real terms, then in a world of inflation they would have to arrange loan contracts so that you pay higher nominal payments later in the contract.

15   Before the crash, nominal interest rates would have been 7–8 per cent, implying a real interest rate of around 1–2 per cent. After the crash, the Bank would have slashed interest rates to around 0.5 per cent, thereby achieving a much bigger nominal interest rate reduction. Moreover, with actual inflation of initially 6 per cent, this would have implied a real interest rate of around −5 per cent. With such a strong stimulus to real aggregate demand, there would have been less need for QE.

16   Many political questions are about redistribution from one group to another. It would not be acceptable if unelected officials made such decisions. But delegating 'technical' decisions has a long history. Recently, it has been recognized that, although monetary policy does have some

distributional implications, these are probably less important than its 'technical function' in stabilizing aggregate demand, which is more effectively pursued by officials who have a clear objective set for them by the government and are then not subject to day-to-day interference by politicians.

17 Other things equal, an increase in the nominal supply must add to prices sooner or later. However, other things are rarely equal. The quantity of money demanded is quite volatile, not merely because of changes in interest rates and output – both affecting money demand – but also because of changes in confidence. Central banks have often tried using money as a leading indicator for inflation but in the short run it is not very reliable.

Chapter 13

1 Long-run aggregate supply and potential output increase. Eventually, monetary policy will accommodate this supply shock in full, allowing aggregate demand to rise by the same amount. Interest rates will be lower. In the short run, the first effect of more workers may be more unemployment. Eventually, this induces existing workers to reduce wage inflation, shifting the short-run supply curve downwards.

2 Monetary policy will begin cutting interest rates since inflation is now below target and output is now below its new level of potential output. Eventually, demand and output are higher and inflation is unaltered.

3 Permanent supply shocks must eventually change the level of output. In the short run, a demand shock will affect inflation and output, moving the economy along a given short-run aggregate supply curve. In the long run, output must revert to potential output, which is unaffected. Inflation will also be unaffected if the central bank sticks to its inflation target and changes interest rates as required.

4 Aggregate demand rises so the Bank raises interest rates. Hence investment may fall if the interest rate effect outweighs the benefit of higher output. Since aggregate demand exceeds potential output (otherwise no reason to have raised interest rates), tax revenue is higher because output is higher.

5 (a) Firms' prices rise too. (b) Consumer incomes rise too.

6 With higher costs, firms' supply curves shift, shifting the short-run aggregate supply curve upwards. If demand is unchanged, this causes a *fall* in output but a *rise* in inflation. The central bank raises real interest rates, and in the short run this reduces aggregate demand in line with the lower aggregate supply. The faster the central bank wants to get inflation exactly back to its inflation target, the more aggressively it has to raise real interest rates and the more output falls in the short run. Ensuring output is below potential output is what brings inflation down again. If permanently higher oil prices lead to a permanent fall in potential output, then monetary policy will have to engineer an even larger reduction of aggregate demand in the short run in order to bring inflation down from its initially high level.

7 Reduced demand for some types of labour, raised demand for others. Temporary mismatch, but eventually skills and wages adjust. Millennia of technical progress would have driven unemployment to 100 per cent if there were any permanent relationship between technical progress and unemployment.

8 (a) Deficient demand in economy. (b) The real wage is too high, for example because of union power or generous welfare benefits, so there is a high level of equilibrium output.

9 (a) By reducing distortions, it may raise equilibrium output. Also this initially raises aggregate demand. The latter effect is faster and probably larger, so boom, and monetary policy raises interest rates to keep inflation on track. (b) The main effect is a boost to aggregate demand, helping restore output to potential output.

10 Teenagers need training from scratch – they lack skills and job experience; teenage wages are not low enough to compensate.

11 (a) Not if equilibrium unemployment. (b) Not if Keynesian unemployment.

12 No. Since we do believe that inflation is damaging, even when foreseen, we should probably draw a long-run Phillips curve with a steep upward slope, implying higher inflation is associated with higher unemployment, even in the long run. Referring to a vertical long-run Phillips curve is a shorthand and implies that inflation is not 'very' damaging over the typical ranges of inflation that we experience.

13 Potential output has historically grown by over 2 per cent a year because of labour force growth and productivity growth through technical progress and capital accumulation. If this continues, actual output growth of 1 per cent will imply rising unemployment. With prolonged recession, investment and capital accumulation will be slower and some discouraged workers will leave the labour force, so potential output growth will slow down.

14 Greece has powerful trade unions, a large public sector, early retirement ages (despite long life expectancy) and inflexible wages. All four would need to be tackled in order to make the Greek labour market more efficient and less of a burden on the public finances.

15 (a) Yes. (b) No. (c) No. In (b) and (c), the Phillips curves are shifting around, so it is hard to detect in the data the downward slope of any particular short-run Phillips curve.

16 (a) Wage and price controls are unlikely to resist market forces for long since there will be mounting pressure to raise wages and prices. At some point, visible inflation will break out. (b) Cut budget deficit, make the central bank independent, and give it a moderate inflation target.

17 A surge of cheap imports is a favourable supply shock that temporarily reduces prices and inflation. Other things equal, it makes life easier for inflation control. But a lack of monetary discipline or an outbreak of trade union pressure could have provided shocks in the opposite direction. Subsequently, Chinese demand for commodities has bid up world prices, an adverse supply shock as far as Western economies are concerned. In principle, independent central banks could have chosen to raise interest rates sufficiently to reduce inflation quickly; in practice, they preferred to adopt a longer horizon for the restoration of low inflation, believing that rapid action would have generated a severe recession that was better avoided if possible. If the credit crunch generates a serious recession, this will bid down inflation again, without any further rise in interest rates.

18 If the main shock to the pension system is that we are all living for longer, extending the retirement age has to be part of the solution. If this is unchanged, it is implausible that people can save enough during their working lifetimes to pay for a much longer retirement.

Chapter 14

1 (a) Balance of payments surplus £2 billion. (b) Reserves rising. (c) Selling domestic currency to buy reserves.

2 (a) Deficit countries are likely to be forced by their creditors into more rapid adjustment. Surplus countries can adjust more slowly if they wish. (b) There is no limit to the foreign assets that a country can build up; simply it is not optimal to save forever if the purpose of saving is eventually to finance additional consumption. Countries running persistent deficits run out of foreign assets and have adjustment forced upon them.

3 (a) and (d) only.

4 Depreciates in (a) and (d), appreciates in (b) and (c). If the initial exchange rate is too low (high), an appreciation is good (bad).

5   Depreciates means falls, and hence becomes worth less. A devaluation entails a depreciation of the exchange rate, but we use the term to denote a decision to reduce the level of a fixed exchange rate.

6   (a) Fiscal policy is looser. (b) Aggregate demand increases. (c) Monetary policy raises interest rates to prevent inflation exceeding the target. (d) An exchange rate appreciation (the opposite of depreciation) would have reduced net exports, thereby offsetting the fiscal stimulus to aggregate demand and removing the need for higher interest rates.

7   Monetary policy is more powerful under floating exchange rates because the interest rate change induces a change in the exchange rate that reinforces the effect on aggregate demand and equilibrium output.

8   (a) Desirable if initially the exchange rate is below its equilibrium level. (b) Undesirable if the exchange rate is already above its equilibrium level.

9   (a) Acquired large stock of foreign assets by having previous years of current account surplus. (b) With large foreign assets, the current account will benefit from large inflow of income from these assets. If the current account is zero, the trade balance must be negative to offset the inflow of income from foreign assets.

10 Having lost cocaine exports, Colombia now has a trade deficit. The real exchange rate will depreciate, reducing imports (including cars from the US) and boosting other exports (including flowers).

11 Current account surplus during industrial revolution, leading to large stock of foreign assets. By late nineteenth century, so much foreign income flowed back from these assets on the current account of the balance of payments that there had to be a trade deficit in order to keep the overall current account broadly in balance.

12 (a) Substantial trade deficit to restore external balance eventually by offsetting the inflow of income from foreign assets. (b) Loss of competitiveness (higher real exchange rate) is the market mechanism that achieves the required trade deficit. (c) Yes. (d) If they had understood economics better, they would have realized that this was inevitable and appropriate. The benefit of foreign assets is that they allow a perpetual trade deficit, enabling domestic use of goods for consumption, investment and government spending to exceed national output.

13 (a) They can, by setting whatever interest rates induce speculators to be content with the level of the pegged exchange rate. (b) Short-run volatility mainly reflects the need to keep restoring two-way traffic of financial flows as opinion of speculators and investors keeps changing.

14 A large one-way flow would mean that the traders who organize the foreign exchange market were being forced to absorb the other half of these deals, in volumes that far exceed their capacity to do so. Their only alternative is to alter the exchange rate quickly to restore two-way traffic, out of which they can take a small commission and earn large incomes because the (two-way) volume is still pretty high. Under fixed exchange rates, eventually it is the central bank that has to be the other half of one-way traffic. If the financial flow is an inflow of foreign exchange, there is no technical limit to the ability of the central bank to print domestic money with which to buy the foreign currency. If the financial flow is an outflow of foreign exchange, the central bank will run out of foreign currency reserves and have to float the exchange rate. And even an inflow cannot last, because it is another country's outflow, and their central bank will run out of foreign exchange reserves.

15 The reason that a large country is less exposed within a monetary union is that, because it is a significant part of the total, the external exchange rate of the union is probably not entirely inappropriate for that country. In contrast, a small country contributes little to the union's aggregate data and may therefore find the external exchange rate quite inappropriate. Competitiveness can still adjust if the small country has flexible wages and prices. When uncompetitive, its wages and prices fall, restoring its competitiveness. Unfortunately, this usually takes a long time and entails a painful recession.

Chapter 15

1 No. The equilibrium exchange rate can be low enough to offset any absolute disadvantage. To enjoy efficiency gains from comparative advantage, the country should allow trade. For example, the UK gains by importing cheap trainers made in China and Dominican Republic – it would waste UK resources to make these in the UK. The same UK resources are better used in making exports with which to finance the imports of trainers.

2 Small countries can't enjoy scale economies without international trade, and for this reason rely on it more and benefit more. Additionally, trade by large countries also bids the world price in an adverse direction from their viewpoint.

3 Wine and cars have high two-way trade based on choice and differentiation; steel is based more on comparative advantage and is one way.

4 (a) No. Government may as well have the tax revenue too. (b) Domestic art buyers gain since prices fall. Domestic artists lose out, so too foreign art buyers. (c) Probably not.

5 (a) Changes in the exchange rate cope with the changes in the average level of absolute advantage, and every country must then have a comparative advantage at something. (b) Not always. The optimal tariff is an example in which a large country gains by a departure from free trade. (c) Fails to exploit comparative advantage and the gains from trade.

6 Technical progress in agriculture (e.g. winter wheat). Application of machinery and fertilizer to raise land productivity. Both augmented supply a lot, driving down the equilibrium price.

7 They require intensive but low-skilled labour, which LDCs have in relative abundance, but do not need very sophisticated technology, and shipping of the finished products is cheap and easy.

8 Debt/GDP ratio stays constant. If output growth then stagnates, debt/GDP ratio starts to grow because of cumulative interest so eventually the country must run a trade surplus to earn foreign exchange to pay interest to foreign creditors.

9 (a) Declining industries in Western Europe, such as shipbuilding, crude steel and agriculture, cause political difficulties when imports flow in. (b) These are precisely the industries in which Central and Eastern Europe were likely initially to have a comparative advantage.

10 (a) LDCs often argue that aid encourages dependence. They want foreign investment, less protection by rich countries, technology transfer and debt relief to wipe out mistakes of the past. (b) Europe would make a net gain from greater exploitation of comparative advantage, even though vociferous particular losers have so far blocked the process.

11 Consumers like variety, but if this is the only argument they should be prepared to pay the appropriately higher price to get it. A cultural heritage may be more like a public good, however, in which case some subsidy may be appropriate. If so, it should take the form of production subsidies not tariffs (principle of targeting again).

12 (a) Suppose relative poverty is defined as x per cent of the average income. By definition, there are always some people in this category, and it cannot be eliminated simply by economic growth for everyone. (b) Number in relative poverty would increase (i) if the definition were tightened (e.g. changed from those below 10 per cent of average income to those below 20 per cent of average income), or (ii) if the dispersion of incomes increased (in which case the average remains unaltered but there are more people in the very rich and very poor groups).

13 Austria is very close to its major trading partners (particularly Germany) and thus faces extensive competition in deciding tax rates, interest rates and regulations; this is why Austria was quite happy to join the EU and adopt the euro. In contrast, New Zealand is shielded by distance from both the US and the EU, and effectively has more scope to make national decisions.

14   (a) The really big migrations (to the US and Australia) took place in the nineteenth century.
(b) Absolute poverty has declined, and there is quite a lot of evidence that international trade helps economic growth, which is the main solution to national poverty.

15   China has principally been aiming to secure the mineral resources that it needs to fuel its rapidly growing economy. Given its scale, and the concentration of some resources in particular African countries, China may eventually have strategic control of several key natural resources, a potential source of concern. Meanwhile, Chinese investment is helping foster growth and development in Africa.

16   When the market is small, it takes a big profit rate to compensate drug companies for the risks they have taken. In principle, with a larger market it now takes a smaller profit per sale to offer the same total reward. Hence, if anything, globalization eases the conflict between the need to provide adequate rewards for risky research and the need to keep the price down so that the poor can afford key drugs. Moreover, if companies making AIDS drugs had *already* been rewarded by their sales in rich markets, there may be no economic case for their having to charge such high prices in new LDC markets.

17   Goods rather than services have historically dominated international trade statistics because these refer to gross outputs not value-added: many countries import resources or partly finished goods, add a bit of value, and then re-export. However, services are the bulk of the world economy, and the digital revolution is making their international trade ever easier. Top of the *Fortune 500 International* is Wal-Mart. Retail supermarkets are classed as providing services not goods.

18   There are probably two important issues. First, if China becomes a sufficiently large share of the world economy, the Chinese government will be forced to take into account things that affect the world as a whole, and its self-interest may lead it to become an effective champion of solutions to problems such as global warming. Second, if there is a phase during which China overtakes the US in economic power, this is potentially the source of global conflict, which may make solutions to global problems more difficult.

19   Internationally-traded carbon permits are the textbook solution to the emissions that create global warming. Those who can easily change behaviour do so, selling their permit to those who cannot cheaply change. The total supply of permits reflects the speed with which the planet wished to tackle the problem. Two issues arise. First, this is an acute version of the 'for whom' question, with big winners and losers. Losers always mobilize, protest and fight. Second, all important countries need to participate if the scheme is to be effective, but there is a considerable incentive to free ride on the efforts of others. Without a world government it is hard to do the right thing.

Chapter 16

1   Germany, France and Holland have high human capital; Greece, Spain and Portugal less so.

2   (a) No. (b) The equilibrium risk premium on riskier bonds exists to prevent capital flows by compensating properly for extra risk. (c) Yes, a monetary union: two firms' bonds pay slightly different interest rates even within the UK.

3   Every member state has one vote on the ECB board. The Stability Pact aims to prevent countries getting into fiscal trouble and then voting for high inflation to help their budget position. Even with tough monetary policy, monetary–fiscal mix matters. With loose fiscal, you need tight money, but then high real interest rates and real exchange rate appreciates to uncompetitive levels.

4   (a) and (b) are favourable to the establishment of a monetary union, (c) and (d) make it much less likely to succeed. Countries with similar industrial structure are more likely to face similar shocks and need the same monetary policy; countries with slow wage and price adjustment cannot use

their domestic labour market to adjust to shocks that the single monetary policy cannot target for their particular country.

5 Within the union, it may be possible for members to trust one another's regulators and allow banks to be regulated in their country of origin. However this trust is quickly tested in an acute crisis. Foreign banks from outside the union probably need to be forced to comply with centrally agreed rules within the union.

6 Since 2008, Ireland has dutifully pursued a vigorous policy of austerity and wage cuts that have so reduced its cost base that it has actually become more competitive than has the UK through external depreciation of sterling.

7 It is a force for lower wages, to the extent that firms are more competitive and less profitable; however, scale economies might also increase labour productivity and allow firms to pay workers more rather than less.

8 (a) Non-tariff barriers are also important. (b) By matching German interest rates in the ERM, countries had already given up most of their monetary sovereignty. (c) Independence from political control is the best commitment to price stability if politicians are the main cause of inflationary policies.

9 If international bond markets are highly integrated, investors expect the same risk-adjusted return everywhere. This means two things. First, governments that exhibit a risk of default are charged an extra risk premium in proportion to the perceived risk. Second, governments of countries whose currency is expected to depreciate have to offer suitably higher interest rates to compensate international investors for the capital loss they expect to make on the exchange rate while holding the currency.

10 Greek currency would depreciate substantially (up to 50 per cent according to some estimates) if it exited the EZ. Foreseeing this, there would be a huge one-way bet in the period immediately prior to exit, with everyone trying to remove money from Greece (and from any other countries which contagion might then affect). This capital flight might bring down the Greek banks and provoke the exit. Whether Greeks themselves win or lose depends on how long the austerity would last if they remain in the EZ. A 50 per cent reduction in living standards after exit, but thereafter with the prospect of improvement, might be less depressing than a nuclear winter within the EZ. Since exit would be accompanied by default, Greece's creditors elsewhere would be hit (but they should probably have recognized they were never going to get paid anyway). The real cost of exit for the rest of the EZ, and the rest of the world, depends critically on whether Greece is the only exit, or whether there are then serious concerns about other countries doing the same thing.

Index

Note: Glossary terms are in **bold** type.